D0086684

Building Construction

Principles, Practices, and Materials

GLENN M. HARDIE

School of Architecture
University of British Columbia

Prentice Hall
Englewood Cliffs, New Jersey   Columbus, Ohio

Library of Congress Cataloging-in-Publication Data

Hardie, Glenn M.
    Building construction : principles, practices, and materials /
  Glenn M. Hardie.
        p.   cm.
    Includes index.
    ISBN 0-13-350570-7
    1. Commercial buildings—Design and construction.   I. Title.
  TH4311.H37   1995
  690′.52—dc20   94-39073
                                                                                    CIP

Acquisitions Editor: Edward Francis
Production Editor: Mary Harlan
Cover Designer: Thomas Mack
Cover Photo: Glenn M. Hardie
Production Buyer: Pamela D. Bennett
Editorial Production Supervision: WordCrafters Editorial Services, Inc.
Text Designer: Laura Cleveland
Illustrations: Bruce Bolinger, Freehold Studio

This book was set in New Aster by BookMasters and was printed
and bound by Courier/Kendallville Inc. The cover was printed
by Phoenix Color Corp.

© 1995 by Prentice-Hall, Inc.
A Simon & Schuster Company
Englewood Cliffs, New Jersey 07632

10 9 8 7 6 5 4 3 2 1

Printed in the United States of America

ISBN 0-13-350570-7

Prentice-Hall International (UK) Limited, *London*
Prentice-Hall of Australia Pty. Limited, *Sydney*
Prentice-Hall Canada Inc., *Toronto*
Prentice-Hall Hispanoamericana, S.A., *Mexico*
Prentice-Hall of India Private Limited, *New Delhi*
Prentice-Hall of Japan, Inc., *Tokyo*
Simon & Schuster Asia Pte. Ltd., *Singapore*
Editora Prentice-Hall do Brasil, Ltda., *Rio de Janeiro*

Contents

Preface and Acknowledgments   vii

CHAPTER 01

Introduction   1

01-001   Prologue   1
01-002   MasterFormat and Layout   5
01-003   The Design/Build Process   12
01-004   Dimensioning   30
01-005   Inspection and Safety   36
01-050   Field Engineering   43
01-500   Temporary Facilities*   53
01-520   Construction Aids   63

CHAPTER 02

Site Work   76

02-100   Preparation   76
02-140   Dewatering   84
02-150   Protection   88
02-200   Earthwork   96
02-500   Paving*   105
02-700   Drainage*   112

CHAPTER 03

Concrete Work   116

03-100   Formwork   116
03-200   Reinforcement   130
03-300   Cast-in-Place Concrete   138
03-350   Concrete Finishing   151
03-370   Concrete Curing   158
03-400   Precast Concrete   163

*Because of the scope of this section, its title has been modified from its corresponding MasterFormat reference.

CHAPTER 04   Masonry Work   170

04-100   Mortar and Accessories*   170
04-200   Unit Masonry   179
04-400   Stone Masonry   192

CHAPTER 05   Metal Work   200

05-050   Metal Fasteners   200
05-100   Steel Framing   212
05-200   Steel Joisting   220
05-300   Steel Decking   226
05-400   Steel Stud Systems*   230
05-500   Metal Fabrications   241

CHAPTER 06   Woodwork   248

06-050   Adhesives   248
06-100   Rough Carpentry   254
06-170   Prefabricated Wood   274
06-200   Finish Carpentry   283
06-300   Wood Treatment   302
06-400   Architectural Woodwork   309

CHAPTER 07   Enclosures   320

07-100   Water and Dampproofing*   320
07-200   Insulation   325
07-300   Shingles and Tiles   332
07-400   Preformed Cladding*   340
07-500   Membrane Roofing   344
07-600   Flashings   355
07-900   Joint Sealing   362

CHAPTER 08   **Openings**   **369**

08-100   Metal Doors and Frames   369
08-200   Wood Doors and Frames   378
08-400   Storefront Systems   383
08-500   Metal Windows and Frames   389
08-600   Wood Windows and Frames   395
08-700   Finish Hardware   400
08-800   Glass and Glazing   415
08-900   Curtain Walling   430

CHAPTER 09   **Finishes**   **435**

09-100   Metal Support Systems   435
09-200   Lath and Plaster Work   439
09-250   Gypsum Plasterboard Systems   448
09-300   Ceramic Tile Work*   456
09-400   Terrazzo Work   462
09-500   Acoustical Treatments   469
09-550   Finished Wood Flooring   476
09-650   Resilient Flooring   484
09-680   Carpets, Underlay, and Trim   491
09-900   Painting and Decorating   498

CHAPTER 10   **Specialties**   **510**

10-001   Manufactured Specialties*   510

Epilogue   **522**

Glossary   **523**

Bibliography   **534**

Index   **540**

Preface and Acknowledgments

1.0 Preface

1.1 In General

This book is the third in a trilogy undertaken by this author in the field of construction practice. The first book dealt with contracts and specifications. The second book dealt with measurement and pricing. This final book of the series deals with materials and methods.

These three books have been written to fit together to provide the novice student with a wide and well-organized range of information on building technology; the intermediate student with a reasonably detailed and in-depth study of a number of discrete but closely related topics, such as construction, contracts, materials, specifications, estimating, and budgets; and the advanced student with authoritative reference works that will ensure that his or her knowledge of practice is appropriate, consistent, and reliable.

1.2 In Particular

This book is *not* a "how to" book for amateurs; rather it is a book on how things are (or should be) done by professionals. The intention is not to develop any special skill in the reader of the techniques of actual construction work, such as carpentry, masonry, painting, or welding. The intention is to improve knowledge of practical methodology used to ensure construction work of an appropriate type for buildings of any function, style, size, or quality, so that proper instructions may be given by middle management personnel to those other artisans who actually build the buildings. This is done through the media of construction drawings, memos, specifications, estimates, and other related documents used in construction contracts. An *Instructor's Manual* is also available from the publisher.

2.0 Acknowledgments

2.1 In General

Acknowledgment is made of the contributions and influences of the many authors, clients, colleagues, colleges, companies, employees, employers, friends, instructors, organizations, peers, professors, students, universities, and the rest from whom I have learned much of the methodology which I have set down in these pages. Acknowledgment is also made of cooperation received from government agencies, professional and trade associations, manufacturing companies, publishers, individuals, and others from whom permission was requested to refer to or to reproduce information of one sort or another for use in this book. Constructive comments made by a number of anonymous reviewers during production were also incorporated into the manuscript.

2.2 Photographs

Regarding photo credits, the origin of each photograph used in the book is indicated in one of four ways:

1. Photos marked "BCIT" were selected (with permission) from two sources at the British Columbia Institute of Technology: the Department of Building (from its collection of instructional graphics) and the Department of Audio-Visual Production (from its collection of promotional graphics).
2. Photos marked "UBC Architecture" were taken by the author in connection with courses taught in the School of Architecture, University of British Columbia, as well as for this book.
3. Photos made available through the publishers of this book are so identified and attributed to their respective origins.
4. Photos obtained from other sources (such as government agencies, manufacturers, construction associations and companies, private design firms, and the like) are identified by the name of the specific organization.

2.3 In Particular

I would also like to thank the following individuals for their specific contributions to the book:

1. Anna Maharajh for her friendship and assistance over many years in developing instructional material for college courses in contracts, estimating, specifications, materials, and methods, much of which was used in various ways in the book.

Anna also prepared the three plot plan diagrams used in Section 01–003.

2. Bruce Bolinger of Freehold Studio for his fine work in preparing all other finished line drawings for this book from very rough draft sketches provided by the author.

3. The lab crew at Action Reprographics in Vancouver for printing virtually all of the black and white photographs.

4. Laura Cleveland of WordCrafters Editorial Services for her editorial skills in the enhancement of the manuscript and the coordination of several components of the final work.

5. Edward Francis of Prentice Hall for taking a chance, securing reviews, arranging a contract, and initiating the publishing process.

6. My wife, Lorraine, who encouraged me to write my first book, put up with me while I wrote the second one and dared me to take the time to write this final one in the series. The book is dedicated to the memory of my parents, James and Maud Hardie.

Glenn M. Hardie
Vancouver, Canada

CHAPTER 01
Introduction

Section 01–001 Prologue

1.0 Introduction

Many books on construction methods and materials deal extensively with the manufacture and classification of building products or systems but do not address the equally important aspects of procedures involving installation. Other books focus more on aspects of design and construction detailing, placing a secondary emphasis on applications. Consequently, students and others entering the construction industry, as well as some already in a specialized portion of the industry, while having relatively good access to information on construction materials and components, may have little knowledge of how buildings are assembled overall from their component parts. Many people also have difficulty grasping the relationships between the various facets of project development, such as design, drafting, specifications, construction, estimating, cost control, contracts, and management. This book will assist such people to a better understanding of many of these issues through the detailed study of construction processes and methodology, following an outline of the building process.

2.0 Organization

2.1 Objectives

The primary objective of this book is generally to identify common construction materials, products, and systems, and particularly to describe in detail the procedures, equipment, and productivity necessary to physically incorporate such materials, products, and systems into buildings. The manufacture and classification of materials, products, and systems are addressed only to the extent required to properly explain and comprehend such incorporation.

A second objective is to present accurate, reliable, and current information on constraints involving efficiency and safety in the delivery, handling, and installation or application of building materials, products, and systems. A third objective is to gather information on a wide variety of building materials, products, systems, and procedures into one source, and to present such complex information in a manner that is conveniently organized and adaptable to a variety of college curricula.

High-Rise Institutional Buildings
Because of the cost of land and the need to be near related services, many businesses, institutions, and condominiums consolidate their operations in multistory framed buildings. (UBC Architecture)

A final objective is to present all of the foregoing matter in a useful, understandable, and pleasing manner, particularly for the instruction of students of architectural design, construction engineering, and building technology, and more generally for the guidance of others, such as draftspersons, junior specification writers, novice construction estimators, and apprentice project managers in the two broad fields of design and implementation.

2.2 Scope

All construction work can be categorized under two main headings: **heavy (or horizontal) construction**, comprising roads, bridges, dams, and the like; and **building (or vertical) construction**, comprising residential and nonresidential construction. Residential construction, which includes individual dwellings and small apartment blocks, is so special-

ized that it can almost be considered as a separate industry. Nonresidential construction consists of commercial buildings, such as large blocks of apartments, retail businesses, restaurants, and medical-dental buildings; institutional buildings, such as banks, colleges, courthouses, hospitals, laboratories, libraries, and schools; and industrial buildings, such as lumber mills, mining structures, manufacturing plants, and concrete batch plants. This book focuses primarily on nonresidential commercial and institutional projects as defined, although much of the content will have direct or modified applications to residential and industrial construction.

2.3 Structure

In the construction industry, the expertise of personnel tends to fall into fairly narrow and well-defined categories. Some of these include architectural design, building services, construction economics, materials purchasing, technical sales, inspection, and site supervision; others include the work of as many as 75 separate building trades (such as concreting and plumbing), embracing the work of about 25 distinct construction crafts (such as cement finishing and pipefitting).

The construction industry can also be conveniently (though only approximately) divided into the four discrete disciplines of architectural, structural, mechanical, and electrical work. The book includes structural and architectural work, such as site preparation and completion; framing in concrete, masonry, steel, and wood; doors, windows, and glass; common enclosures for walls and roofs; typical exterior and interior finishes; and some specialty items. The book excludes mechanical and electrical work, such as air conditioning, electronics, elevators, escalators, heating, lighting, plumbing, power supply, and ventilating. Nor does it deal with other more specialized services, such as audiovisual configurations, food preparation equipment, medical radiation protection, and security systems and vaults. The book also excludes descriptions of movable furnishings used in buildings, such as chairs, desks, drapes, lamps, pictures, rugs, sofas, and tables.

The book is organized on a trade-by-trade basis and covers much of the craft work in about two-thirds of the building trades (the excluded third being concerned with mechanical and electrical work). Regrettably, limitations of space did not permit the inclusion of the work of every structural or architectural trade; some obvious exceptions include blasting, demolition, landscaping, masonry restoration, piling, special doors, and wallpapering.

Low-Rise Commercial Buildings
In suburban and semirural areas, owners and developers can usually afford to spread various retail, residential, or service buildings and related parking areas over larger sites. (UBC Architecture)

3.0 Contents

The content of this book deals with materials, methods, and people, based on procedures common to both the United States and Canada. However, from experience gained and observations made by the author during visits to many other parts of the world (Australia, China, Europe, and elsewhere), it can be asserted that the majority of the design/build processes contained in this book will have applications wherever access to modern construction equipment, machinery, and tools is available. In regions where there is a significantly higher proportion of manual labor to mechanized equipment, some of the procedural suggestions and productivity factors in this book will require modification. In regions where there are extremes of climatic conditions, such as the winter in northern Canada or the summer in the southern United States, modifications to recommendations will also be necessary.

3.1 Regarding Materials

The selection of appropriate building materials, products, or systems to perform any specific construction function in a building involves consideration of a number of related attributes. These include physical size, mass or weight, chemical composition, compatibility with other materials, grade or quality, economic value, comparative durability, functional suitability, aesthetic value, personal preference, fashion or style, manufacture, cost, and availability, among others.

3.2 Regarding Methods

The selection of appropriate construction methods during the building process also involves consideration of a number of related attributes. These include availability of suitable equipment or tools, efficient machine outputs, assembly of a task force, labor productivity and cost, use of union or nonunion crews, methods of delivery and handling, hoisting or scaf-

Architectural Models
Because many clients have difficulties visualizing design drawings in three dimensions, it is not uncommon for designers to have scale models made of proposed buildings. (UBC Architecture)

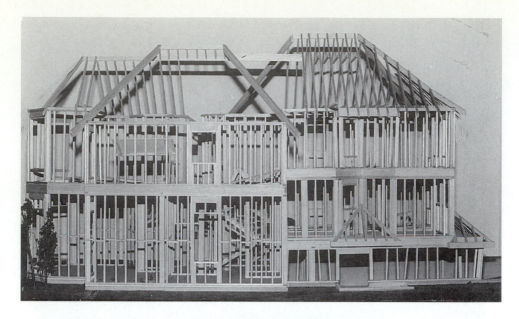

Instructional Models
Because many students have difficulties visualizing building details, it is not uncommon for instructors to use scale models showing a variety of common solutions to construction problems. (UBC Architecture)

folding, techniques and devices for fastening, safety and security, cleanup, and disposal of surplus materials, among others.

3.3   Regarding People

No matter how large or small the project, the process of successfully assembling a building and completing a construction contract involves the individual effort of each fully skilled, semiskilled, or unskilled person doing his or her job in the correct manner, sequence, and time. The largest of buildings are put together piece by piece by individuals, working steadily either alone or in small teams, and working either manually or (more often) with appropriate tools and equipment. Although there may be some moments of high structural drama in the process and sheer architectural magic in the result, there is really no profound mystery to the process by which buildings get built: People get together to do the job. The outcome is a direct function of the skills and attitudes of all of the people involved, from top management to casual help.

Building Morphology
Morphology refers to building shape. Not all buildings are rectangular and level; many are spherical (like this geodesic sphere). Others are circular, triangular, or irregular. (UBC Architecture)

3.4   Regarding Costs

Although the costs of labor, materials, equipment, and tools form an important part of the selection and production processes, cost data have been excluded from the text for two reasons:

1. The rapid fluctuations in prices render such data (and hence such books) obsolete in a relatively short space of time. Current costs can be obtained by the reader from local sources.

2. The sheer magnitude of required data would render the book unmarketable, as it would necessitate comment on about two dozen construction crafts, several hundred items of equipment and

tools, and well over one thousand distinct groups or types of materials and accessories.

4.0 Conclusion

To conclude this prologue, five other features of the book are mentioned because of their pervasive influence.

4.1 Dimensions

Dimensions are given in both metric (or SI or Système International) units and imperial (English or American) units; the reader is referred to Section 01–004 for specific details on dimensioning.

4.2 Meanings

Most technical terms are used correctly in their various contexts throughout this book. While there may be some minor regional variations in definitions, in most cases the meanings of terms will be evident from their specific context. For those words requiring more specific explanation, reference can be made to any good dictionary of construction terminology.

4.3 Gender

As far as practical, the use of gender words has been avoided throughout the book. Wherever the male gender has been used, the female gender may be substituted. However, some words with traditional meanings, such as *journeyman* (meaning a qualified tradesperson) or *manhole* (meaning a covered access panel leading to a buried service), have not yet been modified to reflect new semantic realities; such words are used where appropriate in this book in their traditional sense. Also, female readers should know that many construction associations now cater especially to the interests of women in this industry; inquiries can be made locally.

4.4 References

During preparation of this work, reference was made to hundreds of books, catalogs, codes, lecture notes, monographs, papers, pamphlets, regulations, reports, texts, and so on. While some are mentioned in context here and there in the book, limitations of space prevent reproduction of every title; some are even out of print. However, any well-stocked college or public library should carry sufficient background material to confirm or expand upon the data contained or alluded to herein. Those wishing to contact specific construction organizations can do so by using either of the following books:

1. In the United States, consult the *Encyclopedia of Associations*, published annually by Gale Research, Inc., Detroit, MI 48226.
2. In Canada, consult the *Directory of Associations*, published annually by Micro Media Ltd., Toronto, ONT M5H 1L3.

4.5 Instructor's Manual

Guidelines on using the book as a classroom text have been included in a separate *Instructor's Manual*. This manual includes directions on how to prepare, mark, and grade questions for tests and examinations, plus suggestions for term assignments.

Section 01–002
MasterFormat and Layout

1.0 Introduction

The organization of the chapters of this book is based on *MasterFormat*, which is a reference system for construction information. It was created and is jointly published and updated by The Construction Specifications Institute (CSI) in the United States and its counterpart in Canada, Construction Specifications Canada (CSC). Their current addresses are as follows:

CSI: 601 Madison Street, Alexandria, VA 22314.

CSC: 100 Lombard Street, Toronto, ONT M5C 1M3.

2.0 MasterFormat

MasterFormat is intended to assist with the production, distribution, filing, and subsequent retrieval of construction literature and information of every description on a uniform basis throughout North America. *MasterFormat* consists of 17 major Divisions, each related to a major grouping of construction work or contractual responsibility, and each containing a number of sections. Each section is subdivided into *BroadScope* (primary) titles and *NarrowScope* (secondary) titles, providing a detailed alphanumeric reference point for virtually all construction work and related interests.

The scope of this book primarily covers typical structural and architectural work in commercial and institutional buildings. References to such work are found in Divisions 02 through 10 of *MasterFormat*, and correspondingly in Chapters 02 through 10 of this book. Mechanical, electrical, and other more specialized work is found in Divisions 11 through 16; such work is excluded from this book. Some contractual issues addressed in Division 00 and 01 of *MasterFormat* are included in appropriate contexts throughout the book.

Table 2, excerpted from the 1988 edition of *MasterFormat* and used by permission, shows all 17 divisions, together with the numbers and titles assigned to the BroadScope sections within each division. The numbers of the various trade sections in each chapter of this book will be seen to match their corresponding *MasterFormat* numbers in Divisions 02 through 10.

The purpose of incorporating this excerpt here is to show where the section numbers and titles used in this book came from, and also to permit the reader to start to develop his or her own filing system for the insertion and retrieval of construction information, such as catalogs, pamphlets, lecture notes, and so on, based on *MasterFormat* numbers.

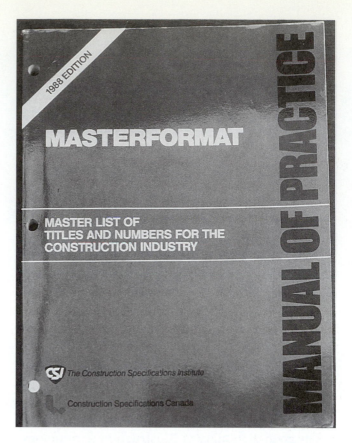

"MasterFormat" ©
MasterFormat is a reference manual having three parts: (1) numbers and titles for Project Sections, (2) detailed recommendations for Section Content, and (3) an alphabetical index. (UBC Architecture)

tended for the preparation of trade specifications in construction contracts. Parts 1.0, 2.0, and 5.0 of each section of this book loosely correspond to some of the data required for parts 1, 2, and 3 of *SectionFormat*; parts 3.0 and 4.0 would not normally be detailed in such contracts.)

3.0 Section Layout

In this book, each trade section in Chapters 02 through 10 presents information of the same type in the same sequence, in five parts, as shown in Table 1. (The layout of sections in Chapter 01 is different, as it is primarily introductory.) Care has been taken to avoid duplication or omission between related sections, to keep the book comprehensive yet concise.

(In addition to *MasterFormat*, there is also a three-part CSI/CSC *SectionFormat* especially in-

4.0 Graphics

Single-line sketches used to illustrate aspects of the text are intended to be general representations of typical instances and not to show particular details of specific merchandise or market examples. Photographs are intended to suggest only general approaches to resolving building technology problems, using actual personnel, processes, equipment, and materials; they are not intended to promote the sale or use of any specific type of equipment, make of material, size of crew, methodology, or safety measure.

Table 1
TYPICAL SECTION LAYOUT

1.0 INTRODUCTION
1.1 General Issues
1.2 Design Aspects
1.3 Related Work

2.0 PRODUCTS
2.1 Materials
2.2 Accessories

3.0 CONSTRUCTION AIDS
3.1 Equipment
3.2 Tools

4.0 PRODUCTION
4.1 Crew Configurations
4.2 Productivity

5.0 PROCEDURES
5.1 Preparation
5.2 Process
5.3 Precautions

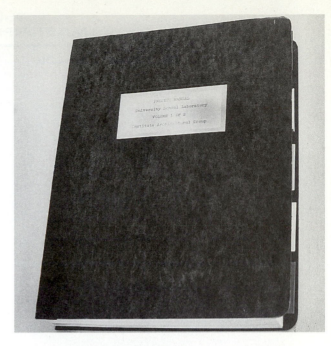

Project Manual
The project manual contains all the documentation for a construction contract, except for the drawings. Most manuals are organized into divisions and sections conforming to MasterFormat. (UBC Architecture)

5.0 Safety Considerations

To avoid repetition, the twin issues of inspection and safety are treated in a comprehensive manner in Section 01–005. Most safe practices are based on common sense and concern for the well-being of oneself and one's working companions. As a general comment, safety on construction sites should be the business of everyone affected.

6.0 Precautionary Note

While productivity factors presented in this book are considered to be realistic and are given in good faith with respect to their magnitudes, no responsibility is assumed by the author or publisher for commercial or other decisions made by readers based on these factors. The factors are intended only to be used as a general guide for students or novices who may have little or no concept of such matters. While they may be useful for academic practice exercises, they are not intended to be used in calculations related to actual construction contracts. In virtually every instance, these generalized factors will require significant modification to suit the special circumstances of a real construction project. Some of these factors represent average or median values, taken from larger ranges of observed possibilities. Others represent the best- (or worst-) case scenario. Almost all require unstated reservations or qualifications before application to actual work. For the foregoing reasons they are not recommended for uses other than the academic exercises described above.

Table 2
MASTERFORMAT LIST

DIVISION 00—BIDDING AND CONTRACT REQUIREMENTS

00010 PRE-BID INFORMATION

00100 INSTRUCTIONS TO BIDDERS

00200 INFORMATION AVAILABLE TO BIDDERS

00300 BID/TENDER FORMS

00400 SUPPLEMENTS TO BID/TENDER FORMS

00500 AGREEMENT FORMS

00600 BONDS AND CERTIFICATES

00700 GENERAL CONDITIONS OF THE CONTRACT

00800 SUPPLEMENTARY CONDITIONS

00950 DRAWINGS INDEX

00900 ADDENDA AND MODIFICATIONS

DIVISION 01—GENERAL REQUIREMENTS

01010 SUMMARY OF WORK

01020 ALLOWANCES

01030 SPECIAL PROJECT PROCEDURES

01040 COORDINATION

01050 FIELD ENGINEERING

01060 REGULATORY REQUIREMENTS

01070 ABBREVIATIONS AND SYMBOLS

01080 IDENTIFICATION SYSTEMS

01100 ALTERNATES/ALTERNATIVES

01150 MEASUREMENT AND PAYMENT

01200 PROJECT MEETINGS

01300 SUBMITTALS

01400 QUALITY CONTROL

01500 CONSTRUCTION FACILITIES AND TEMPORARY CONTROLS

01600 MATERIAL AND EQUIPMENT

01650 STARTING OF SYSTEMS

01660 TESTING, ADJUSTING, AND BALANCING OF SYSTEMS

01700 CONTRACT CLOSEOUT

DIVISION 02—SITEWORK

02010 SUBSURFACE INVESTIGATION

02050 DEMOLITION

02100 SITE PREPARATION

02150 UNDERPINNING

02200 EARTHWORK

02300 TUNNELING

02350 PILES, CAISSONS AND COFFERDAMS

02400 DRAINAGE

02440 SITE IMPROVEMENTS

02480 LANDSCAPING

02500 PAVING AND SURFACING

02590 PONDS AND RESERVOIRS

02600 PIPED UTILITY MATERIALS AND METHODS

02700 PIPED UTILITIES

02800 POWER AND COMMUNICATION UTILITIES

02850 RAILROAD WORK

02880 MARINE WORK

DIVISION 03—CONCRETE

03050 CONCRETING PROCEDURES

03100 CONCRETE FORMWORK

03150 FORMS

03180 FORM TIES AND ACCESSORIES

03200 CONCRETE REINFORCEMENT

03250 CONCRETE ACCESSORIES

03300 CAST-IN-PLACE CONCRETE

03350 SPECIAL CONCRETE FINISHES

03360 SPECIALLY PLACED CONCRETE

03370 CONCRETE CURING

03400 PRECAST CONCRETE

03500 CEMENTITIOUS DECKS

03600 GROUT

03700 CONCRETE RESTORATION AND CLEANING

DIVISION 04—MASONRY

04050 MASONRY PROCEDURES

04100 MORTAR

04150 MASONRY ACCESSORIES

Table 2
MASTERFORMAT LIST (CONTINUED)

04200	UNIT MASONRY
04400	STONE
04500	MASONRY RESTORATION AND CLEANING
04550	REFRACTORIES
04600	CORROSION RESISTANT MASONRY

DIVISION 05—METALS

05010	METAL MATERIALS AND METHODS
05050	METAL FASTENING
05100	STRUCTURAL METAL FRAMING
05200	METAL JOISTS
05300	METAL DECKING
05400	COLD-FORMED METAL FRAMING
05500	METAL FABRICATIONS
05700	ORNAMENTAL METAL
05800	EXPANSION CONTROL
05900	METAL FINISHES

DIVISION 06—WOOD AND PLASTICS

06050	FASTENERS AND SUPPORTS
06100	ROUGH CARPENTRY
06130	HEAVY TIMBER CONSTRUCTION
06150	WOOD-METAL SYSTEMS
06170	PREFABRICATED STRUCTURAL WOOD
06200	FINISH CARPENTRY
06300	WOOD TREATMENT
06400	ARCHITECTURAL WOODWORK
06500	PREFABRICATED STRUCTURAL PLASTICS
06600	PLASTIC FABRICATIONS

DIVISION 07—THERMAL AND MOISTURE PROTECTION

07100	WATERPROOFING
07150	DAMPROOFING
07200	INSULATION
07250	FIREPROOFING
07300	SHINGLES AND ROOFING TILES
07400	PREFORMED ROOFING AND SIDING
07500	MEMBRANE ROOFING
07570	TRAFFIC TOPPING
07600	FLASHING AND SHEET METAL
07800	ROOF ACCESSORIES
07900	JOINT SEALANTS

DIVISION 08—DOORS AND WINDOWS

08100	METAL DOORS AND FRAMES
08200	WOOD AND PLASTIC DOORS
08250	DOOR OPENING ASSEMBLIES
08300	SPECIAL DOORS
08400	ENTRANCES AND STOREFRONTS
08500	METAL WINDOWS
08600	WOOD AND PLASTIC WINDOWS
08650	SPECIAL WINDOWS
08700	HARDWARE
08800	GLAZING
08900	GLAZED CURTAIN WALLS

DIVISION 09—FINISHES

09100	METAL SUPPORT SYSTEMS
09200	LATH AND PLASTER
09230	AGGREGATE COATINGS
09250	GYPSUM WALLBOARD
09300	TILE
09400	TERRAZZO
09500	ACOUSTICAL TREATMENT
09550	WOOD FLOORING
09600	STONE AND BRICK FLOORING
09680	CARPETING
09700	SPECIAL FLOORING
09760	FLOOR TREATMENT
09800	SPECIAL COATING
09900	PAINTING
09950	WALL COVERING

DIVISION 10—SPECIALTIES

10100	CHALKBOARDS AND TACKBOARDS
10150	COMPARTMENTS AND CUBICLES
10200	LOUVERS AND VENTS

Table 2
MASTERFORMAT LIST (CONTINUED)

10240	GRILLES AND SCREENS
10250	SERVICE WALL SYSTEMS
10260	WALL AND CORNER GUARDS
10270	ACCESS FLOORING
10280	SPECIALTY MODULES
10290	PEST CONTROL
10300	FIREPLACES AND STOVES
10340	PREFABRICATED STEEPLES, SPIRES, AND CUPOLAS
10350	FLAGPOLES
10400	IDENTIFYING DEVICES
10450	PEDESTRIAN CONTROL DEVICES
10500	LOCKERS
10520	FIRE EXTINGUISHERS, CABINETS, AND ACCES-SORIES
10530	PROTECTIVE COVERS
10550	POSTAL SPECIALTIES
10600	PARTITIONS
10650	SCALES
10670	STORAGE SHELVING
10700	EXTERIOR SUN CONTROL DEVICES
10750	TELEPHONE ENCLOSURES
10800	TOILET AND BATH ACCESSORIES
10900	WARDROBE SPECIALTIES

DIVISION 11—EQUIPMENT

11010	MAINTENANCE EQUIPMENT
11020	SECURITY AND VAULT EQUIPMENT
11030	CHECKROOM EQUIPMENT
11040	ECCLESIASTICAL EQUIPMENT
11050	LIBRARY EQUIPMENT
11060	THEATER AND STAGE EQUIPMENT
11070	MUSICAL EQUIPMENT
11080	REGISTRATION EQUIP-MENT
11100	MERCANTILE EQUIPMENT
11110	COMMERCIAL LAUNDRY AND DRY CLEANING EQUIPMENT
11120	VENDING EQUIPMENT
11130	AUDIO-VISUAL EQUIPMENT

11140	SERVICE STATION EQUIPMENT
11150	PARKING EQUIPMENT
11160	LOADING DOCK EQUIPMENT
11170	WASTE HANDLING EQUIPMENT
11190	DETENTION EQUIPMENT
11200	WATER SUPPLY AND TREATMENT EQUIPMENT
11300	FLUID WASTE DISPOSAL AND TREATMENT EQUIPMENT
11400	FOOD SERVICE EQUIPMENT
11450	RESIDENTIAL EQUIPMENT
11460	UNIT KITCHENS
11470	DARKROOM EQUIPMENT
11480	ATHLETIC, RECREATIONAL, AND THERAPEUTIC EQUIPMENT
11500	INDUSTRIAL AND PRO-CESS EQUIPMENT
11600	LABORATORY EQUIPMENT
11650	PLANETARIUM AND OB-SERVATORY EQUIPMENT
11700	MEDICAL EQUIPMENT
11780	MORTUARY EQUIPMENT
11800	TELECOMMUNICATION EQUIPMENT
11850	NAVIGATION EQUIPMENT

DIVISION 12—FURNISHINGS

12100	ARTWORK
12300	MANUFACTURED CABI-NETS AND CASEWORK
12500	WINDOW TREATMENT
12550	FABRICS
12600	FURNITURE AND ACCES-SORIES
12670	RUGS AND MATS
12700	MULTIPLE SEATING
12800	INTERIOR PLANTS AND PLANTINGS

DIVISION 13—SPECIAL CON-STRUCTION

13010	AIR SUPPORTED STRUCTURES
13020	INTEGRATED ASSEMBLIES
13030	AUDIOMETRIC ROOMS

Table 2
MASTERFORMAT LIST (CONTINUED)

13040	CLEAN ROOMS
13050	HYPERBARIC ROOMS
13060	INSULATED ROOMS
13070	INTEGRATED CEILINGS
13080	SOUND, VIBRATION, AND SEISMIC CONTROL
13090	RADIATION PROTECTION
13100	NUCLEAR REACTORS
13110	OBSERVATORIES
13120	PRE-ENGINEERED STRUCTURES
13130	SPECIAL PURPOSE ROOMS AND BUILDINGS
13140	VAULTS
13150	POOLS
13160	ICE RINKS
13170	KENNELS AND ANIMAL SHELTERS
13200	SEISMOGRAPHIC INSTRUMENTATION
13210	STRESS RECORDING INSTRUMENTATION
13220	SOLAR AND WIND INSTRUMENTATION
13410	LIQUID AND GAS STORAGE TANKS
13510	RESTORATION OF UNDERGROUND PIPELINES
13520	FILTER UNDERDRAINS AND MEDIA
13530	DIGESTION TANK COVERS AND APPURTENANCES
13440	OXYGENATION SYSTEMS
13540	THERMAL SLUDGE CONDITIONING SYSTEMS
13560	SITE CONSTRUCTED INCINERATORS
13600	UTILITY CONTROL SYSTEMS
13700	INDUSTRIAL AND PROCESS CONTROL SYSTEMS
13800	OIL AND GAS REFINING INSTALLATIONS AND CONTROL SYSTEMS
13900	TRANSPORTATION INSTRUMENTATION
13940	BUILDING AUTOMATION SYSTEMS
13970	FIRE SUPPRESSION AND SUPERVISORY SYSTEMS

13980	SOLAR ENERGY SYSTEMS
13990	WIND ENERGY SYSTEMS

DIVISION 14—CONVEYING SYSTEMS

14100	DUMBWAITERS
14200	ELEVATORS
14300	HOISTS AND CRANES
14400	LIFTS
14500	MATERIAL HANDLING SYSTEMS
14600	TURNTABLES
14700	MOVING STAIRS AND WALKS
14800	POWERED SCAFFOLDING
14900	TRANSPORTATION SYSTEMS

DIVISION 15—MECHANICAL

15050	BASIC MATERIALS AND METHODS
15200	NOISE, VIBRATION, AND SEISMIC CONTROL
15250	INSULATION
15300	SPECIAL PIPING SYSTEMS
15400	PLUMBING SYSTEMS
15450	PLUMBING FIXTURES AND TRIM
15500	FIRE PROTECTION
15600	POWER OR HEAT GENERATION
15650	REFRIGERATION
15700	LIQUID HEAT TRANSFER
15800	AIR DISTRIBUTION
15900	CONTROLS AND INSTRUMENTATION

DIVISION 16—ELECTRICAL

16050	BASIC MATERIALS AND METHODS
16200	POWER GENERATION
16300	POWER TRANSMISSION
16400	SERVICE AND DISTRIBUTION
16500	LIGHTING
16600	SPECIAL SYSTEMS
16700	COMMUNICATIONS
16850	HEATING AND COOLING
16900	CONTROLS AND INSTRUMENTATION

Section 01–003
The Design/Build Process

1.0 Introduction

1.1 Preamble

Before examining the myriad of particular details described in the dozens of trade sections included in this book, those not familiar with common construction industry procedures should review this outline of the design/build process. The title of this section should not be confused with similar titles (such as "own-design-build" or "design-bid-build") used to describe common configurations or relationships between the parties to construction developments.

To ground this discussion of general principles in a particular reality, a hypothetical construction project consisting of a wood-frame building containing 10 large-sized townhouse dwelling units will be used as a vehicle to illustrate issues as they arise. Figure 1 shows a plot plan of the 10-unit townhouse site as it might be presented by the designer for the construction project.

1.2 In General

Briefly stated, potential developers (whether private, commercial, or public) require access to land and to finances, to designers and to builders, and sometimes to customers to buy (or realtors to sell) the finished building.

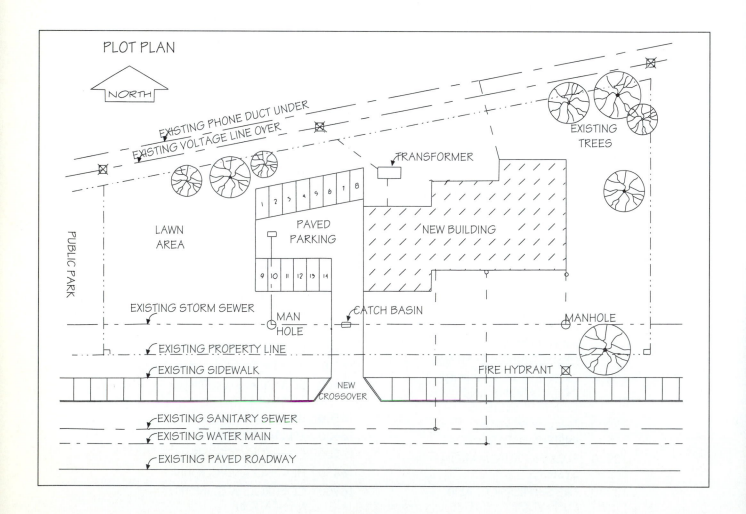

Figure 1 Plot Plan

Ten-Unit Townhouse
This photo represents a typical urban townhouse development of the type described in the accompanying text. It is included here to give a visual focus to the design/build process. (UBC Architecture)

1.3 In Particular

For the purpose of this brief review, the entire design/build process has been divided into three parts: **designing, contracting**, and **building**. Each of these is examined in more detail in Parts 2.0, 3.0, and 4.0 of this section; the process of selling a completed building is excluded.

2.0 The Design Process

2.1 Owner/Developer's Needs

A developer or landowner perceives a need for a building. The need usually arises from commercial, industrial, institutional, or personal requirements for shelter. The first step is to make a feasibility study of the entire proposal to ensure that it is economically viable. If the developer is a private individual or organization, financing may be arranged through a bank or savings and loan agency, a mortgage or trust company, or some other source, such as shareholders, family members, pension or personal funds, or whatever other money is available at a competitive and reasonable interest rate. If the developer is a public agency, such as a government department, a school or hospital board, or perhaps a

county or city agency, financing is usually dependent on tax dollars being allocated to the appropriate budget at the right time and in sufficient amounts. Either way, the amount of money available for the design and construction of the proposed building must be established within a reasonable cost range, so that both designer and developer know the budget constraints. Figure 2 shows an example of typical calculations that might be made at this stage, relative to the townhouse project.

If land is not already owned by the developer, legal steps will be taken to acquire proper title or options to a piece of land for the project, suitable in location, size, type, and zoning. Negotiations then commence between the owner/developer and a designer, such as an architect, engineer, or other specialist.

2.2 Design Process

This process has four distinct stages detailed below. Each stage should include a check on the costs, to confirm that the budget determined in item 8 of Figure 2 has not been exceeded.

Program. The designer receives the developer's subjective needs and personal wishes, clarifies any ambiguities relative to costs and services to be provided, and articulates the proposal into an objective program of possible physical accommodation, based on the preliminary budget calculations.

Schematics. The designer develops a design outline and cost plan for the approved proposal, allocating portions of the budget to the various parts or elements of the developer's general proposals. This activity tends to establish the size and general appearance of the proposed building and the level of quality that can be reasonably specified for the predicted end result, given the budget constraints.

Development. The design of specific elements of the building and particular aspects of construction details are more fully developed, based on the owner/developer's requirements, subsequent refinements, and probable costs and their relationship to the original proposals. This usually results in some modification to both the developer's proposals and the designer's ideas.

Documentation. Relatively finalized design concepts are developed into detailed working drawings, specifications regarding quality of materials and labor, contract conditions regarding rights and responsibilities of the parties to the emergent construction contract (dealing with payments, in-

DEVELOPMENT BUDGETS—METHODOLOGY
(given values are illustrative only)

1. PROGRAM: five units each 150 m²   = 750 m²
           five units each 175 m²   = 875 m²
           rental area (65 x 25 m)   = 1625 m²

2. MARKET RENTAL: small units ($1700 pm)   = $136/m² pa
                   large units ($2000 pm)   = $137/m² pa
   (pm = per month; pa = per annum, market predictions)

3. GROSS ANNUAL INCOME (GAI):

    (a) small units 750 m² @ $136 = $102,000
    (b) large units 875 m² @ $137 = 119,900   = $ 221,900

    DEDUCT ANNUAL EXPENSES (say 25% of GAI
    including an allowance for vacancies)   55,500

    NET INCOME: $ 166,400
    capitalized at 6% (factor 100/6 = 16.7)   × 16.7

4. GROSS DEVELOPMENT VALUE (GDV)   = $2,778,900

5. DEDUCT COSTS:

    (a) land   (estimated) $500,000
    (b) financing (10% of 5a)   50,000
    (c) fees   (5% of GDV)   139,000
    (d) profit   (15% of GDV)   417,000   = $1,106,000

6. AMOUNT AVAILABLE FOR BUILDING AND FEES   = $1,672,900

7. DEDUCT REMAINDER:

    (a) design fee (10% of 6) $167,290
    (b) site costs (5% of 6–7a)   75,310   = $ 242,600

8. RESIDUAL AVAILABLE FOR CONSTRUCTION COST: $1,430,300

9. PROGRAM REQUIREMENTS:

    (a) total small units 750 m²
    (b) total large units 875 m² = 1625 m²
    (c) circulation (say 5%)   = 75 m²
    (d) gross floor area   = 1700 m²

10. MAXIMUM CONSTRUCTION COST ($1,431/1.7)   = $841.76/m²

    The designer should aim for about $800/m² ($80/ft²)

Figure 2 Budget Development

surance, warranties, and so on), and the bidding procedure and format.

Working drawings are normally organized into the following sequence: site plan; structural framing; architectural plans, sections, and elevations; plumbing and mechanical systems; and electrical power distributions and lighting layouts. A project manual should be organized using *MasterFormat* (see Section 01–002) as a guide. Page 1 of the table of contents for the 10-unit townhouse project manual would be arranged as shown in Figure 3. In this figure, one can see the various trade sections applicable to the townhouse project.

```
┌─────────────────────────────────────────────────────────────┐
│                                                               │
│  ┌─────────────────────────────────────────────────────────┐ │
│  │                                                           │ │
│  │         PROPOSED TEN UNIT TOWNHOUSE COMPLEX               │ │
│  │                                                           │ │
│  │             SUTCLIFFE PARK, VANCOUVER                     │ │
│  │                                                           │ │
│  │  JOB NO: 93.05        TABLE OF CONTENTS      PAGE 1 OF 3  │ │
│  │  ─────────────────────────────────────────────────────── │ │
│  │                                                           │ │
│  │  DIVISION 00 BIDDING AND CONTRACT              PAGES      │ │
│  │                                                           │ │
│  │      00-100 Instruction to Bidders               2        │ │
│  │      00-220 Soil Investigation Data              3        │ │
│  │      00-310 Bid Form for Stipulated Price        5        │ │
│  │                                                           │ │
│  │      00-430 Subcontractor Listing                2        │ │
│  │      00-510 Form of Agreement                    3        │ │
│  │      00-610 Form of Performance Bond             2        │ │
│  │                                                           │ │
│  │      00-710 General Conditions of Contract      14        │ │
│  │      00-810 Supplements to General Conditions    3        │ │
│  │      00-851 Drawings Listing                     1        │ │
│  │                                                           │ │
│  │  DIVISION 01 GENERAL REQUIREMENTS                         │ │
│  │                                                           │ │
│  │      01-010 Summary of Work                      2        │ │
│  │      01-021 Cash Allowances                      1        │ │
│  │      01-152 Application for Payment              3        │ │
│  │                                                           │ │
│  │      01-340 Shop Drawings and Samples            2        │ │
│  │      01-370 Schedule of Values                   3        │ │
│  │      01-510 Temporary Services                   2        │ │
│  │                                                           │ │
│  │      01-590 Field Offices and Sheds              2        │ │
│  │      01-710 Maintenance Data                     2        │ │
│  │                                                           │ │
│  │  DIVISION 02 SITE WORKS                                   │ │
│  │                                                           │ │
│  │      02-110 Site Clearing                        2        │ │
│  │      02-200 Earthwork                            4        │ │
│  │      02-400 Drainage                             2        │ │
│  │                                                           │ │
│  │      02-500 Asphalt Paving                       3        │ │
│  │                                                           │ │
│  │  DIVISION 03 CONCRETE WORK                                │ │
│  │                                                           │ │
│  │      03-100 Formwork for Concrete                2        │ │
│  │      03-200 Reinfor~~~~~                         4        │ │
│  │                                                           │ │
│  │  (and so on....)                                          │ │
│  │                                                           │ │
│  └─────────────────────────────────────────────────────────┘ │
│                                                               │
└─────────────────────────────────────────────────────────────┘
```

Figure 3   Sample Table of Contents for Project Manual

3.0 The Contract Process

3.1 Contract Types

Simply stated, there are two basic types of construction contract; each one gives rise to several hybrid forms embracing some of the features of the two basic forms. The two basic types are:

1. **Stipulated sum type**, in which fully detailed information is made available to the contractor, who then decides in advance what it is all worth for him or her to do the complete job. The risk is largely on the contractor in this form, as something may have been overlooked during the estimating phase.

2. **Cost-plus-fee type**, in which fully detailed information is not available to the contractor, who is

Document Generation

Construction contract documents are commonly produced using electronic devices for drafting and word processing. In some smaller firms, drawings and specifications are produced manually. (BCIT Audio-Visual Production)

instead paid for work done as work progresses to completion. The risk is largely on the owner/designer in this form, as neither they nor the contractor knows at the outset what the final cost will be.

For further information on each of these two basic contract types, readers can refer to the following documents, produced, respectively, by the American Institute of Architects (AIA) in Washington, D.C., and by the Canadian Construction Documents Committee (CCDC) in Ottawa, Ontario:

	United States	Canada
Stipulated sum	AIA # A101 and A107	CCDC # 02
Cost-plus-fee	AIA # A111 and A201	CCDC # 03

Two of the hybrid contract types are as follows:

3. **Target price type**, in which enough information can be given to let the job be bid as though it were a stipulated sum contract but the project is run as though it were a cost-plus-fee contract. There is the possibility of sharing savings made if actual final costs do not exceed anticipated or target costs.

4. **Unit price type**, in which detailed quantities of work are calculated by the designer (or by a spe-

cialist cost consultant) and priced by the contractor and the priced job is bid like a stipulated sum contract. As the job progresses, work is remeasured and paid for at the quoted unit prices, allowing for adjustments to measurement and pricing necessitated by variations in the work.

In any event, it is the owner, in consultation with the designer, who usually decides on the type of contract. The contractor seldom has much input into this selection. Regardless of which type of contract is employed, the content of most forms of construction contracts will include detailed description of most or all of the following topics, arranged here alphabetically for convenience of reference:

Addenda. Changes to the bidding documents.

Bonds. Guarantees of performance.

Changes. Adjustments to work in progress.

Disputes. The resolution of disagreements.

Documents. Contracts, drawings, and specifications.

Inspection. Required by designers and authorities.

Insurance. Financial protection for parties.

Legalities. The law of the land.

Parties. The owner, contractor, and, perhaps, designer.

Payments. Process, intervals, and amounts.

Permits. Required authorizations and fees.

Progress. Expectations for completion.

Protection. Legislated safety and other constraints.

Taxes. Imposed by several levels of government.

Time. Definitions of day, week, month, or year.

Warranties. Confirmation of promises.

Work force. Union or nonunion, certified or not.

Work quality. Economy, custom, or premium grade.

The type and contents of the contract will have a marked effect on the final price of the building.

3.2 The Bidding Process

Before bidding on any new work, contractors regularly engage in a process called bid strategy. They assess work already undertaken, the merits or otherwise of the proposed project under review on which they may bid (with regard to contract type, building classification, size, timing, and so on), and its comparison to other projects currently available for bid. They also review such issues as financing, bonding capacity, availability of materials and labor, and market trends in general, among other things. If appropriate, the contractor will then approach the owner/designer to express interest in the project, either by responding to a formal invitation or by direct personal contact.

3.3 Estimating Activity

Once it has been decided to bid on a particular project, the contractor will first acquire a complete set of the proposed contract documents from the owner or designer. The documents are then reviewed by the contractor to determine which parts of the project will be done with the forces directly available to the company and which other parts will be farmed out (or sublet) to subcontractors or suppliers. Each contractor, subcontractor, and supplier bidding on the project will then initiate a process of measurement and pricing of those portions of the work to be done by their own companies, using either standard preprinted stationery forms or a computerized preprogrammed spreadsheet specially designed for this task. The variety of such forms and programs is enormous; any construction estimating book will show appropriate examples.

The general contractor will assemble all the estimates for each portion of the project and from these will put together a final submission in the appropriate bid form. Figure 4 shows the first page of such a completed bid form. It will be seen that this bid figure is well within the initial budget allocation.

Estimating and Bidding
In construction companies, estimators are employed to review the contract requirements and calculate probable costs and times (using electronic spreadsheet and projection programs). (UBC Architecture)

```
        PROPOSED TEN-UNIT TOWNHOUSE COMPLEX

              SUTCLIFFE PARK, VANCOUVER


                      BID FORM

Bidder's Name: Concourse Construction Inc.       Date: 15 DEC 93

Address: 666 Elm Street, Vancouver.             Phone: 555-1234


   To the Owners: ABC Holdings, Inc., 1500 No.3 Road, Richmond


1.   THE STIPULATED SUM

     Having  examined the site, the drawings, the project  manual
and  all  conditions affecting the contract, we hereby  offer  to
furnish  labor, materials, equipment, services, and other  things
necessary to complete the entire work in all particulars, and  to
pay  all  taxes,  fees, permits, premiums  and  all  other  costs
required by the contract documents for the sum of:

   - ONE MILLION THREE HUNDRED FORTY THOUSAND -         Dollars

(  $1,340,000.00  ) in United States funds.

Bidder's Signature: _Glam Hardie_  Title _President_


2.   ADDENDA

     The  following  list  identifies  addenda  to  the  contract
documents  issued  after  the  call  for bids and  before  the  date
fixed for the receipt of bids:
```

Addendum Number	Date of Issue	Number of Pages
1	22 OCT 93	2
2	29 OCT 93	1
3	09 NOV 93	2
4	15 NOV 93	1

```
JOB NO: 93.05  SECTION 00-310  BIDDER'S INITIALS _GH_  PAGE 1 OF 3
```

Figure 4 Sample Bid Form

Occasionally changes have to be made to the documentation during the bidding process. This is accomplished by issuing addenda, instructing bidders to incorporate the changes into the project. Figure 5 shows an addendum for the townhouse project.

In order to make some changes to the contract later, owners and designers often issue fairly detailed tables or lists of alternate, separate, or unit price devices to be included by contractors into their bids. Figures 6, 7, and 8 show examples of such contractual adjustment devices.

```
                    THE ARCHITECTURAL GROUP, INC.
                     1250 West First Avenue, Vancouver
                        (Post Code and Telephone)

                                ADDENDUM

    1.   This Addendum is addressed to all prime contractors who have
         contract  documents  to prepare offers  for  the  undernoted
         project, designed by this office.

    2.   Project Identification:
              Job No.:  93.05      10-Unit Townhouse Complex

    3.   Addendum Identification:
              Addendum No.: 4     Addendum Date: 15 NOV 93
         Contractors  shall acknowledge receipt of this  Addendum  in
         the appropriate space on the Bid Form.

    4.   Document Modification:
         This  Addendum shall become part of the  contract  documents
         for the project identified in Item 2 above.

    5.   Addendum Content:
         Make the following amendments to the documents as issued:
         1.   In Section 04-100, delete references to Type "N" mortar
              throughout and substitute Type "M" mortar therefor.
         2.   In Section 09-900, Paragraph 3.3, amend "two coats" to
              read "three coats."
    _____

    JOB NO: 93.05    SECTION 00-901    ADDENDUM # 4       PAGE 1 OF 1
```

Figure 5 Sample Addendum

3.4 Award of Contract

From the submitted bids, the owner (with the designer's advice and after reviewing the initial budget) will select the most suitable offer and, upon accepting it, brings about the primary contract. The unsuccessful bidders should be informed of the results and thanked for their interest.

A valid construction contract has five primary constituents:

1. **Mutual agreement**, being the acceptance of an offer. Such agreement should be unequivocal and unambiguous, and the deal should be struck between two willing parties, neither of whom is acting under any undue pressure (or duress).

2. **Consideration**, being the exchange of value (the building for the money). Note that the value does not have to be equal on both sides of the deal. A contractor might bid $100,000 on a job which is worth only $90,000 to the owner, and vice versa).

```
ALTERNATE PRICES

The offer entered on Page 1 of the Proposal Form is based on  the
documents issued for bidding purposes. If and when authorized  by
the architect, we shall provide and install the following
alternative items of work on the same terms and conditions.  The
contract amount shall be adjusted by the net amount of the  extra
or credit sums stated below for each item so authorized.

Item 1. To delete Section 09-450 Stone Facings and to  substitute
therefor Section 04-400 Stone Veneers:

     Net Extra:_____($_____)

     or Credit:_____($_____)

Item  2.  To delete single glazing throughout and  to  substitute
therefor double glazing thoughout as specified in Section 08-800:

     Net Extra:_____($_____)

     or Credit:_____($_____)
```

Figure 6 Sample Alternate Prices Form

3. **Genuine intention**, an abstract concept best expressed by hard copy in the form of drawings, specifications, bid forms, and other appropriate documentation that can be used as evidence of what was intended to be done by each of the parties.

4. **Legal capacity**, concerning the status of the parties regarding age, citizenship, mental state, and so on. Nonlegal aspects of capacity have to do with experience, credit rating, ability to do the proposed job, and so on.

5. **Lawful object**, concerning the purpose or object of the building contract. The contract should not contain illegal provisions or be itself a legal contract to construct a building for an illicit purpose or activity.

In awarding a construction contract, the owner (or the designer) should have regard to these elements of contract to ensure that a sound relationship is created between the parties to the contract. Although there is no legislated requirement to have construction contracts prepared in written form, the practical advantages of doing so far outweigh any reason to risk an oral contract. An oral contract may be perfectly valid, but it is often difficult to enforce; written contracts are preferable. If all elements are satisfied, the contract can be signed (and sealed if necessary), and construction can start.

```
SEPARATE PRICES

The offer entered on Page 1 of the Proposal Form is based on  the
documents issued for bidding purposes. If and when authorized  by
the architect, we shall provide and install the following
ADDITIONAL items of work on the same terms and conditions.  The
contract amount shall be adjusted by the net amount of the  extra
sums stated below for each item so authorized.

Item 1. To ADD athletic equipment specified in Section 11-480:

     Net Extra:_____($_____)

Item 2. To ADD smoke detector system specified in Section 16-600:

     Net Extra:_____($_____)
```

Figure 7 Sample Separate Prices Form

UNIT PRICES

The contractor submits the following unit prices to be used to adjust the contract amount for additions or deletions authorized by the architect. The prices include costs for labor, materials, equipments, overhead, taxes, profit and all other costs. Methods of measurement used to determine quantities of work shall be as described in the various Sections identified by number below:

SECTION	ITEM OF WORK	UNITS	ADD	DDT
02-200	machine excavation	m^3		
	machine trenching	m^3		
	machine backfill	m^3		
	hand excavation	m^3		
	hand backfill	m^3		
03-180	formwork to foundations	m^2		
	formwork to walls	m^2		
03-200	rebar in foundations	kg		
	rebar in walls	kg		
03-300	concrete (20 mPa)	m^3		
	concrete (25 mPa)	m^3		

Figure 8 Sample Unit Prices Form

4.0 The Building Process

4.1 Site Startup

One major responsibility of the general contractor or project manager is to lay out the site in an efficient manner so as to be able to conveniently build the building. By site layout is meant the determination of the legal property lines and building dimensions, the establishment of the actual building location and services on the site, the supply of temporary services, the provision of field offices and fences, the demarcation of site areas suitable for storage sheds and parking, and the direction of traffic both onto and off the site. Such work is usually done to accord with survey plans already approved by local authorities for the project in question. Figure 9 shows a layout plan as it might be prepared by the contractor for the townhouse project, corresponding to the designer's approved plot plan, and indicating locations of temporary services and other facilities.

After the site has been laid out on paper, then work can actually commence by physically moving temporary offices and sheds into place, erecting fences and hoardings, connecting temporary services, placing markers and batter boards to locate the new building lines and levels, starting the preliminary accumulations of stored materials, and so on. For further details on field engineering, refer to Section 01–050.

4.2 Procurement of Subcontracts

During the bidding process, the general contractor will receive bids from subcontractors and suppliers for specific sections of the work. Until the general contractor has been awarded the overall contract, he or she obviously cannot accept any of the subcon-

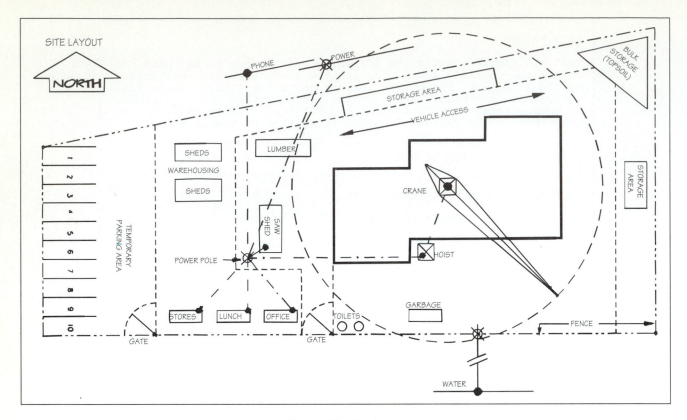

Figure 9 Site Layout

tract bids. Immediately upon award of the overall contract, the general contractor should move quickly to accept the best offers of the various sub-trades and suppliers and sign them up to individual subcontracts, consistent with the objectives of the primary contract. The general contractor should also quickly establish a timetable confirming expected due dates, warranties, payments, penalties, and other details pertinent to each subcontract.

4.3 Construction Procedure

The actual sequence of construction of the project by the various trades involved is usually achieved under the direction of a competent superintendent. He or she should apply the principles of good construction management to the process. It is appropriate to introduce here two aspects of construction management which have a major bearing on the successful progress of any construction project, namely **planning** and **scheduling**.

By dictionary definition, *planning* means the development of a scheme of action, whereas *scheduling* (usually) means a written statement of explanatory details, often in a classified form. In construction terminology, *planning* primarily concerns the arrangement of building activities, whereas *scheduling*

primarily concerns the timing of these activities, and their presentation in tabular or graphical form. A sec-

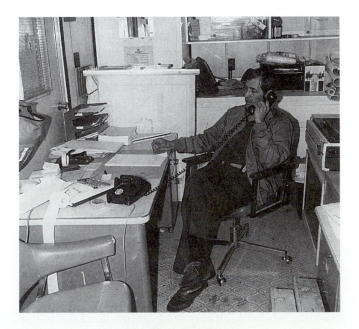

Site Management

The job superintendent has overall control of construction progress. This picture shows a super in a site office arranging contracts by phone for construction of portions of the building. (UBC Architecture)

ondary objective is to produce essentially subjective (or verbal) data converted to a suitably objective (or numerical) form capable of analysis by either humans or machines. Planning and scheduling are usually combined on construction projects by utilizing either bar charts or precedence networks. A simplified example of each is shown in Figures 10 and 11. For more information and detail, as well as alternative ways of organizing construction work, the student is referred to any of several books on construction management.

Figure 12 represents the completed precedence diagram for a small building such as the ten-unit townhouse project.

4.4 Payments

As the work progresses, the contractors require to be paid. In a stipulated sum contract, this process consists of basing regular applications for payment on a schedule of values, agreed upon prior to the start of work. Figure 13 shows a typical schedule; Figure 14 shows a typical application.

In a cost-plus-fee type of contract, there cannot be a prior schedule of values to be agreed upon. Payments are therefore made on the basis of documentation submitted periodically by the contractor to the owner or designer. The key issue in this type of

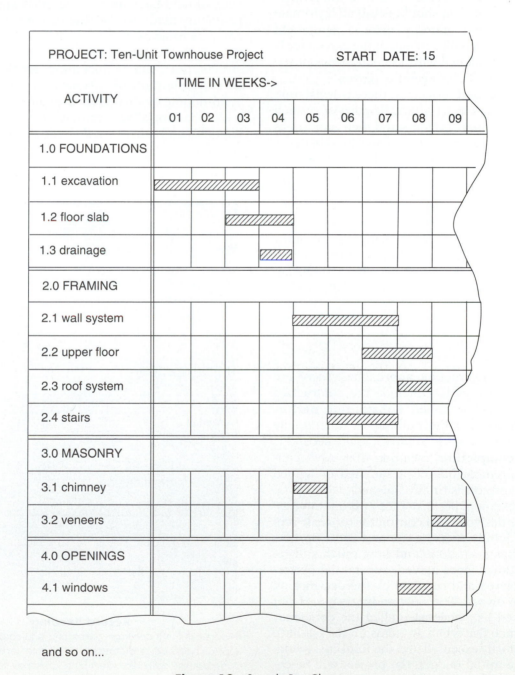

PROJECT: Ten-Unit Townhouse Project   START DATE: 15

ACTIVITY	TIME IN WEEKS->								
	01	02	03	04	05	06	07	08	09
1.0 FOUNDATIONS									
1.1 excavation	▨	▨	▨						
1.2 floor slab			▨	▨					
1.3 drainage				▨					
2.0 FRAMING									
2.1 wall system					▨	▨	▨		
2.2 upper floor							▨	▨	
2.3 roof system								▨	
2.4 stairs					▨	▨			
3.0 MASONRY									
3.1 chimney					▨				
3.2 veneers								▨	
4.0 OPENINGS									
4.1 windows								▨	

and so on...

Figure 10 Sample Bar Chart

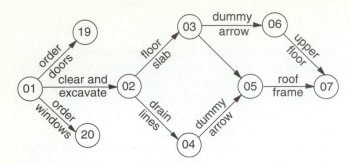

Figure 11 Sample Precedence Network Diagram

contract is the precise definition of what constitutes cost. The documentation should detail all legitimate costs, such as payroll, material invoices, equipment rentals, taxes, and the like, to which the agreed fee is added, all in accordance with the conditions of the construction contract between the parties.

In most states and provinces, there is legislation concerning builders' lien rights. The purpose of such legislation is to protect builders and their employees from doing work on property owned by others for which they may not be paid. Although there are some regional differences, the legislation usually operates by requiring the owner to hold back a percentage (often 10 percent) of money owed to the contractor in each pay period right up to the end of the job, to create a lien fund. If there are no claims filed against the fund, the hold-back money is subsequently released to the contractor after a stated period. Reference to local legislation will provide specific details on this topic.

4.5 Closeout

As the end of construction approaches, there are two significant stages to conclude the contractual process. The first is called **substantial performance**, meaning that the building is functionally operational and ready for occupancy; the second is called **total completion**, meaning that every contractual requirement has been satisfied or agreed upon and the project is finally finished.

When substantial performance is about to be established, the designer and contractor (or their representatives) jointly visit the site and agree on how much work has been done and how much still remains to be done. Once agreed, substantial performance is declared and certified by the designer on behalf of the owner. The outstanding work is put onto an agreed list, variously called the deficiency list or the punch list; when all items on the list have been satisfactorily executed and the final cost reconciled with the initial budget, the project will be declared complete.

Between these two stages, a number of important things happen. The contractor must remove all remaining temporary services, such as site offices, cranes and hoists, rough debris, and so on. All warranties and guarantees required by the contract documents must be furnished by the contractor to the owner. A certificate of occupancy almost always has to be acquired from the city or other government agency; this critical issue should be researched in context with other codes and regulations. Occupancy by the owner may be completed in one stage, or it may be phased in on different parts of the project while the contractor is still working on other parts.

Arrangements also have to be made for the release of hold-back money and other appropriate adjustments made to the final accounts. On large or complex projects, there may be an actual hand-over procedure, in which the outgoing contractor instructs the owner's incoming employees on the correct operation of various services (such as air-conditioning or surveillance systems). On some projects, a janitorial service may be employed to wash windows and mirrors, polish tile work, dust off light

Record Keeping

It is essential that accurate written and photographic records be kept of construction progress. This picture represents a typical page from the daily diary kept by a job superintendent. (UBC Architecture)

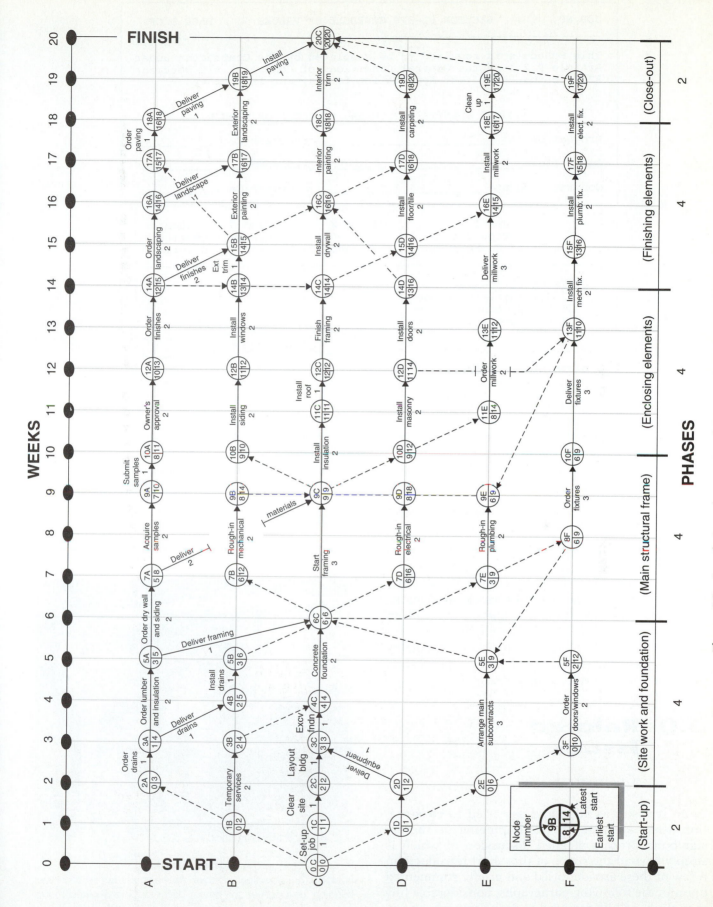

Figure 12 Sample Precedence Network Diagram for a Small Building

25

This Schedule is required to be completed by the Contractor under Article 9.2.1 of the General Conditions of Contract, AIA Document A201, before the first Application for Payment is approved.

PROJECT IDENTIFICATION AND SCHEDULE OF VALUES

Project Title:_____ Contract No:_____

Contractor:_____ Phone No:_____

Contract Amount:_____ Contract Date:_____

Column 1 Section Titles and Numbers	Column 2 Names of Subtrades	Column 3 $ Values of Work	Column 4 Remarks & Notes
DIVISION 01 GENERAL 01-001 Initial Expenses 01-002 Continuing Ditto 01-021 Cash Allowances			
DIVISION 03 CONCRETE 03-100 Formwork 03-200 Reinforcement 03-300 Concrete (cast) 03-400 Concrete (P.C.)			
Carried Forward	to page 2		

Figure 13 Sample Schedule of Values Form

fixtures, remove fingerprints, vacuum carpets, clean out toilets, basins, and bathtubs, stock up toilet accessories with soap and paper, and generally clean up the whole project, to make the building ready for the new owners. Once all of these finalizing processes are finished, the construction contract and the project are considered to be complete.

5.0 Related Issues

5.1 In General

In an industry as large and as varied as construction, there are many issues impinging on the design/build process detailed discussion of which is simply beyond the scope of this short introduction. A few of these are identified and briefly commented upon in the following paragraphs; considerable further study will be required to make one adequately

Coffee Break

In most urban locations, mobile canteens visit construction sites bringing fresh coffee, soft drinks, and snacks for workers to purchase during their break periods. (BCIT Building Technology)

This Application is required to be submitted by the Contractor under Article 9.3.1 of the General Conditions of Contract, AIA Document A201, before Payment will be certified by the Architect.

PROJECT IDENTIFICATION AND APPLICATION FOR PAYMENT

Project Title:_____ Contract No:_____

Contractor:_____ Phone No:_____

Contract Amount:_____ Contract Date:_____

Column 1 Section Titles and Numbers	Column 2 $ Values (TOTALS)	Column 3 Percents Complete	Column 4 $ Values Complete

DIVISION 01 GENERAL
  01-001 Initial Expenses
  01-002 Continuing Ditto
  01-021 Cash Allowances			

16-500 Lighting
  16-900 Controls
  16-950 Testing			

TOTAL VALUE OF WORK COMPLETED	- - - - -		$
DEDUCT:			
1. Retainage (Art S.G.C 15.1)	$		
2. Total of Previous Payments:	$		$
PAYMENT # _____ NOW DUE TO THE CONTRACTOR:			$

Figure 14 Sample Application for Payment Form

knowledgeable about each topic and the other related issues.

5.2 Changes in the Work

In the construction of most buildings, some changes are inevitable, arising from owner's instructions regarding alternatives, the belated discovery of design or construction problems or deficiencies, nondelivery or unavailability of components, building code or safety inspection requirements, and so on. Construction contracts and procedures should therefore permit necessary changes to occur. Figure 15 shows a typical change order form, to suit a change to the townhouse project.

5.3 Computer Applications

Virtually every facet of the design/build process lends itself to computer application. Feasibility studies can be analyzed, promotional brochures and presentation graphics developed, structural and mechanical calculations checked, architectural drawings prepared, specifications word-processed, materials and waste estimated, labor force man-hours balanced, equipment time and costs recorded, payroll and deductions data issued, invoices automatically sent and paid, and so on. Recently, the application of computer technology to robots has been successfully introduced into some actual on-site building excava-

```
                    THE ARCHITECTURAL GROUP, INC.
                    1250 West First Avenue, Vancouver
                        (Post Code and Telephone)


                            CHANGE ORDER

 1.    Project Identification: Job # 93.05  10-Unit Townhouse

 2.    Change Order Identification: No.: 4  Date:   15 NOV 93

 3.    Party Identification & Copy Distribution:

           The Owner:        ABC Holdings, Inc., Vancouver
           The Contractor:   Concourse Construction, Inc.
           Copies to Owner, Contractor, Designer, Superintendent.

 4.    Document Modification:

       This Change Order shall become part of the  contract
       documents for the project identified in Item 1 above.

           a)   Other contracts affected:    none
           b)   Effect on contract time:     none
           c)   Effect on contract cost:     see 5 below

 5.    Authorized Changes:

       Make  the following amendments to the contract on the  terms
       agreed to in the Change Orders listed below:

       1.   Extra Work Order #4 (Formwork)   ADD  $ 4,500.00
       2.   Extra Work Order #5 (Paving)     ADD    1,700.00
       3.   Notice of Deletion #1 (Flagpole) DDT      900.00
           _____

           Total ADDITION to Contract Sum:       $ 5,300.00
           Original Contract Amount:         $ 1,340,000.00
           Revised Contract Amount to date:  $ 1,345,300.00

 6.    Approvals:         (signatures required)          (dates)

       Contractor:   _____  _____

       Owner:        _____  _____

       Designer:     _____  _____

       _____
       JOB NO: 93.05    SECTION 00-902   CHANGE ORDER 4   PAGE 1 OF 1
```

Figure 15 Sample Change Order Form

tion and erection processes. The incursion of the personal computer into almost every aspect of almost every business is one of the major societal shifts of our time. This is particularly true in the construction industry, and this topic is therefore worthy of further study in its own right. Figure 16 shows a computer-generated image of a nonexistent building, and is included here to show just how real such images can appear using currently available technology.

5.4 Organized Labor

If one were to divide the entire construction industry in two halves, one half would comprise most residential building. This half is not significantly involved with union labor, although some specific trades (such as plumbing and electrical) tend to show a higher-than-average proportion of organiza-

Figure 16 Computer Image. This shows the high level of quality, detail, and resolution that can be incorporated into computer-generated illustrations of non-existent (in this case) buildings. (UBC "Digital Folio" 1992 (page 91). Editor: J. Wojtowicz; Illustrator: K. Mah)

Building Progress

A commercial building begins to take shape. Excavation is complete, foundations are in, tower cranes and supplies are ready, and temporary facilities (toilets, etc.) are positioned. (UBC Architecture)

tion. The other half, comprising commercial, institutional, and industrial construction, tends to have a higher proportion of union labor (in trades such as carpentry, ironworking, steel erection, and masonry, as well as plumbing and electrical, to name a few). Although figures vary considerably from region to region and time to time, one might estimate that organized labor in the nonresidential sector comprises between one-third and one-half of this half of the overall work force. Regardless of the specific proportions, the crucial point to be understood is that mixing union and nonunion workers on one site can and will lead to problems, if the issue is not handled very carefully. It is generally better wherever possible to have each site completely union or nonunion, although some interface is inevitable and unavoidable. There have been many books written on topics dealing with labor relations, labor economics, organizational behavior, and the construction unions; a visit to any good public or college library will produce suitable titles.

5.5 Inspection and Safety

The intrusion of public and private authorities with vested interests in safety and security is an increasingly important aspect of the design/build process. Public officials in the form of building inspectors and others appear with increasing frequency on construction sites to check on everything from lunch room lighting to security of storage areas. Representatives of private manufacturing companies visit the site to see that their products are being properly utilized; financial houses send agents to ensure that their money in being well spent; others come to check on almost every other thing imaginable. These two important topics are dealt with in Section 01–005.

5.6 Energy and Pollution Controls

As the costs of energy continue to rise and the effects of environmental pollution are becoming ever more serious, more and more stringent controls are being brought into being to make buildings more energy efficient and environmentally friendly. Two examples will indicate some of the many trends in this direction:

1. Buildings are now being designed to be virtually airtight to ensure total control over the interior atmosphere. Such design requirements can be quantified and subsequently measured (by compression and leakage tests) to ensure compliance with legislation and contractual requirements.

2. Many dangerous products, such as CFC formerly used in refrigeration systems, some plastic insulations, and some synthetic glues, are no longer acceptable. Most city garbage disposal facilities will not accept many toxic waste construction products, such as gypsum board and volatile fluids, in bulk.

Section 01–004 Dimensioning

1.0 Introduction

1.1 In General

In construction materials and products, there are three aspects of dimensions with which one usually has to contend: nominal dimensions, actual dimensions, and manufacturer's tolerances. A simple illustration is found in carpentry work, wherein the common wooden stud has a nominal cross-sectional size (in imperial dimensions) of 2″ × 4″, while the actual size is 1½″ × 3½″, and the lumber mills are permitted to produce two manufactured sizes, depending on whether the wood is seasoned or unseasoned. In masonry, concrete cinder blocks are referred to as having a nominal face area of (say) 200 × 400 mm (using metric units), while the actual dimensions are 190 × 390. The final manufactured sizes of blocks made to conform to either Canadian or American standards will again vary slightly (within stated limits or tolerances) from both the nominal and actual dimensions. It is of course important for all people involved with sizing drawings, specifying products, or laying out buildings to consider this matter of nominal, actual, and manufactured dimensions with some care.

1.2 In Particular

Regardless of whether one is using nominal, actual, or manufactured dimensions, one must also determine whether **metric** or **imperial** dimensions are being used. The metric (or SI) system of measurement is now officially used in virtually every country of the world, with the principal exception of the United States. In the United States, there is a slow but perceptible movement toward official adoption of the metric system, although there is still some resistance to it in the popular marketplace. However, the automobile industry, the pharmaceutical industry, the military and scientific communities, much of the academic community, and the wine industry have already largely adopted the metric system for day-to-day measurement components. It may be of interest to learn that the official standard for linear measurement in the United States, namely the yard of three feet measured on a bar of platinum located in Washington, D.C., is now confirmed by reference to the length of the SI meter, itself standardized to the wavelength of light emitted from a specific element. A brief explanation of the SI metric system follows for the benefit of those who do not encounter it in daily life.

Table 1
METRIC RELATIONSHIPS

Linear Units × 10	Area Units × 100	Volume Units × 1,000
basic = 1 mm	basic = 1 mm²	basic = 1 mm³
10 mm = 1 cm	100 mm² = 1 cm²	1,000 mm³ = 1 cm³
10 cm = 1 dm	100 cm² = 1 dm³	1,000 cm³ = 1 dm³
10 dm = 1 m	100 dm² = 1 m²	1,000 dm³ = 1 m³
10 m = 1 dam	100 m² = 1 dam²	1,000 m³ = 1 dam³
10 dam = 1 hm	100 dam² = 1 hm²	1,000 dam³ = 1 hm³
10 hm = 1 km	100 hm² = 1 km²	1,000 hm³ = 1 km³

2.0 Metric Dimensions

2.1 In General

The metric system is simple, rational, consistent, and coherent, in that all of its parts fit together. It consists of three primary elements: numerical, nominal, and prefix. The **numerical** base is 10; all arithmetical functions are either multiples or decimal fractions of 10. Thus each linear unit is smaller or larger than its predecessor by a factor of 10, each square unit by 100, and each volume unit by 1,000. This is illustrated in Table 1. The **nominal** element identifies each unit by name. In construction material considerations, one must contend with length, mass, capacity, and temperature; the names for the basic units to describe these attributes are meters (m), grams (g), liters (l), and degrees Celsius (°C), respectively. The **prefixes** used in conjunction with these names are shown in Table 2.

2.2 Relationships

The relationship between length, capacity (volume), and mass (weight) is established by considering a cube having sides measuring 10 cm and therefore a volume of 1,000 cm³ (10 × 10 × 10). This volume is called one liter. One liter of cold (but not freezing) water weighs (or has a mass of) one kilogram or 1,000 grams. Therefore, this relationship is established: 1 cm³ = 1 ml = 1g. One gram is about the weight of an ordinary small paper clip. One thousand kilograms of any commodity equals one metric ton.

The metric temperature scale considers water at the point of freezing to be at 0 degrees Celsius and at the point of boiling to be at 100 degrees Celsius. On this scale, the normal temperature for human blood is 37 degrees; 39 or 40 would represent a serious fever. A really hot bath would be around 50 degrees. A cool spring day would be 10 degrees, a pleasant summer day would be 25 degrees, and during a hot spell, temperatures might rise above 35 degrees. On construction sites, care should be taken if temperatures drop below 5 degrees or rise much above 30 degrees Celsius. Incidentally, the Celsius scale and the Fahrenheit scale coincide at 40 degrees below zero, when it is too cold for most people to care.

2.3 Applications

Throughout this book, dimensions are given first in metric units and then in imperial units. Wherever possible, rationalized (or soft) conversions have been used, to make the magnitude of dimensions easier to grasp and therefore more meaningful. A hard conversion simply converts imperial dimensions arithmetically and directly to their metric

Table 2
METRIC PREFIXES

Latin Prefixes			Greek Prefixes		
deci	(d)	means 1/10th	deka	(da)	means 10 times
centi	(c)	means 1/100th	hecta	(h)	means 100 times
milli	(m)	means 1/1000th	kilo	(k)	means 1,000 times

used in the United States) are hard-converted to 1,219 × 2,438 mm, using 25.4 mm to the inch. Soft conversion produces rationalized dimensions of 1,200 × 2,400 mm (as used in Canada). The relationship between plywood sizes and stud spacing must also be rationalized in both systems. For example, typical stud spacing to support plywood panels of standard width in imperial dimensions is 16 in. (because 16 is a factor of 48); similarly, such spacing in metric dimensions would be 400 mm (not 406.33 mm) to fit in with the 1,200 mm width of metric-dimensioned plywood.

3.0 Imperial Dimensions

3.1 In General

The imperial system of measurement is not so much an integrated system as a collection of separate customary ways of quantifying objects, based on traditional precedence.

3.2 Relationships

Relationships (insofar as they exist) among the units are largely arbitrary or arranged for expediency. The main units of linear measure originated from the proportions and characteristics of the human body, such as the length of the foot, the width of the hand,

Planer Mill
After logs have been debarked and converted to rough lumber by sawing, selected joists and studs are cleaned up and brought to accurate dimensions by passing them through planing machines. (BCIT Audio-Visual Production)

equivalents or vice versa, whereas a soft conversion presents corresponding but new dimensions, usually rounded off to produce convenient magnitudes.

For example, the dimensions of a sheet of plywood having imperial dimensions of 4'-0″ × 8'-0″ (as

Steel Deck Mill
Flat steel sheets of selected thickness are forced at medium speed through a system of adjustable rollers which can impart any desired cross-sectional profile and dimension to the sheets. (BCIT Audio-Visual Production)

Table 3
LINEAR AND AREA MEASUREMENT

Linear Measure				Area Measure		
12	inches	= 1 foot		144	square inches	= 1 square foot
3	feet	= 1 yard		9	square feet	= 1 square yard
1,760	yards	= 1 mile		4,840	square yards	= 1 acre
5,280	feet	= 1 mile		640	acres	= 1 square mile

Table 4
VOLUME AND WEIGHT MEASUREMENT

Volume Measure				Weight Measure		
1,728 cubic inches	=	1 cubic foot		16 drams	=	1 ounce
27 cubic feet	=	1 cubic yard		16 ounces	=	1 pound
(144 cubic inches	=	1 board foot)		2,000 pounds	=	1 ton

the distance from the center of the forehead to the tips of the fingers, and so on. Units of volume or capacity measure include the American gallon, which is different in size from the English gallon, because the original measure was abolished and replaced in England, whereas the old measure was retained for use in America. With respect to the measurement of weight, the former English system of ounces, pounds, stones, hundredweights, and long tons (2,240 lb.) has been simplified to some extent in America by use of the short ton of 2,000 lb. and decimal fractions thereof. Readers are referred to any of the many books that have been written on the development of systems of weights and measures for further detail on this interesting and important topic. Tables 3 (Linear and Area), 4 (Volume and Weight), 5 (Liquid and Dry), 6 (Time and Angular), and 7 (Miscellaneous) show American values for various units of imperial measure

Table 5
LIQUID AND DRY MEASUREMENT

Liquid Measure				Dry Measure		
4 gills	=	1 pint		2 pints	=	1 quart
2 pints	=	1 quart		8 quarts	=	1 peck
4 quarts	=	1 gallon		4 pecks	=	1 bushel

Table 6
TIME AND ANGULAR MEASUREMENT

Time Measure				Angular Measure		
60 seconds	=	1 minute		60 seconds	=	1 minute
60 minutes	=	1 hour		60 minutes	=	1 degree
24 hours	=	1 day		90 degrees	=	1 right angle
7 days	=	1 week		4 right angles	=	360 degrees
62 weeks	=	1 year		360 degrees	=	1 circle

Table 7
MISCELLANEOUS MEASURES

Miscellaneous Measures			Imperial to Metric Conversion		
1 gill	=	4 fluid ounces	1 pound	=	454 grams
1 pound	=	7000 grains	1 yard	=	0.914 meters
1 gallon	=	8.330 pounds	1 gallon	=	3.785 liters

4.0 Conversions

4.1 In General

It is occasionally necessary to convert dimensions, weights, or other physical attributes of materials from metric units to imperial units, and vice versa. Some of the factors used for such conversions for frequently encountered units are listed in Table 8, together with their reciprocals. Some examples follow the table.

4.2 In Particular

For example, 1 m³ equals 1.31 yd.³, whereas 1 yd.³ equals 0.76 m³. To convert temperatures, multiply degrees C by 1.8 and add 32; for example, 10 degrees C equals (10 × 1.8 = 18 + 32 =) 50 degrees F. Conversely, subtract 32 from degrees F and multiply by 0.56; 50 degrees F equals (50 − 32 = 18 × 0.56 =) 10 degrees C. For an approximation, one can double degrees C and add 30, or deduct 30 from degrees F and divide by two (−10 C × 2 = −20 + 30 = 10 F;

(a)

(b)

(c)

Product Marketing
Most building products are packaged: (a) steel cans of contact cement, (b) paper bags of portland cement, and (c) plastic sacks of mortar cement. (BCIT Building Technology)

Table 8
METRIC/IMPERIAL DIMENSION CONVERSION

Metric Units	Factor	Reciprocal	Imperial Units
	→	←	
Degrees C (+ 32)	1.8000	0.5556	Degrees F − 32
Lineal meters	1.0936	0.9144	Lineal yards
Square meters	1.1956	0.8361	Square yards
Cubic meters	1.3079	0.7646	Cubic yards
Hectares	2.4711	0.4047	Acres
Kilograms	2.2046	0.4536	Pounds
Kg/m^3	0.0624	16.0184	Lb./ft.^{3}
Kilometers	0.6314	1.6094	Miles
Liters	0.2642	3.7854	Gallons (U.S.)
Liters	0.2200	4.4560	Gallons (U.K.)
Tonnes	1.1023	0.9072	Tons (short)*
Tonnes	1.0161	0.9842	Tons (long)*

* A short ton = 2,000 lb.; a long ton = 2,240 lb.

and 10 F − 30 = −20 × .5 = 10 C). For an explanation of the board foot system used to convert imperial-sized lumber from length to volume measure in carpentry work, refer to Section 06–100 (Part 4.2). Finally, a note of caution is included here regarding the fact that while there is no difference between one square unit (metric or imperial) and one unit square, there is a considerable difference between ten square units and ten units square. "Ten square feet" equals a geometric shape *A* containing 10 ft.^{2} of area; "ten feet square" equals a square *B* having sides each 10 ft. long and containing 100 ft.^{2} of area, an area 10 times as large as *A*. Clearly, one must be careful about how one expresses quantities, regardless of the units selected.

Bulk Supplies
Many building materials (such as the sand and gravel shown stockpiled here) are provided in bulk in loose form. These are ordered by volume or weight, depending on local practice. (BCIT Building Technology)

Section 01-005
Inspection and Safety

1.0 Introduction

A book on construction procedures requires some mention of inspection and safety. There would be not much point in specifying methods to be followed or standards to be achieved if no inspections were undertaken to confirm compliance with contractual requirements and legislated obligations.

2.0 Building Inspection

2.1 Preamble

The following items represent aspects of building inspections worthy of examination at the preliminary, interim, or final stages of the overall construction process.

2.2 In General

Regardless of the specific construction process being examined, building inspectors will usually check on the following procedural aspects of construction work:

Adherence to material or system manufacturer's instructions for proper preparation, use, or application of building products.

Allowances permitted by manufacturing and installation processes.

Appearance of surfaces exposed to view (free of imperfections, blemishes, or defects).

Conformity with contract documentation.

Cracking: some is acceptable; some is not (it depends on the trade).

Drawing development for shopwork or layout.

Guarantees: examination of relevant documents.

Handling of materials on site.

Preparation of surfaces and work areas, where appropriate.

Materials: provision of correct products or systems.

Safety: compliance with regulations.

Samples: testing and reporting on same.

Storage of materials on site.

Subsequent trades: proper preparation for such work.

Utilization of correct types of materials.

Unless otherwise specified, it is a general expectation that construction work will be installed square and true, level or plumb, tight and secure, and neatly cut and fitted where necessary, so as to operate or function properly. In many cases, cut edges and fastenings are required to be concealed from view with trim or capping pieces. Work formed to special angle, bevel, circle, curve, or slope should be correctly set out to accurately produce the intended effect.

2.3 In Particular

In addition to the foregoing generalities, inspectors will examine the specific categories of work as described in the various trade sections of this book for most or all of the features indicated as good practice (or as precautions to watch out for) in each of these sections. There are many comprehensive guides to construction inspection published, to which readers may also refer, one example of which is the *Construction Inspection Manual*, published by Building News, Inc., Los Angeles, CA 90034.

3.0 Safety Inspection

3.1 Preamble

The topic of safety can be divided into two subtopics: safety in building **design** and safety in construction **procedure**. Safety in design is beyond the scope of this book; safety in procedure is primarily a function of workplace issues and as such is addressed in this section.

3.2 Safety Issues

Virtually every construction **activity** has some safety components. At the most basic level, all construction workers should be in reasonable mental and medical health, in good physical condition, and have had training (or at least proper instruction) in the tasks expected of them. They should be dressed in clothing appropriate to their work, and should avoid working with untied shoelaces, long hair, loose caps, ill-fitting boots, or torn or ragged shirts or pants. Ornamental finger rings, wrist bracelets, and necklaces (as well as slings, casts, or bandages) can all be hazardous, as they can catch in equipment or cause one to falter.

Virtually every construction **trade** has some safety problems. For example, many workers doing drywall and plastering like to use leg stilts to reach high places. Properly used, they are safe, but they can lead (and have led) to serious injury. Workers in the painting, roofing, and stucco trades frequently use and move ladders in their work; they don't always secure these ladders in position in the prescribed manner. Steel erectors often complain that the use of safety belts can cause them more problems than would the accidents that might arise from not using them; they also often prefer to use soft-soled canvas "sneakers" instead of steel-toed shoes. Some excavators occasionally skimp on proper shoring when digging pits or trenches, and cases have occurred where workers have been buried alive as a result. Carpenters should use proper waist aprons to hold their tools and accessories, and should not store small nails and tacks in their mouths (as many do), regardless of how convenient it may be to spit them out one at a time for nailing. Steel stair pans, intended to be filled later with concrete or terrazzo, should be temporarily filled with plywood boards to prevent people tripping on the edges of the pans. Guy wires temporarily supporting parts of the building frame should be tested for tension before release. Care must be taken with cranes and hoists not to exceed rated load or speed capacities or to over-reach recommended radii. And so it goes on, through the rest of the 60 or 70 trades one might encounter on larger institutional projects. In construction, there are many large and vital gravitational, physical, electrical, and other natural forces at work, which workers ignore at their peril. Safety is everyone's business.

Virtually every construction **site** has safety concerns. It is a good practice (and in some regions a re-

First Aid Post

At suitable locations or where required by law, there should be clearly marked cabinets with suitable medical supplies, fire extinguishers, warning air-horns, stretchers, and flashlights. (BCIT Building Technology)

quirement) for the general contractor or project manager to develop a safety plan and post copies of it for the benefit of all persons on the site. The plan (which would be similar to Figure 9 in Section 01–003) should indicate most or all of the following elements:

1. The property lines bounding the site.
2. Surrounding streets and access to and from the site.
3. The position of the building under construction.
4. The position of all semipermanent cranes and hoists.
5. The location of first-aid facilities and phones.
6. The location of firefighting equipment and hydrants.
7. Offices, storage, parking, and other restricted areas.

8. Rules of conduct to promote safety and avoid accidents.

9. Phone numbers of emergency services and personnel.

3.3 Safety Inspection

Regardless of the specific construction process being examined, safety inspectors should check on the following aspects of construction work:

Cleanup and disposal of debris, especially toxic wastes.

Conformity with legislated requirements and local regulations, especially of hazardous work such as blasting or demolition.

Tools and equipment: correct use of appropriate devices.

Trade practices relative to the specialty under review.

Safety requirements such as protective clothing, barricades, harnesses, lights, and warnings.

Construction workers should consider the safety of themselves, their work colleagues, and the general public.

Safety Harness
When work has to be done at open edges of floor slabs on high buildings, workers should be secured to safety life lines. (UBC Architecture)

3.4 Safety Legislation

In response to obligations to the general public and requests from the building industry, governments and other public agencies have developed fairly stringent legislation and regulations to control the safety of construction activities. Most regional or local governments model their safety legislation through state or provincial occupational safety boards to more or less meet or indeed exceed the standards set by federal agencies.

In the United States, the Occupational Safety and Health Administration (OSHA), a branch of the federal Department of Labor in Washington, is the governing agency. Descriptions of construction safety standards are listed in U.S. government publication OSHA 2207 (revised 1991 edition) entitled *Construction Industry Safety and Health Standards* (29 CFR Subparts 1926/1910).

In Canada, there is a corresponding authority: the Occupational Safety and Health Branch (OSHB) of the federal Department of Labour in Ottawa. Most provinces have their own Occupational Safety and Health Act (also referred to as OSHA) or one similar to it. Canadian OSHB requirements are generally consistent with the U.S. OSHA standards. Some OSHB section titles (corresponding to OSHA titles) have been selected from the Canadian Labor Code (published by Butterworth's Canada Ltd., revised 1991 edition) as mentioned in Part 3.7 following.

3.5 OSHA Sections (United States)

In this paragraph, some OSHA sections have been selected as being representative of general safety issues affecting most of the trades detailed in this book. The appropriate OSHA Subpart 1926 title is shown opposite each alphabetical subpart:

Subpart A   General

Subpart B   Interpretation

Subpart C   Safety and Health

Subpart D   Environmental Controls

Subpart E   Personal Protection

Subpart F   Fire Protection

Subpart G   Signs and Barricades

Subpart H   Materials Handling

Subpart I   Tools (Hand & Power)

Subpart J   Welding & Cutting

Subpart K   Electrical

Subpart L   Scaffolding

Subpart M   Openings (Floors & Walls)

Subpart N   Cranes, Derricks, Hoists

Subpart O   Mechanized Equipment

Subpart P   Excavations

Subpart Q   Concrete & Masonry

Subpart R   Steel Erection

Subpart S   Underground Work

Subpart T   Demolition

Subpart U   Blasting

Subpart W   Roll-Over Protection

3.6 Specific Issues (United States)

In this paragraph, specific safety issues, selected from the foregoing OSHA subparts, are listed alphabetically. In some cases, items have been paraphrased or edited for brevity or clarity, and are thus not exhaustive; in every case, reference to the original source is made. Each entry title is followed by its appropriate OSHA decimal reference number:

Barricades (.202)

1. Barricades for traffic control shall conform to the specified standard (ANSI D6).

Breathing Protection (.103)

1. Wherever there is a hazard of any kind to respiration, breathing equipment shall be provided by the employer.

2. Depending on the type of hazard (oxygen deficiency, gas, dust, etc.), specific equipment is described and required.

Eye Protection (.102)

1. Eye and face protection is required wherever work presents potential injury.

2. Such protection must conform to a specified standard (ANSI Z87) and be kept clean and serviceable.

3. Workers who wear corrective lenses must use goggles which will accommodate their vision requirements.

4. There are special requirements for welders and others using radiant energy.

Preventive Practices
Measures can usually be taken to prevent accidents from occurring. In this photo, an extension ladder is seen chained to scaffolding to prevent significant slippage (and theft). (BCIT Building Technology)

Fire Prevention (.151)

1. Care shall be taken to eliminate sources of ignition (faulty electrical devices, poorly maintained or improperly positioned gas-powered engines or heaters, careless cigarette smoking, etc.).

2. Consideration shall be given to the placement of temporary buildings, storage areas, and access roads, to minimize fire risks and maximize fire-suppression response capabilities.

Guardrails, Handrails, Covers (.500)

1. A standard wood guardrail shall be 42 in. high. It shall consist of a 2 × 4 smooth top rail, a 1 × 6 intermediate rail at midpoint, a 1 × 4 toeboard at bottom, 2 × 4 vertical posts spaced not to exceed 8 ft., and supports. It shall resist a pressure of 200 lb. applied laterally to the top rail.

2. Specifications are also given for temporary guardrails made of structural or tubular steel.

3. Openings in floors shall be guarded by a standard rail or a hinged cover or both. Where access is necessary, the access shall be offset to prevent people walking directly into the open space. Manhole openings shall have the permanent manhole cover or a temporary cover in place except when directly in use.

4. Wall openings, where the sill of the opening is less than 3 ft. above the floor and the drop on the other side is 4 ft. or more, shall be guarded with a standard rail.

5. Open-sided floors or platforms more than 6 ft. above adjacent levels shall be guarded with a standard rail. In special cases, construction runways 18 in. wide may have the rails removed from one side for temporary convenience.

6. Roof openings shall be guarded as described for floor openings. Covers shall support a weight of 200 lb.

7. Safety training is mandatory for all employees working on roofs where there is a risk of falling over the edge.

Head Protection (.100)

1. Helmets (hard hats) are required where there is risk of injury from impact, falling or flying objects, or electrical shock.

2. Helmets shall conform to a specified standard (ANSI Z89).

Hearing Protection (.101)

1. If noise levels exceed those in OSHA .52 (see **noise levels**), hearing protection is mandatory.

2. Ear protection devices inserted into the ear shall be individually determined by competent acoustical personnel.

Housekeeping (.25)

1. Work areas and passageways shall be kept clear of scrap lumber and other debris.

2. Combustible debris shall be safely removed at regular intervals.

3. Appropriate containers shall be provided for the collection, separation, and removal of debris.

Illumination (.26)

1. Construction work areas—5 foot-candles.
2. Storage and passageways—3 foot-candles.
3. Site offices, lunch rooms—10 foot-candles.
4. First-aid rooms—30 foot candles.

Materials Disposal (.252)

1. Material dropped outside the building more than 20 ft. shall be slid down through an enclosed chute.

2. Material dropped inside the building shall be routed to a receiving area, completely barricaded and posted with warnings.

3. Disposal by burning shall comply with local regulations.

4. Solvents and flammable materials shall be stored in tightly covered containers.

Materials Handling (.251)

1. Rigging equipment shall be inspected at the start of each shift.

2. Rigging equipment shall not be loaded beyond its rated capacity.

3. Chains, links, shackles, hooks, and ropes shall be checked for wear.

Materials Storage (.250)

1. Materials shall be stacked so as to prevent accidental collapsing, falling, rolling, or sliding.

2. Safe load limits shall be posted and observed.

3. Noncompatible materials shall be kept separate.

4. Necessary passageways shall not be blocked with stored material.

5. Specific guidelines shall be followed for storing materials used in carpentry, masonry, and steelwork.

Unsafe Material Storage

Many building products are flammable or volatile. This picture shows a potentially hazardous collection of paint cans, drop cloths, and equipment in an enclosed storage area. (BCIT Building Technology)

Noise Levels (.52)

1. For an eight-hour day, a continuous level of 90 dBA or less is required.

2. For higher levels, exposure times must be reduced.

3. Variable levels and intermittent higher peaks require special arrangements.

Safety Belts (.104)

1. Wherever workers might fall any appreciable distance and thus injure themselves, individual safety belts and lifelines (each having a breaking strength of 4,000 lb.) are required.

2. Lifelines must be secured above the work level to a structural member capable of sustaining a load of 5,400 lb.

Sanitation (.51)

1. Drinking water shall be in adequate supply, clearly marked.

2. Common drinking cups are prohibited.

3. Toilets—one seat-type for up to 20 workers; one seat-type and one urinal-type for up to 40 workers.

Scaffolding—Definitions (.452)

1. There are no less than 36 definitions of significant terms relative to scaffolding types and components listed in this subpart.

Scaffolding—General (.451)

This is a very extensive subpart covering 18 pages in the OSHA handbook. A few highlights have been excerpted below:

1. Footings and anchorages of scaffolds to buildings shall be solid.

2. Design, erection, assembly, connection, moving, altering, and dismantling shall be under the control of competent personnel.

3. Guardrails and toeboards shall be provided at open sides and ends of platforms more than 10 ft. above grade.

4. Safe access shall be provided to all levels.

5. Mobile scaffolds shall be braced and designed to prevent overturning or accidental movement.

6. Specific requirements relative to the following trades are detailed: carpentry, decorating, formwork, plastering, masonry, roofing, and window installation, as well as scaffolding for work in large and small areas.

Safe Signaling

Proper signals between crane operators and others are imperative. In this picture, a clear and correct signal is given by an authorized worker to the operator to start to raise a load. (BCIT Building Technology)

Signals (.201)

1. Where signs or barricades are not sufficient to provide protection, competent flagmen or signalers shall be utilized.

2. Signaling must conform to specified standards (ANSI D6.1).

Signs and Tags (.200)

1. Danger signs shall be used only where an immediate hazard exists.

2. Other informational signs (such as exit, traffic, safety, and instructional) shall be posted at all appropriate places.

3. All signage and tags must conform to the various standards specified.

Tools—General (.300)

1. Tools shall be appropriate to the task and maintained in safe condition.

2. Guards on tools so equipped shall be used.

3. Persons using tools shall wear appropriate personal protection.

Tools—Manual (.301)

1. Wrenches with sprung jaws permitting slippage shall not be used.

2. Impact tools with heads mushroomed by wear shall not be used.

3. Wooden handles shall be tight and free of cracks or splinters.

Tools—Power (.302)

1. Handheld power tools shall have pressure-control finger switches.

2. Switches with locking features must be able to be released with one move of the switch finger.

3. Power tools shall not be raised or lowered by pulling on their electrical cords or air hoses.

4. Fuel-powered tools (like chainsaws) shall be stopped when refueling.

5. Powder-actuated tools (like stud guns) shall only be operated by personnel so certified.

6. Loaded or powered tools shall not be left unattended.

3.7 OSHB Sections (Canada)

In this part, some OSHB sections have been selected from Part 2 of the Canadian Labor Code (1991 edition).

Subpart 1   General

Subpart 2   Building Safety

Subpart 3   Temporary Structures & Excavation

Subpart 4   Elevating Devices

Subpart 5   Pressure Vessels

Subpart 6   Lighting Levels

Subpart 7   Sound Levels

Subpart 8   Electrical Safety

Subpart 9   Sanitation

Subpart 10   Hazardous Substances

Subpart 11   Confined Spaces

Subpart 12   Safety Devices & Clothing

Subpart 13   Tools & Machinery

Subpart 14   Materials Handling

Subpart 15   Recording & Reporting

Subpart 16   First Aid

Subpart 17   Safe Occupancy

3.8 Specific Issues (Canada)

Specific safety issues in Canada are essentially identical to the U.S. OSHA requirements. For more detail, readers should refer to the OSHB publications and to OSHA or workers' compensation board (WCB) regulations in force in every province.

4.0 Other Work

Items for inspection and safety of work in sections not listed herein can be inferred from those that have been listed, as well as from the more detailed descriptions of scope, procedures, and precautions contained in each trade section of this book, in the OSHA and OSHB reference books, and in state and provincial WCBS requirements. Inquiries can also be made to the National Institute for Occupational Safety and Health (located at 5600 Fishers Lane, Rockville, Maryland) for information on dangerous construction site substances.

Section 01-050
Field Engineering

1.0 Introduction

1.1 General Issues

This section describes the preliminary surveying activities involved in positioning the building and its various parts both horizontally (relative to property lines) and vertically (relative to known elevations). Only the briefest of outlines is given, to introduce some simple and practical field engineering procedures, and to draw attention to some significant elements of this part of the building process.

In practice, this aspect of construction work must be done by personnel who are skilled (and if necessary licensed) in this type of activity and who are prepared to take legal responsibility for the outcome of their survey procedures. If particularly complex, the layout work is best done by a licensed surveyor. Simpler projects can often be laid out by skilled and experienced trades foremen or journeymen, usually employed directly by the general contractor or project manager. This is distinct from work done by separate subcontractors as described in most of the remaining sections of this book. The more complex survey procedures involved in the subdivision of land or the establishment of legal property boundaries by professional land surveyors are beyond the scope of this book.

1.2 Design Aspects

From a construction perspective, the primary design requirement is to ensure that such surveys place the proposed building (and its major features) in the correct position on the correct building site. This is necessary to avoid subsequent legal or economic problems arising out of encroachments onto adjacent property, conflicts with contractual or legislated requirements, or improper interfacing of any of the many facets of the actual construction work, which can result in disputes between owners, designers, contractors, or suppliers. A secondary design requirement is to get confirmation that all given data (such as property lines) on which site surveys will be based are also correct and reliable.

A third aspect of design involves the limitations which zoning ordinances (with related setback, building area, and height restrictions) can have on the positioning of buildings on land. Where zoning is in force, it creates an additional spatial boundary (inside the existing legal property boundaries) required to be determined by survey, within which the building must be located. The building designer may also need to do some topographical investigation of the site, to determine contour levels and other geophysical features (such as cliffs or streams). He or she will have to work out problems of sun angles and views, drainage and water sources, wind directions and other climatic issues, and power and servicing, and to consider vegetation (such as shrubs and trees) relative to its removal or retention in the final building scheme. It is often a good practice to locate the best part of the building in the worst part of the site, so as to reserve the best part of the property for activities (such as parking, gardening, or recreation) which go on around the building. Like professional land surveying, such elements of building design are also beyond the scope of this book on construction procedures.

1.3 Related Work

Work closely connected to this section is described in the following sections, to which reference should be made:

01–003   The Design/Build Process

01–004   Dimensionng

02–100   Preperation

02–200   Earthwork

03–100   Formwork

2.0 Products

As this work involves only processes that are best described as belonging to administrative or managerial services, no permanent building materials or accessories are involved.

3.0 Construction Aids

3.1 Equipment

The following items of equipment are representative of those likely to be encountered in typical field engineering for many ordinary building projects. Some are illustrated in sketches; others are shown in accompanying photographs.

Batter Boards. These are rough wood frames, set up and leveled outside the corners of the proposed building location, and onto which nylon lines can be attached to indicate the precise location of the building (see Figure 1).

Chains. These were formerly used by surveyors before accurate steel tapes became generally available. They consisted of a series of bent-wire metal links, strung together to produce a chain of known length (usually 66 ft. but sometimes 100 ft.) having intermediate marker-tags to indicate regular subdivision of the overall length into tenths, twelfths, or other convenient increments. An area 1 (66-ft.) chain wide by 10 chains long (66 ×660 lf) equaled 43,560 sf or 4,840 sy, which is 1 acre.*

Leveling Tube. This consists of an ordinary plastic garden hose (or a number of such hoses linked end-to-end) having a short clear glass or plastic tube inserted at each end through which the water level in the filled hose can be seen.

Levels. There are three common types:

1. The **builder's level** consists of a small telescope, able to rotate horizontally through a complete circle and fixed over a horizontal plate accurately graduated into 360 degrees (and parts thereof) (see Figure 2).
2. The **carpenter's level** consists of an open metal frame, having its longer sides parallel to each other and supporting small glass vials partially filled with liquid; these indicate if the device is held truly in the horizontal or vertical plane.

*The abbreviations lf, sf, and sy are used alternatively for ft. (linear feet), ft.² (square feet), yd. (linear yards) and yd.² (square yards) throughout this book where it is desirable to distinguish linear from square measurement.

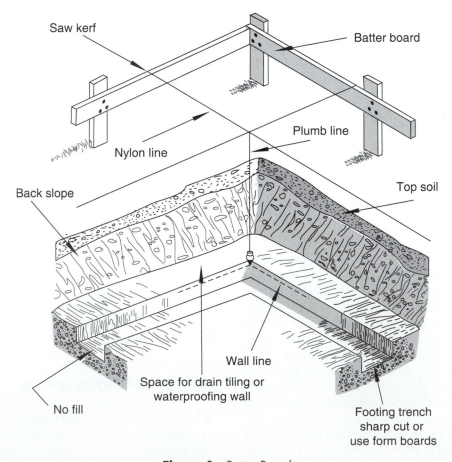

Saw kerf

Batter board

Plumb line

Nylon line

Back slope

Top soil

No fill

Space for drain tiling or waterproofing wall

Wall line

Footing trench sharp cut or use form boards

Figure 1 Batter Boards

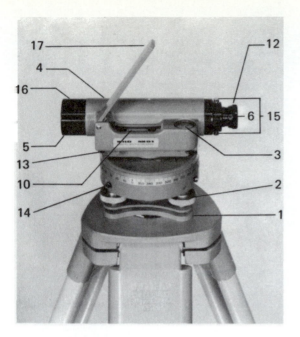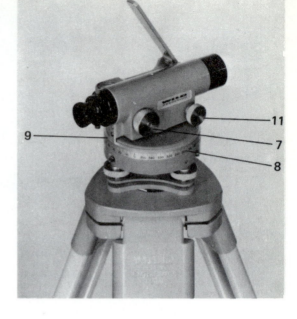

1. Base plate	7. Focusing knob	13. Tubular level adjusting screw
2. Leveling screw	8. Horizontal circle	14. Adjusting screw for leveling screw
3. Circular level	9. Horizontal circle vernier	15. Cross-hair adjusting screws
4. Telescope	10. Tubular level	16. Sunshade
5. Objective lens	11. Horizontal motion tangent screw	17. Bubble viewing mirror

Figure 2 Builder's Level

3. The **transit-level** is similar to the builder's level, but its telescope can also be tilted vertically through any angle up to 45 degrees (and parts thereof) above the horizontal plane.

4. There is also a new range of electronic leveling devices coming onto the market, some of which feature automatic readout of levels and others which use laser light to mark points of equal elevation or to establish truly vertical orientations (see Figure 3).

Lines. These consist of monofilament or woven nylon cords, having minimal shrinkage or stretch; they are used to lay out the lines of the proposed building, as described later. Ordinary string or twine should not be used for this purpose.

Markers. These consist of short wood or metal posts, painted white and tapered at one end so that they may be easily driven into the ground using a small hammer or mallet. For precise marking, a small nail can then be driven into the top or a neat pencil mark can be made on the side of the marker post.

Plumb bob. This device consists of a small steel or lead weight, rounded on top, pointed at the bottom, and having a hook to which a string can be attached

to suspend the bob vertically over a marker or other surveyed point.

Rods. There are two common types:

1. A vertical **leveling rod** consists of an interlocking sectional or telescoping-type pole, up to 5 m or 15 ft. in overall length, and usually graduated either in meters or feet and fractions thereof. Some models have a movable target plate attached, to facilitate accurate reading of values on the rod from some distance away (see Figure 4).

2. A horizontal **measuring rod** consists of a sectional or collapsible wood or metal rod (similar to a carpenter's folding ruler) opening up to 2 m or 6 ft. overall, with appropriate fractional subdivisions.

Squares. There are two types:

1. The **set square** consists of a large triangular wood or metal frame, having the outside dimension of its three sides in the ratio of 3:4:5. The longest side is usually not less than 2 m or 6 ft. in length.

2. The **tee square** consists of two wood or metal arms, each not less than 2 m or 6 ft. long, with one

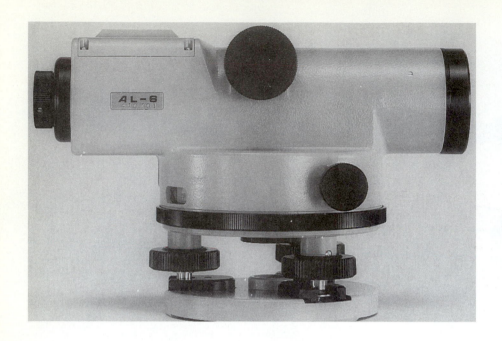

Figure 3 Automatic Level

arm arranged to be at a true right angle to the center point of the other arm.

Tape measures. There are two types:

1. The **carpenter's tape** consists of a long retractable band of thin painted flexible steel, marked with customary metric or imperial measurements, and having one end secured inside a button-operated, spring-loaded metal case. Overall lengths are commonly available up to 15 m or 50 ft.

Field Survey
A surveyor uses a transit on a tripod to note positions and elevations of various points critical to the proposed layout of the building on the property. (UBC Architecture)

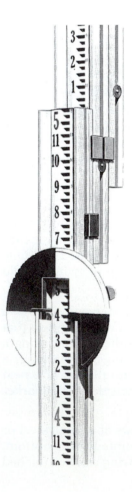

Figure 4 Leveling Rod

Figure 5 Theodolite

4.0 Production

4.1 Crew Configuration

Field engineering work is usually done by crews of two people, one called the instrumentman or surveyor and the other the rodman or survey assistant. The surveyor sets up and operates the survey instruments, holds and reads one end of horizontal measuring tapes, and records appropriate dimensions, calculations, and notes in data books. The assistant holds vertical measuring devices such as rods or graduated staffs, as well as the other end of horizontal tapes, chains, or wires, at designated points on the site some distance away from (and as directed by) the surveyor. Both may be required to do some minor clearing of grass, brush, or tree branches, to

2. The **surveyor's tape** is similar to the carpenter's tape but of heavier unpainted steel and having manual crank retraction (instead of spring-loading) inside a leather- or vinyl-bound case. Overall lengths are commonly available up to 30 m or 100 ft.

Theodolite. This is a general-purpose surveying instrument, consisting of a telescope mounted on a pivotal frame and capable of exceedingly precise measurement of any angle (between two distant points viewed from the location of the instrument) in both the vertical and horizontal planes (see Figure 5).

Tripod. This is a portable three-legged collapsible stand, used as a mounting platform for other instruments such as levels, sighting devices, theodolites, and transits (see Figure 6).

3.2 Tools

The tools are those of the surveyor and include small hammers and screwdrivers, light axes and saws, flashlights, and a variety of colored pens, pencils, chalks, and plastic tapes to highlight specific features of the work on site or in data books.

Leveling Rod

An assistant holds the leveling rod vertically over the point being surveyed to permit the surveyor to take a sight. The rod is moved slowly back and forth to ensure the best reading. (UBC Architecture)

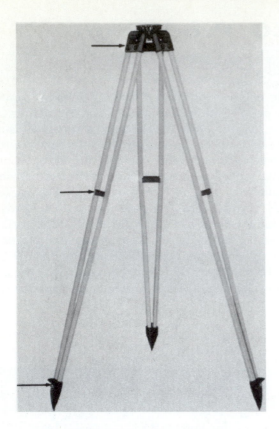

Figure 6 Instrument Tripod

ensure unimpeded sight lines or open spaces for point markers.

4.2 Productivity

Under normal and average conditions (i.e., reasonably level land, minimal obstruction, easy access to reliable reference points, and good weather), an experienced survey crew should be able to lay out a small residential building in one-half to one full working day. Larger but simple single- or double-story commercial buildings on regularly shaped and properly surveyed city lots may take one to two working days. More complex institutional or high-rise buildings may require two or more crews, and they may spend the equivalent of several working days laying out various portions of the work, working intermittently.

5.0 Procedures

5.1 Preparation

With regard to building lots, there are a number of possibilities that can occur which will affect the field engineering process:

1. The property shape may be simple (square, rectangular, or triangular) or complex (circular, irregular, or a combination).

2. The building layout may have to commence from only one known point, or from two or indeed many known points.

3. The lot topography may be simple (level or evenly sloped) or complex (stepped, irregularly sloped, or a mix of features).

4. The land may be cleared or covered with vegetation (such as bushes, crops, tall grasses, or trees) or other obstructions.

5. The time of year, the severity of climate, and the type of contract will also affect the survey work.

As a result of the foregoing, judgments first have to be made as to how the layout work will generally proceed, what instruments and measuring devices will be required for the survey process, under what site conditions (of access, mud, weather, etc.) the work will be done, and how long this part of the overall building project will probably take.

Second, it is necessary to discover the location and check the accuracy of the various external reference points given on which the internal site survey will be based. These may be in the form of wooden pegs, metal pins, or other markers already surveyed into true positions by other professionals. It is recommended that some acceptable form of certification as to the accuracy of given references be secured by the survey crew before layout work commences.

Third, some point of known elevation, such as a city or county fire hydrant or manhole cover, must be discovered, from which the proper elevation of the proposed building can be established. This point is called a *bench mark* by surveyors. Data regarding bench marks can usually be obtained from local government records.

Fourth, it is usually necessary to set up temporary batter boards. The initial location of these devices can be roughly established by simply pacing off the approximate distances from the known survey lines to points approximately 1.5 m or 5 ft. beyond the outside dimensions of the proposed building position; the final location of the boards will be precisely determined as the survey proceeds. After the boards have been leveled (as described later), small notches are sawn into the top edges of the boards to secure nylon marker cords in precise positions. Refer to Figure 7.

5.2 Process

There are two basic approaches to field engineering:

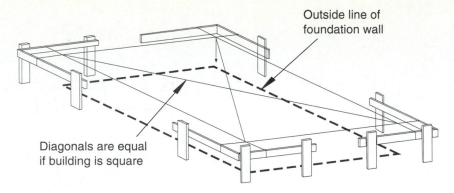

Outside line of
foundation wall

Diagonals are equal
if building is square

Figure 7 Initial Positioning of Batter Boards

1. Using **simple devices**, such as tapes and lines, on small and simple sites, or

2. Using **survey instruments**, such as levels and rods, on larger or more complex sites.

In some instances, a combination of the two approaches can be used. In each approach, there are two primary components (or objectives) to the layout survey process:

1. Determination of the geographical location of the proposed building in the **horizontal** plane, and

2. Establishment of the correct elevations for various portions of the building in the **vertical** plane.

In the unusual event that the coordinates and elevation of only one known survey point are given, magnetic north may be determined using a compass accurately calibrated to permit a true north line to be established relative to the known survey point and the proposed building site. From (and along) this line, measurements may then be made to establish the building lines, using either of the approaches described subsequently. Suitable for use with simple rectangular plots and buildings, the key to this approach is the use of the geometric right triangle, having the lengths of its three sides in the ratio of 3:4:5. This results in a triangle with one right (or 90-degree) angle between the two shorter sides. The triangle can be an actual physical entity, accurately made out of fairly long flat pieces of wood or metal, or it may just be measured marks precisely made on nylon lines or indeed made right on the surface of the earth, floor, or paving slab.

To illustrate and exemplify some of the procedures described in this section for use on typical projects, reference is made to the 10-unit townhouse project described in Section 01–003. The following assumptions have been made:

1. That zoning restrictions require the building to be set back a minimum of 15 m or 50 ft. from the front and side property lines as shown in Figure 8.

2. That the land has been cleared of obstructions, and that the topography is reasonable level and free of significant features such as ravines, cliffs, or bluffs.

3. That specific instructions on how to set up and calibrate survey instruments and other measuring devices are not necessary, as the object of this section is merely to describe the nature of typical survey site work and not to develop skill in the tasks.

Layout Using Simple Devices

1. To establish the **horizontal** location (Figure 8): A measuring tape and nylon line are required. Starting at point A, establish a line to point B. Measure along line AB to a point I exceeding the required

Measuring Tape

A typical surveyor's tape, made of flexible weatherproof nylon-coated steel, mounted in a carrying frame complete with a rewind crank. This example comprises 30 m (about 100 ft). (UBC Architecture)

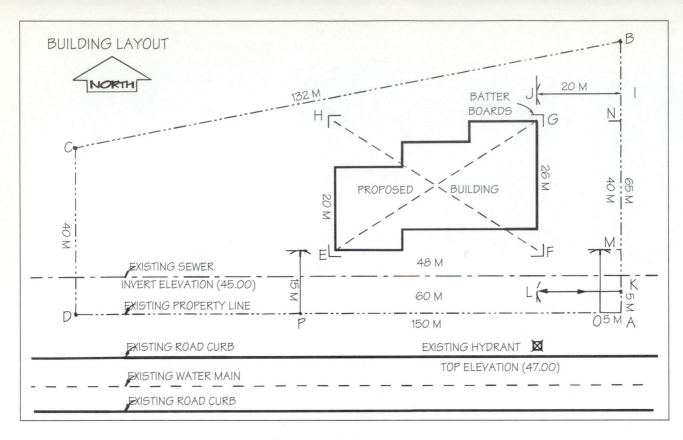

Figure 8 Building Layout

BUILDING LAYOUT

NORTH

setback and the overall depth of the building. At point I, swing an arc IJ with the tape equal to the sideyard setback. Measure along AB to a point K at a distance less than the required frontyard setback, and swing an arc KL with the tape equal to the side-yard setback. Move along the front line AD a distance equal to the sideyard setback and sight a tangent line to touch the highest points of both arcs IJ and KL. This establishes the building side line; string nylon cord between the batter boards along this line. Then repeat this process to establish the building front line. The intersection of these two lines dictates the location of point F; measure the overall dimensions of the building along both lines to establish points E and G. Using the tape to swing additional arcs or using the right-triangle technique, set off point H. To confirm the accuracy of the resulting rectangle, measure the lengths of diagonals EG and FH; they should be equal.

2. To establish the **vertical** elevation (Figure 9): A leveling tube and a long wood or metal marker stake are required. Fill the tube with water. Align the water level at one end of the hose with the level of a known bench mark. Move the other end of the tube to any point (within the length of the hose) where an elevation is required to be established, such as at the top of the nearest batter board. Drive the marker stake truly vertically into the ground and mark a

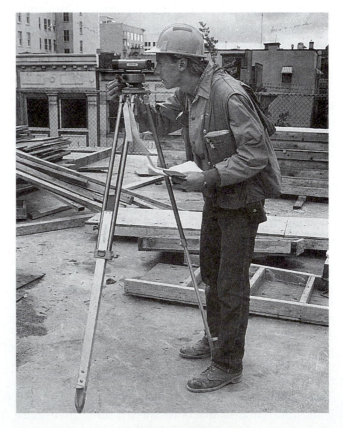

Site Leveling

A field engineer uses a builder's level to take readings at various points to ensure that the building is being erected with floors and other components at the correct elevations. (UBC Architecture)

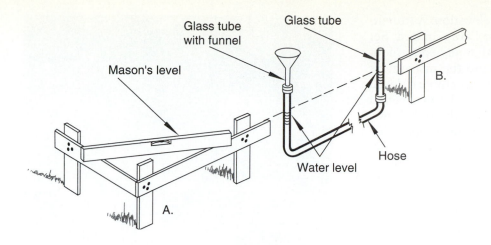

Figure 9   Leveling System

point on the stake equal to the water level in the hose. This will determine the elevation at this point on the marker stake to be the same as the original hydrant elevation. From this mark, measurements may be made up or down the stake to fix other elevations, such as the top of the batter board. All other required points of elevation (such as the tops of the other batter boards) can be similarly established by repeating the leveling process. Once the tops of all batter boards have been aligned at one known elevation, then vertical measurements can easily be made at any required point along the marker lines to determine various excavation depths, footing levels, drain inverts, and so on, around the building.

Layout Using Survey Instruments

   1. To establish the **horizontal** location (refer to Figure 8): A transit-level instrument, a measuring tape, and a plumb bob are required. Accurately locate the instrument over point A and level it. Rotate the instrument telescope until point B is sighted and lock it in; this is called the fore-sight. Measure along the line of sight AB a distance AM, equal to the required frontyard setback. Use the plumb bob to mark point M on the ground and move the instrument to that point. Sight point B again, then unlock and rotate the instrument telescope 180 degrees back toward point A, thus confirming the alignment; this is called the back-sight. Rotate the telescope 90 degrees toward point F and measure out the correct distance to both points F and E along the line of sight, using the plumb bob to drop the measured mark from the line of sight to the ground. Move the instrument to point N and repeat the confirmation, alignment, and measurement processes to set out points G and H. To confirm the accuracy of the resulting rectangle, measure the lengths of diagonals EG and FH; they should be equal. A check of the setbacks at points E and H should also be made, to con-

firm the building position relative to the property lines. Allowance must be made for significant slopes or other irregularities in the land (by stepping the sight lines up or down) as well as for excessive sagging in tapes and/or lines, caused by measurement over long distances.

Laser Level
This electronic device emits a rotating narrow beam of coherent light, thus permitting contractors to establish known points of equal height in various parts of any building. (UBC Architecture)

2. To establish the **vertical** elevation: A transit-level instrument and a leveling rod are required. Set up, level, and lock the instrument at any convenient spot within the building site where the instrument telescope is slightly above the benchmark level. Place the rod vertically on top of a known bench mark; read and record the height on the rod shown by looking through the instrument telescope. This reading (called the back-sight) will be added to the elevation of the bench mark to determine the elevation of the instrument. Move the rod to any new point for which a desired elevation is required, such as at one corner of the proposed new building or the invert level for a proposed new sewer line. Rotate the instrument telescope to sight on the vertical rod at its new location; read and record the height now shown on the rod. This reading (called the foresight) will be subtracted from the elevation of the instrument, to determine the elevation at the foot of the rod. The process is then repeated for all other points around the site for which height or depth data are required. In multistory construction, the elevation and levelness of each floor must be established by measuring the height from one level to the next and then using the transit-level instrument to determine elevations at various points as necessary. It is also possible to use other more sophisticated electronic devices (such as laser levelers) to rapidly and accurately perform this critical task.

5.3 Precautions

Care should be taken to mark and protect surveyed points, batter boards, and layout lines. Valuable survey instruments, measuring devices, and data books should not be left unattended in the field, at site offices, or in unlocked vehicles. All measuring devices should be kept clean and dry, and they should be

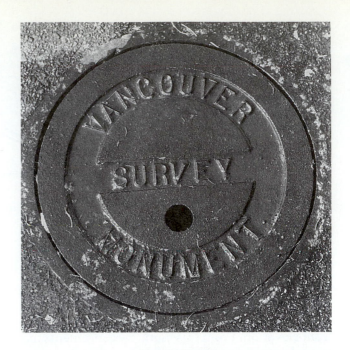

Bench Mark
Beneath this framed sidewalk cover, a point with known coordinates has been established by local authorities for use by builders to establish accurate connections to city services. (UBC Architecture)

tested and calibrated from time to time to ensure their continuing accuracy. It is poor practice to relocate theodolites or levels while they are still attached to their tripods; this puts undue strain on the threads of the leveling screws. Survey crews must use common sense and caution when working on loose shale or scree, in ice and snow, around derelict or unfinished buildings, or in dense bush or other hazardous terrain. An accurate record of all survey data received as well as new data generated (by measurement and calculation) for the site layout should be kept on file along with other contract documents.

Section 01–500
Temporary Facilities

1.0 Introduction

1.1 Organization of Information

The last two sections of Chapter 01 deal generally with the provision of things (as distinct from processes) required to enhance the efficient prosecution of construction work at the job site. This section (01–500) deals with aspects of temporary facilities, barricades, and field offices. The next section (01–520) deals with aspects of **construction aids** such as equipment and tools.

There are of course many detailed aspects of site administration, such as approval of shop drawings, record keeping, processing of change orders, organization of subcontractors at the site, preparation of deficiency lists, and so on; most of these are addressed in Section 01–003 (The Design/Build Process).

2.0 Temporary Facilities

Some temporary services are required on every building site to permit construction to proceed; most of the services commonly encountered on commercial and institutional building projects are described below in alphabetical order. In most construction contracts, the responsibility for making arrangements for the provision of temporary services is placed by the owner on the general contractor or project manager. The manner in which the various subcontractors use and pay for such services are many and varied, but all fall into two broad categories: Services are either provided **free** (in which case the subcontractors do not include such costs in their bids) or services are provided on a **user-pay** basis (back-charged to each subcontractor in proportion to the amount of use made by each for each service). Fuel and other servicing or maintenance costs must be included in estimates.

First Aid (Figure 1). Most local authorities require first-aid services to be provided on site in proportion to the number of people working on the project and in relationship to the distance to the nearest emergency hospital. A designated area or a separate room is required to be set aside at the site for this purpose, equipped with a list of prescribed medical supplies, such as antiseptics, bandages, blankets, scissors, splints, stretchers, thermometers, and so on, and staffed by personnel having current first-aid certification. On small jobs, the staffing would not be full-time, but instead one or more of the workers would be required to have the correct first-aid certification in addition to other credentials

(a) First aid room

(b) Site lunch room
Safety and Comfort
Large projects usually provide temporary accommodation for several worker functions. In many cases, legislation or union agreements make such facilities mandatory. (BCIT Building Technology)

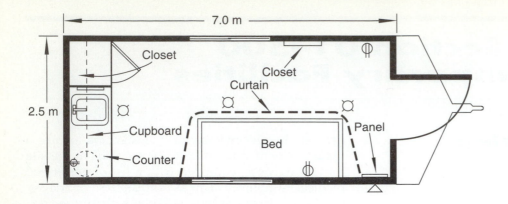

7.0 m

2.5 m

Closet

Closet

Curtain

Cupboard

Counter

Bed

Panel

Figure 1 First-Aid Office

necessary to do his or her trade work. Such personnel usually receive a bonus payment for maintaining up-to-date first-aid credentials.

Garbage Disposal. This is usually achieved in one of two ways: by strategically locating several small steel or reinforced plastic bins or containers around the site, or by vertically installing temporary large-diameter, heavy-duty metal or plastic sectional chutes at convenient locations at the edge of each floor. These bins or chutes can be periodically emptied into a larger mobile dumpster for off-site disposal. On most construction projects, the various subcontractors are made responsible by the general contractor or project manager for removing garbage and debris created by their own work.

Heat (Figure 2). Power for temporary heating is derived from two principal sources: electricity (either public or private—see below) or propane gas. As electric heat is usually quite expensive and also has some limitations of location, it is more common to encounter gas heat. Electric heat is best provided in the form of welded-steel, oil-filled radiators with immersion coils or enclosed heating elements with motor-driven fans. Gas heat is best provided in the form of salamanders (see Glossary), from which heat outputs up to one million Btus can be achieved.

As the construction of the building progresses, it may be possible and permissible to tap into the permanent heating system to provide some temporary heat using removable and relocatable radiators, convectors, or grilles suited to the permanent system. Exterior openings in the building structural frame should be temporarily closed with removable covers to conserve energy losses. Before final handover of the newly constructed building to the owners, it may be necessary to replace filters or other parts which have become used or worn during the construction process.

Light (Figure 3). Most temporary lighting used in construction is electrical. There are two primary purposes for temporary lighting: to illuminate work areas in day time, and to improve security at night time. Poles, panels, conduits, wires, lighting fixtures, bulbs, and other fittings are usually provided by the general contractor or project manager through the

Garbage Disposal
Construction debris can be collected in a transportable scow for disposal at a dump. This picture also shows how sectional plastic, metal, or wooden chutes can facilitate handling of debris (UBC Architecture)

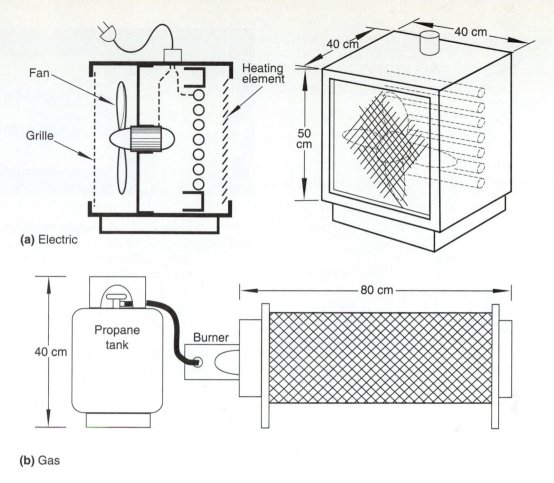

(a) Electric

(b) Gas

Figure 2   Temporary Heat

direct employment of an electrician qualified to do the work. Permits separate from the primary one are not usually required for such secondary work.

Phone (Figure 4).   Installation of a telephone is usually done at the site office by the local telephone company at the request of the contractor or manager. Permits are seldom required to be obtained. The contractor provides any poles and panel boards necessary for supporting and securing the wires or phone equipment. The normal type of service is the same as for any other business, with installation fees and monthly billings. It is possible to request that extra-loud bells be connected to site office phones, so that incoming call signals may be heard outside the office. Various types of extensions and answering or recording devices can also be rented or purchased for connection to the phone equipment, as well as remote electronic pagers, cellular or radio phones, beepers, and fax machines.

Power (Figure 5).   Electrical power is required to run many kinds of equipment and tools on construction sites. Tower cranes and hoists require

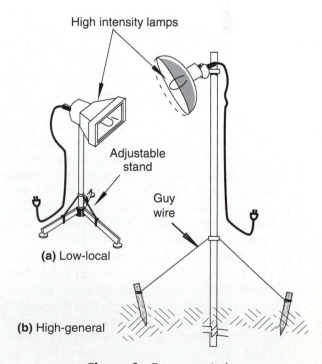

(a) Low-local

(b) High-general

Figure 3   Temporary Light

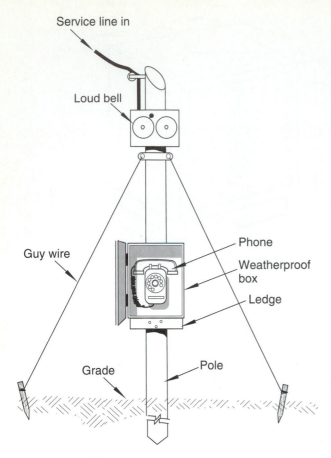

Figure 4 Temporary Phone

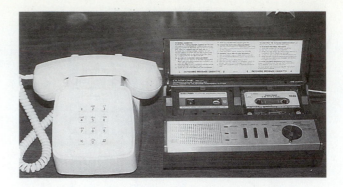

Phone and Answering Machine
This simple device is typical of many that can record all incoming phone calls and also play back a prerecorded outgoing message to give information. Fax machines are also used on sites. (UBC Architecture)

power at 440 volts; table saws and large heaters require 220 volts; other devices, such as hand drills, lights, routers, and portable saws, require at least 110 volts. Power can be derived from two main sources: local public utility companies or privately owned generators.

1. **Public**. It is usually necessary to make an application to the utility company or other local authority (such as city hall) for a permit to have the power safely connected and delivered to a panel through a meter. The contractor is usually responsible for supplying and erecting poles and panels to which the utility company can secure its equipment. Once the service is connected, it is then up to the contractor to employ electricians to run feeder wires to subpanels located wherever necessary around the construction site.

2. **Private**. Contractors may either purchase, rent, or lease gas- or diesel-powered electrical generators, having outputs varying between 600 and 6,500 watts, depending upon power requirements which are determined by adding the power ratings of the items of construction equipment requiring to be energized. Such generators are usually used only until such time as the perma-

nent electrical supply for the building can be brought or restored to the site.

Signage (Figure 6). Most building sites necessitate a number of signs to indicate specific things. For example, the site itself usually has to be identified for two reasons: to let the public know what is being built, and to enable people who have to visit the site to locate it correctly. There are also aspects of advertising and public relations involved in such signage, and these signs can often cost several hundreds (or thousands) of dollars to construct, maintain, and remove. Within the site, signs are often necessary to designate temporary facilities, traffic directions, parking and storage areas, multiple floor levels, hazardous conditions, and so on. Provision, coordination, and maintenance of signage (and accompanying permits) are usually the responsibility of the general contractor or project manager.

Toilets (Figure 7). There are three approaches to handling this aspect of procedure:

1. Digging deep holes beneath a wooden seat, surrounded by wood or canvas screens in a remote part of the site, where permitted by law;
2. Providing temporary chemical toilets enclosed in plywood or plastic cabinets, where required by law;
3. Using parts of the permanent toilet system in the building under construction or renovation.

In the third instance, provision must be made to protect and clean such parts periodically and upon completion of the project. With increasing numbers of women working on construction sites, considera-

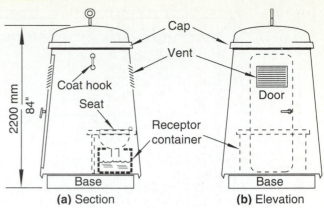

Figure 7   Temporary Chemical Toilet

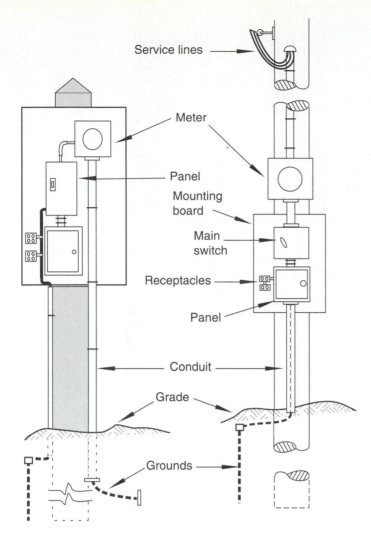

Figure 5   Temporary Power

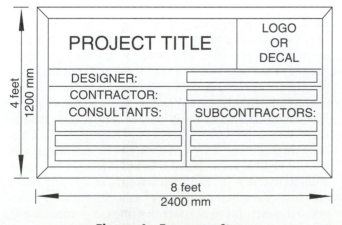

Figure 6   Temporary Sign

tion must be given to providing separate toilet accommodation and restrooms for their exclusive use.

Water (Figure 8).   There are several ways in which water can be provided for temporary use on a site. It can be delivered by tank truck, it can be tapped from local fire hydrants, it can be obtained by connection to local water mains (usually done directly by local authority workers up to the property line of the site), streams can be diverted, wells can be drilled, and rainwater can be collected in barrels. In almost every case, a permit is required to authorize the use of significant quantities of publicly provided water for construction purposes.

Work Platforms (Figure 9).   It is occasionally expedient to build fairly substantial temporary platforms from which workers can operate safely and efficiently. An example is illustrated in Figure 9. Such facilities should be structurally sound within themselves and securely fastened to the permanent building frame during use. (See also Staging in Section 01–520.)

3.0   Fences and Barricades

There are two aspects to this topic: barriers required **by law** as safety measures and barriers required **for convenience** to prevent theft, to conceal unsightly building processes from the public, or to contain work operations within a restricted area.

Barriers required by law are usually prescribed in detail in local or national building codes, as well as OSHA regulations or WCB legislation (see Section 01–005). They are intended to prevent workers and the public from unwittingly entering hazardous areas and also to avoid potentially harmful incidents

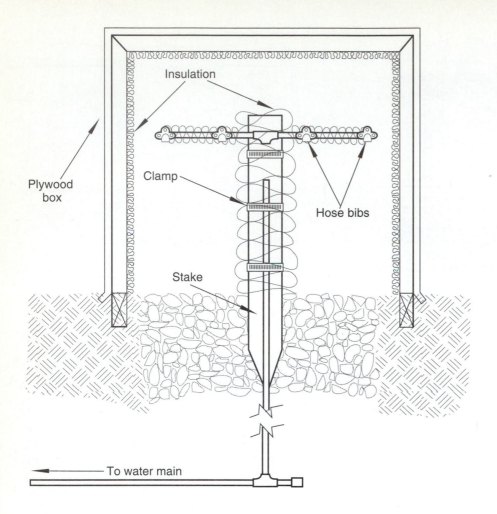

Insulation

Plywood
box

Clamp

Hose bibs

Stake

To water main

Figure 8 Temporary Water Supply

Temporary Water Supply

Plenty of fresh water is needed for virtually every building project. In this instance, water pipelines to various parts of the construction site are connected to a city fire plug. (BCIT Building Technology)

by providing nets or deflectors to intercept falling objects, for example. Barriers required for convenience are usually specified by the building owner or designer in the construction contract documentation, or else they are provided by the general contractor to achieve the objectives outlined above.

Fences (Figure 10). These are usually built of braced wood supports and plywood or fiberboard panels, although chain link fences are occasionally used where security is of greater concern. Fences may be built in situ or prefabricated ready for rapid assembly at the site; they may be painted or decorated or they may be left unfinished. If a building project has a permanent fence specified, portions of the fence can often be built early in the process to serve the same purpose as a temporary fence. It is usually necessary to provide swinging or sliding gates for access through the fence at strategic locations; gates should be able to be locked. In solid fences, it is possible to insert or leave small cutouts as viewing ports (so that so-called "sidewalk superintendents" can watch construction activity in progress—apparently, this is a neverending fascination). In some urban ar-

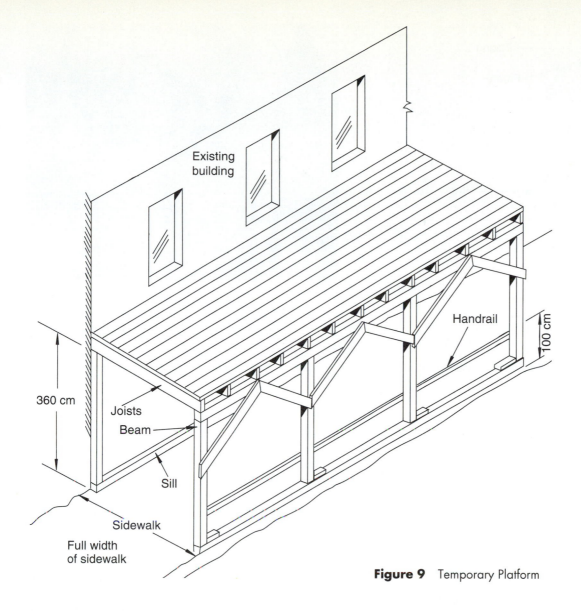

Existing building

360 cm

Joists

Beam

Sill

Sidewalk

Full width of sidewalk

Handrail

100 cm

Figure 9 Temporary Platform

eas, lighting is required to be provided on temporary fences and barricades at night.

Fences are often consolidated with covered walkways, the framing for which should leave a clear passageway having a width of about 1.5 m or 5 ft. and a height of about 2.5 m or 8 ft. The roof of such walkways should slope toward the site to deflect debris and water away from adjacent public roadways, and guide rails should be attached on each side to direct the flow of pedestrian traffic. If field offices are going to be located above the covered walk, then the framing design must be properly engineered to withstand the anticipated loads.

Barricades (Figure 11). It is customary (where not legally necessary) to provide temporary guardrails around the edges of all open-sided floors, walkways, runways, and balconies. These guardrails consist of wood members or ropes sufficiently strong

to resist the force of a person weighing about 100 kg or 200 lb falling against them. Such barriers should have a top rail about 1.0 m or 3.5 ft. above the floor, a toeboard (to prevent tools from slipping over edges), and an intermediate rail halfway between the other two rails.

Small openings in floors or roofs should be covered with plywood panels secured in position. Safety nets can also be rigged beneath such openings to catch any items that may fall through. Openings leading into elevator shafts should be solidly closed off with plywood panels when elevator workers are not actually working in the shafts.

4.0 Field Offices

The provision and use of temporary field offices and storage sheds depends on a number of factors,

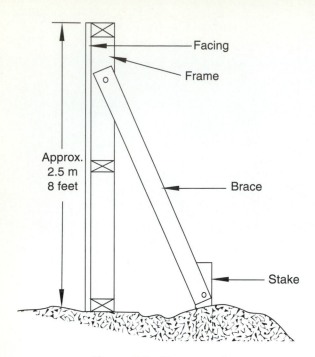

Figure 10 Temporary Fence

Temporary Fencing
Before construction starts, fencing (or hoarding) is often built to enclose the site for safety, security, and privacy. (BCIT Building Technology)

such as the size of the project, the location of the work, the necessity to have full-time on-site supervision, the need for shelter for personnel or security for documents or goods, legislation governing the provision of first-aid rooms, and union agreements governing the provision of lunch rooms, among other needs of the owners, designers, contractors, and on-site personnel.

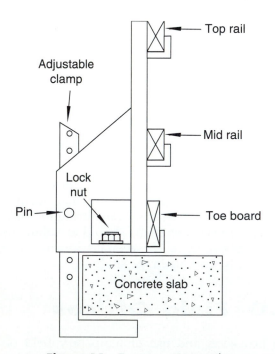

Figure 11 Temporary Barricade

It is necessary to locate temporary buildings on the site where they will not impede the construction processes of materials delivery, storage, preparation, assembly, and installation. While it is usually possible to relocate such buildings if necessary, it is obviously less expensive to put them in the right position in the first place.

Field Offices (Figure 12). These can consist of simple wooden sheds or shanties, mounted on skids or wheels for easy removal. They are now more commonly encountered in the form of weatherproof insulated metal trailers specially manufactured or modified for the purpose. Such offices should be relatively secure against unauthorized entry and be fitted with operable windows. They should be equipped with serviceable furniture, such as chairs, desks, filing cabinets, drawing boards, stools, shelves, and storage cupboards. Adequate lighting, heating or air conditioning, and janitorial services must be supplied. A stock of suitable stationery items, such as memo pads, letterhead paper, envelopes, paper clips, pens, pencils, staplers, and the like is usually required. A telephone is a necessity; an answering or call-recording device is a convenience. A computer terminal, a plotting device, and a fax machine are often needed for the use of site office management personnel.

Such offices are best located close to the main entrance to the site and if possible where they also have a general overview of the main work areas and other storage sheds. Field offices may be rented,

Temporary Barricades
Barricades are often necessary for physical safety or as a warning at openings in floors or walls. Ribbons and ropes are sometimes used until more solid barriers can be installed. (BCIT Building Technology)

readily assembled for use and knocked down for removal, similar to the ones shown in Figure 12. The benefit of using sectional modules is that such sheds can be enlarged or reduced to accommodate changing needs or spaces.

They should be weatherproof, able to be secured against unauthorized entry, and should protect materials and equipment stored in them from loss or damage from likely sources, such as theft, water, or heat. In general, the provision and maintenance of temporary storage sheds is the responsibility of each subcontractor; the location of the sheds is the responsibility of the general contractor or project manager. As the project under construction develops, spaces within the new building are often allocated by the contractor or manager to subcontractors to use for temporary storage of supplies and equipment. In appearance, such sheds are similar to the temporary field offices described above, but would have simpler interior finishes, probably no insulation, and little if any furniture, other than shelving, storage racks, or lockable chests.

It is also possible to buy, lease, or rent fully equipped mobile trailers containing storage lockers, wash basins, flush toilets, lighting, heating, and even showers for the use of workers at the site, so that workers can wash up and store their work clothes when they quit work at the end of a shift.

leased, or purchased. Contracts for rent or lease of such trailers usually include delivery and placement of the unit at the start of work and its removal off the site at or before the end of the project. Sizes range between 2.5 and 3.0 m or 10 and 12 ft. wide and lengths of 3 and 15 m or 12 and 50 ft. long. They are usually put into position and removed by crane or tow truck.

Storage Sheds. These usually consist of prefabricated sectional metal or wooden units that can be

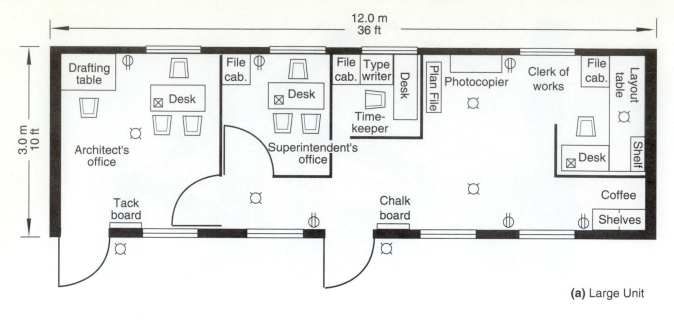

(a) Large Unit

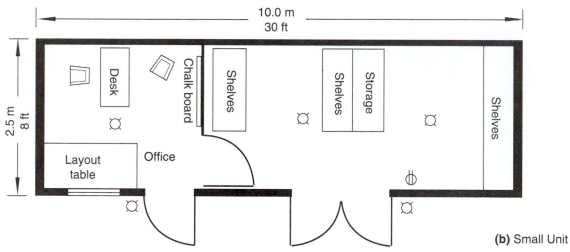

(b) Small Unit

Figure 12 Field Offices

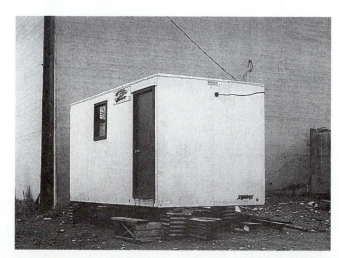

Site Offices

Temporary site offices and storage facilities are almost always required. Limitations of space sometimes make it necessary to locate offices over a city sidewalk or in nearby buildings. (BCIT Building Technology)

Section 01–520
Construction Aids

1.0 Introduction

1.1 General Issues

Mechanical aids in the form of plant, equipment, and tools are necessary to build any construction project. By definition, *plant* means relatively large, immobile pieces of machinery and often the buildings that house such machinery, such as one finds in gravel pit or concrete batch operations. *Equipment* means heavy but relatively mobile operable machinery, such as concrete mixers, conveyers, and power screeders, as well as nonmachinery items, such as ladders and scaffolding. *Tools* means lightweight powered or manual devices, such as chisels, drills, hammers, and saws, capable of operation by one person and necessary to do the work of that person. (See Figure 1.)

Further discussion of *plant* is beyond the scope of this book; *equipment* and *tools* are the subject matter of this section.

1.2 Organization of Information

As with almost everything to do with the construction industry, the range of equipment and tools that could be considered under the title of *Construction Aids* is enormous, indeed probably infinite. They could easily fill a book on their own, and many subject-specific books have already been written about all sorts of aspects of particular construction aids.

For the more general purposes of this book, a rigorous selection has been made from the range of available aids, to present some useful (though limited) information about typical types of equipment and tools used by the trades commonly encountered on commercial and institutional buildings. These items have been listed in this section for two reasons: first, to identify, describe, and illustrate some of these items for the benefit of students who may not be familiar with them; and second, to minimize repetition throughout the rest of the book, as the work of different trades often requires use of the same or very similar tools and equipment.

2.0 Equipment

Operating Equipment. This consists of items that do actual construction work. It includes backhoes, cement mixers, compressors, concrete buggies, paving machines, power screeders, table saws, and welding machines, among others. For specific detail, see Part 3.0 of any of Chapters 02 through 10.

Administrative Equipment. This consists of items necessary to run the business side of construction at the site. It includes chairs, computers, desks, field offices, filing cabinets, office accessories, telephones and pagers, typewriters, and the like. For specific detail, see Section 01–500 of this chapter.

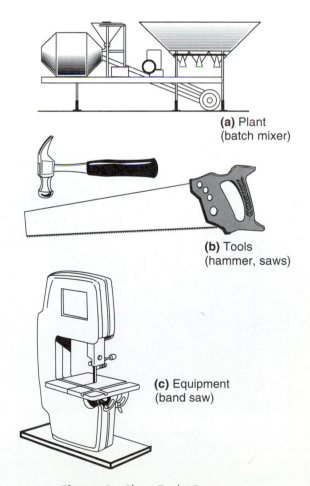

(a) Plant
(batch mixer)

(b) Tools
(hammer, saws)

(c) Equipment
(band saw)

Figure 1　Plant; Tools; Equipment

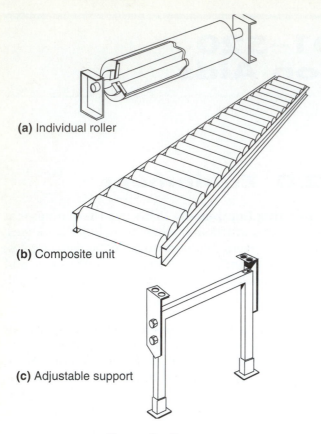

(a) Individual roller

(b) Composite unit

(c) Adjustable support

Figure 2 Conveyor

Conveyor Belts

These come in a wide range of sizes and configurations, for sale or lease. This photo shows a small gas-powered portable conveyor belt in the yard of an equipment rental company. (UBC Architecture)

Ancillary Equipment. This consists of items that permit workers and operating equipment to get access to do their work or assist in construction processes in some other general way. Specific descriptions follow.

1. Conveyers (Figure 2). These are devices designed to move materials either horizontally, vertically, or up an incline, on either a continuous or an intermittent basis depending on the type of machine.

2. Cranes (Figure 3). These are devices used to raise construction materials in unit loads from grade

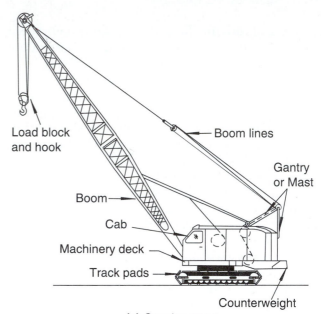

Load block and hook

Boom lines

Boom

Gantry or Mast

Cab

Machinery deck

Track pads

Counterweight

(a) Crawler crane

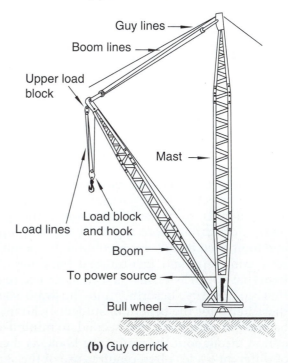

Guy lines

Boom lines

Upper load block

Mast

Load lines

Load block and hook

Boom

To power source

Bull wheel

(b) Guy derrick

Figure 3 Cranes

(a) Tower crane

(b) Mobile crane

(c) Hiab crane

(d) Articulated crane

Cranes

Self-raising tower cranes are commonly used for high-rise construction. Articulated cranes can be used in restricted spaces. Some larger mobile cranes can reach to heights of 30 stories. (UBC Architecture)

to higher levels. There are two basic styles: fixed and mobile. Fixed (or tower) cranes usually stay in one position throughout the construction process, although there is a modified form called the climbing crane, which can be raised on its vertical axis (by hydraulic jacks and ratchets) as the building increases in height; such cranes are often stabilized with guy wires. Mobile (or conventional) cranes are mounted either on tracks, trucks, or wheels; they are usually stabilized with special antisway bars protruding from the base. Some mobile cranes can reach as high as a 30-story building. Cranes may be hydraulically or electrically powered. A standardized system of clear manual or electronic guidance signals must be adopted by all personnel involved in the use of cranes to ensure their correct and safe movement in every direction and at every speed. Care must be taken during any operations involving physically moving the crane from one location to another, to avoid contact with power sources or eccentric loading that could cause a collapse.

3. Hoists (Figure 4). These are similar to light-duty passenger elevators, and consist of a vertical arrangement of rails, guides, safety enclosures, and gates, collectively called the *mast*. The mast accommodates a counter-balanced car or cab which is raised and lowered by cables attached to special heavy-duty, electric traction motors, gears, and drums, and controlled by a button signaling device located either in the cab or at grade level. Hoist

masts are usually located on the outside of the project under construction, although it is sometimes possible to locate them in interior permanent elevator shafts. Maximum cab speed is about 500 m or 1,500 ft. per minute, and capacity is the equivalent of five or six people of average size and weight. Hoist heights seldom exceed 80 stories, and they can take as long as four days to assemble ready for use. Some hoists are authorized for use only with materials; personnel are forbidden to ride in such restricted hoists.

4. Ladders (Figure 5). There are four basic types used: extension, step, sectional (or trestle), and roll-away; each may be made of hardwood or lightweight metal. In every case, ladders should be solidly constructed, well maintained, correctly placed, and secured in position.

5. Scaffolds (Figure 6). These are wood or metal (or a combination) devices intended to pro-

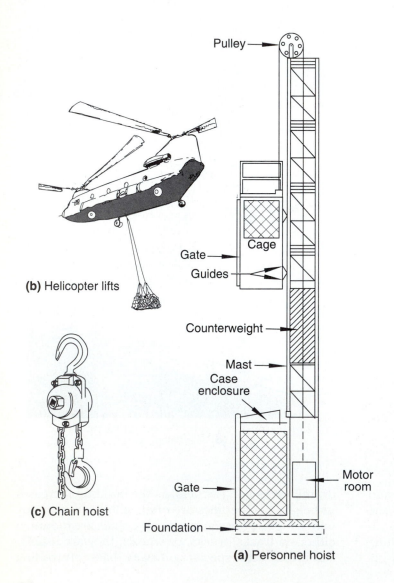

(b) Helicopter lifts

(c) Chain hoist

(a) Personnel hoist

Figure 4 Hoists

Hoists

There are many ways to raise materials and workers from grade level to higher elevations. Some are semipermanent, while others can be easily moved around according to need. (UBC Architecture)

vide a temporary platform for work operations above grade level. There are two broad categories: access and support; access permit personnel and supplies to be brought close to the desired place of work, and support are used to sustain heavy loads in place until they can support themselves, such as beneath concrete floors. Access scaffolds can be categorized in a number of ways, some of which are illustrated in this section.

In some Far Eastern countries, bamboo is extensively used for scaffolding on buildings of considerable height. The author has visited buildings 20 stories and higher under construction in China, completely scaffolded full height in tied bamboo.

6. Skips and Scows (Figure 7). These are large rectangular reinforced steel bins, used for the collection of garbage, debris, and waste from the site, and capable of being detached from and easily remounted onto truck beds for transportation from the site to an authorized dumping area.

7. Staging and Gantries (Figure 8). This is similar to scaffolding in purpose, but usually consists of a small adjustable platform suspended by cables attached to the top of the building. It is capable of being raised or lowered either manually or elec-

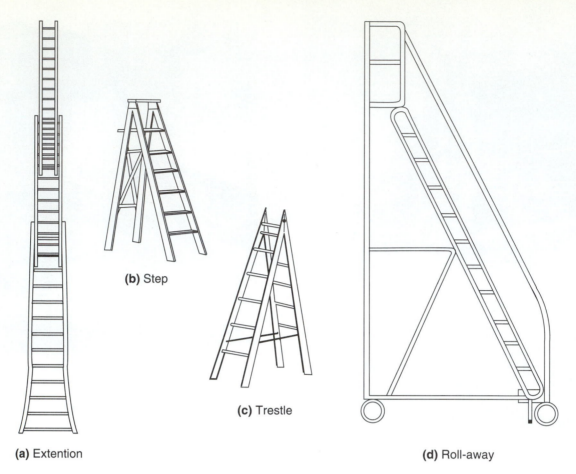

(b) Step

(c) Trestle

(a) Extention

(d) Roll-away

Figure 5 Ladders

Platforms

Adjustable platforms and gantries are often utilized to provide rapid and convenient access to work positions. Strict safety guidelines accompany the use of all such equipment. (UBC Architecture)

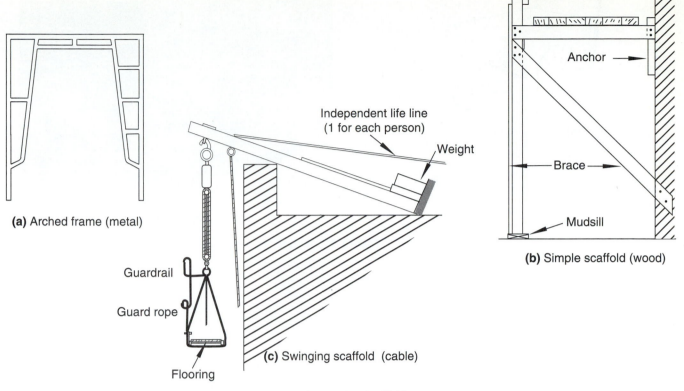

(a) Arched frame (metal)

Independent life line
(1 for each person)

Weight

Guardrail

Guard rope

Flooring

(c) Swinging scaffold (cable)

Guard

Anchor

Brace

Mudsill

(b) Simple scaffold (wood)

Figure 6 Scaffolds

Scaffolding

Work on the exterior surfaces of buildings (such as painting or caulking) frequently requires the installation of temporary sectional scaffolding to support safe catwalks for workers. (UBC Architecture)

trically, and is used by glaziers, painters, window washers, and others doing work on the external surfaces of buildings.

8. Trucks (Figure 9). These comprise a large variety of vehicles, ranging all the way from general, light-duty panel vans and pickups to specialized heavy-duty dumpsters, pups, and forklifts. A few typical models are illustrated in this section as being representative of many such vehicles used by construction companies.

Mobilization Equipment. This involves the use of certain items of road-worthy and highway-licensed equipment to transport other pieces of less mobile construction equipment from an off-site storage yard or warehouse to the job-site before the start of part of a construction project requiring such equipment, and returning it (if necessary) on conclusion of that part of the work. They include barges, flatbed trucks, specialized trailers, tow trucks, and on occasion, helicopters, among others.

3.0 Tools

As mentioned in Part 1.2 above, the range and variety of tools used in construction is colossal. It is not practical nor particularly useful (even if it were possible) to list, describe, or illustrate every type of

(a) Skip

(b) Scows

Figure 7 Skips & Scows

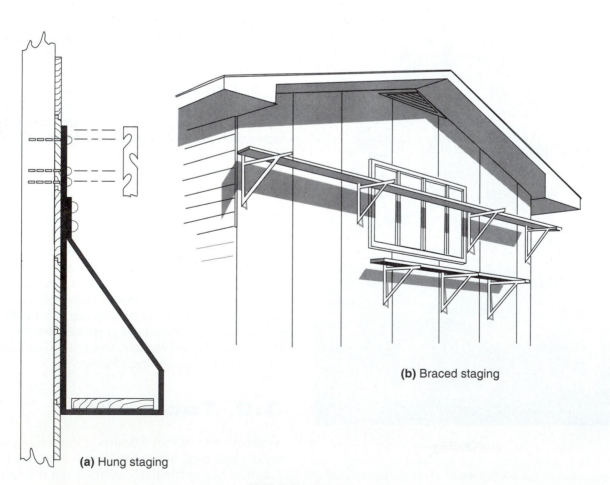

(a) Hung staging

(b) Braced staging

Figure 8 Staging

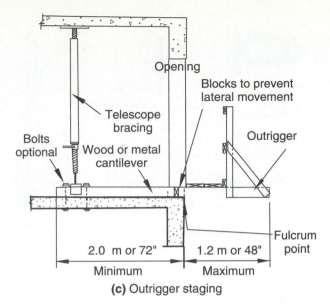

Opening

Blocks to prevent
lateral movement

Telescope
bracing

Bolts
optional

Wood or metal
cantilever

Outrigger

Fulcrum
point

2.0 m or 72"
Minimum

1.2 m or 48"
Maximum

(c) Outrigger staging

Figure 8 (continued)

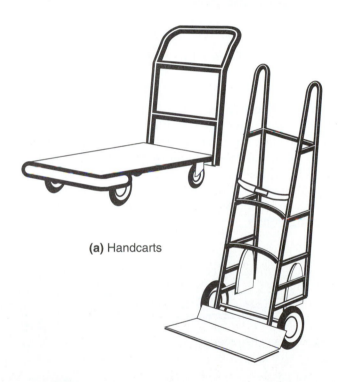

(a) Handcarts

tool. Instead, the general topic has been subdivided for convenience into the broad categories noted below. Students are urged to make themselves familiar with the tools mentioned in each category and to compare and relate them to the tools detailed for each of the trades throughout the rest of the book. A few of the tools, representative of each category, are illustrated in this section. To avoid duplication and to permit students to make their own observations in the field, tools mentioned elsewhere in the book are not specifically illustrated, although many are shown in use in the photographs which accompany each section.

Clamping Tools (Figure 10). These are used to hold two or more pieces of material together, either temporarily or permanently. They include clamps (spring and screw types), come-alongs (used to

(b) Pup truck

(c) Panel Van

(a) Pick-up truck

(d) Dump truck

Figure 9 Trucks

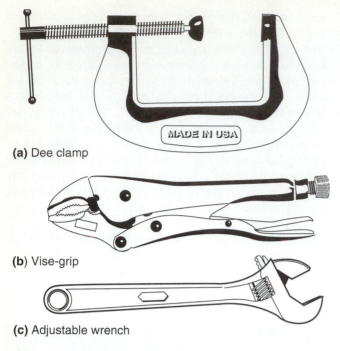

(a) Dee clamp

(b) Vise-grip

(c) Adjustable wrench

Figure 10   Clamping Tools

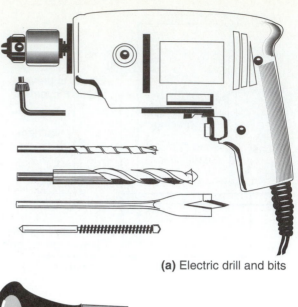

(a) Electric drill and bits

(b) Hand awl

Figure 12   Drilling Tools

tighten straps), jigs of various sorts, pliers, lifters, miter boxes, staplers, and vise-grips, among others.

Cutting Tools (Figure 11). These are used to separate parts of materials from their parent bodies. They include chisels, cutters (for bolts, glass, and wire), files, knives, planes, nippers (for trimming tiles), rasps, scissors, shears, manual and power saws, and tin-snips, among others.

Drilling Tools (Figure 12). These are used to make holes or grooves in materials. They include awls, braces, bits, drills, punching devices, and routers, among others.

Driving Tools (Figure 13). These are used to apply force to components to tighten or loosen them. They include allen keys, hammers (such as ballpeen, claw, and tile), jimmies, mallets (of rubber, steel, or wood), nail-sets, powder-drivers, screwdrivers (such as flathead, Phillips-head, and nuthead) and wrenches (such as adjustible, slip, and torque type), among others.

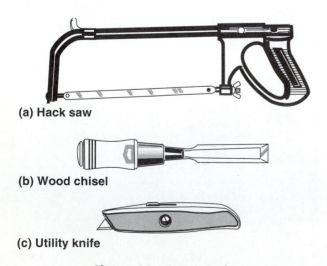

(a) Hack saw

(b) Wood chisel

(c) Utility knife

Figure 11   Cutting Tools

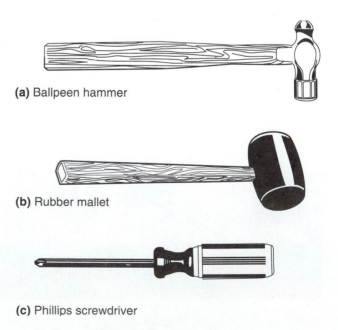

(a) Ballpeen hammer

(b) Rubber mallet

(c) Phillips screwdriver

Figure 13   Driving Tools

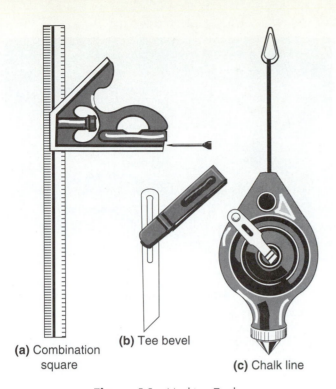

(a) Combination square

(b) Tee bevel

(c) Chalk line

Figure 14 Marking Tools

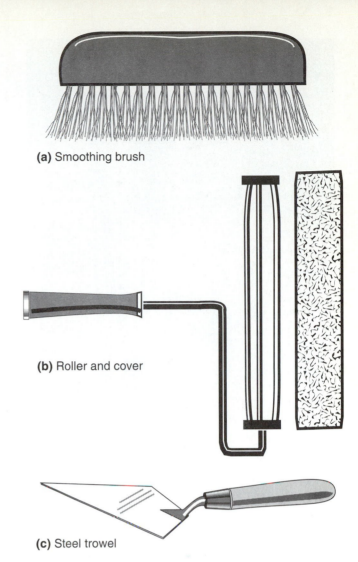

(a) Smoothing brush

(b) Roller and cover

(c) Steel trowel

Figure 15 Spreading Tools

Marking Tools (Figure 14). These are used to set out and mark materials ready for clamping, cutting, drilling, or driving. They include chalk-lines, compasses, dividers, levels, measuring tapes, pencils, plumb bobs, scribers, squares, tee bevels, tee squares, and templates, among others.

Spreading Tools (Figure 15). These are used to distribute or shape products or materials such as mortar, paint, powders, and the like. They include brushes, darbies, floats (of wood or steel), masonry jointers, putty knives, rollers (for paint and adhesives), screeds, shovels, spades, sponges, squeegees, rakes, and trowels, among others.

Miscellaneous Tools (Figure 16). These are used for a variety of activities or purposes such as clean-up, gathering, holding, leveling, and preparation. They include buckets, brooms, dustpans, hawks, hods, paint spinners, sandpapers, scrapers, sharpeners, stirring sticks, straightedges, toolboxes, wire brushes, and perhaps work aprons, among others.

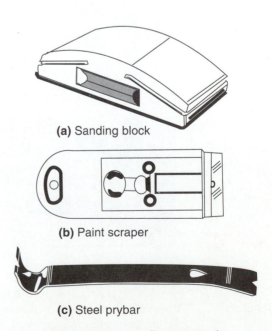

(a) Sanding block

(b) Paint scraper

(c) Steel prybar

Figure 16 Miscellaneous Tools

Miscellaneous Aids

It is impossible to illustrate every kind of construction aid here. These representative photos show two manually operated hydraulic jacks and one gas-powered mobile concrete buggy. (BCIT Building Technology)

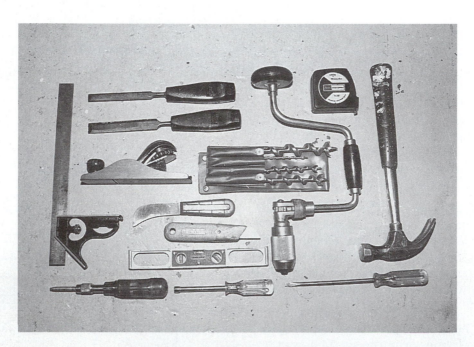

(a) Carpentry

Assorted Hand Tools

These four pictures show an assortment of typical tools used by four of the more common construction trades. Many of these same tools will be used by other trades not illustrated. (UBC Architecture)

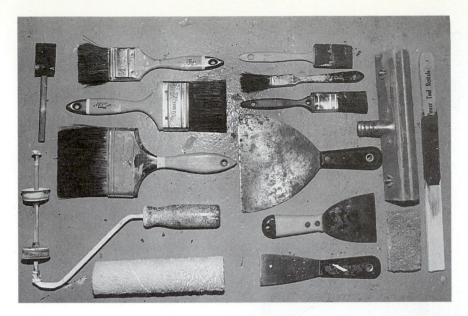

(b) Painting

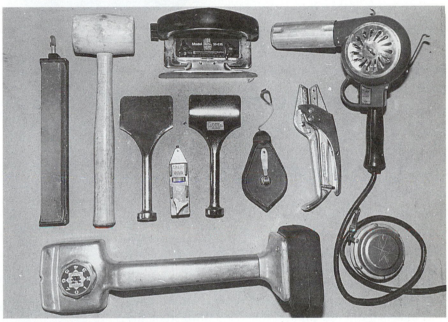

(c) Carpeting

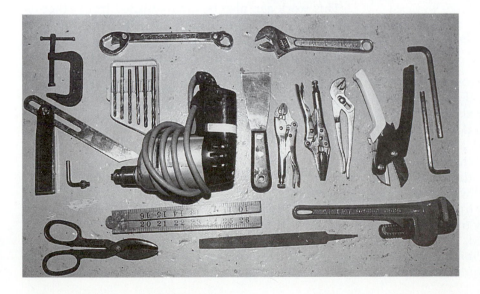

(d) Metal working

Section 01–520   Construction Aids

75

CHAPTER 02
Site Work

Section 02–100 Preparation

1.0 Introduction

1.1 General Issues

It is usually necessary to do some preparatory work on almost every new building site before construction work commences. Large trees may have to be felled, stumps and roots removed, smaller shrubs and bushes cut down, and loose vegetation, rubbish, and debris gathered up and disposed of in some authorized manner.

1.2 Design Aspects

The primary aspect of design in this context lies in determining which parts of the natural on-site vegetation have to be permanently removed off site; which parts have to be temporarily taken down, set aside, and later replaced; and which parts are intended to remain untouched and undamaged throughout construction operations. Consultation with the landowner or a designated landscape consultant will usually clarify the design intention. On parts to be preserved, some means is necessary to identify trees, shrubs, or other features not to be disturbed; colored chalk marks, plastic tapes, and canvas ribbons can serve this purpose. Permits are often required from local

authorities before clearing can commence. Consideration must be given to access and exits for vehicles and equipment at the site.

The work of this section can be distinguished from similar work described in other sections as follows:

Section 02–150   Protection

Section 02–200   Earthwork

This work can also be distinguished from other aspects of site preparation involving special techniques used to alter the quality of the ground on which the new building will stand. The primary objective of these techniques is to improve the bearing capacity of the ground by consolidating the soil particles through the removal of water or soft clay, using weights, or powered dynamic compaction. Three are listed below:

1. One such patented technique is called *vibroflotation*, in which loose gravel fills are mechanically compacted by the forced insertion and careful withdrawal of heavy-duty vibrators.

2. A second patented technique is called *geo-paction*, in which loose gravel soils are consolidated by simply dropping a large (25-ton), flat steel weight

Demolition
It is often necessary to clear construction sites of obstructions. This photo shows a six-storey brick building being demolished by wrecking ball; the hose is used to control dust. (UBC Architecture)

repeatedly at intervals across the site and removing the water thus displaced.

3. A third technique involves *preloading* the entire site with sand, applied to a depth of 1 to 2 m or 3 to 6 ft. (depending on circumstances) and left in place for several months, to compress water out of the subsoils. Further consideration of such specialized procedures is beyond the scope of this book.

1.3 Related Work

Work closely connected to this section is described in the following sections, to which reference should be made:

01–050 Field Engineering

02–140 Dewatering

02–200 Earthwork

02–500 Paving

2.0 Products

As the work of this section deals primarily with naturally existing things (such as trees, stumps, bushes, and the like) located at the site, there are few materials or accessories normally required to be provided. Following are some possibilities that may be encountered from time to time:

Explosives. Sometimes blasting is a necessary part of land clearing to remove large or stubborn tree stumps; refer to Section 02–250 in *MasterFormat* for more detail on this topic.

Poison. Occasionally it is necessary to kill off roots and stumps in the earth. A variety of liquid and powder soil-poisoning agents are available to do this work, although there are serious ecological and procedural problems to be considered and resolved before such hazardous chemicals are used. As all such products must be used in strict accordance with manufacturers' directions and governmental regulations, none of them will be listed in this section.

3.0 Construction Aids

3.1 Equipment

The primary pieces of equipment used in connection with this work are briefly identified below. The first two are described in more detail in Section 02–200.

Bulldozer. This may be fitted with a sharp blade attachment instead of a bucket, used to push over or cut off trees near the ground; it may also be fitted with a large steel rake.

Backhoe. This is usually fitted with a toothed bucket and used to pull out small stumps and roots.

Cables. These are usually made from stranded steel, with reinforced galvanized steel eyelets or hoops braided into one or both ends. They are stronger and easier to handle than chains.

Chains. The standard logging or tow chain consists of heavy-duty welded steel links, having a simple round hook at one end and a specially designed grab hook at the other end.

Clearing
Unwanted trees and bushes can be cut down and set aside for disposal. Top soil is cleared, ready for stripping (before construction) and replacement or sale (after construction). (UBC Architecture)

Fan. A heavy-duty gas- or electric-powered fan is used to increase airflow to promote burning of wooden debris.

Rake blade. This is an attachment for the bulldozer, consisting of an open rectangular grid of heavy, solid steel bars that act like a large sieve or rake.

Shredder/chipper. This machine has a large steel hopper into which small cut branches, twigs, and leaves can be thrown against rapidly rotating blades, powered by a gas motor connected to a large weighted flywheel which imparts powerful inertial forces to the blades. The whirling blades reduce the vegetation to a form of mulch and eject the particles into a bin.

Tree-cutter. This is a tractor-mounted device, having metal arms capable of gripping the trunks of small- to medium-sized trees and large, powerful, scissor-type blades capable of cutting through the trunk just above ground level. The vertical cut tree can then be moved, turned horizontally, and placed on site or on a truck bed as desired before the grip is released (see Figure 1).

Winch. This is an accessory usually attached to a bulldozer or heavy trucks. It consists of a steel drum, powered by the bulldozer or truck engine, capable of being rotated to wind in or pay out heavy-duty rope or steel cables.

3.2 Tools

Some tools commonly used in this work are described below:

Block. This consists of two or more pulley wheels, set on an axle in a steel block, and is intended to give

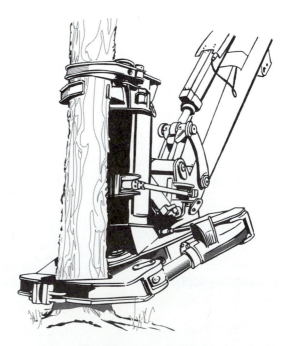

Figure 1 Trunk Cutting

improved mechanical advantage to various configurations of ropes or cables being used to remove trees or stumps.

Chainsaw. This consists of a flat steel plate, up to 1 m or yd. in length, used as a guide for a continuous chain having sharp saw teeth fastened to it at regular intervals. The plate is fastened to the casing of a small portable gas or electric motor, which is the power source for the rotating chain.

Choker. This is a length of cable with a loop on one end, capable of being passed around the trunk of a tree or stump and cinched up tight so that the tree or stump can be dragged out of position.

Root-hook. This is a short wooden or steel shaft having a steel hook at the end, used to push under lateral root systems to pull them out of the ground.

Wedge. This is literally a small wedge-shaped block of mild carbon steel or hard neoprene plastic, used to pry sawn or split surfaces of wood apart, primarily to control the direction of fall of a whole tree or parts of it.

Burning Wood Waste
Many localities permit burning of wood debris on site. The piled cuttings may burn naturally; occasionally forced-air fans can be used to assist controlled burning in windrows or ditches. (BCIT Building Technology)

Discarding Waste
If burning is not practical, tree trunks can often be bucked and stacked for sale as lumber or cordwood. Alternatively, wood debris may be chipped, shredded, and dumped off-site. (UBC Architecture)

4.0 Production

4.1 Crew Configuration

Crew sizes usually range from two to four people, usually involving at least one with forestry skills, one with carpentry skills, and a couple of semiskilled workers, experienced in this phase of development.

4.2 Productivity

It takes about 60 minutes for a skilled faller to manually clear, cut, and fell a medium-sized tree under average conditions, and about 100 to 120 minutes to trim and buck the felled tree, using a chainsaw.

It takes about 30 minutes for a machine operator using a bulldozer to get into position and fell a medium-sized tree. Although this is twice as quick as manual work, it could also cost twice as much, as much work remains to be done once the tree is on the ground. Felled and trimmed trees can be moved to a central area for more rapid bucking into shorter lengths.

Shrubs, bushes, and small trees are usually removed by bulldozer at the rate of about one every 30 seconds; occasionally some stubborn ones might take up to 4 or 5 minutes. A tractor-mounted rake should be able to clear and grub 1 hectare or 2 acres of land in two days. Manual labor to grub up medium-sized roots will require between 10 and 15 man-hours per stump.

5.0 Procedures

The varying circumstances encountered at each separate site will obviously dictate the precise procedure to be followed in each specific case. Nevertheless, it is possible to group basic clearing operations into the following four types: tree felling, stump grubbing, shrub removal, and general cleanup.

5.1 Tree Felling

If really large trees, or large quantities of medium-sized trees, are encountered on a construction site, it may be advisable to retain the services of professional tree fallers to accomplish the task safely and efficiently; the detailed procedures and specialized equipment used by such personnel are beyond the scope of this book. For the purposes of this section, medium-sized trees shall be considered to be between 15 and 25 m or 50 and 75 ft. tall.

It is often possible to top taller trees (that is, cut off sections in lengths of about 2 m or 6 ft. starting from the top) to bring each tree down to a more manageable height, usually to avoid damage to neighboring property. For smaller trees, or small quantities of medium-sized trees, it is usually possible for the general contractor to do the work directly, by renting appropriate equipment and hiring trained personnel.

The sequence of activity for manual felling is as follows:

1. A cutting pattern is determined by examining the lean of the trees and the direction in which they may be naturally inclined to fall or have to be felled because of obstructions. Generally, on sloping sites, it is best to work from the lower levels upward, and to fell the trees downward. The vertical height and width of each tree indicate the minimum horizontal space on the ground that the felled tree will occupy.

2. All debris and brush around the base of the trees must be removed, for three reasons: to allow proper access for tools and equipment, to avoid interference with the direction of fall of the tree, and to permit several quick and safe exits for the fallers. If the stumps are to be removed later, care should be taken to cut each tree off sufficiently high above ground to provide good leverage when pulling the stump out.

3. The first cut in the tree, called the under-cut, is made on the side nearest to the intended direction of fall. It is a vee- or wedge-shaped cut, with the top plane horizontal and the bottom plane sloping downward, and should extend inward between one-quarter and one-third of the diameter of the tree trunk at that point.

4. The next cut, called the back-cut, is made on the side remote from the direction of fall, about 50 mm or 2 in. above the top of the under-cut. The back-cut is extended through the trunk until the tree starts to fall, at which moment the saw should be removed and the fallers should quickly stand clear. This will usually occur before the front of the back-cut overlaps the back of the under-cut, the result being that the remaining uncut wood in the middle of the trunk will largely control the general direction of the falling tree.

5. If it is necessary to change the natural direction of the fall, wedges can be inserted into the back-cut and cables can be attached to the higher members of the tree, to control the direction (though not the rate) of descent.

6. Finally, the felled tree is trimmed of useless branches and then bucked or cut into serviceable lengths and the pieces stacked, ready for use as firewood, for sale to a lumber mill, or for other disposal.

For machine removal using a tree-cutter, see Part 3.1 Equipment. For machine removal using bulldozers and blades, see Part 5.3 Shrub Removal.

5.2 Stump Grubbing

The stump is the piece of the tree between the root system and the cut line. Grubbing is the act of removing the stump and root system after the tree has been felled. Stumps are more easily removed from loose sandy soils than from stiff clay soils.

There are five principal techniques used to grub stumps efficiently; all of them involve considerable force. The techniques are pushing, pulling, digging, blasting, and grinding. In some regions, grubbed stumps may be buried on site, with permission; elsewhere, they must be removed off site and properly disposed of in an authorized manner.

Pushing. The dozer blade is set to contact the stump about 30 cm or 12 in. above the ground. In

low gear, the dozer pushes the stump until the roots appear out of the ground below the blade. The dozer is backed off, the blade is lowered beneath the exposed roots, and the process is repeated until all roots on one side are free. The process is then repeated on the opposite side of the stump, until the entire unit is free of the ground. Sometimes gentle rocking of the dozer against the reverse pressure be-

Improving Property
If it is desired to retain but relocate existing valuable trees, a truck-mounted hydraulic root ball remover can be used. A gas-powered stump grinder rapidly reduces small stumps to mulch. (UBC Architecture)

ing exerted by the stump will help to free particularly stubborn root systems.

Pulling. A small wedge is cut about 30 cm or 12 in. above the ground on the side opposite the proposed line of pull. One end of a chain or cable is fitted into the wedge cut and choked around the stump; the other end is attached to a dozer or a winch, both capable of exerting great pulling power. To use the winch, the dozer must be facing away from the stump and be locked in place using its brakes in addition to an anchor line attached to some other permanently fixed point, so that the stump, the dozer, and the fixed point are all aligned.

To remove excessively large stumps, it is sometimes necessary to provide a system of pulley blocks to increase the pulling force. One pulley is located on the line between the winch and one fixed point. A second pulley can be located on the line between the first pulley and a second fixed point. A third pulley can be connected to the second pulley by a sling block. A choker cable is connected from the sling block to the stump to be pulled. The effect of this arrangement is to increase the maximum pulling force by a factor of four, as shown in Figure 2.

Digging. A trench is cut by a bulldozer or backhoe on all four sides of the stump, down to the level of the underside of the main root system; during this process, the smaller roots are also cut through. A short ramp is then dug to permit the dozer or backhoe blade to get under the main root system from one side. Once the stump has been loosened and raised to the level of the surrounding ground, it can be temporarily supported by blocks of wood until the dozer or backhoe can move around to pull it aside in some other way.

Blasting. There are two common techniques: mud-capping and splitting, shown in Figure 3. In mud-capping, a small hole is made in the soil among the root system, a small charge of 40 percent dyna-mite is inserted with a fuse attached, and a layer of mud is then used to cap the hole. Upon detonation, the stump will be blown out of the ground. In splitting, a small stick of dynamite is inserted into a drilled hole in the body of the wooden stump, attached to a fuse, and then capped. Upon detonation, the wood is split and the root system disturbed to the point of removal.

Grinding. A special machine is used to grind what is left of the stump in the ground, to reduce it to a level below that of the finished grade.

5.3 Shrub Removal

For machine removal of shrubs, bushes, small trees, and similar vegetation, bulldozers with blades can be effectively used. On one pass in one direction with the blade high enough to provide good leverage, the vegetation is uprooted and pushed over. If roots protrude, the dozer can be backed off, the blade lowered, and the roots then pushed out. On a second pass in the opposite direction, again with the blade lowered, the dozer will push over and pull out most of the items missed or incompletely moved on the first pass. If small- to medium-sized trees are being pushed over by machine, care should be taken not to get the dozer caught up on the emerging root systems of trees as they overturn ahead of the machine. There are also bladed machines which can dig out small trees completely by their roots.

Another method used to clear shrubbery, undergrowth, and small trees (having trunk diameters less than 40 cm or 15 in.) is to secure a heavy chain about 25 to 30 m or yd. long to the rear of two bulldozers of equal power and weight. The two dozers then proceed at identical speeds in a parallel direction about 10 to 15 m or yd. apart, dragging the chain along the ground between and behind them. This has the effect of ripping all small plants and bushes out by the roots as the chain passes over them.

5.4 General Cleanup

For machine removal of surface vegetation and minor debris, bulldozers with blades usually start around the outer perimeter of the site and work in a spiral toward the center, pushing stripped materials in front of them. If the ground is very rough and uneven, there will be a loss of productivity as the blade will not be in uniform contact with the surface of the ground. If burning is permitted, it is best done quickly in long windrows (see Figure 4) rather than slowly in single large bonfire piles.

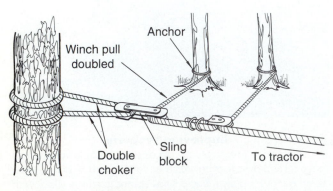

Figure 2   Pulley Systems

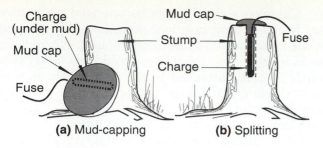

Figure 3 Mud-Capping and Splitting

(a) Mud-capping

(b) Splitting

Shallow trenches can be dug, the trash, slash, and debris to be burned laid or pushed into the trenches, and then fresh air, forced by a fan, directed through lightweight ductwork with outlets at intervals onto the debris to assist the burning to occur faster, at a higher temperature, and with less smoke. If burning is not permitted, then the debris must be hauled away in dump trucks.

5.5 Precautions

Personnel should not stand in the line of falling trees or in front of moving equipment. A sharp lookout should be maintained to avoid injury from whiplash or spring-back, which may occur when tension in a tree trunk or branch is suddenly relieved. Similarly, when chains or cables are under tension, they may snap with deadly force; therefore personnel should be kept out of the line and distance of possible recoil, or else they should be protected by cages. Individuals have been regrettably but literally cut in two or decapitated in such accidents.

Consideration should be given to developing appropriate warning signals for use by operational personnel, to aid communications on the job-site, and to arrange for any necessary temporary diversions of traffic or service lines, on or adjacent to the site. Where blasting is contemplated, care should be taken to remove any stones or rocks near the explosive charges that could inadvertently become dangerous projectiles upon detonation.

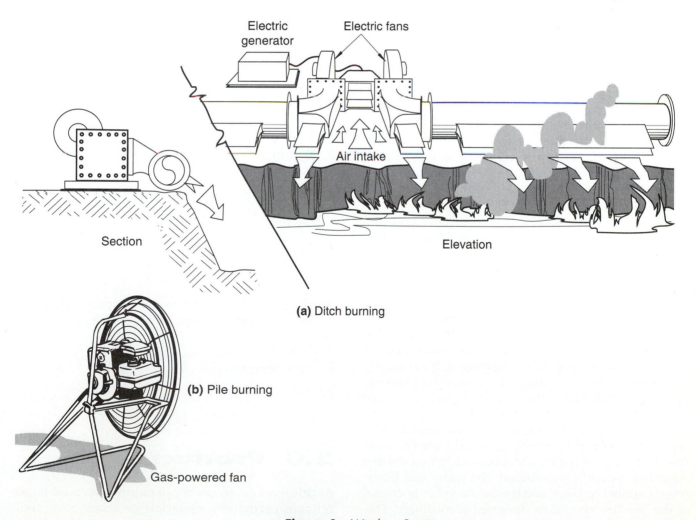

(a) Ditch burning

(b) Pile burning

Figure 4 Windrow Burning

Where soil- or plant-poisoning chemicals are used, manufacturer's directions and legislated restrictions must be reviewed, understood, and strictly followed. Where burning of slash or debris is permitted and contemplated, care must be taken to prevent the fire or sparks from getting out of control, and to provide adequate firefighting equipment and personnel. Fuels used to ignite such fires should have a low flash point, such as kerosene or diesel fuel; white gas or gasoline, which can be explosive upon ignition, should not be used.

Chainsaws should only be operated when they are in the cutting position; they should be stopped while being moved from place to place. When using tools to top trees, the tools should have safety lanyards or cords attached to the faller's belt, to prevent them from falling to the ground, to avoid damage to the tools or injury to workers, and also to save time of having to climb down to retrieve them. Wooden handles of hand tools should be of smooth, straight-grained hardwood without defects and should be securely attached to the metal parts of such tools.

Section 02–140 Dewatering

1.0 Introduction

1.1 General Issues

Without question, water is essential to life; without it, animal and vegetable life would perish. One can also say that with too much of it, life and its activities can become imperiled. Water is the most important single natural element with which designers, builders, owners, and humans in general have to contend. Water is one of the most fundamental and pervasive aspects of nearly all building design and procedure. It is largely because of water that we design and construct buildings, to shelter ourselves from water in its many forms (such as vapor, rain, hail, sleet, snow, and ice) and to control or restrain the flow of water and moisture to our advantage (by the use of vapor barriers and plumbing, heating, and ventilating systems).

It frequently happens that sites proposed for buildings have water problems associated with them: there is either too little or too much. If too little, then usually a well can be dug or a pipeline brought to the site, to deliver as much water as necessary first to build the building and then to operate it. If too much, then some form of drainage or dewatering system must be considered, either on a temporary or permanent basis.

In general, the dewatering systems described in this section would be effective only during the construction stage of the building project. When the dewatering system is terminated, the water will likely return, sooner or later, and the below-grade portions of the building should be designed accordingly. The design of sites requiring permanent dewatering is beyond the scope of this book, as is description of some of the more esoteric dewatering systems, such as electro-osmosis of fine-grained soils.

In simplest terms, dewatering is the process of removing surface water or extracting subsurface water from a building site. There are several ways that this can be done; these will be examined later in this section. There are four primary design reasons that dewatering might be contemplated:

1. To predrain the soil.
2. To control or reduce the levels of ground water.
3. To remove or deflect surface water.
4. To improve the bearing capacity of the earth materials at foundation level.

1.2 Related Work

Work closely connected to this section is described in the following sections, to which reference should be made:

02–100   Preparation

02–200   Earthwork

2.0 Products

As this work is temporary in nature, there are no significant permanent materials or accessories applicable to this section.

3.0 Construction Aids

3.1 Equipment

Some of the following pieces of equipment may be encountered:

Centrifugal pumps. These are usually electric or gasoline powered, having outputs ranging from 50 to 5,000 liters or 20 to 2,000 gallons per minute.

Drills. There are two types: hand-held and boom-track. Both are powered by compressed air.

1. Hand-held drills, sometimes called sinker drills or jack hammers, weigh between 15 and 30 kg or 30 and 70 lb, and are capable of drilling holes to a depth of 3 m or 10 ft.
2. Track drills are of two types: high speed and low speed. High speed drills are not often used for construction work; low speed boom-track drills can drill down to 15 m or 50 ft.

Risers. These are lengths of galvanized steel tubing, threaded at the ends, used in well-point systems to connect between the well-point tips and the header pipes.

Sump pumps. These are usually electric or gasoline powered, having outputs ranging from 150 to 2,000 liters or 50 to 500 gallons per minute.

Trucks. Regular road-worthy vehicles are used to transport the system components from yard to site and back; they should be equipped with hydraulic arms for handling heavyweight components. Occasionally, tank trucks may be required to transport water onto or off the site.

Well-point tips. These consist of short steel pipes, prepared for threaded connection to the riser pipes, approximately 15 cm or 6 in. in diameter. The bottom is fitted with a heavy-duty ball valve device and a filter screen, as shown in Figure 1.

3.2 Tools

Adjustable wrenches, hammers, measuring tapes, carpenter's levels, and the like may be required from time to time, to lay out and connect various component parts.

Sump Pumps

Shown are two small submersible electric pumps used to keep trenches and pits free of small quantities of water. Larger gas-powered pumps are also available for more severe conditions. (UBC Architecture)

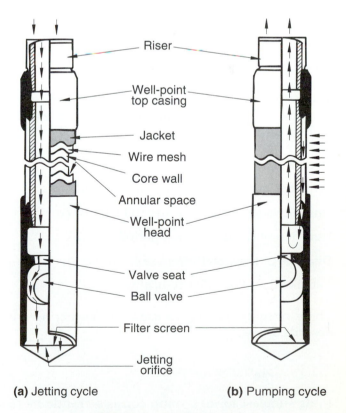

Riser
Well-point top casing
Jacket
Wire mesh
Core wall
Annular space
Well-point head
Valve seat
Ball valve
Filter screen
Jetting orifice

(a) Jetting cycle   **(b)** Pumping cycle

Figure 1   Well-Point Tips

4.0 Production

4.1 Crew Configuration

Normally, a foreman, a journeyman or qualified plumber, and a semiskilled helper would form a crew for this work.

4.2 Productivity

With respect to digging of pits and trenches for use as sumps by hand or machine, details are given in Section 02–200. With respect to well-pointing, because of the many variables in job-site conditions, equipment availability, and crew efficiencies, it is impractical to give precise data for every eventuality that may be encountered. Instead, a simple example is given to indicate likely productivity involved in preparing for dewatering a small site, to provide some indication of output:

Example: Installation and removal of 100 m or yd. of header with 60 well-points at 1.5-m or 2-yd. intervals plus two pumps would take a typical crew about four days. Once started, the system must be continuously operated to keep the water levels under control. It is prudent to keep a spare workable pump, some well-point tips, and a few extra sections of riser pipe at the site, in case of system failure.

5.0 Procedures

There are a number of considerations to be taken into account before deciding which dewatering technique to employ in a given situation:

Overall size of the project.

Investigation of the soil and subsoil conditions.

Quantity and quality of water to be removed.

Duration of the dewatering period.

Disposal of the water removed from the site.

The likelihood of water returning.

Three primary techniques used for dewatering are described next.

5.1 Sumps

In its simplest form, a sump consists of little more than an artificial depression (such as a trench or a

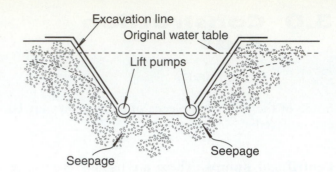

Figure 2 Simple Sump

pit) in the ground where free water can accumulate through gravitational force, as shown in Figure 2. Sumps work best in soils that are relatively impervious to water; more porous soils permit the water to disperse with less control. Water in the sump can be removed by use of a sump pump and lengths of hose to direct the flow of water for disposal.

5.2 Wells

In simplest terms in this context, a well is a hole drilled into the earth, as shown in Figure 3. Wells can be shallow or deep, narrow or wide, single or multiple. The dividing line between shallow and deep is defined at about 8 m or 25 ft. Common diameters for construction wells range from 100 to 1,000 mm or 4 to 36 in. Single wells are usually used for test purposes to determine water quantities and levels; multiple wells are used to effectively drain portions of construction sites. Through gravitational force, wa-

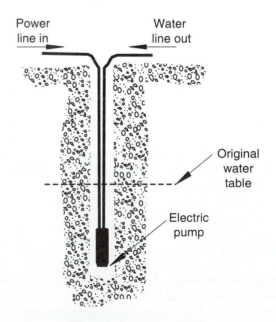

Figure 3 Simple Well

Pumping Process
The pump is placed in the trench or pit with a rope attached to aid recovery. Suitable electric power and a discharge hose are connected and the unit is then switched on. (BCIT Building Technology)

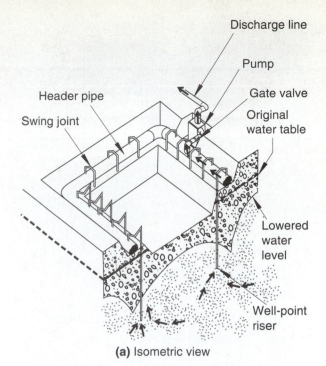

(a) Isometric view

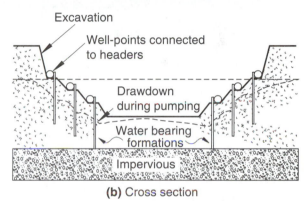

(b) Cross section

Figure 4   Well-Point Layout

ter will seep into the well shaft; submersible electric pumps can be lowered to the bottom of the shaft to force the water up and out.

5.3 Well-Points

The well-point system consists of a lateral collection or header pipe having a diameter between 20 and 40 cm or 8 and 16 in. that is placed around the perimeter of the site or portion to be dewatered, connected through swing joints to a number of vertical well-point risers located at intervals of about 1.5 to 2 m or 4 to 6 ft. along the header which are of appropriate length (or, more correctly, depth) as determined by a soils analysis. Well-point tips are attached to the lower end of each riser. For general layout, see Figure 4.

To install the system in reasonably soft and permeable soils, a centrifugal pump is used to force water under pressure along the headers, down the well-points, and out through the ball-valves, causing the well-point riser pipes to sink to predetermined depths. In stiffer, harder soils, a larger-diameter hole can be predrilled using conventional drilling equipment, a continuous metal sleeve inserted, the well-point riser pipe placed in the sleeve, and fine sand run in between the sleeve and the pipe, after which the sleeve is withdrawn.

To extract water through the system, a centrifugal pump is used to create a powerful vacuum in the headers and riser pipes, thus causing atmospheric pressure to force water out of the soil and into the riser pipes, through the filter screens, along the header, and into a surface discharge pipe. The water thus removed can be directed to any location where it cannot seep back into the drained area of the site, or it can be trucked off site.

5.4 Precautions

One primary restriction concerns the discharge of water removed from the site, as care must be taken not to damage or adversely disturb adjacent properties through altered flows of water. The drying and shrinking of dewatered soils can cause slippage and subsidence. The discharge of excessive amounts of water onto neighboring properties can cause damage from flooding and decay. Conversely, removal of

Dewatering System

Larger water problems require larger pumping solutions. This photo shows a perimeter piping system (equipped with branches and valves at intervals) connected to a central pump. (BCIT Building Technology)

Well Points

Well points are drilled and steel pipes are connected to the central system at each branch to extract water under high pressure from any established depth below grade. (BCIT Building Technology)

water from the site under development can cause reduction in quantities of water being available on adjacent properties, with consequent risk of legal claims, if the amounts of water necessary for living, agriculture, or manufacturing processes on these adjacent sites is adversely affected.

Section 02–150 Protection

1.0 Introduction

1.1 General Issues

Protection of excavated areas is necessary for two good reasons:

1. Most cities, towns, counties, and municipalities require it, to protect the public and the workers; and

2. Prudence suggests that it is better to prevent accidents from happening than to try to rectify their results later, through payment of either costs of replacement, monetary damages, medical expenses, or all three.

Consequently, there are a number of systems used to prevent property damage or personal injury from occurring as a result of excavation activities in trenches, pits, or banks, either during work in progress or upon completion. Such systems usually involve shoring, sheeting, or underpinning; this terminology is explained as follows:

1. The word *shoring* is borrowed from a term describing the protection used to prevent erosion of

the "shore" side of a breakwater. Currents of water swirling around the outer end of such a breakwater would rapidly wash away any unprotected materials on the leeward or shore side, so slabs of stone or concrete are used to minimize such effects. Similarly, shoring is used in construction processes to eliminate or reduce the potentially dangerous effects of soil erosion after excavation has occurred.

2. The word *sheeting* is self-evident; it means any broad, thin mass of material used as a covering. In construction, sheets of plastic or canvas are sometimes draped over the face of excavated surfaces to prevent erosion by rainwater; sheet pilings are sometimes constructed to form a type of solid retaining wall to prevent collapse of a steep or high excavated face.

3. The word *underpinning* means a system of permanent new supports inserted under an existing foundation or wall, to permit alterations to the foundation or wall itself or to immediately adjacent property.

1.2 Related Work

Work closely connected to this section is described in the following sections, to which reference should be made:

02–200   Earthwork

06–100   Rough Carpentry

Trenches
Deep trenches can be made safe by inserting sheeting and cross-braces cinched together as shown in this photo. OSHA and most WCB regulations are stringent and specific in this regard. (UBC Architecture)

2.0 Products

2.1 Materials

Basic materials are of wood, steel, plastic, or shotcrete.

Wood. All wood members should be a botanical softwood such as fir, hemlock, or spruce, and should be of a good structural grade, sound and free of defects that might impair strength or suitability. It is not usually necessary to treat members with wood preservatives, provided they are not left in place for extended periods of time. Thick plywood is occasionally used for close sheeting.

Steel. Steel for bracing, stringers, and sheeting should be of good commercial quality and be specially designed and treated for the various purposes intended.

Plastic. Large sheets of plain or fiber-reinforced polyvinyl chloride plastic are frequently used to cover exposed surfaces of excavated areas.

Shotcrete. This is a concrete-like material (also known as gunite), made from a mixture of rapid-setting cement, sand, water, and admixtures, sprayed under high pressure onto exposed excavated embankments or faces.

2.2 Accessories

Accessories such as bolts, washers, shims, screws, nails, cleats, and the like should be purpose-made and treated for use in such work and specially selected having regard to the specific conditions of use anticipated.

Vertical Sheeting
Open faces of shallow excavations usually can be protected by sloping the sides. Deep vertical faces require sheeting, shown here to be anchored steel piles restraining solid timber planks. (UBC Architecture)

3.0 Construction Aids

3.1 Equipment

The most common piece of equipment used in this work is the hydraulic or pneumatic jack in place of the wooden or steel brace.

3.2 Tools

The tools used in this work are the same as those used for ordinary carpentry work, described in Section 06–100.

4.0 Production

4.1 Crew Configuration

This work is normally done by carpenters and their helpers. A typical crew might consist of two skilled carpenters, two semiskilled helpers, and one or two unskilled laborers.

4.2 Productivity

In shoring, consider a trench about 2 m wide, 3 m deep, and 30 m long (or approximately 6 ft. wide, 10 ft. deep, and 100 ft. long), requiring to be braced on both faces with wooden open shoring placed at 1-m or 3-ft. intervals, using pneumatic jacks. This would entail about 200 m² or 2,000 ft.² of shoring. It would take two carpenters and one helper about 20 man-hours to install this quantity of this system, and another 4 man-hours to strike it or remove it. This can be reduced to 10 m² or 100 ft.² per man-hour for installation and 50 m² or 500 ft.² per man-hour for removal, working under ideal conditions. For poor conditions, these data can be reduced by a factor of up to 20 percent.

In placing plastic sheets, productivity might be figured at around 100 m² or 1,000 ft.² per man-hour.

Shotcrete output is about 50 percent that of plastic sheeting.

5.0 Procedures

5.1 Systems

There are two protective systems commonly encountered in excavation work: closed sheeting and open shoring. Both systems consist of diagonal or cross-bracing members which support horizontal stringer members, which in turn restrain vertical supporting members that are in actual contact with the material to be supported. These verticals are set either side by side in close butt contact or interlocking with each other, called closed sheeting (see Figure 1), or spaced apart at intervals, called open shoring (see Figure 2).

Plain sheeting involves the placement of plastic sheets, described later.

5.2 Components

The components of this work are as follows:

Bracing. In open-face excavations, there are three parts to the bracing members: the strong back, the brace, and the picket. Where excavations occur in trenches, the brace members and pickets may be replaced with a steel screw jack of appropriate size and strength. Bracing should always be cut slightly oversize and then be tightly wedged into position, with no joints in any of the parts.

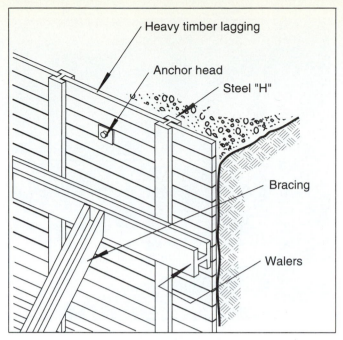

(a) Basic system

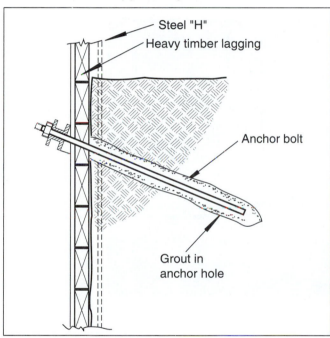

(b) Anchor device

Figure 1 Closed Sheeting

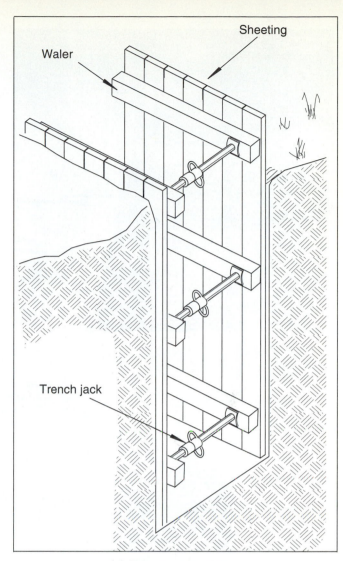

(a) Telescope bracing

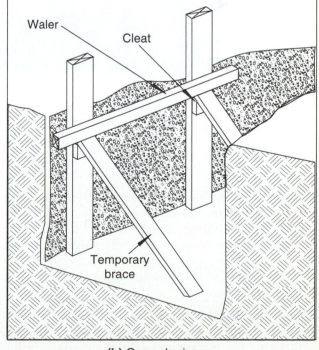

(b) Open shoring

Figure 2 Shoring Types

Embankments
Open faces of excavations can sometimes be protected with plastic and wire mesh or gunited concrete. Stockpiles of loose earth can be protected from erosion with heavy-duty tarpaulins. (BCIT Building Technology)

Stringers. These members, also called walers or ribs (from historical origins having to do with wooden boat building), usually run the length of the excavated face or faces at vertically spaced intervals depending on the amount of support necessary. Care should be taken to offset joints at ends of walers in successive levels.

Closed sheeting. Vertical members are fitted in one piece between the stringers and the excavated surfaces to be supported, with their edges either closely butted if of wood or interlocked if of steel, to prevent noncohesive materials such as sand or gravel from slipping into the excavated areas.

Open shoring. Vertical members are similarly fitted in one piece between the stringers and the surfaces to be supported, but they are spaced horizontally at a predetermined distance apart, depending on the cohesiveness of the soils such as clay or hardpan to be supported.

Bracing

Buildings under extensive renovation (as in this example) need portions braced as a precaution against collapse. Steel stiffeners are bolted through available openings. (UBC Architecture)

5.3 Sequence

In general, sheeting and shoring operations commence from the top down. Sheeting and shoring should extend from a point 30 cm or 12 in. above the grade level to the lowest possible level of each excavated area. Sheets or shores are temporarily placed, small cleats are secured to support the walers if necessary, walers are tacked to sheets or shores, and braces are installed. Conversely, during striking or extraction operations, lower bracing and walers are removed first, working upward to the top of the excavation.

Care should be taken to keep all upright members essentially plumb, within 10 degrees of the vertical. Diagonals should be at about 45 degrees, with long members intermediately subbraced for stiffness. Ends of brace members should not bear directly on the shoring or sheeting members, as they may pierce them after loads are imposed.

5.4 Other Techniques

Plain sheeting is done by simply rolling out plain or reinforced plastic sheet from the top down, taking care to fasten sheets securely at top edges and to overlap and secure sheets at vertical edges (see Figure 3).

Shotcreting is done by carefully spraying the liquid concrete mixture onto the prepared surfaces to be coated, taking care not to dislodge any of the parent material (see Figure 4).

Underpinning is done by carefully removing small sections of earth in sequence under the foundation or wall to be supported, and then quickly inserting a new construction system designed to sustain the old load (see Figure 5). Hydraulic jacks or piles can be used to temporarily support the existing structure while the new construction is undertaken.

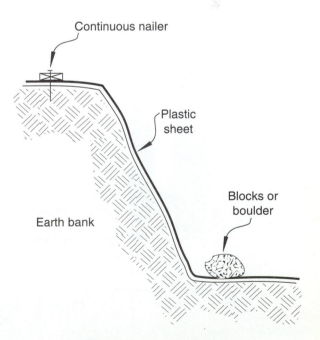

Figure 3 Plastic Sheeting

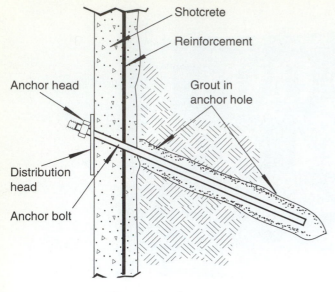

Figure 4 Shotcreting

Labels on figure: Shotcrete, Reinforcement, Anchor head, Grout in anchor hole, Distribution head, Anchor bolt

5.5 Backfilling

For safety and convenience, backfilling should be completed as soon as possible after excavation protection is removed. In particularly deep excavations, it is a good practice to commence partial backfilling at the lower levels before all bracing is removed from the upper levels. For further detail on backfilling, see Section 02–200.

5.6 Precautions

A check should be made of the types of earth and soil about to be excavated. If necessary, a soils engineer or geologist may be consulted to determine the nature of the materials to be encountered at various levels between the initial grade and the underside of footings, foundations, or below-grade floor slabs. All shoring and sheeting should be placed in such a way that:

1. It will not interfere with subsequent construction operations, such as the installation of formwork, reinforcing steel, or service pipelines;

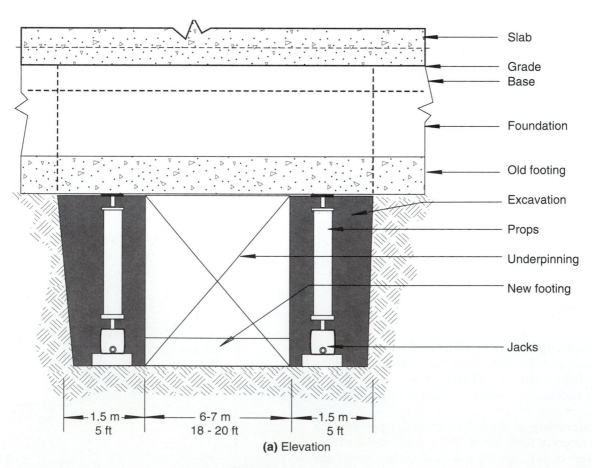

Labels on figure: Slab, Grade, Base, Foundation, Old footing, Excavation, Props, Underpinning, New footing, Jacks

1.5 m / 5 ft   6-7 m / 18 - 20 ft   1.5 m / 5 ft

(a) Elevation

Figure 5 Underpinning

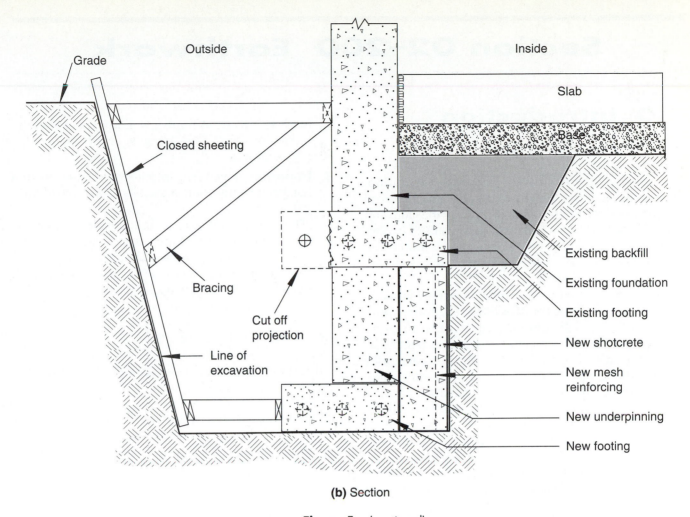

Outside | Inside

Grade

Slab

Base

Closed sheeting

Bracing

Cut off projection

Existing backfill

Existing foundation

Existing footing

New shotcrete

Line of excavation

New mesh reinforcing

New underpinning

New footing

(b) Section

Figure 5 (continued)

2. No joints are located in places that might significantly weaken the composite assembly;

3. Minimal disturbance to the cut faces occurs; and

4. It can be removed easily (if necessary) after it has served its purpose.

All protection systems should be periodically checked by a responsible and knowledgable person to ensure that safe conditions are maintained. Any voids occurring behind the sheeting or shoring should be filled. Ladders should be provided to permit personnel to enter and leave excavated areas without climbing on the protection systems.

Section 02–200 Earthwork

1.0 Introduction

1.1 General Issues

The title *Earthwork* generally embraces excavation, placement, stabilization, and compaction of natural earth materials at the site, including the addition and disposal of earth. The term *earth* as used in construction is generally held to mean the softer soil portions (as distinct from the harder rock portions) of the crust of the earth.

Excavation can be subdivided into two main categories: large-volume (bulk or mass) excavation, and other types of small-volume excavation, such as required for trenches, pits, and post holes. Some major factors affecting excavation in both categories include the nature of the material to be excavated, the types of equipment and tools available, the skill of the excavation machine or tool operators, and the general conditions of work at the site. As it is often very difficult to describe the precise character and extent of the natural soil materials likely to be encountered during excavation procedures, a number of contractual problems can arise as a result of poorly or ambiguously worded specifications.

Because of the large number of variables, some of which are virtually ungovernable, excavation work must be considered as one of the financially riskier of the construction trades.

1.2 Related Work

Work closely connected to this section is described in the following sections, to which reference should be made:

01–050   Field Engineering

02–100   Preparation

02–150   Protection

02–700   Drainage

2.0 Products

2.1 Earth Materials

Earth or soil materials encountered in excavation work are naturally very varied. However, they can be classified first under two broad headings:

1. **Native.** This term implies soil materials that are indigenous to (i.e., existing in or on) the site being excavated.
2. **Imported.** This term implies new material that has been brought onto the site from some external source.

The primary criteria to be considered prior to soil excavation are moisture content and layer structure of the soils likely to be encountered during the excavation processes. These criteria are determined for each site by doing a soils analysis.

2.2 Soil Types

All earth soils can be further classified as one of two types:

1. **Cohesive** or solid soils which include clay, conglomerate, hardpan, loam, rock, shale, and silt.
2. **Noncohesive** or loose soils which include boulders, glacial till, gravel, and sand.

Underground services, buried debris, and other geologic categories of soil are also occasionally encountered during excavation in urban and rural areas. In most regions, archaeological artifacts of any significant historical interest uncovered during excavation processes are protected by a variety of national and local laws; such finds should be reported to the appropriate authorities.

2.3 Swelling and Shrinking

When solid earth materials are loosened by digging, they usually occupy more volume than before; conversely, when excavated materials are compacted, they may take up less volume than before. These phenomena are called *swelling* and *shrinking* (also known as bulkage and shrinkage), and each category of material has its own factors. Using metric units, if ordinary soil is known to weigh 1,250 kg/m³ in its natural solid state and is found to weigh 1,000 kg/m³ in its loose state after excavation, the swell factor is (1,250/1,000-) 1.25 or 25 percent, and the shrink factor is (1,000/1,250-) 0.80 or 20 percent. Note that the two factors are not the same, assuming 100 percent compaction. Another way of expressing the same re-

General View

Excavation can involve just a few small holes or trenches, or can take up much of a city block. Vehicle access into and out of large excavated areas must be considered and later removed. (UBC Architecture)

sult is to say that ordinary soil weighing 1,250 kg/m³ in its natural state and capable of being compacted to 80 percent of its original volume will weigh (1,250 × 1.25-) 1,562 kg/m³ in its compacted state, because 1.25 is the reciprocal of 0.80. When soil is disturbed by excavation, evaporation of moisture usually occurs; upon compaction, there is also a breakdown of smaller particles. These two factors cause higher density (or smaller volumes) of recompacted material. See Figure 1.

3.0 Construction Aids

3.1 Equipment

As earthwork invariably has to be done in place at the site, it does not lend itself to the economies and more rigid controls of factory production techniques, and it is also subject to all the many vagaries of weather and climate. At the same time, unlike much of other building technology processes occurring on site, earthwork tends to be equipment intensive, and there is a great variety of equipment suitable for almost every conceivable earthwork project. Brief descriptions of most of the main types of excavation equipment and tools follow.

Backhoe. This machine looks similar to and functions much like a normal farm tractor, with a light-duty diesel or gasoline engine and four pneumatic-tired wheels (small at the front and large at the rear), and is equipped with an adjustable hydraulic arm at the rear which operates a bucket or scoop of various capacities, together with mechanically extendible stabilizing legs at each side. It is used for general excavation and trenching work. See Figure 2.

Bobcat. This is a small, lightweight, highly maneuverable machine, with a light-duty gas engine, usually mounted on four small pneumatic-tired wheels of equal size, and equipped at the front with a relatively small-capacity bucket or scoop on hydrauli-

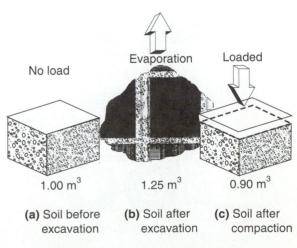

Figure 1 Swelling and Shrinking

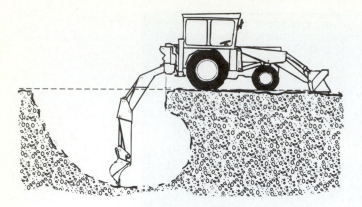

Figure 2   Backhoe

Figure 4   Bulldozer (UBC Architecture)

cally operated arms. It is often used on small jobs in place of a backhoe. See Figure 3.

Bulldozer. A bulldozer is usually larger and more powerful than a backhoe, with a heavy-duty diesel engine, track mounted as distinct from wheeled, and capable of being fitted at the front with a variety of shovels, blades, or scoops of varying capacities to move large quantities of soil around. It is used to strip topsoil and generally to push quantities of earth and soil around on the site. See Figure 4.

Clamshell. The power source for this machine is a large, heavy-duty diesel engine, mounted on a movable, tracked chassis, capable of rotating through 360 degrees, and fitted with a lengthy, steel-framed

boom to which a clamshell bucket is attached and controlled by strong cables from an enclosed cab. The clamshell consists of two large, heavy steel cups, hinged at the top and with interlocking teeth along the bottom edges; it is dropped into the soil in the open position, forced shut, and then raised to remove the soil. The whole rig is then rotated over to a truck or dump, and the bucket is opened to release the excavated load. This machine is not encountered in any but the largest of excavation projects. See Figure 5.

Compactor. This device usually takes the form of a large steel drum, having a central axle attached to a steel frame, and intended to be towed behind or pushed in front of a bulldozer, truck, or tractor. The drum may be either empty or filled with water, con-

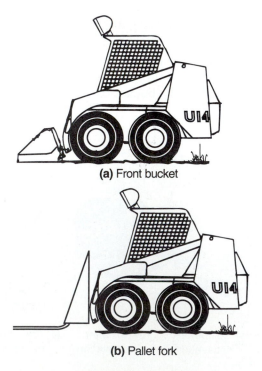

(a) Front bucket

(b) Pallet fork

Figure 3   Bobcat

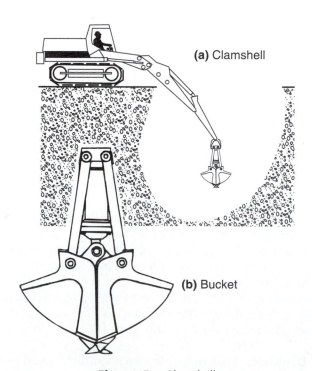

(a) Clamshell

(b) Bucket

Figure 5   Clamshell

Figure 6 Compactor

Figure 8 Front-End Loader (UBC Architecture)

crete, or other substances. It may either be smooth faced or have projections on its surface; this latter type is known as a "sheep's foot" roller, because each of the projections has a vague resemblance to the foot of a sheep. A special form of compactor is called the "wobbly wheeled" roller, and consists of a series of five or six large, heavy, rubber-tired wheels loosely mounted side by side in line on a single axle. As the device moves over the ground, the wheels wobble slightly from side to side and thus compact the soil more effectively. It is used, of course, for compaction of earth and soil. See Figure 6.

Dragline. Basically the same as the clamshell, the dragline has a cable arrangement which causes a heavy-duty bucket to be dragged down into, through, and then up out of the soil to be moved. It is seldom encountered on normal projects. See Figure 7.

Front-end loader. This machine is a cross between a backhoe and a bulldozer. The power source is usu-

ally a light-duty, tractor-like machine, with hydraulic arms at the front to operate buckets or blades of various sizes and configurations. These machines often also have a backhoe device attached at the rear. It is used for general light excavation work. See Figure 8.

Hydraulic shovel. This piece of equipment is a diesel-powered, hydraulically operated shovel, mounted on a specially prepared truck bed. The shovel is mounted at the end of a telescoping boom, capable of being extended or withdrawn to any distance within the limits of the machine, and also of being rotated through about 90 degrees either side of the central axis of the telescoping arm. It is used mostly for fine though rapid grading work on embankments, ditches, and the like. Such machines are popularly called "gradalls," although the word "Gradall" is actually the copyright brand name of one specific manufacturer. See Figure 9.

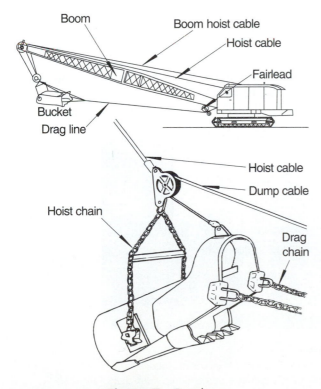

Figure 7 Dragline

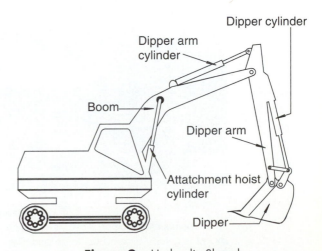

Figure 9 Hydraulic Shovel

Figure 10 Post-Hole Digger (BCIT Building Technology)

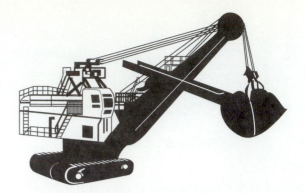

Figure 11 Power Shovel

Post-hole digger. This is a device shaped like an auger or corkscrew, occasionally used manually but more frequently attached to the rear of a bulldozer or backhoe for power operation. As the name implies, it is used to quickly dig accurately placed and dimensioned holes. See Figure 10.

Power shovel. As the name implies, this is a heavy-duty power source, similar to the clamshell in size and operation, but instead of having an open steel-frame boom, it has a primary, fixed, closed steel shaft to support a secondary, sliding steel shaft, to which the bucket or scoop is attached. Both shafts are raised, lowered, and otherwise maneuvered by a complex arrangement of pulleys and cables. Such shovels are available in two basic configurations: those that dig by cables pulling the bucket away from the cab, and those that pull the bucket toward

the cab. They are used for general-duty to heavy-duty excavation work. See Figure 11.

Ripper. This is a single-toothed device that can be fitted to the front or back of a bulldozer to permit paving or graveled surfaces to be ripped up or loosened to minimal depths. See Figure 12.

Scraper. This machine looks like a very large diesel-powered tractor, with the operator's cab mounted on four or six large pneumatic-tired wheels, and having a large, heavy-duty, steel blade mounted on a hydraulically adjustable frame in front of the vehicle, midway between the rear and two additional steerable forward wheels. It is used to scrape off thin layers of earth or soil. See Figure 13.

Tamper (powered). This consists of a metal housing, containing a small gas engine which drives an eccentric cam which converts the rotary motion of the engine into a vertical oscillation, causing the whole device to bounce up and down on a broad rectangular base plate, thus compressing the ground below. See Figure 14.

Power Shovel

A tractor-mounted power shovel is commonly used for average-sized excavation jobs. Here, a shovel is quickly digging out large quantities of stiff clay and loading it into a dump truck. (UBC Architecture)

Figure 12 Ripper

Trencher. This is a light-duty, track-mounted power source similar to the bulldozer, but instead of having a blade or bucket, it is fitted with an adjustable cutting device that can be raised, lowered, or moved from side to side. The cutting device consists of small steel cups, fastened to a circular wheel or to a continuous ladder-type belt; earlier models utilized a vertical boom arrangement. They are specially made to dig trenches quickly and accurately. See Figure 15.

Trucks. Heavy-duty, diesel-powered trucks are used to haul earth materials from or to the construction site. They usually have a hydraulically powered lifting feature, permitting the box of the truck to be tipped up to any desired angle to cause the load to be dumped out through a tailgate. They should also be capable of reaching and maintaining reasonable highway speeds when fully loaded.

Figure 13 Scraper (UBC Architecture)

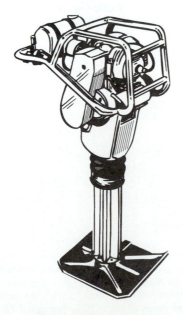

Figure 14 Tamper

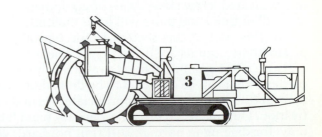

Figure 15 Trencher

3.3 Tools

The following tools are commonly used in this work:

Auger. This is a vertical wood or metal shaft with a double circular blade at the bottom and a crossbar handle at the top, suitable for digging postholes.

Jimmy or prybar. This is a vertical steel shaft, having a point at one end and a narrow, chisel-like blade at the other, suitable for loosening soil, stones, or small boulders.

Shovel. This tool consists of a vertical wood or metal shaft with either a straight or slightly curved blade at the bottom, and either a plain straight handle or a "D" handle at the top, suitable for trimming sides and bottoms of pits or trenches.

Tamper (manual). This consists of a vertical wood or metal shaft with a broad, heavyweight, flat base, suitable for tamping or compacting disturbed soil or paving.

4.0 Production

4.1 Crew Configuration

Most excavation equipment and tools can be operated by one person working with a helper. On medium-sized commercial or institutional projects, two crews might be involved, with one person delegated to act as foreman. On projects involving more than normal amounts of shallow trenching, additional helpers may be brought on site to do hand trimming.

4.2 Productivity

There are two aspects to productivity in this section.

Manual Output. It will be obvious that a large number of factors exist that will influence productivity in excavation work. The weather, the period of year, the time of day, the nature of the materials being excavated, crew sizes, types of equipment available, all of these and more will have their effect.

In this part of this section, some typical labor productivity outputs are listed to give readers a general idea of the amount of manual and machine work per hour that can be expected to be done under normal conditions by crews of appropriate size and motivation. Outputs listed in Table 1 are for hand labor only, for digging in normal, stiff (but not hard) clay or soil, as noted:

Table 1
TYPICAL LABOR OUTPUTS

Type of Work	Output per Man-Hour	
	m³	yd.³
Small pits	0.4	0.6
Large pits	0.6	0.8
Trenches	0.8	1.0
Postholes	0.3	0.5
Backfilling	1.8	2.0

Where general grading and squaring of bottoms of trenches or pits is done by hand, allow about 2 m² or 2.5 yd.² per man-hour.

Machine Output. Table 2 shows typical productivity figures for the some of the pieces of excavation equipment described previously, when used for ordinary excavation operations in normal earth soils. Excavation output is a function of bucket size, machine lift capacity, and efficiency.

It should be noted that the machine outputs listed are intended for the different types of work described for the equipment in Part 3.2; there is no implication intended that a bulldozer is necessarily more efficient than a backhoe just because a bulldozer appears from the data in the table to be able to move more dirt per hour. It is unlikely that a bulldozer would be used to do work that might better be

Table 2
TYPICAL EQUIPMENT OUTPUTS

Type of Machine	Output per Hour* (m³ or yd.³)
Bobcat	30
Front-end loader	50
Backhoe	70
Gradall	90
Bulldozer	110
Power shovel	130
Trencher	150

*Quantities are given as bank measure, that is, net before loosening through excavation, and on the assumption that the bucket size is 0.75 m³ or 0.75 yd.³. The factors also allow for inefficiency of about 15%; that is, a 0.75 m³ bucket will pick up only about 0.65 m³ of material on each pass.

done by a backhoe, and vice versa. Conversely, it can be deduced from the data that a trencher will be about twice as efficient as a backhoe if the job in hand involves only trenching, whereas a trencher would be useless for other types of excavation work at which backhoes excel.

Where a medium-sized bulldozer is used to do light clearing or vegetation stripping, allow about 100 m² or 1,000 ft.² per hour.

5.0 Procedures

The excavation process consists of a number of components, each of which is briefly described in approximate chronological order or sequence below. Some of the elements are more fully detailed in other related sections (identified in parentheses).

5.1 Digging

Inspection. Before any excavation activity commences, proper investigations should be conducted to determine soil types and characteristics likely to be encountered, moisture content, probable climatic conditions, necessary permits, and location of disposal sites.

Clearing. This involves the removal and disposal of small trees, shrubs, and bushes, as well as minor debris lying around the site. (Section 02–100)

Stripping. This involves the removal and storage or disposal of loam, topsoil, or other overburden.

Loosening. Chemical blasting or mechanical disturbance of solid earth or rock material may be required before digging can commence.

Excavating. This is mass or bulk digging to reduce ground elevations to lower levels, to accommodate building foundations or basements below grade. Holes for fence posts may also be considered here.

Trenching. This involves digging out trenches to create space for strip foundations, drain lines, or other services, usually just below the bottom of the mass or bulk excavation.

Trimming. This involves the removal of minor projections or filling of minor hollows in exposed surfaces of excavated areas.

Dewatering. This is the removal from the site of water from any source, such as rain, snow, melted ice, underground streams, burst pipes, and high water tables. (Section 02–140)

Protection. This is the provision of shoring, fencing, barricades, and other devices to prevent damage

to the excavation work and injury to the workers doing the excavation work or to the passing public. (Section 02–150)

5.2 Finishing

Filling. Filling involves packing native or imported materials, such as gravel, earth, or soil, into trenches and pits and around foundation and basement walls.

Grading. This involves moving earth or soil around to produce level, graded, or contoured surfaces to conform to the proposed elevations for the new building.

Finishing. This is final preparation of the graded surfaces, ready to receive paving, landscaping, seeding, sodding, or other treatment.

Disposal. This involves transportation and dumping of excavated material in excess of the need for backfill. In some localities, burning of small amounts of debris on site is permitted.

5.3 Precautions

As in much of building technology, safety in excavation work is very much a function of common sense and caution. In general, reasonable preliminary investigations should be made at the job-site before excavation work is undertaken. Such investigations may range from little more than a superficial visual examination of conditions at the site to the commis-

Telescopic Grader
This tractor-mounted diesel-powered machine has an hydraulically controlled telescopic arm to which various buckets or blades can be attached for digging, scraping, or finishing. (UBC Architecture)

Deep Drilling
Many buildings (such as service stations and warehouses) have powerful (if slow) hydraulic elevators. These require a deep shaft to be drilled to accept the lift-ram and casing tubes. (UBC Architecture)

Backfilling
After work has been done in service trenches, foundation pits, and other basement excavations, excavated (or imported) material is carefully deposited in compacted layers. (BCIT Building Technology)

sioning of detailed soils reports to be undertaken by geological specialists. There are two basic reasons to make sufficiently detailed examination: to determine the load-bearing and moisture-retention characteristics of the soil materials for structural design purposes, and to determine the best way to remove and replace these materials.

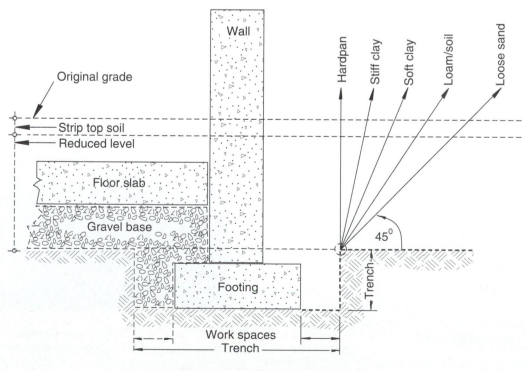

Figure 16   Slope Allowances

Some specific safety considerations relative to excavation processes in this section are as follows:

1. The sides of trenches and pits should be sloped outward from the bottom levels at an angle close to the natural angle of repose of the type of material being excavated; see Figure 16.

2. Ladders should be provided to permit easy entry to and exit from any excavated areas deeper than 1.5 m or 4 ft.

3. Avoid dumping excavated materials too close to the edges of excavated areas, as this might cause a cave-in. Similarly, avoid letting heavy equipment, such as dump trucks, come too close to the edges of excavated pits, trenches, or banks.

4. As far as practical, try to prevent or minimize the amount of water running down or onto excavated surfaces, as the characteristics of earth soils are rapidly, significantly, and almost always adversely affected by moisture.

5. Warnings and barricades must be positioned to prevent unwary people or equipment from accidentally falling into excavations.

6. It is imprudent to probe the earth with sharp poles or sticks if one does not know what is under the surface. A buried water or gas pipe service line may be punctured by such careless procedures, with possibly dangerous and certainly costly results.

Section 02–500 Paving

1.0 Introduction

1.1 General Issues

The title *Paving* includes surface coverings of prepared and graded site areas, using asphalt, brick, concrete, gravel, stone, tile, and a variety of synthetic products such as are used in athletic surfacings like running tracks and tennis courts. Related curbs and gutters, sealers, sealants, and pavement markings are usually included with this work in construction contracts, although they are excluded from this particular section in this book, being adequately covered in other sections.

There is some slight ambiguity in the use of the words *concrete paving* because concrete is a general term for a mixture of coarse and fine stone aggregates held together by a binder; the binder may be either hydrated portland cement, petroleum or asphaltic cement, or some other natural or synthetic product. In general, though, **concrete** paving is considered by most people to have a portland cement binder, and **asphalt** paving to have a natural or synthetic asphaltic, bituminous, or petroleum binder. Concrete paving is described in Section 03–300; asphalt paving is described in this section.

1.2 Design Aspects

Good paving design requires that the finished product be able to withstand the anticipated rigors of traffic and weather at the job-site; the correct selection of an appropriate paving system for specific traffic-use conditions is therefore critical. There are five broad traffic-use categories to consider, relative to normal construction activities:

1. **Heavy duty.** To withstand all types of vehicles, such as on major roads, dock-sides, and warehouse or industrial ramps.

2. **Medium duty.** For heavily loaded delivery trucks, such as on suburban roads and urban public or private parking lots.

3. **Light duty.** For cars and light delivery vans, such as on residential driveways and sidewalks.

4. **Very light duty.** For pedestrians and bicycles, such as in play parks, tennis courts, and other athletic areas.

5. **No traffic.** For appearance or protection only, such as for landscaping and embankment protection.

Consideration must also be given to the maxi-

Concrete Paving
Conrete sidewalks and curbs are often used to finish on-site vehicle parking areas. Curbs are usually installed using concrete extrusion machines; slabs are poured, screeded, and cured. (UBC Architecture)

mum single-axle loads anticipated from traffic of the anticipated types. There are six basic paving options from which to choose, relative to the possible traffic conditions described above:

1. **Gravel only.** For all traffic conditions.
2. **Gravel with oil.** For light traffic (driveways, parking).
3. **Concrete on gravel base.** For medium to heavy traffic.
4. **Asphalt on gravel base.** For light to medium traffic.
5. **Paving brick or tile.** On sand, gravel, concrete, or asphalt base, for very light to light traffic conditions.
6. **Soil-cement mixtures.** For airport runways and ramps, reservoir linings, and similar heavy construction functions, beyond the scope of this book.

In general, the quality of asphalt paving is deter-

mined by achieving the right combination of two complex properties:

1. **Durability,** which is a function of the resistance of the asphalt cement to oxidization and volatilization, as well as to physical wear and tear, and the ability of the cement to adhere to the aggregate particles and thus to bind them together.
2. **Curing time,** which is determined by a combination of rate of evaporation of the volatile solvents in the asphalt mix, the temperatures of the mix and the surrounding atmosphere, the surface area exposed to weather, and wind speed and chill factors.

A key element of good design involves the provision of adequate drainage below, around, and on top of the paving surfaces. Poor drainage may result in frost-heave or washout of the base, or ponding of water and ice on the surface, with attendant problems.

Attention must therefore be paid to the provision of proper base courses and the development of level or sloping surfaces to direct the flow of water off the paving.

Other aspects of good design include the following:

1. The necessity to allow for expansion and contraction of the paving under normal anticipated use.
2. The location and quality of drainage frames and gratings.
3. The texturing of paving surfaces to provide for good traction and appearance.
4. The sealing of surfaces to retard deterioration from chemical and physical influences (spilled gasoline, tire skids, etc.).
5. Proper procedures and conditions to ensure correct curing of the paving mixture.

1.3 Related Work

Work closely connected to this section is described in the following sections, to which reference should be made:

02–700   Drainage (gratings)

03–300   Cast-in-Place Concrete (pavings and curbs)

06–100   Rough Carpentry (wooden curbs)

09–300   Ceramic and Tile Work (pavings)

09–900   Painting and Decorating (traffic markers)

2.0 Products

2.1 Materials

The materials used for asphalt paving are as follows:

Aggregate, coarse. Crushed stone, gravel, or slag, conforming to specifications of the American Society for Testing Materials (ASTM) and the Canadian Standards Association (CSA).

Aggregate, fine. Natural sand or fine gravel, conforming to CSA or ASTM specifications.

Asphalt, basic. A dark brown or jet black cement-like bituminous material, occasionally occurring naturally, but more often synthetically produced through the petroleum cracking process.

Asphalt, cut-back. Asphalt cement diluted with one of three solvents having different rates of volatilization:

1. Heavy lubricating oil: slow curing.
2. Kerosene or diesel oil: medium curing.
3. Petroleum distillate: rapid curing.

Mineral Fillers. Very finely graded materials, such as pulverized cement, limestone, mica, sand, and sometimes asbestos fibers.

Road oil. A slow-curing grade of heavy petroleum oil.

Seal coat. A fine asphalt mixture thinly applied to the surface of existing asphalt paving.

2.2 Accessories

There are very few accessories used in connection with this work:

Curbs. Made of asphalt, concrete, steel, or wood; see related work in Sections 03–400 Precast Concrete, 05–500 Metal Fabrications, and 06–100 Rough Carpentry.

Gratings. Heavy-duty cast iron covers and frames; see related work in Section 02–700 Drainage.

Marker paint. A heavy-duty rubberized paint; see related work in Section 09–900 Painting and Decorating.

2.3 Mixing

The word *gradation* refers to the proper sizing of the aggregate particles used to make the asphaltic concrete mix. Table 1 shows the approximate percent-

Table 1
AGGREGATE PARTICLE SIZES

Mesh Size		Percent Base	Percent Top
mm	in.		
75	3.00	100	100
50	2.00	80	100
25	1.00	60	75
10	0.30	40	50
5	0.15	20	35
1	0.05	10	20

ages of particles of various sizes recommended for use in asphalt base and top-course mixtures, in terms of quantities passing mesh apertures of the stated dimensions.

Asphalt used for normal paving weighs approximately 1,750 kg/m^3 or 3,500 lb./yd.^{3}. The reason a more precise value cannot be given is that the mass or weight to some extent depends on the density or degree of compaction.

3.0 Construction Aids

3.1 Equipment

Equipment falls into three broad categories: transportation, application, and compaction.

Transportation. Equipment used for transport in paving operations includes:

Drums. Asphalt is delivered in drums of approximately 200-liter or 50-gallon capacity, constructed of steel of thicknesses shown in the following tabulation for asphalt of the stated grades.

Gage	Asphalt Grade
28	< 85
24	85–100
18	> 100

Trucks. These should be of suitable size, have tight and clean metal boxes, and be capable of being covered by soft tarpaulin or metal lids. They should also be insulated where necessary to prevent premature cooling of the mixture. The inside of the truck box should be lightly oiled or soaped before loading with the asphalt mix to prevent the mix from sticking to the box surface.

Application. Equipment used for application of paving materials includes:

Brooms. These are of both manual and machine type, and are used to clean surfaces to be paved prior to start of paving.

Heaters. These are tanks having hot oil or steam coils by which the asphalt is heated prior to spreading or laying.

Kettles. As the name suggests, these are small metal pots with handles, used to manually transport small quantities of hot asphalt over short distances.

Paving machine. This is a self-propelled device, consisting primarily of a diesel engine connected to driving tracks, and mounted on a frame that supports a hopper to receive the mix, a motor-driven screw- or auger-like device to spread the mix, and a system of rollers and guides to permit laying down a continuous ribbon of asphalt of any given composition, width, and thickness.

Pulverizer. This machine is used to break down scarified material into smaller particle sizes.

Scarifier. This device is used to rip up or reshape existing paved or unpaved surfaces, ready to receive new material.

Spreader. There are three types: hopper, vane, and whirl. Each type is attached to the rear of a truck carrying the bulk asphalt mix. In each case, the asphalt is moved by gravity from the truck box into the device and then spread either by spiral auger, by guiding vanes, or by rotating disc, respectively, to produce a layer of asphalt paving of the required thickness before compaction.

Curbing machine. This is a machine not unlike a paving machine, but which can extrude a ribbon of softened asphalt through a preformed metal die (like squeezing toothpaste out of a tube).

Compaction. In general, proper compaction of each stage of the layering process of paving greatly improves the strength and durability of the overall finished product. Equipment is as follows:

Rollers, rubber-wheeled. These usually have a bank of three, four, or five wheels across the front and a second bank of four, five, or six wheels in the rear.

Rollers, steel-wheeled. These usually have one large steel roller drum in front and either one or two

Asphalt Paving (Manual)
The hot asphalt mix is dumped in place from wheel barrows, screeded to establish thickness, raked smooth, and then rolled by hand or by lightweight motorized machine. (BCIT Building Technology)

steel drums in the rear, arranged side by side or in tandem.

Tampers. These consist of large, heavy steel drums, having many metal cylindrical protrusions in rows like feet, and intended to be towed by a bulldozer over the area to be tamped.

Vibrators, plate. These machines operate by transferring mechanical energy from an eccentric cam to one or more flat plates or shoes in contact with the surface of the gravel or concreted material to be compacted. Some smaller units can be manually directed, whereas larger units require power propulsion and a steering mechanism.

Vibrators, wheeled. These machines, weighing anywhere from 3 to 10 metric tonnes, consist of large-diameter steel rollers, usually arranged in tandem, to which controlled vibratory energy is transmitted.

4.0 Production

4.1 Crew Configuration

Crew sizes naturally vary, depending on the time constraints of the job and the type of equipment involved. There can also be as many as three and even more unions involved in having one asphalt-spreading machine efficiently operated, as it requires machine operators, truck drivers, laborers, and managers to get the job done, not to mention mechanics to keep the equipment repaired.

4.2 Productivity

To give some idea of productivity, consider the provision of simple asphalt paving to create a paved parking lot beside a suburban retail market; the area to be paved measures 30 x 65 m or 100 x 200 ft., resulting in 1,950 m² or 20,000 ft.². A typical crew to place the gravel subcourse, 100 mm or 4 in. thick, would require three people, two called rakermen and the other the foreman; they would take about 8 hours to prepare the gravel base. The crew to place the asphalt, 50 mm or 2 in. thick, would involve six people, namely one foreman, two rakermen, one roller operator, and one or two helpers; they would take about 4 to 5 hours to complete the paving.

Table 2 gives some general productivity data for typical operations encountered in asphalt paving work.

5.0 Procedures

There are two primary elements to be considered in the construction of a typical asphalt paved surface: preparation of the base and application of the surfacing. A cross section of a typical paved roadway is shown in Figure 1.

5.1 Preparing the Base

Following are the stages in preparing the base for asphalt paving:

1. **Sub base.** The areas to receive paving are stripped of organic material, cleared of obstructions or debris, and compacted as necessary.

Asphalt Paving (Machine)
The hot asphalt mix is extruded to the correct thickness from a motorized paving machine, trimmed by hand at edges, and then compacted with a lightweight mechanical roller. (BCIT Building Technology)

2. **Base course.** Graded gravel is selected, placed, spread, and compacted to a thickness of 100 mm or 4 in.

3. **Paving base.** The surface of the base course is cleaned and primed; then asphalt of specified composition and quality is spread at a temperature about 150 degrees C or 300 degrees F, to a thickness of 75 mm or 3 in.

Table 2
TYPICAL OUTPUTS FOR ASPHALT PAVING

Work Type	Output per Day		Crew Size	
	m²	yd.²	Skilled	Helper
Base, gravel: 100 mm or 4 in.	90	100	1	2
Prime coat	1,650	1,800	1	1
Base, asphalt (spread by hand):				
50 mm or 2 in.	90	100	1	2
100 mm or 4 in.	50	60	1	3
Tack coat	1,800	2,000	1	1
Form curbs:				
By hand	30 m	30 ly*	1	2
By machine	90 m	100 ly*	1	3

*Linear yard.

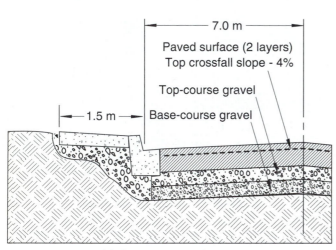

(a) Cross section of paving

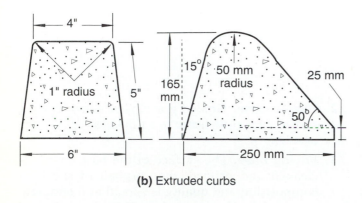

(b) Extruded curbs

Figure 1 Typical Pavement

5.2 Applying the Finish

Following are the stages in applying the finish to a paving base:

1. **Paving finish.** If necessary, the surface of the paving base is cleaned and primed; then asphalt of specified finer composition and higher quality is spread, to a thickness of 50 mm or 2 in. It is important to note that none of the equipment used to spread or compact the asphalt paving materials can remain in one place for any length of time, as unacceptable indentations will almost certainly occur.

2. **Painting traffic directional signs.** See Section 09–900.

3. **Sealing.** A very fine mixture, sometimes consisting of asphalt and sand or coal tar pitch, but occasionally consisting of vinyl or epoxy resins, is misted, sprayed, or flooded onto the surface of the paving finish layer and allowed to cure. Its purpose is to seal small cracks and to fill small voids, to render the surface more impervious to attack by oil and gasoline spills and frost.

4. **Forming curbs and bumpers.** See related work in Sections 03–400, 05–500, and 06-100 for concrete, steel, or wooden curbs, respectively. Asphalt curbs are usually extruded by machine.

5.3 Precautions

Most of the critical safety issues related to asphalt products have to do with their manufacture, as dis-

Stone Paving

Many variations are possible. In this example, split flagstones have been bedded in a concrete base, then grouted by hand with a coarse sand-cement mortar between the pieces. (UBC Architecture)

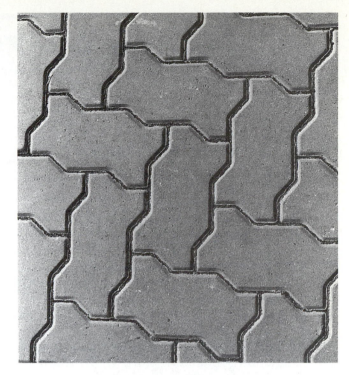

Brick Paving

Plain bricks, thick clay tiles, or patented interlocking units (as shown in this photo) can be bedded on leveled and compacted sand and laid in close contact to form patios or walks. (UBC Architecture)

tinct from their application. While it must be recognized that asphalt products are toxic, flammable, and on occasion explosive, the primary safety problems in their day-to-day use in paving systems stem from heat and pressure. The asphalt material usually has to be heated to fairly high temperatures to permit it to be poured and molded, and thus can cause serious burns if mishandled. Furthermore, the heavy mobile equipment used to compact the asphalt is not easily maneuverable and also is designed to induce considerable pressure; these factors can easily lead to serious accidents if care is not taken by all concerned.

The fumes given off by hot asphalt may over a lengthy period of exposure be detrimental to the health of those who constantly breathe significant concentrations of such fumes. Good ventilation and masking are also necessary to minimize the inhalation of dust particles. Surplus waste asphaltic products must be disposed of in an acceptable and authorized manner.

In general, asphalt paving cannot be satisfactorily laid under wet or freezing climatic conditions. Care should be taken not to splash asphalt onto parts of the building project not scheduled to receive such treatment, as it is extremely difficult to satisfactorily and economically remove such visual blemishes.

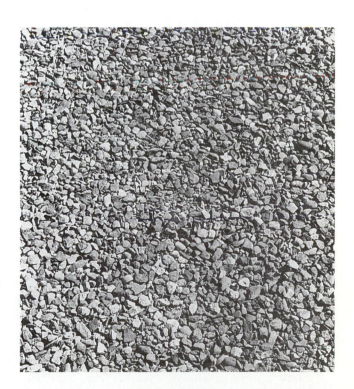

Gravel Paving

Some sites require temporary (and occasionally permanent) driveways or walkways made of compacted gravel. Gravel is placed in layers, blinded with fine sand, then rolled, watered, or oiled. (UBC Architecture)

Section 02–700 Drainage

1.0 Introduction

1.1 General Issues

Building drainage can be considered under two main headings: **sanitary drains** and **storm drains.** Sanitary drainage involves raw sewage passing through closed but vented pipe systems with air traps to septic tanks or treatment plants; storm drainage involves fairly fresh rainwater runoff passing by gravity through untrapped pipes or open ditches to some off-site disposal area.

Sanitary drainage as defined above falls under the jurisdiction of plumbing work (in Division 15 of MasterFormat), and thus will not be dealt with further in this book. Although it is possible to design combined sanitary and storm drainage systems, this section deals with separate storm drainage as described above and detailed below.

1.2 Design Aspects

The primary object of any storm drainage system is to stabilize soil conditions by controlling moisture content in the earth. Such control can reduce water tables, hydrostatic pressures, and possible soil movements, while increasing the bearing capacity of the soil to sustain loads transmitted to it through foundations.

There are two major categories of storm drainage:

1. **Temporary drains** are often necessary to keep the building site reasonably free of water during

   the construction period; they usually involve open ditches and French drains.
2. **Permanent drains** are usually required to permit the building to function properly for the purposes intended during its life span; they involve pipes of various types, manholes and covers, cleanouts and catch-basins.

Such simple drainage systems can be distinguished from more complex systems involving sumps, pumps, wells, and well-point drainage, described in more detail in Section 02–140. Refer to Figure 1 which contrasts simple sanitary and storm drain systems.

1.3 Related Work

Work closely connected to this section is described in the following sections, to which reference should be made:

01–050   Field Engineering
02–140   Dewatering
02–200   Earthwork
02–500   Paving

2.0 Products

2.1 Materials

Drainpipes are usually made of one of three materials: clay, concrete, or plastic. Asbestos pipes are no

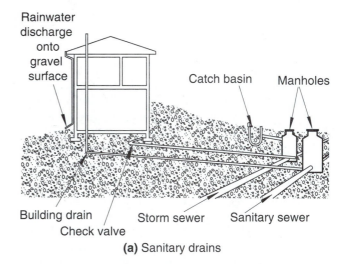

(a) Sanitary drains

(b) Storm drains

Figure 1   Drainage Layout

longer used; metal pipes are usually classified with plumbing work.

Clay. These pipes, also known as agricultural tiles, are first dry-pressed in a mold, then fired in a kiln, as for bricks. They are available with plain butt or collared ends, and are usually unglazed, in contrast to sewer pipes. Inside diameters can vary between 50 and 150 mm or 2 and 6 in. Straight pieces are usually about 30 cm or 12 in. long.

Concrete. These pipes are precast from a mixture of cement, sand, and water, poured into steel forms, and steam-cured. They are slightly porous. Straight pieces are usually 30 cm or 12 in. in diameter and 1.2 m or 4 ft. in length.

Plastic. These pipes are machine-molded or extruded either from polyvinyl chloride (PVC) or polyethylene (PE) plastic. PVC is more resistant to pressure but less resistant to impact than PE, especially at low temperatures. Common diameters vary between 50 and 100 mm or 2 and 4 in.; larger diameters are available. Lengths can range up to 200 m or yd., as these pipes are produced in continuous coils.

All three types are available in straight pieces, 45- or 90-degree bends, branches, and tees, and also with solid or perforated wall styles. Plastic pipes may have either smooth or corrugated walls. End caps and cover plates are also available in concrete and plastic.

2.2 Accessories

There are very few accessories involved in storm drain work, beyond a few pieces of cedar wood to support the bottoms of pipes in alignment, some small pieces of brick or block to stabilize the pipe system during backfill, and small pieces of normal asphalt roofing felt placed over the open joints at ends of pipe pieces to prevent silt and gravel from being washed into the pipes. Catch-basin covers, gullies, and similar drain gratings and frames are invariably made of heavy-duty cast iron material.

3.0 Construction Aids

3.1 Equipment

For descriptions of backhoes, tampers, and trenching machines used in this work, see Section 02–200 Earthwork.

Sanitary Drain

Patented units of plastic or vitrified clay are assembled according to maker's recommendations, installed to conform to project specifications, and pressure-tested to city standards. (BCIT Building Technology)

Storm Drain

Open clay (or perforated plastic) drain tiles are carefully aligned in a prepared ditch or trench, with joints covered with asphalt paper to exclude dirt, then covered with clean gravel. (BCIT Building Technology)

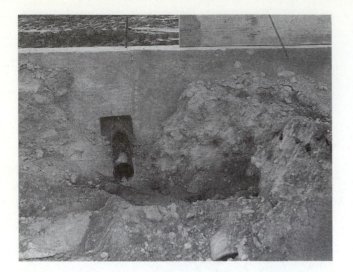

Temporary Drain

Most building sites have water disposal problems. This picture shows a drain and hole left in a concrete retaining wall to permit water to safely discharge into a runoff trench. (BCIT Building Technology)

3.2 Tools

The following tools are used in construction of drainage systems:

Drain scoop. Used to remove raised portions of earth in the trench bottom that might interfere with the pipe alignment.

Hoe, lateral. Used for making small adjustments to trench depths.

Hook, correction. Used to align pipe ends in the trench.

Hook, laying. Used to place the pipe piece in the trench.

Pipe tongs. Used for removing bits of broken pipe.

Soil pincer. Used for removing small amounts of earth from around the pipe beds.

Spade, dee-blade. Used for general manual excavation and backfill.

Spade, long-blade. Used for digging out deep and narrow portions of the trench.

4.0 Production

4.1 Crew Configuration

On most jobs, the drain crew will consist of one journeyman foreman and two helpers. If machine exca-

vation of trenches is required, then a backhoe or trenching machine operator will also be necessary.

4.2 Productivity

There are five basic operations involved: layout, digging the trench, preparing the trench bottoms, laying the pipes and fittings, and backfilling. If one considers a drain line 100 m or yd. in length and of average width (0.5 m or yd.) and depth (1.0 m or yd.), then the crew would take about 2 hours to lay out, 4 hours to dig the trench by machine, about 8 hours to prepare and compact the bottoms, about 24 hours to lay and connect the pipe, bends, branches, and accessories in place, and about 2 hours to backfill the trench by machine at the end (4 hours if the earth has to be compacted).

5.0 Procedures

As mentioned, drainage systems can be categorized as temporary or permanent; both are described here:

5.1 Temporary Drains

The simplest form of temporary drain is the open ditch, as shown in Figure 2. Ditches can be effectively used in sites having soils of medium permeability and being more or less level, where the ditch will be slightly sloping along its longitudinal axis not in excess of 1 in 100. Such ditches can be dug by hand labor, but are more often and more efficiently formed using a power backhoe fitted with a bucket of the correct size and profile for the proposed ditch. The sides of such ditches should slope outward in the ratio of 1.5:1.0; the bottoms may be either flat or veed. Some hand finishing of backhoe cuts is almost always necessary.

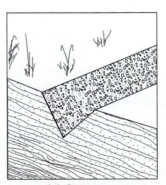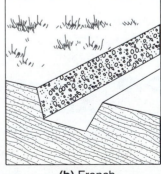

(a) Open   **(b)** French

Figure 2 Open and French Ditches

A modified version of the open ditch is the French ditch or drain, more commonly used on sites where there is more of a slope and the soil is less permeable. The French ditch is best located parallel to and some reasonable distance downslope from the area to be kept dry. It is dug by hand or backhoe to form a shallow trench, approximately rectangular in cross section, and then it is filled with coarse gravel. The object is to let surface water wash over the ground and down through the gravel into the ditch, where it collects and drains away to a deeper sump or dry well or other disposal area, above the natural water table level for the site as a whole.

5.2 Permanent Drains

The location of the drain line is determined by need, survey, and inspection. Wood stakes are set out to establish the line and elevation of the trench. If a drain line 100 m or yd. long has to have a slope of 0.1 percent, the top of the downstream stake must be 10 cm or 4 in. below the top of the upstream stake.

The trench is dug by hand or machine to the required depth and gradient. Dimensions vary; widths are generally between 40 and 60 cm or 16 and 24 in.; depths for manual digging seldom exceed 1 m or yd., although machines can easily dig trenches as deep as 2 m or yd. The selected pipe type and its accessories are brought to the site and laid in the bottom of the trench, by hand or by machine, with or without drain gravel, as called for in the specifications. The pipe may be stabilized by small brick or concrete blocks or by wooden pegs during the backfilling process. Footing or perimeter drains are laid in the trenches already dug for the building foundations.

5.3 Precautions

A check should be made to ensure that the proper invert levels and fall lines have been established before filling in around new drainage systems. Care must be taken not to disturb the installed drainage system during filling operations. If required by law, a pressure or smoke test can be made to discover any leakage.

CHAPTER 03
Concrete Work

Section 03–100 Formwork

1.0 Introduction

1.1 General Issues

Although it is certainly possible to pour concrete in a freeform manner, almost all concrete used in buildings requires to be molded to produce some specific shape desired by the designer. The assembly of temporary panels and accessories that do such molding is generally called formwork. The temporary support system that holds the formwork in place is generally called falsework.

Formwork consists of a system of strong panels made of wood, metal, plastic, or other materials (such as plaster or fiberglass) stiffened by a wood or metal frame, held together with a variety of ties, clips, wedges, and special nails, and braced in position with a series of vertical or diagonal adjustable jacks or supports comprising the falsework. The formwork panels can be textured or modeled in a variety of ways, either directly or with inserted linings, to impart an enhanced appearance to the finished concrete surfaces exposed to view upon removal of the forms. The specific design of formwork and its supporting falsework will naturally vary, depending on which part of the concrete building is to be formed, such as the side of a wall, the edge of a floor slab, the faces of treads in a stairway, and so on. Figure 1 shows typical wall formwork.

If one reviews the economics of a typical reinforced concrete structural system for a multistory commercial or institutional building, it becomes clear that there are two key factors involved:

1. The single most costly element in such work usually involves the formwork; on average, this cost may amount to as much as one-half of the total cost of the concrete system. Furthermore, if one reviews the economics of formwork, it soon becomes clear that the single most costly element of formwork usually involves the labor to fabricate and erect it; on average, this cost may amount to as much as one-third of the total cost of the formwork system. Bearing this in mind, it is appropriate to consider ways to reduce the cost of labor for formwork by simplifying the design of both the concrete and the formwork.

2. The other key factor is reuse, i.e., the number of times that a particular formwork or falsework component or composite can be utilized. The proper combination of these two factors (labor cost and reuse) can make a significant difference to the construction budget.

116

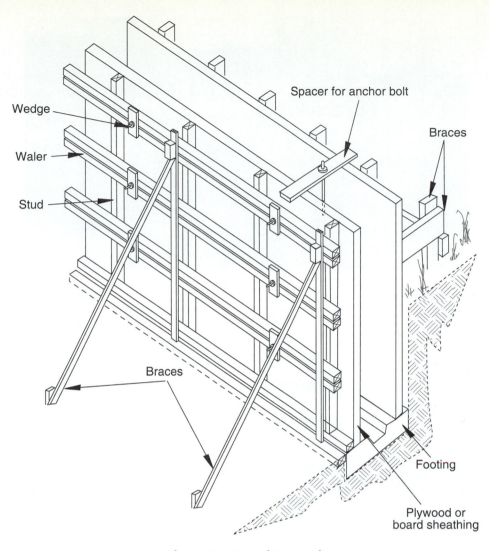

Figure 1 — Labels in figure:
Wedge
Waler
Stud
Braces
Spacer for anchor bolt
Braces
Footing
Plywood or board sheathing

Figure 1 Typical Formwork

While considering economic issues, it should be mentioned that because formwork is usually made from common building materials, many of which are subsequently incorporated into the permanent building structure on many projects, some estimators and superintendents record formwork costs as *material* cost. Because of its temporary nature, it is more appropriate to account for formwork costs in the same category as other *equipment* costs, and to recover its cost on the basis of first cost, use, depreciation, and salvage value, similar to a pickup truck or a concrete mixer.

1.2 Design Aspects

Formwork serves a number of purposes. It molds or shapes the concrete; it determines the position and alignment of the concrete member; it assists with the setting and curing process of the concrete; it permits exact reproduction of significant building elements;

it allows economical duplication of expensive labor-intensive components.

Formwork and related falsework should be designed by a knowledgeable person, and it should exhibit a number of specific characteristics. It should be strong and stable, as it must be able to withstand live loads such as the movement of personnel and equipment on top of it, the force of plastic concrete being poured into it, and the effects of rain, snow, or wind; as well as dead loads, such as the weight of reinforcing steel and concrete plus its own weight. Formwork and falsework should be reusable where possible or necessary and easily assembled, erected, demounted, and transported.

The key factor in formwork design is the correct determination of the pressure to which the forms will be subjected as the concrete is poured into position. The pressure will be a function of the thickness and depth of the concrete to be restrained by the form. This will in turn dictate the thickness of the

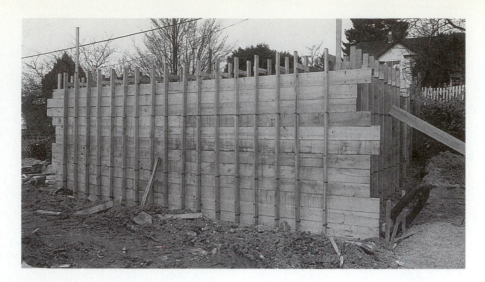

Wall Forms

On small jobs, formwork is often made from sheathing boards which will be reused to line framed walls. On large projects, it is customary to use large sheets of plywood and metal ties. (BCIT Building Technology)

formwork panels, the spacing of formwork ties, and the size of supports and braces. While these parameters can be calculated from first principles, it is customary to determine them from tables of precalculated data, published for this purpose in construction estimating reference books.

1.3 Related Work

Work closely connected to this section is described in the following sections, to which reference should be made:

01–050	Field Engineering
03–200	Reinforcement
03–300	Cast-in-Place Concrete
03–400	Precast Concrete

2.0 Products

2.1 Materials

The materials used to fabricate formwork and falsework can be categorized under the following broad headings:

Metal Products.   Steel and aluminum are common.

Steel is used in three forms: in large, flat, stiffened sheet form panels; in square- or rectangular-shaped steel pans for forming ribbed (one-way) or waffle (two-way) joisted slabs; and in tubular form in welded scaffolding and telescopic jacks used in falsework.

Aluminum is used in two principal forms: as prefabricated waffle pans and as chords in long-span, open-web joists for falsework. Ordinary domestic steel and aluminum "tin cans" of various sizes are frequently used as pots to form small openings for vents and pipes.

Plastic Products.   Materials such as fiberglass, plaster, and styrofoam which can be molded or sculpted are used to create special ornamental and decorative shapes in concrete. The molded plastic materials are usually fastened to the inside of regular wood or metal forms before concrete is poured. Occasionally, ordinary glass "pop bottles" are used to form small holes for pipes. Where rigid insulation is to be left in place in contact with concrete surfaces, such as in foundation walls, the insulation board itself often is used as the form panel. Occasionally, concrete itself is used as a form material, for example where new work is being placed beside existing work.

Wood Products. Dimension lumber is used for supports for form panels. Softwood plywood sheets and tongue-and-groove sheathing boards are used to make form panels. Hardboards and particleboards, factory-tempered with drying oil, are sometimes used to form fine patterns on concrete surfaces. A specially treated, fiber-reinforced paper is used to make continuous circular tubes for forming concrete columns of various diameters.

2.2 Accessories

A number of accessories are used in conjunction with the principal formwork materials; these can be categorized as follows:

Chemicals. These consist of oils and emulsions of various sorts, such as lanolin, mold cream, paraffin, petroleum jelly, oleic acid, and other so-called release agents; they are used to prevent the concrete from adhering to the form surface.

Fasteners. A large variety of anchors, aligners, bolts, brackets, clamps, drift pins, eyes, hangers, nails (box, common, and double-headed type), pins, screws, spreaders, stirrups, straps, ties, and yokes are utilized in formwork and falsework (see Figure 2).

Liners. These are materials that are nailed, stapled, or glued to the insides of form panels to alter the surface appearance of the poured concrete. Liners may be made from flexible sheet rubber or cardboard, semirigid elastomers like polyethylene and polyvinyl, or rigid materials such as gypsum, fiberglass, or styrene. Occasionally, plain plastic sheeting is tacked to the inside of formwork, to ensure good separation and to impart a random mottled ornamentation to the concrete surface.

3.0 **Construction Aids**

3.1 Equipment

As much of this work *is* equipment, only a few additional items need to be identified, such as high-reach ladders, metal hoppers that can be attached to form-

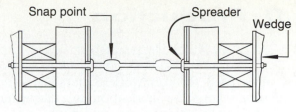

(a) Snap tie with washer spreader

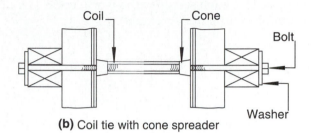

(b) Coil tie with cone spreader

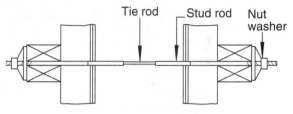

(c) Stud rod (she-bolt) tie

Figure 2   Formwork Accessories

work to assist with the placement of concrete, and motorized, rotary wire brush devices to rapidly clean form panels. If slip-forming is to be employed, then a system of hydraulic or pneumatic jacks will be required to be provided, as described in Part 5.2.

3.2 Tools

As the fabrication, erection, and stripping of formwork and falsework is essentially carpentry work, the tools usually encountered are those of the carpenter, such as electric saws and drills, plumb bobs, and mallets. In addition, there are some specialized tools used to tighten or loosen formwork and falsework accessories, such as crowbars, pullers used to strip form panels, aligners used to align studs and walers, drift pins used to align holes in studs and forms, and tie-removal cranks effectively used to break off ties below the concrete surface.

4.0 Production

4.1 Crew Configuration

Crew sizes used for formwork sectors are often arranged as follows: for fabrication: two carpenters and one helper; for erection: two carpenters and two helpers; and for stripping: one carpenter and two helpers. For large projects, two or more crews may be utilized for each sector of the work, under the direction of a carpenter-foreman.

4.2 Productivity

As it is customary to measure and price formwork on the basis of concrete surfaces formed, factors given in Table 1 are expressed in terms of contact area fabricated in one hour. Factors represent typical and straightforward formwork being executed on commercial and institutional buildings under normal market and climatic conditions. For complex configurations, small jobs, or inclement weather, the factors can be decreased by up to 25 percent.

For erection and installation operations, the factors can be increased by an average of 35 percent; for stripping operations, the factors can be increased by about 400 percent. To say the same thing in other words, if it takes 60 minutes to fabricate an area of formwork, it will probably take about 45 minutes to install it for the first time, with a proportional reduction in time developing for repeated reinstallation of the same piece. If it takes 45 minutes to install an area of formwork, it will take about 10 to 12 minutes to carefully strip the same area of formwork after the concrete has cured.

Table 1
PRODUCTIVITY IN FORMWORK

Type of Work (Fabrication)	Contact Area per Hour m²	ft.²
Bases, isolated	1.0	10.0
Beams, horizontal	3.0	30.0
Bulkheads, lineal	3.5	35.0
Columns, circular	2.5	25.0
Columns, rectangular	2.0	20.0
Edges, slab-on-grade	1.5	15.0
Edges, suspended slab	1.0	10.0
Features, ornamental	0.5	5.0
Footings, pier	3.0	30.0
Footings, strip	1.0	10.0
Openings, edges	1.5	15.0
Slabs, rib pan	1.0	10.0
Slabs, suspended	2.0	20.0
Slabs, waffle pan	1.5	15.0
Slip forming	2.0	20.0
Stairs, landing	1.0	10.0
Stairs, riser	0.5	5.0
Stairs, soffit	1.5	15.0
Walls, foundation	3.5	35.0
Walls, shear	3.0	30.0

5.0 Procedures

5.1 Preparation

Fabrication. An area of the job-site should be set aside for a small carpentry mill, close to the construction area, and with sufficient room for supplies to be delivered and fabricated forms to be stored. Wood or form plastic panels are measured and cut to size, supporting plates and studs are attached, and holes for ties and other items passing through the forming system are drilled.

Preliminaries. Work areas should be cleared free of debris and construction equipment not required for the work of this section. Surfaces on which mudsills are going to rest should be checked for firmness and load-bearing capacity. Rented or purchased factory-made metal or plastic formwork and falsework components such as joists or pans should be selected from manufacturers' catalogs. Components, equipment, and tools should be gathered together at the construction location, ready for use.

5.2 Process

Falsework Erection. There are two common situations encountered: where the falsework is erected before (precedent to) the formwork, as in vertical and horizontal supports for suspended slabs, and where the falsework is erected after (subsequent to) the formwork, as in diagonal supports for vertical wall forms. Both are described:

Precedent (Figure 3.1). The horizontal shoring base is normally made of lengths of heavy timber, called mudsills; they spread the point loads of the jack supports across a larger area. Mudsills must be solid, securely positioned, and free of settlement. Care

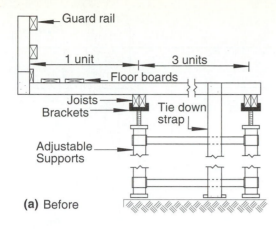

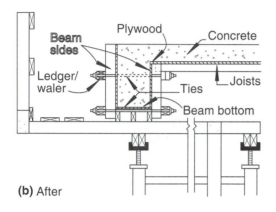

Figure 3.1 Precedent Falsework

Falsework

Formwork has to be rigidly secured in position to prevent movement or collapse. This is achieved by the use of falsework in the form of diagonal braces for walls or upright jacks for slabs. (BCIT Building Technology)

should be taken not to place mudsills on uneven, wet, or frozen ground, or in any place where running water could wash away the ground under them. Vertical single or scaffold-type shores must be plumbed and tightly secured in position, using wedges at top or bottom, or adjustable threaded jacks, so that each shore carries its share of the load. Wedges can be temporarily toenailed in position. Horizontal solid or open-web members are then installed to carry the form panel loads to the vertical supports.

Subsequent (Figure 3.2). Diagonal braces are loosely positioned, then bolted connections are made at the top end to the outside of the wall form. The bottom end is secured with wedges or pins driven into the ground or secured to floor slabs. Then the threaded sleeves are tightened to secure the wall form in correct position, taking care not to drive it out of alignment.

Formwork Erection. As with so much of building technology, the permutation of possible variations in formwork materials types, sizes, and arrangements is virtually infinite. This is also one of the few areas in construction where contractors are given essentially free reign to devise suitable methods to achieve required results. However, the topic

does permit identification of common and typical configurations likely to be encountered on normal construction projects; some of these are described as follows:

Bases (Figure 4.1). These usually consist of a solidly made enclosed wood or metal box, cut to the exact

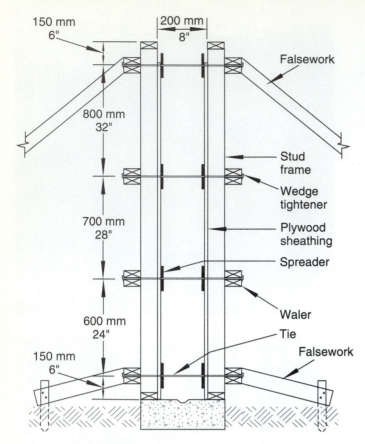

Figure 3.2 Subsequent Falsework

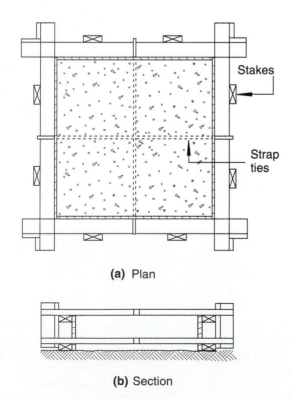

(a) Plan

(b) Section

Figure 4.1 Bases

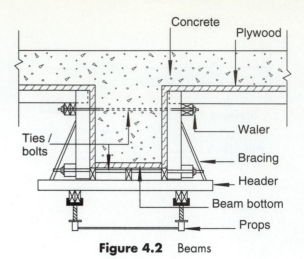

Figure 4.2 Beams

dimensions of the desired concrete base usually braced on the outside and sometimes across the top.

Beams (Figure 4.2). These usually consist of a bottom plate the exact width of the beam and two side plates to determine the beam depth. The sides are made to be removable before the bottom plate.

Columns (Figure 4.3). If square or rectangular in horizontal cross section, they are formed using vertical plywood panels held in place with horizontal adjustable metal straps. If circular in cross section, they are usually formed with a single continuous fiberboard cylinder of appropriate diameter and length.

Fly forms (Figure 4.4). These are formed with large sheets of wood or metal, secured to the tops of open-web wood or metal joists, and arranged to be capable of easy placement, removal, and relocation by crane on successive floors of highrise buildings.

Footings (Figure 4.5). These are formed with long lengths of plywood or lumber, supported at intervals with braces across the top and at the sides.

Foundations (Figure 4.6). These are formed using prefabricated wood or metal panels, separated, secured, and aligned by form ties, and supported by diagonal braces.

Openings (Figure 4.7). For windows and doors, continuous strips of wood or metal are placed inside the surrounding formwork panels at the heads, jams, and sills to form the openings. For pipes and conduits, small metal rectangular or circular cans of appropriate size can be nailed inside the formwork to create a passageway.

Rib slabs (Figure 4.8). These consist of an assembly of long, narrow, shaped steel or aluminum pans,

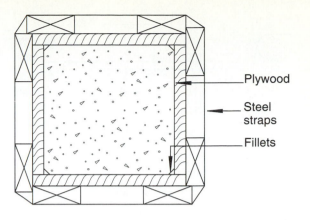

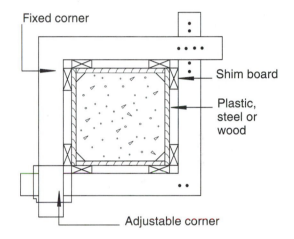

Plywood

Steel
straps

Fillets

Fixed corner

Shim board

Plastic,
steel or
wood

Adjustable corner

Figure 4.3 Columns

Wall Gang Forms

Large repetitive areas can be economically formed using smaller form panels ganged together. Gang forms are quickly transported, installed, removed, and cleaned ready for reuse. (UBC Architecture)

Figure 4.4 Fly Forms

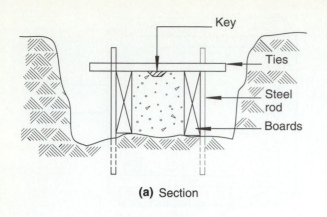

(a) Section

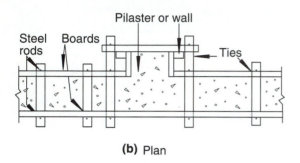

(b) Plan

Figure 4.5 Footings

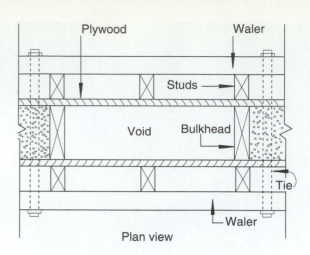

Plan view

Figure 4.7 Openings

usually supported on an open framework of longitudinal horizontal supports.

Setbacks (Figure 4.9). This is a point or line where the vertical plane of one surface of a wall is abruptly offset by a short distance.

Slabs on grade (Figure 4.10). The edges of these slabs are formed in a manner similar to footings.

Slip-forms (Figure 4.11). These are large wood or metal panels which are attached to hydraulic or

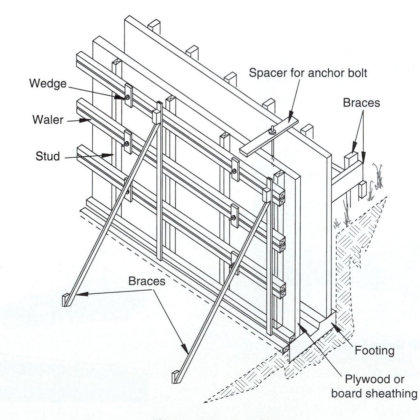

Figure 4.6 Foundations

Chapter 03   Concrete Work

Slab Fly Forms

On buildings with repetitive floor slab design, it is economical to use large fly form assemblies which are secured below slabs before concreting, then "flown" up to the next level. (UBC Architecture)

of a building, or perhaps a cantilevered canopy at the outside of a building.

Waffle slabs (Figure 4.14). These consist of an assembly of shaped rectangular steel or aluminum pans of various sizes and configurations, usually secured in position on top of a fully boarded platform.

pneumatic jacks which force the panels to rise upward at a predetermined rate and direction. (For further detail on slip-forming, see later in this part.)

Stairs (Figure 4.12). These consist of (usually wood) sloping soffit forms to create the underside of the staircase and landings, in conjunction with horizontal but angled boards, cut and braced to suit the run and rise of the treads forming the steps.

Suspended slabs (Figure 4.13). These are large wood or metal panels, usually connected together to make sufficient formed area to cover one whole floor

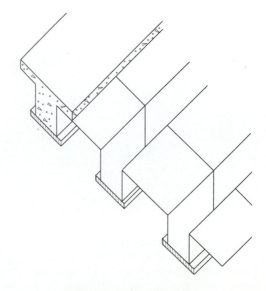

Figure 4.8   Rib Slabs

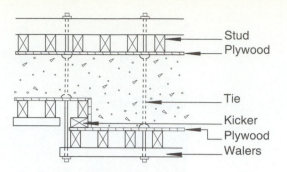

Figure 4.9 Setbacks

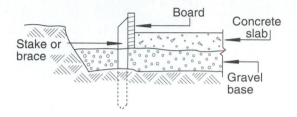

Figure 4.10 Slabs on Grade

Column Forms

Depending on shape and size, concrete columns can be conveniently formed using preassembled and supported sheets of wood, metal, plastic, or tempered hardboard. (UBC Architecture)

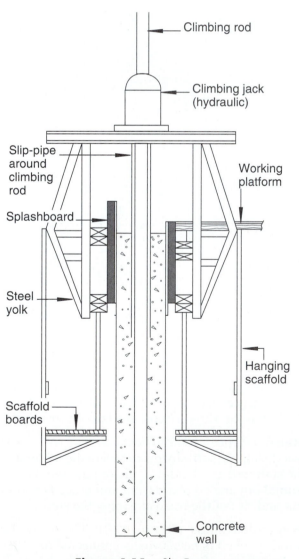

Figure 4.11 Slip-Forms

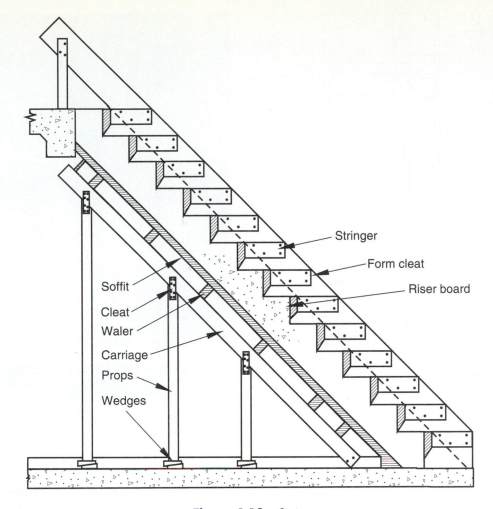

Figure 4.12 Stairs

Stringer
Form cleat
Riser board

Soffit
Cleat
Waler
Carriage
Props
Wedges

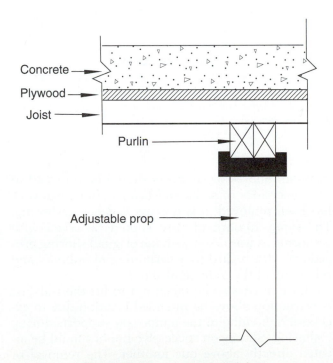

Concrete
Plywood
Joist
Purlin
Adjustable prop

Figure 4.13 Suspended Slabs

Walls (Figure 4.15). These are generally similar to formwork for foundations, described above.

Inspection. Both during and after assembly and before concreting commences, the entire formwork and falsework system should be inspected by knowledgeable personnel. If the falsework system is rented, the rental company should be notified to come and inspect installation of its own components. The entire installation should be checked for adequacy, accuracy, and cleanliness by a responsible person.

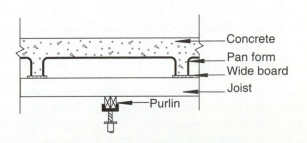

Concrete
Pan form
Wide board
Joist
Purlin

Figure 4.14 Waffle Slabs

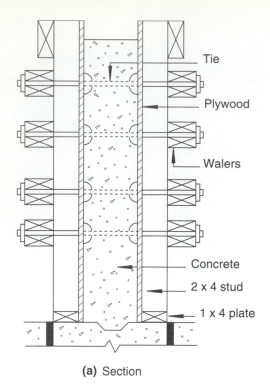

(a) Section

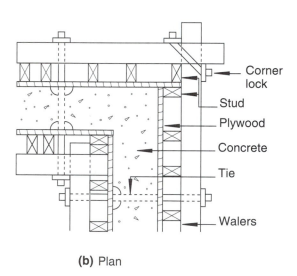

(b) Plan

Figure 4.15 Walls

Typical Features

Most concrete buildings require beams to support slabs and spaces or cavities to be blocked out for mechanical services. The photos show typical arrangements before concreting commences. (UBC Architecture)

After concrete has been poured, the system should be inspected again, to ensure that no damage or misalignment has occurred or is likely to occur in the system.

Stripping. Stripping should not commence until the inspector gives approval, based on consideration of the results of laboratory tests of the poured and cured concrete in the various parts of the structure. Stripping should be arranged to be done so that no damage to the concrete is sustained. Falsework pressure should be reduced by removing wedges or slackening threaded sleeves, and formwork panels should be released and eased away or dropped out of

position. Shores or supports should be returned to the undersides of slabs and beams after formwork has been removed; this process is called reshoring. The same amount of care should be taken with reshoring as was taken with the original shoring procedure, with regard to ascertaining plumbness and reliability of the individual shores.

Care must also be taken not to lift the finished construction above its intended location due to excessive tightening of the temporary supports during reshoring. Shores on successive floors should be located directly above one another. The removal of shores should only be done on the instruction of a re-

Chapter 03   Concrete Work

sponsible person, after having ascertained that the concrete construction so supported can now adequately support its own weight and that of any other loads likely to be imposed on it. Stripped forms should be cleaned free of concrete deposits as soon as possible, then they should be recoated with form oil. Supports and shores should also be repaired, cleaned, and oiled as necessary. If formwork and falsework units are to be stored for a period of time, they should be stacked off the ground and under cover, and at a slight angle to permit water runoff.

Slip-Forming. This special and uncommon forming method involves pouring concrete into forms which are continuously moving upward at a rate sufficient to permit the concrete to set and cure enough to sustain its weight and retain its shape before the formwork passes on; a general configuration is shown in Figure 4.11 above. The object is to permit continuous pouring of concrete over extended periods, such as may be necessary in the construction of grain elevators, observation towers, concrete cores of steel-framed buildings, and so on. The height of the formwork panels is usually 1.2 m or 4 ft. and the rate of climb is usually 0.3 m or 1 ft. per hour. There are six principal parts to the system: the jacks and pumps which cause the system to rise, the steel climbing post up which the system rises, the steel yokes or framework braces which support the formwork panels and work platforms, the walers which stiffen the panels, the sheathing and splashboards which form the panels, and the working platforms for the concretors and finishers.

5.3 Precautions

Most failures of formwork and falsework systems stem from ignorance of basic structural theory. There is a general misconception that formwork design is unimportant because it is only temporary and therefore does not require the same degree of engineering knowledge and skill that are imparted to the permanent structure. There have been too many tragic and unnecessary deaths and serious injuries caused by the collapse of improperly designed formwork and falsework, which refute this argument. Many state, provincial, and municipal jurisdictions now require that formwork and falsework designs be checked by a registered professional structural engineer before their construction and use. Most regulations about working in and around formwork and falsework include a ban on people working directly under formed areas when concrete is actually being poured.

Nontypical Features

Most buildings have design or ornamental features requiring special formwork arrangements to produce desired results. The photos show forms for a curved slab edge and a flight of stairs. (UBC Architecture)

Ornamental Formwork
There are many ways to impart ornamental texture to concrete surfaces. One is to use simple straight wood or metal profiles; another involves finely modeled foamed plastic shapes (see text). (UBC Architecture)

Only properly specified, certified, and identified materials should be used for formwork and falsework. Damaged or distorted supports should not be used. Care should be taken with assembly and disassembly of components. Inadequate bracing, overloading, or eccentric loading should be avoided. The ground underneath mudsills should be examined for stability. Reshoring (the replacement of falsework supports after formwork has been removed) should be done carefully. The forms should not be removed too early, before the concrete structure has attained sufficient confirmed strength to sustain its own weight and any additional loads imposed on it. Strong batter boards, ropes, or railings should be provided at all open edges where a person might fall an appreciable distance and thereby suffer injury.

Section 03–200 Reinforcement

1.0 Introduction

1.1 General Issues

Concrete is strong in compression but weak in tension. For this reason, any portion of a concrete structure (such as a slab, beam, or column) that may be subjected to significant tensile forces beyond what the plain concrete can naturally sustain will require to be reinforced in some way. One common way to do this is to introduce steel bars, rods, wires, or woven mats into the concrete mass. Such components are collectively referred to as reinforcement or "re-steel"; bars and rods are also called "re-bar"; woven mats are sometimes called meshes, grids, or mats.

1.2 Design Aspects

As stated, concrete is relatively good at resisting compressive forces or loads, but not so good at resisting tensile forces, that is, those forces which tend to pull it apart. Part of the explanation for this feature of concrete is that the primary compressive strength of concrete comes from the stone particles from which it is made, while the tensile strength cannot ultimately exceed the ability of the hydrated cement paste to glue the aggregate ingredients together in a solid mass.

By comparison, steel is strong in compression but it is also strong in tension. As the concrete cures and hardens toward achieving its designed compressive strength, it can form a tight bond around embedded reinforcing steel members, thus giving a structurally homogeneous characteristic to the composite whole. The concrete mass can then resist the compressive forces, while the steel reinforcing members sustain the tensile forces, resulting in a considerably more efficient and refined and less costly structural system than otherwise would be the case. In some designs, some of the steel is also required to carry some of the compressive forces. To enhance the bond between the concrete and the steel, the bars, rods, or wires are usually deformed, that is, they have ridges or grooves formed in their surfaces during manufacture (see Figure 1 for one example); plain or non-deformed steel rods are often used to make up two-directional open-weave mats.

A slight uniform coating of rust on the surface of reinforcing steel members is acceptable, indeed some say desirable; loose, flaking, or deep pockets of rust are not acceptable and must be removed before fabrication or installation in concrete members. Care must be taken during fabrication processes not to bend the steel members to radii so small as to cause damage to the integrity of the steel; in such cases, heating may be required before bending, although excessive heating can also change the characteristics of the member. The spacing of reinforcing steel members relative to each other, to the formwork, or to other components should not be so close that they might prevent the largest pieces of concrete

Stockpile
Lengths of rebar are selected from stock in the steel yard and placed by overhead crane on rollers, ready to move along to the bending or shearing machines shown next. (BCIT Building Technology)

aggregate in the mix from being properly consolidated into position. Most building codes are quite specific about limiting such parameters of rusting, bending, and placing, as well as other parameters regarding grading, cutting, and splicing of members.

1.3 Related Work

Work closely connected to this section is described in the following sections, to which reference should be made:

03–100   Formwork

03–300   Cast-in-Place Concrete

03–400   Precast Concrete

2.0 Products

2.1 Materials

Reinforcing products for concrete construction can be categorized under two broad headings: separate bars and integrated fabrics.

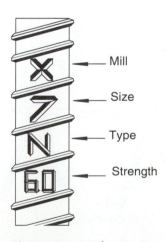

Figure 1   Reinforcing Bar

Bars. These may be made of new billet steel or reconstituted axle or rail steel.* They may be in the form of either round rods or flat bars and either plain (smooth) or deformed (ridged), as shown in Figure 1. They are graded on the basis of their yield stress: values of 300, 400, and 525 megaPascals (mPa) or 40, 60, and 75 thousands of pounds per square inch (kpsi) are typical. Round deformed rods are encountered in nominal diameters ranging between 10 and 55 mm (in eight steps) or between $^3/_8$ and 2 $^1/_4$ in. (in eleven steps), with 10M or #4 bars being most common.

Fabrics. These consist of an arrangement of plain bright or galvanized steel wires of various diameters, laid out parallel to and usually equidistant from each other to form either a square, rectangular, or triangular grid pattern, as shown in Figure 2, with the intersecting points of the grid either interwoven, welded, or wire-tied. They are described on the basis of the pattern created, such that a fabric designated in metric units as $100 \times 200 - MD25 \times MD25$ would indicate a rectangular grid having deformed wires with a cross-sectional area of 25 mm² spaced 100 mm apart in one direction and 200 mm apart at right angles. In imperial units, the designation might be 4 × 8 × 10/12, indicating spacings of 4 and 8 in. for the 10 and 12 gauge wires respectively. Roll dimensions vary between widths of 2.0 and 2.5 m or 6 and 8 ft. and lengths of 30 and 60 m or 100 and 200 ft. Cut flat sheets 6 m or 20 ft. long are also available.

2.2 Accessories

Connections. These consist of an assortment of plain or threaded steel sleeves, filled or malleable splices, and tie wires of various sizes and gauges; they are used to transfer the load from one bar, rod, or wire to its neighbor.

Supports. These consist of an array of small concrete blocks, metal bolsters, plastic chairs, steel dowels, and other inserts intended to restrain the reinforcing steel in specific locations during the concrete pouring operations, to ensure correct positioning in the final composite reinforced concrete structure, as shown in Figure 3.

*Plastic reinforcing bars made of high-strength polymers are now also available in some localities; as this technology develops, more such products will be encountered.

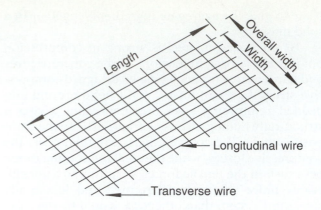

Figure 2 Welded Fabric

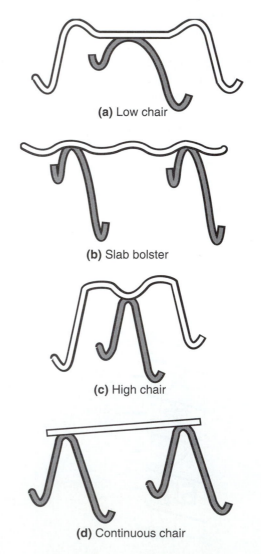

(a) Low chair

(b) Slab bolster

(c) High chair

(d) Continuous chair

Figure 3 Supports and Chairs

3.0 Construction Aids

3.1 Equipment

Because this work involves bending, cutting, and welding of steel, some of the equipment involved is of a personal nature, while the rest is of an impersonal nature. Personal equipment includes special work gloves, goggles, helmets, hard-wearing coveralls, and steel-toed shoes. Impersonal equipment includes fixed or movable electric, hydraulic, or pneumatic machines for bending, cutting, and welding steel. Other items of equipment include cranes and conveyors for moving steel in bulk at the fabrication plant. (See Figure 4.)

3.2 Tools

As this work involves bending, cutting, and welding steel of various types, shapes, and thicknesses, the tools encountered are those of the ironworker or steel fabricator. In addition to the hand tools common to most trades, these workers require to use heavy-duty bolt cutters, acetylene torches, wire cutters, and hickey bars used to bend rods or pipes.

4.0 Production

4.1 Crew Configuration

Personnel involved in reinforcing steel operations can be subdivided according to two main divisions of the work.

Fabrication. The crew often consists of a craneman, a unionized ironworker (called a shearliner) for the cutting machine, a unionized ironworker (called a bender) for the bending machine, and apprentices and yardmen to move the steel around.

Installation. The crew for rods and bars usually consists of a foreman, one or two rodmen, and a helper or two. The fabrication of welded wire fabric by bending and cutting usually involves one unionized ironworker and two helpers. The installation of welded wire fabric sheets usually requires at least two helpers because of the size and weight of the sheets or rolls, working under the direction of a journeyman rodman.

4.2 Productivity

In general terms, for every metric ton (1,000 kg) or imperial short ton (2,000 lb.) of reinforcing steel stock, fabrication takes between 3 and 4 man-hours and placing takes between 8 and 9 man-hours. Some representative factors for typical reinforcing operations are shown in Table 1 for typical work involving reinforcing steel members on normal commercial or institutional construction projects. For heavy steel or complex configurations, the factors can be decreased by up to 25 percent.

5.0 Procedures

5.1 Preparation

There are two components to preparation for reinforcement. The first is the fabrication of the steel

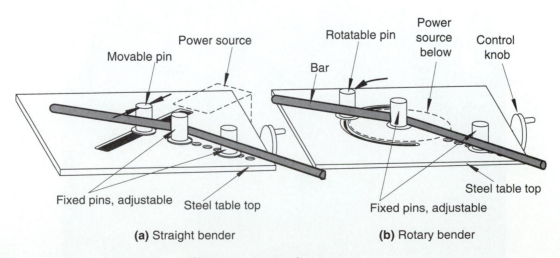

(a) Straight bender   **(b)** Rotary bender

Figure 4 Bar-Bending Equipment

Table 1
PRODUCTIVITY OF INSTALLATION OF REINFORCEMENT

Type of Work	Output per Hour	
RE-BAR	tons (metric or short)	
Unloading	0.50	
Sorting	0.35	
Bending	0.25	
Placing:		
Slabs	0.20	
Walls	0.15	
Columns	0.10	
Beams	0.05	
FABRIC	m^2	ft.^{2}
Fabricating	40	400
Placing:		
Slabs	20	200
Walls	10	100

members; the second is the preparation of areas into which reinforcement will be placed.

Fabrication. There are three elements to this process: cutting, bending, and delivery. During fabrication, care must be taken not to get any grease, oil, paint, or water onto the steel.

  1. Cutting. Reinforcing steel is moved by crane from yard stockpiles to the cutting or shearing line; a conveyor moves the steel past the hydraulic or pneumatic shearing blade. As the rods or bars are cut, each piece is color-coded or tagged to indicate

Cutting Machines
Selected bars are measured and cut to length, according to project specifications. Bars of large diameter are machine cut; smaller rods can be sheared through with heavy-duty bolt cutters. (BCIT Building Technology)

Chapter 03   Concrete Work

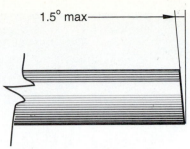

Figure 5 Cut Ends of Bars

its length. Any additional cutting required to be done at the site can be carried out using an acetylene torch or bolt cutters. Cut ends of bars or rods should be not more than 1.5 degrees off the square (see Figure 5).

2. Bending. Precut bars are placed on a steel table, pressed against a restraining pin, and bent by rotating a foot-operated, hydraulic-powered roller through a predetermined arc. The lighter the bar, the smaller the roller. Up to eight bars can be bent simultaneously; some machines are semiautomated with computer controls. Bending is classified as light if the rods or bars are thin and they are not bent at more than six points along their length; otherwise it is classified as heavy bending (for cost-estimating purposes). Any additional bending required to be done at the site can be carried out using a portable bender or a hickey. Any special fabrication involving oversize bars, hot bending, square-cutting bar ends, or other nontypical features will result in additional costs because of the necessity for making adjustments to equipment.

3. Delivery. After fabrication, the ordinary or special steel is marked for identification, bundled and loaded onto flatbed trucks (having regard to traffic regulations governing the overall sizes and weights of loads), and delivered to the job-site. When the steel arrives at the site, it is unloaded from the delivery vehicle, usually by means of a hydraulic arm mounted on the truck, and dropped where required on the site area, usually on dunnage at ground level. The site crane will then pick up selected bundles and move them closer to their final position, either below, at, or above grade level. The bundling wires are then cut with wire cutters, and the bundles are sorted out as necessary.

Preparation. Areas in formwork or foundations scheduled to receive reinforcement should be cleaned free of debris and water. Construction equipment not required for the work of this section should be removed. Sufficient working space should be left around and within such areas to permit insertion of the reinforcing steel in its fabricated form.

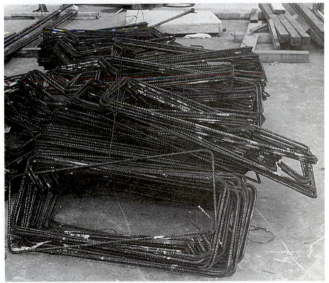

Bending Machines

Bars (cut to length) are then bent to shapes required by the project design. Bars of large diameter are machine bent one at a time; smaller rods can be done in bundles or even manually. (BCIT Building Technology)

For large continuous rolls of welded wire fabric, a heavy-duty spindle can be rigged at the site to store the roll and support it as it is being unrolled for cutting. Both before and after reinforcing steel work is done, a careful inspection of the work and site conditions is usually required and must be made by knowledgeable and responsible personnel; not to do so involves grave risk of subsequent structural failure with attendant legal problems.

5.2 Process

The placement of reinforcing steel can be considered under two broad headings, corresponding to the basic types of materials used: **rods and bars** and **sheets and mats**. All must be dry just before concrete is poured, to avoid interference with the concrete hydration process. (For hydration, see Section 03–300.)

Rods and Bars. After reviewing drawings and specifications, each individual previously bent and shaped rod is selected from the cut bundles, carried manually into position, and installed in foundations, walls, slabs, columns, or beams as required. Any bolsters, blockings, or chairs necessary to align the steel are placed and secured at this time, either simultaneously with or just prior to the placement of the steel members. If lapped, welded, or coupled splices are required to join the ends of rods to each other, they are also installed as the members are being put in place. The various components are then tightly wired together, using a variety of special knots with loose wire ends trimmed off (see Figure 6).

Sheets and Mats. After consulting the drawings and specifications, the sheets are either selected or cut (using wire cutters) to size from the roll and manually carried into position, starting with whole sheets around the outer edges of the area being reinforced and working toward the center; this ensures that any small cut strips are not located at the edges. Ends and sides of sheets or mats can be overlapped (by any multiple of the member wire spacings) and tied with 18-gauge wire, if areas to be thus reinforced exceed sheet dimensions. Specifications or building codes usually detail the permissible locations and configurations of overlapped joints. The sheets and mats can be easily bent to almost any desired configuration required by the structural design. All offcuts, scraps, and ends of tie wire must be removed manually or by blowing with compressed air hoses.

Openings are usually formed by cutting the fabric back along the line of the opening edges and installing additional rods or wires to reinforce the edges of the opening. In slabs, the reinforcing fabric can be draped in such a manner as to be continuously located in the tension zones; alternatively, the

Placing Rebar
Column steel is usually preassembled horizontally (one floor at a time) and raised to the vertical by crane. Wall and floor steel is placed manually in position, piece by piece. (UBC Architecture)

fabric can be cut, with separate sheets appropriately placed in tension zones. Staples and ties are used to hold the fabric in correct position.

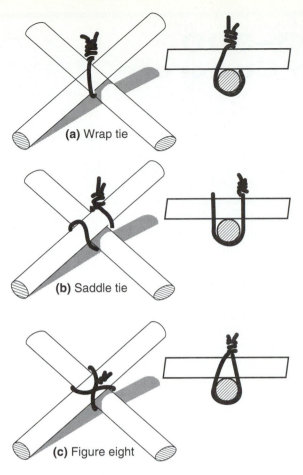

(a) Wrap tie

(b) Saddle tie

(c) Figure eight

Figure 6 Wire Knots

Accessories

Common accessories used with reinforcing steel are chairs or stools (of various shapes and heights) and tie wire (of various gauges) to keep bars in position during concreting operations. (BCIT Building Technology)

5.3 Precautions

From the point of view of design, the vital relationship between all components in a reinforced structure gives rise to very stringent regulations contained in most building codes concerning the selection and placement of the reinforcing steel. From the point of view of fabrication and installation, the work of this trade involves the use of relatively dangerous pieces of powered equipment and heavy materials, which if handled improperly can result in serious injury or property damage. Much of this work is regulated by legislation and union requirements.

Reinforcing steel must be protected from excessive rusting and from accidental applications of grease, oil, or paint. The formwork into which the steel is placed must be protected from damage such as perforation or distortion during placement operations. Workers must be protected from injury caused by sharp protrusions or burrs such as may occur on the ends of cut steel members. Care must be taken by the workers as they move about on decks covered with a myriad of intersecting steel bars.

Clean-Up

After the reinforcement is in place and secured, and just before concreting commences, compressed air is often used to clean the steel and the formwork free of loose scraps and debris. (UBC Architecture)

Section 03–300
Cast-in-Place Concrete

1.0 Introduction

1.1 General Issues

Concrete is one of the most widely used of construction materials in North America; it is also one of the most narrowly understood of materials. In some regions of the continent, concrete is referred to as "mud," and is treated with about as much respect, notwithstanding the fact that the chemical processes occurring in the setting and curing of concrete are among the most sophisticated of any encountered throughout the construction industry. This lack of understanding does not arise from a lack of information; there is an abundance of excellent literature concerning concrete technology. Some of the difficulties relative to concrete appear to arise from the fact that, although the physical ingredients appear to be obvious and simple, their chemical relationships are obscure and complex. Nevertheless, if some basic facts about the design, mixing, and placing of concrete are understood and implemented, concrete of acceptable and predictable quality can be repeatedly produced.

In general, there are three attainable objectives relative to the use of concrete in construction; these are adequate strength, reasonable durability, and acceptable appearance. **Strength** is a function of the quality of materials and their physical and chemical relationships. **Durability** is a function of resistance to physical or climatic wear and tear and chemical attack by acids or salts. **Appearance** is a function of materials selection and mechanical or chemical surface treatments.

On a minor matter of terminology, one often hears people (who should know better) referring to "cement" sidewalks or "cement" blocks, to mention a couple of examples. It should be realized that *cement* is a powder, used to make *concrete* sidewalks and blocks, in conjunction with other ingredients. Because of the pervasive aspect of construction contracts and the possibility of misunderstandings (and therefore disputes) arising throughout building technology processes, it is wise to use all such technical terminology accurately.

Aggregate Storage

Ingredients for concrete are usually stored in large concrete or steel silos raised so that trucks can fit into position below hopper gates through which the ingredients pour under control. (BCIT Building Technology)

1.2 Design Aspects

The notes on concrete design included in this section do not constitute an exhaustive discourse on all aspects of the topic; they are simply intended to present readers with sufficient knowledge to appreciate some of the precautions required to be taken when mixing and placing concrete in bulk. The solution of design problems involving aesthetics or engineering using concrete as a material is beyond the scope of this book.

Two broad aspects of concrete design are **ingredients** and **proportioning**.

Ingredients. The ingredients of concrete primarily consist of coarse aggregate, such as crushed hard rock; fine aggregate, such as clean sand; factory-made portland cement powder; and clean fresh water. Other secondary ingredients may be added to alter the characteristics of any specific mixture, such as entrainment of air, rate of curing, resistance to moisture, prevention of freezing, uniformity of color, and so on. (See Figure 1.)

Proportioning. The proportions of ingredients in concrete involve three ratios:

1. The water/cement ratio. Part of the strength of any concrete mix comes from the ability of the portland cement to literally glue or cement the ingredients together. In its powder form, cement has no adhesive quality; however, when mixed with water, the powder is chemically converted into a gel or crystal-like structure having very high adhesive properties. It follows that, in general (and within limits), the more cement introduced into a concrete mix, the stronger will be the final product. The quantity of cement in any given volume of concrete is called the *cement factor*; it is expressed as a percentage of the volume. Closely related to the cement factor is the ability of the cement to react properly with the amount of water used to make the chemical conversion. This reactive process is called *hydration*. In simple terms, the amount of water should be just sufficient to exactly convert all of the powder to gel. Too little water, and some free powder may be left over; too much water, and some free water may be left over.

2. The coarse/fine aggregate ratio. While it is theoretically possible to build structures of pure cement, the cost would be prohibitive; this is one reason that aggregates are used in concrete mixes. Another reason is that what we really want to do is build a structure using small pieces of inexpensive stone, and the cement is necessary to glue the stone pieces together. The stone comes in the form of inert aggregate, of which there are two primary categories: coarse and fine; both are described in Part 2.1.

The basic concept in proportioning aggregates for concrete involves some understanding of the nature of granular materials. In any given volume of any specific granular material, such as $1 m^3$ or $yd.^3$ of coarse gravel, there will be a proportion of solid material to void air space between the particles, perhaps in the ratio of 80:20. That 20 percent of void space can be filled with finer aggregate, such as sand, which in turn will have a proportion of solid to void space, again perhaps in the ratio of 80:20. The ratio of solid to void space can be simply determined by carefully filling a container of known volume with dry aggregate, and then topping it off with water. The water is then decanted or poured off into another measuring container to determine its volume. That volume, expressed as a percentage of the volume of the original container, indicates the percentage of void space.

3. The paste/aggregate ratio. The void space in the finer aggregate can be filled with a cement and water paste to glue the whole composition together. The maximum amount of cement possible to be introduced into any given volume of concrete mix without increasing the final mix volume cannot be greater than the volume of void space not already displaced with aggregate. To a large extent, this will dictate the ultimate compressive strength of the concrete, usually expressed in newtons/m² or lb./in.². The strength of any specific mix of concrete will be a function of the amount and quality of cement available to bind the ingredients together, combined with the ability of the stone aggregates to resist compressive forces.

In arithmetical terms, if one starts with a given volume of $1 m^3$ or $yd.^3$ of coarse gravel having a solid/void ratio of 80:20, then the 20 percent void space can be filled with fine aggregate. If the fine aggregate also has an 80:20 ratio, then the residual volume available for the cement/water paste cannot exceed 20 percent of 20 percent which is 4 percent or $1/25$ of the original volume. This will largely dictate the strength (or weakness) of the concrete. The only practical way to significantly change the strength would be to select aggregates having other ratios, such as 70:30, 65:35, and so on, thus increasing the residual volume available for cement and additives.

Miscellaneous Issues. Concrete is strong in compression and weak in tension. Therefore wherever tension is expected to be encountered, reinforcing members of one sort or another are introduced into the design. Reinforcement for concrete is described in Section 03–200. Concrete in its initial form (before it sets) is plastic in nature; it can be and usually has to be molded or formed to produce some desired configuration. Formwork for concrete is described in Section 03–100.

To ensure consistent results in concrete mixes, proportions of all ingredients are best measured by **weight** and not by **volume**. However, proportions for concrete mixes are often given in the format of one part cement to a higher number of parts of fine aggregate and coarse aggregate, such as one part cement, two parts sand, and four parts gravel. In such a format, the parts referred to are **parts by volume**. A typical mixture might be written out as a 1:2:4 mix;

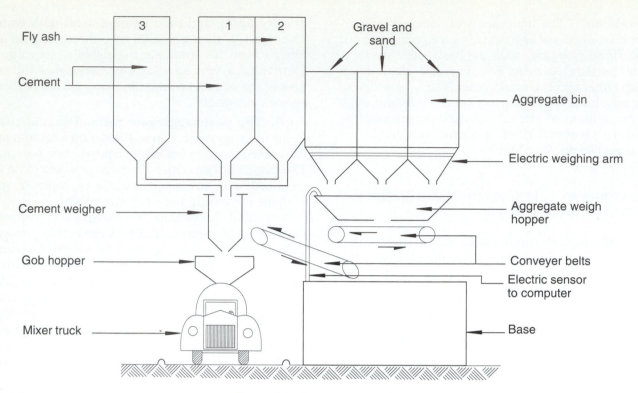

Figure 1 Concrete Proportions

a variation might be a 1:3:7 mix. Some typical values are shown in Table 1.

In most construction contracts, the desired compressive strengths of concrete for the various parts of the building are specified in megaPascals (mPa) or pounds per square inch (psi); it is then up to the contractor to produce a mixture that will meet the specification. Some typical values would be in the range of 15 to 20 mPa or 2,000 to 2,500 psi, although there is a trend toward higher values. Concrete of different strengths delivered to any one construction site can be color-coded using water-soluble additives to ensure that the right concrete ends up in the right place.

Proportions to produce concrete of various predicted strengths are best established by reference to empirical tables, published by the Portland Cement

Association, among others. The values for proportions in these tables have been established by experience and testing. Though important and interesting, the general topic of testing concrete by both destructive and nondestructive means is beyond the scope of this book, because most of it is done off site in specialized materials testing laboratories. However, one simple site test is called the slump or wetness test, shown in Figure 2.

In this test, a metal cone, open at both ends, is placed on a level platform and filled with concrete which is tamped with a steel rod to ensure uniform compaction. The cone is then removed and placed beside the molded concrete, and the difference in height between the cone and the mold is noted. This distance is called the *slump* of the concrete; in most normal circumstances it should be around 75 mm or 3 in., with a small tolerance either way as permitted by concrete codes. It should be noted that this test is not a test of potential concrete strength, but merely an indication of the quality (and, if repeated, the consistency) of the uniformity of the mix and wetness of the ingredients.

When determining the amount of water to add to cement to ensure proper hydration, the amount of water that may already exist in the aggregates should be determined and subtracted from the overall amount of water to be added. The amount of water can be determined by weighing a sample of the damp aggregate, drying it, reweighing it, and com-

Table 1
CONCRETE STRENGTHS AND TYPICAL PROPORTIONS

Strength				
mPa	psi	Cement	Sand	Aggregate
15	2,000	1	2	4
		1	—	6
20	2,500	1	1.75	3
		1	—	4.75

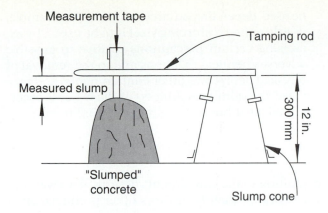

Figure 2 Cone Slump Test

paring the two results. Conversely, it is also important that some additional water is allowed to offset the amount that may be absorbed by dry and porous aggregates, so as to maintain the correct amount of water for hydration. Once the chemical action of hydration has commenced, concrete should not be retempered (made more workable) by adding water.

It has been found that the workability and durability of concrete is greatly enhanced by the introduction of a small percentage of aerating chemicals to produce millions of microscopic air bubbles within the mixture. These bubbles act first as lubricants to improve the homogeneity or uniformity of the concrete mix and its placement; secondly, they interrupt the development of capillary (or hairlike) passages near the surface, where moisture might collect and freeze and thus cause deterioration of the consolidated mass. The process is referred to as air entrainment.

1.3 Related Work

Work closely connected to this section is described in the following sections, to which reference should be made:

03–100   Formwork

03–200   Reinforcement

03–350   Concrete Finishing

03–370   Concrete Curing

2.0 Products

2.1 Materials

The three primary ingredients of concrete are aggregates, cement, and water.

Quality Control
The quality, quantity, and rate of delivery of ingredients in each silo is carefully controlled so that each batch delivered to the trucks is of predictable composition and strength. (BCIT Building Technology)

Aggregates. There are two types and two grades.

1. **Types.** Aggregates made of solid stone such as granite, sandstone, or other bedrock material are described as being of standard weight; they weigh approximately 2,400 kg/m³ or 160 lb./ft.³. Aggregates made of porous stone such as pumice, perlite, or other expanded material are described as being lightweight; they weigh approximately 1,800 kg/m³ or 120 lb./ft.³.

2. **Grades.** Aggregates having a maximum granule size of less than 6 mm or ¹/₄ in. (such as sand) are considered to be fine grade; those having larger particles (such as gravel) are considered to be coarse grade. The upper size limits of coarse aggregate largely depend on the maximum size of concrete members and the minimum spacing of reinforcing members, as the aggregate must be able to pass between the reinforcing bar members.

Cement. Most cement used in North America is a factory-made product called portland cement. It is a kiln-fired, powdered, light-gray-colored mixture consisting of about 64 percent calcium carbonate, 24 percent silica, 7 percent alumina, 4 percent ferrous oxide, and 1 percent other trace elements. Powdered bulk cement weighs approximately 1,500 kg/m³ or 100 lb./ft.³. There are three types of cement in **common** use; another three types have more **specialized** uses.

1. **Common use.** These are normal portland (Type 1), modified or slow-setting portland (Type 2), and high-early-strength portland (Type 3). All cements can and usually do have air-entrainment chemicals added during manufacture (see Part 2.2 Accessories); if so, they should have the letter "A" after the type number (e.g., Type 1A).

2. **Special use.** These are low-heat portland (Type 4), sulfate-resistant portland (Type 5), and specialty portlands (unnumbered), such as white cement for architectural finishes and masonry cement which has some lime added to it to improve workability (see Section 04–100).

Water. Water used for concrete must be clean and free of significant amounts of acids, alkalis, or other chemical ingredients that might react adversely with the cement. There are two types:

1. **Fresh water** running from public water mains is preferred, although drinkable water from other sources may be acceptable. Water from swampy or brackish sources should not be used.

2. **Saltwater** taken from the ocean may sometimes be used, depending on circumstances (for example, if little or no reinforcing steel is to be used), by exercising certain precautions relative to possible adverse chemical reactions and to the removal of physical debris and other contaminants, and provided the salinity (saltiness) of the water is ascertained, as it has to be within certain limits.

2.2 Accessories

In addition to the constituents described above, concrete work frequently involves other products, all of which can be broadly categorized under two headings: **additives** which are mixed into the concrete and **accessories** which are used in conjunction with the plastic concrete. Some common items are described as follows:

Additives. As mentioned in Part 1.2, the secondary ingredients of concrete consist of additives of various sorts, used to alter the characteristics of the mixture of the primary ingredients. Some of the more common of these are alphabetically listed and described below. Stated percentages are approximate and relative to cement volume, unless otherwise stated.

Accelerator. Calcium chloride at 2 percent rate; it can reduce the setting time of concrete by up to 25 percent.

Air entrainer. Stearates or aluminum hydroxide at 0.5 percent rate; it can increase the life expectancy of concrete by as much as 100 percent and sometimes more.

Coloring agent. Various metallic oxides at 10 percent rate; these can change the normal gray color of cement to several attractive primary or secondary colors.

Dampproofer. Stearic acid compound at 2 percent rate; it can reduce capillary attraction of moisture in concrete voids by 90 percent.

Pozzolan. Natural volcanic or siliceous material at 10 percent rate; it can reduce heat generation and expansion in concrete by 15 to 20 percent.

Retarder. Calcium sulfate or zinc oxide at 2 percent rate; it can slow hydration (for example during hot weather) by as much as 15 percent and sometimes more.

Water reducers (also called plasticizers). Carboxylic acids, lignosulfonates, and others, applied at selected manufacturers' recommended rates; they can reduce the amount of water necessary for hydration by up to 20 percent.

Delivery
Concrete, delivered by ready-mix truck, is off-loaded into steel hoppers ready for raising to its final location by crane. Timing of such operations is critical; the concrete is setting. (BCIT Building Technology)

Placing
The hopper is positioned by the crane operator, a gate valve in the base of the hopper is opened, and the hopper is moved around slowly until all of the concrete has been placed. (BCIT Building Technology)

Accessories.   These are products used in conjunction with concrete, either by surface application or insertion.

Abrasive. Fine Carborundum granules, sprinkled onto and troweled into concrete floor surfaces, according to maufacturers' directions; intended to improve traction.

Hardener. Magnesium fluosilicate, applied as described above for an abrasive; intended to improve wearability.

Laitance reducer. Silica powder, applied as described above for an abrasive; intended to reduce the formation of cement paste on top of worked concrete surfaces.

Water-stop. Butyl, neoprene, or vinyl rubber preformed strip; 3 mm or 1/8 in. thick and in various widths up to 25 mm or 10 in.; intended to be inserted into concrete construction joints to prevent the passage of water, as shown in Figure 3.

3.0 Construction Aids

3.1 Equipment

The equipment described in this section is of particular concern to the work of this trade.

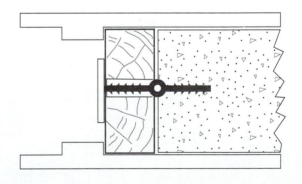

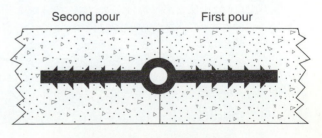

Figure 3   PVC Water-Stop

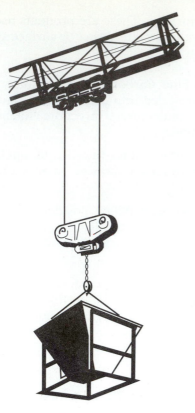

Figure 4.1 Concrete Bucket

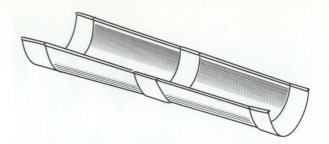

Figure 4.3 Concrete Chute

Buckets (Figure 4.1). There are two basic types: roll-over and constant-attitude; both are intended to be used in conjunction with cranes or hoists. They consist of a large steel container, up to 9 m³ or 10 yd.³, having a lever-operated trapdoor at the bottom and a surrounding metal frame to which hooks and guys can be attached.

Carts (Figure 4.2). An assortment of small and large manual and motorized wheelbarrows are available; most have steel bodies and one, two, or three rubber-tired wheels.

Figure 4.2 Concrete Cart

Chutes (Figure 4.3). These consist of sheet-steel or steel-lined wooden, open, semitubular sections, having a round-bottomed configuration, and large enough to permit concrete to slide along inside without spilling over the edge. Sections vary between 1.2 and 2.4 m or 4 and 8 ft. in length.

Conveyers (Figure 4.4). These consist of a continuous, durable, nylon-canvas, rubberized plastic belt, 400 to 600 mm or 16 to 24 in. wide, stretched between and supported by steel pulleys separated by a metal frame, equipped with a loading hopper, and powered by a small gas or electric motor. Lengths vary between 12 and 18 m or 40 and 60 ft.

Hoppers and sleeves (Figure 4.5). These consist of a heavy-duty, reinforced, rubberized canvas tube, fitted to the underside of a bucket to direct the concrete flow into a cart or a narrow opening, such as the top of wall or column forms.

Mixers. A large steel drum equipped with a set of angled internal blades, set to rotate on a slightly inclined vertical axis about 20 times per minute, and powered by a gas or electric motor. Mixing machines are usually categorized by the number of bags or sacks of cement needed to make a drum-full of concrete; they are thus called 6-sack or 12-sack mixers.

Pumps (mechanical) (Figure 4.6). These consist of a gas-, diesel-, or electric-powered, auger- or piston-type pump which receives the premixed concrete through a hopper intake and forces it to its destination through a system of steel or rubber pipes about 20 cm or 8 in. in diameter. Although some of the larger machines can pump concrete considerable heights and distances, most commonly encountered pumps will accommodate maximum heights of about 100 m or 330 ft. and maximum horizontal distances of about 300 m or 1,000 ft. There are some limitations on concrete slump and aggregate size.

Pumps (pneumatic) (Figure 4.7). These are often referred to as gunite pumps. They consist of a compressed air pump which loads cement and aggregates through a hopper, then moves the dry concrete

Figure 4.4   Concrete Conveyor

ingredients through a hose to a nozzle, where they are mixed with pressurized water just prior to placing. The mixture is called *gunite*.

Vibrators (Figure 4.8). These consist of a small rotary power unit, a flexible hose enclosing a flexible shaft, and a handling head having an eccentric cam which rotates and causes vibration of the head in the approximate range of 1,000 cycles per minute. They are used for consolidating concrete around reinforcing steel and in corners.

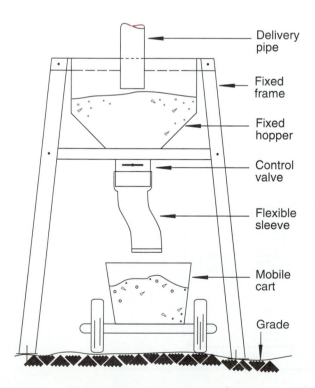

Figure 4.5   Hoppers and Sleeves

Delivery pipe

Fixed frame

Fixed hopper

Control valve

Flexible sleeve

Mobile cart

Grade

Pumping

On low-rise (and some high-rise) buildings, it is expedient to place concrete using equipment which pumps it through hydraulically controlled pipe booms to its final position. (BCIT Building Technology)

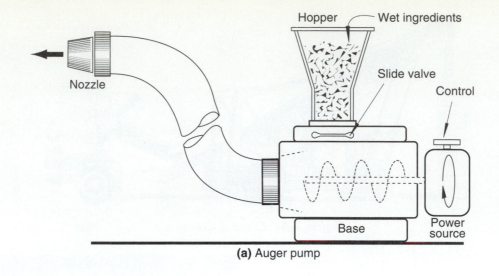

(a) Auger pump

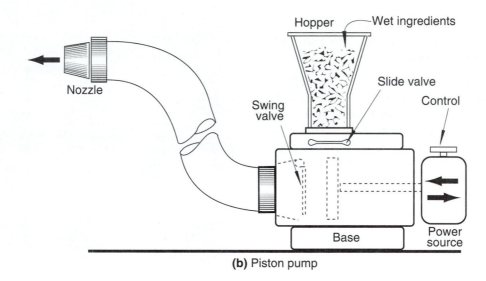

(b) Piston pump

Figure 4.6 Mechanical Pumps

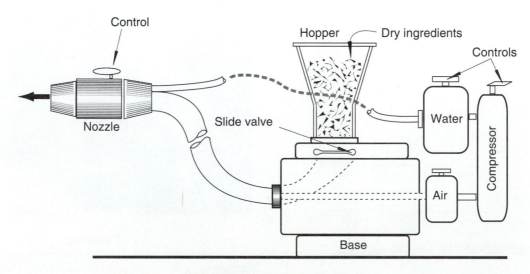

Figure 4.7 Pneumatic Pump

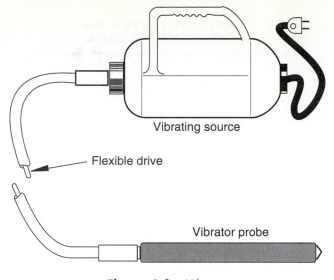

Figure 4.8 Vibrator

3.2 Tools

The tools described in this section are of particular concern to the work of this trade.

Rakes. These are similar to ordinary garden rakes, having long wooden handles and wide steel-toothed heads.

Screeds (Figure 5). These are long wooden or steel blades, having handles attached at each end, and used to strike off concrete at tops of slab levels, established by wood boards or metal pipes.

Shovels. An assortment of sturdy shovels, spades, and hand trowels are used in the work of this trade.

Finished level

Sub-base level

(a) Wood board on pegs   (b) Metal pipe on supports

Figure 5 Screeds

4.0 Production

4.1 Crew Configuration

Because of the enormous scope of variable methodology in concrete work, crew sizes can vary all the way from one person to literally dozens of people. Most concrete crews consist of several skilled workers acting in concert with some semiskilled and even unskilled helpers. On a small commercial project, one might find one or two semiskilled persons engaged in mixing or transporting concrete, in addition to three or four skilled persons handling, placing, and screeding the concrete. On a large institutional project, one might find a semiskilled crew involving two or three persons operating pumping, conveying, or hoisting equipment to keep a larger crew of seven or eight skilled persons busy handling, placing, and screeding concrete for a number of days. The rates quoted for ready-mix concrete usually include the cost involved in providing personnel to manufacture and deliver the mix.

Table 2 gives some representative and typical crew sizes for common concrete work of various kinds. The factors can be combined by simple addition where more than one type of work is performed or more than one crew is assigned on one project.

4.2 Productivity

As with crew sizes, the extraordinarily large number of variables encountered in concrete work will permit only a brief review of some typical productivity factors to be included in this book. To give some idea of the magnitude of possible data on the productivity factors of concrete construction, one well-known

Table 2
CREW SIZES FOR CONCRETING

Type of Work	Crew Size	
	Skilled	Unskilled
Bucketing	3	2
Carting	—	1
Chuting	2	1
Conveying	4	2
Handling	3	1
Mixing	1	1
Pumping	2	1
Screeding	3	—
Vibrating	2	—

reference book* allocates well over 100 tightly written pages or approximately 10 percent of the entire book to the topic. Productivity factors listed in Table 3 assume reasonably large and straightforward commercial and institutional construction projects, where a high degree of mechanization and crews of average size can be utilized and concrete volumes average around 100 m³ or yd³ per floor. The type of work involves the placement, handling, compaction, and leveling of ordinary cast-in-place concrete around previously placed reinforcement in prefabricated wooden formwork.

For example, an experienced seven-person placing crew should position and consolidate about 4 m³ or yd³ of concrete in suspended slabs in 1 hour. An experienced mixing crew should be able to machine-mix and deliver about 15 m³ or 16.0 yd³ of concrete in 1 hour. If only floor work is being done, then it will take about four placing crews to keep one mixing crew fully occupied during that phase of the project. Other permutations are of course possible.

5.0 Procedures

5.1 Preparation

There are two primary aspects of preparation for concreting with which to contend: **procedures for mixing** and **preliminaries for placing**.

Procedures for Mixing.   There are three common techniques:

1. By hand. A large sheet of plywood is laid level as a mixing platform. A layer of cement is spread over a layer of sand, and then both layers are mixed dry to a uniform distribution. The mixture is arranged into a saucer-like shape and water is carefully poured into the center by bucket and turned into the surrounding mixture by shovel. Coarse aggregate is then added, the whole mixture is gently worked for two or three minutes until a uniform color and texture is achieved, and then it can be left to mature for a minute or two. The platform is unloaded by shoveling the concrete mix into wheelbarrows.

2. By machine. All of the dry ingredients are loaded by shovel or chute into the mouth of the drum of a concrete mixer and mixed dry for a few minutes. Water is then added to the drum by hose or bucket; on larger machines, a water tank equipped with a

*The Building Estimator's Reference Book (Chicago: Frank R. Walker Company Publishers), 331–443.

Table 3
PRODUCTIVITY IN CONCRETE WORK

Type of Work	Output per Man-Hour	
	m³	yd.³
Foundations, mass	0.90	1.00
Walls, basement	0.80	0.90
Walls, above-grade	0.70	0.80
Slabs, on-grade	0.60	0.70
Slabs, suspended	0.50	0.60
Slabs, waffle	0.40	0.50
Columns, vertical	0.33	0.40
Beams, horizontal	0.25	0.30

measuring gauge is attached to the machine to deliver accurate quantities of water to the mix. Rotation should continue for about one minute for each cubic meter or yard of concrete being made, after the water has been added. Drums are usually unloaded either by tilting them around their vertical axis, by reversing rotation, or both; some horizontal types are loaded from one end and discharged from the opposite end.

3. By batching. Two batching processes are used: dry and wet. In dry batching, the ingredients are stored in bulk in large silos, proportioned by computer-controlled machines in hoppers, and dumped dry into a ready-mix delivery truck either before or while water is added. In wet batching, the concrete is mixed in bulk at the central batch plant before being dumped into the truck and delivered to the site. The drum and discharge mechanism on the ready-mix truck works on the same rotation principle as the drum on a machine mixer, but the axis of the drum is usually slightly inclined from the horizontal. Water can be added and the drum rotation speed altered by the driver-operator depending on varying parameters of concrete design, climatic conditions, distance, and traffic speed. The drum should rotate for about one minute for each cubic meter or yard of concrete in the drum, although more than 100 rotations between the introduction of water and final delivery is seldom advisable.

Preliminaries for Placing.   Before placing concrete, care should be taken to remove debris and unnecessary construction equipment from areas where the concrete work is to be done. Proper access by the relatively heavy concrete equipment to the placement areas should be considered. Bottoms and sides of trenches should be examined to see that they are firm and clean and, in particular, free of water. Formwork and falsework configurations should be checked to ensure that they are complete, sound, and correctly arranged. Other work to be embedded in concrete, such as reinforcing steel, anchor bolts, electrical conduits, and so on, should be properly installed, completed, and checked before concrete work starts. Preliminary consideration should be given to the organization of the crew and the manner in which work of various types should proceed.

5.2 Process

Methods of on-site placement of concrete will vary, depending on the location and type of the building under construction, the various types and quantities of concrete to be placed, and the location of concrete in the building. To make some obvious comparisons, low-slump concrete being poured into shallow below-grade foundations for a small farm building can be deposited quite differently from high-slump concrete required to be raised to roof slab levels in a multistory office building. Concrete being placed in horizontal floor slabs and beams will be placed and handled differently from concrete being poured into vertical forms for columns, even though the type of concrete may be the same in both locations. Concrete of different strengths can be colored for identification.

Placement methods used in normal building construction procedures can be categorized as follows. (Photographs accompanying this section show some of the methods.):

Bucketing. Concrete is placed into buckets for vertical movement from grade to higher levels. Useful where the supply of concrete should be maintained at a steady but intermittent rate.

Carting. Concrete is placed into manual or motorized wheelbarrows for horizontal transportation around the site. Useful where small amounts of concrete are required to be deposited some distance from the main deposits.

Chuting. Concrete can be slid down inclined chutes, to avoid dropping the product through an excessive height likely to cause segregation. Useful where concrete is being poured into deep wall-forms.

Conveying. Concrete can be rapidly and continuously transported on the level or up an inclined plane not exceeding 35 degrees, using one or more conveyors in tandem. Useful where a continuous supply of concrete is required at some distance from where the concrete is first brought onto the site.

Working
The concrete is worked to make sure it fills formed spaces without segregation of ingredients. This picture shows concrete being poured and vibrated around rebar in a perimeter beam. (BCIT Building Technology)

Handling. Concrete almost always requires to be manually (but carefully) shoved around and consolidated into its final position using floats, rakes, screeds, and shovels.

Vibrating
This picture shows a typical portable concrete vibrator. Note the motor device, the grounded electric cord, the flexible cable drive, and the vibratory hand-held probe. (BCIT Building Technology)

Spreading

After placing from pump nozzle or hopper, the plastic concrete is spread around using rakes and shovels, taking care not to separate ingredients and to fill all voids. (UBC Architecture)

Screeding

After spreading, the concrete on horizontal or inclined slabs is screeded to bring it to its intended thickness. Metal shovels and long wooden screed boards are used for this phase. (UBC Architecture)

Floating

After screeding and before the concrete achieves its initial set, the surface is brought to a reasonably smooth and level plane by wood floats as shown, ready for final finishing. (UBC Architecture)

Pumping. Concrete can be efficiently, rapidly, and continuously raised to levels above grade or over intervening obstruction through the use of special sectional pipes and concrete pumping equipment. Useful where a continuous supply of concrete is required at a considerable height or distance from the delivery source, often at street level.

Screeding. Concrete in slabs can be struck off at any specific level by the use of screeds preset to determine the desired thickness or level of the slab.

Vibrating. Concrete can be consolidated around reinforcing steel and into corners by the use of vibrating equipment and probes specially designed for this task. Useful to ensure rapid consolidation of concrete in bulk or large volume, but note the precautions stated in Part 5.3.

Finishing. See Section 03–350.

5.3 Precautions

Any concrete not used within about 90 minutes from the time water is first added to the mixture should be discarded and the equipment used to make it should be thoroughly cleaned to remove all traces of cement. Precautions should be taken to avoid overmixing, which can alter the characteristics of the aggregate particles and the hydration process. During the placement process, the primary precaution to be exercised is to prevent segregation of the ingredients of the concrete which may occur through excessive, prolonged vibration, vigorous handling, or dropping

Concrete Topping
Many structural decks, whether made of wood, steel, concrete or other material, require a fine concrete topping applied to improve finish, fire-resistance, or acoustical separation. (UBC Architecture)

the plastic concrete mix any significant distance. Concrete should be gently deposited as close to its final resting place as possible. Prolonged contact with concrete chemicals can damage human skin.

Section 03–350
Concrete Finishing

1.0 Introduction

1.1 General Issues

Concrete finishing is a matter of considerable importance. Apart from any issues of objectionable aesthetic appearance, improperly finished surfaces will be less likely to withstand the effects of weather and wear imposed on many concrete surfaces during the life of the building. For these two reasons (appearance and durability), it is appropriate to consider the methodology required to produce concrete finishes of acceptable quality.

1.2 Design Aspects

The entire topic of concrete finishing can be generally considered under three headings.

Applied Finishes. Paint or stain is often used to enhance the appearance of an otherwise drab and essentially colorless structure. There are several reasons why a concrete topping may be applied to a concrete structural slab: finer tolerances in leveling can be achieved, longer and better wear can be assured, color can be more easily imparted, and service pipes or conduits can be embedded in the topping, to name a few.

Chemical Finishes. These often involve alterations to the natural setting or curing characteristics of the ingredients of the concrete mix, thus permitting further work to be done on the surface to achieve desired effects. They can also involve imparting color or durability to the surface of traveled areas by the addition of selected pigmented, metallic, or mineral powders and pastes.

Physical Finishes. Designers and owners often require or desire specific textures to be imparted to building surfaces, for either aesthetic or utilitarian purposes, such as ornamental fluting on vertical columns and walls, traction ribbing on a sloping ramp or driveway, or rough broom finishes to improve the bonding of waterproof membranes to concrete roof decks, to mention three examples.

1.3 Related Work

Work closely connected to this section is described in the following sections, to which reference should be made:

03–100   Formwork

03–300   Cast-in-Place Concrete

03–370   Concrete Curing

2.0 Products

2.1 Materials

Depending on the technique selected for finishing concrete, the nature of materials will vary. Materials commonly encountered are categorized as follows; their uses are explained in Part 5.2:

1. **Chemical products.** These include salt crystals, silicone solutions, calcium chloride, pozzolans, and a wide variety of colored oxide pigments, patented cement densifiers, and metallic or mineral epoxy resin hardeners, all in granular, paste, powder, and liquid forms, and usually combined with other chemicals to reduce water retention and improve dispersion.
2. **Paint products.** Refer to Section 09–900.
3. **Topping ingredients.** Refer to Section 03–300.

2.2 Accessories

The materials used as accessories to this work include various grades of hard and sharp sands for sandblasting and fresh clean water for waterblasting.

3.0 Construction Aids

3.1 Equipment

Equipment for concrete finishing falls into two categories (see Figure 1):

1. Machines capable of manipulating concrete in its plastic state, such as powered concrete pumps, screeds, floats, and trowels.
2. Machines capable of cutting or abrading concrete in its cured state, such as compressors, hoses, bushhammer bits and chisels, grinding machines, and sandblasters.

3.2 Tools

As this work involves handling of concrete mixtures, the primary tools are those of the concrete finisher. They include brushes, darbies, edgers, groovers, hand trowels, wood floats, and assorted rakes and shovels.

(a) Power float   (b) Power saw

Figure 1   Finishing Equipment

4.0 Production

4.1 Crew Configuration

Crew sizes for concrete finishing work naturally will vary, depending on the type of work to be done. The finishing of surfaces such as slabs and walls may involve one or two skilled cement finishers applying chemicals or wielding tools. The placement of toppings can give rise to many permutations; however, to give one example, the crew used to place 250 m² or 2,500 ft.² of topping 38 mm or 1½ in. thick on one job-site consisted of one foreman for 2 hours, four semiskilled workers placing concrete for 2 hours, two skilled cement finishers troweling for about 12 hours, and a pump truck operator standing by for 2 hours.

4.2 Productivity

The factors shown in Table 1 relate to the finishing techniques described in Part 5.0, and indicate prob- able productivity on plain horizontal surfaces on normal commercial or institutional projects of aver- age size and complexity. For work on plain vertical surfaces, factors can be reduced by up to 20 percent. On complex surfaces, factors can be further reduced by about 20 percent.

5.0 Procedures

5.1 Preparation

In every case, a key element of preparation involves establishing the rate of curing of the concrete sur- face to be finished. Some techniques require that work start before curing commences, while others require a state of partial or even total curing. Areas to be finished should be cleared free of debris and construction equipment or formwork not required in connection with this work. Areas being finished should be barricaded off from the rest of the build- ing structure to prevent unauthorized traffic that might damage the structure or the finishes. Areas scheduled for painting should be cleaned free of dust, grease, and oil. Areas scheduled for separate topping should be treated with an appropriate chemi- cal bonding agent. If necessary, areas scheduled for bushhammering, sandblasting, or waterstripping should have protective tarpaulins hung to contain the dust, water, and noise.

5.2 Process

As stated in Part 1.2, the topic of concrete finishing embraces three subdivisions: applied, chemical, and physical.

Applied Finishes. These include paints and top- pings.

   1. Paints. For detailed discussion of paint ap- plications, refer to Section 09–900. Most paint fin- ishes should not be applied until after the concrete has thoroughly cured.

   2. Toppings. This technique involves a micro- cosm of general concreting technique, for which see Section 03–300. Toppings are mixed like concrete (but using finer aggregates), delivered by pump or chute and spread where required, and then screeded, floated, and troweled smooth, either manually or by machine. Screeding establishes the thickness of the topping, as shown in Figure 2; floating removes any minor hills or valleys, and troweling produces a smooth, dense, and hard finish, as shown in Figure 3. Toppings may be either integral or bonded. Inte-

Table 1
PRODUCTIVITY IN CONCRETE FINISHING

Type of Work	Area Done per Hour	
	m²	ft.²
Applied finishes:		
Paint:		
Cleaning	30	300
Applying	15	150
Topping (38 mm or 1.5 in.):		
Placing	100	1,000
Finishing	20	200
Chemical finishes:		
Integrally worked	15	150
Superficially applied	30	300
Physical finishes:		
Formed:		
Brushed	20	200
Molded	(see 03–100)	
Troweled	15	150
Machined:		
Blasted	6	60
Ground	4	40
Hammered	2	20

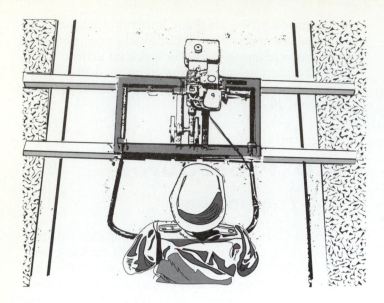

Figure 2 Screeding Slabs

gral toppings are applied before the substrate is cured; bonded toppings are applied after the substrate has been cured, using a patented bonding agent or a fine cement/sand slurry. In both cases, the substrate must be clean, damp, and slightly roughened. It is also possible to apply paint, chemical finishes, or ornamental mineral surfaces integrally or superficially to the topping as appropriate and as desired.

Chemical Finishes.   These include **integral** treatments which are applied while the concrete or topping is being placed, and **surface** treatments which are applied after the concrete or topping has cured.

Figure 3   Troweling Slabs

1. Integral treatment. Rock salt crystals can be scattered on the concrete surface, troweled in, and then washed out by dissolution after the concrete has cured, leaving a random pitted effect. Colored pigments and/or metallic or mineral hardeners can be uniformly dusted on or shaken out over the surface, carefully troweled or brushed in, and left to set and cure, to improve durability and traction. Chemical accelerators can be poured or sprayed on to alter the timing of the set of the concrete at and just below the surface, which is then washed and brushed to remove the unset cement paste on the surface, revealing the underlying texture and color of the aggregate.

2. Surface treatment. The simplest surface treatment consists of washing with water containing a mild detergent and then brushing the concrete surfaces. Silicone solutions in the ratio of about 5 percent silicone to 95 percent water can be handsprayed over vertical concrete surfaces to reduce moisture penetration for periods of up to several years. Patented liquid hardeners that combine with the lime in the cement to form a hard dense surface skin can be applied by carefully flooding and brushing horizontal areas requiring to be treated, at intervals of several years.

Physical Finishes.   These include **formed configurations** and **mechanical abrasions,** described as follows:

1. Formed configurations. This category includes four distinct techniques:

    a. Dashing (Figure 4). The surface of the concrete may be seeded with mineral or other inert granules before it has cured; these granules

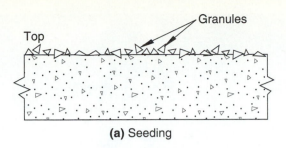

(a) Seeding

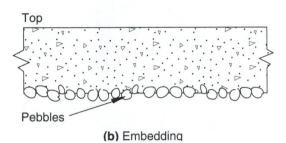

Pebbles

(b) Embedding

Figure 4 Dashing Concrete

Broom Finish
The surfaces of many concrete slabs require a textured finish to improve traction (on driveways) or enhance bonding (on roof tops). A simple texturing technique is brooming. (BCIT Building Technology)

are embedded into the concrete by lightly darbying the surface of the granules to ensure good and uniform adhesion. An alternative technique involves distributing the granules in a formed frame, and then pouring a thin layer of concrete on top. The layer is later removed from the forms, thus producing small ornamental precast concrete panels, ready for fastening to the structural frame of the building.

b. **Troweling** (Figure 5). The exposed surfaces of concrete slabs or toppings and the tops of walls and beams usually require to be brought to a reasonably smooth or even and level state. This is achieved by a combination of fine screeding and either manual or mechanical troweling of the concrete before its final set.

c. **Brushing** (Figure 6). This process usually follows the troweling process. In it, stiff brooms

or brushes are worked across the uncured concrete or topping surface to create a textured or patterned effect.

d. **Molding** (Figure 7). When plastic concrete is poured into a mold or form, its surface will obviously adopt the shape of the mold; it is for this primary reason that forms are used. However, the form may be of either plain or ornamental configuration. It is a relatively simple matter to secure ornamental panels made of molded metal, plaster, steel, wood, or other material inside the forms as liners before the concrete is poured, to impart an aesthetically pleasing relieved design to surfaces of con-

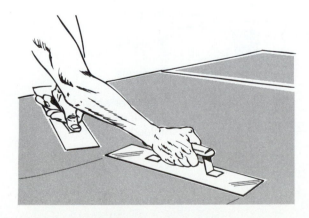

Figure 5 Troweling Concrete

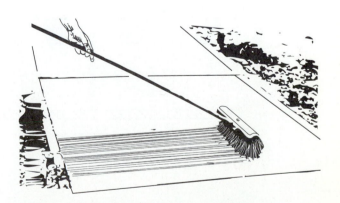

Figure 6 Brushing Concrete

Power Troweling

A smooth finish can be quickly achieved over large surface areas of concrete by using a gasoline-powered rotary trowel. (Note that this worker is not wearing proper protective clothes.) (BCIT Building Technology)

Bushhammering

A pleasing though expensive finish on concrete can be achieved by chipping off a thin layer at the surface, exposing the natural beauty of the aggregate ingredients. (BCIT Building Technology)

crete that may be exposed to view. For more detail, refer to Section 03–100.

2. **Mechanical abrasions.** This category includes four distinct techniques; some design specifications call for a mixture of these techniques:

   a. **Bushhammering** (Figure 8). Compressed air is used to drive a vibrating cutting bit or chisel point against the cured surface of the con-

crete, the objective being to expose the natural beauty of the stone aggregate particles used in the concrete mix by removing about 3 mm or $1/8$ in. of the surface concrete.

   b. **Grinding** (Figure 9). This technique is similar to that used for terrazzo work; for more detail, see Section 09–400.

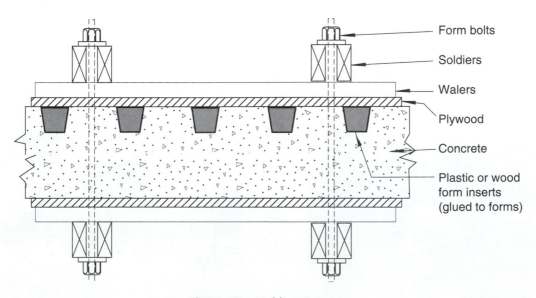

Form bolts

Soldiers

Walers

Plywood

Concrete

Plastic or wood form inserts (glued to forms)

Figure 7   Molding Concrete

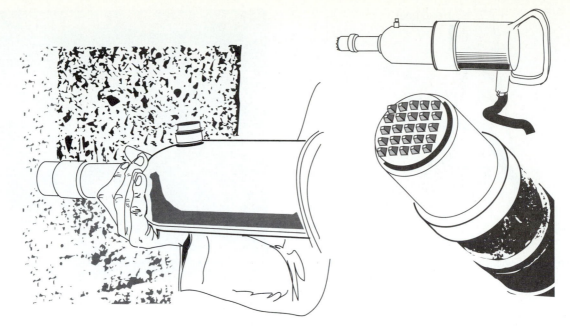

Figure 8 Bushhammering

c. Sandblasting (Figure 10). Compressed air is used to blow sharp and hard particles of specially selected abrasive sand through an adjustable nozzle against the cured surface of the concrete, the objective being to remove minor discoloration and paste from the surface to a depth of about 1 mm or $1/16$ in.

d. Waterblasting. This is a modified version of sandblasting using high-pressure jets of water to achieve the same objective. This technique is useful where the generation of excessive dust particles and loud noise must be avoided.

Grinding

Minor imperfections on concrete can often be removed by simply grinding the surface with a carborundum disc. Workers need eye and breathing protection for this operation. (UBC Architecture)

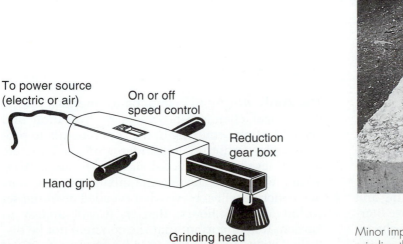

Figure 9 Grinding Concrete

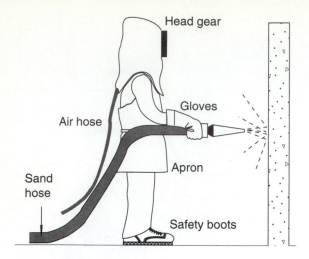

Figure 10 Sandblasting with Protective Clothing

Cutting and Coring
It is often expedient to cut or drill through concrete slabs after they have set and cured. A variety of heavy-duty water-cooled saws and drills can be rented to suit specific needs. (UBC Architecture)

5.3 Precautions

Parts of this work involve the use of pressurized equipment and toxic chemicals. Most local authorities have regulations governing such equipment and materials, to prevent or reduce hazards both to the operators and to the environment.

For personnel doing bushhammering and sandblasting work, protective clothing consisting of coveralls, hand gloves, eye goggles, and a breathing mask are recommended (see Figure 10). Portions of the building structure not scheduled for concrete finishes often have to be protected by masking or covering with tarpaulins or sheets. Consideration must be given to protecting the public around the site and other personnel on the site from harm arising from finishing operations involving pressurized equipment causing dust to be generated in high volume or particles to move with high and dangerous velocity.

Section 03–370
Concrete Curing

1.0 Introduction

1.1 General Issues

Curing involves procedures to ensure that sufficient water is retained to permit complete hydration of the cement in a concrete mix. (For a discussion of hydration, refer to Section 03–300.) The proper curing of concrete is as important as the proper mixing and placing of concrete; improper curing can have literally disastrous effects if it adversely affects the chemical processes which impart adhesion strength to the concrete.

1.2 Design Aspects

The word *curing* used in this context means allowing the critical chemical processes of hydration and crystallization occurring in the concrete mix to proceed under optimum conditions until the concrete has achieved its predicted design strength. After adding water and starting the mixing process, normal concrete will achieve what is called its *initial* set within about 3 hours; that is, it will appear to harden. It is important that the concrete not be disturbed by traffic for at least 24 hours after its initial set. Several days later, if properly cured, the concrete will achieve what is called its *final* set. It will then continue to develop toward its final design strength over a period of 25 to 30 days, and indeed can continue to cure beyond that period. Under factory conditions, and using artificial means of curing, it is possible to accelerate this process from 30 days to about 30 minutes in some circumstances.

The ideal temperature range for proper **natural** curing is between 10 and 25 degrees C or 50 and 80 degrees F. At temperatures below this range, the early strength is seriously delayed, while at temperatures above this range, the rate of evaporation of surface water is greater than the rate of hydration. In **artificial** curing, where control can be exercised over every aspect of the process, higher or lower temperatures may be utilized.

During very hot, dry weather, a false set (also called a *flash* set) may occur if the ingredients are not cooled before mixing; conversely, during very cold weather, a false set (also called a *failed* set) may occur if the ingredients are not heated before mixing. Later in this section, techniques are suggested to cope with hot and cold weather curing.

1.3 Related Work

Work closely connected to this section is described in the following sections, to which reference should be made:

03–100   Formwork

03–300   Cast-in-Place Concrete

03–350   Concrete Finishing

03–400   Precast Concrete

2.0 Products

2.1 Materials

Materials used for curing fall into two categories: those used integrally (**chemicals**) and those used superficially (**coverings**).

Chemicals. These consist of a variety of rubber emulsions, pozzolans, resins, stearates, and waxes, all marketed under various trade or brand names. They are available in liquid or powder form and in colorless, white, or black shades. The object is to temporarily cover a concrete surface with a waterproof skin or membrane. Colorless types usually have a fugitive (or disappearing) dye added, so that one can see if an area has been properly covered with the product. Coverage will vary, depending on the

porosity of the concrete surface and the strength of the applied solution. Some chemicals, such as calcium chloride and calcium sulfate, are added directly into the concrete mix to either accelerate or retard, respectively, the rate of hydration and thus the rate of curing of the concrete mass.

Coverings. These fall into two groups:

1. **Sheet goods.** These consist of large rolls of heavy-duty woven burlap or cotton cloth, fiberglass-reinforced polyethylene plastic, waterproof kraft building paper, and even special electric blankets (for cold weather work). They can all be treated to reflect or absorb light and heat energy and to resist fire and rotting. Rolls can have widths of 1 to 6 m or 3 to 20 ft. and lengths up to 30 m or 100 ft.
2. **Loose goods.** These consist of a variety of natural materials, such as clean earth (free of organic material), hay, sand, sawdust, and straw.

2.2 Accessories

The only accessories used for this work involve a few small blocks or clamps to hold the curing covers in place.

3.0 Construction Aids

3.1 Equipment

On-site curing procedures involve the use of light hand pumps, heavy-duty water hoses, nozzles, and sprays, and a few buckets and assorted brushes. Factory curing procedures involve provision of an extensive system of steam pipes and heat generators.

3.2 Tools

Apart from a few sharp knives to cut sheet goods, some simple measuring devices to proportion and mix curing compounds, and some shovels and rakes to spread loose materials around, no specialized tools are required for this work.

4.0 Production

4.1 Crew Configuration

One semiskilled person is required for mixing and spraying chemical compounds. Two helpers working under the direction of an experienced concrete finisher are required to handle large sheet goods or to spread large quantities of loose goods over areas to be cured. On large projects, crews can be doubled.

4.2 Productivity

Productivity in this work is a function of the coverage capacity of the materials being used to control the curing process. For most of the liquid chemical products, coverage averages about 8 m² per liter or 300 ft.² per gallon, and they can be applied at the rate of about 10 liters or 2 gallons per hour. Sheet goods can be spread at the rate of about three rolls per hour and removed at about three times that rate.

Heavyweight loose goods (such as earth and sand) can be spread by hand at the rate of about 1 m³ or 1.5 yd.³ per hour and removed at about twice that rate; lightweight goods (such as hay or straw) can be handled about twice as fast as heavyweight. The use of machines for spreading and removal will increase productivity by a factor of two or three. For areas to be ponded, the perimeter curbs can be built at the rate of about 5 m or yd. per hour and removed at about twice that rate; the area can be shallow-flooded at the rate of about 200 m² or yd.² per hour and drained at about the same rate. Some of these data are summarized in Table 1.

5.0 Procedures

5.1 Preparation

Areas to be cured should be cleared of all debris and construction equipment not required for this work.

Table 1
PRODUCTIVITY IN CURING CONCRETE

Type of Work	Area per Hour	
	m²	ft.²
Spraying chemicals	60	600
Spreading sheets	180	1,800
Removing sheets	500	5,000
Laying heavy material	20	200
Removing heavy material	40	400
Laying light material	40	400
Removing light material	80	800
Flooding areas	200	2,000
Draining areas	250	2,500

Material quantities should be carefully checked to ensure provision of adequate supplies and sources.

During hot weather, the cement can be stored in a refrigerated or air-conditioned warehouse, the aggregates can be cooled with cold water, and crushed ice can be added as part of the water proportion. In prolonged periods of exceptionally hot, dry weather, it is possible (though expensive) to cool the formwork by running refrigeration pipes along the outside of the panels. It is also possible to enclose the formwork with plastic sheets and pump in chilled air.

During cold weather, a chemical accelerator can be added to the cement to raise the heat of hydration, the aggregates can be heated, and warm water can be used for the mix. In freezing weather, it is possible to insulate and/or provide steam-heat pipes to the formwork, and to enclose the formwork with plastic sheeting and pump in warmed air. It is also possible to electrify the reinforcing steel, which (through resistance) will raise its temperature. This latter technique is obviously expensive and potentially hazardous, and for these reasons it is not recommended for use in normal construction.

5.2 Process

Procedures of curing concrete can be grouped into **natural** and **artificial** methods.

Natural Methods. There are three methods commonly encountered:

1. Covering. There are three variations of this method: leaving the forms in place, using large sheets or blankets, and spreading layers of loose material. If time permits, vertical formwork for walls and columns can be left in place until the concrete has cured; they can be kept damp by means of a soaker hose placed along the top edges. Otherwise, vertical and horizontal concrete surfaces can be covered with sheet goods as described in Part 2.1 Materials. Sheets should be fully and tightly overlapped at all internal edges and secured at intervals with small blocks or clamps; they should also extend over the outside edges of slabs by a distance equal to about twice the thickness of the slab. On horizontal surfaces, loose materials such as clean earth, hay, sand, sawdust, or straw can be laid in uniform layers sufficiently thick to minimize the risk of being blown away (say between 50 and 100 mm or 2 and 4 in.). The object is to retain the moisture in the concrete by keeping the covering materials in uniform contact with the concrete surface and uniformly dampened by spraying clean water on them. Consideration must be given to removal and disposal of the covering materials after curing is complete;

Figure 1 Curing by Covering (UBC Architecture)

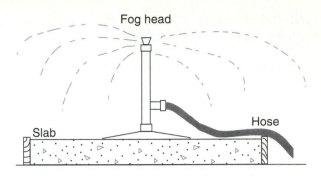

Figure 2 Curing by Fogging

Water Spray

A worker lightly and carefully sprinkles clean water from a hose to keep the surface of poured concrete slabs moist. (BCIT Building Technology)

some covering materials can also discolor or deteriorate concrete surfaces through incidental chemical action. See Figure 1.

2. Fogging. In this method, water is forced through a fine nozzle to produce a mist or fog of moisture above or around the concrete surface. Care must be taken to prevent erosion of the concrete by keeping the size of water droplets very small and the rate of flow at a low level. A modification of fogging, called spraying, involves the use of common garden lawn sprinklers, although this method can cause more significant erosion than the fogging method. The water temperature should be close to that of the concrete surface. See Figure 2.

3. Ponding. In this method, the concrete slab is gently flooded and kept covered with clean fresh water to a depth of at least 50 mm or 2 in. until it is cured. The water is contained by forming an upstanding watertight wood or metal ridge or earth berm around the perimeter of the slab. The temperature of the water should be within 10 degrees of the temperature of the concrete, to prevent stress. Care must be taken to arrange for the proper discharge and disposal of the water after the concrete is cured. See Figure 3.

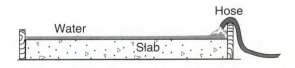

Figure 3 Curing by Ponding

Artificial Methods. There are also three artificial methods commonly encountered:

1. Chemicals. These are usually in liquid form; they are applied using low-pressure spraying equipment to the concrete surfaces. Surfaces should be moist but not covered with free water. The curing cover is good for about 3 or 4 days, but then may have to be repeated; after 14 days, its effectiveness is zero. It might be noted that most of these chemical curing compounds if not thoroughly cleaned off will prevent or at least interfere with subsequent bonding of additional concrete, toppings, or paint finishes applied to the cured surface. See Figure 4.

2. Steaming. This method is normally restricted to concrete plant application. Concrete is poured into steel molds, allowed to take on its initial set, then covered with waterproof tarpaulins. Steam under normal atmospheric pressure is then introduced through a series of perforated pipes shown in Figure 5. If the entire system is pressurized to accelerate the process by raising the temperature, the process is called *autoclaving*.

3. Dry heating. This method is identical to steaming, except that the steam is passed under pressure through a series of finned pipes outside the molds or forms, developing radiant heat which is maintained at about 50 degrees C or 120 degrees F for about 4 hours. Fogging is also required to maintain correct moisture levels within the molds. The concrete is then allowed to return to ambient temperature before being removed from the mold.

Chemical Spray
A worker uses a long nozzle to apply liquid curing chemical under pressure to seal the surface of a concrete sidewalk. (Canadian Portland Cement Association)

5.3 Precautions

Most specifications describing aspects of concrete work contain stringent clauses dealing with proper procedures for curing. These should be read, understood, and applied.

Formwork Curing
One of the most common methods of curing concrete is simply to leave the formwork in place and keep it damp by lightly sprinkling the system with clean cool water from time to time. (UBC Architecture)

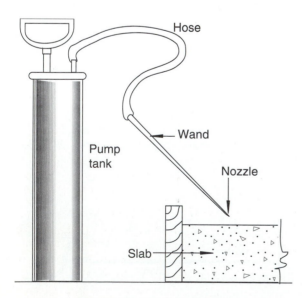

Figure 4 Chemical Spray

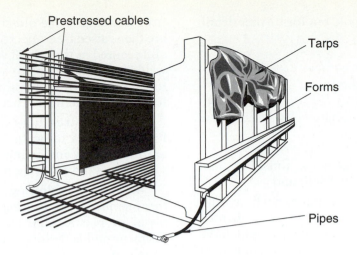

Prestressed cables

Tarps

Forms

Pipes

Figure 5   Curing by Steam

As this work is not particularly hazardous, little needs be said about protection, other than to caution that some of the chemicals used for curing are toxic or corrosive, requiring protective clothing and face protection to be worn. Care should be taken to check the compatibility of the curing compounds or materials with the concrete on which they are going to be used, as some reactions can be anticipated. For example, some types of hardwood sawdust contain acids which can actually destroy the cement paste at the surface of the concrete mix. A small test area should be prepared and examined before widespread use of any curing compound.

Section 03–400
Precast Concrete

1.0 Introduction

1.1 General Issues

Precast concrete is well named: It is concrete which is cast in forms or molds, finished, and cured **before delivery** to its final position in any structure. The precasting may be done off site at a concrete manufacturing plant, or it may be done on site in an area specially allocated for this purpose.

There are three primary advantages to using precast units in a concrete structural frame. First, the degree of control over every stage of the fabrication of the concrete product is greater in a manufacturing plant than at most construction sites. Secondly, production of units may proceed in any sequence, independent of the order of construction, and at usually significantly higher rates. Thirdly, all the units for one building could be precast simultaneously (although this is unlikely to happen in practice). In contrast, for cast-in-place concrete, the fabrication of beams for the lower floors must precede that for the upper floors. A cost analysis can and should be made to determine the financial implications of both processes before design decisions to use one or the other system are finally made. Such calculations are beyond the scope of this book, but for further detail, see the reference below.*

1.2 Design Aspects

There are two primary aspects to precast concrete design:

1. The proportioning, placement, finishing, and curing of the concrete mix itself; and
2. The assembly of the precast unit as a whole, with regard to the relationships between the concrete, the reinforcing members, the molds in which the precast units are made, and the attachment of each unit to the building structure.

For more detail on the first aspect, refer to the first five sections of this chapter; this section will deal with the second aspect.

Precast concrete can be made in several categories. Plain precast concrete is unreinforced and is therefore seldom encountered in structural designs, except for small block units, such as one finds in concrete block or brick walls and in paving systems in patios or courtyards. Simply reinforced precast components are commonly encountered in the form of structural members such as lintels, sills, and jambs, as well as in the form of building components such as car bumpers, manhole covers, paving curbs, and sewer pipes.

Prestressed and posttensioned precast members (described in more detail in Part 5.2) are often encountered in the form of beams, columns, girders, slabs, and walls, as well as in sandwich-lift floors and tilt-up wall panels.

1. In **sandwich-lift slabs**, all the horizontal floor slabs for a building are precast in position at grade level, one on top of the other, like the layers in a multi-decker clubhouse sandwich. Separation chemicals or plastic sheets are placed between each slab, and after all of the concrete is cured, the individual slabs are separately raised (top one first) by winched cables and guiding rails and secured into their final elevated positions to the permanent structural steel or concrete frame of the building.

2. In **tilt-up construction**, the nonloadbearing exterior walls of a building, such as for a warehouse, are precast horizontally or flat on the prepared floor slab, which has been treated with a bond-breaking chemical to prevent the new concrete of the wall from bonding to the old concrete of the floor. They are then raised by crane, rotated through 90 degrees, and secured in their final vertical position, either by welded or bolted clips to a structural steel frame or to each other by welding the tab ends of the reinforcing steel members together.

3. In **prestressing**, some of the compression forces expected to occur in the concreted member are induced by imparting tension to the reinforcement *before* the concrete is cast around it.

4. In **posttensioning**, the forces are induced in the member *after* casting, by introducing hollow metal or plastic pipe sleeves into the precasting forms or molds (before concrete is poured) through which the reinforcing rods or wires are later threaded and then stretched. In both prestressing and posttensioning, the tension forces are very slowly induced into the reinforcing steel components by heavy-duty hydraulic jacks attached to their ends; just how this is done is explained in Part 5.2.

1.3 Related Work

Work closely connected to this section is described in the following sections, to which reference should be made:

03–100   Formwork

03–200   Reinforcement

03–300   Cast-in-Place Concrete

03–350   Concrete Finishing

03–370   Concrete Curing

2.0 Products

2.1 Materials

The materials for precast concrete are virtually identical to those described in Sections 03–100, 03–200, and 03–300. In addition, seven-strand woven steel wire ropes are often used for reinforcement in prestressed and posttensioned concrete precast for buildings.

2.2 Accessories

The accessories for precast concrete are virtually identical to those described in Sections 03–200 and 03–300. In addition, there is a wide variety of specialized devices, such as metal yokes or collar clamps and plastic tubes or ducts, used in pre-

---

*See Glenn M. Hardie, *Construction Estimating Techniques* (Englewood Cliffs, N.J.: Prentice Hall, 1987).

stressed and posttensioned concrete to permit the compression or tension in each completed concrete member.

3.0 Construction Aids

3.1 Equipment

For equipment used in the manufacture of precast concrete units, refer to Part 5.1. For equipment used in the installation of precast units, refer to Part 5.2.

3.2 Tools

The tools used for this work are the same as those described in Part 3.2 of each of the five previous sections of this chapter.

4.0 Production

4.1 Crew Configuration

Crew sizes are discussed separately for the **manufacturing** and the **installation** phases of this work.

Manufacturing. There could be anywhere from 50 to 200 people involved in the direct production of precast concrete units for construction projects, depending on the size of the concrete manufacturing plant. As all of these people are not necessarily working on production for any one construction project, it is difficult to give meaningful detail relative to crew sizes that may be allocated to the manufacture of specific units for a particular construction project. It can, however, be said that, as a general guide, the production of an average-sized prestressed beam (such as might be incorporated into a bridge ramp or a parking structure) would probably involve about four or five skilled workers, with a couple of semiskilled helpers working intermittently for the best part of a full day. The crew would likely be working on more than one unit at a time.

Installation. The erection and connection of typical precast units such as beams, columns, and slabs in a building will involve a crew consisting of the crane operator, a guidesperson, three or four skilled workers, such as carpenters, masons, or ironworkers, and one or two helpers. Installation of precast plank floor decks might involve a crew of three ma-

sons and three helpers. For manual installation of smaller units such as manhole collars, sewer pipe sections, or paving curbs, a smaller crew of one or two skilled cement finishers with a semiskilled helper may prove to be sufficient.

4.2 Productivity

The data shown in Table 1 are deliberately limited but are nevertheless representative of realistic productivity factors for the placement of the components listed. The components listed were selected from those typically found in commercial or institutional buildings of average quality and complexity. The quantities given represent the number of individual components of average size and weight that can be installed, after manufacture and delivery, in one hour.

5.0 Procedures

5.1 Preparation

There are two components to preparation of work in this section: **manufacture** and **groundwork**.

Manufacture. Methods of making the two basic types of concrete units (other than concrete blocks) are described below:

1. Plain or simply reinforced precast units. Manufacture of such concrete units is not unlike that of cast-in-place concrete, although much greater attention is paid to control of the precast manufacturing environment. Another significant difference

Table 1
PRODUCTIVITY IN PRECAST CONCRETE PLACEMENT

Component Type	Quantity per Hour
Beams, double-T	1
Beams, single-T	2
Collars, manhole	1
Columns, single	1
Curbs, paving	5
Floor planks, narrow	15
Floor planks, wide	10
Joists, floor	1
Pipes, sewer	4
Wall panels, tiltup	1

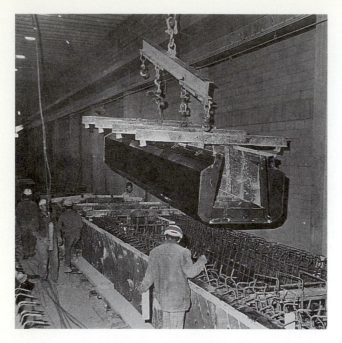

Factory Production
Precast components are usually factory fabricated. Here, the metal outer forms are complete, the rebar has been positioned, and the inner form is being placed before concreting commences. (BCIT Building Technology)

of this chapter for details of the manufacturing process.

2. Prestressed and posttensioned units. A section of the plant or site is set up as a stressing bed; the bed should be longer than the longest anticipated precast unit length. In some plants, the beds extend for several hundred meters or yards, to permit the formation of multiple units simultaneously; the units are separated later. At each end of the bed, strong steel vertical sections or plates (called stressheads) are installed in massive and solid concrete foundations. Between the end stressheads, a prefabricated removable and reusable steel form, made to the cross-sectional profile and length of the precast concrete beam, column, or slab to be formed, is placed. The form can have pipes attached to assist with steam or radiant heat accelerated curing, to permit the expensive formwork and hydraulic equipment to be used more frequently.

For **pre-stressing**, the steel tendons are unrolled from a drum, passed through properly located holes in the stressheads, clamped at one end, attached to a hydraulic jack at the other end, and tensioned. The form is then filled with concrete which is vibrated, finished, and cured overnight or to conform to specifications. The tension is then released from the jacks and the ends of the tendons protruding from the cured concrete units are burned or sheared off, if necessary. See Figure 1.

is that the concrete is removed from the forms in manageable-sized units and then transported some distance to its final destination for installation. To avoid repetition, refer to the five previous sections

Stockpiling
Precast units are delivered on flatbed trucks, off-loaded by crane, and stockpiled at site. This flight of precast steps awaits installation; note lifting eye-rings at top and bottom. (BCIT Building Technology)

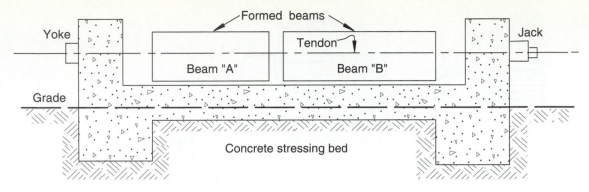

Figure 1 Prestressing

For **posttensioning**, metal or plastic tubes or ducts to carry the steel tendons are installed between the stresshead ends, supported and securely fastened in correct position by a light reinforcing steel cage along the length of the unit. The tubes may be depressed in the center to improve the strength of the posttensioned strands. The forms are installed, and the concrete is poured, finished, and cured as above. The ducts are then flushed clean with water and dried with compressed air, and the reinforcing tendons are threaded through. See Figure 2.

The tendons are then clamped with wedge-shaped bell-collars at one end of the unit and attached to stresshead hydraulic jacks (see Figure 3) at the other end. Tension is induced, and more collars are attached between the unit and the stresshead to maintain the tension in the tendons within the unit. Excess tendons are then burned or sheared off if necessary, and cement grout is forced into the ducts to completely fill and seal them against corrosion.

Groundwork. Work areas to receive precast units should be clean and free of debris or construction equipment not required for the work of this section. Adequate clear and safe access to the general site area, to temporary storage areas on site, and to the specific final location of the precast units must be made available at appropriate times. Bearings, beddings, foundations, plates, or seats on which the precast units rest or to which they will be attached must be properly designed, completely installed, and securely fastened before precast units are installed.

5.2 Installation

Precast concrete units are usually large, heavy, and relatively fragile before installation. They therefore require to be handled by skilled operators using heavy-duty equipment with considerable care. There are two primary elements: **delivery, erection,** and **connection.**

Delivery. Precast units of every type are usually delivered to the building site on flatbed trucks (except for sandwich-lift slabs and tilt-up wall units which are made on site).

Erection. There they are lifted by cranes with slings attached to eyebolts or hooks preset at strategic points in the precast units for this specific purpose. The units may be temporarily stored on site or moved directly to their final locations in the structure.

Connection. The precast units are slowly and carefully raised or lowered into their final position, where skilled workers join prefabricated connections by bolting, riveting, or welding, depending on design requirements.

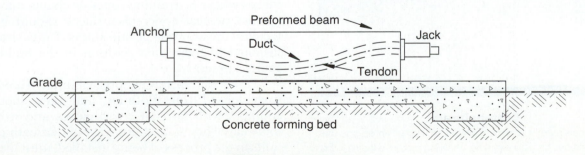

Figure 2 Posttensioning

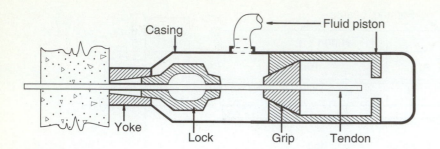

Casing — Fluid piston

Yoke — Lock — Grip — Tendon

Figure 5 Hydraulic Jack

Installation

Units are retrieved by crane from site stockpiles, raised into position, and bolted or welded to the structural frame as required by the project specification. (BCIT Building Technology)

5.3 Precautions

There are two general precautions relative to the work of this section: one concerns protection of the precast units themselves, and the other concerns the safety of the personnel installing them. The units are heavy, cumbersome, and relatively fragile until finally installed; they require careful handling to prevent damage to themselves or to adjacent building components.

Precast units must be protected from severe climatic elements such as freezing, ice, rain, hot sun, or strong wind until they are completely cured and ready for installation. They should be stored off the ground and under cover, with wooden separators inserted to prevent units from touching each other. If necessary, they should be crated or otherwise secured during delivery. Slings and hooks should be attached only at points designed for the purpose. Places where restraining ropes or chains may chafe against precast concrete surfaces should be protected with wood or plastic shims. Units should be installed in their final position in the building as soon as practical.

Personnel installing precast units should not wear loose-fitting clothing, and they should be equipped with hard hats, work gloves, and protective footwear. They should not walk underneath precast units in the process of being installed, until they have been adequately secured in position.

Custom Design

Precast panels readily lend themselves to almost unlimited and innovative artistic design. This example, showing a marine theme in bas-relief, enhances a fishing union office building. (UBC Architecture)

Tilt-Up Panels
Slabs on grade are cleaned, perimeter forms are placed, and concrete is poured and cured. Later, with wedge and sledge, the seal is broken and lifting shackles are attached to raise panels. (UBC Architecture)

Temporary Support
After tilt-up panels are raised and before they are permanently fastened to the building frame, temporary diagonal braces are secured by bolts to the main floor slab. (UBC Architecture)

Section 03–400   Precast Concrete

CHAPTER 04
Masonry Work

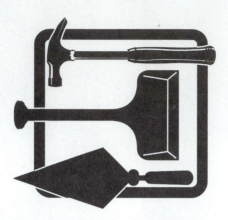

Section 04–100
Mortar and Accessories

1.0 Introduction

1.1 General Issues

Simply stated, mortar is the glue that holds masonry units and accessories together. It secures each masonry unit (whether made of brick, block, stone, glass, or plastic) into composite walls or veneers. It also provides space to permit the embedding of reinforcement rods and bars and other accessories either horizontally or vertically between the masonry units. Grout is a specialized form of mortar, used to fill cavities or voids in masonry work. Because of their close association in masonry, this section will combine mortar, grout, and related accessories together as a matter of convenience; *MasterFormat* lists them separately. Attention is also directed to the correct spelling of the word *masonry*; it is frequently misspelled *masonary* or *masonery*.

1.2 Design Aspects

Some of the basic design principles of mortar have to do with its **ingredients, purposes, workability, compressive strength,** and **accessories.**

Ingredients. Mortar consists of four ingredients: cement, sand, lime, and water. The relationship between the ingredients is critical for predictable and satisfactory end results. The selection of specific relationships depends on the type of masonry, its location in the building, and its exposure to the elements. There are five common types of mortar specified by the American Society for Testing Materials (ASTM) from which to choose, each designated by a letter, M, S, N, O, or K (allegedly taken from the word <u>MAS</u>O<u>N</u>W<u>OR</u>K). They are listed in Table 1 in order of decreasing strength, along with their proportions of ingredients by volume. Sufficient water must be added to achieve proper hydration of the cement, as explained in Section 03–300. In Type K mortar, the proportion of lime content is very high; this results in low strength offset by ease of workability. Recommendations of proportions for ingredients of mortar contained in ASTM C270 for the United States differ in very minor ways from CSA A179M for Canada. For example, the U.S. standard refers to damp sand, whereas the Canadian standard refers to dry sand. For more specific details, refer directly to these standards.

Grout consists of portland cement, sand or fine gravel, and water; it seldom contains lime. Propor-

Table 1
MORTAR TYPES AND PROPORTIONS

Type	Proportions			Suggested Uses
	Cement	Lime	Sand	
M	1.00	0.25	2.50–3.00	Foundation work.
S	1.00	0.50	3.50–4.50	Reinforced walls.
N	1.00	1.00	4.50–6.00	Chimneys, veneers.
O	1.00	1.50	6.50–9.00	Ordinary masonry.
K	1.00	1.00	2.50–4.00	Nonloadbearing use.

tions vary, depending on specifications. It serves one primary purpose: to fill voids in masonry.

Purposes. Mortar serves four major purposes:

1. **Adjustment** suggests the ability of the mortar to accommodate minor irregularities or imperfections in the masonry units as they are installed in the wall system.

2. **Appearance** has two aspects: color and texture. Colors are imparted by the addition of very intense chemicals; texture is achieved by physically working the mortar as it is placed between the units, to produce protruding, flush, or recessed joints, as described in Part 5.2.

3. **Bonding** in this context means the adhesion of the mortar to the masonry units.

4. **Embedding** involves the placement of reinforcement or other accessories into mortar joints between masonry units.

Workability. One of the key issues in good mortar design is workability; this is largely achieved by controlling the lime content, to produce mortar which is neither too lean nor too fat. Care must be taken when increasing the lime content to balance the tradeoff between increased workability (which improves productivity and quality of installation) and declining strength and durability, as the lime imparts neither to the mortar. Another significant issue is water retention, as many masonry units (such as clay bricks) are relatively dry and porous, thus tending to absorb moisture from the mortar, usually with detrimental results.

Compressive Strength. The compressive strength of mortar is a direct function of the cement content and the quality of the aggregates. In general, mortar bond strength also increases in proportion to cement content, as does durability, although this latter characteristic is more affected by the proportion of air-entrainment chemicals in the mix.

Accessories. These consist of reinforcement and ties of various sorts. As in concrete design, the relatively high compressive and bonding strength of cement mortar is coupled with the high tensile strength of steel to produce a composite which can resist potentially disturbing vibrations caused by various factors such as earth tremors, gusting winds, explosive blasts, and traffic, as well as thermal movement. Mortar joints between masonry units must be sufficiently wide to accommodate any reinforcement embedded in the joint and to provide suitable cover around the reinforcement to protect it and to provide for proper bonding, as shown in Figure 1.

In simple block or brick masonry, the horizontal bars are laid in the mortar beds and connected by vertical stirrups where necessary. In reinforced grouted masonry, the reinforcement is assembled in the form of a grillage or flat cage, placed in the space between two wythes of brick or blockwork and then grouted after the wythes have been built up by a few courses. In filled-cell masonry, vertical rods are

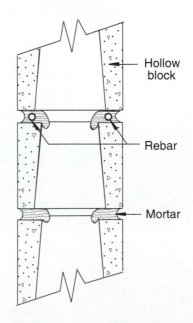

Figure 1 Mortar Cross Section

(a) Site mixing

Mortar Mixing
On small jobs, mortar can be conveniently mixed on site in small batches. For large projects, factory-made mortar is preferred for uniformity, economy, and the ease of bin handling. (BCIT Building Technology)

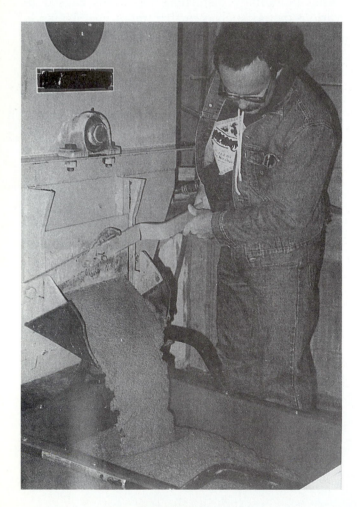

(b) Plant mixing

threaded down through the hollow cores of the masonry units, as shown in Figure 2, which are then filled with grout.

1.3 Related Work

Work closely connected to this section is described in the following sections, to which reference should be made:

03–300   Cast-in-Place Concrete

04–200   Unit Masonry

04–400   Stone Masonry

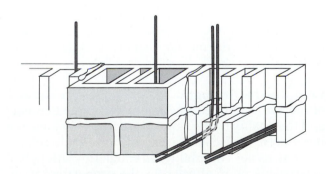

Figure 2   Reinforcement in Cores

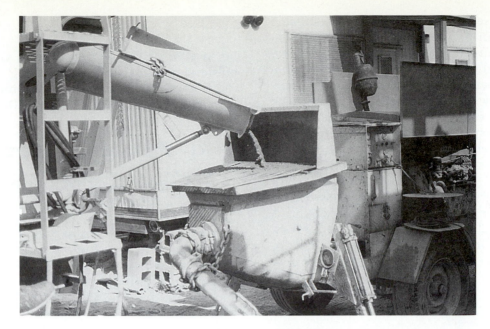

(a) Pump machine

2.0 Products

2.1 Materials

As stated, there are four primary materials encountered in mortar mixes:

1. **Cement.** Common portland cement as described in Section 03–300 (Type 1, 2, or 3 or air-entrained Type 1A, 2A, or 3A). White cement should be used in conjunction with limestone masonry units to prevent staining.
2. **Lime.** Hydrated calcium carbonate; Type S as defined by ASTM is preferred.
3. **Sand.** Clean, washed, sharp, fine-grain material.
4. **Water.** Clean, fresh, cold, potable water.

Masonry cement is a factory-composed mixture of selected cement and hydrated lime, often with other additives such as air-entrainment chemicals, pozzolans, and resins intended to improve durability, plasticity, and water retention.

2.2 Accessories

The main accessories used in conjunction with mortar are **additives** to change the characteristics of the mortar and masonry **reinforcement** members of various sorts; some of the more common of these accessories are described.

(b) Placement nozzle

Mortar Delivery
Mortar can be delivered to the site in bulk (like concrete), deposited into the hopper of a pump machine, and placed directly into masonry units (a bond beam is shown in this case). (BCIT Building Technology)

Additives. These are mostly organic or inorganic chemicals used in powdered or liquid form to enhance air entrainment, coloration, setting rates, water retention, and workability. They should seldom exceed about 5 percent of the total volume of mortar, because they contribute little to the ultimate strength of the mortar. Calcium chloride is used as an accelerator to speed up setting; sulfonated lignin salt is used as a retarder.

Reinforcements. These are mostly in the form of plain steel rods or welded laddered or trussed composites of various weights, widths, and lengths. A large variety of plain or galvanized steel anchors, clips, dowels, nailing inserts, straps, and ties are also available to bond various parts of masonry construction together or to other parts of the building structural frame.

3.0 Construction Aids

3.1 Equipment

For mortar, equipment similar to that described in Section 03–300 is used. For reinforcement, equipment similar to that described in Section 03–200 is used.

3.2 Tools

For mortar work, the mason uses an assortment of bolsters, brushes, mallets, pointing tools, and trowels. For preparation of reinforcement, the mason uses tools as described in Section 03–200.

4.0 Production

4.1 Crew Configuration

Mortar. Applying mortar will require a team of about four or five, using one skilled person to mix the mortar, one or two unskilled helpers to transport the mortar in wheelbarrows and do cleanup work, and one or two masons laying the masonry units with the mortar.

Grouting. Applying grout pumped from a truck will require a team of about four, using two masons to place the grout and guide the hose nozzles, one mason to do the compaction, and one helper, not including the truck crew which usually involves two skilled workers.

Accessories. Placing accessories will require a team of about three, using one or two masons to cut,

Mortar Application
A mason uses a steel trowel to apply fresh mortar to a dampened brick; this process is known as buttering. The mortar should be stiff enough to stick to the brick (or block). (BCIT Building Technology)

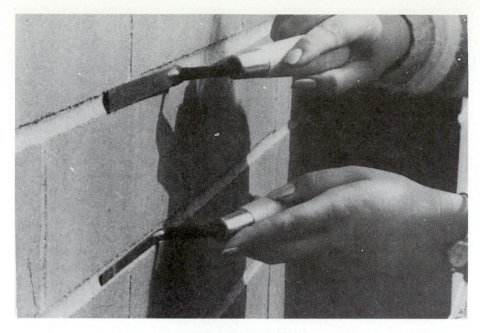

Joint Finishing
After excess mortar has been struck off and the joint mortar has achieved initial set, an assortment of hand tools can be used to impart density, smoothness, and shape to the joints. (BCIT Building Technology)

place, and secure the components, and one or two helpers to move materials and equipment around the site as necessary.

4.2   Productivity

Data presented in this part relate only to the production of mortar and grout, application of grout, and installation of accessories; factors for laying masonry units of various types are given in other sections of this chapter.

Mortar.   One skilled mortar maker should be able to produce about 1 m³ or yd.³ of mortar or grout every 2 hours. Ready-mix mortar and grout is also available in bulk, mixed as described in Section 03–300; such mortar usually has a retarder added to extend the working period of the mortar from 2 to 3 hours before the initial set occurs.

Grouting.   A crew of three or four workers should place about 1 m³ or yd.³ of grout every half-hour.

Accessories.   The placement of any given quantity of reinforcement or other components is not really significant in itself, as such work must naturally be done in conjunction with the laying of masonry units, as described in other sections. In lightly rein-

forced masonry walls, reinforcement work causes no significant reduction in output; in heavily reinforced walls, there may be a slight drop in production amounting to perhaps 5 or 10 percent in the factors given for placement of masonry units.

5.0 Procedures

5.1 Preparation

Mortar ingredients have to be mixed in appropriate proportions before use; reinforcement has to be cut and bent as necessary before installation. Preparation of both facets of masonry work is described below. All work should proceed in areas which have been cleared free of debris and construction equipment not required for the work of this section.

Mortar.   Regardless of which type of mortar is selected, the mixing operation is the same. The dry ingredients are usually measured carefully by **volume** and not by **weight** (in opposition to concrete proportioning). The ingredients are then mixed together either manually or by machine, essentially the same as described in Section 03–300 for concrete mixing. For large projects, ready-mix concrete trucks can be utilized. Care should be taken to avoid using too much sand or too much water to make the mortar "go further." Mortar should not be mixed in temper-

(a) Masonry to suit rebar

(b) Rebar to suit masonry

Reinforcement

Sometimes masonry units have to be cut and fit to accommodate reinforcing steel bars and rods. Occasionally, the rebar has to be cut and fit to suit the masonry. Codes govern. (Canadian Masonry Contractors Association)

atures below 5 or above 30 degrees C or below 40 or above 85 degrees F, without taking some precautions appropriate to the prevailing temperature and humidity conditions. Mortar not used within two hours of initially adding water to the mix should be discarded. Because of the uncertainty of results, retempering of stiffening mortar with additional water is not considered by this author to be a good practice, although it is permitted in some areas. When ready, the mortar is then usually loaded into wheelbarrows or buckets to be quickly delivered to the masonry location.

Reinforcement. Rods, ladders, and trusses are measured; then burned, cut, sawn, or sheared to length; and bent to shape as necessary by hand or by machine as described in Section 03–200. Small accessories such as anchors, clips, connectors, and the like are removed from their delivery cartons, sorted, and adjusted as necessary.

5.2 Process

The placement of mortar, grout, and accessories each have their own requirements.

Mortar. After the location of the masonry walls or veneers has been established (as described in Section 04–200) and the mortar and masonry units have been delivered to the workplace, the mason places a small quantity of the mortar onto a tray or platform from which the mortar is then dispensed by trowel onto the masonry units. A layer of mortar about 13 mm or 0.5 in. thick, called the *bed*, is placed over the entire surface on which the wall or veneer will stand. A layer of mortar is then applied to the vertical face of the masonry unit and it is placed in position on the uncured bed. When the unit has been approximately placed, mortar is squeezed from the joints by gentle pressure on the unit to push it into its final position. Then, depending on the kind of mortar joint required (see Table 2), the excess mortar may be quickly and neatly struck off with a trowel. Some masons prefer to "butter" one end of each unit before it is placed in the wall; others prefer to apply the mortar to the end of a previous unit already placed in the wall. Mortar beds should not precede the lay-ing of units by too great a distance, to reduce the loss of bonding power that can occur through absorption and evaporation.

There are a number of configurations commonly practiced by masons to finish off mortar joints; these are alphabetically listed and shown in cross section in Table 2.

Grouting. Grouting can be done in one of two ways: low-lift or high-lift. In low-lift, the grout is placed and manually compacted by tamping after a few courses of masonry units have been built up; in high-lift, all of the grouting is done at once, using compressed air hoses to assist with the compaction

Table 2
TYPICAL MORTAR JOINTS

Type	Profile	How Formed
Beaded		Using a concave trowel.
Flush		Rubbed with sacking.
Raked		Mortar raked out.
Rodded		Pressed with a rod.
Stripped		Removal of form strip.
Struck		Cut with trowel tip.
Tucked		Pressure on units.
Veed		Using a vee-tip trowel.
Weathered		Cut with trowel tip.

Construction Aids

All trades use aids as well as tools to simplify and ease their work. This example shows an adjustable manual hod for lifting, moving, and placing several clay bricks at once. (BCIT Building Technology)

of the grout in the void spaces after the entire wall has been raised to its finished height. High-lift is usually cheaper and faster to do, but perhaps the end result is not as thorough.

Accessories. All reinforcement or other components are manually placed in position, tied with wire or otherwise secured to the structural frame of the building as necessary, and carefully embedded into the mortar or grouted so as to be completely enclosed. Long lengths can be lapped and tied as required by building codes or manufacturers' recommendations.

5.3 Precautions

Masonry work is not overly hazardous, but it does involve the use of machinery, sharp tools, heavy loads, platforms, and work done in locations that are exposed to the elements. Furthermore, much of masonry work is done from scaffolding at various heights; a number of legislated regulations will therefore apply, creating some constraints on procedures and budgets. Most national and local building codes have fairly strict requirements regarding the proportioning of ingredients for mortar and the placement of masonry accessories, particularly for reinforced masonry construction in areas of potential earthquake activity.

Because some of the ingredients of mortar are potentially corrosive or toxic, gloves and goggles should be worn at all times while preparing the ingredients. Portions of the building structure not scheduled for masonry work have to be protected from damage caused by accidental spillage of mortar or careless handling of masonry units or accessories. Care should also be taken to prevent mortar from staining the visible surfaces of masonry units, as it is almost impossible to completely remove such stains without damage to the surface of the units. Dry powdered products such as cement and lime can be stored in the paper bags in which they are delivered for fairly long periods, provided they are kept cool and dry. Accessories should be protected from dampness which might cause rust and from uneven or excessive loading which might cause deformation.

Section 04–200   Unit Masonry

1.0 Introduction

1.1 General Issues

While it is possible to construct certain types of open-framed buildings without walls, most buildings have walls of one sort or another. Walls of buildings serve several purposes: they can support loads such as upper floors and roofs; they can resist loads such as earthquakes or wind forces; and they can provide loads to give mass or weight to all or portions of buildings requiring acoustical separation or those in areas subject to radiation. They can establish boundaries to areas or volumes for reasons of privacy, security, or economy; they can keep the natural effects of weather outside and any desirable artificially controlled climate inside. They can also provide opportunities for the support and concealment of building services such as electrical conduits and plumbing pipes, and can create surfaces either beautiful in themselves or suitable for decoration.

Historically, walls have been built using one or more of many locally available materials, such as adobe, dung, clay, glass, marble, metal, mud, plaster, plastics, stone, vegetable matter, wattle, and wood, among others. One approach frequently encountered in modern times and countries is the use of standardized unit masonry, which comprises walls built with (usually) factory-made blocks, bricks, or tiles commonly made of either adobe, clay, concrete, glass, or plastic. Such work is the subject matter of this section; walls built of fieldstone and veneer marble are described in the next section of this chapter. Concrete walls are described in Chapter 03; metal walls in Chapter 05; wood walls in Chapter 06; drywall, plaster, and stucco walls in Chapter 09. Walls made of more esoteric materials (such as cardboard, pop bottles, dried camel dung, palm leaves, and so on) are regrettably beyond the scope of this book.

Masonry units can be placed either monolithically or in large or small component units, and either singly or in composite arrangements.

1.2 Design Aspects

For the purposes of this section, aspects of wall design using unit masonry are classified under the headings of **categories, patterns,** and **quality.**

Categories.   There are four main categories of walls:

1. **Loadbearing walls** are designed to support loads other than their own weight.
2. **Nonloadbearing walls** are usually intended to function simply as self-supporting partitions.
3. **Curtain walls** are literally hung from a separate concrete or steel structural frame to form a sort of lightweight external envelope to the building.
4. **Masonry veneers** are applied to cover the structural frame of the building like a close-fitting ornamental skin.

Patterns.   There are six main bond patterns commonly encountered in unit masonry work: American bond, English bond, Flemish bond, garden wall bond, running bond, and stacked bond. These basic patterns are shown in Figure 1; variations of each are occasionally encountered.

Masonry units can be inserted into wall elevations in any one of five primary orientations, to create desired structural, or aesthetic effects; they are called header, rolok, shiner, soldier, and stretcher. See Figure 2.

In recent years, there has been a trend toward the use of modular units. These are bricks and blocks sized to fit into modules dimensioned on the basis of 100 mm or 4 in. including the mortar joint between units. A typical metric modular concrete block having nominal dimensions of 200×400 mm, laid with 10-mm joints, would therefore have actual face dimensions of 190×390 mm; similarly, an imperial modular block nominally $4'' \times 8''$ laid with $3/8$-in. joints would have actual face dimensions of $3^5/8'' \times 7^5/8''$. (See Figure 3).

Because of the relatively small and uniform size of most masonry units, a considerable degree of design flexibility is available to architects and engineers to solve structural or aesthetic problems using unit masonry instead of concrete, steel, or wood.

Quality.   In general, walls should be built true to plumb and plane, to follow the design layout precisely and to incorporate the selected bond pattern. Unit masonry walls are usually built in straight lines both horizontally and vertically, but it is also possible to build them in curves, slopes, or steps to suit

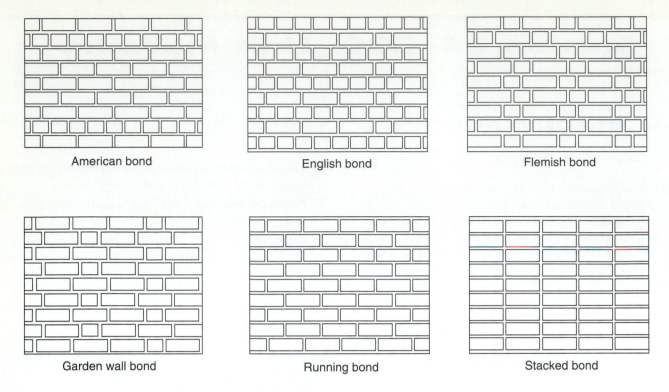

| American bond | English bond | Flemish bond |

| Garden wall bond | Running bond | Stacked bond |

Figure 1   Six Bond Patterns

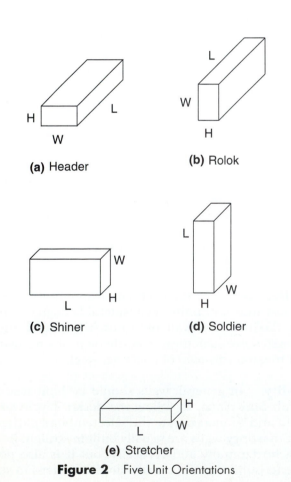

(a) Header

(b) Rolok

(c) Shiner

(d) Soldier

(e) Stretcher

Figure 2   Five Unit Orientations

the designer's objectives. Consideration should be given to the size, texture, color, and weight of the units selected and their relationship to the quality of mortar (required by codes) and the type of mortar joint (required by the designer).

Wherever practical, specially manufactured units should be used to form corners, headers, jambs, lintels, sills, openings, or other structural or ornamental features in unit masonry work. This avoids the additional costs of labor and waste cutting standard units to fit into irregular modules, and it improves appearance. Recent developments in high-bond adhesives are permitting innovative solutions to unit masonry design problems, for example, by allowing brick or block units to be prefabricated into fairly large composite panels ready for securing to the structural frame in a manner similar to that used for precast concrete panels.

In long lengths of masonry walls, it is good practice (and in many cases a code requirement) to introduce control joints every 5 to 7 m or 15 to 20 ft. to permit some movement in the structure without cracking of the walls, as shown in Figure 4. Such joints usually take the form of a straight vertical break in the wall plane, and are achieved by the use of interlocking male and female masonry units in conjunction with some packing and caulking materials (see Section 07–900) to render the joint watertight.

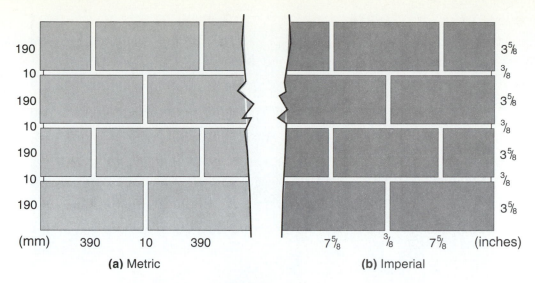

190					$3\frac{5}{8}$
10					$\frac{3}{8}$
190					$3\frac{5}{8}$
10					$\frac{3}{8}$
190					$3\frac{5}{8}$
10					$\frac{3}{8}$
190					$3\frac{5}{8}$

(mm)   390   10   390 $7\frac{5}{8}$ $\frac{3}{8}$ $7\frac{5}{8}$ (inches)

(a) Metric   **(b)** Imperial

Figure 3   Modules

1.3 Related Work

Work closely connected to this section is described in the following sections, to which reference should be made:

01–050   Field Engineering

03–300   Cast-in-Place Concrete

04–100   Mortar and Accessories

07–600   Flashings

07–900   Joint Sealing

Figure 4   Control Joint

2.0 Products

2.1 Materials

Modern masonry units may be categorized under two primary headings: **fired** and **cured**. Units in both categories may be made in either solid or hollow form as plain or decorated bricks, blocks, or tiles, and with either glazed ceramic or unglazed finishes. Dimensions and grading rules for typical units are also discussed.

Fired.   There are two basic groups: **clay** and **glass**.

1. Clay. These units consist of selected clays formed by one of three methods: **soft-mud** (30 percent moisture) using wood or metal forms, **stiff-mud** (15 percent moisture) using extrusion dies and wire cutters, or **dry-press** (10 percent moisture) using hydraulic presses and steel forms. The method of manufacture imparts significantly different structural and aesthetic characteristics to the end product. Units formed by all three methods are then fired under strict control in brick kilns to produce common bricks, custom bricks, engineering bricks, face bricks, fire bricks, and oversize bricks, among others. Colors range from light yellow into reds, browns, and black. Clay bricks are graded according to their resistance to weathering: SW for resistance to severe weathering, MW for resistance to medium weathering, and NW for no resistance to weathering.

Stockpiling

Masonry units (such as bricks and blocks) are usually palletized at the factory after manufacture and delivered to the construction site wrapped in plastic for protection. (UBC Architecture)

2. Glass. These units consist of either two pressed-glass hollowed shapes fused together or one solid formed glass block; edges have a factory-applied coating of grit to improve mortar bonding. They are available in clear, colored, etched, glazed, patterned, or prismatic forms. They are not suitable for loadbearing applications.

Cured. There are four basic groups: **adobe, concrete, gypsum,** and **sand-lime.**

1. **Adobe.** These are units made from sundried mixtures of clay, fibers, and binders, formed in wood or metal boxes. Colors range from light beige to dark brown.

2. **Concrete.** These are machine-formed, steam-cured units made to rigorous standards of composition, size, and weight. There are two common grades: S for general use and N for veneers. Colors are naturally light to medium gray; pigmented units are also available.

3. **Gypsum.** These units are made of a mixture of gypsum with vegetable fibers as a binder; they are primarily intended to be used as a backing block in nonloadbearing plastered partitions.

4. **Sand-lime.** These units are made from a mixture of 90 percent selected silica and 10 percent hydrated lime; they are formed semidry in presses and hardened by steam-curing. Colors are light gray to silver gray.

Dimensions. Although there is as yet little standardization of sizes in unit masonry in North America, Table 1 shows the commonly applied names and approximate nominal dimensions of selected typical masonry units as a general guide; for actual dimensions for use in design or construction, refer to manufacturers' catalogs and to the recommendations of the Brick Institute of America.

Grades. Masonry units are usually graded according to their ability to withstand specific exposures in use, such as exterior or interior, loadbearing or otherwise, fire resistance, and above or below grade.

Isometric sketches of typical concrete blocks and clay bricks are shown in Figures 5.1 and 5.2, respectively.

2.2 Accessories

Accessories used in conjunction with unit masonry may be categorized under two broad headings: **mortar and associated reinforcement** and **specialty units.** Mortar and reinforcement is described in detail in Section 04–100.

Specialty Units. These constitute a large variety of specially made blocks, bricks, and tiles, used to form bond beams, caps, copes, corners, headers, jambs, junctions, lintels, sills, stringcourses, and similar special structural or ornamental features. Some of

Table 1
DIMENSIONS OF SELECTED MASONRY UNITS

Type of Unit	Nominal Dimensions					
	Length		Width		Height	
	mm	in.	mm	in.	mm	in.
Bricks:						
Adobe	450	18.0	300	12.0	100	4.00
Common	225	9.0	113	4.5	60	2.50
Facing	190	7.5	90	3.5	55	2.25
Fire	225	9.0	113	4.5	60	2.50
Jumbo	300	12.0	150	6.0	100	4.00
Norman	290	11.5	90	3.5	55	2.25
Norwegian	300	12.0	100	4.0	80	3.20
Oversize	250	10.0	80	3.3	80	3.25
Paving	150	6.0	150	6.0	06	0.25
Roman	290	11.5	90	3.5	40	1.50
SCR*	300	12.0	150	6.0	65	2.66
Split	225	9.0	113	4.5	30	1.25
Blocks:						
Concrete, large	400	16.0	200	8.0	200	8.00
Concrete, small	200	8.0	100	4.0	100	4.00
Glass, large	300	12.0	100	4.0	300	12.00
Glass, small	200	8.0	100	4.0	100	8.00
Gypsum	750	30.0	100	4.0	300	12.00
Tiles, large	300	12.0	300	12.0	300	12.00
Tiles, small	200	8.0	50	2.0	150	6.00

*Structural Clay Research.

the types commonly encountered are illustrated in Figure 6. Blocks, bricks, and tiles of any specific size, shape, or appearance can be specially ordered, if the quantity is sufficiently large to justify the additional expense.

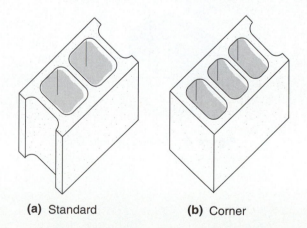

(a) Standard   **(b)** Corner

Figure 5.1 Typical Blocks

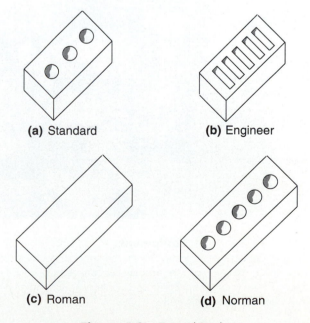

(a) Standard   **(b)** Engineer

(c) Roman   **(d)** Norman

Figure 5.2 Typical Bricks

Equipment
On large projects, it is common for the general contractor to provide exterior scaffolding. The masonry subcontractor provides all other machinery. Note stockpiles and waste pile. (Canadian Masonry Contractors Association)

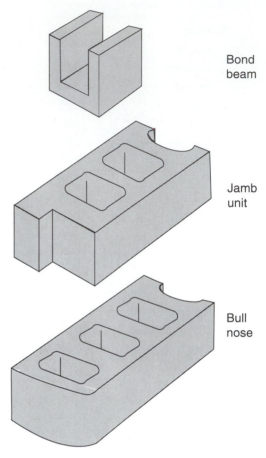

Bond beam

Jamb unit

Bull nose

(a) Concrete blocks

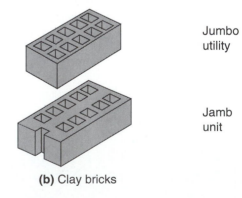

Jumbo utility

Jamb unit

(b) Clay bricks

Figure 6 Some Specialty Units

Concrete Blocks
Mortar is placed on the outer shell faces of the blocks and the succeeding course is carefully placed, with excess mortar being squeezed out of the joints and struck off. (BCIT Building Technology)

3.0 Construction Aids

3.1 Equipment

The equipment used for the mortar part of the work of this section is described in Section 04–100, Part 3.1; the equipment described below is in addition to the mortar equipment:

Light scaffolding is required to reach the higher portions of the work; such scaffolding should be set on wood mudsills to prevent sinking, and care should be taken to reinforce the scaffolding as necessary to sustain the heavy loads of the masonry units and mortar during construction operations.

Masonry saws are frequently used to cut units. They consist of a metal frame to support an electric motor used to drive a carborundum- or diamond-tipped circular saw blade, and a platform on which the unit to be cut can be placed and maneuvered.

3.2 Tools

The tools applicable to the mortar work of this section are described in Section 04–100, Part 3.2; in addition is the following:

Story poles are wood or metal rods on which the heights of each masonry course are marked to maintain alignment and proper level of each course of units. See Figure 7.

4.0 Production

4.1 Crew Configuration

For a discussion of crew sizes for unit masonry, refer to Section 04–100, Part 4.1.

4.2 Productivity

Productivity in masonry is dependent on a number of components: design of the wall, type of mortar joints, skill of the workers, suitability of the weather, quality of supervision, and adequacy of materials supply, among others. There are therefore no absolute standards that one can apply to the prediction of productivity in this trade. The work of the mason is relatively intensive compared to other trades, as the mason tends to stay in one place and work at the task directly in front of him or her, in contrast to (say) a carpenter whose work involves considerably more movement around the immediate place of work and the job-site in general. It will be obvious

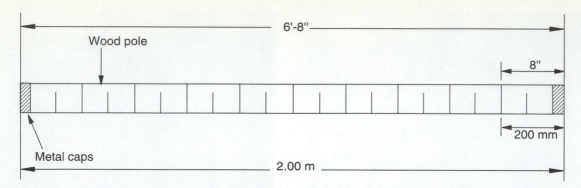

Figure 7 Story Pole

that on large, straightforward projects such as schools or warehouses with simple plain walls, output will be much greater than on small complex projects with more intricate bonding, such as churches, motels, or residences.

Although masonry **work** is best measured in terms of superficial area, masonry **productivity** is usually best expressed in terms of numbers of units laid within a given period. Factors given in Table 2 represent outputs likely to be achieved on normally reinforced projects of medium size and complexity, such as suburban shopping or commercial centers or college or similar institutional buildings, built during periods of good weather and using one of the standard masonry bonds, such as Flemish or garden wall.

5.0 Procedures

5.1 Preparation

Areas scheduled to receive unit masonry should be clean and free of debris and construction equipment not required for the work of this section. Cutting of masonry units can be done by scoring the unit on the front face with a chisel along the line of the desired cut, and then striking it sharply on the rear face with a hammer. Units can also be cut using a masonry power saw, where speed, repetition, accuracy, and cost are considerable factors. Holes and recesses in units can be cut by hand using chisels or drilled by machine using appropriate bits.

5.2 Process

To enhance clarity and avoid repetition, some general principles of unit masonry methodology will be described first, followed by particular aspects appropriate to specific types of units.

General Principles. Masonry walls may be built completely using one type of unit or as a composite of two or more types (see Figure 8); they may be built

Table 2
UNIT MASONRY OUTPUT*

Type of Unit	Output per Man-Hour
Bricks:	
Adobe	100
Common	150
Facing	125
Fire	25
Glazed	50
Jumbo	100
Norman	100
Norwegian	75
Oversize	100
Paving	150
Roman	100
SCR**	75
Skintled	50
Split	125
Step	25
Blocks:	
Concrete, large	50
Concrete, small	75
Concrete, glazed	50
Concrete, ornamental	25
Glass, large	15
Glass, small	20
Gypsum	75
Tiles, large	50
Tiles, small	75

*Numbers over 25 are rounded to the nearest 25.
**Structural Clay Research.

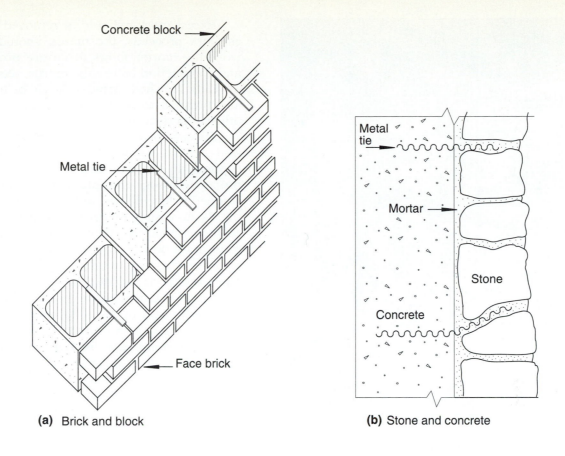

(a) Brick and block

(b) Stone and concrete

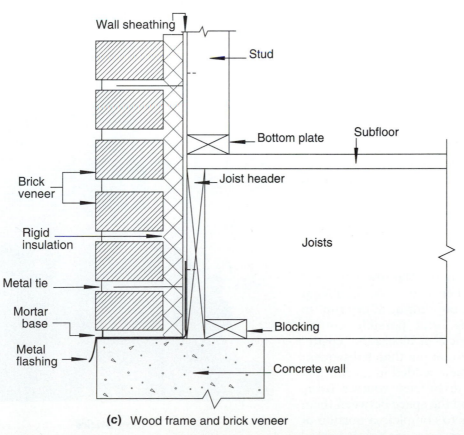

(c) Wood frame and brick veneer

Figure 8 Typical Composite Sections

Excess mortar should be removed immediately; as work proceeds, the mason should periodically work the mortar joints to ensure proper profiling and compaction before the mortar sets (see Section 04–100). Finished surfaces should be lightly washed and brushed to remove minor surface debris and other imperfections.

Special consideration must be given to the location of doors, windows, and other openings or interruptions to the masonry wall, to ensure that the proper accessory units are correctly selected and positioned below, above, and at each side of the opening as necessary to permit proper structural and aesthetic bonding. In general, door and window frames are best positioned and temporarily braced prior to masonry work being completed around them. Intersections between walls in different planes are usually connected by interbonding of the masonry units and by the additional use of small flat metal tie-bars inserted into the joints to transfer forces between the walls. Care must also be taken with control joints, to ensure that the joints are correctly located, that units are properly bonded on each side of the joint, and that mortar does not unintentionally bridge the gap deliberately created by the control joint units.

As walls progress in height, it is frequently necessary to provide temporary bracing to support them against sudden wind loads or other lateral forces

Glass Blocks

Glass blocks are placed using techniques common to both concrete blocks and clay bricks. Mortar bed is placed, blocks are embedded, mortar is buttered on sides, and excess struck off. (UBC Architecture)

one, two, three or more units wide, called wythes; they may be built using only one bond pattern throughout or in combinations of patterns, such as English bond in single courses separated by three or five courses of running bond, for instance. Walls may also be built solidly or with a cavity in the vertical central plane; the purpose of the cavity is to improve insulation values and to reduce opportunities for the passage of moisture.

It is good practice to lay out the first course of blocks, bricks, or tiles between two significant corners or openings of the building as a "dry run" to check alignment, spacing, and possible cutting of units. Some call such bricks or blocks the "costly" units, as they take longer to set out than subsequent units. The first course is then bedded in mortar, the corners or jambs are built up by a few courses, using a story pole and a level, and the space between them is then filled in with units to complete a portion of the wall. The units and accessories are lightly tapped into place using a mason's trowel, avoiding excessive movement to avoid disrupting the mortar bond.

Clay Bricks

Mortar is buttered onto the brick units, the bricks are pressed into position, they are checked for line and level, and excess mortar is struck off. (BCIT Building Technology)

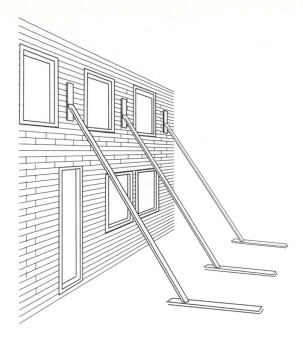

Figure 9 Temporary Bracing

for glass blocks than for other masonry, because the blocks are nonabsorptive.

c. **Tile.** Only units rated for exposure should be used for external walls. Tiles are often used as backup in composite walls having face brick veneers. The masonry bond should be arranged so that there are no open tile cells exposed upon completion of the work.

during construction. In general, the process consists of inserting a wood or metal nailing block into a mortar joint high up the wall, driving a peg into the ground at about the same distance out from the base of the wall, and securing a diagonal wood or metal brace to connect between the block and the peg to form rigid but adjustable triangulation, as shown in Figure 9.

Particular Aspects. In addition to the foregoing generalities, some specific issues relative to working with particular types of units are given for reference.

1. **Block work:**

   a. **Concrete.** The thicker edge of the face shell of each block should be upward to provide maximum bedding for the mortar. In general, mortar is placed only along the outside shells and not on the inside webs forming the cores. There are some dimensional limitations to areas scheduled for block walls. Blocks are generally laid dry.

   b. **Glass.** Special consideration must be given to the detailing at heads, jambs, and sills in glass block areas, to permit some thermal movement and to avoid loads being transferred to the glass. Patterned blocks must be laid to produce the correct visual effect. There are some dimensional limitations to areas scheduled for glass block or brick construction. During installation, mortar has to be stiffer

(a) Brick corner

(b) Block intersection

Building Process

It is customary, in both blockwork and brickwork, to set out corners and jambs first and to build up a few courses before filling in the remainder. Joints may be tooled at this point. (BCIT Audio-Visual Production)

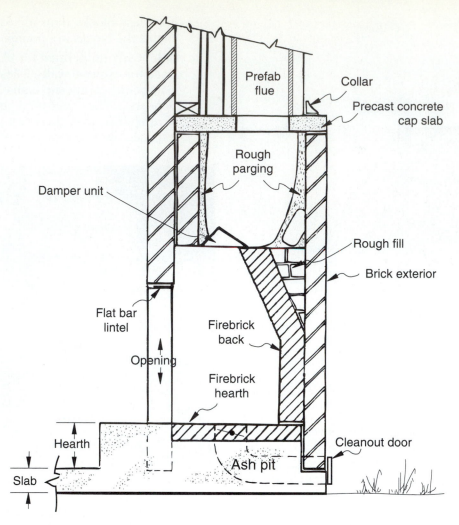

Prefab
flue

Collar

Precast concrete
cap slab

Rough
parging

Damper unit

Rough fill

Brick exterior

Flat bar
lintel

Firebrick
back

Opening

Firebrick
hearth

Hearth

Cleanout door

Ash pit

Slab

Figure 10 Fireplace Construction

2. Brick work:

a. Common. Although there is conflicting opinion on this point, it is felt that these are best laid with the frog upward, to ensure that it will be filled with mortar. Bricks are generally lightly wetted (but not soaked) before laying, to reduce water absorption from the mortar.

b. Face. There are some limitations on heights of unsupported veneer facings beyond about three stories; check local building codes for details. Spacing of ties is of considerable importance. Rapid removal of mortar spilled onto exposed faces is recommended. Light dampening of facing units is recommended prior to laying, to remove dust, reduce suction, and improve bonding.

c. Fire. Fireplace design is a highly developed masonry specialty. The relationships between the hearth opening, the vent shaft, the damper, the smoke shelf, and cleanout features are critical. Solid foundations are essential; smoke

tests are advised during construction. A section through a typical fireplace is shown in Figure 10.

d. Used. Salvaged bricks should not be used for structural work; they do, however, lend themselves well to decorative veneer work if care is taken to properly clean the surfaces to be remortared to ensure an adequate bond. Imitation used brick is also available.

5.3 Precautions

Workers involved in machine cutting or manual breaking of masonry units should wear eye and ear protection. The selected masonry units should be delivered to the site well in advance of their required installation, and stored under cover to minimize the absorption of excessive moisture. Units in temporary storage should not be stacked too high, to prevent accidental overturning, causing damage or injury.

(a) Clay brick running bond

(b) Glass block stack bond

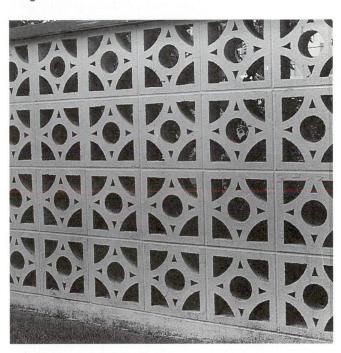

(c) Ornamental screen block

Bonding
In all forms of unit masonry, proper bonding of the units is critical to preserve structural integrity, minimize waste and save time, and to enhance visual appearance. (UBC Architecture)

Section 04–400
Stone Masonry

1.0 Introduction

1.1 General Issues

Much of the center of our planet consists of molten magma. Near the surface, the magma has cooled sufficiently to form a sort of stone skin or crust. As a result of evolutionary processes occurring over several billion years, this crust now consists of a variety of stone types. These types of stone can be classified by their basic geologic origins as either **igneous**, **metamorphic**, or **sedimentary**. The first is caused by solidification from a former molten state; granite is an example of such stone. The second is caused by changes brought about through various combinations of heat, pressure, and moisture occurring below the crust of the earth; marble is an example of such stone. The third is caused by settlement and solidification of organic or inorganic particles on top of the crust, such as shell fragments, eroded sand, clay, or other materials over long periods of time; limestone is an example.

Many stone types occur in combinations of two or more of the above three basic categories, and they can also be classified in terms of being solid or porous. Slate is an example of a stone which is metamorphic, sedimentary, and solid; pumice is an example of a stone which is igneous, sedimentary, and porous. Igneous stone tends to be very hard, metamorphic stone tends to be less hard, and sedimentary stone is usually relatively soft and therefore more easily worked (and damaged) compared to the other two types.

Since earliest recorded time, stone has been used as a building material, for a variety of reasons: It is readily available in most regions of the world, many types of stone are comparatively easy to work to desired shapes, it has generally good compressive strength, it affords good protection from the climatic elements, and, being a natural material, it offers a wide range of aesthetically satisfying colors and textures.

This section will detail aspects of natural stone masonry in two basic forms: rough-cut shaped blocks made of solid stone, such as granite used in freestanding or composite walls, and fine-cut polished panels made of thin stone, such as marble used in applied veneers.

1.2 Design Aspects

For the purposes of this section, aspects of wall design using stone masonry can be classified by **category, pattern,** and **quality.**

Categories.   There are four, identical to those already described in Section 04–200, Part 1.2.

Patterns.   There are two main bond patterns commonly encountered in stone masonry work: ashlar and rubble. Both may be of coursed or random configuration. Some basic patterns are shown in Figure 1; variations of each are frequently encountered.

If stone masonry is to be used in composite walls in conjunction with unit masonry, the stone blocks should be sized to fit into standard clay or concrete masonry dimensions or modules.

Quality.   In general, walls should be built true to plumb and plane, to follow the design layout precisely and to incorporate the selected bond pattern. Like unit masonry walls, stone walls are usually built in nominally straight lines both horizontally and vertically, but it is also possible to build them in curves, slopes, or steps to suit the designer's objectives. Consideration should be given to the size, texture, color, and weight of the stones selected and their relationship to the quality of mortar (required by code) and the type of mortar joint (required by the designer). Wherever practical, specially cut units should be used to form corners, jambs, lintels, sills, openings, or other structural or ornamental features in stone masonry work; this will improve both the appearance and the ability to fit other building components, such as windows and doors, into openings.

In long lengths of stone masonry walls, it is good practice (and in many cases a code requirement) to introduce control joints every 7 to 8 m or 20 to 25 ft., to permit some movement in the structure without cracking of the walls. Such joints usually take the form of a straight vertical break in the wall plane, packed and caulked as described in Section 07–900.

Stone should not be used in locations likely to be subjected to extremes or rapid changes of temperature. Particular care should be taken to ensure that any metal embedded in masonry mortar is com-

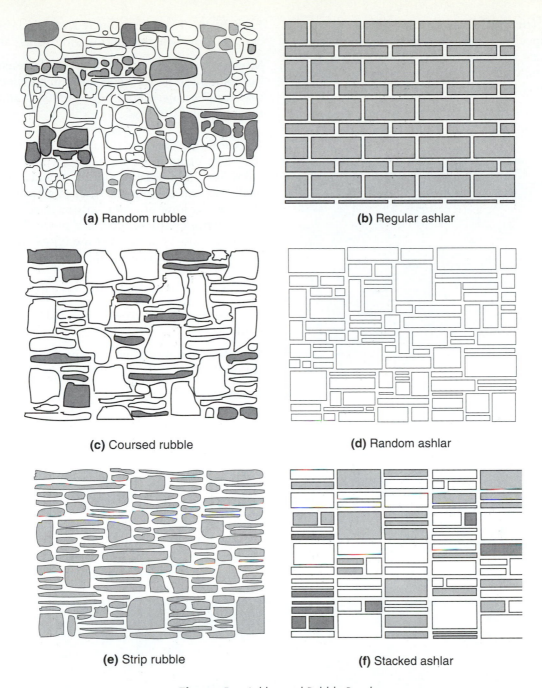

(a) Random rubble

(b) Regular ashlar

(c) Coursed rubble

(d) Random ashlar

(e) Strip rubble

(f) Stacked ashlar

Figure 1   Ashlar and Rubble Bonds

pletely sealed to prevent rusting; there have been some serious accidents and resultant lawsuits arising out of such failures of metal components in masonry work.

1.3   Related Work

Work closely connected to this section is described in the following sections, to which reference should be made:

03–300   Cast-in-Place Concrete

04–100   Mortar and Accessories

2.0 Products

2.1 Materials

Types of stone can be categorized in several ways.

Market Title.   Stone can be categorized on the basis of its end uses:

Dimension (or building) stone. Stone cut and squared to specified (and, to a limited extent, standardized) sizes, used for floors, jambs, panels, sills, stairs, veneers, walls, and general purposes. The exposed face may be rough, textured, or smooth.

Fieldstone. Rough stones of various types, sizes, and shapes, used for exterior walls and embankments.

Flagstone. Thin, irregularly shaped slabs, used for countertops, hearths, patios, sidewalks, and stairs.

Monumental stone. Similar to dimension stone, but usually in larger sizes and cut to special shapes and finishes, used for monuments, statuary, grave markers, and the like.

Geologic Origin. Stone can be categorized on the basis of its material name, type, hardness, and color. It should be remembered that as stone is a naturally occurring material, there will always be some slight variations of color, grain, hardness, and texture, giving character to each piece. Following is a list of the most common stone types encountered in contemporary construction:

Granite. Igneous; very hard; very light to dark gray.

Limestone. Sedimentary; soft; beige, medium gray, white.

Marble. Metamorphic; medium; wide variety of colors.

Sandstone. Sedimentary; soft; beiges, browns, reds.

Stockpiling

In urban areas, most stone masonry contractors will carry a wide variety of stone products, local or imported, and natural or artificial. Stockpiles are palletized and strapped for shipping. (UBC Architecture)

(a) Limestone blocks

(b) Marble veneers

Table 1
TYPICAL ASHLAR DIMENSIONS

Dimension	mm	in
Thickness	90–100	3.5–4
Length	300–1,800	12–72
Height	60, 125, 190	2.25, 5, 7.75

Schist. Metamorphic; hard; light to dark grays and greens.

Slate. Metamorphic; medium; light to dark grays and blues.

Traprock. Igneous; hard; dark gray to deep black.

Travertine. Sedimentary; medium; wide variety of colors.

Ashlar Dimensions. Some common dimensions for ashlar units are shown in Table 1.

Marble Grades. The Marble Institute of America identifies four commercial marble grades: A, B, C, and D, where A has the most uniform characteristics and D the least uniform; in practice, A grade is often the least expensive of all the grades. The Institute also recommends six commercial finishes for marble: split-face, sawn, sanded, grit-abraded, honed, and polished, where split-face is the roughest surface and polished is the smoothest.

2.2   Accessories

Most of the accessories used in conjunction with stone masonry come in the form of noncorrosive metal anchors, angles, bars, bolts, clips, cramps, dowels, pins, shims, straps, and ties.

3.0 Construction Aids

3.1 Equipment

For a detailed description of equipment used for the work of this section, refer to Section 04–200, Part 3.1.

3.2   Tools

For a detailed description of tools used for the work of this section, refer to Section 04–200, Part 3.2.

4.0 Production

4.1 Crew Configuration

Apart from minor stone facings or simple chimneys on residences which might require the attention of not more than one mason and one helper, most stone masonry jobs will require a crew consisting of two or more stonesetters, several semiskilled helpers sorting and moving stone blocks and scaffolding, and possibly a crane or forklift operator to move the heavier units.

4.2   Productivity

The factors affecting productivity in stone masonry are many and varied. In general, it can be said that, compared to unit masonry, productivity factors in stone masonry are not high. The nature, location, and extent of the work, the quality of the material, the conditions under which the work is done, and the skill of the crew, among other things, will all naturally influence the outcome. As with many other trades, only broadly representative figures for work of average quality and quantity done under good conditions by skilled masons can be given in Table 2, all of which will require significant modification before application to actual work.

Table 2
PRODUCTIVITY IN STONEWORK

Type of Work	Area per Hour	
	m²	ft.²
Ashlar, coursed	0.20	2.0
Ashlar, random	0.25	2.5
Carving, fine	0.05	0.5
Carving, machine	0.15	1.5
Carving, rough	0.10	1.0
Marble, trim	0.50	5.0
Marble, veneer	1.00	10.0
Rubble, coursed	0.30	3.0
Rubble, random	0.35	3.5
Letters, incised	2 letters	

(a) Boasting and chipping   **(b)** Building and bonding

Stone Block Work

The mason selects each stone piece based on size, color, and texture, then works it to shape using mallets and chisels. A base is prepared, guidestrings secured, and stones are built up. (BCIT Building Technology)

5.0 Procedures

5.1 Preparation

Preparation for stonework involves three main elements: **quarrying, finishing,** and **setting up.**

Quarrying. Depending on their geologic type, stones are quarried from their original sites by a number of techniques:

Blasting. This process produces random-sized, irregularly shaped boulders from solid stone beds through the use of explosives.

Heating. A sharply focused, high-temperature flame is continuously directed onto the rock to heat it along a predetermined line, then cold water is simultaneously introduced to crack it open using thermal forces.

Cutting. This process involves the use of saws or wires, mechanically driven to cut through the stone like cutting through a loaf of bread.

Drilling. This process involves boring a number of holes at close intervals along a straight or curved line and removing the material between them to create an open plane.

Wedging. Steel wedges may be hammered into the rock face; alternatively, holes may be drilled for the insertion of dried wood wedges which are then soaked to cause them to expand, thus splitting the rock between the holes.

In all five techniques, there is considerable waste, as the split does not always occur just where it is proposed by the mason. Much of the waste can be converted by further reduction to produce graded gravels and stone dust of marketable quality.

Finishing. Once quarried, the stones are usually further reduced in size by sawing or splitting; then they are finished in one of several ways:

Boasting. This involves roughly trimming the natural split faces of the stone with a chisel, to make them more uniform. See Figure 2.

Sculpturing. This involves skilled hand-tooling by an experienced sculptor, usually working from a model.

Tooling. This involves imparting a texture of ribbing, dimpling, or other pattern to the stone surface either by hand tool or machine tool.

(a) Cutting to size

(c) Finished installation

(b) Grinding and polishing

Stone Veneers

These make popular finishes for floors and walls in offices, shopping malls, and institutional buildings. The panels usually have smooth faces and textured backs for bonding to subbases. (UBC Architecture)

(a) Chiseling

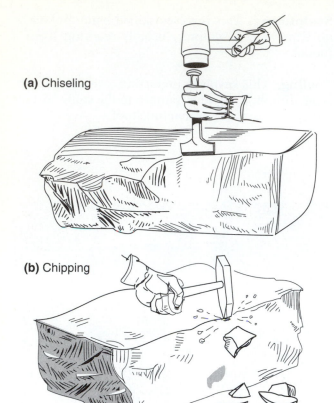

(b) Chipping

Figure 2 Boasting Stone Blocks

(a) Random rubble

(b) Coursed ashlar

(c) Fitted dry stone

Polishing. This involves rubbing or honing previously cut surfaces to produce a fine, smooth, flat or curved surface.

Setting Up. There are several elements associated with this part of the process:

Areas scheduled to receive stone masonry should be clean and free of debris and construction equipment not required for the work of this section.

Foundations for stone masonry should be made of either concrete or large stones carefully embedded and with joints filled with mortar.

Mortar used for stone masonry work generally has slightly less lime in it and is thus stiffer than that used for unit masonry work. Stone pieces should be soaked (with free surface water removed) before being laid into the wall, to avoid suction of moisture out of the mortar.

Shop drawings are recommended (except for random rubble work) before stone masonry work is commenced, to show each piece of finished stone in its final location and to indicate proposed methods of fastening. Components can then be identified so that they are placed where intended by the drawing.

Stone Bonds

There are probably as many ways to arrange stone bonds as there are stones to arrange. Most require the use of mortar, but it is possible to cut, stack, and fit stones in a "dry" state. (UBC Architecture)

Substrates or backup walls should be dampproofed before stone veneers are applied.

As walls built with stone involve the use of natural material, it is a good practice to specify that some small trial panels be made before the entire wall is built, so that the overall effect of the selected stones and mortar joints can be studied and modified, if necessary. These panels can be built in their final location, so that when one is found to be acceptable, it can remain in position to form the standard for the rest of the work, while the others are demolished and removed off site.

5.2   Process

The procedure in this type of work is essentially the same as that described in Section 04–200, Part 5.2, except that greater skill and attention to detail is required to achieve a suitable appearance in stone masonry than in unit masonry, largely because of the greater variations in dimensions. It is also less usual to "butter" the stone or marble blocks with mortar, and there is often more need to "slush" or fill joints with mortar, due to the irregular shape of many of the stone blocks. Because the size and weight of the stone or marble pieces are often greater than one or two workers can conveniently handle manually, it is quite common to utilize lifting tackle and slings of various sorts to assist with the placement of units, as shown in Figure 3.

Depending on the bond pattern selected for the stone wall, pieces should be selected on the basis of size and suitability for their place in the wall, to produce the smallest practical joints while allowing for some movement, and to achieve the best match of color, grain, and texture.

5.3   Precautions

Restrictions on activities described in Part 5.3 of Sections 04–100 and 04–200 equally apply to the work of this section.

(a) Cutting to size

(b) Installing tiles

Stone Tiles

Factory-made stone tiles of uniform dimension and thickness are available in many areas. They are cut, fit, and set much like ceramic tiles. Note temporary spacer nibs between tile units. (UBC Architecture)

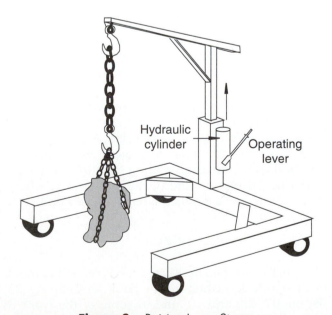

Figure 3   Raising Large Stones

Hydraulic cylinder

Operating lever

CHAPTER O5
Metal Work

Section 05–050
Metal Fasteners

1.0 Introduction

1.1 General Issues

Virtually all building components have to be fastened to other components. In particular, components made of one material may be fastened to (and by) other components made of either identical or different materials. The possible permutations are extensive.

Fastenings are not in themselves the subject of a separate construction trade (with the possible exception of welding); they are instead incorporated as an integral part of construction works described in several other sections. For this reason, the format of this section has been modified to eliminate inappropriate parts and to minimize repetition of other sections.

1.2 Design Aspects

The primary design considerations in fastenings are the establishment of physical adequacy, chemical compatibility, and acceptable appearance. Careful consideration must be given to the correct selection of fastenings of suitable type and strength, and to the matching of metal materials and metalized coatings so as to avoid electrolytic potential developing between two or more components that will be in contact with each other for a prolonged period. The reason is that if such conditions occur, then one component will likely corrode adjacent components over time, ultimately causing failure of the fastening system.

A secondary design consideration involves choice between fastenings that are exposed to or concealed from view or weathering. Methods of fastening cover a wide range of choices, including bolting, braising, crimping, nailing, riveting, screwing, soldering, stapling, and welding, among others; many of these are detailed later in this section.

1.3 Related Work

The work described in this section is related to much of the work described in this book, in Chapters 03, 05, 06, 07, 08, and 10, and to some of the work in Chapter 09 (such as plasterboard construction).

2.0 Fastening Devices

The main categories of fastening devices include **bolts, nails, rivets, screws,** and **staples**; each is described below. Within each category, several distinct types are listed; each type is usually available in a variety of sizes and shapes. Most metal fasteners are made of steel of one type or another, although some are made from aluminum, brass, bronze, copper, and other metals. Most are unfinished (called *bright*), though some are cement coated, oiled, painted, plated, or otherwise treated where required for particular protective or decorative effects.

The great majority of fasteners used in construction are now installed using powered devices. Precautions should therefore be taken to use these devices correctly as recommended by their manufacturers, to avoid injury to people or damage to property. Care should also be taken to select the length of fasteners relative to the thickness of the components to be fastened. The correct selection and use of fasteners and their accessories in structural situations should always be confirmed by reference to appropriate technical data published by the relevant institute for steel or wood construction.

2.1 Bolts

Bolts consist of a straight, solid, cylindrical, metal shank, having a head of any of several standard configurations molded on one end and a standard thread turned on the shank; they are used in construction to connect structural members using friction caused by pressure. Most bolts require to be used in conjunction with corresponding accessories, such as nuts to induce pressure and washers to distribute or absorb friction in various ways.

Bolts include the following types, among hundreds of others; some of the more common are shown in Figure 1:

Anchor. These have threaded shanks without heads; they are embedded in concrete or masonry foundations, ready to secure subsequent framing.

Carriage. These have oval heads with the shank squared below the head to prevent the bolt from turning.

Expansion. These have two components—a regular bolt and a soft metal expandable shield. As the bolt is tightened, the shield expands to create sufficient holding pressure on the surrounding material.

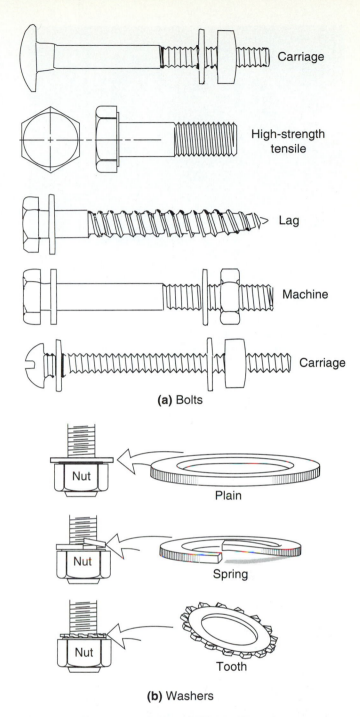

(a) Bolts

(b) Washers

Figure 1 Types of Bolts and Washers

Field. These are bolts that are used temporarily to connect structural members in position until permanent fasteners are installed and secured.

High-strength or high-tensile. There are three types, each distinguished by its carbon content and identified by an ASTM number on the head. Such bolts are usually relative strong, short, and stubby.

Machine. These are similar to high-strength bolts, but are usually much longer and thinner.

Bolting (Steel to Steel)
A worker is shown using an air hammer gun to tighten bolts on a structural steel beam. Such work is best done with an assistant to manage the air hose and hand up accessories. (UBC Architecture)

Stove. These have flat or round heads and are often threaded along the entire shank if less than 50 mm or 2 in. long.

Toggle. These are small, lightweight bolts fitted with a pivoted spring-loaded or gravity-activated wing which rotates to secure the bolt in position.

Unfinished. These are similar in appearance to high-strength bolts but are generally made of low-carbon steel, and are intended for lightweight fabrications.

Methodology for bolts usually requires that a hole, slightly larger than the shank of the bolt, be drilled through all the components to be fastened, a bolt of appropriate length, strength, and profile inserted into the hole, washers placed over the protruding threaded end of the bolt, and a nut of suitable size and shape threaded on by hand. The nut can then be tightened to the point of refusal using hand, power, or torque wrenches as required by circumstances.

2.2 Nails

There are two main classes of nails, resulting from different methods of manufacture: wire (produced from rolls of wire) and cut (stamped from sheets of

metal). The three main parts of the ordinary nail are the head, the shank, and the point; each can vary. Heads can be broad or narrow, flat or oval, or countersink; shanks can be thick or thin, smooth, grooved, or ringed; and points can be shaped like a chisel, a diamond, or a needle, among others. Nails are usually specified by reference to their type,

(a) Drilling bolt holes

(b) Column bolts in position

Bolting (Steel to Concrete)
A heavy-duty drill with specially hardened bit is used to drill bolt holes in concrete. Bolts are then inserted and secured with grout, melted sulfur, or other specified method. (UBC Architecture)

Table 1
SOME NAIL SIZES AND LENGTHS

Penny Number	Shank Length (in.)
2	1
6	2
10	3
20	4

length, and shank diameter. In Canada, nails are described in imperial or metric sizes using their dimensions; in the United States, nails are described by weight or pennyweight; some examples are shown in Table 1.

Nails include the following types, among thousands of others; some of these and others are shown in Figure 2:

Annular-ring. These have parallel rings formed along the shank, intended to improve holding power. They are used to secure drywall panels, floorboards, and shingles, among other components.

Box. These are small common nails.

Brad. These are small, thin wire nails, used for fine finishing work, such as cabinetry and casework.

Nailing
This photo shows a section of "ganged" finishing nails taken from a continuous roll. The roll is placed in the magazine of a compressed air-gun which fires each nail into its position. (UBC Architecture)

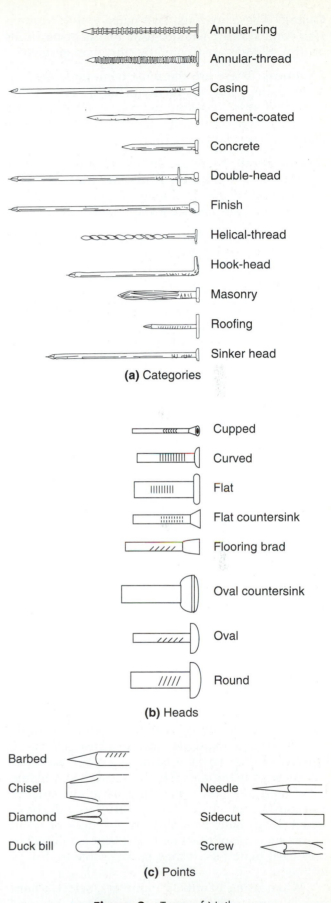

(a) Categories

(b) Heads

(c) Points

Figure 2   Types of Nails

Casing. These are long, thin nails, with a countersink conical head, and are used for securing siding or trim. Shanks are frequently ringed or spiraled.

Common. These are the most commonly encountered nails, having medium-sized, flat heads, straight shanks, and diamond points. They are available in a large variety of sizes and are used for all kinds of general construction.

Double-head. These are similar to common nails, but they are intended for temporary use, such as in concrete formwork or bracing. They have a second head to facilitate easy removal.

Finish. These are short and thin, and usually have a small, rounded, barrel-shaped head suitable for driving in flush with the surface. They are used in paneling and cabinetwork.

Masonry. These are made of hardened steel, with strong stubby heads and sharp points. They are used to fasten wood blocks and plates to concrete or masonry substrates.

Panel. These are short and thin, often with very small heads colored to match hardwood or plastic veneers which they secure in position.

Powder-set. These are made of hardened steel, and are driven using powder-activated guns. They are used where high strength and holding power is a consideration.

Roofing. These have large flat heads, short shanks, sharp points, and are usually cadmium-plated or galvanized. They are used to secure membrane roofing felts to wood or plastic decks.

Spikes. These are similar to common nails, but much larger. They are often used to fasten wood decking to joists.

Tacks. These are usually small cut or cast nails, often tempered and sterilized, and used for fastening upholstery, carpets, and other fabric materials in position.

Methods for nailing involve consideration of the type of service conditions expected in use, such as required holding power, weather or other exposure, thickness of materials relative to length and diameter of nails, and aesthetics. In general, the smallest nail consistent with satisfactory service should be selected. Keep nails well away from edges or weaknesses such as splinters or knots. When nailing into very hard materials, it may be advisable to drill pilot holes.

When using handheld hammers, select a hammer of appropriate size and type and hit nails squarely on the head until they are flush with the material surface. With finish nails, stop hammering when the nailhead is just proud of (above) the surface, and complete the sinking using a nail-set.

When using powder-activated guns, select the appropriate gun, nail, and cartridge strength. Press the gun nozzle firmly and completely against the material surface; do not attempt to override safety locks. Check the backing material to make sure that the energy from the shot will be fully absorbed and that the nail will not pass completely through the components to be fastened.

2.3 Rivets

Rivets are a subset of fasteners in which a short stud with a shaped head on one end is inserted into a preformed hole and pulled up tight, and the other end is then deformed to produce a second head which secures the composite arrangement in position.

Rivets include the following types, among others; some examples are shown in Figure 3:

Button-head. This is the most common kind of rivet, having a short stubby shank and a round head on one end. It is heated to red-hot temperature, inserted into the rivet hole, and the protruding end hammered down to form a second button-head.

Chemical-expansion. These are one-piece devices, having a hollow shank filled with an explosive. When detonated by heat or electricity, the shank walls expand to tightly fill the hole.

Countersink. These are similar to button-heads, except that the heads and rivet-hole ends are countersunk to achieve a flush installation upon completion.

Flathead. These are a variation of button-heads, in which the newly formed head is hammered flat but not quite flush with the material surface.

Pop-type. These have a shank with a preformed head on one end and a stem through the center of the rivet shank, attached to the head on the far side. A gripping tool is attached to the stem. By exerting force on the stem through the tool, a new head is formed on the side remote from the tool; the stem is then removed and discarded.

Methods for riveting require drilling a hole in the materials to be fastened, slightly larger in diameter than the rivet selected for use. The rivet is inserted into the hole from one side, pulled or pushed up tight against one head, and the second head is formed on the other end of the rivet shank by striking hot rivets with a hammer or pneumatic rivet gun, forming cold pop-rivets with a plier-like device, or screwing in a threaded companion head. The energy used to form

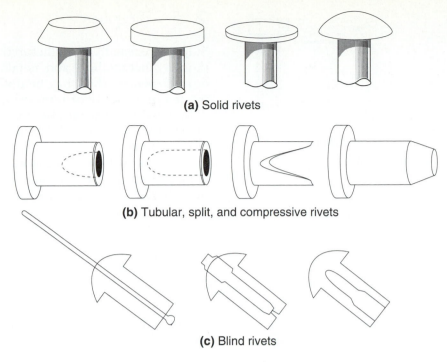

(a) Solid rivets

(b) Tubular, split, and compressive rivets

(c) Blind rivets

Figure 3   Types of Rivets

the head also causes the shank of the rivet to expand slightly and tightly fill the predrilled hole.

2.4   Screws

Screws generally have four main portions: the head, one-third plain shank, two-thirds threaded shank, and the point. Screws are usually described by reference to their shank diameter in wire gauge, length, type, and head. The shape or profile of the head may be bugle, fillister, flat, hexagonal, oval, pan-type, round, or square, among others. Screws are manufactured with plain (slot), cross, square (Robertson), or star (Phillips) slots in their heads, prepared to take the tip of a manual or powered driving device. The points may be either plain pin for wood applications or slotted for metal applications. Although screws are more expensive to buy and to install than nails, they have some advantages: They have higher holding power, cause less damage to the materials they secure, generally look better, and are easier to remove.

Screws include the following types, among many others; some examples are shown in Figure 4:

Drywall. These usually have completely threaded shanks and bugle-shaped heads with star slots. The threads are alternatively high and low to increase holding power.

General or wood. These are intended for general use. They are mostly flat countersink type, and are

available in hundreds of combinations of head, shank, and point sizes and configurations.

Lag. These are large, heavy-duty screws formed with a square or hexagonal head for driving with a wrench or nutdriver instead of a screwdriver.

Machine. These have straight shanks, no points, and are usually threaded right up to the underside of the head.

Masonry. These are similar to drywall screws but are larger and made of toughened steel, capable of being driven into holes predrilled in concrete or masonry surfaces.

Self-tapping. These are similar to machine screws but have sharp pin or slotted points capable of cutting through soft metal to form a self-threaded slot during installation.

Methods for using screws require drilling a shank hole corresponding to the diameter and length of the unthreaded portion of the shank, followed by a narrower pilot hole corresponding to the inner diameter and length of the threaded portion of the shank. For flush installation, a countersink profile must be drilled at the top of the shank hole corresponding to the diameter of the screwhead. All holes should be slightly narrower than the corresponding portions of the screw to be installed. Depending on the type of slothead, a manual or powered screwdriver with the correctly selected bit is then used to install the screw.

2.5 Staples

Staples are usually manufactured from steel wire, although other methods and metals are also used. Like other fasteners, they may be unfinished, coated, or treated in a variety of ways. Staples are commonly designated by their proposed end use and specified in terms of wire gauge, leg length, crown width, and point profile.

Staples include the following common types, among dozens of others and indeed variations of those listed; some examples are shown in Figure 5:

Chisel point. This cut ensures that the staple legs will stay parallel during driving into soft materials.

Divergent point. This cut ensures that the staple legs will spread out during driving into fibrous materials.

Spear point. This cut ensures optimum penetration when driving into hard materials.

Methods for stapling always involve the use of manual or powered staplers. Either type should accommodate a cartridge-loading device to facilitate the supply of staples to the work point. Staple guns may be powered either by compressed air or by electricity. They can be activated or fired by trigger or by touch against the work surface.

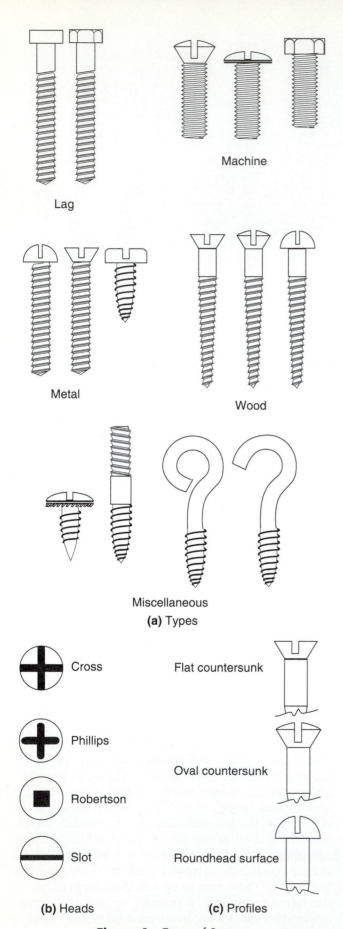

(a) Types

(b) Heads

(c) Profiles

Figure 4 Types of Screws

Lag

Machine

Metal

Wood

Miscellaneous

Cross

Phillips

Robertson

Slot

Flat countersunk

Oval countersunk

Roundhead surface

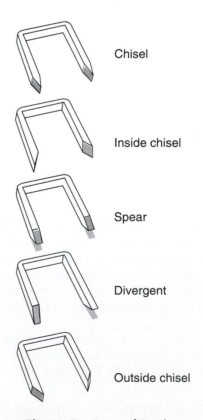

Chisel

Inside chisel

Spear

Divergent

Outside chisel

Figure 5 Types of Staples

Chapter 05 Metal Work

3.0 Fastening Processes

Major categories of fastening processes for metals include **brazing, soldering,** and **welding.** Within each category, the primary types are listed.

3.1 Brazing

In general, this process involves the gluing together of two heated parent metals, using a third nonferrous molten metal alloy as an alloying adhesive. The temperatures are not as high as those encountered in welding (about 500 degrees C as compared with 3,500 degrees) so there is less distortion of the parent metals. Brazed joints are stronger than soldered joints, but they are not usually as strong as welded joints. Brazing metals consist of a variety of alloys, such as aluminum, silicon, copper, phosphorus, magnesium, and silver. Heat-resisting types are also available. Naturally, care must be taken to select brazing materials that are chemically compatible with the parent materials to be thus joined. Brazing alloys are available in a variety of combinations, such as aluminum-silicon, copper-phosphorus, copper-zinc, and others.

Common **factory** brazing techniques include the following:

Dip. The parent and brazing metals are submerged in a bath of molten salts.

Furnace. The parent and brazing metals are secured in place, then the entire assembly is heated in an enclosed furnace.

Induction. Electrical induction creates heat high enough to melt the brazing metal.

Resistance. Electrical resistance and physical pressure create heat throughout the joint in which the brazing metal has already been positioned.

Torch. A gas-generated flame is directed onto both the parent and brazing metals, causing them to fuse together.

To perform common **site** brazing, the parent metals are clamped in position and cleaned, and the joint to be brazed is filled with a flux material. Heat is applied from a gas torch or electrical source until the flux melts. A metal brazing rod is then inserted into the molten flux, causing the rod to melt and flow to fill the joint by displacing the flux. After an undisturbed cooling period, excess flux is removed by chipping and wirebrushing, and the joint can then be ground smooth if required.

3.2 Soldering

Soldered joints are often encountered at joints in metal roof flashings, in ornamental or utilitarian metal panel work such as rangehoods and countertops, in commercial kitchen and store fittings, and wherever positive electrical connections are required. Such joints can be watertight, but they are not very strong; they should not be used where significant impact, shear, tension, or vibration is anticipated.

Solder commonly used in construction is an alloy of 50 percent lead and 50 percent tin. Other solders consist of varying proportions and mixtures of antimony, lead, silver, and tin. Solders are available in the form of bars, ingots, slabs, tapes, and wires, among others. All solders are used in conjunction with fluxes of three generic types: corrosive, noncorrosive, and neutral, utilizing chlorides, rosins, and mild acids, respectively.

There are three common soldering techniques encountered in construction; each involves relatively low temperatures, usually not exceeding approximately 300 degrees C or 600 degrees F:

Iron. A pointed metal block (the "iron") with an insulated handle is heated either by an internal electric element or by an external flame, then applied to the heated joint simultaneously with the soldering material and a fluxing material. The iron is used to control and shape the molten solder. The joint may also be left unheated during soldering; this produces a "cold" joint.

Sweat. The parent metal pieces are carefully heated with a gas blowtorch, causing the prefluxed, preapplied solder to spread throughout the joint or seam. The profile or shape of the work pieces usually controls the spread of the solder.

Torch. This method is similar to the sweat method, except that the solder and flux are applied as in the iron method.

In addition to the foregoing methods, there are several factory applications in soldering that embody techniques akin to welding processes, where automatic repetition of standardized soldered joints becomes economically feasible.

3.3 Welding

Welding involves the interatomic bond or fusion of the metal molcules, either between two parent pieces of metal to be joined or between them and a third piece introduced as a filler. The principal agent involved is usually heat, although pressure and friction can also be applied in some techniques.

Shop Welding

As mentioned in the accompanying text, there are many methods and techniques used in welding processes. Most of these are available to work done off-site in steel fabrication plants. (UBC Architecture)

Welding is a relatively rapid, clean, neat, quiet, and economical method of joining two pieces of metal together. There are more than 30 different industrial welding processes available, including welding by explosion, by friction, by pressure, and by the use of ultrasonic sound energy. The processes commonly encountered in construction have been selected for discussion below. Wherever possible, welding is best done at the fabrication plant and not at the construction site. The main problems encountered in site welding include adequate control of temperature and moisture levels and difficulty of access to the final workplace. Some arrangements are shown in Figure 6.

Welding processes involve three main categories: **arc, beam,** and **gas.**

Arc. Some common processes are:

Flux-core arc weld (FCAW). A continuous metal filler wire having a core of fluxing and deoxidizing agents is used as an electrode, being slowly passed along the joint to be welded.

Gas-metal arc weld (GMAW). Heat is generated by an electric arc created between a consumable metal electrode moved rapidly against the work piece; no flux is required.

Gas-tungsten arc weld (GTAW). An electric arc is created between a tungsten electrode and a metal filler rod, with gases (such as argon and helium) used to form a shield around the weld.

Metal inert-gas weld (MIG). Another name for GMAW welding.

Submerged arc weld (SAW). An electric arc causes heat to melt a moving filler metal and flux shield against the metal pieces to be joined; the filler is submerged in the shield.

Tungsten-inert-gas-weld (TIG). Another name for GTAW welding; often used to weld aluminum pieces.

Wire-fed weld (WFW). Another name for GMAW welding.

Site Welding

Site welding presents additional problems, more hazards, and less certain environmental conditions. Nevertheless, it is still a popular process, used to connect structural steel members. (BCIT Audio-Visual Production)

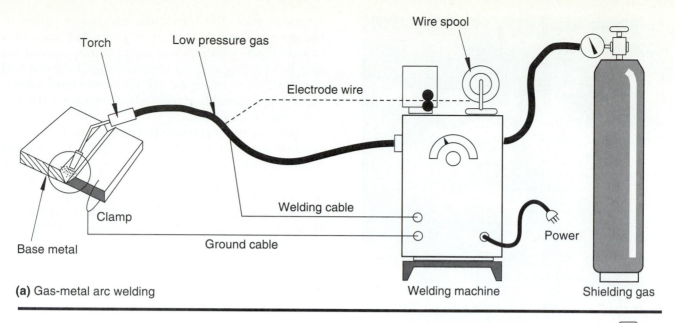

(a) Gas-metal arc welding

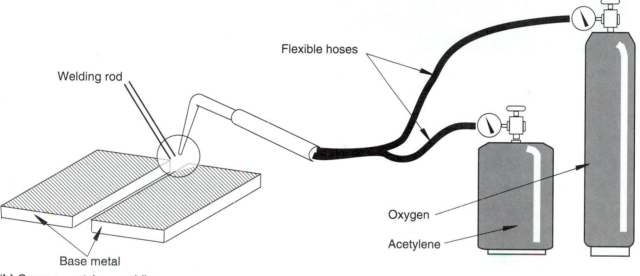

(b) Oxygen-acetylene welding

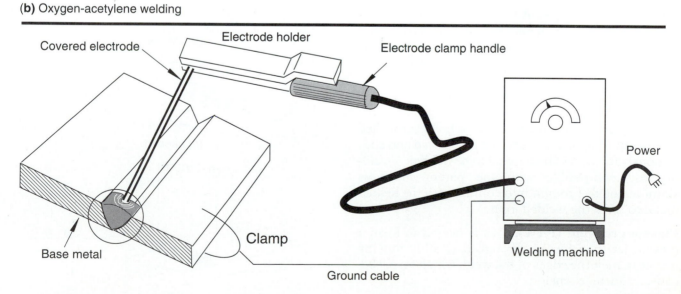

(c) Shielded-metal arc welding

Figure 6 Welding Arrangements

Welding Machine
To do electric welding on site, it is necessary to have reliable portable diesel-powered machines capable of continuously producing the correct amount and type of voltage and current. (UBC Architecture)

Beam. Some common processes are:

Electron-beam weld (EBW). A continuous beam of accelerated electrons is electronically focused on the joint to be welded as the metal is intermittently moved past the electron beam.

Pulsed-laser weld (PLW). A repeated pulse of coherent light energy from a ruby rod is focused through a lens onto the metal parts to be joined as they are steadily moved past the light beam.

Gas. Two common processes are:

Oxyacetylene gas weld (OAGW). A controlled mixture of oxygen and acetylene gas is fired and continuously focused to heat metal to be welded. A welding rod compatible with the parent metal is simultaneously brought into contact with the heated metal to form the welded joint.

Plasma arc weld (PAW). Gas is heated to form a plasma jet then forced through a steadily moving nozzle to melt the edges of the weld, which forms because of surface tension.

Of the foregoing processes, FCAW, GMAW, and GTAW are frequently used to join metals at con-

struction sites; the remainder are better suited to factory applications at present. One other process is called "flash" welding and incorporates instant fusion by creating a direct resistance arc between two metal pieces to be joined. All processes have advantages and disadvantages, details of which are beyond the scope of this book.

Each of the foregoing processes can be used to produce several types of welded joints, of which the most common are listed below; some examples are shown in Figure 7. Each type of joint can be designated on construction drawings by a unique symbol according to a letter-and-line system developed in 1958 by the American Welding Society (AWS) and updated several times since.

Butt. The two pieces to be welded are placed side by side in the same plane, edges are cut to a slight bevel, and the weld is poured in and ground smooth.

Edge. The two pieces are placed back-to-back and parallel to each other, and the weld is run along their matching edges.

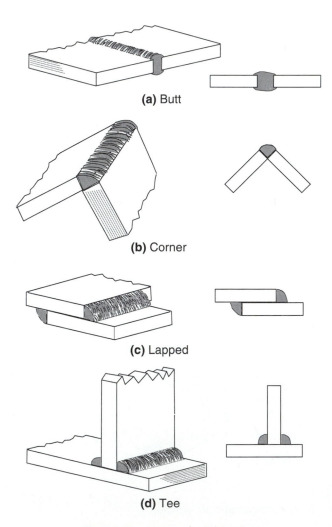

(a) Butt

(b) Corner

(c) Lapped

(d) Tee

Figure 7 Types of Weld Joints

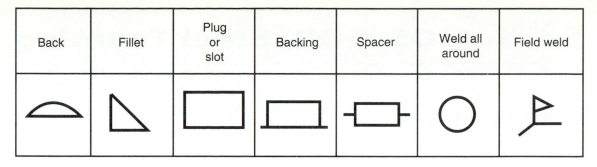

Back	Fillet	Plug or slot	Backing	Spacer	Weld all around	Field weld

Figure 8 Types of Weld Symbols

Fillet. The two pieces are abutted, usually at an angle up to and including 90 degrees, edges are machined flat for a tight fit, and weld material is then added in a triangular cross-sectional continuous or intermittent bead.

Groove. This is similar to a butt joint but having square instead of beveled edges.

Lapped. The two pieces to be welded are overlapped by a small margin, and a small and usually continuous fillet weld is created along one or both edges of the lapped joint.

Plug. Small circular holes are drilled at intervals along one edge of one piece of metal; the piece is then lapped over the other piece, and the holes are filled with molten weld metal.

Stud. This is a semiautomatic electric-arc technique for rapidly welding threaded studs to webs or flanges of columns and beams.

Tack. This joint is similar to the fillet weld joint, but occurs at intermittent points along the junction of the two pieces being thus connected.

The characteristics of a good weld include uniformity, straightness, consistency in section and profile, cleanliness, and minimal penetration or deformation of the parent metals. The strength of the weld should approximate the strength of the original metals.

The various types of welds required for any specific application are represented on construction drawings by symbols standardized for use throughout the steel fabrication industry. A few representative welding symbols are shown in Figure 8; for a complete list, consult the American Institute of Steel Construction (AISC) or refer to AWS standard A2.4–86.

For further information on welding equipment, features, processes, safety, techniques, and types, the reader is referred to any of dozens of excellent textbooks on the subject, available in most bookstores and libraries.

3.4 Other Processes

In addition to the foregoing processes, it is also possible to join some metals to other materials in some situations by using high-strength contact-bond glues, as noted in Section 06–050, and by crimping or otherwise carefully deforming the metal components to a greater or lesser extent to achieve a friction fit. Separate removable clamps, brackets, and vise-grip pliers can be used for temporary fastenings.

Metal can also be cut using an oxyacetylene gas cutting process (OAGC). A controlled mixture of oxygen and acetylene gas is fired and continuously focused to heat the metal to be cut. Then a fine jet of pure oxygen is directed onto the metal to produce the cut.

Patented Connectors
A wide assortment of specialized fastening devices is available. In this example, the intersections of the framing members are connected with specially cast aluminum hub blocks. (UBC Architecture)

Section 05-100 Steel Framing

1.0 Introduction

1.1 General Issues

Metals of various types are used in the construction of many portions of many buildings. Consequently, there is some ambiguity in terminology arising out of the overlapping of work of closely related metal trades. To conform to *MasterFormat*, this section *Steel Framing* includes structural elements of rolled steel (or other metals), including related temporary or permanent bracing members and accessories. It does not include metal items incidentally fastened to or supported by such structural members, such as steel door frames, aluminum windows, curtain wall systems, and so on. It also does not include lightweight metal framing (in the form of steel studs) used to form interior partitions or exterior furrings. Such related work is described in other sections identified in Part 1.3.

1.2 Design Aspects

Consideration of some design aspects of this work will also help to clarify its scope. Steel framing normally consists of an arrangement of vertical columns or posts, horizontal primary girders, secondary beams or joists, and diagonal braces or inclined friction dampers. All of these components are specifically engineered, fabricated, assembled, and connected to serve as the main structural frame of a particular building. Such engineering will take into account the dead loads and live forces in the form of bending, compression, flexure, shear, and tension expected to be sustained by the various components as a result of building function and use, traffic vibrations, earth tremors, wind loads, and expansion and contraction. The manner of transmitting such forces through the joints or connections in the system must also be determined by the structural engineer.

The beams or joists transmit the loads from the floors to the girders, thence to the columns, and so down to the foundations and into the earth. If it is intended that the rigidity of the structural frame is to be sustained by itself, then the members and the connections between them must be specially designed to resist the turning or bending moments likely to be encountered. It is often necessary to cut or cope the top flanges at the ends of beams or joists, so that they may finish flush with the upper surface of the top

flange of the primary girders to which they are attached, as shown in Figure 1.

Cuts, holes, or other voids through structural steel members should be designed by a structural engineer and positioned under the guidance of a building technologist. It is common for steel-framed structures to be completed with steel or composite decking, as described in Section 05-300.

1.3 Related Work

Work closely connected to this section is described in the following sections, to which reference should be made:

01-050   Field Engineering

03-300   Cast-in-Place Concrete

05-300   Steel Decking

05-400   Steel Stud Systems

2.0 Products

2.1 Materials

Steel is a metal alloy, composed primarily of iron (about 95 percent or more) but having a significant amount of carbon and lesser amounts of manganese and other trace elements carefully selected and proportioned to achieve various effects. The iron ore and other elements are combined in a smelting process and then poured out into ingot molds. The ingots are then reheated as necessary and passed through several sets of heated rollers or extruders to

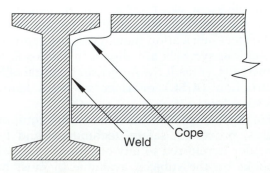

Figure 1   Cut or Coped Flanges

produce the desired cross-sectional configuration, dimensions, and lengths for structural shapes, plates, and bars. Cold-rolled steel is also available, usually in the smaller dimensions and in thin sheet form. One should be aware of various **types** and **shapes** of steel products.

Types. There are two broad categories of commercial rolled steel encountered in construction:

1. **Carbon steels.** These include low carbon (under 0.25 percent carbon); medium carbon (0.25 to 0.50 percent); and high carbon (above 0.50 percent but not exceeding 2.0 percent). So-called wrought irons and mild steels are essentially medium-carbon steels. Steel having in excess of 2.0 percent carbon would be more suitable for casting as distinct from rolling.

2. **Alloy steels.** These are usually identified by the name of the significant alloy metal, such as boron, chromium, cobalt, copper, nickel, and vanadium, among others. As with carbon, the percentages of metal alloyed with the steel are very small.

Shapes. Typical shapes and sizes of some selected rolled carbon steel sections are shown in Table 1, as being representative examples. For a fuller description and a wider range, consult the data lists in AISC (American Institute of Steel Construction) or CISC (Canadian Institute of Steel Construction) and the product catalogs of any national steel manufacturer. The designations used to indicate the W, M, S, and C members consist of the letter symbol for the specific shape, the nominal web depth in milli-meters or inches, and the mass expressed (in metric) in kilograms per meter or (in imperial) in pounds per foot. For each nominal depth listed, most manufacturers will make a range of varying weights (masses).

There are also combination profiles, such as HP for bearing piles, MC for miscellaneous channels, and WT for wide columns.

The designations used to indicate the L, T, Z, and more specialized hollow square, rectangular, or circular (HS and HR) sections consist of the letter symbol for the shape together with the significant outside dimensions in millimeters or inches, as shown in Table 2. Most manufacturers offer a wide range of sizes within each letter designation.

Combinations. It is of course possible to combine various shapes and qualities of steel components to make up composite columns, girders, beams, and

Table 1
TYPICAL STRUCTURAL STEEL SHAPES

Shape	Type	Designation	Dimensions	
			Metric	Imperial
	Wide flange	W	460 × 177	18 × 114
	Miscellaneous	M	360 × 25.6	14 × 17.2
	Standard beam	S	610 × 179	24 × 120
	Channel	C	380 × 74	15 × 50

Table 2
SPECIAL STRUCTURAL STEEL SHAPES

Shape	Type	Designation	Dimensions	
			Metric	Imperial
L	Angle	L	200 × 150	8 × 6
T	Tee	T	460 × 223	18 × 9
Z	Zee	Z	75 × 167	3 × 6.5
☐	Hollow rectangle	HS	127 × 63.5	5 × 2.5
◯	Hollow round	HR	73 (diam.)	2.875 (diam.)

joists as necessary. Such composite units are often referred to as box beams, plate girders, or trusses, among other titles, depending on their specific configurations. Consideration should be given to possibly adverse side effects when dissimilar metals are joined.

Because of the process that was used to rationalize metric shapes, there are fewer intermediate sizes now available in Canada. The additional sizes included in the imperial selections in the United States are not necessary for most Canadian buildings, all of which have to conform to the uniform Canadian National Building Code, which is itself a rationalized metric document. In the United States, there are at least four distinct building codes, applicable to various parts of the country, all of which are expressed in imperial units and terms; greater variety is therefore appropriate for the U.S. situation.

2.2 Accessories

Most structural metal framing involves the modification of standard manufactured components to fit nonstandard projects. Consequently, there are no significant accessories to consider in connection with the work of this section, other than metal fastenings as described in Section 05–050. One might say that whatever steel accessories there may be are integral parts of the components being otherwise fabricated to accommodate specific design criteria.

3.0 Construction Aids

3.1 Equipment

A primary piece of equipment used in steel framing is the crane. Cranes used for this work should have at least 45-metric-ton or 50-short-ton capacity; higher capacities are available if necessary. There are many types of cranes available, but the ones most commonly used for this work (and other construction operations) are illustrated and described in Section 01–525.

A secondary item of equipment frequently encountered in steel framing is the welding machine, described in Section 05–050. A surveyor's transit or

Stockpiles
Prefabricated steel components are delivered to site and stock-piled in a convenient location. A crane is used to raise and transfer pieces from the stockpile to the building frame. (UBC Architecture)

surveyor's level is frequently required to line up, level, and plumb framing members; these instruments are described in Section 01–050.

Most of the large items of equipment used by steel erection companies are either leased or rented; it is usually too expensive to purchase and maintain such items. A tower crane could easily cost a quarter of a million dollars.

3.2 Tools

The tools required for this work are those of the iron-worker, and consist of a variety of drills, drift pins, plumb bobs, shears, steel tapes, tin-snips, vise-grips, and various wrenches, such as the impact or torque type, the expandable jaw type, and the spud wrench.

4.0 Production

4.1 Crew Configuration

Workers in this field are generally well-trained, highly skilled, and often unionized, all of which results in comparatively high labor costs. A typical

welding crew consists of five or six ironworkers, of whom one would act as foreman while another would act as welder, together with an equipment operator to work the crane and an oiler to maintain the equipment and stockyard supplies. On large projects, two such crews might be efficiently utilized, with an additional welder and perhaps a general foreman.

Although **riveting** is not as common in construction as it once was, some types of plate girders still use rivets for their assembly. A crew of three workers would heat, move, and place the rivets. An additional worker would operate a compressor for the rivet gun, used to flatten the rivet heads. Such work is often done at the fabrication shop, instead of at the site.

For **bolting**, the total crew would be divided into two components: one for erection and the other for connection; each would have its own foreman.

4.2 Productivity

There are five elements to this work:

Drawings. The production of shop drawings (necessary for the fabrication of the steel components) can be considered on the basis of number of detail drawings to be made or tons of steel to be erected. For this purpose, the metric ton (1,000 kg = 2,220 lb.) and the imperial short ton (2,000 lb. = 900 kg, approximately) can be considered to be similar in magnitude. Using experienced drafting personnel, drawings produced manually for normal commer-

Steel Erector Tools
This photo shows an assortment of typical tools used by steel erectors; they include a webbing belt and canvas pouch to hold drift pins, spud wrenches, and mallets, among others. (UBC Architecture)

cial or institutional projects will take about one day per sheet or two hours per ton on average; drawings produced electronically will take about one-third of these time factors. Detailing for simple or repetitive industrial buildings will take somewhat less time; more complex buildings will naturally take more time.

Fabrication. The manufacture and fabrication of steel framing components involves the use of highly specialized plant, equipment, and labor forces. As the end product is essentially the same as any other manufactured building component, it is beyond the scope of this book to give a detailed analysis of the internal economics of the processes. However, it can be stated that typical fabrication rates in a well-equipped plant may average around 3 tons per hour for work of normal complexity. Table 3 gives a brief summary of fabrication data as a general guide to production of some of the more common components encountered in typical steel-framed construction.

Painting. Shop-painting of fabricated components involves semiskilled labor using spray equipment to prepare for and apply one coat of rust-inhibiting paint to the surface of each member. On average, one metric ton of fabricated steel yields approximately 20 m² of surface area; similarly one short ton yields approximately 200 ft.² of area. It takes one person just over 1 hour to apply 2.0 liters of paint to 20 m² or 0.5 gallon to 200 ft.². After each component has been painted, it is identified by felt marker or paint stencil to ensure its correct placement in the building frame; this takes about 2 or 3 minutes per item.

Delivery. Fabricated, painted, and identified components are usually delivered by flatbed trucks in quantities varying between 5 and 15 tons in weight and usually not exceeding 15 m or 40 ft. in length. Times obviously will vary in proportion to the distance between the fabrication shop and the construction site, the size of the loads, and the volume of traffic encountered by the delivery vehicles.

Erection. The erection of steel frame components involves the use of heavy equipment such as derricks or cranes and fairly large and specialized crew configurations as outlined above. In general, it can be expected that on typical and straightforward commercial or institutional projects of medium to large size, about 2 tons of metal framing will be erected and connected by each crew per hour. Table 4 gives a slightly more detailed distribution for specific framing components. As will be understood, the lighter-weight components usually have more parts per ton than the heavier-weight members and therefore take longer to erect on a unit-weight basis. To put it another way, one component may weigh 1 ton and take 1 hour to install, whereas four small components may weigh 0.25 ton each but each may take perhaps 0.5 hour to install, for a total of 2 hours.

5.0 Procedures

5.1 Preparation

Before any metal is cut, shop drawings are usually prepared by skilled drafters (directly employed or retained on contract by the steel erection contractor) from the original contract drawings, to show the exact fabrication and assembly of each component part of the structural framing system. Such drawings should be approved by the structural engineer responsible for the overall design. Each piece is then selected from stock, drilled, punched, coped, and combined with others as necessary at the steel fabricating plant. Any additional connections are attached to each piece before delivery, to simplify field erection procedures. If any large holes have to be cut through the components, additional reinforcing

Table 3
OUTPUT FACTORS FOR FABRICATING STEEL MEMBERS

Building Component	Fabrication (hours/ton)
Angle and beam framing	1
Complex plate columns	4
Heavy built-up girders	5
Light braces and struts	2
Simple wide-flange columns	3

Table 4
OUTPUT FACTORS FOR ERECTING STEEL MEMBERS

Building Component	Erection (hours/ton)
Angle and beam framing	3
Complex plate columns	2
Heavy built-up girders	1
Light braces and struts	2
Simple wide-flange columns	2

Placing Columns
These workers are guiding a steel column as a crane slowly lowers it to its final position on its prepared base plate. The column will be temporarily braced until secured and connected. (UBC Architecture)

bars or channels are welded on to restore the structural integrity of the member.

The fabricated steel components are then coated with a rust-inhibitive paint, such as zinc chromate or lead oxide, and then marked to identify the piece and its orientation and place in the final structure according to the contract drawings and specifications. Components are finally loaded onto a flatbed truck by crane and delivered to the job-site.

5.2   Process

Upon arrival at the site, the structural framing components are unloaded by crane from the delivery trucks, checked for damage in transit, and arranged in a stockyard area of the site specially set aside for this purpose. Damaged components should be rejected and removed from the site immediately. The stockyard should be located within the radius of the main tower crane or climbing crane serving the general construction of the building.

Before installation commences, field measurements should be taken to ensure accuracy in the placement of all fabricated steel components. A wire sling and a tag line are attached to each component in the stockyard in turn. The sling is used to raise the component by crane; the tag line is used to control its direction during the lift. Several small components may be raised simultaneously, provided there is sufficient space to temporarily store them at the higher level. Each component is swung into position, temporarily secured by bolts, drift pins, or guy wires, plumbed or leveled as necessary with a surveyor's transit, and then permanently connected as specified for the design.

Although each project will vary, most structural steel erection on highrise buildings follows the general pattern described below. Engineered anchor bolts of suitable size, strength, and number are first embedded into the concrete foundations. Bearing or base plates, to be attached to the ends of vertical column members and having oversized holes corresponding to the anchor bolts, are then placed over the anchor bolts, washers and nuts are applied, and the whole assembly is then adjusted and shimmed as necessary to ensure correct positioning. When they are level and secure, the space between each plate and the foundation is then fully packed with special concrete grout. See Figure 2.

Vertical columns for the first lift (called a tier) are then erected on the bearing plates. If there is to be more than one tier, the length of the columns is usually such to permit them to extend about 60 cm or 24 in. above the column-to-beam connection at the upper end of each column, to avoid interference at such critical joints. Columns in succeeding tiers are subsequently butted on to the tops of lower columns, using reducer plates where necessary. Horizontal beams at each tier or floor level are positioned

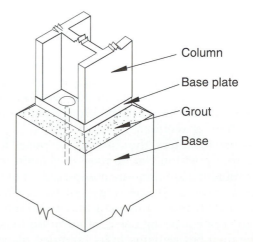

Figure 2   Grouted Base Plate

(a) Curved beams

(b) Straight beams

Placing Beams

A crane is used to move and support straight or curved beams while steel workers make temporary connections. After the beam system is complete, permanent fastenings will be installed. (UBC Architecture)

between the columns and either pinned in place or secured to a prepared seat, using clips and bolts or welds as necessary. The framing for two floors would probably be completed throughout the length and breadth of the building, then the crane would be moved up and the next two floors similarly assembled. Once the primary structural frame at each level or in each bay or wing of the building is completed, secondary steel components such as stairs, minor joists, decking, clips for curtain wall panels and the like, can start to be positioned and secured as described in other sections.

In some instances, the crane which raised a component into position can be used to sustain it until the permanent fastenings are completed. In other instances, temporary braces or guy wires may have to be attached to the component and to suitable anchors to create a triangular configuration to ensure that the member remains in its intended place during the remainder of construction. See Figure 3.

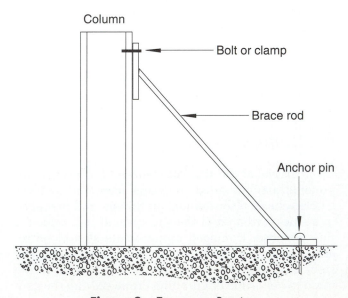

Figure 3 Temporary Bracing

(a) Bolt detail

Bolt Fastening

Special high-strength bolts and nuts are used to connect steel components. Manual, electric, or pneumatic machines can be used to drive the nuts to their code-specified torques. (BCIT Building Technology)

(b) Bolt technique

5.3 Precautions

In all buildings under construction, there is a risk of collapse, but incomplete column and beam structures are particularly vulnerable to this hazard. Therefore, steel-framed buildings require to be very securely stayed and guyed during the erection process. Temporary connections need to be carefully designed and executed to sustain the forces and loads likely to be encountered. Braces and guy wires should be properly attached and tensioned at every step of the process. Work should not proceed in areas immediately below portions of the building where steel framing is being installed. Temporary supports should not be removed until tests confirm stability of the permanent frame.

Metal frame construction using hollow rectangular, square, or circular column and beam components is essentially similar to the process described above, except to note that such construction is usually considerably lighter to handle and faster to erect and connect. Such construction is often encountered in single-story lowrise buildings, such as commercial shopping centers, warehouses, small school or service buildings, and the like.

(a) Weld finish

(b) Weld detail

Weld Fastening

In this photo, a steel column has been temporarily clipped and bolted, then permanently fastened with a deep weld. After welding is complete, excess material is ground off by machine. (UBC Architecture)

Section 05–200 Steel Joisting

1.0 Introduction

1.1 General Issues

One of the advantages of utilizing metal in buildings is the inherent economy of being able to carry large building loads in small structural members. In particular, one of the advantages of using steel joists of one kind or another is that it is usually very economical to thus span spaces to support horizontal floor, ceiling, or roof systems (of concrete, metal, plastic, or wood) between the vertical supports such as columns or walls to create the required planes in the building. Steel joists are frequently encountered in such situations either exclusively or in a mixture of two basic types: solid web or open web. Solid web joists are described in Section 05–100; this section describes open web types.

1.2 Design Aspects

Most horizontal beams are designed to resist forces of compression, tension, bending, and shear imposed on them by the building structure and its use. The object is to design a beam with the upper portions in compression and the lower portions in tension, with enough stiffness in the system to resist bending and enough strength in the materials to resist shear.

In addition to the structural advantages gained by the use of such joists, there are benefits to the installation of mechanical, electrical, and other services which can often be fitted inside the spaces created by the open webs of the joists. Open web joists are usually designed and manufactured to have a small upward camber, intended to offset expected deflection when the floor or roof loads are ap-

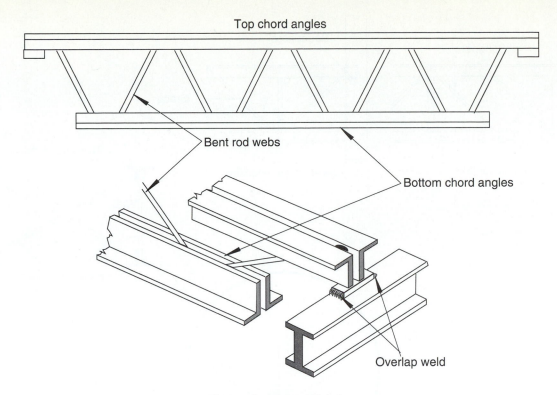

Top chord angles

Bent rod webs

Bottom chord angles

Overlap weld

Figure 1   Open Web Joist

plied to the joist system. Figure 1 shows a typical arrangement.

1.3   Related Work

Work closely connected to this section is described in the following sections, to which reference should be made:

05–100   Steel Framing

05–300   Steel Decking

2.0 Products

2.1 Materials

Open web joists consist of two continuous top and bottom chords, held apart by intermittent angled web members fastened to the chords. The chords may be made of hot-rolled or cold-formed angle, bar, channel, or tubular components, while the web components are usually made of solid metal rods.

Joists are available in two types: **unified** joists which consist entirely of metal components, either of steel or aluminum; and **composite** joists which

may have metal chords with wooden webs, or vice versa. Most joist manufacturers make standard joists in specific categories of length, strength, and type, according to recommendations of the Steel Joist Institute (SJI). Nonstandard joists can be designed and manufactured on special order. Some typical and approximate joist designations and characteristics are shown in Table 1; for actual dimensions and structural performance, refer to the SJI or manufacturers' published tables. The word *interval* used below signifies the increments between the minimum and maximum dimensions available.

Special deep web beams (designated as DLJ and DLH) having web depths up to 2 m or 72 in. and spanning distances of up to 45 m or 144 ft. are also available from some manufacturers. Other designations, such as "K" series joists, are also encountered.

2.2   Accessories

Accessories used in conjunction with open web joists consist of setting plates used to distribute the joist loads to supporting members, wall clips to attach the ends of joists to walls, metal shims used to permit accurate and true alignment of the joists between supports, and high-tensile bolts with washers and nuts, used to fasten the joists in position. Some are shown in Figure 2.

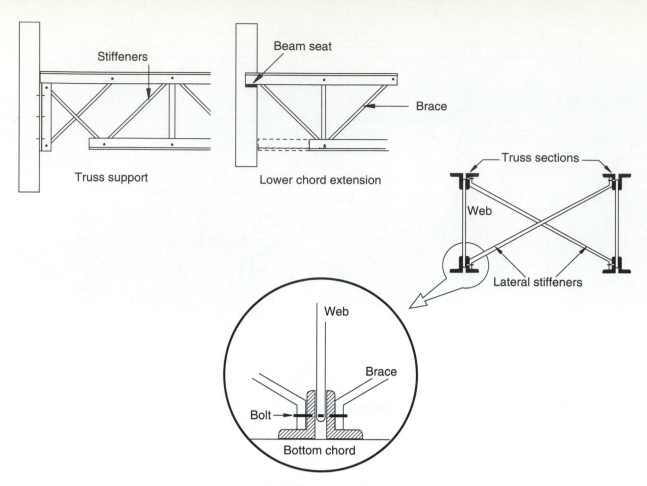

Figure 2 Joist Accessories

Table 1
JOIST DESIGNATIONS AND CHARACTERISTICS

Characteristic	Designation	Dimensions
Web depth	J & H	Minimum: 200 mm or 8 in.
		Maximum: 600 mm or 24 in.
		Interval: 50 mm or 2 in.
	LJ & LH	Minimum: 450 mm or 18 in.
		Maximum: 1.2 m or 48 in.
		Interval: 100 mm or 4 in.
Span length	J & H	Minimum: 4 m or 12 ft.
		Maximum: 18 m or 60 ft.
	LJ & LH	Minimum: 8 m or 24 ft.
		Maximum: 30 m or 96 ft.
Yield point	J & LJ	250 mPa or 36,000 psi
	H & LH	350 mPa or 50,000 psi

3.0 Construction Aids

3.1 Equipment

The equipment required for the work of this section is identical to that described in Section 05–100 Steel Framing.

3.2 Tools

The tools required for the work of this section are identical to those described in Section 05–100.

4.0 Production

4.1 Crew Configuration

The erection of open web metal joists on most medium-sized commercial projects will involve a single crew, consisting of one foreman, one ground rigger to attach slings and tag lines, three or four ironworkers or beam persons, one helper to move light equipment and supplies, and a crane operator. This work is done by specialist subcontractors for the general contractor.

4.2 Productivity

The sequence of selecting a typical joist, rigging it, hoisting and positioning it, and finally securing it, takes about 6 minutes. However, as the final fastening process can occur simultaneously with the preceding elements, the actual elapsed time can get down to about 3 minutes per joist, after the first few joists have been installed and a working rhythm established. Labor productivity in this work is usually expressed by the weight of steel erected. On simple commercial construction, an experienced crew should lay about 1 ton per person per day; on complex institutional work, the crew might lay only about 0.5 ton per person per day.

5.0 Procedures

5.1 Preparation

The installation of metal joists usually follows very closely behind the completion of erection of the structural components (such as columns, beams, or walls) required to support them. For this reason,

joists are usually prefabricated at a plant off site, coated with a rust-preventative paint if necessary, and delivered in bundles ready to be put into their position in the building frame. The bundles are checked and sorted in a temporary storage area after delivery on flatbed trucks to the site. A crane at the site is usually used to off-load the trucks.

(a) Stockpiling

(b) Retrieval

Preparation

Prefabricated joists are delivered on flatbed trucks and stockpiled on site. Crane slings are then attached to selected assemblies, ready for raising to their intended locations. (BCIT Building Technology)

(a) Raising

(b) Lowering

Installation

Joists are swung up by crane and guided into place by workers holding tag lines. Joists are carefully aligned and spaced and then lowered into their intended positions. (BCIT Building Technology)

(a) Aligning

(b) Connecting

Positioning

Bolt-holes in the joist truss are aligned with corresponding holes in the supporting member using a pointed drift-pin. Bolts or welds are then used to secure the trusses in place. (BCIT Building Technology)

Composite Members
Trussed long-span joists are not always made solely of steel. Composite arrangements of steel, wood, and bolts are also popular, as shown in this illustration. (Trus-Joist Corporation)

5.2 Process

By reference to the construction drawings and to identifying tags, each joist is selected, fitted with a wire rope sling and a tag line, and raised by crane to its intended position. One end is lowered onto the building frame first, aligned by an ironworker using a spud wrench or pinch bar, and temporarily bolted in position. The other end of the joist is then lowered and the temporary fastening process is repeated. The joist is then finely aligned, shimmed if necessary, and permanently secured in position, either with additional bolts or, in some cases, by welding. This entire process is repeated with the rest of the joists to complete the required framing system. If required by the structural design, lateral bracing may then be installed longitudinally between the joists. Once the joist is temporarily but safely secured, the rigger can climb along the joist to release the sling; on long joists, a self-releasing system of hook and cable is more conveniently used.

5.3 Precautions

The design and installation of open web joists is governed by building codes in every part of the continent. One main area of concern during erection of joists involves the system of signals used between the foreman and the crane operator to ensure safe movement of material. In most states and provinces, such systems are devised and authorized by OSHA or WCBs, with which strict compliance is required by law. Some typical signals are shown in Figure 3.

Care has to be taken to prevent damage to the joists during handling. The rigging must be placed so as to preclude the possibility of the joists bending or warping during hoisting, and the tag lines must be used to prevent joists from bumping into any part of the building structure during erection procedures, until final placement in position. Figure 4 shows a typical arrangement.

Workers climbing on the joists to make the connections in this type of work frequently wear good-

(a) Hoist load   (b) Raise boom   (c) Use whipline

Figure 3 Typical Safety Signals

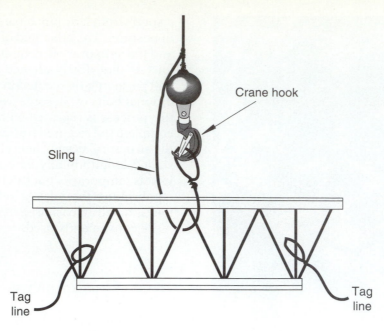

Crane hook

Sling

Tag line

Tag line

Figure 4 Sling Points and Tag Lines

quality, tightly laced, lightweight, rubber-soled, canvas shoes (called "sneakers") to enhance their agility and safety. They also use chinstraps on their hard hats to prevent the hats from falling off when they bend over. Such workers seldom wear safety harness; some say the dangers so posed are greater than the risks incurred without harnesses. It is a point on which authoritative opinion should be sought.

Section 05–300   Steel Decking

1.0 Introduction

1.1 General Issues

Metal decking consists of large, preformed, corrugated panels, usually made of steel (factory galvanized or primed-coated), although aluminum and stainless steel panels are also available. It is manufactured and delivered in standard-sized sheets. It is relatively inexpensive to buy and easy to handle, cut to shape, and fasten in place.

1.2 Design Aspects

Steel decking is normally incorporated into the design of a building to provide a continuous horizontal diaphragm to improve lateral structural stability and to enhance resistance to the spread of fire; it simultaneously provides an excellent base for suspended flooring or roofing systems and space for building services; it can also be used effectively in inclined or curved ramps. Such multiple functions can have distinct and beneficial effects on budgets, as well as enhancing aesthetic effects.

Steel decking is most often encountered in conjunction with structural steel framing or long-span open web steel joists, to which it is easily attached by riveting, spot-welding, or bolting. Because of its ribbed or corrugated cross-sectional profile (as shown in Figure 1), such decking is exceptionally strong and rigid in relation to its weight. It is capable of spanning considerable distances and sustaining substantial loads, provided the deck system and supports have been properly designed by knowledgeable engineering personnel.

Flooring in conjunction with steel decking usu-

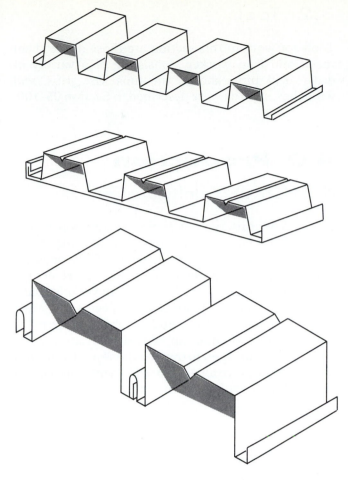

Figure 1 Metal Deck Profiles

ally consists of a layer of poured concrete (see Chapter 03) with an applied topping or other finish, such as resilient tiles or carpets (see Chapter 09). Roofing usually involves the application of rigid insulation boards followed by a built-up roofing system (see Chapter 07).

1.3   Related Work

Work closely connected to this section is described in the following sections, to which reference should be made:

03–300   Cast-in-Place Concrete

05–100   Steel Framing

05–200   Steel Joisting

07–200   Insulation

07–500   Membrane Roofing

2.0 Products

2.1 Materials

The entire range of steel decking products can be considered under two broad headings: **configurations** and **dimensions**.

Configurations.   There are two basic categories of panels:

1. **Single-sheet** panels consist of flat sheets of metal, cold rolled through special dies to produce a pan having a curved or angular corrugated cross-sectional profile.

2. **Cellular** panels are similar, except that they have an additional sheet of flat sheet metal seam-welded to the underside of the corrugations of a formed single sheet, thus increasing strength and rigidity while forming a series of continuous hollow cells suitable for housing cables, conduits, pipes, or other building service utilities. A variation of the cellular panel consists of two separate channeled panels seam-welded to the underside of a flat sheet. Both categories have their long edges prepared for interlocking connection to adjacent panels; ends may be cut square or prepared for nesting into a succeeding panel. Some typical profiles are shown in Figure 1.

Dimensions.   There are two primary categories:

1. **Regular decking.** The gauge of metal used for regular metal decking varies between 18 for heavy-duty or long spans and 22 for light-duty or short spans. The depth of corrugation can vary from about 35 mm or 1.5 in. to about 60 mm or 2.5 in. The width of corrugation is usually 150 mm or 6 in.; panels are manufactured in multiples of one, two, three, or four full corrugation widths. Lengths vary between 4.5 m or 15 ft. and 9.0 m or 30 ft.

2. **Long-span decking.** The gauge of metal used for long-span deck pans varies between 14 and 18. Pan width is normally 300 mm or 12 in.; pan depth varies between 110 mm or 4.5 in. and 190 mm or 7.5 in.; pan length varies between 6.0 m or 20 ft. and 9.0 m and 30 ft.

2.2   Accessories

Accessories for decking fall into two categories:

1. **Trim.** Although not required on every project, trim used in conjunction with metal decking may

include long, narrow, flat or shaped galvanized steel or aluminum sheet material compatible with the decking, used to neatly finish the decking system as perimeters or cut edges, as cant strips, and as capping pieces.

2. **Fastenings.** The other main class of accessories is a variety of bolts, screws, washers, and clips, used to secure the deck components in position (for details, see Section 05–050). After the decking is installed, small, hard steel studs are sometimes installed (usually by welding) as supports for reinforcing steel rods or fabrics, if the design requires such treatment. It can be argued that such studs are part of the reinforcement system and not part of the deck, but it should be remembered that the system has to function properly as a whole, from both the structural and contractual point of view.

3.0 Construction Aids

3.1 Equipment

Equipment for work in this section would include a truck-mounted crane, extendible ladders, and a welding machine.

Stockpiling
The deck panels are raised by crane to appropriate levels and then distributed by hand to their approximate final position. (UBC Architecture)

3.2 Tools

Tools for work in this section are those of the sheet metal and iron worker, consisting of a variety of drills, drift pins, shears, tin-snips, vise-grips, and wrenches, such as were described in Section 05–100.

4.0 Production

4.1 Crew Configuration

On work of this type, it is not uncommon to encounter crew sizes of four workers, consisting of two ironworkers, a welder, and a helper. The ironworkers handle, measure, and fit the steel; the welder cuts and fastens the decking; the helper moves materials, equipment, and tools around as necessary. Most medium to large jobs would involve two or more crews, with a foreman appointed from among the qualified journeymen to oversee the work. Crane and truck operators are also required to deliver and move materials and equipment in bulk.

4.2 Productivity

Although factors will vary, depending on crew size and capability, the weather, job-site conditions, and the complexity of the installation, it is probable that about 10 m² or 100 ft.² of single lightweight or long-span roof deck will be able to be installed in about 30 minutes. The same unit area of floor deck, being usually slightly heavier, should take about 40 minutes. For cellular deck, the above time factors can be increased by about one-third.

5.0 Procedures

5.1 Preparation

It is customary for detailed shop drawings to be prepared by the deck installation company from the contract drawings prepared by the structural designer. These drawings should show the proposed layout of panels in each area of the portions of the structure to be decked, and indicate where cuts and reinforcements are to be made and the fastening techniques proposed. Shop drawings should be approved by the structural designer before work commences. The ironworkers at the job-site then review the drawings relative to the work to be done to judge the most economical way of laying out the panels and fastenings.

Modifying

Standard panels are measured, marked, then cut to shape or size as necessary using a carborundum-bladed saw. Workers wear approved ear-plugs to protect their hearing. (UBC Architecture)

(a) Conventional arc welding

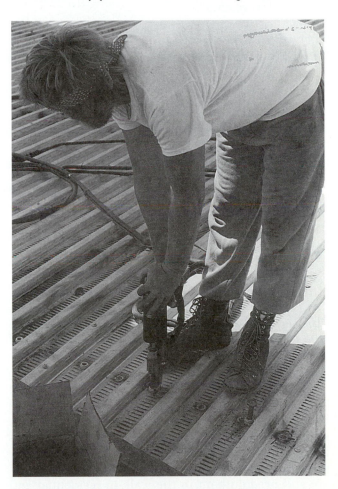

(b) Patented fastening device

Installation

Panels are placed into position, lapped as necessary, and secured by bolting or more commonly by spot-welds, using either conventional arc devices or patented fastening devices. (UBC Architecture)

5.2 Process

Deck panels are raised by crane, hoist, or forklift to the deck level in bulk and spread around in such a way as to avoid unduly heavy or eccentric loading on the structural frame at any one point. Panels are loosely placed in their approximate final position, with the longitudinal corrugations usually at or near to right angles with the supporting framework below. They are then measured and cut to size or shape as necessary, repositioned, and fastened in place as described below. Wherever possible, each deck panel unit should span at least three structural supports; end joints are also best positioned over supporting members.

Openings for service pipes or other building features passing through the deck are usually also positioned and cut out at this time. All openings measuring more than 150 mm or 6 in. in their smallest dimension should be reinforced; if less than 450 mm or 18 in., reinforcement is usually done by the deck installer by welding on some additional deck material; larger openings should be properly framed by the structural steel erector before the deck is positioned.

Fastening may involve fusion spot-welds or screws, placed through the lower valley of the corrugations, to secure the deck to the supporting steel at usually not less than 400 mm or 16 in. on center, or greater if the spacing of supports or the design otherwise dictates. Adjacent edges of sheets may be interlocked and secured by welding, screwing, or crimping at intervals of about 1.0 m or 36 in. If required and so specified, the deck installer may be responsible for supplying and installing such accessories as cant strips, flashings, perimeter trim, and capping pieces to match the deck material.

5.3   Precautions

This work involves some hazards. Most of it is performed at some height above grade; the material is fairly bulky and can be awkward to handle in windy conditions; cut steel deck components have very sharp edges; welding and other powered equipment is extensively utilized; rain and ice can add to the normal difficulties. Most jurisdictions have fairly specific safety regulations regarding work of this type. Workers should be properly qualified to do this work and be equipped with appropriate clothing (devoid of loose or flapping parts), hardhats, eye and hand protection, and safety-toed shoes. Those workers doing welding require even more specific protection and certification relative to that part of the work.

Personnel should not work in areas immediately below locations where decking is being installed, in case pieces should fall. Installation is seldom affected by adverse weather conditions involving normal heat or cold. Care must be taken to avoid humid or wet conditions that might contribute to condensation, freezing that may produce ice, wind blowing on large metal panels, or very high temperatures causing problems of expansion or contraction and making jointing and fastening more difficult.

Section 05–400
Steel Stud Systems

1.0 Introduction

1.1 General Issues

This section is identified by its popular term—*steel stud systems;* a more formal term is *lightweight steel framing*. In *MasterFormat*, it is listed under *cold-formed metal framing*.

Around the middle of the 20th century, steel studs began to replace wood studs in framed walls in buildings. Now, virtually all commercial and institutional building projects in the larger urban centers incorporate steel studs for selected interior partitions and exterior framed walls; wood studs are still predominant in the walk-in residential and walk-up apartment building sectors of the construction industry.

It is a common practice for the trade that erects steel stud framing also to install metal lath systems. However, to avoid repetition, the installation of lathing is excluded from this section, as it is described in Section 09–200.

1.2 Design Aspects

In general, steel studs simply replace wood studs, for both loadbearing and nonloadbearing interior partitions and exterior walls, spandrel panels, service recesses, dropped ceilings, furred walls, and other infill framing. Top tracks are secured parallel to and directly above the floor track and the studs placed vertically in between, as described in more detail in Part 5.2. Chases or recesses for mechanical, plumbing, or other services can be easily configured using steel stud systems.

Steel studs have some design advantages over wood studs, in that they are

Lighter in weight for comparable sizes.

Easy to handle, cut, shape, and secure.

Free from warp, rot, and creep.

Immune to attack by fungus, insects, or vermin.

Fireproof (they cannot burn, but they can bend).

(a) Exterior

(b) Interior

Major Applications

In many regions, steel studs are replacing wood studs for framing systems in large commercial projects. This example shows a suburban shopping mall completely framed in steel. (UBC Architecture)

More uniform in profile and length.

Provided with holes precut to permit the easy passage of braces, cables, conduit, or other small service pipes. They also lend themselves better than wood to some degree of prefabrication. Some disadvantages of steel studs in comparison to wood are:

They are less yielding.

They transmit sound more readily.

It is not so easy to fasten other materials to them.

They have a higher longitudinal coefficient of expansion.

They can rust if not properly treated and protected.

They are (in some opinions) less pleasant to work with.

Furthermore, care must be taken when using galvanized steel studs in conjunction with other materials, to avoid electrolytic action and to avoid unintentional electrical grounding.

In particular, consideration must be given to anticipated loads on both the X and Y axes of steel stud members, as well as their potential to resist wind or shear loads and torsional or flexural buckling. (For an explanation of structural terminology, refer to any handbook on structural engineering.)

The length of unsupported vertical studs of any given cross-sectional dimension and metal thickness is usually governed by portions of local or national building codes. Studs of longer length require to have lateral support or stiffening. Steel stud walls are laid out in the same manner as wood stud walls, with the bottom track accurately placed relative to the required centerline of the framed partition or wall. Care must be taken to ensure that unanticipated loads from the building structural frame are not accidentally transferred to the steel stud system, except where a loadbearing system has been deliberately incorporated. In regions prone to earthquake and where required by local building codes, allowance should be made for possible building movement in addition to the normal tolerances.

On exterior applications, the rain-screen principle of design, as it applies to construction detailing in general and to exterior steel stud framing in particular, should be given appropriate consideration. The principle involves recognition of the fact that outside air pressure tends to drive moisture into and through small crevices in the exterior skin or cladding of buildings. The moisture travels inward (and usually downward) as a result of a combination of several natural phenomena, such as capillary action, gravitational attraction, surface tension, and velocity. The solution is to arrange the construction details to permit equalization of the pressures outside and inside the exterior skin to defeat the tendency,

thereby preventing moisture from reaching the inner skin of the structure. For some typical details related to this principle, refer to Figure 1.

One other design advantage of steel studs over wood studs is the relative ease with which a steel stud system can be disassembled without significant damage or debris, should it become necessary to relocate a portion of the wall or ceiling system to suit the changing needs of building owners or tenants. It is usually desirable to acoustically seal interior steel-framed partitions with a compressible foam strip of some sort, placed between the perimeter track and the supporting structural surface. Similarly, it is usually necessary to seal exterior framed systems with a waterproof gasket secured between the framing components and the building structure. For all but the very simplest of applications, it is considered prudent to retain the services of a competent structural engineer to advise on design relative to light-weight steel framing.

1.3 Related Work

Work closely connected to this section is described in the following sections, to which reference should be made:

03–300   Cast-in-Place Concrete

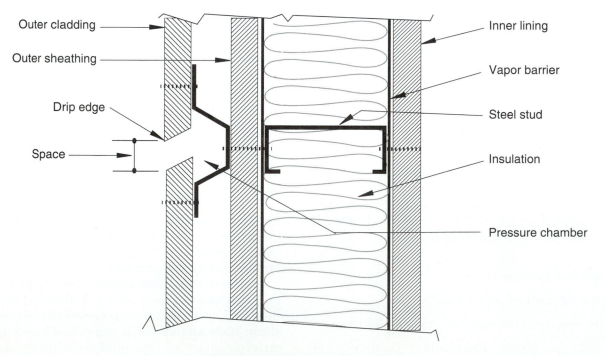

Figure 1 Rain-Screen Principle

06–100   Rough Carpentry

06–170   Prefabricated Wood

07–200   Insulation

09–200   Lath and Plaster Work

09–250   Gypsum Plaster Board Systems

2.0 Products

2.1 Materials

Following are several aspects of materials used in steel stud systems.

Components. Steel studs and tracks are manufactured from cold-rolled light- or heavy-gauge sheet steel, protected from rust with a galvanized coating after manufacture, to conform to the general profile shown in Figure 2. Studs have small openings cut out of their flanges at regular intervals to allow for the passage of bracing, piping, or wiring. Runners and channels are shop-fabricated, finished, and cut to length identically to the primary steel studs and tracks, but to smaller dimensions, more suited for furring and strapping applications.

Dimensions. Studs are normally 2,400 mm or 96 in. long; longer lengths are available. Tracks are normally at least twice as long as studs. Some stock sizes for component widths and depths are given in Tables

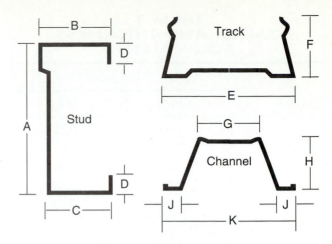

Figure 2   Stud, Track, and Channel

1 and 2; components with nonstandard dimensions can be specially ordered if the project is large enough to warrant the change.

Standards. Components should conform to the following standards:

United States: ASTM A591 (Steel Sheet, Cold Rolled, Zinc Coated)

Canada: CAN3–S136 (Cold Formed Steel Structural Members)

Stockpiles
Steel studs of various dimensions and lengths are strapped into bundles and delivered by truck to the site. They are raised to upper levels by the building hoist and carried in manually. (UBC Architecture)

Table 1
GAUGE AND THICKNESS EQUIVALENTS

Gauge	Thickness* mm	Thickness* in.
12	2.65	0.104
14	1.90	0.074
16	1.55	0.060
18	1.20	0.047
20	0.91	0.036

* Bare metal thickness; add 0.03 mm or 0.001 in. for galvanized zinc coatings. In some regions, the thickness of the various stud framing members is indicated by use of a color-coding system.

Table 2
DIMENSIONS OF COMPONENTS

Stud Width mm	Stud Width in.	Stud Flange mm	Stud Flange in.
41	1$5/8$	35	1$3/8$
64	2$1/2$	33	1$5/16$
92	3$5/8$	Track Flange	
102	4	mm	in.
152	6	29	1$1/8$
203	8	35	1$3/8$

2.2 Accessories

The following accessories are used in steel stud systems:

Braces. Lightweight, flat-bar galvanized steel straps, in lengths up to 6 m or 20 ft.

Hangers. For horizontal ceilings: wire, 3.6 mm or 9-gauge for lightweight systems or close hanger spacing; rods, 4.8 mm or $3/16$ in. for heavy systems or wider hanger spacing.

Inserts. Recessed butterfly type or as recommended by steel stud manufacturer to support hangers.

Lath. Refer to Section 09–200.

Rivets. Small steel pop-rivets occasionally used to secure studs to tracks or runners to studs.

Screws. Self-drilling or self-tapping hard steel types of various lengths and gauges, used to join components.

Sealing tape. Fine vinyl foam gaskets; 6 mm or $1/4$ in. thick and 12, 19, or 25 mm or $1/2$, $3/4$, or 1 in. wide; rolled in various lengths, depending on the manufacturer.

Tie-wire. 16-gauge (1.6-mm or .064-in.) or 18-gauge (1.2-mm or .048 in.) soft annealed galvanized steel wire, for tying runners.

3.0 Construction Aids

3.1 Equipment

Equipment used to perform the work described in this section is as follows:

Punch fasteners are used to join two pieces of sheet metal, by cutting a rectangular hole in both pieces and rolling the cut edges of the hole over to secure the joint.

Radial arm saws are often used to cut multiple bundles of studs, tracks, or channels to appropriate lengths before installation.

Scaffolding or motorized scissor-lift platforms are often necessary to give access to work at higher levels.

3.2 Tools

Tools described in this section are of particular concern to the work of this trade; such tools are largely those of the carpentry trade, outlined in Section 06–100, with the addition of the following:

Hacksaws. Used to cut through steel studs and plates where necessary.

Plumb bobs. Used to accurately transfer the bottom or floor track layout to the ceiling level.

Powder-guns. Cartridge-powered hand tools used to drive hardened concrete nails through sheet metal components to secure them to the building frame.

Screw gun. An electric-powered hand tool (like a drill) used to drive Phillips-head screws to preset depths, to fasten metal or other components together.

Tin-snips. Heavy-duty, hard steel scissors, capable of cutting thin sheet metal by hand.

4.0 Production

4.1 Crew Configuration

Crew sizes for steel stud work are generally small, usually consisting of one or two journeyman carpenters or lathers, with perhaps one semiskilled helper. On larger projects, two or more crews might be employed.

4.2 Productivity

There are two ways in which productivity is practically expressed in steel stud work: by area of framing and by length of component parts; some representative examples are given in Tables 3 and 4, respectively.

The costs of constructing stud framing with steel appear to be marginally lower than with wood. In every case, however, a check estimate should be made to determine which is the cheaper system for a given installation.

5.0 Procedures

5.1 Preparation

Work should proceed under good natural or artifical lighting conditions. Floor, wall, and ceiling areas scheduled to receive stud framing work should be swept clean and be free of water, dirt, dust, and debris. Structural substrates (surfaces) should be checked to ensure a firm basis for supports and connections. Chalk-lines should be snapped against the

Preparation
Individual studs are easily and quickly cut to length as necessary using a light-duty table saw. Minor adjustments to studs can also be made using handheld tin-snips. (UBC Architecture)

Table 3
PRODUCTIVITY FACTORS (IN AREA) IN STEEL STUD WORK

Type of Work	Area per Day	
	m²	ft.²
Walls, framed:		
Exterior	40	400
Interior	45	450
Add lathing	120	1,200
Ceilings, suspended:		
Runners and channels	13	130
With channels only	15	150
With stud framing	35	350
Add lathing	100	1,000

substrates to indicate the correct alignment of floor, wall, and ceiling tracks. Laser equipment can also be utilized for this purpose. Positions of openings should be determined prior to commencement of work. Component parts should be cut or selected to correct lengths, bundled, and moved into convenient locations adjacent to the place where the work will be done.

5.2 Process

The installation sequence for typical framing systems comprises these four stages: **tracking, studding, ceiling,** and **furring.**

Table 4
PRODUCTIVITY FACTORS (IN LENGTH) IN STEEL STUD WORK

Component Part	Length per Hour	
	m	ft.
Tracks:		
Floor	15	50
Ceiling	13	40
Studs:		
End and corner	20	60
Intermediate	25	80
Soffit framing	20	60
Accessories:		
Acoustic seal	30	100
Cross-bracing	50	150
Blocking and girts	15	50
Lathing	(see Section 09–200)	

(a) Floor runners

(b) Wall plates

Installation

The lines of framing are laid out and marked on floor and wall surfaces. Floor, ceiling, and wall-end runners are power-fastened to the structural frame of the building. (UBC Architecture)

Tracking. This concerns the installation of the lower and upper tracks to which the studs will be secured.

Lower

Measure the width of the track, make a mark on the floor offset by half that width, and note on which side of that mark the track will be placed. Measure the net distance to the finished faces within each room or area, to allow for drywall or other face paneling to be applied over the stud framing, and adjust track locations accordingly. Snap a chalk-line to confirm the stud wall location, then locate door and other openings. Secure the track with steel nails or screws to wood or with a powder-gun and concrete nails to concrete surfaces. Spacing of fasteners should not exceed 600 mm or 24 in. along the lengths, and be not more than 50 mm or 2 in. from track ends. Form plain butts at ends and corners; do not form miters at junctions.

Upper

Transfer the floor layout to the ceiling level with a plumb bob, level and shim if necessary, and then snap corresponding chalk-lines. Secure the top tracks as described for floor tracks.

Studding. This concerns the installation of the vertical studs into the horizontal tracks. See Figure 3.

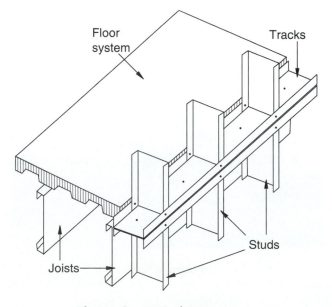

Figure 3 Vertical Arrangement

(a) Using tin snips

(b) Using vise clamps

Curved Framing

Framing is not always erected in simple flat planes. Here, a bottom runner is snipped at short intervals, gently bent by hand, clamped to vertical studs, and secured with pop-rivets. (UBC Architecture)

Interior

Cut studs to be 8 mm or $\frac{1}{3}$ in. shorter than floor-to-ceiling height, taking care to ensure that the punched-out holes for bracings and services will be aligned after installation of studs. Insert each stud into the floor track at the specified horizontal spacing (usually 600 mm or 24 in. on center), swing it upright to fit into the upper track with a slight twisting motion to ensure a tight friction fit, and accurately plumb vertical. Check alignment of punchouts, then secure the studs to the tracks at top and bottom by screwing, pop-riveting, or neatly crimping metal to metal. Where necessary to provide a thicker wall frame to accommodate plumbing pipes or other services, provide for a double row of stud framing, of equal or unequal thicknesses, cross-tied to each other.

Exterior

Proceed as described for interior studs, but note that work often must be done from one side of the framing only, namely the interior of the building. Wherever extra-long studs are required, such as might happen where the combined height of an exterior wall and related spandrel panels exceed the normal stud length, it is possible to telescope one stud inside another (having the identical profile) to create an overlapped joint. The joint length should be four times the stud width or at least 200 mm or 8 in. in length, and should be tightly fastened with screws located 25 mm or 1 in. from each end of the overlap. Some specifications prohibit such extended studs.

Openings

Provide track material cut to length to form heads and sills at door and window openings as necessary, to support the cut ends of intermediate stud members. Ensure that studs on each side of openings extend full height for solid fastening to bottom and top tracks.

Ceiling. This concerns the preparation of a horizontal plane, ready to receive plasterboard or other panel boards. Such planes can be achieved either by using **hangers, runners, and channels,** or by using studs horizontally positioned (**soffit framing**). See Figure 4.

Hangers, Runners, and Channels

If it is required to create some space between the

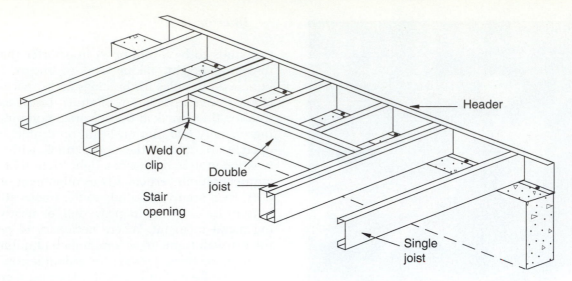

Figure 4 Horizontal Arrangement

structural soffits and the ceiling plane below, proceed as follows:

At cast-in-place concrete soffits, provide inserts embedded in soffit formwork before concrete is poured.

At precast concrete soffits, provide inserts installed and grouted into holes drilled after the concrete component has been placed.

At steel deck soffits, pass the upper ends of hanger rods through predrilled holes, and form a pigtail twist on the upper end.

At steel joist soffits, tie the hanger ends around portions of the steel frame members, at positions acceptable to the structural engineer.

At wood deck soffits, proceed as for steel deck soffits, or loop the upper ends of hangers into threaded steel eyehooks, screwed into the underside of the decks.

At wood joist soffits, drill holes through the joists at least 75 mm or 3 in. above the underside of each joist, bend and pass the upper end of the hanger rods through the holes, then bend the ends down at least 100 mm or 4 in.

In every case, select inserts or hooks of sufficient size and strength to sustain the anticipated design loads. Check to make sure that both the upper and lower ends of wires or rods are properly secured so that they cannot unravel under designed loads. The sizes of inserts or holes which have to be provided to secure the ends of the rods or wires must be selected to suit the size or gauge of the hanger. The layout pattern of the hangers must be arranged to suit the spacing and configuration of the runners and channels they are intended to support (as indicated in Tables 5 and 6).

As it is usually proposed to attach lath or other panels to ceiling frames, it is necessary to provide and install main runners and cross-channels to which the panels may be fastened.

1. Main runners. These are usually set out at spacing indicated in Table 5 to form a square grid pattern, commencing and finishing within 150 mm or 6 in. of all perimeters to support the edges of cross-channels or panels. They are tied to the bottom ends of the hangers at the correct elevation, either with a twist in the wires or a bend in the rods. If it is

Table 5
SPACING ON CENTER OF HANGERS AND RUNNERS

Hangers		Main Runners	
mm	in.	mm	in.
1,200	48	900	36
1,000	42	1,000	42
900	36	1,200	48

Table 6
THICKNESS AND SPACING ON CENTER OF CROSS-CHANNELS

Thickness		Spacing	
mm	in.	mm	in.
13	1/2	400	16
16	5/8	600	24
19	3/4	800	32

Repetitive Framing

There is usually repetitive work in building construction. It is therefore expedient to mass-produce repetitive components (such as these furred duct frames) prior to final installation. (UBC Architecture)

necessary to overlap ends of runners, the overlap should be not less than 300 mm or 12 in., and the overlaps should be tied with tie-wire or screwed not less than 50 mm or 2 in. from the end of the overlap. It is evident from Table 5 that the closer the runners, the wider the hanger spacing, and vice versa.

2. Cross-channels. These are usually set out at spacing indicated in Table 6 to form a rectangular grid pattern, to suit the sizes of the selected lath or panels. The grid should commence and finish within 150 mm or 6 in. of all perimeters. It is evident from Table 6 that the spacing of the cross-channels is related to the stiffness (or thickness) of the lath or panels intended to be supported. If a double layer of lath or panels is required (say for fire protection), then

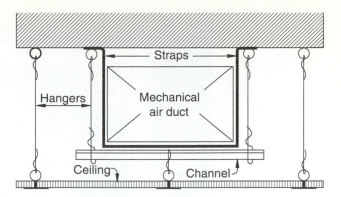

Figure 5   Soffit Arrangement

the minimum spacing is probably best, in the absence of other specific directions from the lath or panel manufacturer.

Soffit Framing

It is also possible to produce horizontal framing using regular stud members where circumstances prohibit the use of runners and channels, such as at the underside of wide heating ducts or across open areas or at other locations where hangers cannot be attached to structural elements of the building. These stud members should be cut to full length to bridge the gap in one piece, and should be double-screwed to supporting components, such as upper tracks which are themselves firmly secured to the vertical structural frame of the building. See Figure 5.

Table 7 gives some representative approximate spacings and spans for two widths of such members. Stud thickness should be 0.5 mm or 25 gauge minimum, and thicker where necessary. While Table 7 gives factors for single configurations, it is of course also possible to double each stud, thus increasing the span distances by about 25 percent; check with stud manufacturers for specific details of actual safe span factors.

Table 7
SPACING AND SPANNING
OF SOFFIT MEMBERS

Spacing		Span Length			
		63-mm or 2¹/₂-in. width		92-mm or 3⁵/₈-in. width	
mm	in.	mm	in.	mm	in.
300	12	2,400	96	2,700	105
400	16	2,200	90	2,500	100
600	24	1,900	80	2,200	90

(a) Raising frames

Specialty Framing

Every project has some minor structural anomalies requiring special consideration. This example shows erection and connection of a canopy frame for a picture window in a commercial building. (UBC Architecture)

(b) Plumbing frames

Accessories

Once the framing members have been erected and secured in position, the final task is to install a variety of accessories to accommodate electrical, mechanical, hardware, and other devices. (UBC Architecture)

Furring. This word refers to applying secondary framing members required to support finished plane surfaces in the building design (such as at dropped ceilings or ductwork) in addition to planes created by the primary structural frame of the building. Steps are as follows:

1. **Strapping.** Commence stud strapping at not more than 100 mm or 4 in. from horizontal or vertical edges, and continue with parallel straps across areas to be furred at not exceeding 400 mm or 16 in. on center; secure strapping with nails or screws—do not use tie-wire.

2. **Blocking.** Wherever fixtures (such as chalkboards, mirrors, vending machines, washbasins, and the like) have to be mounted against steel stud walls, blocking pieces consisting of cut lengths of tracking or studding have to be fitted into the stud frame system in the correct positions as indicated by the project drawings and secured with screws or nails, before the lath or paneling is installed. Similarly, junction boxes for electrical outlets and switches and other supports for mechanical devices have to be installed and secured in correct locations by screwing them to the tracks, studs, or blocking pieces.

3. **Lathing.** Refer to Section 09–200.

Other Items. These concern items of work such as the following, relative to specific design requirements:

Acoustic taping. Acoustic tape should be lightly compressed by hand and continuously adhered to the tracks before their installation; take care not to disturb or damage the tape while the tracks are being fastened in position.

Bracing. Some specifications or codes call for diagonal or lateral bracing straps to be laced through the punched-out service slots in steel stud framing members. These straps can be screwed or wired to the stud and track members at ends and at intermediate supports.

Cleanout. Spaces within steel stud framing should be cleaned out prior to installation of insulation or finishing materials.

Waterproof taping. Waterproof tape should be installed as described above for acoustic tape.

5.3 Precautions

This work is not particularly hazardous, apart from the normal risks and difficulties associated with working from ladders and scaffolding, using power-activated tools to cut and fasten the components, and handling long or heavy studs or tracks having sharp edges and corners. Precautions should be taken before firing powder-activated guns, to avoid injuries to people or damage to property caused by flying debris.

Cut ends of galvanized steel should be painted with a rustproof primer before installation. Workers should wear hardhats, eye protection, work gloves, and steel-toed boots. Care should be taken not to damage the edges or alignments of tracks, studs, or other components after installation. Care should also be taken not to damage the work of preceding trades during the processes involved in doing the work of this trade. All such damage must be rectified before subsequent work proceeds.

Section 05–500
Metal Fabrications

1.0 Introduction

1.1 General Issues

In every building, there are many standard metal items (such as frames, doors, ducts, pipes, windows, and so on) that can be satisfactorily classified in divisions of *MasterFormat* other than 05. Within Division 05, there are many specific building elements made with standard products (such as structural steel work, steel decking, and long-span joists) that are sufficiently discrete to merit separate sections of their own; some of these are dealt with elsewhere in this chapter. But there is a residual of custom-made metal items occurring in almost every building (such as small specialized frames, metal clips or brackets, brick support angles, service access covers and ladders, pipe rails, weather bars, and the like) that are by their general nature difficult to classify, and these are popularly referred to as *miscellaneous metals* and *metal specialties*, among other terms. *MasterFormat* designates all such items under its title of *Metal Fabrications*, and this convention will be followed in this book.

1.2   Design Aspects

The key word in the preceding paragraph is *custom-made*. If a specific metal item (such as an aluminum flagpole or a cast-iron drain cover) can be selected out of a manufacturer's catalog, delivered to the site, and installed at the building site with minimal or no modification, then by definition it is not a *metal fabrication*; it is a manufactured specialty and classified elsewhere under *MasterFormat*, perhaps in Division 10 or one of the other divisions.

In contrast, if some standard metal items, such as flat or angle bar steel and plate are selected and then cut, machined, and assembled to suit a special design unique to the subject building (such as a wrought iron balustrade or perhaps a frame to support a storage tank) and delivered for installation, then by definition these would be considered as *metal fabrications* and would be included in this division and section of *MasterFormat*.

Some items of metal fabrication are an essential part of other building components, such as clips and angles necessary to secure or support windows or curtain walls; such metal devices are not normally detailed on the contract or working drawings for the overall project, although they should show up on shop drawings. Other metal devices, such as non-typical reinforcement, supports for tanks or bins, purpose-made frames for louvers and grilles, access ladders in elevator pits, and so on, do have to be indicated in some overt manner either on the contract drawings or in the project manual, to ensure their inclusion in the contract for the project.

1.3   Related Work

Work closely connected to this section is described in the following sections, to which reference should be made:

05–050   Metal Fastening

Many other sections*

---

*Work in this section often has a close connection with work in many other sections, arising out of the need for various metal items to be custom made to support or connect other building components. It is therefore not deemed appropriate to list the titles of all such additional

2.0 Products

2.1 Materials

The materials most commonly encountered in metal fabrications are aluminum and steel in various forms and shapes; these metals are described in the corresponding Part 2.1 of the following sections of the book, to which reference may be made (to avoid repetition).

Aluminum. See Section 08–400.

Mild steel. See Section 05–100.

Stainless steel. See Section 07–600.

Other materials more occasionally encountered are listed below:

Copper. See Section 07–600 for commercial sheet and strip copper. Alloys of copper include brass which is a mixture of copper and zinc, and bronze which traditionally was a mixture of copper and tin but is now more commonly available in alloys with manganese, nickel, phosphorus, silicon, and other materials.

Lead. See Section 07–600 for commercial lead.

Zinc. This metal, prepared electrolytically from zinc blende ore, is mostly used as an anticorrosion protective coating on other metals, such as steel shapes and plates. It is not used in significant quantities in angle, plate, rod, or sheet form in construction projects, although some use is made of zinc in die-casting for special shapes, such as in items of finish hardware or special trim.

2.2 Accessories

Accessories encountered in conjunction with metal fabrications include a wide assortment of metal bolts, buttons, nuts, rivets, screws, sleeves, spacers, washers, welds, and similar fasteners, more specifically described in Section 05–050. The principal precautions to exercise in this regard are in the selection of the correct size and type to be compatible with the metals to be fastened together.

specific sections here, as has been done in other sections of the book. However, some examples are listed in Part 5.2 as an indication of the kinds of metal devices often encountered in buildings in conjunction with the work described in other sections.

3.0 Construction Aids

3.1 Equipment

For details of specific pieces of equipment required to fabricate metal items, refer to Part 5.2. In addition to such equipment, the metal fabricator will also have a need for truck transportation to move the products from plant to site. Such vehicles are often equipped with a light electric crane or hydraulically powered tailgate to facilitate loading and unloading of heavy items.

3.2 Tools

The tools required for this work consist of a composite of those described for ironworkers in Section 05–100, carpenters in Section 06–100, and sheet metal workers in Section 07–600.

4.0 Production

4.1 Crew Configuration

The labor component of metal fabrications comprises two main elements:

Fabrication. Most purpose-made metal devices for construction projects are made in a light industrial shop or plant; because of this, the processes involved are usually similar to those used in the manufacture of other factory-made commodities. As stated in other sections, it is beyond the scope of this book to investigate industrial and manufacturing processes in detail, although it may be said that in factories there is usually a greater proportion of machinery over manual labor, and greater control can be exercised over environment, supplies, quality, and production.

In a typical metal-fabricating shop, one or more crews, each consisting of perhaps up to three people (an ironworker, a sheet metal fabricator, and a semiskilled helper), will be assembled to attend to and operate the various machines which do the actual cutting and forming of the metal components, all under the direction of a supervisor. In addition to the actual production crew, it is usually necessary to have a competent draftsperson available to prepare and print shop drawings, although in many cases this element is contracted out to companies that specialize in this kind of work. It might be noted in passing that many items (such as joist hangers and masonry reinforcement devices) that are generally

considered by construction personnel to be within the ambit of work in this section are also in fact mass-produced in large-scale factories.

Installation. To install metal fabricated items or devices at the site, crew sizes are generally quite small, perhaps consisting of only one or two skilled tradespersons, such as ironworkers, sheet metal workers, or carpenters, working with occasional assistance from semiskilled helpers, and often in close conjunction with larger crews engaged in other work, such as the erection of structural concrete, steel, masonry, or wood framing, or perhaps the installation of specialties, such as toilet cubicles, conveyors, mechanical systems, and similar work.

4.2 Productivity

Typical fabrication rates in a small but well-equipped plant may average around 2 tons per hour for work of normal complexity. Installation may vary between 0.25 and 0.75 tons per hour. Table 1 gives a brief summary of data as an approximate guide to the fabrication and installation of some common components encountered in metal fabrications. One difficulty encountered which prevents determining such data with greater accuracy arises from the fact that few construction companies specifically distinguish the costs of installing fabricated metal components from the costs of installing the other building components of which the metal devices form only a part.

5.0 Procedures

5.1 Preparation

In almost every case, metal fabrication items require to be produced from shop drawings prepared by a specialist metal subcontractor. These detailed drawings are produced by a draftsperson extracting data from the contract drawings which indicate the general nature of the items to be fabricated. The draftsperson may be employed directly by the metal company or temporarily hired from an outside firm of specialists. The shop drawings are then presented to the designer for general approval before fabrication, delivery, and installation of the items.

Once the drawings have been approved, the specifics of manufacturing tolerances can be considered by the metal fabricator, and the components for each item can then be prepared, cut, assembled, fastened, and finished as necessary, either at the factory or at the site as appropriate.

Table 1
APPROXIMATE PRODUCTIVITY OF METAL FABRICATIONS (TONS PER HOUR)

Building Component	Fabrication	Installation
Anchor clips	0.5	0.5
Bar products	2.0	1.0
Beams and columns	1.5	0.5
Frames for tanks	1.5	0.5
Guards and frames	1.0	0.5
Gusset plates	1.5	1.0
Ladders, steel	1.5	0.5
Railings, pipe	1.5	0.5
Stairs and rails	1.0	0.5
Tanks and bins	1.5	1.5

5.2   Process

While it would be impractical to describe how to make every miscellaneous metal item that conceivably could be required for any building, it is possible to list the basic processes by which metals are usually **fabricated** by being cut and shaped, to describe some techniques of general **assembly** of components, and to identify some representative **examples** of specific fabricated items commonly encountered in typical buildings.

Fabrication.   The primary processes are listed in alphabetical order as follows:

Bending. Metal bars, rods, and tubes can be bent in a number of ways, by stretching them around a fixed and shaped form block, by drawing them around a

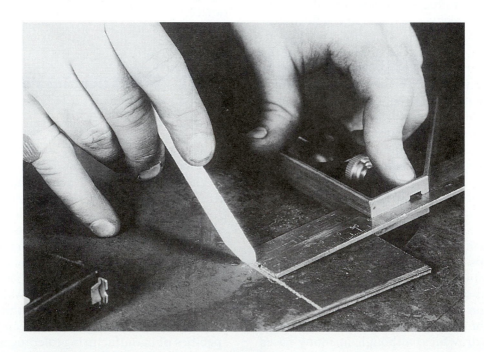

Marking
A set-square and chalk are used to mark out lines on light gauge steel plate. The plate will be later cut to size and shape by burning with acetylene gas or shearing by guillotine machine. (BCIT Audio-Visual Production)

Post Stirrup
Many standard components are available from stock to solve specific construction problems, such as this steel column stirrup used to secure the bottom of a post and keep it free from damp. (BCIT Building Technology)

Custom Framing
Almost every building requires some custom steel framing. In the example shown, workers are installing a special frame to support custom made fascia/sign panels on a commercial building. (UBC Architecture)

Precast Panel Connector
Buildings to which precast panels will be attached require metal plates corresponding to inserts in the panels for welded or bolted fastenings. One is shown installed inside the formwork. (BCIT Building Technology)

movable form block, by rolling them between a system of rollers, and by extruding them through hollow rotating heads.

Burning. Metal can be cut using a high-temperature flame, generated by burning oxyacetylene or other appropriate gas under controlled conditions.

Drilling. Metal components can be drilled in much the same manner as wood, using a power drill and hardened steel bits, to produce circular holes or elongated slots for the insertion of fastening or other devices.

Fastening: Refer to Section 05–050.

Forming. This process is a combination of several of the other processes, involving bending, pressing, and rolling of metal products to form shapes or profiles other than their original ones.

Machining. This general term refers to the cutting of metal in a rotating or reciprocating powered lathe or jig, to produce smooth ends, grooves, rings, or other features in the metal components as may be required by any specific construction design.

Pressing. This process requires the use of a press brake, on which long or wide sheets or plates can be bent under mechanical pressure to form corners or bends of almost any desired radius.

Punching. This process is similar to shearing, in that the metal to be punched is placed between a shaped die-block and a powered punch which forces the piece to be punched out down into the die and out of the parent member. The size and shape of both the die and the punch should be kept within fine tolerances for best results. Punching is often used to produce small square or rectangular openings in metal components.

Reaming. In some cases, holes through metal are punched slightly less than the final diameter required to receive fastenings; they are then reamed out by a rotating blade which cuts away the excess metal to produce a hole of exactly the correct size, with clean and smooth edges.

Ornamental Trim

Some metal fabrications are purely decorative, as shown in this example made from welded mild steel angles and rods, to which an aluminum-alloy automobile hubcap has been bolted. (UBC Architecture)

Custom Components

Most projects require some specialized metal items. In this example, mild steel sections and rods have been shaped and welded together to form a pair of simple yet attractive gates. (UBC Architecture)

Rolling. In this process, metal of one thickness is passed between smooth, patterned, or contoured rollers to produce metal of thinner or more uniform thickness, larger area, denser composition, or patterned appearance.

Sawing. Many metals can be sawn by hand or by machine, using reciprocating hacksaws or jigsaws equipped with specially toughened saw blades.

Shearing. Metal to be sheared is placed between a rigid straight-edged die and a powered blade which cuts down and along at a predetermined angle, much as scissors are used to cut paper. Rough cut edges can be burned, filed, or shaved smooth.

The fabricated metal items frequently require to be protected, often by applications of rust-inhibiting primers and occasionally by suitable cardboard boxes, wooden crates, or plastic bags, to facilitate handling and provide protection from physical damage during delivery to and storage at the site.

Assembly. Once the metal components have been fabricated by one or more of the processes listed above, they are ready either for composite assembly or for immediate finishing before installation as necessary and decorative finishing if appropriate.

Composite assembly may be entirely manual in the case of a few small lightweight items; they are simply put together on a workbench or on the shop floor. Larger, heavier, or repetitive items may require to be set up in special jigs or other restraints of some sort, to facilitate handling of framing components while other components are being fitted and fastened to them, and also to ensure accuracy of shape, dimension, and repetition in the finished composition.

Finishing of individual or composite items may involve dipping, plating, spraying, or other protective or decorative process (metal finishing is excluded from this book; refer to *MasterFormat* Section 05–700). Items fabricated with ferrous metal components generally require to be at least rustproof-primed, regardless of any other proposed finish.

Examples. Some representatives of specific custom-made metal items commonly encountered in typical buildings are listed in Table 2 by their *MasterFormat* division numbers. Divisions not listed are considered by the author to contain less significant amounts of such purpose-made fabricated metal items. Illustrations of many of these items are given in other sections.

5.3   Precautions

In most regions, there are strict regulations governing the conditions under which metal work should be done. Metalworkers should wear properly fitting protective clothing, such as steel-toed boots, leather or canvas aprons, work gloves, and especially eye and ear protection. They should remove all personal ornaments, such as bracelets, neckties, rings, wristwatches, and similar items that could get accidentally in moving machinery. Similarly, long hair should be constrained inside a cap or headband.

Table 2
EXAMPLES OF CUSTOM-MADE METAL ITEMS

Division	Fabricated Items
03	Clips for precast concrete components. Expansion joint plates and covers. Reinforcing steel bolsters.
04	Lintel plates and bonding bars. Heavy-duty flashing plates. Shelf angles for masonry.
05	Bumper posts and rails. Gusset plates for structural framing. Pipe railings and steel stairs.
06	Connections for wood posts and beams. Foot scraper bars and joist hangers. Metal brackets for wooden benches.
07	Frames for equipment enclosures. Storm clips for metal flashings. Weather bars at doors and windows.
08	Anchors for curtain wall systems. Mounting clips for frames at openings. Window security guards and enclosures.
09	Mat recess frames and stair nosings. Metal supports for furred spaces. Purpose-made lathing systems.
10	Clotheslines and games posts. Framing for canvas awnings. Supports for toilet partitions.
13	Access ladders and handrails. Monorail beams and supports. Specialty items for vaults.
14	Elevator hoistway and divider beams. Framed supports for conveyors. Metal trim around shaft openings.
15	Framed supports for tanks and bins. Louvers, vents, and grilles. Sleeves for pipe openings.
16	Cabinet enclosures for appearance. Framed supports for motors and fans. Grilles for protection of equipment.

CHAPTER O6
Woodwork

Section 06–050 Adhesives

1.0 Introduction

1.1 General Issues

Fastening devices and processes used in both metal-work and woodwork were described in Section 05–050. In this section, attention will be focused on the use of adhesives in carpentry in particular and in other work in general. Like Section 05–050, the format of this section has been modified to eliminate unnecessary parts.

By definition, an *adhesive* is a material having sticking or clinging properties, such that it may bond the surfaces of other materials together. Adhesives are variously and popularly referred to as cements, glues, gums, and pastes. Adhesives do not include patented hooked-fabric materials such as Velcro™ and similar fastening strips, which are occasionally encountered in buildings in conjunction with carpets, draperies, display panels, or canvas covers or awnings.

Adhesives technology has taken some remarkable strides in the past few years. Compared to the recent past when choice was limited to a few products made from natural ingredients, there is now a wide range of adhesives made from synthetic materials, some with astonishing capabilities. Many of these products have become available for construc-

tion through spinoff technology from the aerospace industry, wherein sophisticated materials have been developed for airframes, spacesuits, window sealants, and wing laminations. Some beneficial attributes of these newer products are high strength, long life, good stability, and low weight; resistance to creep, decay, heat, and moisture; short curing times, absence of odor, lower cost, and higher performance.

1.2 Design Aspects

In many cases, the attributes mentioned above permit designers to consider the use of smaller or thinner structural members, larger or heavier covering panels, longer or more shapely clear spans, and faster construction processes, among other benefits. Aspects of good design with adhesives include the necessity to have precise knowledge of adhesive materials and the service conditions under which they will be expected to perform. Typical situations might require accommodation of the forces of cleavage, compression, impact, movement, shear, tension, or vibration.

Some design applications might require resistance to creep, moisture, or heat; while others might be concerned with speed and cleanliness of application and rapidity of curing as main criteria. Cost, of course, is usually a significant factor in construction design decisions. Most adhesives used in construction are strong in tension, shear, and compression, but relatively weak in resistance to cleavage and peeling.

Good design will involve consideration of the compatibility of materials, curing times and temperatures, and the correct application technique necessary to ensure proper bonding. Adhesives used in construction should be selected and applied in accordance with the recommendations of the adhesive manufacturer, bearing in mind the recommendations of the makers of the products intended to be adhered. There is greater control over adhesives applied in a factory situation than those applied at the construction site. Although virtually all species of wood can be satisfactorily glued together, open-grain hardwoods are often more difficult to glue than close-grain softwoods; some hardwoods (such as beech, birch, and maple) are more difficult to glue than other hardwoods (such as mahogany, oak, and teak). Tests may be required to find the best adhesive to solve a design problem.

1.3 Related Work

The work described in this section is related to much of the work described in Chapters 03 through 10 of this book. Some typical uses of adhesives in construction include repairing damaged goods and joining components such as cabinets, carpets, ceramic tiling, claddings, floor systems, glazing systems, glued-laminated members, heavy timbers, insulation materials, metal fascias, paneling and trim, plastic laminates, precast concrete, prefabricated masonry and other panels, roofing systems, sandwich spandrel panels, sidings, stressed-skin plywood panels, trusses, underlays, vapor barriers, and wall coverings. Adhesives are used in rough and finish carpentry and in woodwork in general.

2.0 Classification and Selection

2.1 Classification

Adhesives are commercially available in the form of thin films, thick liquids, light powders, small pellets, and heavy solids in stick and rope form. They are also obtainable in a variety of colors as well as grays ranging from black to white; however, being usually concealed from view, color is not often considered to be significant. They can be classified in a number of ways, three of which are as follows: by

material origin, by **curing temperature,** and by **moisture resistance.**

Material Origin. This determines the compatibility of adhesives with the components being so fastened. (In case of doubt, a test for compatibility can be performed.) There are two categories:

1. **Organic or natural materials** such as casein and protein glue (made from animal or fish byproducts), starch or cellulose (such as the traditional flour and water pastes, tannin, and lignin), rubber cement and latex, and gums such as manila, rosin, and shellac. Most are fire resistant; many are water soluble.

2. **Inorganic or synthetic materials** such as acrylic, asphalt, butadiene, epoxy, furan, neoprene, polyurethane, polyvinyl, phenol, resorcinol, Thiokol, and urea (all made from various chemicals, oils, and plastics). Many so-called contact-bond adhesives are one or another of these types. Some are flammable; most are water resistant.

Many commercial adhesives contain a solution of formaldehyde (CH_2O), an extremely poisonous chemical. Such adhesives frequently have to be heated before use, and good ventilation is essential during application. They also tend to be expensive but are considered highly appropriate for many construction applications, because their performance

Wood Framing
Adhesives are often used in good quality wood framing to improve structural strength and reduce movement. It is also common to glue floor sheathing to joists to eliminate squeaking. (BCIT Building Technology)

advantages outweigh their application drawbacks. They are usually unsuitable for on-site applications, because of heating requirements.

Curing Temperature. This determines the suitability of adhesives for factory or site application. There are three categories:

1. **High heat,** requiring application in excess of 70 degrees C or 160 degrees F; exclusively for factory application.
2. **Medium heat,** requiring application between 70 and 30 degrees C or 160 and 80 degrees F; mostly for factory application and highly controlled on-site conditions.
3. **Low heat,** requiring application below 30 degrees C or 80 degrees F; suitable for on-site application.

Moisture Resistance. This determines the solubility of the adhesive in service conditions. There are three categories:

1. **Nonmoisture resistant,** intended for use in completely moisture-free conditions.
2. **Moisture resistant,** which can resist the effect of intermittent water in the form of water vapor.
3. **Waterproof,** which can withstand free water pressure for extended periods of time.

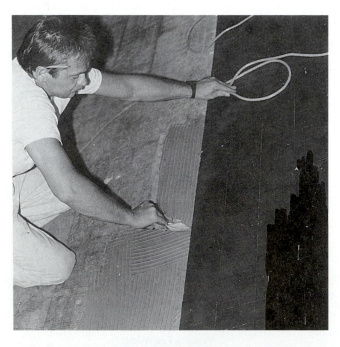

Floor Finishes
Most floor finishing materials are fixed to subfloors using patented adhesives. The glue is usually spread and leveled with a trowel then allowed to cure for a short period. (UBC Architecture)

2.2 Selection

Before describing specific applications, some general aspects of selection of adhesives alluded to in Part 1.2 can be identified for specific consideration:

Compatibility with the materials to be adhered.

Ease of mixing and applying.

Sufficient time available after mixing to permit proper working.

Shortest practical curing time.

Simplest practical curing process.

The need for resistance to moisture (or otherwise).

Freedom from harmful side effects of any type.

Economic considerations, such as availability, productivity (or workability), and cost will also have a bearing on the selection process, as do the relationships between the generic types of adhesives, the forms in which they are commercially available, the required methods of application, and the preferred uses, as summarized in Table 1 later. In many cases the materials used to make adhesives for construction are the same materials that are used to make plastics for construction, raising issues of compatibility requiring investigation.

3.0 Application

There are about as many techniques of adhesive application as there are types of adhesives. Of course, not all adhesives are used in construction; of those that are, not all are suitable for on-site application. This part describes application devices and procedures likely to be encountered on site; factory processes are beyond the scope of this book. To ensure satisfactory results in either category, reference should be made in every instance to the specific recommendations of the selected adhesive manufacturer regarding proper application of the particular product.

3.1 Tools and Equipment

Devices. The devices used in connection with on-site adhesive application are relatively simple and inexpensive; some of the more common ones are as follows:

Brushes of various sizes, similar to those used to apply paint and wallpaper, are often used to spread adhesives efficiently.

Table 1
CONSTRUCTION ADHESIVES
AND THEIR APPLICATIONS

Type	Form	Application	Common Uses
Animal	Liquid	Pressed hot	Furniture
Asphalt	Emulsion	Unpressed cool	Flooring
Casein	Powder	Pressed warm	Carpentry
Epoxy	Paste	Unpressed warm	Wood, metal
Melamine	Powder	Pressed warm	Cabinets
Neoprene	Mastic	Pressed hot	Metal joints
Phenolic	Liquid	Pressed hot	Plywood
Polyvinyl	Emulsion	Pressed warm	Millwork
Resorcinol	Liquid	Pressed warm	Glued-laminated members
Starch	Paste	Unpressed cold	Wall coverings
Urea	Liquid	Pressed cold	Wood veneers

Clamps, made of wood or steel, can be used to hold components together or in position while the applied adhesive cures.

Glue guns are used to electrically heat solid sticks of glue to softening point; they are handled similarly to soldering irons.

Putty knives have long, narrow, pliable steel blades attached to a wooden or plastic handle; they are used both to apply adhesives and to remove excess adhesive from surfaces.

Rollers, similar to those used to apply paint, are often used to quickly spread adhesives over large areas.

Sandbags are often used to provide temporary pressure on materials during the adhesive curing period. Such bags should be made of tightly woven canvas or solid plastic material, to prevent the sand contents from leaking out.

Spray guns of either compressed air or airless type can be used to spread fine liquid adhesives rapidly and uniformly.

Stirring sticks, made of wood, plastic, and occasionally metal, are used to mix adhesives and catalysts.

Trowels are frequently used to spread adhesives; such tools can have either smooth or serrated edges.

Dispensers. Most adhesives are dispensed directly from the containers in which they are supplied and delivered to the site; however, some (such as the two-component types) require mixing, heating, or other preparation before application. The thinner liquid adhesives can be applied by spray or brush; thicker, more viscous gums and pastes can be applied by roller or trowel. Sheet goods (such as wall coverings and carpets) usually require a uniform spread of adhesive using rollers, whereas unit goods (such as acoustic or ceramic tiles) can often be secured by placing a dab of adhesive on the backs at the corners using a putty knife. For more detail on applications for specific materials, refer to other sections of the book.

3.2 Application Techniques

Adhesive techniques can be classified by their **type** and by their difficulty of **application:**

Type. **Thermosetting** adhesives involve chemical reactions, sometimes with a catalyst, and usually with applied heat and/or pressure, whereas **thermoplastic** adhesives involve evaporation of a solvent, usually at room temperature.

Application. The main considerations are requirements for combinations of pressure and heat. On-site pressure can be considered as the force attainable by the use of ordinary carpenter's clamps or braces and manually placed weights or rollers. On-site heat can be considered as ranging from being slightly warmed (by hand or by the sun) to significantly heated (by propane gas or electrical power). Adhesives should not be applied during extremely cold, hot, or wet weather. Good ventilation to assist curing, remove vapors, and aid breathing is a requirement during all adhesive processes.

Four combinations of pressure and heat are discussed.

No Pressure, No Heat

In the following applications, no heat or sustained pressure is applied, beyond the initial force necessary to put the products properly in position. Such simple processes are very convenient.

1. Two-part epoxy glues consist of two components mixed cold: a base resin and an activating catalyst. The reaction takes about 5 minutes to develop full strength. Such glues require extreme care to ensure proper proportioning and mixing and they take some time to cure, but are otherwise ideal for many construction applications. Surfaces should be slightly roughened, with the active adhesive applied by spatula or brush to both areas to be bonded at ambient temperatures. The surfaces to be bonded are then quickly brought together and left to cure. Mixing tools, applicators, and containers are usually discarded after use.

2. Premixed, solvent-based, inorganic adhesives are frequently used to attach ceramic wall tiles to mortar or drywall surfaces. Such adhesives are poured or ladled onto floors and walls, spread with a serrated-edge (notched) trowel to establish uniform thickness, and tiles embedded before final curing occurs.

Structural Features
Glues can be used to permit designers to create unique structural forms. In this instance, the shaped laminations for a curved stair stringer have been glued and clamped in place. (BCIT Building Technology)

Walls and Ceilings
Many types of boards, panels, and ceiling tiles are secured in position with patented adhesives. The glue is usually applied in small daubs or patches to the rear face before installation. (BCIT Building Technology)

3. Premixed, water-based, organic adhesives are frequently used to attach wallpapers and vinyl cloths to wood or plaster substrates. Such adhesives are uniformly and thinly spread by brush or trowel over the back surface of the paper or cloth pieces to be applied, which are then positioned on the wall substrate and smoothed out by light rolling or brushing on the surface exposed to view.

Some Pressure, No Heat

In the following applications, no heat is required, but some temporary or permanent pressure is applied to sustain the products properly in position.

1. Polyvinyl acetate (or white glue) is a common, inexpensive, nontoxic adhesive product, best applied by uniformly brushing in a thin coat on one or both surfaces, followed by light clamping until cured. In its cured state, it tends to be brittle and thus susceptible to cracking. Brushes can be washed in water after use.

2. One-part elastomeric adhesives consist of rubber-based compounds. They form a flexible but reliable bond and are particularly useful in large applications, such as for securing plywood flooring to joists or panel boards to studs. Some of these products are mildly toxic if inhaled or swallowed. They are easily applied by being squeezed ready-mixed out of a tube (like toothpaste), using a reusable caulking gun device. Pressure can be applied by temporarily nailing or permanently screwing the flooring or wall panels to their supporting frames.

3. Liquid asphalt adhesives are specially formulated for use with resilient flooring tiles. Adhesive is poured or ladled onto the floor, quickly spread by squeegee, then struck off to a uniform thickness by serrated trowel, ensuring that at least 75 percent of the floor surface is covered. Tiles are carefully laid on top of prepared glued surfaces, lightly shoved into final position, and then continuously rolled or sandbagged to impart a slight pressure during the curing period.

Some Heat, No Pressure

In the following applications, some heat is required to assist the application process, but temporary or permanent pressure to sustain the products properly in position is usually redundant. Such processes are less convenient for site applications.

1. Rubber-based adhesives (often called contact cements) are very effective for use in fastening sheets of plastic laminate to millwork bases. The glue is slightly warmed, spread by brush or roller on both surfaces to be bonded, and allowed to cure for several minutes until dry but tacky to finger touch. Extreme care must be taken when bringing the two surfaces together, because more than half of the final bond strength will be achieved immediately upon contact; subsequent adjustment or movement is practically impossible without destroying the bond. Clamping is unnecessary. Such adhesives are quite toxic, and prolonged contact can cause skin and lung irritations.

2. Resorcinol-formaldehyde adhesives (also called structural binders) are often used in the manufacture of glued-laminated wood members because of their great strength and excellent resistance to the effects of moisture. Because the application temperatures are quite high (being well above the boiling point of water), they are not well suited to on-site uses. Some of them also require temporary clamping.

Finishing Features

Glues are often used to permit simple fastening of otherwise complicated components. In this instance, a curved strip of solid clear plastic is being glued to the front of a receptionist desk. (UBC Architecture)

Some Pressure, Some Heat

In the following applications, higher temperatures and sustained pressure are required to ensure proper bonding. Such complex processes are usually not convenient for site application.

1. Animal and casein glues are (now less often) used for the assembly of cabinets and furniture. They are occasionally encountered in on-site assembly of fine architectural woodwork such as courtroom benches and staircases.

2. Melamine, neoprene, and phenolic resin glues are used in factories to assemble plywood and metal sandwich panels.

3. Urea-formaldehyde adhesives, though strong, do not have very good moisture resistance, and are therefore not recommended for permanent exterior locations without appropriate chemical modification. They are often used to secure plastic laminates to substrates. Because they take a fairly long time to cure properly, clamping is required.

The content of the foregoing paragraphs is partially summarized for reference in Table 1 showing some construction adhesives, their common forms, their suggested application methods, and their customary uses:

There are a number of other adhesives (e.g., polymers such as acrylics, polyurethanes, and silicones) which are mostly used as admixtures in other cementitious products (such as concrete, grout, and mortar) to enhance the strength, moisture-proofing, and weathering properties of these other products. Their function is to bind together the particles of the materials to which they are added in an improved and approved manner.

3.3 Cleanup

Occasionally, excess and unwanted material will spill over or become lodged on a surface intended to be free of adhesive, requiring a cleanup operation. In general, the more quickly one can react to the spill, the better the probable result; it is therefore good practice to keep a supply of appropriate solvents close to the workplace. Depending on the adhesive selected, cleanup can be achieved by using one or more of a variety of liquid solvents, as follows:

For organic adhesives: alcohol, kerosene, turpentine, water.

For inorganic adhesives: acetone, benzene, toluene, xylene.

Gasoline should NEVER be used as a solvent or cleaner.

Solvent application is normally achieved by impregnating a clean cloth with the selected solvent, lightly dabbing or rubbing the affected areas, rinsing off any residue of adhesive or solvent, and allowing surfaces to air dry. If uncertain of results, a small area in an obscure location or a sample component can be tested before applying the solvent to the larger surfaces. Good ventilation is necessary, regardless of the solvent selected. Care should be taken to ensure that solvent materials do not adversely affect the main body of adhesive intended to remain.

Finally, it should be noted that it is also often possible to physically burn, chisel, grind, plane, or sand excess adhesive off the surface of many building components, provided such action does not impair the intended strength, durability, or appearance of the components intended to remain in service.

Section 06–100
Rough Carpentry

1.0 Introduction

1.1 General Issues

The word *carpentry* originates from Latin and specifically meant to build wooden wagons or *carpenta*; it now means generally to build with wood. Rough carpentry is one specialized division of carpentry work, being basically structural in nature and usually intended to be concealed from view in most types of building construction. The work of this trade comprises construction of the basic frame of essentially wooden buildings (or the wooden parts of buildings made primarily of other materials), such as floors, decks, walls, ceilings, and roof systems, as well as related structural arches, beams, bracings, lintels, and posts.

Rough carpentry work also embraces portions of other sections, such as the construction of temporary shoring and protection for excavation work (see Section 02–150) and the fabrication and erection of wooden formwork for concrete work (see Section 03–100). Although solid wood decking is considered by *MasterFormat* to be part of rough carpentry, it is described elsewhere in this book (Section 06–170) because of its closer relationship to prefabricated post and beam construction. Steel stud systems, though viewed as part of carpentry work in many regions, are assigned to light structural framing by *MasterFormat*, and are therefore described in Section 05–400.

The precise division of work between the sections listed in this chapter is not always as clearcut in practice as it may seem to be in this book. To a limited extent, an arbitrary though hopefully logical allocation of some information has been made, to improve clarity and to avoid repetition. In the real world of construction contracts, local practice will dictate the proper distribution of work in this discipline.

1.2 Design Aspects

The use of wood in building construction is an ancient tradition. Properly handled, wood can provide an exceedingly durable frame lasting for hundreds of years, as evidenced by the continuing existence of wooden buildings constructed in Europe at the time of Shakespeare (16th century) and in America after the arrival of the Pilgrim fathers at Plymouth Rock (17th century). It should be mentioned in passing, though, that most modern wooden buildings have an economic life not exceeding 50 years (representing about 2 percent depreciation per year) on the average, after which they are demolished or removed to make way for improvements. In some cases, demolition occurs as the result of material deterioration through neglect or poor design, but in most cases, most of the wood in such buildings is still perfectly sound—the buildings are demolished for economic reasons.

With respect to designing in wood in buildings, there is one good practical rule to remember: Because of the way trees grow (i.e., upward), wood shrinks **across** the grain much more than **along** the grain. For this reason, care must be taken to allow for significant movement wherever structural wood members are placed in horizontal positions relative to their longitudinal axis, such as the depth of beams, joists, plates, and rafters compared to the length of vertical bucks, cripples, posts, and studs. Although flakeboard, hardboard, particleboard, and plywood panels are relatively stable in this regard, allowance must still be made at edges for some lateral moisture movement parallel to the plane of the panel. Moisture content in softwood used in construction should not exceed 19 percent, which is the technical dividing line between so-called *dry* or seasoned lumber and *wet* or "green" lumber.

There are two major approaches to designing buildings using wood as the primary structural component: **frame and brace** construction and **post and beam** construction. This section deals with frame and brace construction; the next section deals with post and beam construction, including solid wood decking.

Frame and brace construction comprises two major techniques of wood design: **platform** framing and **balloon** framing. Both consist of floor systems, wall systems, ceiling systems, and roof systems. The first of these techniques is very common (indeed almost universal) in North America and will be explained in some detail below; the second is relatively uncommon because it is less economical (it requires more personnel, equipment, and time) and therefore will be only briefly outlined in this section.

With respect to the general brevity of description of design in this part of this section, it should be remembered that this is a book about construction methodology, not construction detailing; many other books deal much more extensively and authoritatively with details of carpentry framing. For specific design requirements regarding grades and species of wood as well as dimensions and spans for joists, rafters, and lintels; sizes and spacings of studs, stiffening of framed members; wall plates and firestoppings; sheathing types and thicknesses, and so on, reference should be made to local building codes and practice.

Platform Framing. In this technique, the floor system rests on a sill plate and extends to the outermost edge of the building, forming a platform on which the exterior and interior wall system can be initially assembled, temporarily braced, and permanently supported. These floor and wall systems can be repeated upward for three or four stories, depending on local regulations and design requirements. The ceiling system is installed on top of the uppermost wall plates, followed by or in conjunction with the roof system. For details of installation of these various framing systems, see Part 5.2. See Figure 1.1.

Balloon Framing. In this technique, the wall studs rest directly on the sill plate and extend upward for the full height of the wall, usually not exceeding two stories; the lowest floor joists also rest on the sill plate adjacent to the studs. The studs are notched for the insertion of a horizontal plate to support the upper floor joists. Depending on floor loading, an additional cripple may be installed to carry the upper floor loads down to the sill plate. Floor and wall frames are blocked or bridged for stiffness and firestopping, and sheathing is applied to form the interior floor and exterior wall planes. The ceiling and roof systems are identical to those described above for platform frame construction. The primary advantage of balloon frame construction is the avoidance of significant shrinkage at the intersection of vertical walls and horizontal floor platforms, particularly useful if the exterior veneer of the building consists of uninterrupted areas of stucco plaster or masonry. See Figure 1.2.

In both of the framing techniques described above, there is the obvious necessity to cut out and

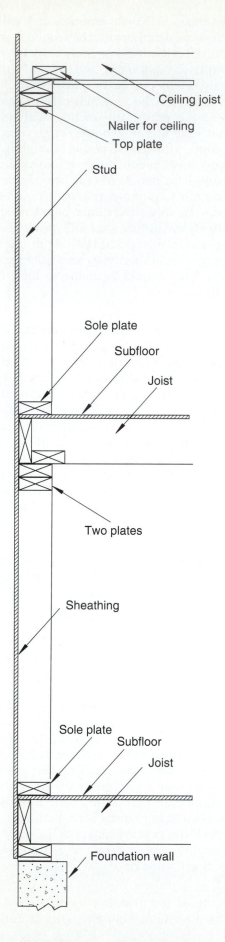

Figure 1.1 Platform Framing

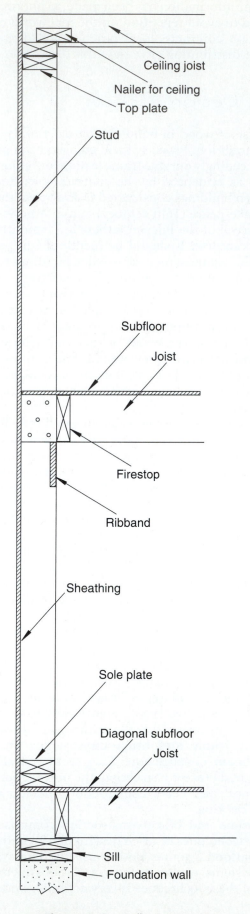

Figure 1.2 Balloon Framing

(a) Forklift loading

(b) Flatbed delivery

Materials Delivery

Dimension lumber and sheet plywood (or particleboard) for rough carpentry framing is usually pre-cut and prepackaged at the timber mill and delivered in bulk on pallets by flatbed truck. (BCIT Building Technology)

frame around openings for stairwells in floor systems, doors and windows in wall systems, and skylights, chimneys, and vents in ceiling and roof systems. In general, headers, joists, lintels, or studs around openings are doubled, as are top plates for loadbearing walls. In many regions, studs at corners are at least doubled, often tripled, not only for strength but also (where required) to provide solid backing for securing the edges of wall linings on both interior and exterior faces of the wall. Holes must also be left, cut out, or drilled for plumbing pipes, electrical cables, and other building services or components.

1.3 Related Work

Work closely connected to this section is described in the following sections, to which reference should be made:

01–050	Field Engineering
02–150	Protection
03–100	Formwork
06–170	Prefabricated Wood
06–200	Finish Carpentry
06–400	Architectural Woodwork
07–200	Insulation
09–000	Finishes

2.0 Products

2.1 Materials

Wood is an abundant naturally occurring material, fairly strong relative to weight, fairly elastic yet stiff enough to be useful, easily worked, and relatively inexpensive. Being organic, wood is susceptible to attack by fire, fungus, insects, moisture, rot, and vermin. The products used for rough carpentry work, although mostly made from wood or wood byproducts for obvious reasons, are quite varied in their specific forms and characteristics. Wood occurring naturally, from which comes the lumber used in rough carpentry, is either **softwood** or **hardwood**; **plywood** is a manmade composite:

1. **Softwood** trees are evergreen, have narrow needles, and produce cones; they tend to grow tall and straight. They have a fairly close grain in cross section, and tend to be mostly used for structural purposes in rough carpentry work. Some examples of common softwoods include cedar, fir, hemlock, larch, pine, and spruce. Sizing and grading of building products made from softwood are described later in this section.

2. **Hardwood** trees are described in Section 06–200, Part 2.1.

3. **Plywood** is a composite manmade material, in which thin continuous laminations of wood are peeled from selected logs and then glued and laid in (usually) odd numbers of plies, having their grains running at right angles to one another. The assembled laminations are then heat-treated, pressed, and trimmed to exact thicknesses and sizes. The reason for having an odd number of plies is to produce a balanced system about the central core to minimize warpage and to ensure that the face grains on both sides of the finished product run in the same direction. Plywood grading is described later in this section.

Lumber. The purpose in grading softwood lumber is to determine the suitability of each cut piece for specific end uses. Experienced graders look at each piece as it passes them on the sawmill green chain, directly assess its overall characteristics measured against the known requirements for each grade, and mark it accordingly. The wood is cut into nominal lengths varying between 2.4 and 8 m or 8 and 24 ft., rising in increments of 60 cm or 24 in.

The cut wood is initially graded into three major categories:

1. **Structural lumber,** intended for specific engineered applications.
2. **Yard lumber,** intended for general construction use.
3. **Shop lumber,** intended to be further reduced to produce high-quality boards for use in cabinetwork, furniture, and trim.

Yard and shop lumber is graded visually; structural lumber is graded by machines which test its resistance to specific stresses. In all softwood grading systems, the highest quality is listed first, the lowest last. Within each grade, an allowance is made for some minor mixing of species; for example, in a mill order for a load of douglas fir, there may be a few pieces of spruce or hemlock.

On-Site Saw Mill
It is customary to set up a central location on site for the efficient trimming of dimension lumber to fit the building. A table saw is located over a strong bench and beneath a canopy. (BCIT Building Technology)

U.S. Grading Standards

In the United States, there are several authorities having jurisdiction over softwood grading. One of these was the National Bureau of Standards (NBS), now replaced by the National Institute of Science and Technology (NIST); it publishes Voluntary Product Standards, one of which (VPS 20–70) deals with lumber grading. There are several regional authorities, such as the Western Wood Products Association (WWPA) and the West Coast Lumber Inspection Bureau (WCLIB), both of which use grading systems essentially consistent with the national standards, although specific titles may vary. The primary grading subdivisions of VPS 20–70 follow:

1. **Boards.** In this category, boards are divided into two primary grades:

   a. **Appearance** grades are classified as follows:

      Selects: B and better, C, D.

      Finish: Superior, prime, E.

      Paneling: Clear, #2 common, #3 common.

      Siding: Superior, prime.

   b. **Sheathing** grades are classified as follows: No. 1, No. 2, No. 3, No. 4, No. 5 common.

2. **Dimension lumber.** In this category, dimension lumber is graded as described under Canadian Grading Standards below.

3. **Timbers.** In this category, heavy beams, posts, and stringers are graded into select structural, No. 1, No. 2, No. 3.

Canadian Grading Standards

In Canada, softwood lumber is graded under a system developed by the National Lumber Grading Authority (NLGA); this system is consistent with the U.S. standard mentioned above (VPS 20–70). In particular, dimension lumber commonly encountered in rough carpentry work is subdivided into five primary grades, three of which have secondary grades, as follows:

1. **Structural framing.** This grade is intended for light wooden structures which require engineering analysis. There are four secondary grades: select structural, No. 1, No. 2, and No. 3; each is assigned factors indicating its structural function in terms of bending, shear, and so on. The first two are intended for use where visual appearance may also be a factor.

Wood Products
The variety and availability of wood products is immense. Some examples of dressed dimension lumber, composite joist members, and patented fiber-oriented beams and posts are shown. (Trus-Joist McMillan)

2. **Light framing.** This grade is intended for general construction of standard wood-framed buildings. There are three secondary grades: construction, standard, and utility. The first two are entirely suitable for standard joists, rafters, ridge boards, and so on; the utility grade might be best used for rough bases, blockings, and nailers.

3. **Stud lumber.** This grade is solely intended for use as vertical studs and to be concealed from view in quality work. There are no significant secondary grades. In many localities, such stud lumber can be purchased with precision end trimming (called PET lumber by some), cut to suit the exact size between bottom and top plates in framed construction.

4. **Joist and plank.** This grade is similar to the first one, but is intended for larger structures having heavier members. Like the first grade, there are four secondary grades, with identical names: select structural; No. 1, No. 2, and No. 3.

5. **Appearance framing.** As the name implies, this grade is intended for use where fine architectural appearance is significant; it is also the most expensive grade. Each piece is virtually free of defects of any kind, especially visual blemishes. There are no secondary grades.

   In all of the foregoing grades (except appearance), there is also an **economy** grade, suitable only for limited use in unimportant and nonstructural temporary work. Design values are assigned to all dimension grades except economy.

Plywood.   Plywood is available in two basic categories, **exterior** and **interior**, distinguished by the type and quality of the glue used to bond the laminations. Edges may be plain butt, tongue-and-groove, or beveled. In both categories, there are four classes, as follows:

1. **Softwood.** Also known as plain or standard plywood, having all core and face laminations made of softwood. It is graded as shown below.
2. **Hardwood.** Similar to standard plywood, but having the face laminations of selected hardwood veneers. It is described in more detail in Section 06–200.
3. **Overlaid.** Similar to standard plywood, but having a resin-impregnated melamine paper face-bonded to one or both faces. There are two classes: medium- and high-density overlay.
4. **Specialty.** Refer to Section 06–200.

Plywood products are usually stamped on their back faces or edges by the producing mill to show maker's name, species groups of woods, grades of veneers, whether suitable for interior or exterior use, and so on. The basic grades for softwood plywoods used in the United States and Canada are shown below.

U.S Grading

One U.S. system uses letter grades, such as A–A, A–B, A–D, and B–D. Softwood plywoods are graded on the basis of the quality of face and back laminations; inner plies are usually "D" quality.

Canadian Grading

Softwood plywoods are graded by a system of words and numbers to indicate quality, species, origin, number of plies, and so on. The system uses phrases like "good 2 sides," "good 1 side," "select (2 types)," "overlaid (2 types)," and "sheathing (2 types)." In this context, the word "good" means free of objectionable defects and "select" means very good quality all around.

Dimensions

Standard sizes for most plywood panels are nominally 1,200 × 2,400 mm or 48 × 96 in.; thicknesses

commonly range from 6 to 19 mm or ¼ to ¾ in. Other sizes and thicknesses can be ordered.

Standards

In the United States, plywood quality is governed by PS–1 (66) and CS–45 (55), among others. In Canada, plywood quality is governed by CSA O–121 and O–151, among others.

Other Products.   In addition to the dimension lumber and plywood described above, there are many other products in common use in wood construction. Some of these are described.

Particleboard

There are three principal groups of particleboard used in rough carpentry work:

1. **Hardboards.** These are mostly used for finish carpentry, and are therefore described in Section 06–200.
2. **Pulpboards.** These boards consist of small wood chips or cellulose particles, formed with specially selected resins under heat and pressure to produce large, thin, flat sheets or panels which are in some cases not as durable or strong as hardboard panels. There are two main categories (exterior and interior); there are three density grades (A, B, and C), with two strength classes in each grade. Surfaces can be finished with plastic coatings or laminates, colored paints or stains, or other treatments. Pulpboard is often used as a backing for laminate-faced cabinetwork and cork tackboards and as a core for doors and lightweight partitions, among many other uses.
3. **Waferboards.** These boards consist of small wood wafers, cut explicitly for this purpose from debarked aspen logs and bonded with a waterproof phenolic resin under rigidly controlled factory conditions. In some types, the wafers are deliberately aligned or oriented during manufacture and are thus known as oriented strand boards (OSB) or oriented wafer boards (OWB). Such boards exhibit a high degree of uniformity, strength, and appearance. They serve many of the same purposes as plywood.

Standard sizes for most particleboard products are 1,200 × 2,400 mm or 48 × 96 in. For pulpboard, thicknesses range from 3 to 50 mm or ⅛ to 2 in. Thicknesses for waferboard are similar to those for plywood, listed above. Approximate average weights of standard full-sized panels are shown in Table 1; variations will be caused by different wood species, glue types, panel sizes, and moisture contents.

Table 1
APPROXIMATE WEIGHT OF PARTICLEBOARD AND PLYWOOD

Type	Panel Weight kg	Panel Weight lb.
Hardboard:		
Thinnest	5	12
Thickest	12	25
Pulpboard:		
Thinnest	8	18
Thickest	80	180
Waferboard:		
Thinnest	12	27
Thickest	35	80
Plywood:		
Thinnest	15	35
Thickest	40	90

Building Papers

There are several types of building papers used in rough carpentry work:

Dry kraft paper. Made from a mixture of treated wood pulp and shredded paper, dried and rolled into large sheets.

Asphalt sheathing paper. Similar to dry kraft paper, but saturated with asphalt to improve its damp-proofing capabilities.

Reinforced building paper. Similar to asphalt sheathing paper, but reinforced with glass fibers to improve strength; such papers are usually laminated in two or more layers.

Black waterproof paper. Similar to reinforced paper, but made from jute fibers, rolled and pressed, saturated and coated with refined tar, then laminated.

Plastic-coated paper. Similar to black waterproof paper, but omitting the tar and with one or both sides coated with plastic.

Rolls of sheathing papers are 2.4 × 90 m or 8 × 300 ft. Standard roll sizes for other papers are 3 m or 10 ft. in length and either 0.9, 1.2, or 1.5 m or 3, 4, or 5 ft. in width.

Vapor Control Products

This is a rapidly developing segment of building technology, involving two basic material categories:

1. **Vapor retarders.** These have some permeability of moisture, air, or gases, and include asphalt sheathing paper as described above as well as thin polyethylene plastic films, which are available in either transluscent or mat form in various thicknesses and qualities.

2. **Vapor barriers.** These have virtually zero permeability. For situations requiring a high degree of resistance, barriers of denser polyvinyl and other plastics are available.

Both categories are available in rolls having widths of approximately 2, 3, 4, and 5 m or 6, 8, 12, and 20 ft., and lengths virtually to order.

2.2 Accessories

Many of the accessories used in rough carpentry have been described in more detail in other sections, to which reference can be made to avoid repetition:

Metal fasteners: Section 05–050

Steel studs: Section 05–400

Adhesives: Section 06–050

Plastic laminates: Section 06–200

Wood preservatives: Section 06–300

3.0 Construction Aids

3.1 Equipment

This work often requires the use of portable air compressors to operate staple guns and air hammers, electric planes, radial arm saws, and jigsaws, as well as a variety of scaffolding or motorized scissor-lift platforms to give access to work at higher levels.

3.2 Tools

Common carpentry tools are required for this work, as well as an assortment of augers, awls, calipers, chisels, files, markers, miterboxes, planes, rasps, routers, sanders, saws, squares (combination, framing, set, and try), stair gauges, and wrenches of various kinds and sizes.

4.0 Production

4.1 Crew Configuration

Carpentry crews can vary all the way from one trades-person working alone up to four or five journey-man carpenters, working with one or two helpers, under the supervision of a full-time carpenter fore-man. An average crew might consist of two or three carpenters, with one of them designated as a part-time foreman, working in conjunction with one carpenter's apprentice. There is an increasingly higher proportion of power-assisted tools being utilized in commercial carpentry work; this is having the effect of improving production. On large projects, two or more crews may be allocated to various parts of the work; in some cases, a crane operator and crane may be required to move heavy components such as roof trusses or beams into position. Productivity factors given next assume the use of power tools wherever practical.

4.2 Productivity

This part is divided into three portions: an expla-nation of **lumber volume measures, productivity in general wood framing,** and **productivity in panel work.**

Lumber Volume Measure. Most reference books used by estimators show labor productivity factors for rough carpentry framing in volume units; most lumberyards also quote lumber prices in volume units. The units are either **cubic meters** in metric measure or **board feet** in imperial measure. It is necessary to understand these material units to make sense of rough carpentry productivity times and costs.

Metric Measure—Cubic Meters

In metric measure, calculations are based on **actual** dimensions. To convert linear meters (m) of lumber to cubic meters (m³), multiply the cross-sectional area of the piece by its length. For example, a common stud measures 38×89 mm and is 2.4 m long. Its volume is therefore (0.038 m $\times$ 0.089 m $\times$ 2.400 m) 0.008 m³; if there are 30 such studs, the total volume is (0.008 m³ $\times$ 30) 0.24 m³. Conversely, to find out how many meters of 89×89 mm fence posts one might get out of 10.0 m³ of treated cedar, divide the volume (10 m³) by the cross-sectional area (0.089 m $\times$ 0.089 m = 0.008 m²) to produce the total length of 1,250 m. If one knows that each post is (say) 2.5 m long, then one can divide 1,250 by 2.5 to find that

there are 500 pieces in the bundle. To confirm that this is correct, multiply all dimensions by the quan-tity (0.089 m $\times$ 0.089 m $\times$ 2.5 m $\times$ 500) to produce (approximately) 10 m³.

Imperial Measure—Board Feet

In imperial measure, calculations are based on **nomi-nal** dimensions. To convert linear feet (lf) of lumber to board feet (bf), divide the cross-sectional area of the piece in nominal inches by 12 and multiply the result by the length of the piece in feet. For example, a single fir rafter, $2 \times 8''$ and 24 lf long, contains $(2 \times 8 = 16 / 12 = 1.33 \times 24)$ 32 bf. If there are 31 such rafters, the total volume is (32×31) 992 or ap-proximately 1,000 bf. Conversely, to convert board feet to linear feet, divide the total board feet by the cross-sectional area divided by 12. For example, to find out how many linear feet of $2 \times 4''$ studs there might be in 160 bf of lumber, divide 160 by $8/12$ (or 0.67) to produce the answer, 240 lf. If each stud is 8 lf long, then there are 30 studs in that bundle. To confirm that this is correct, check by multiplication $(2 \times 4 = 8 / 12 = 0.67 \times 8 \text{ ft.} \times 30 \text{ pc.} = \text{approximately}$ 160 bf).

Dimension Equivalents

The abbreviation fbm* stands for foot board mea-sure. One thousand board feet is called 1 Mbf (as "M" means 1,000 in this context), and prices are often quoted by suppliers on this basis. The letter "C" is used to signify 100, as in Csf, meaning 100 square feet. It is also sometimes useful to know dimensions in metric units that correspond to imperial units. Some examples of common lumber dimensions are given in millimeters in metric and inches in imperial in Table 2.

To convert cubic meters of dimension lumber approximately to board feet, first multiply the quan-tity by 35.314 to determine cubic feet, then multiply the result by 12.005 to determine board feet (or mul-tiply once by 423.945 [35.314 $\times$ 12.005]). Con-versely, to convert board feet approximately to cubic meters, first multiply by 0.084 to determine cubic feet, and then by 0.028 to determine cubic meters (or 0.084 $\times$ 0.028 = 0.002352). For example, 15 m³ = $(15 \times 35.314 \times 12.005)$ = 6,360 bf; conversely, 6,360 bf = $(6,360 \times 0.084 \times 0.028)$ = 15 m³. The results are accurate to within 0.5 percent.

Productivity in Framing. In Table 3, productivity factors for work in dimension and board lumber are

---

*fbm is an equivalent term for bf.

Table 2
EQUIVALENT LUMBER DIMENSIONS

Metric (mm)	Imperial (in.)	
Actual	Nominal	Actual
38 × 64	2 × 3	1.5 × 2.5
38 × 89	2 × 4	1.5 × 3.5
38 × 140	2 × 6	1.5 × 5.5
38 × 184	2 × 8	1.5 × 7.25
38 × 235	2 × 10	1.5 × 9.25
38 × 286	2 × 12	1.5 × 11.25

given in approximate man-hours per unit volume, unless otherwise stated. Work is assumed to be done on medium-sized projects under normal working conditions.

Productivity in Panels and Sheets. In Table 4, productivity factors for work in panels and sheets are given in approximate man-hours per unit area, unless otherwise stated.

5.0 Procedures

5.1 Preparation

An area of the site close to the center of carpentry activity is selected to set up the on-site sawmill. Suit-

Table 4
PRODUCTIVITY IN PANELS AND SHEET GOODS

Type of Work	Man-Hours per Area (10 m² or 100 ft.²)
Plywood panels:	
Subfloors, small	1.0
Floor decks, large	0.5
Walls, exterior	1.2
Walls, interior	1.0
Roofs, flat	1.4
Roofs, sloped	1.6
Hardboards	1.8
Particleboards	1.5
Sheet goods:	
Building papers	0.3
Vapor barriers	0.5

Table 3
PRODUCTIVITY IN FRAMING MEMBERS

Type of Work	Man-Hours per Volume	
	m³	Mbf*
Western platform framing:		
Floors, framed:		
Plates	10	24
Joists	8	18
Bridging	25	60
Walls, stud:		
Exterior, simple	13	30
Exterior, complex	17	40
Interior, simple	10	25
Ceilings, framed	8	18
Roofs, framed:		
Flat, simple	9	20
Sloped, simple	13	30
Sloped, complex	17	40
Balloon framing:		
Walls:		
Exterior, simple	17	40
Exterior, complex	21	50
All other framing	(as for western platform)	
Other work:		
Blocking	21	50
Furring	25	60
Sheathing		
Floors, joisted	7	15
Walls, horizontal	8	18
Walls, diagonal	9	20
Roofs, flat	9	20
Roofs, sloped	13	30
Strapping:		
Floors	15	35
Walls	17	40
Ceilings	19	4

*1 Mbf = 1,000 × 0.002352 = 2.352 m³; or 1 m³ = 423.945/1,000 = 0.424 Mbf.

able quantities of assorted dimension lumber, decking, roof trusses, sheathing boards or plywood, rough hardware, and other components are assembled in covered stockpiles or sheds close to the sawmill.

Lumber, decking, and panels should be stored flat and level, with protection from dampness and provision for air to circulate; finished faces, edges, and corners should be protected from damage. These components are selected, measured, and cut according to the project drawing and specification requirements, then set aside for later incorporation into the building frame. Small items, such as rough hardware, can be moved around the site by hand or wheelbarrow; larger items, such as loads of lumber or plywood, can often be conveniently moved around and raised into position by forklift tractor or by the construction crane.

There are several methods to secure the building frame to the foundation; one common way is described in this paragraph. Before the framing can be started, 13-mm or $1/2$-in. threaded steel anchor bolts are set into the tops of the concrete foundations, spaced at about 1.5-m or 5-ft. intervals. A continuous strip of asphalt sheathing paper is then placed over these bolts and pressed down onto the top of the foundation; alternatively, a plastic sill sealer may be used. A wooden sill plate is prepared with holes drilled to correspond to the bolt spacing, placed on top of the paper, and secured in position with washers and nuts. Care must be taken to ensure that the sill plate is level and on solid bearing throughout its entire length. See Figure 2.

5.2 Process

The methodology used to construct **platform-framed** floors, walls, and roofs is outlined in detail in this part. Some additional aspects of **balloon framing** are also described, followed by some comments on **other items** of rough carpentry work.

Platform Framing

Floor System

The lowest floor joists are selected or cut to length, then placed by hand at 400 mm or 16 in. on center (oc), to span between foundation wall sill plates. Joist ends are lined up; a header joist is placed across the ends and nailed to them. Intermediate joints are allowed to overlap; openings at hatches or stairwells are framed. Blocking or cross-bridging is inserted to stiffen the joists at midpoints if required by code.

After checking to ensure that the frame is square and level, the floor frame is then toenailed to the sill plate at 300 mm or 12 in. oc. The subfloor, usually consisting of tongue-and-groove plywood 19 mm or $3/4$ in. thick, is laid down by hand, lightly tapped to ensure a good fit (but not too tight, to allow for moisture movement), and secured to the frame by gluing and/or machine nailing at not less than 150 mm or 6 in. oc. At any point where the sill plate is interrupted, metal joist hangers should be installed to support the joists. See Figure 3.

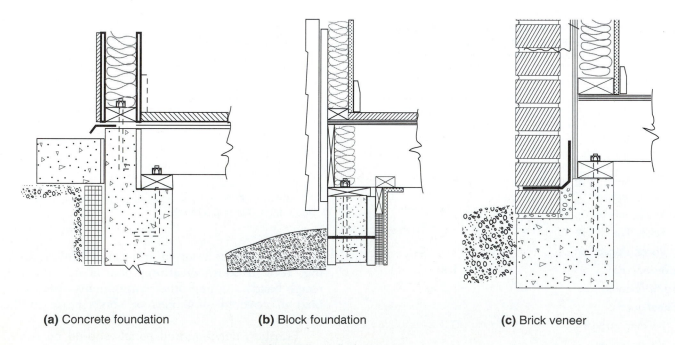

(a) Concrete foundation   **(b)** Block foundation   **(c)** Brick veneer

Figure 2 Sill plate Sections

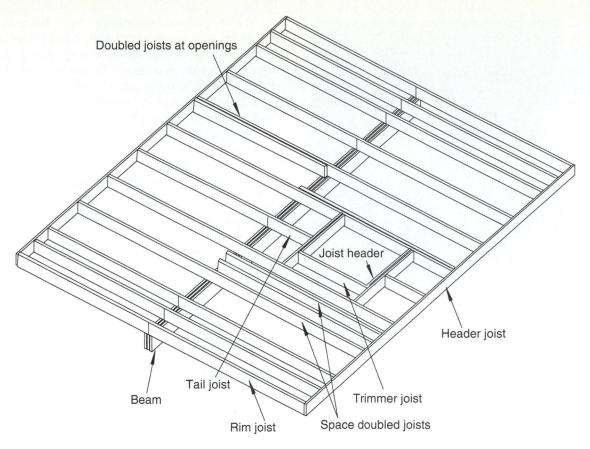

Doubled joists at openings

Joist header

Header joist

Beam

Tail joist

Rim joist

Trimmer joist

Space doubled joists

Figure 3 Floor System

(a) Basic framing

(b) Cross bridging

Framed Floor Systems

Floor joists are laid out according to the building plan. Joists and trimmers are doubled where necessary. Cross bridging is used to stiffen joists and minimize effects of warping. (BCIT Building Technology)

Joist Hangers
Where floor or ceiling joists abut headers or trimmer joists, metal joist hangers are often used for support. There are many types and shapes; the ones shown here are simply nailed. (BCIT Building Technology)

Wall System

Studs are selected from stock or cut to length, then placed by hand at 400 mm or 16 in. oc, horizontally on top of the finished floor platform. Ends are lined up, and top and bottom plates are nailed in position. Openings for doors and windows are framed as necessary; girts or blockings are installed where necessary to stiffen the framing. Sheathing for exterior walls is applied as described above for floor sheathing; openings in sheathing are cut out by electric saw.

Walls without sheathing may have diagonal braces let into the studs or flat metal straps applied to the surface of the studs, at a 45-degree angle to help stiffen the structure. The entire wall system is then raised by hand to the vertical plane, positioned, plumbed, temporarily braced, and secured to the floor platform with common nails at 30 mm or 12 in. oc. Interior unsheathed framed walls are similarly constructed and raised, with a second continuous top plate added to tie the system together and distribute upper floor or roof loads. See Figure 4.

Roof System

This part of the structure can be one of two forms: sloped or flat. Each can be completed in one of two ways: site construction or prefabrication. Both forms and processes are described.

Sloped Roofs

1. Using **site construction,** ceiling joists are raised by hand and placed at 400 mm or 16 in. oc to rest on and be nailed to the upper wall plates. The ridge board is then raised and temporarily braced, and the rafter members are cut and fitted between the ceiling joists and the ridge. Framing at gables, hips, and valleys is completed next, followed by the installation of necessary primary collars and ties and secondary cross-bridging, blocking, firestopping, and framing around openings. Depending on the roofing system selected (refer to Section 07–500 for suggestions), the roof frame can then be finished either with continuous sheathing or by the installation of spaced continuous battens. A typical arrangement is shown in Figure 5.

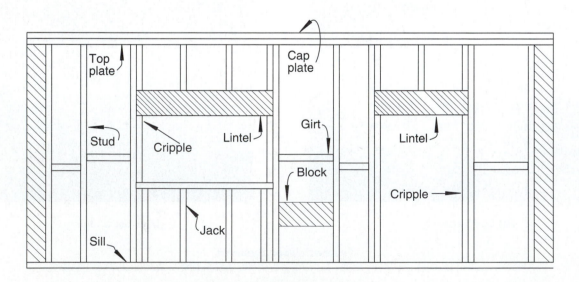

Figure 4   Wall System (Platform)

Lower Wall Systems
A dampproof course is laid to separate the wall plate from the concrete. Vertical studs are raised, toenailed to the plate, and finished with a double top plate to distribute forces. (UBC Architecture)

(a) Foundation detail

(b) Simple framing

(a) Assembly

(b) Erection

Upper Wall Systems
Upper framed wall systems are assembled on the flat floor deck, raised manually into position by a work crew, temporarily braced, and then permanently fastened to the floor framing. (BCIT Building Technology)

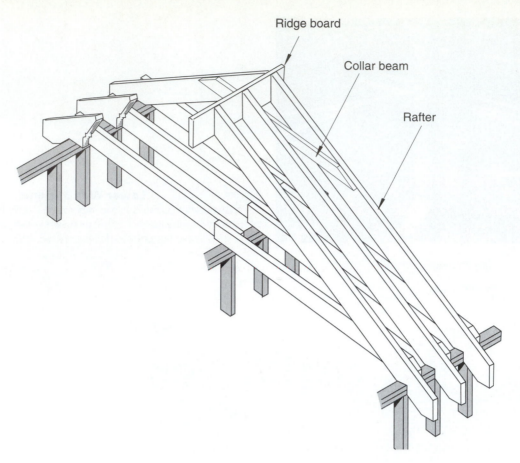

Figure 5 Sloped Roof Framing

(a) Truss stockpile

(b) Trusses positioned

Roof Systems
Because of high labor costs, many roof framing assemblies are factory assembled, delivered by truck, stockpiled, and installed by forklift, as shown here. (BCIT Building Technology)

2. Using **prefabrication,** the trusses are raised by derrick or crane, temporarily braced, and placed at not more than 600 mm or 24 in. oc on the upper wall plates to which they are secured by nailing. Gables, hips, valleys, ridges, and openings are individually framed on site as described in the preceding paragraph.

Flat Roofs

1. Using **site construction,** flat roofs are assembled as described above for platform-framed floors, with one modification: a slight slope must be imparted to the system, to facilitate the drainage of rainwater off the roof system. This can be accomplished in one of two ways: Either tapered or feathered slips are secured to the tops of the horizontal joists or rafters before the sheathing is applied; or the wall frames at one side of the building can be made to be slightly higher than those at the opposite side by installing an additional wall plate. A typical arrangement is shown in Figure 6.

2. Using **prefabrication,** open web trusses or closed web joists are installed; for details, refer to Section 06–170. Slopes must be imparted as described in the preceding paragraph.

Balloon Framing

Floor System

The lowest floor joists are cut and placed as decribed for platform-framed floors. Joist ends are lined up with the outside edge of the sill plate; no header is used. Blockings are inserted, openings are framed, and after wall studs have been erected, floor sheathing is applied as before.

Wall System

Studs are cut to length for the full wall height, notched for the upper floor plate or ribband, and laid out on level ground; the continuous ribband and top plate are installed, then the entire assembly is raised (by hand, derrick, or crane) vertically alongside the ends of the horizontal joists, resting directly on the sill plate. The studs are temporarily braced, and the upper level of floor joists are installed, using scaffolding. Firestopping and blockings are inserted, and the upper floor sheathing is then installed as described for platform framing. If required, permanent diagonal bracing is let into the studs before the temporary bracing is removed. Exterior wall sheathing is then applied, with openings framed and cut out all as previously described. See Figure 7.

Roof System

This part of the structure is constructed essentially as previously described under platform framing.

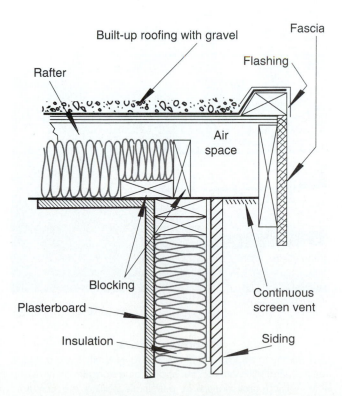

Figure 6 Flat Roof Framing

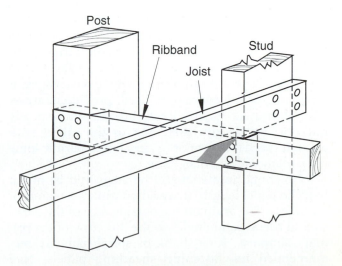

Figure 7 Wall System (Balloon)

Other Items

Blocking

It is frequently necessary to provide either continuous or intermittent softwood blocking to secure or support other building components, such as edges of roof membranes, metal door frames in concrete walls, or surface-mounted or recessed metal wall cabinets. In many cases, such blockings have to be treated with preservatives, as described in Section 06–300. The blocking pieces are cut to length and then either spiked to wood frames, screwed to steel studs, or powder-fastened to concrete slabs or walls.

Furring

This usually consists of short pieces of light timber, cut and fitted together to create a rigid frame to support finished wood, gypsum, or metal paneling, to provide a false vertical plane or dropped horizontal or sloped ceiling. Its purpose is to locate the finished surface at a short distance away from the basic structural frame of the building, to provide space for electrical, mechanical, plumbing, or other services to be concealed from view. In some cases, furring is used for purely visual purposes, relative to the design of the building spaces. In some regions, furring (or strapping) is used to level the undersides of joist systems before applying ceiling boards.

Sheathing

This item is used to stiffen the building frame and to form the planes of floors, walls, and roofs, ready to support subsequent finishes, such as flooring, drywall, stucco, and shingles. It occurs in two basic forms:

1. **Panels.** Panel sheathing consists of sheets of plywood or particleboard, manually laid either in flat or sloped planes or shaped to suit barrel vault, parabolic, or other curved or domed surfaces. It is best to use sheets with tongue-and-groove edges; if plain butt-edged boards are used, provide intermediate aluminum H-clips. Each sheet should be neatly but not too tightly fitted one to the other, with enough space (1.5 mm or $^1/_{16}$ in.) left to permit some movement without distortion.

Panel end joints should be staggered by about half the panel length, to avoid continuous planes of weakness. The grain on the outside face of the panel should run at right angles to the direction of the primary supports. Ring-shank or spiral nails are recommended for fastening sheathing panels. Nail length should be about three times the thickness of

the sheathing; nails should be spaced at 150 mm or 6 in. oc along edges and at 250 mm or 10 in. oc along intermediate supports. Nailheads should be driven flush with or set slightly below the sheathing surface. If air-powered staples are used, reduce the spacings by about 25 percent. Plywood sheathing should be sawn face up when using a table saw, face down

(a) Placing T+G board

(b) Securing boards

Sheathing Floors

T&G sheathing boards are cinched up fairly tightly using a sledge hammer. End joints are recommended to be staggered where possible. Gluing and manual or pneumatic nailing are common. (BCIT Building Technology)

(a) Wall sheathing

(b) Roof sheathing

Sheathing Walls and Roofs

Plywood or particleboard is commonly used on walls and roofs as sheathing. Panels can be secured manually as shown or by using automatic nailing guns. Metal clips are sometimes used. (Trus-Joist McMillan)

when using a manual power saw, with the blade set to protrude about 13 mm or ¹/₂ in. in each case.

2. Boards. Board sheathing consists of long lengths of thin, flat rough-sawn lumber, having either plain or tongue-and-groove edges, secured to the structural framing in either a horizontal or diagonal (45-degree) pattern, with every board double-nailed with common nails to every bearing point.

Use coated nails in exterior work. Board edges should be slightly separated to permit movement, and board ends should be supported by framing. Ends of boards at corners and open edges should be neatly trimmed off flush with the supporting framing.

(a) Drilling bolt holes

(b) Forklift truch and sling

Preparing Posts and Beams

Before erection by forklift, posts and beams are prepared by cutting to length, then using a heavy-duty long-bit electric drill to make suitable bolt holes at correct locations. (UBC Architecture)

(a) Parapet wall

(b) Furring for services

Customized Features

Most wood-framed buildings have many specialized features. Perimeters of flat roofs may require a small parapet and cant strip for flashing. Furring creates spaces for services. (BCIT Building Technology)

Strapping

This consists of long flat pieces of softwood (vertically or horizontally positioned) nailed, screwed, or powder-fastened to concrete or masonry walls at regular intervals of about 400 mm or 16 in. oc. Strapping forms a rigid true base for the subsequent installation of panels made of plywood, gypsum, or metal, while permitting some minimal ventilation behind the panels. Additional pieces are secured at tops and bottoms, as well as behind all intermediate joints in the subsequent panels, to provide adequate support at all edges of the panels. Strapping lumber is frequently treated with wood preservatives, as described in Section 06–300. Floor sleepers are installed in a manner almost identical to wall strapping.

Vapor Control

This may be achieved by paper or plastic film as described in Part 2.1, depending on the project design and specification. In general, such sheet products are carefully unrolled (to avoid rips or tears) and spread smoothly under slight tension across the area to be protected, with edges overlapped about 100 mm or 4 in. (and tucked and glued in top-quality work). The entire installation should be stapled or nailed in position at not more than 400-mm or 16-in. intervals in both directions. Edges of cutouts for openings, vents, or service outlets should be carefully sealed with masking tape or adhesives.

(a) Checking plumb

(b) Checking square

(c) Checking level

Framing Process

It is essential for functional, economic, and legal reasons that buildings are accurately located and properly built. Contractors must check work to ensure compliance with contracts. (BCIT Building Technology)

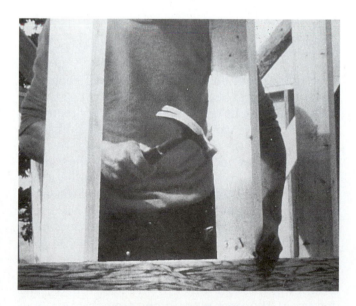

Miscellaneous Details

The technique of attaching studs to wall or ceiling plates by driving common nails in at an angle is called toenailing. For economy, short stud lengths can be toothed and glued together. (Trus-Joist McMillan)

Seismic Control

Building codes are increasing requirements for structures to resist earthquakes. This picture is representative of a wide range of specialty products designed with such restraint in mind. (UBC Architecture)

5.3 Precautions

The assembly and erection of rough carpentry require involvement with the building frame during a particularly fragile stage of its construction; precautions must therefore be taken to avoid personal injury and property damage. The general principles of triangulation should be utilized to temporarily but securely brace unfinished wood-framed systems.

The structural loads commonly encountered in carpentry work can be quite high, and the work often requires the use of sharp or powered tools and considerable force. Untreated rough carpentry work should be protected or isolated from excessive or prolonged wet or damp conditions. Large amounts of heavy material should not be carelessly placed in concentrated loads on unbraced floors, ceilings, or roofs.

Section 06–170
Prefabricated Wood

1.0 Introduction

1.1 General Issues

Frame and brace construction with sheathing was described in Section 06–100; post and beam construction with decking is described in this section. According to *MasterFormat*, this section includes glued-laminated members and prefabricated wooden trusses and joists, together with their connections. Although decking is assigned by *MasterFormat* to Section 06–100 Rough Carpentry, in this book such decking will be described in this section, because of its normally close relationship to the prefabricated wood products used in typical post and beam construction.

Post and beam systems are often incorporated to accommodate design requirements for wide uninterrupted spans to support floors or roofs in most commercial, many institutional, and some larger residential buildings. They are also effectively used in many industrial and farm buildings, as well as in covered outdoor tennis courts, aircraft hangars, boat marinas, and ice hockey rinks and other sports arenas.

Traditional manufacturing processes (such as GluLam™) produce posts, beams, and arches made of a factory assembly of carefully selected, graded, tested, shaped, and machined kiln-dried softwood lumber pieces. The assemblies are glued together under controlled heat and pressure, cured and cooled, and the surfaces finally sanded and sealed. Newer manufacturing processes (such as ParaLam™) involve the longitudinal alignment of selected and premixed wood fibers in special synthetic resins, continuously extruded through metal dies of predetermined cross-sectional dimension and shape. The extrusions are cooked and cured in industrial microwave ovens and then cut off to virtually any desired length. Some ceiling, floor, and roof joists consist of a patented prefabricated assembly of glued-laminated longitudinal chords separated by vertical plywood webs. These patented products are made by specialized companies (such as TrusJoist™) using state-of-the-art manufacturing techniques (such as MicroLam™) to produce prefabricated wood products of exceptionally high and uniform quality. While they are functionally efficient, they are not inexpensive.

1.2 Design Aspects

There are several design advantages to be achieved by using post and beam systems. They can have high strength-to-weight ratios relative to other materials or products; they can be fabricated to suit almost any required building configuration, shape, or size; they can be easily cut and drilled on site; and they can be rapidly erected and installed. They also offer excellent resistance to damage by fire; they provide good acoustical, thermal, and electrical insulation; they are not subject to corrosion; and they can exhibit the natural beauty of the species of woods used in their manufacture as part of the building decor.

Some disadvantages include susceptibility to deterioration through attack by insects, fungus, and dampness, if proper precautions are not taken. Special care must be taken during delivery and installation maneuvers to avoid damage to relatively fragile surfaces, edges, and finishes. Particularly large or heavy members may encounter limitations with re-

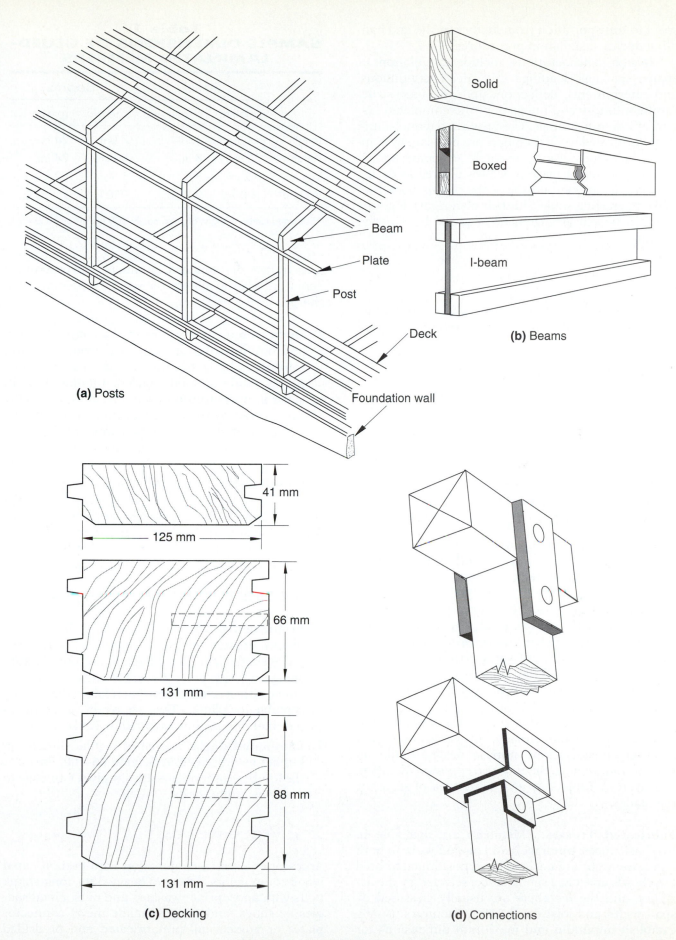

(a) Posts

Beam
Plate
Post
Deck
Foundation wall

(b) Beams

Solid
Boxed
I-beam

(c) Decking

41 mm
125 mm
66 mm
131 mm
88 mm
131 mm

(d) Connections

Figure 1   Posts, Beams, and Decks

spect to transportation from factory to site and handling during installation procedures.

Design considerations include calculation of spans, spacings, loadings (live, dead, continuous, and intermittent), deflection, and adequate structural continuity and integrity of the completed system, among other things. The design and manufacture of prefabricated wood members are now largely computerized in most plants, for safety, economy, and efficiency; details of these processes as well as design calculations are beyond the scope of this book (but make interesting studies in their own right). Figure 1 shows a typical arrangement of posts, beams, and decking.

1.3 Related Work

Work closely connected to this section is described in the following sections, to which reference should be made:

03–300   Cast-in-Place Concrete

06–100   Rough Carpentry

07–500   Membrane Roofing

2.0 Products

2.1 Materials

Materials for post and beam systems can be considered in three categories: **laminated members, fabricated trusses,** and **deck systems.**

Laminated Members.   Post and beam members are available in three stress grades (bending, flexure, and shear), two service grades (interior and exterior), and three appearance grades (industrial, paint, and quality grade). There is a cost variable of approximately 10 percent between each of the three appearance grades.

Dimensions and shapes are theoretically unlimited, but manufacturing, transportation, and erection considerations impose design limits on lengths and weights. Sizes of two common members are given in Table 1 to give some idea of scale for the reader.

Fabricated Trusses.   Members are available in two basic types: **open web** and **closed web.** In both types, the webs are designed and positioned to hold the chords apart at a set distance, selected by the designer, and the members are usually classified by span width and joist depth. Manufacturers usually establish minimum and maximum dimensions for

Table 1
SAMPLE DIMENSIONS OF GLUED-LAMINATED MEMBERS

	Posts		Beams	
	metric	imperial	metric	imperial
Length	3.5 m	12 ft.	7.0 m	24 ft.
Height	20 cm	8 in.	60 cm	24 in.
Volume	0.2 m^3	8 ft.^{3}	1.9 m^3	72 ft.^{3}
Weight*	100 kg	240 lb.	950 kg	2,160 lb.

*Softwood lumber weighs approximately 500 kg/m^3 or 30 lb./ft.^{3}.

their range of standard products; purpose-made items are also available on special order at extra charge.

1. **Open web** members consist of a continuous top and bottom solid or laminated wooden chord, separated by intermittent diagonal webbing pieces, made of solid wood or tubular steel. In general, open web roof trusses are additionally categorized by their configuration (either by the title of their shape or by the name of their original designer), some of which are shown in Table 2. Standard spans can range up to 25 m or 80 ft.

2. **Closed web** members also consist of two wooden chords, separated by a continuous vertical plywood panel web. Lengths can range up to 15 m or 50 ft.; clear spans can range up to 6 m or 20 ft. depending on lateral spacing. Joist depths vary between 17.5 and 35 mm or 7 and 14 in.

Deck Systems.   Materials fall into two categories:

1. **Preformed Decks** consist of solid fir or cedar planks, dressed flat and machined to provide either a single or double tongue-and-groove feature along each side and returned at ends. In most regions, either select or commercial grades are acceptable for planks. They are readily available in nominal dimensions as noted in Table 3.

2. **Laminated decks** consist of regular dimension lumber as described in Section 06–100, Part 2.1; the lumber components are simply set on edge to form the laminations.

2.2 Accessories

Accessories used in conjunction with prefabricated wood components consist of heavy-duty, long-shank bolts with appropriate washers and nuts, metal saddles or shoes, and purpose-made metal connector plates or gussets, all prefabricated and predrilled

Table 2
SOME COMMON CATEGORIES
OF ROOF TRUSSES

Title	Shape	Name	Design
Crescent		Fink	
Bowstring		Howe	
King-post		Pratt	
Scissors		Warren	

ready for installation. Decks are normally secured in place with heavy-duty spiral nails or galvanized steel spikes.

3.0 Construction Aids

3.1 Equipment

Light cranes with wire-rope slings or highrise forklifts are used to raise the members into position. Ladders and scaffolding are also required to permit access for workers to make the necessary joint connections. Heavy-duty hammer drills are used to cut holes through members; excess ends of members can be cut off with chainsaws. Steel cables with tension adjustments are used to temporarily restrain or brace members in position during erection procedures. Surveyor's levels and transits are used to ensure proper alignment of members and accessories.

3.2 Tools

Heavy-duty electric drills with elongated bits are used to cut holes for bolts and spikes. Heavy-duty electric saws are used to cut small notches or rebates in sides or edges of members where necessary. Hemp or nylon ropes are used as tag lines to guide members into position. Other tools used are those of the carpentry trade.

Table 3
NOMINAL DIMENSIONS OF
PREFORMED DECK PLANKS

Units	Thickness	Width	Length *
Metric	50, 75, 100 mm	100, 150, 200 mm	2–6 m
Imperial	2, 3, 4 in.	4, 6, 8 in.	6–20 ft.

*Most orders will include an assortment of planks of random length between the parameters stated.

Stockpiling
Prefabricated wood posts, beams, and trusses are delivered by flatbed truck and stockpiled on site. When needed, they are raised and moved into position by a forklift using slings. (BCIT Building Technology)

4.0 Production

4.1 Crew Configuration

Crew sizes vary from two persons (one journeyman and a helper) required to install lightweight prefabricated joists and decking by hand in a wood-framed residence or apartment building, to four persons (one foreman, one carpenter, one semiskilled helper, and a laborer) to install a post and beam system in a medium-sized commercial project, such as a service station or a drive-in restaurant. On a major institutional building, such as a school or a shopping center, a crew of six (a crane operator, a carpenter foreman, two journeymen, two semiskilled helpers, and one laborer) could be used to install large and heavy glued-laminated arches.

4.2 Productivity

Laminated Members. Using a crew of four, simple, lightweight glued-laminated posts and beams can be raised and secured into position (either manually or with light equipment) in about 5 minutes each. Using a crew of six, heavy or complex arches or trussed glued-laminated frames can take up to 15 minutes each to be positioned, installed, and secured. Expressed another way, one can anticipate installing between 5 and 10 m³ or 175 and 350 ft.³ of light-

weight members and between 10 and 15 m³ or 350 and 525 ft.³ of heavyweight members per 8-hour day. The apparent lower productivity for the lighter-weight members is caused by the fact that there are more of them per unit weight; they therefore take longer to install. On large-scale, simple, and repetitive work, improvements in productivity up to 100 percent can be expected to be achieved over the factors given.

Fabricated Trusses. Using a crew of two, lightweight closed web joists can be manually positioned and secured in about 3 to 5 minutes each. Using a crew of four and light equipment, medium-weight open web fabricated trusses can be raised and secured in place in about 5 to 10 minutes each. As few such trusses could be classified as heavyweight, no useful productivity factors are given in this section. Furthermore, unlike laminated members, there is no useful comparable volume factor applicable to fabricated trusses.

Deck Systems. A crew of two should install large unobstructed areas of lightweight plain wood decking of preformed tongue-and-groove construction at the rate of approximately 30 m² or 300 ft.² per 8-hour day. Heavyweight or laminated decking will reduce productivity by up to 20 percent; small areas and complex shapes will also reduce productivity. On large commercial installations, two or more crews might be utilized for efficiency and speed.

5.0 Procedures

5.1 Preparation

Careful planning of the delivery, storage, erection, and connection of post and beam system members should be given high priority, because of the relatively high costs involved if errors arise. Contractors must take time to work out the precise sequence in which the most efficient assembly will occur. The members are usually delivered by truck from the plant where they were made, so arrangements must be made to permit the trucks to drive in as close to the building frame as possible. Preassembled members should be vertically positioned during transit and be secured by chains or straps; care must also be taken to prevent distortion of members during transit or handling. Whenever possible, members should be lifted off the trucks and placed directly into their final positions, without intermediate handling. A large assembly area is sometimes required on site so that members can be fastened together after off-loading but before erection and installation; this is essential for larger members that cannot be shipped in one piece. Drilling of members for bolt fastenings or pipe passages is best done directly at the site and not previously at the plant, to ensure accuracy of fit and to minimize chances for errors. Bolt holes are best drilled before erection; pipe holes are best cut out after erection.

Special consideration must be given to the proper positioning and dimensioning of all holes or cuts made in chords, flanges, or webs of prefabricated wood members, strictly in accordance with the recommendations of the member manufacturer or structural designer; improper cutting can seriously weaken such members, possibly resulting in structural failure.

5.2 Process

Methodology in this section can be considered under two broad headings: **light construction** (primarily done by hand) and **heavy construction** (primarily done by machine). Both are simple.

Light Construction. This methodology can be readily understood by examining its three primary components: the **posts,** the **beams,** and the **decking.**

The Posts

The vertical posts are positioned and erected by hand, plumbed approximately by eye and then accurately by instrument. A preformed template or jig is often used to ensure accurate spacing between the posts, both at bottom and top. Temporary diagonal braces (made either of wire cables or flat wood strips), connected to turnbuckle tension rings, are

Installation
The prefabricated members are predrilled for connections (and other building requirements) before placing. One difficulty is to provide adequate structural integrity during erection. (BCIT Building Technology)

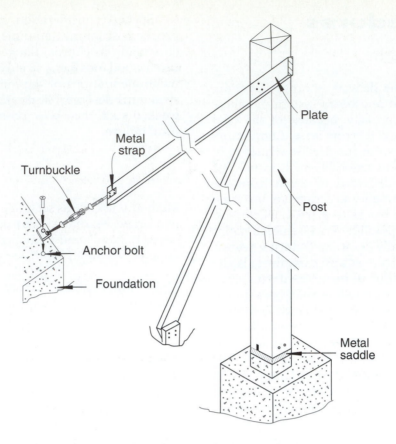

Figure 2 Temporary Bracing

secured to keep the posts truly plumb and in position. The post bases are secured to their respective base plates or saddles at the bottom end. See Figure 2.

The Beams

Scaffolding is erected around the posts or ladders are placed against the braced posts to provide access to the upper beam connections. The horizontal beams are then raised by hand or sling and secured on the post tops or saddles using purpose-made joint fasteners. Permanent braces or blockings are then installed where necessary, before the temporary braces are removed. A check should be made of the tension in temporary braces before they are finally or completely released, to protect against collapse of the system.

Where trusses are used instead of regular joists or solid decking, they are raised by hand or by light derrick, spaced at precalculated centers along the beams (in post and beam construction) or upper bearing plates (in frame and brace construction), and secured by nailing or screwing at ends to bearings. Lateral bracings, blockings, or firestoppings are installed as necessary or as required by codes to stiffen and complete the assembly, ready to receive floor or roof sheathing. See Figure 3.

The Decking

The successful installation of satisfactory wood decking involves knowledge of a number of elements of good design. First, all deck planks or pieces must cross at least one support, and wherever possible, they should span over two or more supports. Second, joints are best located over supports, or where this is unattainable, at least within the end third between supports; avoid joints in the middle third of a span. Third, all joints in adjacent pieces should be longitudinally offset by at least 600 mm or 24 in. Minimize any tendency for joints to line up one with another at lateral intervals less than longitudinal intervals. See Figure 4.

For **preformed** decking (thicker than 50 mm or 2 in.), each plank should be predrilled and spiked to its neighbor at not more than 750 mm or 30 in. oc. The system should be headnailed to bearings at not more than 60 mm or 2.5 in. oc. Thinner decks are not predrilled; they are toenailed directly to the supports. Intermediate end joints should be returned or splined.

For **laminated decking,** each piece of lumber should be spiked to its neighbor at not more than 450 mm or 18 in. oc. The system should be toenailed to bearings at every lamination.

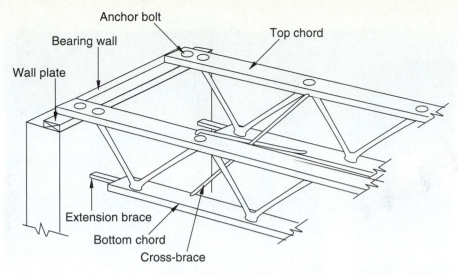

Figure 3 Truss Placement

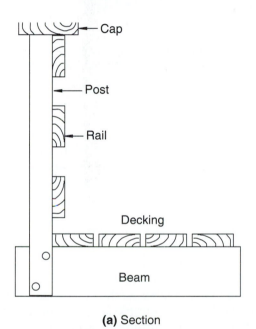

(a) Section

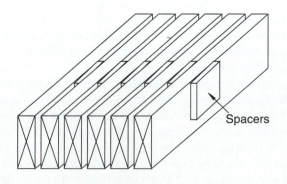

(b) Alternative

Figure 4 Decking Layout

For **spaced decking,** refer to Section 06–200 Finish Carpentry.

Heavy Construction. The general methodology is similar in principle to that described above for light construction. The primary difference is that because of the larger sizes and weights of the members, equipment such as highrise heavy-duty forklift trucks and tractor-mounted or wheeled mobile cranes are used to move, erect, position, and temporarily support the various members. Bracing, scaffolding, and connections are as described above for light framing.

Finally, all of the work described in this section should be considered in close conjunction with the carpentry work described in Sections 06–100 and 06–200, as on most projects the general contractor would consider the installation of prefabricated wood members and decks to be part of his or her direct responsibility.

5.3 Precautions

There are some truly dangerous elements in the erection and connection of post and beam systems, due to the ease with which eccentrically loaded or poorly braced posts, beams, and trusses can be toppled, often with disastrous results. The type and positioning of scaffolding and ladders used in conjunction with prefabricated wood members requires considerable care and thought to avoid the risk of accidental dislodgment of personnel, equipment, or members. Temporary bracing of the uncompleted structure is an essential component of protection, as unframed buildings are more prone to failure during erection than regularly framed buildings—the posts and

Temporary Bracing
Diagonal bracing is used extensively to ensure stability and accuracy during the erection processes. The bracing is removed after permanent connections have been completed and inspected. (BCIT Building Technology)

Connections
Connections between prefabricated wood components are often made with custom-designed steel holsters and stirrups, prepared for and complete with appropriate bolts and nuts. (BCIT Building Technology)

beams can collapse in domino fashion, each one taking down an adjacent one. Designers should not mix design calculations, metal connections, or wood products from one manufacturer with those of another.

Personnel doing this work often prefer not to wear hardhats, because the work requires frequent looking up and leaning down, causing the hats to fall off. Chinstraps can often solve this problem. Many workers also prefer to wear soft-soled sneakers instead of regular work boots; they claim that this permits them to be more nimble and surefooted as they move about on the scaffolding and framing.

There are vehicle limitations in most regions concerning the maximum sizes and weights of loads that can be transported by truck over public highways and roads. Prefabricated wood members often approach such limits, and special permits may be required to move loads that exceed limitations or impede other traffic.

Prefabricated wood members must be protected from dampness or water from any source, as moisture can seriously weaken the strength of members, as well as distort shapes and damage facial appearances. During handling and temporary storage, care must be taken to prevent physical damage (such as nicks, cuts, or dents) from occurring, because these can also reduce the strength and impair the appearance of members.

Section 06–200
Finish Carpentry

1.0 Introduction

1.1 General Issues

Finish carpentry is another specialized division of general carpentry work. Whereas rough carpentry was described as being essentially structural in nature, finish carpentry (as the title suggests) is basically aesthetic in nature and is usually intended to be exposed to view upon completion in most types of buildings. To put it another way, much of finish carpentry is intended to conceal much of rough carpentry, as well as the rough or cut edges of other trade work, such as drywall, roofing, or building services. The work described in this section is sometimes referred to as *finished* carpentry or *finishing* carpentry; some mistakenly call it *finnish* carpentry, although this work has little to do with Finland. According to *MasterFormat*, the correct title is *finish* carpentry.

Opinions differ in various geographical regions regarding the scope of finish carpentry; in general, it comprises the supply and installation of all finished woodwork throughout the building. Some examples of **exterior** work would include wood or composition siding and trim, spaced decking, porch finishes (excluding paint or stain), gutters, eaves, fascias, and standard wood moldings around windows and doors. Some examples of **interior** work would include baseboards and other running (or continuous) trim, residential and commercial wood or plastic countertops, plain plywood convector cabinets and drapery valances, standard wood paneling, simple glazed partitions and borrowed lights, ordinary plastic laminates, and standard moldings or trim used in conjunction with finishing inside doors, windows, stairs, and often the work of other trades.

Finish carpentry can also include the *installation only* of prefabricated wood items (such as factory-made door assemblies, windows and frames, counters and cabinets, stairwork, and the like) fabricated, assembled, and supplied as described in other sections of this book. While opinions may differ as to the scope of finish carpentry, all will agree that the general carpentry rule of "measuring twice before cutting once" is especially applicable to the work of this section, as much of it involves the use of expensive finishing materials and the necessity to achieve fine appearance.

1.2 Design Aspects

Some general design aspects of building with wood applicable to the work of this section were dealt with in Part 1.2 of Section 06–100; these are not repeated here. Because of the large number of building components that can fall in the realm of finish carpentry but have been covered in other sections (and to be consistent with *MasterFormat*), this section of this book deals primarily with four building elements: exterior siding, interior paneling, plastic laminates, and running trim. Significant aspects of design for each of these elements are outlined in a short segment immediately preceding the description of methods in Part 5.2. For other finish carpentry work not included here, refer to Other Work in Part 5.2.

In general, one might say that much of finish carpentry, similarly to rough carpentry, involves the selection and installation of standard wood products, with minimal modification to suit specific site conditions, in contrast to architectural woodwork (Section 06–400) which is usually highly modified and specialized to suit the particular needs of building designers and owners.

1.3 Related Work

Work closely connected to the work of this section is described in the following sections, to which reference should be made:

06–100   Rough Carpentry

06–170   Prefabricated Wood

06–400   Architectural Woodwork

09–900   Painting and Decorating

2.0 PRODUCTS

2.1 Materials

Because of the close connection between finish carpentry and many other construction trades, some materials, products, and grades used for the work of this section have been specified elsewhere, and are not repeated here. Reference can be made to the following sections for materials in addition to those discussed in this part:

Pulpboard and panel siding: Section 06–100

Softwood paneling: Section 06–100

Posts, beams, and decking: Section 06–170

Cabinets, shelves, stairwork: Section 06–400

Plastic Laminate.   This material is a composite of layers of impregnated fine kraft papers compressed to form a structural backing or core and having an integral decorative surface. Inexpensive phenolic resins are usually used for the core layers, whereas more costly melamine resins are used for the surface layers.

Categories

Laminates may be categorized as high pressure (resulting in thin, hard-wearing, decorative surface panels) or low pressure (resulting in thicker, softer, shaped or molded plastic covers).

Sizes

Typical panels are 1,200 × 2,400 mm or 48 × 96 in.; oversize panels can be as large as 1,500 × 3,600 mm or 60 × 144 in.; smaller panels may be cut from larger ones. Typical thicknesses range from 1.5 to 25 mm or $1/16$ to 1 in.; thinner and thicker products are also available. A specially thin but durable laminate about 1 mm or $1/24$ in. thick is produced for post-forming (factory) use.

Grades

Several products are made for specific end uses, as listed in Table 1, with typical approximate thicknesses.

Options

Color and pattern choices are virtually without limit, with new designer fashions being introduced on an annual basis. Plain or decorative thin metal foils can also be factory laminated to the plastic surface for special effects.

Makers

Many companies manufacture plastic laminate materials. Some of the better-known copyright brand names are Arborite, Formica, Panelyte, Textolite, and WilsonArt, among many others of comparable quality.

Hardwood.   There are two main categories of wood species: softwood and hardwood. Softwood is described in Part 2.1 of Section 06–100.

Hardwood trees are deciduous, have broad leaves, and produce fruit; they also tend to grow in more irregular shapes than softwood trees, resulting in cut straight pieces of shorter maximum lengths. Most hardwoods have a more open grain in cross section and tend to be mostly used for aesthetic purposes in finish carpentry and architectural woodwork. In general, hardwood is less susceptible (though not impervious) to attack by fire, fungus, insects, moisture, rot, and vermin than softwood.

Examples of common hardwoods used in construction include alder, ash, birch, cherry, cottonwood, elm, hickory, maple, magnolia, mahogany, oak, rosewood, sycamore, teak, and walnut. More exotic species include balsa, ebony, ironwood, jarrah, and lauan. Many of the common species are indigenous to North and Central America; the others are imported, for reasons of ecology or economy, from other regions.

Table 1
PLASTIC LAMINATE GRADES

| Grade | Purpose | Thickness | |
		mm	in.
Backing sheet	To prevent vapor penetration.	0.75	0.03
Balancing sheet	To stabilize panels or doors.	0.85	0.04
Cabinet liner	To improve utility/appearance.	1.5	0.06
General-purpose	For high-impact installations.	1.5	0.06
Post-forming	For preformed shelves/counters.	1.3	0.05
Vertical	For low-impact walls or doors.	0.75	0.03

Sizes

Hardwood flitches vary from 1.2 to 5.0 m or 4 to 16 ft. In general, the larger sizes are much more expensive than smaller ones.

Grades

The grade of each cut piece is established by inspection of the amount of clear surface on its most defective side, categorized as follows: firsts, seconds, selects, and commons. Grades are further separated into No. 1, 2, 3A, and 3B. The amount of clear face per piece can vary from 100 percent for No. 1 firsts to 90 percent for FAS (firsts and seconds) down to as low as 25 percent for No. 3B commons. One additional grade is called sound wormy, which is identical to No. 1 common but permits clean, natural wormhole patterns as a decorative feature of the appearance of the wood.

Finishes

Pieces may be ordered rough cut, semifinished, or surfaced (machine finished) on one or both faces.

Thicknesses

Standard approximate dimensions are given for some representative saw-cut pieces, surfaced (as distinct from rough cut) on both faces:

Metric sizes: in approximately 3-mm increments in eight stages from 4.75 to 45 mm, then in 13-mm increments in four stages from 57 to 95.25 mm.

Imperial sizes: in approximately $^1/_8$-inch increments in eight stages from $^3/_{16}$ to $1^3/_4$ in., then in $^1/_2$-inch increments in four stages from $2^1/_4$ up to $3^3/_4$ in.

Other sizes and thicknesses may be obtained by special arrangement with local hardwood lumbermills.

Veneer-cut pieces are available in thicknesses varying from about 2.5 to 6 mm or about $^1/_{10}$ to $^1/_4$ in.

Plywood. Plywood in general was described in Section 06–100; as stated, there are four broad categories:

1. **Softwood** (or standard) plywood is described in Section 06–100. As some softwood plywoods are used in finish carpentry, the related grading standards are repeated for convenience in this section.
2. **Hardwood** plywood is similar to standard softwood plywood, but has face laminations consisting of selected hardwood veneers, cut in a variety of ways as described under Veneers below.
3. **Overlaid** plywood is similar to standard plywood, but has a resin-impregnated melamine paper face-bonded to one or both faces. There are two classes: medium-and high-density overlay.
4. **Specialty** plywood can be prepared to any special order, for example by having coatings factory applied, patterns impressed on faces, grooves run to simulate joints, surfaces sandblasted or wire-brushed, or panels oversized to achieve particular architectural effects.

Plywood products are usually stamped on their back faces or edges by the producing mill to show maker's name, species groups of woods, grades of veneers, whether suitable for interior or exterior use, and so on.

U.S. Grading

Softwood plywoods are graded on the basis of the quality of the face and back laminations; the inner plies are usually "D" quality. In Table 2, the letters refer to the quality of laminations permitted in the grade. The grades given are simply representative of the system used; other grades are available. Hardwood plywoods are listed to show the two exterior grades first and the two interior grades next. There are five grades of hardwood veneer (select or custom, good, sound, utility, and backing).

Canadian Grading

Softwood plywoods are graded by a system of words and numbers to indicate quality, species, origin, number of plies, and so on. Hardwood plywoods are graded using a color band system on their edges: red for good, blue for sound, and black for backing. In Table 3, the word "select" means very good quality all around, "good" means free of objectionable de-

**Table 2
SELECTED U.S.
PLYWOOD GRADES**

Softwood Plywood	Hardwood Plywood
A–A	Technical—Special uses
A–B	Type I—Waterproof
A–D	Type II—Weatherproof
B–D	Type III—Nonweatherproof

Table 3
SELECTED CANADIAN PLYWOOD GRADES

Softwood Plywood	Hardwood Plywood
Good 2 sides	Good both sides
Good 1 side	Good 1, sound other
Select (2 types)	Good 1, backing other
Overlaid (2 types)	Sound both sides
Sheathing (2 types)	Sound 1, backing other

fects, "sound" means firm and solid but not necessarily visually attractive, and "backing" means the lowest quality acceptable for the purpose.

Dimensions

Standard sizes for most plywood panels are nominally 1,200 × 2,400 mm or 48 × 96 in.; thicknesses commonly range from 6 to 19 mm or $1/4$ to $3/4$ in. Other sizes and thicknesses can be ordered from plywood manufacturing plants.

Standards

In the United States, plywood quality is governed by PS–1 (66) and CS–45 (55), among others. In Canada, plywood quality is governed by CSA O–121 and O–151, among others.

Plywood Veneer Types

Depending upon how the hardwood log is passed through the cutting blades, veneers may be one of the following types, some of which are shown in Figure 1:

Back cut. The half-log is reversed in the cutting lathe.

Plain sliced. The half-log is parallel sliced.

Quarter sliced. The quarter-log is sliced at right angles to its outside perimeter.

Rift cut. The quarter-log is mounted off center and rotated against the cutting blade.

Rotary cut. The full log is rotated against the blade.

Plywood Veneer Patterns

Depending upon how the cut veneer pieces are placed next to each other on the visible surface, veneer pat-

terns may be any one or combinations of the following types, some of which are shown in Figure 2:

Book. Every second piece is reversed or inverted.

Butt. Pieces are butted end-on to the next piece.

Center. Veneer joints occur on center lines of pieces.

Random. Pieces are deliberately mismatched.

Running. Pieces are deliberately sequence-matched.

Slip. The opposite of book matched.

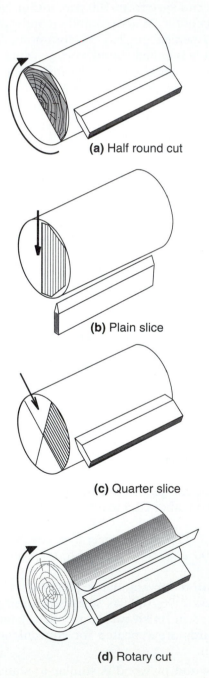

(a) Half round cut

(b) Plain slice

(c) Quarter slice

(d) Rotary cut

Figure 1   Types of Veneer Cuts

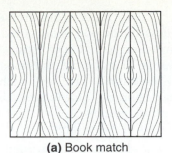

(a) Book match

(b) Center match

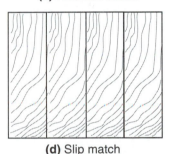

(c) Random match

(d) Slip match

Figure 2 Veneer Patterns

Hardboards. These boards consist of fine cellulose fibers, formed with specially selected resins under heat and pressure to produce large, thin, flat, fairly strong sheets or panels.

Categories

There are two hardboard categories: **basic** and **prefinished.** Both are available in plain or perforated form, with striated or rolled patterns imprinted or impressed on one or both faces.

1. **Basic** panels are available in a variety of qualities, such as standard, tempered, and industrialite; each has its own characteristics of performance.

2. **Prefinished** panels are available in two forms: Class 1 exhibits good resistance to abrasion, heat, moisture, and staining, and is intended for heavy-duty commercial installations; class 2 is intended for lighter-duty domestic applications. Prefinished panels can have factory-applied colored coatings of enamel, paint, stain, or vinyl.

Dimensions

Standard sizes for most panel products are 1,200 × 2,400 mm or 48 × 96 in. For hardboard, standard thicknesses are 3.0, 4.5, and 6.0 mm or $1/8$, $3/16$, and $1/4$ in.; other sizes and thicknesses are available.

Wood Siding. Most wood siding is made of cedar, pine, or redwood, with fir, spruce, and poplar occasionally used. Siding is usually delivered from the mill in strapped bundles containing up to 12 pieces and total (combined) lengths of up to 60 m or 200 ft. Random lengths are normally available, from 2 to 5 m or 6 to 16 ft.; specified lengths cost slightly more.

Grading

See Section 06–100, Part 2.1, U.S. Board Lumber Grading Standards. In general, so-called clear grades are the best but most costly; grades having designations such as "A" or "B" usually permit some minor defects, like tight knots or dry sap stains.

Types

Types of siding include the following, named for their cross-sectional profile; some are shown in Figure 3.1.

Bevel. Having one machined face and one rough face, with plain edges, in cross-sectional sizes ranging from 13 × 100 mm or $1/2$ × 4 in. up to 19 × 300 mm or $3/4$ × 12 in. One special type of partial bevel board is known as *anzac.*

Board-and-batten. Plain sawn or dressed boards arranged vertically, usually of 25-mm or 1-in. nominal thickness and 300-mm or 12-in. nominal width, with battens of matching thickness and 100 mm or 4 in. wide. Wider boards and narrower battens are also available.

Channel. Having faces and edges parallel, all surfaces machined, and shiplap recesses run on one or both edges. In cross-sectional sizes ranging from 25 × 100 mm or 1 × 4 in. up to 25 × 300 mm or 1 × 12 in.

Drop. Similar to bevel, but having the lower edge shiplapped to improve speed of installation and

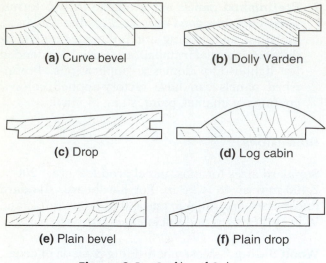

(a) Curve bevel   **(b)** Dolly Varden

(c) Drop   **(d)** Log cabin

(e) Plain bevel   **(f)** Plain drop

Figure 3.1   Profiles of Siding

weather protection; in sizes similar to channel siding. Also known as clapboard in some regions. Dolly Varden siding is one variation.

Tongue-and-groove. Similar to channel siding, but having tongue-and-groove edges instead of channels. Often arranged diagonally.

Figure 3.2 shows typical siding elevations as seen from the exterior of the building.

Trim. There is a very large variety of wood, metal, and plastic moldings used for trim associated with finish carpentry, as shown in Figure 4. Each is available in prepackaged bundles, usually in lengths of about 6 m or 20 ft. Some typical characteristics of such moldings are described below:

1. **Wood.** Usually made from dressed clear fir or pine, unless hardwood is specified to match related hardwood paneling or fixtures; available in a wide range of standard and nonstandard sizes and cross-sectional profiles, such as squares, flats, half-rounds, quarter-rounds, and ogee curves, among others. A variety of paint or plastic finishes is also available.

2. **Metal.** Usually made of extruded anodized aluminum or acrylic-painted rolled steel, in a variety of sizes and colors, and in flat, curved, C-, F-, or U-shaped profiles.

3. **Plastic.** Usually made of extruded colored semirigid polyvinyl; otherwise as described for metal trim.

Other Products. There is a large number of specialty or patented panel products, made from wood particles, chips, or pulp by manufacturers located all over North America, distributed nationally or locally, and sold under copyrighted proprietary or trade names (such as Aspenite, Masonite, and others). Readers are advised to make inquiries locally to determine what is currently available.

2.2 Accessories

Some accessories used in conjunction with finish carpentry are described in other sections as noted:

Adhesives: Section 06–050

Fasteners: Section 05–050

Hardware: Section 08–700

Preservatives: Section 06–300

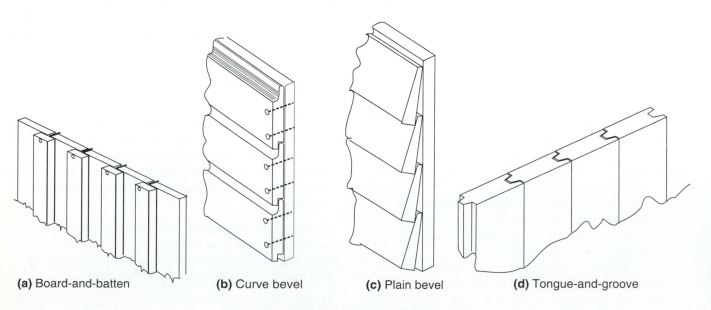

(a) Board-and-batten   **(b)** Curve bevel   **(c)** Plain bevel   **(d)** Tongue-and-groove

Figure 3.2   Elevations of Siding

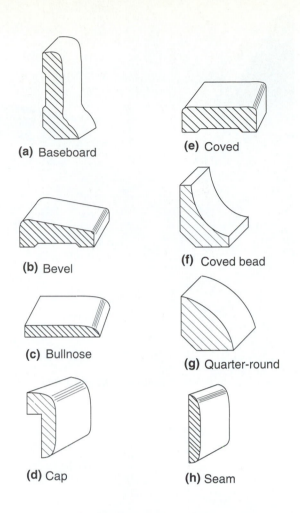

(a) Baseboard

(b) Bevel

(c) Bullnose

(d) Cap

(e) Coved

(f) Coved bead

(g) Quarter-round

(h) Seam

Figure 4 Profiles of Trim

3.0 Construction Aids

3.1 Equipment

For a description of equipment used specifically in carpentry work, refer to Section 06–100.

3.2 Tools

For a description of tools used specifically in carpentry work, refer again to Section 06–100.

4.0 Production

4.1 Crew Configuration

Finish carpentry is generally labor intensive, compared to other trades. It is not unusual to have a crew

of as many as six people on one site, consisting of one foreman, four journeymen carpenters, and one apprentice or semiskilled helper. On large complex projects, several crews might be assembled. Each field crew may be backed up with another crew of equal size at the millwork shop, preparing the finished materials for delivery.

(a) Table saw

(b) Bench saw

Tools and Equipment

Normal carpentry tools are used to prepare and install finish carpentry items. Portable and adjustable electric saws are particularly useful for rapid and accurate cutting of components. (UBC Architecture)

4.2 Productivity

As stated in Part 1.2, this section deals only with finish carpentry related to selected aspects of exterior wood siding, interior wood paneling, plastic laminates, and running trim; approximate and average productivity factors are therefore given in Table 4 only for items of work related to these four units of work; factors for some other finish carpentry work can be extrapolated from these data. For productivity of other woodwork, refer to the corresponding Parts 4.2 in the other sections listed in Parts 1.3 and 5.2, Other Work.

5.0 Procedures

5.1 Preparation

To prepare surfaces or framing to receive finish carpentry work, all previous temporary coverings, dust,

(a) Scaffolding

Table 4
SELECTED FINISH CARPENTRY PRODUCTIVITY

Unit of Work (in Area)	Output per 8-Hr. Day	
	m²	ft.²
Exterior wood siding:		
Horizontal bevel or drop	40	400
Vertical board and batten	35	350
Diagonal tongue-and-groove	30	300
Nondirectional sheeting	50	500
Interior wood paneling:		
Fielded panel or wainscot	10	100
Prefinished plain sheets	40	400
Butted or lapped planks	30	300
Plastic laminate work:		
Simple planes	20	200
Countertops	10	100
(In Length)	m	ft.
Running trim, exterior:		
Door and window moldings	80	250
Fascias and plates	70	200
Nailers or straps	110	350
Running trim, interior:		
Door and window moldings	80	250
Base and chair molds	100	300
Metal trim	30	100

(b) Preparation bench

Preparation

Where necessary, scaffolding is set up on the outside of the building under construction. A fixed bench or saw table can facilitate preparation of repetitive components, such as siding. (UBC Architecture)

glues, or paint should be removed, with rough surfaces planed or sanded smooth where necessary and wiped with a damp cloth or vacuumed clean. Good natural or artificial lighting should be provided, and work should proceed in dry conditions and at average (not extreme) levels of temperature and humidity. A check should be made to ensure that all necessary grounds, blockings, strapping, vapor barriers, and similar preparatory work are complete and ready to receive finish carpentry work. In renovation work, care should be taken to ensure that old surfaces to be covered (such as tile or plaster) are solid and sound, with all loose parts removed or secured.

Exterior Wood Siding. Before installing siding, check to ensure that all necessary wood and/or paper sheathing is properly positioned and secured. For horizontal applications, install starter strips or courses as necessary to provide the correct weathered angle to the siding system. For vertical applications, check to ensure that continuous horizontal strapping is properly leveled at the correct intervals. For diagonal applications, the required angle (usually but not always 45 degrees) is calculated and then snapped onto the sheathing or supports with a chalkline at frequent intervals. For all siding applications, install blocks or plates as necessary at changes of direction or to support ends of pieces at joints. Check to ensure that all metal or plastic flashings are cor-

rectly designed, carefully fabricated, and properly positioned to be integrated with the selected siding system.

Interior Wood Paneling. Before installing paneling, the panel pieces and sheets should be temporarily stored for a few days in the location where they will be finally installed. This permits them to adapt to the ambient temperature and humidity levels, which should be around 20 degrees C or 70 degrees F, with moisture content in the wood around 10 percent. Allowance must be made for temperature and moisture movement of all components in paneled systems. Check to ensure that all panel joints will occur over solid backings, and that electrical switch boxes, vents, and other outlets have been properly positioned in the rough framing. Examine pre-installed air or vapor barriers for satisfactory installation. For vertical board paneling, horizontal strapping is necessary at top, bottom, and in between at about 400 mm or 16 in. oc. If it is proposed to locate paneling finish over concrete or masonry walls, such walls will also require to be strapped with wood or metal strips first. Take care to securely install such strapping level, plumb, and true to plane, using shims as necessary.

In high-class work, fully dimensioned and detailed shop or layout drawings should be prepared from the contractual working drawings, to discover

(a) Lower levels

(b) Upper levels

Exterior Siding

Installation of siding usually commences at the lowest levels and work proceeds upwards. Special care is taken at ends and corners, with levels being checked from time to time. (BCIT Building Technology)

and solve possible assembly problems in advance of cutting and fitting the expensive component members. Most paneling for better-quality commercial, institutional, and residential construction is pre-manufactured in a millwork shop and then delivered to the site ready for installation with only minimal site modification.

Plastic Laminates. Before installing laminates, the dimensions of areas to be covered are measured, the laminate sheets are selected, the dimensions are transferred to the backs of sheets, and then the pieces are cut slightly oversized, to allow for exact trimming later. Short or curved cuts may be made with a sharp carpenter's utility knife, pressing against a metal straightedge or template; longer cuts may require the use of a power saw with a fine-tooth blade, running against an adjustable metal (or hard plastic) guide rail. Special skill is required to cut the material cleanly without excessive chipping; in general, saw teeth should cut into the decorative side of the material. A drill and bit can be used to make small holes for screws or other fasteners; a saber or keyhole saw can be used to make larger cutouts for kitchen sinks, plumbing pipes, electrical outlets, and the like. Careful preparation of the surfaces onto which the laminate will be placed is important, because imperfections will later "ghost" or transmit through the laminate.

Running Trim. Before installing trim, check to ensure that all siding, paneling, drywalling, or other work to which the trim has to be applied has been properly completed. Open up the trim bundles, check for suitability and for defective pieces, then temporarily store them for a few hours in the areas where they will be finally installed, to permit the pieces to adapt to prevailing temperature and humidity conditions.

5.2 Process

The following paragraphs each detail first some general aspects of basic design prior to describing particular issues concerned with installation, relative to each of the four finish carpentry elements selected for review.

Exterior Wood Siding

Design

Design of siding involves selection of one (or more) of four basic arrangements: horizontal, vertical, diagonal, or nondirectional, as shown in Figure 5. Depending on the configuration, selection then has to

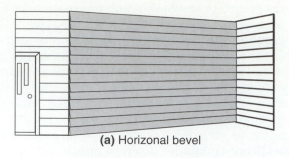

(a) Horizonal bevel

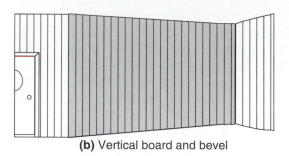

(b) Vertical board and bevel

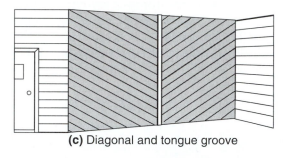

(c) Diagonal and tongue groove

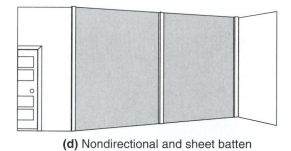

(d) Nondirectional and sheet batten

Figure 5 Siding Patterns

be made from among many appropriate siding components, some of which are listed in Part 2.1. Selection of siding components involves consideration of component size, shape, length, and cost; freedom from defects such as splits, loose knots, cupping, or damage; and aesthetics regarding color and texture

(a) Caulking edges

(b) Power nailing

Exterior Trim

It is common to apply a narrow bead of caulking compound around the perimeter of openings (at windows and doors) before applying the specified trim manually or with power nailers. (BCIT Building Technology)

as well as finishing characteristics when using paints, preservatives, or stains.

Components

Components of narrow and medium width perform best in conditions of moderate moisture change. Siding systems should be kept clear of earth or water contamination at or near grade levels, and provision should be made to permit water deflection and air circulation at edges, ends, and openings in siding systems. To improve the appearance of the finished installation, consideration should be given to aligning siding components to coincide with other features of the building, such as at openings and changes of plane. If preserved wood siding is used, cross-cut ends should be similarly treated to avoid exposure. In many localities, there are building code restrictions on both the design and the installation of siding systems. If continuous wood sheathing is not required (by code or specification) to be provided behind a siding system, it is good practice to provide a membrane of asphalt-impregnated sheathing paper or plastic house-wrap, overlapped 100 mm or 4 in. at all edges, to prevent wind blowing through the system.

Fastening Devices

Fasteners, such as nails and staples, should be corrosion resistant and chemically compatible with the selected siding material. Wherever practical, fastenings should be concealed from view and weather exposure, but they should be positioned and installed so as to permit adequate movement of the siding material due to changes in moisture content. Sinker-head nails are often used for main siding pieces, while casing or finish nails are used to secure siding trim.

Installation

Installation of siding will naturally vary depending on the arrangement and components selected. In general, siding components should be installed in one full-length piece wherever possible or in the longest practical lengths, to minimize joints. Joints should occur only over supports to which the ends of pieces can be secured. A choice can be made between regular or random spacing of joints, and care must be taken to avoid water penetration at all joints.

Typical Configurations

As will be readily understood, the number of possible permutations of alignments and components is very large. Each of the four basic alignments is described below and illustrated in Figure 6, using one typical choice of siding component; other configurations can be inferred from the ones that are given. Trim used with siding is described later.

1. Horizontal, using bevel siding. Starting at the bottom of vertical planes, boards are leveled and installed horizontally with each course overlapping the previous course by 25 mm or 1 in. Boards are usually nailed at intervals corresponding to the stud framing spacing on which the wall is supported. Uniform board intervals are established using a previously marked story pole.

2. Vertical, using board-and-batten siding. Starting at one end or outside corner of vertical planes, boards are plumbed and installed vertically on horizontal strapping, with each board spaced about 13 mm or 1/2 in. apart from its neighbor. Narrow boards can be single-nailed to each strap; wider boards require double-nailing to prevent warping. Uniform board intervals are established using a sticking piece. Narrow battens are then symmetrically positioned to cover the board joints and nailed in place. Two simple variations of the common batten-on-board system are board-on-board and reverse board-on-batten.

3. Diagonal, using tongue-and-groove siding. Starting at one lower corner of vertical planes, the shortest length is angle-cut to fit into interior corners and straight-cut to overlap at exterior corners. Pieces are installed with the tongue side uppermost, and

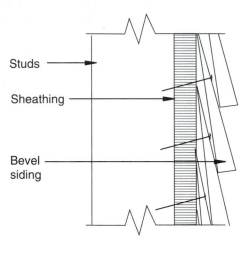

(a) Horizonal bevel

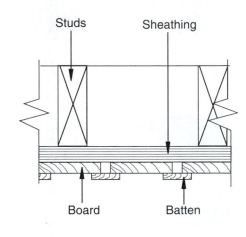

(b) Vertical-board-and-batten

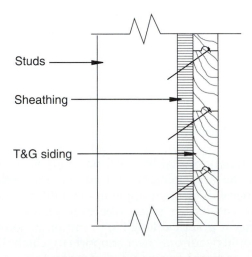

(c) Diagonal tongue-and-groove

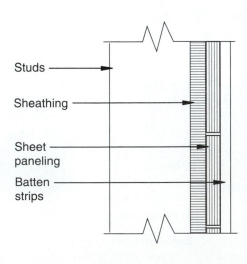

(d) Nondirectional sheeting

Figure 6 Siding Sections

Exterior Soffits
The horizontal undersides of building projections are called soffits. In framed wood buildings, soffits are usually completed with plywood, metal, or wood veed paneling to match the siding. (BCIT Building Technology)

nailed countersunk, "off the feather" (that is, on the tongue so as to conceal the nailheads from view), at stud spacings. On completion, a chalk-line is snapped along the location of wall ends or openings, a wooden or metal saw guide is temporarily positioned, and a power saw is used to trim off excess lengths.

4. Nondirectional, using sheet paneling. This process is virtually identical to that for interior paneling, described below.

Other Systems

There are, of course, many types of materials other than wood used for exterior siding on buildings.

Some of these include factory-colored sheets of anodized aluminum, solid vinyl, and acrylic-coated steel, the supply and installation of which are largely governed by the specific instructions of the manufacturer of the selected siding material, although the basic principles are not unlike those described in this section. Further information on some of these systems, as well as on wood shingles and shakes, is included in several sections in Chapter 07.

Interior Wood Paneling

Design

Most typical paneling falls into one of three primary categories (see Figure 7):

1. Fielded. This consists of solid horizontal or vertical framing members, having grooves or rebate slots run on edges, and either solid wood or veneered plywood infill panel members, usually having edges beveled to fit into precut slots on edges of framing members.

2. Sheet. This consists of full-sized veneered plywood sheets, cut to length or scribed to slope or curve where necessary, and usually installed vertically against stud-framed or strapped walls. Panels are occasionally glued directly to drywall bases.

3. Plank. This consists of vertical or horizontal strips of solid softwood or hardwood, often tongued and grooved along edges and returned across ends of pieces. If required, a small vee profile can be routed along visible edges to enhance joint appearance. Pieces may be of irregular widths and lengths or of equal widths and (usually) full length (height of area to be paneled) in one piece. It is also possible to install such material in diagonal or herringbone patterns for more dramatic visual effect. Another characteristic to be considered is whether the designer wants a knotty or clear appearance in the finished work; this will be determined by the species and grade of wood selected.

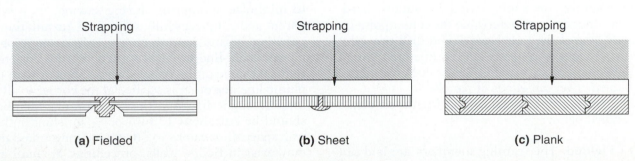

(a) Fielded　　　　**(b)** Sheet　　　　**(c)** Plank

Figure 7　Paneling Types

(a) Curved flight

(b) Tread detail

Stair Construction

Stairs can be in straight or curved flights. They can be delivered premanufactured or in components for site assembly. They can also be built from scratch using stock materials. (BCIT Building Technology)

Installation

Installation of wood paneling is a function of the particular type of paneling desired. Glue is often used in conjunction with nails, screws, staples, or clips to secure paneling; fastenings are usually concealed from view. Use finish nails of smallest adequate size where exposed to view, and set them below the surface. Nailing patterns are best started at the center of panels or pieces and worked out toward the edges or ends; where nailheads are set below the surface, the small nailhead holes can be filled with putty colored to match the selected wood species and grade.

At openings for vents, switches, outlets, hardware, or other devices, determine the center point on the back face of the panel, mark and drill tiny pilot holes at corners, and neatly cut out openings with a fine saber saw, ensuring that the device coverplates will indeed cover cut edges of panels.

The three primary categories identified above are detailed below:

1. Fielded. The framing members are laid out and installed to form a regular and pleasingly proportioned grid to support the infill panels and accommodate openings, such as at doors, fireplaces, and windows. Junctions of framing members are normally plain butted and glued, with specifications for higher-class installations demanding half-lapped or mortise-and-tenon joints. The infill panels are prepared, cut to size, and carefully inserted and glued into the framing members according to the panel design and specification, having regard to the appearance and orientation of the grain of the wood or other characteristics of the visible surfaces. Finally, perimeter trim is installed as described below.

2. Sheet. Veneered sheets should be cut face up with a table saw and face down with a portable saw, to minimize splintering during sawing, with both parent and cut pieces fully supported. Installation of paneling begins in one corner, after snapping a plumb chalk-line to ensure a true vertical orientation. One edge of the panel sheet is aligned with the plumb line; the other is scribed at the corner to allow for any slight irregularities in framing. Members should be cut about 12 mm or $1/2$ in. shorter than wall space dimensions to offset any unevenness that may exist in floors, walls, or ceilings. A small gap should be left between panels (about 3 mm or $1/8$ in.

(a) Installing

(b) Trimming

Interior Paneling
Sub-base walls are framed and rough-finished as necessary to receive the selected paneling. Paneling may be installed in large standard sheets, small preformed panels, or in single strips. (BCIT Building Technology)

Interior Soffits
The interiors of most buildings require some framing and furring or boxing to conceal mechanical ducts and other services. Soffits and faces can often be finished to match wall paneling. (UBC Architecture)

for large or wide panels and about 1.5 mm or $1/16$ in. for small or narrow pieces) to allow for movement. Wherever possible, nail off the feather; where not possible, use finish nails with heads colored to match veneers. Panels should be installed in one piece full height to avoid or minimize end joints. Finally, perimeter trim is installed as described.

3. Plank. Before installing components, measure the length of the wall and divide by the width of the boards, to ensure that the end boards will not be too thin. Plumb a true vertical, and align the first board in a corner against the plumb line, scribing if necessary against the adjacent wall plane. Proceed to install remaining boards snugly but not too tightly, each against its neighbor. Finally, perimeter trim is installed as described below.

Plastic Laminate

Design

Design of plastic laminate installations involves careful preparation of the surfaces onto which the laminate will be placed as explained in Part 5.1 Preparation; consideration of the proper matching of patterns, grains, textures, and colors; elimination or selection of the best location for joints; and selection of the most appropriate means of finishing or trimming at edges and changes of planes. Consideration must also be given to the type of adhesive; the amount of thermal, moisture, and physical movement likely to occur in the substrate and laminate; and the balancing of the number of laminations about the central plane or core to avoid warp. Work done on curved or irregular surfaces requires the use of special techniques (often involving heating, back-cutting, and routing) to avoid splitting or cracking the finished laminate surface; such specialized work will not be described here.

Plastic laminates used in construction may be considered to be one of two types:

1. Laminate sheets can be easily applied on typically horizontal locations, such as countertops, display windows, room dividers, and so on; at vertical locations, such as wall panels, existing doors, cabinet gables, and so on; or on sloping planes, such as at stairwells, organ lofts, store millwork fittings, and so on. Countertops are usually post-formed, that is, the front edges and rear upstanding backsplash portions of the laminate material are formed to a curve by heating and shaping to a specified radius by a specialized piece of post-forming equipment at the shop, and then bonded to a shaped core of compressed particleboard, prior to delivery. See Figure 8.

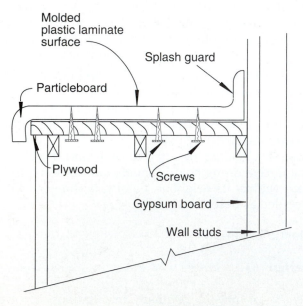

Figure 8 Postformed Countertop

2. Solid plastic panels, used in balustrade rails, shower stalls, stair treads, and so on, can be installed using screws, bolts, or appropriate adhesives. The process is much the same as for any other item of finish carpentry using comparable solid wood components. The solid plastic pieces are carefully measured, neatly cut to length using table saws with high-speed fine-tooth blades, drilled as necessary for screw or bolt fastenings to wood or metal framing members, and simply placed into their final positions. Solid plastic panels can also be inserted into wood glazed partitions or metal curtain wall systems in much the same manner that panels of glass might be installed. For further details on this application, refer to Section 08–800.

Installation

Installation of plastic laminate sheets or panels may be done on simple planes or on complex surfaces such as interior or exterior curves, domes, dished or beveled planes, and many other irregular surface profiles. Such intricate and nontypical work is done in the shop and is excluded from this introductory study. For details of precise methodology for such work and for information on shop applications involving the use of highly specialized machinery and production techniques, the reader is referred to any of several books and manuals readily available in libraries and from laminate suppliers. Preformed plastic-covered countertops are simply cut to length, mitered where necessary, and secured to the cabinet frames by gluing and back-screwing.

At the job-site, the installation of thin plastic laminate sheets or panels on simple plane surfaces involves five phases:

1. Preparation. See Part 5.1.

2. Adhesion. Contact adhesive is applied by brush or trowel to completely and uniformly cover the surface of the substrate and the rear face of the panel, according to the adhesive maker's directions. Use more than one coat if necessary, especially along edges. Allow to air cure, usually between 30 and 60 minutes, and remember, contact adhesives are well-named. The general test for readiness is that the surfaces are dry and slightly tacky to the touch. See also Section 06–050.

3. Placement. Once the glue is cured and before each panel is positioned, it is advisable to insert thin flat separator sticks (at about 30-cm or 12-in. intervals and stretching the full width of the panels) between the substrate and the rear face of the panel to avoid making the final contact before ready to do so. Carefully align and position the panel, then slowly remove the first stick along one edge, press

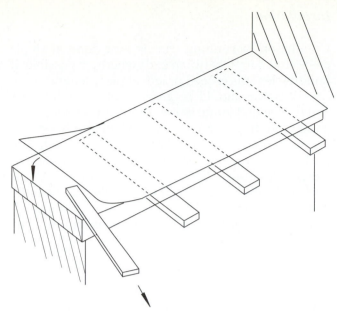

Figure 9 Laminate Adhesive Separators

evenly for contact, and progressively remove the remaining sticks in sequence, taking care not to dislodge the panel from its intended final position and pressing continuously from the first edge to the end, to prevent air bubbles from forming. On small horizontal or sloped surfaces, sheets of waxed paper can be effectively used as a separator instead of sticks. See Figure 9.

4. Finishing. Starting in the center and working out toward the edges, apply moderate force using a heavy smooth roller to remove air bubbles and to ensure uniform contact throughout. At edges, a rubber mallet can be used effectively to lightly tap on a padded wood block to enhance the bond. Excess adhesive should be quickly removed using a solvent and a clean cloth as recommended by the adhesive or laminate maker.

5. Trimming. Overhanging or overlapping edges are easily trimmed by hand with a file or by using an electric router or sanding machine, taking care not to crack the panels or to chip the edges. Exposed edges can be finished in one of two ways: by applying a matching strip of laminate cut to the correct width and glued in position, or by applying a plain or colored metal, plastic, or wooden bead with mitered corners and plain butt ends where appropriate; such trim can be screwed or glued in position. See Figure 10.

Renovations

A number of proprietary foam-backed plastic laminate wall panel sheet goods and accompanying

moldings are available for use in alteration work where owners may wish to quickly and cheaply cover over old tilework, cracked plastered walls, or other unsightly surfaces. Information on the supply and installation of such products is readily available from most local lumberyards and home improvement suppliers.

Running Trim

Design

Design of running trim generally involves the selection of pieces on the basis of appropriate quality and suitable cross-sectional profile. Most lumbermills produce a variety of standard profiles, some of which are shown in Figure 4; nonstandard profiles are available upon special order.

Ends and Joints

All ends and joints in finish carpentry work, including trim, should be supported over solid bearings or backing, wherever possible. Open ends of trim may be either straight-cut or returned, meaning that the shaped cross-sectional profile (if any) is returned across the straight-cut end. Corner joints may be either plain butt, coped, or mitered. Intermediate straight joints may be either plain butt or beveled. In general, it is best to avoid permitting intermediate joints to occur at center points or too near the ends of pieces. If joints are unavoidable, place them at corners or changes of direction; in long straight lengths, place joints at one-third points along each length.

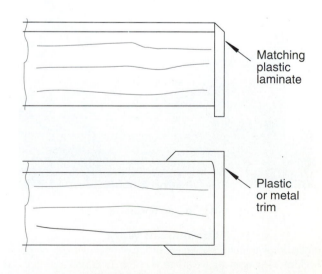

Matching plastic laminate

Plastic or metal trim

Figure 10 Edges and Trim

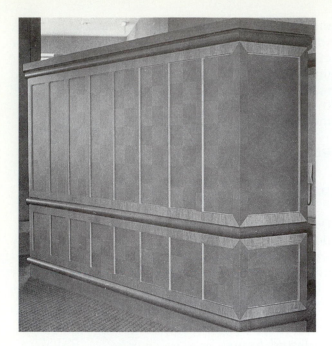

(a) Telephone screen

(b) Column enclosure

Commercial Work

Public areas in public buildings are often finished with carpentry work of very high quality. One purpose is to enhance appearance; another is to reduce maintenance. (UBC Architecture)

Installation

Installation of running trim is best done in single pieces full length between ends wherever possible; if building lengths exceed practical piece lengths, then consideration should be given to both the location and type of end joints as mentioned in the preceding paragraph. In general, trim pieces are premeasured, precut, fitted at one end, aligned and fitted at the opposite end, checked for position, and then secured either with finish nails manually applied, staples pneumatically applied, or glue brushed or sprayed on, depending on the contractual requirements. Running trim occurs on both **exterior** and **interior** surfaces of buildings.

Exterior. In siding application, corner trim pieces are common at both interior and exterior corners. They may be applied either before the siding, in which case the siding pieces are cut to butt against them, or after the siding, in which case the boards conceal the cut ends of the siding. Typical arrangements are shown in Figure 11.1. At doors and windows, casing trim is used to conceal the rough frames and the cut edges of siding or other finishing materials. Trim is also used extensively at edges and ends of roof systems, to form eaves, fascias, soffits, barge boards, and the like.

Interior. In paneling applications, trim is used to conceal or enhance the unavoidable joints at edges or ends of standard- or maximum-sized panels. Typical applications are shown in Figure 11.2. At doors and windows, casing trim is used to conceal the rough frames and the cut edges of abutting drywall or other paneling. Additional trim used at windows includes the stool (a thick horizontal board across the full width at the bottom of the window) and the apron (a thinner vertical plate installed beneath the stool). Trim called base molding and shoe molding is used extensively at junctions of floors and walls. Other trim is frequently used at junctions of different finishes on floors, walls, or ceilings, and at changes of plane.

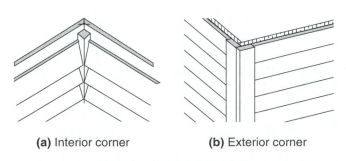

(a) Interior corner   **(b)** Exterior corner

Figure 11.1   Exterior Trim

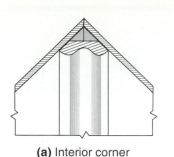

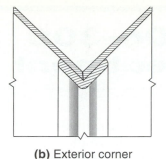

(a) Interior corner   **(b)** Exterior corner

Figure 11.2   Interior Trim

Flooring: Section 09–550

Finishing: Section 09–900

5.3 Precautions

Much of the commentary included in Part 5.3 of Section 06–100 pertains to the work of this section. In general, finish carpentry work is less hazardous than rough carpentry work, in that the structural frame of the building is usually fairly secure before finish carpentry work starts, and much of this work is done on the inside of the building. Nevertheless, difficulties can be encountered in handling large and unwieldy sheets or panels or long lengths of trim and doing work on scaffolding on the outside of buildings, particularly during windy or wet weather.

Many products used for finish carpentry are fairly delicate or brittle, and are often easily cracked, chipped, or scratched; most are factory prefinished. They therefore require care in handling and storage at the site. Most require to be placed under cover and to have protection from dust, dirt, moisture, staining, and adverse weather conditions; particular consideration should be given to kiln-dried components. Panels and stiff sheets should be stacked vertically on edge in narrow racks, permitting easy removal without disturbing adjacent panels and to prevent panels from sagging. Running trim and other long moldings should be stacked horizontally so as to avoid breakage or warpage.

Other Work. In some regions or contracts, other items of woodwork are included in composite finish carpentry specifications. As previously stated, to conform with *MasterFormat* and to avoid repetition, the preparation, fabrication, and installation of such related or similar woodwork is detailed elsewhere in this book, as follows:

Solid and spaced decking: Section 06–170

Cabinets, shelves, stairwork: Section 06–400

Shingles and tiles: Section 07–300

Doors and frames: Section 08–200

Windows and frames: Section 08–600

Residential Work

High-quality finish carpentry work is frequently installed in residences to enhance visual appeal and improve resale value. Components may be factory fabricated, ready for on-site assembly (UBC Architecture)

Section 06–300
Wood Treatment

1.0 Introduction

1.1 General Issues

Wood treated with preservatives was originally used in industries other than building, such as farming, mining, railroading, and shipbuilding, in situations where fine appearance and continuous or close human contact were of secondary consideration. Its extensive use in building construction is of relatively recent origin, largely occurring since World War II. As demand has increased for inexpensive but durable wood-framed housing, improved technology has produced more suitable preservative products which are cleaner, longer lasting, and safer to use.

Being of organic origin, untreated wood is subject to deterioration and attack from a number of sources. In general, there are four primary elements that contribute to decay in wood: air, feeders, heat, and water; elimination of one or more of these elements will significantly reduce the potential for decay. In particular, there are a number of natural agencies that contribute to decay, such as aging and fire, although fungi, insects, and vermin also play an important role in the destruction of wood products. As people who purchase and use such products have an understandable interest in protecting their investment, the construction and chemical industries have developed a considerable body of theoretical knowledge and applied science relative to this issue. The result is that there is now a large variety of products and processes capable of responding to almost any wood treatment need, an increasing awareness of new design possibilities using treated wood, and therefore a large and growing market for treated lumber. Also, in these ecologically enlightened times, research into biodegradable preservatives is proceeding apace. Wood protected by in-depth treatment is described in this section; wood protected by surface treatment is described in Section 09–900.

1.2 Design Aspects

In Section 06–100, it was explained that if wood members are properly handled both in design and in production, the aging process need not be a significant factor; indeed, some members actually improve with age to a limited extent, although most will more likely slowly deteriorate. Rapid deterioration is usually the result of attack by other agencies. Fire destroys wood by converting its coherent carbohydrate structure into discrete noncohesive particles of carbon and other chemicals and gases. Water can destroy wood in two ways: directly by dissolving its fibrous structure and indirectly by supporting the growth of harmful fungi. These wood-rot fungi occur in two main groups: dry (such as *Merulius lachrymans*) and wet (such as *Coniophora cerebella*). Although the spores of both need moisture for their generation, the dry-rot fungus reduces wood to a dry powdery state, whereas the wet-rot fungus flourishes best in a continuously moist environment, reducing wood components to a wet mushy state. Both states seriously detract from the structural integrity, utility, and appearance of wood products.

Insects, such as ambrosia beetles, carpenter ants, furniture and powderpost beetles, termites, and similar borers, destroy wood by simply chewing their way through it. Although such insects are to be found throughout North America and can become a problem wherever they occur, they are more commonly encountered in the warmer southern regions then in the cooler northern regions. Wood can also be damaged by small animals, such as birds, mice, raccoons, rats, and squirrels, many of whom like to make their nests in spaces inside the floors, walls, ceilings, and roofs of wood-framed buildings. Even domestic animals such as cats, dogs, and hamsters can take their toll on wood, as many homeowners know to their cost; the activities of humans are excluded from this study.

The attempt to use chemicals to preserve wood from deterioration can precipitate design problems of other kinds. Preservatives can have negative effects on the strength, appearance, or other integral attribute of wood components, as well as causing possible incompatibility with adhesives, metals, paints, plastics, and other materials frequently used in conjunction with wood members. Some chemicals can also adversely affect humans and animals who may be allergic or otherwise sensitive to their effects. Additionally, one must have ecological concern for the general planetary environment when using chemicals in construction.

In addition to the foregoing generalities, there are certain specific aspects of design that contribute to wood deterioration; if these are understood, then satisfactory measures can be adopted to resist their effects. The problems can be broadly classified as follows: the nature of wood **products**, the building **positions** in which they are placed, and the **environment**.

Problem products. Wood which is damaged, diseased, immature, open grained, unseasoned, or untreated.

Problem positions. Wood fully enclosed in concrete, masonry, or plaster; wood in contact with damp earth or wet metal; wood exposed to physical wear and tear; wood capable of being accessed by insects or other fungal organisms; and wood placed near open flames or other sources of high heat.

Problem environments. Strong sunlight and harsh weather; inadequate ventilation; areas of continuous high heat and humidity; periodic immersion in water; subjection to freeze/thaw cycles; and salt-water exposure. Untreated wood is durable in cold dry environments.

As well as problems of poor design, there are also numerous construction failures with which to contend, such as blocked drains, overflowing gutters, leaking or overheated pipes, rising dampness (through capillary action), broken flashings, and peeling paint, among others.

Treated Foundation Walls
A gravel base is prepared. A treated wood sill plate is secured in position. A section of wall is framed up using treated wood plates and studs. (Canadian Wood Council)

The solutions to such problems are to select the correct kinds of wood, apply appropriate preservatives, place the pieces in proper positions, and control the surrounding environment within limits known to be acceptable. Despite such precautions, accidents may still happen.

Some major applications of treated wood in building design are to be found in foundations and sill plates; below-grade basement walls; concrete formwork; exterior balustrades, decking, and stairs; cant strips and edge blocking in roofing systems; exterior wood siding; rough bucks for doors and windows; strapping and furring; wood thresholds; and border boards, fences, steps, and retainers in landscaping projects. Treated wood frequently has either a pale green or dark brown color which may affect the application of subsequent decorative coatings. Pressure-treated wood is usually more uniform in appearance than manually treated wood, and the probable life of the impregnated wood pieces can be increased by a factor of 10 over that of superficially treated members in most cases, the economic effects of which can be readily calculated. Figure 1 shows a cross section through a treated wood foundation.

1.3 Related Work

Work closely connected to this section is described in the following sections, to which reference should be made:

02–150	Protection
03–100	Formwork
06–100	Rough Carpentry
06–170	Prefabricated Wood
06–200	Finish Carpentry

2.0 Products

2.1 Materials

Most wood preservatives used in construction are derivatives of copper, sodium, or zinc. Arsenic, derived from copper and well-known to be very toxic, is a common preservative ingredient in one of its many forms; properly handled, it is relatively safe. Some of the more common preservatives used in construction are listed in Part 5.2.

There are three primary classes of wood treatment products, categorized by their vehicle types: **gas-borne, water-borne,** and **oil-borne.** Gas-borne preservatives are seldom encountered in construction projects, and are therefore not included in this

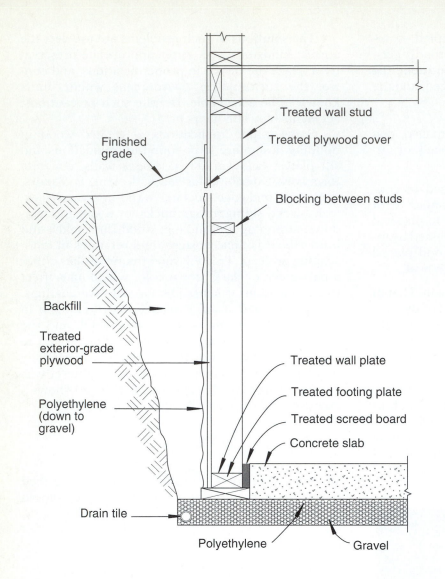

Figure 1 Treated Wood Foundation

study. The other two classes can be further sub-divided into products applied **in plant** and those applied **on site**.

Water-Borne. The vehicle is usually fresh water. These products are considered by many designers to be more suitable for use in buildings, because of their ease of handling, lack of objectionable odors, and paintability. However, being water-borne, they do cause the wood to swell, and allowance must be made for this fact.

In-plant types. Copper arsenate, compounded with other chemicals (chrome and ammonia), forms the bulk of permanent nonsoluble preservatives used in commercial applications.

On-site types. Compounds of zinc chloride and copper sulfate are frequently used in semipermanent manual applications. Being water soluble, they have a relatively short effective duration.

Oil-Borne. The vehicle is usually a light volatile petroleum product, such as diesel oil or kerosene. Some designers reject their use because of possible side effects.

In-plant types. Compounds like pentachlorophenol and copper or zinc naphthenate are used in commercial applications.

On-site types. Creosote, which is a nonsoluble byproduct of coal distilled from coal tar, is sometimes used in semipermanent manual applications.

As mentioned in Part 1.1, there are many companies manufacturing a large variety of wood preservative products. While it is impractical to list them all, some of the better-known companies and products have patented trade names as follows: Boliden, Cafco, Celcure, Chemonite, Greensalt, Koppers, Osmosalt, Tanalith, Timber Specialties, Wolman, and Wood-Tek. Many products are identified by their makers using letters and numbers indicating their composition, such as CCA, C–50, K33, or Copper–8. Inclusion in or exclusion from the foregoing list implies no judgment as to the worth of any or all such products or the companies which make them; the list is simply representative.

Solutions of mineral spirits, silicones, and various paints and stains are also utilized on construction sites to moisture-proof various wood and masonry surfaces, such as cedar siding and concrete blockwork. Some of these treatments are described in Section 09–900.

2.2 Accessories

There are no significant accessories used with preservatives.

3.0 Construction Aids

3.1 Equipment

The off-site treatment of wood is essentially a factory operation; description of the equipment used is therefore beyond the scope of this book. There is no equipment used in on-site application.

3.2 Tools

On-site application of wood preservatives requires use of brushes and spray guns as described in detail in Section 09–900.

4.0 Production

4.1 Crew Configuration

For on-site applications, a preservative crew might consist of one or two semiskilled workers, brushing, spraying, or dipping pieces as required.

4.2 Productivity

For on-site applications, a semiskilled person applying preservatives by brush might achieve the outputs indicated in Table 1.

For spray applications, the above factors can be increased by a factor of about 10. Manual application is best kept to a minimum because of the dangers of using some of the products, the difficulties of ensuring uniform and satisfactory results, the gen-

Table 1
PRODUCTIVITY OF MANUAL APPLICATION OF PRESERVATIVES

Type of Work	Output per Hour	
	m²	ft.²
Fence posts	8	80
Sill plates	10	100
Decking or stairs	12	120
Plywood panels	15	150

erally high waste factors, and the risk of damage to other work underway or adjacent.

5.0 Procedures

5.1 Preparation

Before preservation, wood to be treated should be cut, dressed, drilled, milled, planed, or otherwise shaped as necessary. Defective portions should be cut out and discarded. Wood should be well seasoned and air dried under cover for several weeks prior to treatment. Although more expensive, kiln-dried lumber can also be used. While it is possible to steam cure green (i.e., uncured) lumber to save time, it is not recommended, because of the potential loss of strength and straightness. Some dense close-grained woods like fir or pine have to be mechanically incised by a slitting machine to enhance the penetration of preservatives beneath the surface. In every case, just prior to treatment, moisture content of the wood should be determined, and wood members should be cleaned free of dirt or dust, grease or oil, and loose knots or splinters.

5.2 Process

Procedural issues can be reviewed under two broad headings: **selection criteria** and **application techniques.**

Selection Criteria. The following list gives some general information on specific products to aid in the selection of wood preservative and fire-resistive treatments. In every case, it is recommended that detailed consultations be held with local wood treatment specialists before adopting any specific protective regime. Products are listed alphabetically using generic titles:

Ammonium phosphate. Water soluble; fire resistive; can be integrally colored, or wood can be painted after curing.

Copper arsenate. Good for wood in contact with damp earth or saltwater; can be painted or stained after curing; very toxic—avoid contact with people, animals, or food products.

Copper chromate. Good for wood in water; can be painted after curing; some resistance to borers.

Copper naphthenate. Can be painted after curing; effective in landscaping projects; use 2 percent solution below grade, 1 percent above grade.

Copper sulfate. Water soluble; shortlasting if used outdoors or in contact with free water; fire resistive.

Creosote liquid. For exterior use only; wood cannot be painted later; strong, longlasting odor; suitable for bottoms of fenceposts and wood foundations; effective against most insects and borers; flammable and toxic; 50 percent solutions are common.

Floor Sheathing
Plywood or particleboard sheathing is installed to act as the floor membrane. Tongued and grooved board, glued and nailed to sleepers will result in a serviceable residential floor. (Canadian Wood Council)

Treated Sleepers
A floor system is developed, first by spreading overlapped plastic vapor barrier over the gravel, then using treated dimension lumber as sleepers to support floor sheathing. (Canadian Wood Council)

Pentachlorophenol. A compound involving chlorine and carbolic acid; if dissolved 5 percent in a clear solvent, wood can be painted later; effective against most fungi and insects, but not against borers.

Quinolinolate. Also called copper–8; safe for use on wood above grade in contact with animals and food, such as on sundecks and exterior stairs; can be stained or painted after curing.

Sodium silicate. Similar to ammonium phosphate; fire resistive.

Zinc arsenate. Similar to copper arsenate, but preferably used in predominantly drier conditions.

Zinc chloride. Similar to copper sulfate; fire resistive.

Zinc naphthenate. Similar to but not quite as good as copper naphthenate; avoid contact with damp earth.

Application Techniques

Plant Impregnation

The impregnation of wood with preservatives is essentially a factory process and although beyond the scope of this book to describe in detail, a brief outline follows. There are two pressure processes involved, both utilizing sealed tanks and taking some hours to complete: One uses positive pressure, the other uses negative pressure. In each process, the prepared lumber is loaded onto small purpose-made railcars and run into a steel tank about the size of a railway boxcar. In one process, preservative is forced under pressure into the cells of the wood (Figure 2); in the other, a vacuum is created in the cells, upon release of which the preservative is drawn into them (Figure 3). In either process, the cells may be full of preservative or empty (being merely coated) upon completion, at the discretion of the manufacturer. Two of the commonly used empty-cell pressure processes are known by the names of their inventors, Lowry and Rueping, respectively. In general, empty-cell treatments are less expensive and have less tendency to leach out in service.

A nonpressure process called diffusion involves immersion of prepared lumber in a warm (or hot) bath of selected water-borne preservatives for a few days, then removing and rinsing the lumber before immersing it in a second identical but cool (or cold)

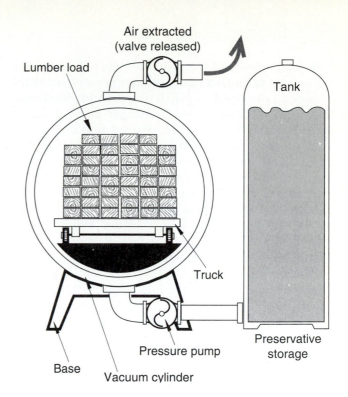

Figure 3   Pressure Preservation

solution for a few more days, all under strict temperature control. The treated wood is then removed, drained, rinsed, dried, stacked, loosely covered, and left to mature for several weeks, before delivery. Another nonpressure process called deluging involves jet-sprays to apply preservatives on prepared lumber passed through a short tunnel, similar to a carwash.

Site Application

The on-site application of preservatives in the field can be done in one of three successively better ways: first, by brushing or spraying to saturate the wood with the selected preservative; second, by dipping or submerging each piece of prepared wood in a bath or tub of preservative for a short time, measured in seconds or minutes; and third, by steeping the pieces in preservative for a longer time, measured in days or weeks.

Miscellaneous Issues

In every process, tests should be conducted to confirm that the proper levels of preservation have been achieved. In each case, excess preservative should be allowed to drain off the wood surfaces before installation in the building. Untreated wood surfaces exposed after on-site cutting or drilling require to be coated by liberally flooding with a preservative compatible with the original, before installation.

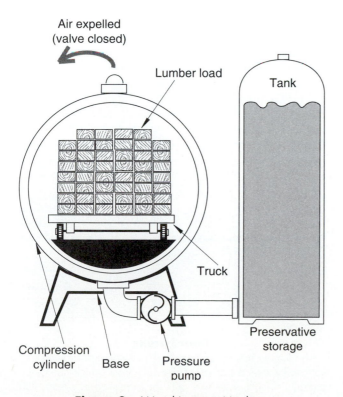

Figure 2   Wood Incising Machine

5.3 Precautions

Unused portions of treated wood such as cut ends should not be burned, as combustion can frequently produce poisonous gases. It is recommended that they be buried in a safe and legal place. Unused preservatives should not be poured into city sewer lines or storm drains without permission. Many disposal dumps require special certificates and will charge fees before accepting such waste products. Hazardous products usually require to be carefully stored under lock and key on construction work-sites.

Workers applying preservatives should wear long-sleeved shirts and gloves. Particular care should be taken to prevent prolonged skin contact with the chemicals or the preserved wood; open cuts or sores should be cleaned and covered. The fumes generated by preservatives should not be inhaled. Eye and ear protection should be worn, and chemi-cals accidentally splashed into eyes or ears should be flushed away with water. If such chemicals are ingested, a licensed physician or certified first-aid attendant should be consulted immediately. Spraying should be limited and controlled, and should not occur during windy weather.

Field tests or literature research should be conducted to ensure that preservative chemicals are compatible with other materials with which they will be in contact, especially structural fastenings and decorative finishes. For example, it is generally good practice to use galvanized or coated nails in treated wood used externally. Surfaces that may be adversely affected by chemicals leaching out of treated wood should be separated from the same by appropriate slip sheets. Surfaces not to be treated should be masked or covered with kraft paper or polyethylene sheeting.

Exterior Structures

Treated dimension lumber is an excellent material to use for many unfinished outdoor framed structures. The illustration shows a secure enclosure for boat storage at a community center. (UBC Architecture)

Boardwalks

Treated lumber has long been used for exterior boardwalks. The illustration shows a portion of one such walk which has been in constant use in a waterfront park for more than 25 years. (UBC Architecture)

Section 06-400
Architectural Woodwork

1.0 Introduction

1.1 General Issues

Like rough carpentry and finish carpentry, architectural woodwork is another specialized subdivision of general carpentry work. It includes most purpose-made wooden artifacts. Some examples include cabinets, counters, and shelving units; church pews, confessionals, organ lofts, screens, and altars; courtroom benches, tables, railings, bars, and witness boxes; glazed hardwood partitions; laboratory benches and fume cabinets; wood stairs and railings; ornamental balustrades; and retail store fitments. While serving primarily utilitarian functions, architectural woodwork can also impart aesthetic values to a building space, by adding beauty, dignity, and character. Coming as it usually does toward the conclusion of the project, such work is often done in close conjunction with work described in other sections, such as finish carpentry, wood doors and windows, and many of the finishing trades, such as flooring, plasterboarding, and painting.

The types of architectural woodwork items are naturally as diverse as the needs of building owners; for this reason, it is impractical to describe every conceivable item. Instead, a selection has been made of some of the more complex of typical architectural woodwork items that one might encounter in a medium-quality institutional or commercial building, such as an apartment building, a school or hospital wing, an office block, or even a substantial residence. It should be possible to infer the probable design processes and installation procedures for most other unspecified simpler items by studying the ones given.

1.2 Design Aspects

Because of the diversity of the various building components that fall under the title of *Architectural Woodwork*, significant elements of design for each of the selected items are outlined in a short paragraph immediately preceding the description of methods in Part 5.2. Virtually all architectural woodwork is intended for interior installation. Furthermore, the great majority of architectural woodwork items are factory made, prefinished, and delivered to the site for final assembly and installation, with only minimal on-site adjustment. Detailed descriptions of the processes by which such items are factory made and finished are beyond the scope of this book; site finishing of wood items is described in Section 09-900.

Some generalities of grading apply to the work of this section as a whole. Because much of architectural woodwork consists of an assembly of wood, plastic, and metal components of varying qualities, it is impractical (and indeed unnecessary) for the buyer to specify the precise quality of each component, when the owner, designer, or end-user is really only concerned with the overall quality of the completed unit. With this in mind, the approach to grading of factory-fabricated millwork adopted by most architectural woodwork-manufacturing associations endeavors to establish three broad bases of quality, **economy, custom,** and **premium,** all generally as described below. Each grade is cumulative, i.e., each grade incorporates all of the good features of the prior grade, but adds some refinements. Manufacturing associations also define acceptable softwood and hardwood shop-lumber grades and sizes, as well as the qualities of construction and materials, such as joints, core components, face veneers, door types, and hardware permitted to be used.

1. Economy. The primary consideration is functional utility; appearance (though not ignored) is of secondary consideration. Provided all components are sound and serviceable, paint-grade plywood, untrimmed door edges, and simple (though strong) hardware and construction are the norm. Items manufactured to conform to this grade are intended for use in service or functional locations, such as warehouses, storage areas, machine shops, and country cabins.

2. Custom. Though utility and serviceability are still considered to be important, some aspects of appearance are given greater prominence. For example, hardwood veneers may be selected for clear finishes on cabinet faces and doors may be edge-trimmed. Items manufactured to conform to this grade are intended for use in average or typical projects, such as stores, schools, ordinary homes, and apartment buildings.

3. Premium. First-class serviceability and appearance are of prime importance. Usually top-quality hardwood veneers and hardware are selected for portions exposed to view. Items manufactured to conform to this grade are intended for use in high-quality projects, such as benches and witness-boxes in courtrooms, information booths in better-quality shopping malls, glazed partitions in reception areas of successful legal or medical offices, cocktail bars and registration desks in public areas of major hotels, and cabinetry and millwork fittings in finer residential or retirement homes.

1.3 Related Work

Work closely connected to this section is described in the following sections, to which reference should be made:

06–100   Rough Carpentry

06–200   Finish Carpentry

08–200   Wood Doors and Frames

08–600   Wood Windows and Frames

09–000   Finishes

2.0 Products

2.1 Materials

Many of the materials used for the work of this section have been described in sufficient detail elsewhere in the book; to avoid repetition, reference is made to the appropriate sections below. In general, materials described in this Part 2 relate only to the woodwork items selected for detailed discussion in Part 5.0.

Softwood lumber and plywood: Section 06–100

Hardwood lumber and plywood: Section 06–200

Plastic laminates: Section 06–200

Cabinet Units. These consist of an assembly of shop lumber, softwood and hardwood plywoods, plastic laminates, nails, glues, and hardware.

Shelves. These can be made from almost any finish or select grade of solid wood, plastic-veneered softwood plywood or natural-veneered hardwood plywood, or laminated particleboard or flakeboard. Many lumber supply yards sell prefabricated shelves, requiring only to be shipped and installed, though some may have to be cut to length to fit into specific areas.

Stairs. Hardwood—oak and maple; softwood—southern pine and hemlock; cedar—for exterior work; generally economy grades for concealed work, select grades for work exposed to view.

2.2 Accessories

These include obvious things such as glues, hardware, moldings, nails, screws, and the like. More de-

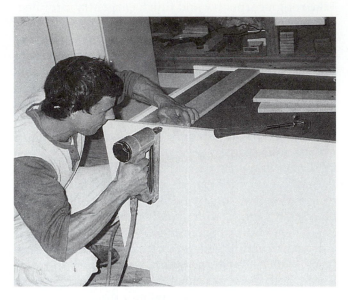

(a) Assembly

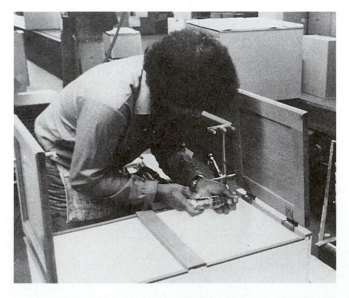

(b) Hardware

Millwork Manufacture

Millwork units (such as cabinets, shelving, and so on) are factory-made from precut components. Gables, shelves, doors, and supports are secured, ready for delivery and installation. (BCIT Building Technology)

tailed information is to be found on accessories used in conjunction with architectural woodwork in the sections listed below:

Adhesives: Section 06–050

Fasteners: Section 05–050

Hardware: Section 08–700

Moldings: Section 06–200

3.0 Construction Aids

3.1 Equipment

For a description of equipment occasionally used in connection with architectural woodwork, refer to Section 06–100.

3.2 Tools

For a description of tools generally used in architectural woodwork, refer again to Section 06–100.

4.0 Production

4.1 Crew Configuration

The installation of most architectural woodwork items is done with small crews of perhaps one or two journeyman finishing carpenters and one semi-skilled helper. On larger projects, or to install larger objects, two or more crews may be used, with a working foreman in overall charge of production.

4.2 Productivity

In the following paragraphs, all productivity factors are expressed in journeyman carpenter hours, unless otherwise stated.

Cabinets. A typical kitchen base cabinet about 90 cm or 3 ft. high by 100 cm or 3.5 ft. long will take about 1.0 man-hour to place and install; an upper wall cabinet will take about 0.5 man-hour; an angled corner unit will take about 1.5 man-hours. If cabinet doors have to be fitted into frames, allow 0.5 man-hour per door; if doors are surface mounted and can overlap frames, allow 0.25 man-hour per door. For first-class work, increase all of the foregoing factors by 50 percent. For placement of countertops, see Section 06–200.

Shelving. In open continuous configurations, such as book or store shelving, one carpenter can lay out, erect, and install about 3 m^2 or 30 ft.^{2} of shelving per hour; in confined closets, decrease production by about 50 percent. To install clothes rails below closet shelving, allow about 15 minutes per rail unit.

Stairs. To lay out, cut, erect, and connect on site a flight of simple interior open stairs will take about 8 man-hours; a flight of closed stairs will take about 12 man-hours. To factory fabricate a flight of closed stairs will take about 3 to 4 man-hours; to erect such a preassembled flight will take 2 to 3 man-hours. To lay out, cut, erect, and install an intermediate landing will take about 6 to 8 man-hours. To lay out, cut, and install a simple wood handrail on brackets at both sides of stairwells will take about 2 man-hours per flight. To prepare and assemble a simple wood balustrade for open stairs using precut components will take about 5 or 6 man-hours per flight. The foregoing factors are for straight uninterrupted work of average quality; for first-quality work, or for curved, angled, or other configurations, add about 50 percent to each of the foregoing times. A flight of prefabricated wood spiral stairs should be installed in about 10 to 12 man-hours, including the accompanying preformed curved balustrade; simple basement, porch, or sundeck stairs and railings should be able to be installed in about half that time.

5.0 Procedures

5.1 Preparation

Good artificial or natural lighting and adequate control of both temperature and humidity are essential to achieve acceptable levels of quality in fine work of this type. Control of excessive noise and dust generation is also desirable, especially during alteration work in otherwise occupied buildings. Shop drawings of manufactured woodwork items should be prepared and reviewed, to ascertain the correct assembly, location, installation, and connection of the various items. Adequate and safe temporary storage space should be set aside within the building to take delivery. Sufficiency of the items should be checked as they arrive at the site. The storage space should be close to but not immediately in the location proposed for final installation, to avoid duplicate handling; on large projects, the delivery vehicle (such as an enclosed trailer) can sometimes be used for temporary storage. The distribution of delivered items throughout the project is often best done at night or on weekends, after the other trades have finished work for the day. Time should be allowed for wood

(a) Laminate bender

(b) Stockpiled units

items to adjust to the new ambient atmospheric conditions pertaining to the project, before installation.

Prior to the delivery or installation of architectural woodwork, the areas of the building intended to receive such work should be cleaned free of debris, dirt, grease, and moisture. A check should be made of all prior work, such as roughed-in services, supports or braces, paneling or drywall lining, painting or decorating, and carpeting or other flooring, to ensure that everything is in readiness for the work of this section to begin.

5.2 Process

In this part, installation methodology for a number of selected items of architectural woodwork is described in some detail, as being representative of

Countertop Manufacture

Countertop and splashback cores are usually made of shaped particleboard to which a plastic laminate surface is glued. The assembly is then heated, bent to shape, trimmed, and stockpiled. (BCIT Building Technology)

many other similar items. Some specific design considerations for the selected items are also described, in addition to the generalities mentioned in Part 1.2.

Cabinet Units

Design

The design of wood counters and cabinets is the responsibility of the manufacturing company (for standard products) and the designer and owner (for custom-built products). There are two basic approaches to cabinet construction: **box frame** and **casework.** Each manufacturer will have its own detailed solution to specific design problems. Cabinets are usually factory finished.

1. For **box-framed** units (see Figure 1), a base section (consisting of a dimension lumber frame supporting a plywood platform) is built on the floor, and a plywood backing section is secured to the rear wall. Thick plywood end gables and intermediate panels are secured to the base and backing, and a face frame of clear dressed wood members is attached to the front to support the drawers and doors, which are installed last.

2. For **casework** units (see Figure 2), a carcass frame of dressed softwood or hardwood is con-

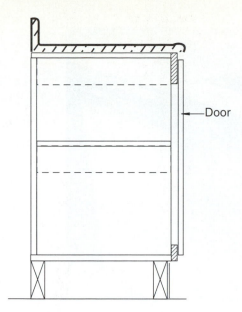

Figure 1 Box-Framed Cabinets

structed first, to which thin plywood base, back, and gable panels are attached by staples and glue. Face framing is not required, as the drawers and doors can be installed directly onto the carcass.

3. The installation of cabinet hardware (such as drawer glides, hinges, and latches) is described in Section 08–700.

Installation

The installation of wood counter and cabinet units is usually the responsibility of the general contractor, although it is frequently delegated to a separate la-

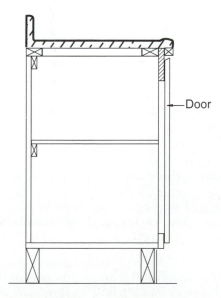

Figure 2 Casework Cabinets

bor subcontractor, independent of the millwork supplier. There are three main components to the work: **sorting, placing,** and **finishing.**

1. Sorting. The units are moved by hand or by small trolley or wheeled dolly from storage to location. The installer unpacks and assembles them

(a) Site assembly

(b) Installation

Cabinet Installation

Individual units are ganged with others, glued, clamped, and screwed together. The composite assembly is manually positioned and fastened to predetermined supports in the wall behind. (BCIT Building Technology)

(a) Installed counter

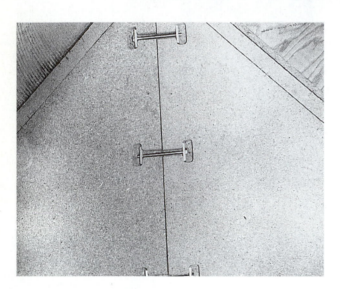

(b) View beneath counter

Completed Installation

Counter corners can be angle cut, routed out, glued, and bolted together on the underside, as shown. Typical kitchen units can be finished with custom-cut plastic laminate veneers. (UBC Architecture)

the cabinets are fastened to the screw strips. Before permanent fastening, a final check is made to ensure that units are square, plumb, level, and centered where appropriate, using concealed wedge shims as necessary.

3. Finishing. Countertops* are then cut, fitted, and installed on base units, usually in one piece between changes of direction, with mitered or butted joints at changes and finished returns at ends. Tops are usually secured to the unit frame by glueing and back-screwing from the underside, taking care not to penetrate the upper exposed surfaces. Drawers and doors are returned to their positions and secured in place. Where necessary, infill pieces of wood trim can be installed at tops or ends to close off open spaces and to conceal shims, blockings, or screw strips. Remaining cabinet hardware is then installed.

Shelving

Design

The design of wood shelving is relatively simple. It consists of a system of boards of (possibly) varying

ready for final installation; doors and drawers are usually removed to lighten the load during installation. The installer then lays out the space to receive the items, by neatly and accurately marking their positions on floors and walls. Tops of units should be level, even though floors or walls may not be exactly true to plane.

2. Placing. Upper wall units are usually installed before base units to permit workers to stand in close to the wall; if base units are installed first, they can be used to support temporary platforms to aid installation of upper units. Corner units are best installed before intermediate units; multiple units are connected to each other before installation, by temporary clamps and permanent screws. Screw strips are fastened horizontally to the wall studs, and

---

*Because the fabrication of plastic laminate countertops is frequently done directly at the site as part of finish carpentry, this work is described in this book in Section 06–200, Part 5.2.

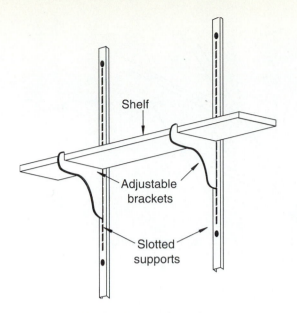

Figure 3 Shelf Brackets

types, widths, and thicknesses, horizontally installed on vertical wood, metal, or plastic brackets or supports, spaced so as to preclude significant deflection in the loaded shelf units.

Installation

The installation of shelving (see Figure 3) involves mounting the brackets or supports in positions where they can be secured to studs or other framing or backing within the wall. Shelves are then selected for size or cut to length and placed on top of the supports. Finishes on open shelf ends are usually returned (or completed) to improve their appearance.

Stairs, Balustrades, and Handrails

Design

The design of stairs and railings is governed by several factors: local building codes and regulations, the nature and type of the building under consideration, the specific use proposed for the stair, safety and comfort, the space and budget available, the skill of the stair carpenters, and the desires of the owner or designer, among other things; some design elements are indicated in Figure 4. The component parts of a typical stair consist of stringer supports, treads and risers, landings, and balustrades and/or handrails, as shown in Figure 5.

The composite assembly of components enabling people to physically climb from one level of the building to the next is called a flight of stairs. The void or open space in the building where the stair is located is called the stairwell.

The topic of stair design is dealt with under the following headings: **manufacture, layout,** and **dimensioning.**

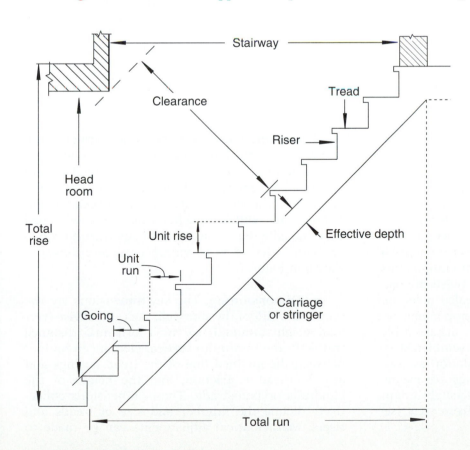

Figure 4 Stair Design

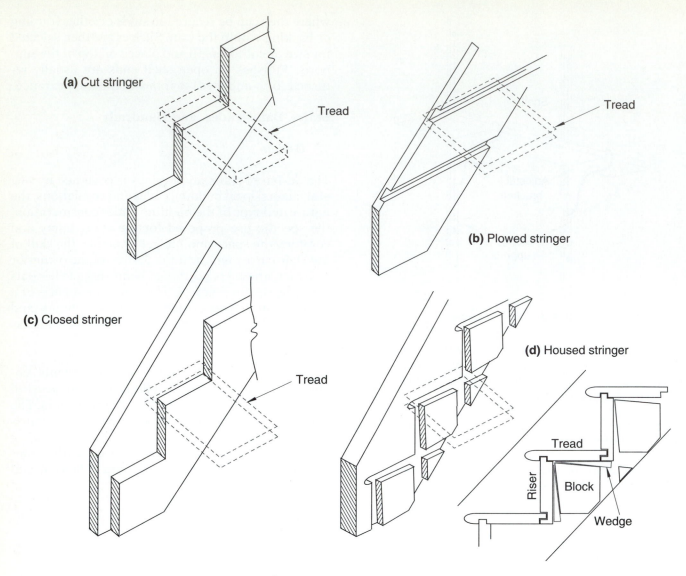

(a) Cut stringer

Tread

(b) Plowed stringer

Tread

(c) Closed stringer

Tread

(d) Housed stringer

Tread

Riser

Block

Wedge

Figure 5 Stair Construction

1. Manufacture. The fabrication of components for stairs and railings is briefly described as follows. The raw woods are debarked, milled to regular shapes and lengths, end-joined and glued up to produce clear or knot-free members of more useful dimensions, which are machine trimmed to size. These composite pieces are then planed, turned, routed, cut, bent, and sanded into specific shapes to form treads, risers, balusters, or other components. Newel posts, transitions, ramps, and twists are usually fastened to each other by concealed bolts and glue. For simple configurations, components are shipped in knocked-down form for on-site assembly; for complex stairs, components are assembled at the factory ready for delivery and installation as composite units. Wood stairs and railings are usually site-finished to permit minor repairs to slightly damaged components to be concealed from view (see Figure 6).

2. Layout. Flights can be either straight run, curved, or spiral; long runs should be interrupted with landings. Winders should be avoided; where unavoidable, they should be located at the bottom of runs. Closed stairs are constructed between two enclosing walls, with simple handrails for safety; open stairs usually have balustrades constructed on one or both sides. Some typical configurations are shown in Figure 7.

3. Dimensioning. The key dimensions are the required width of the stairwell, the ratio of rise (vertical height attained) to run (horizontal distance traveled), the minimum vertical clearance required between the inclined line of the tread nosings and any overhead restriction, and the height of the handrails or balustrade. These dimensions collectively dictate the number and size of treads and risers. Mathematical adjustments can be made to

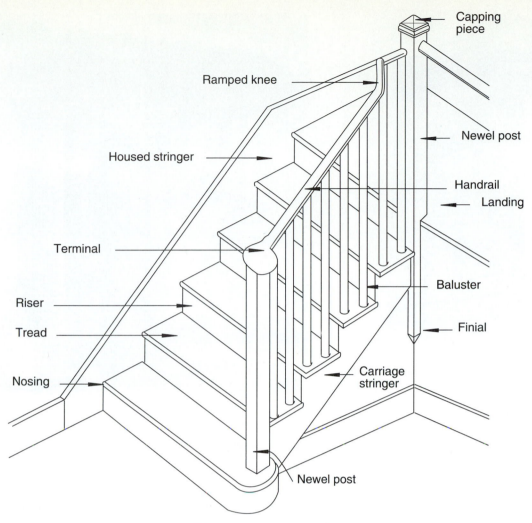

Figure 6 Stair Terminology

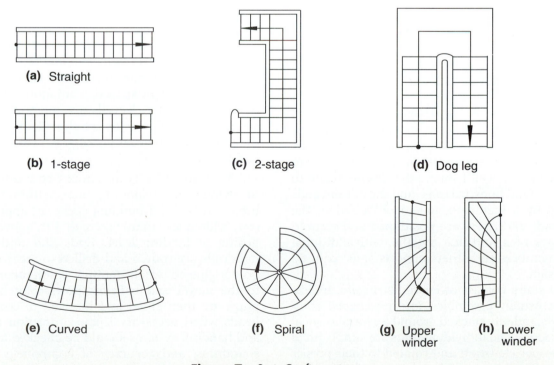

(a) Straight

(b) 1-stage

(c) 2-stage

(d) Dog leg

(e) Curved

(f) Spiral

(g) Upper winder

(h) Lower winder

Figure 7 Stair Configurations

(a) Decorative window

(b) Ornamental entrance

Ornamental Woodwork
The entrance and windows of this mall restaurant have been enhanced by the judicious use of high quality solid and veneered architectural woodwork in conjunction with other materials. (UBC Architecture)

produce various ratios and dimensions; while such calculations are beyond the scope of this book, they can be found in any good book on carpentry detailing.

Installation

The installation of typical stairs, balustrades, and handrails is generally as follows:

1. Stairs. After being designed, laid out, and cut, the components are put in place, either pre-assembled as a composite unit, or built piece by piece. Either way, the stringers have to be secured to the top header or well frame, adjustments made to ensure that tread lines are level, and the bottom ends restrained by a kickplate, nailed or bolted to the floor. Treads and risers are positioned and secured with wedges, pins, and glue, together with additional carriage members and other supports or as required by the design.

Spiral stairs consist of curved stringers, treads, and risers usually assembled into pie-shaped composite units, radially stacked around a central vertical axis or support. The individual units are simply lifted to their proper elevation and rotated to their proper orientation. Each is secured at the vertical axis.

Wood basement, porch, and sundeck stairs usually consist of plain straight cut stringers supporting solid treads without risers. Stringer bottoms placed on concrete or brick should be separated from direct contact, to avoid the risk of rot.

2. Balustrades. Holes of correct size and shape are drilled or cut in treads and landings ready to receive newel and baluster posts where necessary. Balusters should be spaced at not more than 100 mm or 4 in. on center. Newels are mortised to receive steps and rails. Post ends are glued and inserted into the holes, and the tops are aligned, ready to receive handrails.

3. Handrails. These should be located parallel to stringers and landing lines within the height limits set by local building codes, at approximately (but seldom less than) 90 cm or 3 ft. above the tread nosing or landing level. Ends and undersides of handrails are routed and drilled to receive recessed bolt or glued dowel fastenings which secure the rails to the newel and baluster posts. Matching wood plugs are then glued and inserted to conceal bolt-heads, where necessary. Upon completion, balustrade and handrail systems should be checked for rigidity, soundness, and accuracy of component lines and positions.

Other Woodwork. The majority of other architectural woodwork items, such as mentioned in Part 1.1, are factory made and prefinished, requiring minimal adjustment before final installation. Such items are simply carefully carried into position, shimmed, leveled, or straightened as necessary, and secured with concealed screws or glues to prevent movement.

5.3 Precautions

Premanufactured woodwork items should be packaged and crated to prevent damage during transit and should be left in their delivery packaging until close to the time of final installation. Other work already completed should be protected from damage that may be caused during woodwork assembly and installation procedures. Workers should wear face masks during sawing and sanding operations and eye protection during fastening operations. Adequate ventilation should be provided during gluing and finishing operations.

Custom Work

Many buildings require wood components of such high quality that they can be considered as architectural woodwork. Units are factory-assembled into a few pieces for on-site installation. (UBC Architecture)

Special-Purpose Units

Specialty buildings often have some purpose-made ornamental wood components, such as this church pulpit, made with solid oak panels and moldings and decorated with hand-crafted inserts. (UBC Architecture)

CHAPTER 07
Enclosures

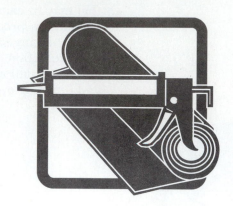

Section 07–100
Water and Dampproofing

1.0 Introduction

1.1 General Issues

The presence of water is one of the most pervasive problems with which designers and builders have to contend. In construction, water is a daily fact of life; there is often either too much of it or too little of it. It is also a fact that the exterior fabrics or the interior mechanical or plumbing systems of almost every completed building leak to some limited extent, much to the annoyance of building designers, owners, and occupants, and of the contractors who may be called back to fix the problems and the consequent mess. For the foregoing reasons, specific care should be taken with the selection, installation, and maintenance of good-quality waterproofing and dampproofing systems to control water in the general building environment. The specific problems of water control relative to mechanical and plumbing systems is beyond the scope of this book; such things are dealt with under Division 15 of *MasterFormat*.

In the context of this section, the term *waterproofing* means the provision of a barrier to prevent the passage of water in its liquid form, such as might be required in a foundation system below grade

level. The term *dampproofing* means the exclusion of water in its vapor form, such as might be required in a wood-framed exterior wall.

1.2 Design Aspects

Water has to be dealt with in construction in each of its states—liquid, vapor, and solid. Designers attempt two things: to keep uncontrolled water (in its free forms of hail, ice, rain, sleet, snow, streams, and vapor) outside of the building, and to control the water inside the building in liquid form (by installing pipes and valves in plumbing systems) and in vapor form (by adjusting humidity levels and ventilation openings in mechanical air distribution or conditioning systems). Controlled water is also used extensively in many construction processes, such as concrete work, masonry, plastering, and terrazzo, and arrangements have to be made to ensure the proper supply, absorption, conversion, evaporation, release, or disposal of water so used.

In buildings for winter sports like skating, ice hockey, and curling, water is of course required to be controlled in its solid form of ice, usually maintained by the provision of a refrigeration system in the floor

320

under the ice pad. It should be noted, however, that water in the form of uncontrolled ice can be very destructive of textured or porous building fabrics, primarily because of the expansion incurred during the freeze/thaw cycle. Any given volume of water expands upon freezing, with the resultant development of enormous forces if the volume is constricted in any way, such as in a pipe or a small crevice or crack in a masonry or concrete surface. The result is usually a fracture of the containing vessel or fabric to a greater or lesser extent, and such damage can be cumulative and ultimately disastrous if not remedied.

With respect to waterproofing, water weighs 1 kg/liter or 8.33 lb./gallon; it can therefore exert considerable hydrostatic pressure in large quantities. For this reason, a good drainage system should always be considered as part of the waterproofing system and should divert water away from the structure. Failure to do so may result in cracked foundations, leaking basements, or lifted floor slabs.

With respect to dampproofing, warm air can hold more moisture than cool air. When the temperature is reduced, moisture in air condenses. It is for this reason that vapor barriers require to be installed in buildings on the warm side of insulation systems, so that the moisture does not condense within the insulation at the dew point (the point or plane in the wall where warm and cool air meet) and thereby reduce its effectiveness. The insulation should keep the temperature of the air on the warm side high enough to prevent significant condensation from occurring on the vapor barrier surface. Dampproofing systems are required to be applied to the outsides of basement and foundation walls below grade levels, to deter the ingress of moisture through the structure and into the building. Figure 1 shows the dew point in a typical exterior wall.

1.3 Related Work

Work closely connected to this section is described in the following sections, to which reference should be made:

02–200   Earthwork

02–700   Drainage

03–300   Cast-in-Place Concrete

06–100   Rough Carpentry

07–200   Insulation

07–500   Membrane Roofing

2.0 Products

2.1 Materials

Materials for this work can be classified under the two broad headings already identified:

Waterproofing. Materials used for this purpose are intended to resist the passage of water in liquid form. Two categories are commonly encountered:

1. **Sheet products.** There is a large variety of large, thin prefabricated sheets of asphalt-impregnated paper, butyl rubber, lead, neoprene, polyvinyl chloride (PVC), and similar durable materials, ready for installation. Many companies also produce metal-clad, asphalt-core sandwich panels and sheets for this purpose.
2. **Coating products.** These include asphalt, coal-tar pitch, and a variety of solutions containing fibers such as glass or asbestos or expandable ingredients such as oxidized iron or bentonite clay.

Dampproofing. Materials used for this purpose are intended to resist the passage of water in vapor form. Three categories are commonly encountered:

1. **Paint** barriers consist of one or more thin coats of thick asphalt paint, butyl rubber, coal-tar pitch, epoxy resin, or silicone solution.
2. **Paper** barriers are made of plain asphalt-impregnated kraft paper, sometimes reinforced with long glass fibers. They are available in continuous rolls in widths of 1 m or 3 ft.
3. **Plastic** barriers are made of thin sheets of polyethylene (PE), 0.1 mm or 0.004 in. (4 mils) thick and supplied in continuous rolls in widths varying from 2 m or 6 ft. up to 6 m or 20 ft. wide. (The word *mil* in this context means 0.001 in.)

2.2 Accessories

Some waterproofing or dampproofing systems require adhesive plastic tapes and rustproofed nails and staples to secure them in position.

3.0 Construction Aids

3.1 Equipment

Compressors with hoses, nozzles, and bits are used to prepare surfaces and to pump waterproofing and dampproofing materials.

3.2 Tools

Heavy-duty brushes, trowels, and utility knives are commonly used to cut and shape membrane materials and to apply coatings.

4.0 Production

4.1 Crew Configuration

Crew sizes normally consist of one or two skilled applicators, with one semiskilled helper to move materials and equipment as required. On large projects, two or more crews may be required.

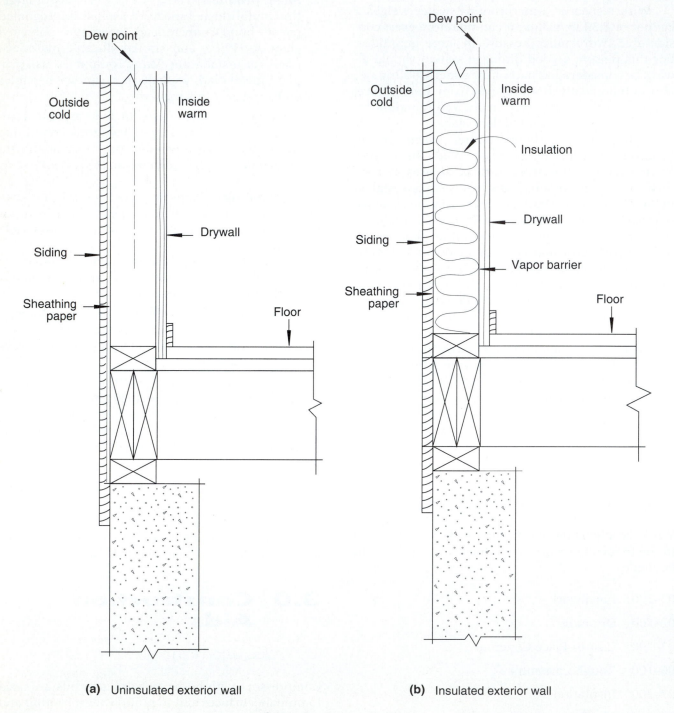

(a) Uninsulated exterior wall   (b) Insulated exterior wall

Figure 1 Exterior Sections

4.2 Productivity

As much of this work is done in comparatively confined areas and spaces, productivity is often not as high as might otherwise be expected. Table 1 shows factors for preparatory work and for application of waterproofing and dampproofing on typical projects of average size and complexity.

5.0 Procedures

5.1 Preparation

The process starts with the removal of all materials, equipment, and debris not associated with or required for the work of this section. Building areas scheduled to receive waterproofing or dampproofing should be clean, dry, firm, and properly cured. They should be free of dust, loose particles, or sharp projections; concrete or masonry surfaces should be roughened as necessary by sandblasting or jackhammering to provide a good bond or fit between the structural frame and the selected waterproofing or dampproofing system. Gravel subbases under concrete floor slabs should be "blinded" (finished or topped off) with fine gravel or sand and rolled smooth and level.

Priming

Most treatments (whether on floors, walls, or roofs) require the subbase to be cleaned and then primed with an appropriate primer/sealer, ready to receive the selected proofing system. (UBC Architecture)

Table 1
PRODUCTIVITY FACTORS FOR MOISTURE-PROOFING

Type of Work	Area per Hour m²	Area per Hour ft.²
Preparation:		
Cleaning concrete	5	50
Roughening concrete	2	20
Priming wood decks	40	400
Preparing stud walls	80	800
Waterproofing:		
One-layer lead sheet	2	20
Two coats clay or mastic	3	30
Three-ply built-up membrane	4	40
Four coats iron oxide	5	50
Dampproofing:		
One-coat thick paint	10	100
One-ply polyethylene sheet	50	500
One coat silicone spray	40	400
Two-ply asphalt paper	30	300

5.2 Process

Waterproofing. There are two areas commonly requiring treatment:

1. **Basement walls** (see Figure 2). These can be treated in one of three ways:
   a. A membrane consisting of two or three plies of asphalt and felt or other synthetic material is built up as described in Section 07–500.
   b. A membrane consisting of emulsified asphalt or clay is sprayed on in layers to any desired thickness.
   c. A membrane consisting of prefabricated waterproof panels is assembled in position and secured with nails or clips.

2. **Floor slabs** (see Figure 3). These can also be treated in one of three ways:
   a. A membrane consisting of heavy PVC or butadiene sheets is positioned, with all edges overlapped 150 mm or 6 in. and sealed with a proprietary adhesive.

Figure 2 Waterproof Vertical Wall

b. A membrane consisting of two or three plies of asphalt and felt or other synthetic material is built up as described in Section 07–500.

c. A membrane consisting of sheet lead (weighing 20 kg/m² or 4 lb./ft.²) having lapped soldered joints is placed on a prepared smooth concrete base.

Dampproofing. There are four areas requiring treatment:

1. **Foundations.** One or two coats of heavy, thick, waterproof paint are applied by brush or spray to the exterior wall surfaces.

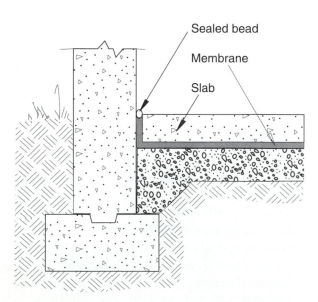

Figure 3 Waterproof Horizontal Slab

Sealed bead
Membrane
Slab

2. **Concrete floors.** A layer of heavy PVC sheet is uniformly spread over a prepared gravel base, overlapping all edges by about 150 mm or 6 in.

3. **Walls.** For stud walls, a layer of light PE sheet is uniformly spread over the wood or metal framing, overlapped 100 mm or 4 in. at all edges, and stapled in place. For masonry or concrete walls, proceed as described above for foundations.

4. **Roof decks.** Two layers of asphalt-impregnated building paper are hot-mopped into position as described in Section 07–500.

(a) Checking

(b) Installing

Membrane Application

In horizontal systems, the sheets are rolled out to check alignment, then rerolled and relaid with asphalt or patented sealer by brushing or mopping to ensure contact and remove air bubbles. (UBC Architecture)

Paint Coat Application
Where moisture conditions are not severe, a one- or two-coat spray or brush application of asphalt paint may suffice. Care should be taken regarding neatness at the finished grade line. (BCIT Building Technology)

Openings for devices such as pipes, conduits, light switches, electrical outlets, and the like passing through waterproofing or dampproofing systems should be carefully sealed after the devices are positioned.

Protection
After the proofing system is complete and cured, backfilling of trenches may commence. Plastic, hardboard, or paper can be used to protect membranes from damage during backfill. (BCIT Building Technology)

5.3 Precautions

All waterproof or dampproof membranes located in areas below grade are liable to be damaged during backfilling of earth or gravel. Consideration should therefore be given to protection by placing inexpensive hardboard or plywood sheets between the membrane and the fill.

Section 07–200 Insulation

1.0 Introduction

1.1 General Issues

Insulation work in construction includes applications in electrical systems, in mechanical installations, and in other construction. Insulation used in electrical and mechanical work is beyond the scope of this book. Insulation used in other construction can be subdivided into the following broad categories: placement of **rigid boards** onto foundations, roofs, and slabs; insertion of **flexible batts** into floors, walls, and ceilings; and troweling, spraying, or blowing prepared **granules, foams, pastes, or powders** onto or into parts of the building frame. These applications are discussed in this section. The amount and type of insulation in buildings is usually determined by a combination of factors involving building location, building codes, owner's requirements, designer's recommendations, and product availability and cost.

1.2 Design Aspects

Heat loss or gain through building systems is measured in **metric** units as joules per second per square meter per degree (J/s/m²/°C); or in **imperial** units as British thermal units per hour per square foot per degree F (Btu/hr./ft.²/°F). Heat loss or gain calculations are based on the relationships between the resistance and the conductivity of each of the particular materials comprising a composite floor, wall, or roof system in any building; such calculations are beyond the scope of this book. Good insulation design involves uniformity of appropriate material types and thicknesses and continuity of the system to completely isolate one side from the other. The provision of adequate vapor barriers (described in Section 07–100) on the warm side of the insulation is also critical to the maintenance of good insulation properties in most cases.

The purpose of insulation is to control the passage through building components of energy in any of several forms, such as flame, electricity, heat, light, sound, magnetism, or radiation. In particular, insulation materials can be used to contain electrical energy in wires, thermal energy in pipes, light energy in windows, sound energy in rooms, fire energy in industrial processes, and radiation energy in laboratories. They are also commonly used to keep heat or cold in or out of entire buildings or parts thereof.

All construction materials restrict or permit the passage of energy to some extent. Specific resistance of any material will vary directly with its thickness, while conductivity varies inversely with thickness. Materials having significantly low factors of heat conductivity (below 0.5 kJ [Kilojoules] or 0.5 Btu) are classified as thermal insulators. Plastic insulation products require to be protected from exposure to ultraviolet radiation.

In general, metal products have little or no value as insulators, while masonry and concrete products are of low value. Wood products are of medium value, while fibrous or chemically foamed products (of mineral, plastic, animal, or vegetable origin) are usually of high value, as is entrapped air.

1.3 Related Work

Work closely connected to this section is described in the following sections, to which reference should be made:

05–050   Metal Fastening

07–100   Water and Dampproofing

07–500   Membrane Roofing

2.0 Products

2.1 Materials

Insulation materials can be generically categorized into five groups.

Rigid Insulations.   These are made from foamed or beaded plastics such as polyurethane, polystyrene, or polyisocyanurate, from asphalt-impregnated wood fiberboard or chipboard, and from foamed resin-bonded glass fiber. They are available in boards between 13 and 100 mm or $1/2$ and 4 in. thick, having face dimensions between 60 and 120 cm or 2 and 4 ft. wide and 1.2 and 4.8 m or 4 and 12 ft. long. Some have reflective plastic or metallic film laminated to one or both faces.

Flexible Insulations.   These are made either from bonded glass fibers or bonded mineral wool. They are available in either blanket or batt form and in paper-enclosed or plain form. Batt insulations are produced in a variety of sizes and thicknesses, ready to fit into standard spacings between studs and joists, such as 400 and 600 mm or 16 and 24 in. wide. Some have integral vapor barriers attached to one side, ready for stapling to the structural frame of the building; others have a layer of aluminum foil laminated to one side to reflect heat.

Foamed Plastics.   These are normally two-component systems of polystyrene or polyurethane, in which one component acts as a catalyst to cause a chemical action in the other, resulting in the generation (within seconds) of an aerated foam product, suitable for pumping or pouring into building cavities.

Loose Particles.   These consist of cleaned and graded fractions of common aerated minerals, such as mica, perlite, vermiculite, and blown slag, as well as cork granules, diatomaceous earth, and occasionally sawdust. They are packaged in bags, ready for hand pouring or machine blowing into position between wall studs or floor or ceiling joists.

Sprayed Materials.   These usually consist of aggregations of cementitious or resinous products, gypsum fibers, and expanded shales or vermiculites, reduced to powder form and activated by the addition of water (in carefully specified quantities) at the site to form a thick cream or paste, suitable for spray or trowel application as appropriate.

2.2 Accessories

The accessories used in conjunction with insulations comprise a large variety of adhesives, anchors, clips, nails, staples, tapes, and vapor barriers. These are all described in other sections of this book.

3.0 Construction Aids

3.1 Equipment

Pumping equipment of suitable size and output is necessary for sprayed-on or blown-in insulation. One of these machines is illustrated in Figure 1.

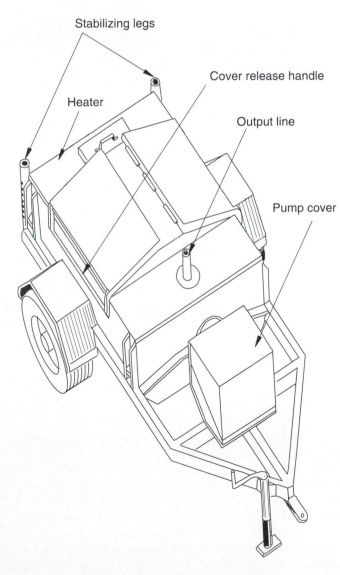

Figure 1 Pumping Equipment

3.2 Tools

Operators installing insulation require a variety of light saws, utility knives, shears, and staplers in their work.

(a) Checking stud framing

(b) Inserting batt insulation

Wall Batts
The wood or metal framing system should be checked to ensure that it is complete and ready for insulation. Fiberglass or mineral wool batts are unrolled and gently pushed into position. (Owens-Corning Canada)

4.0 Production

4.1 Crew Configuration

Most types of insulation can be installed by one skilled person, such as a carpenter or roofer, or by a semiskilled laborer, working under guidance. On large projects, a helper may be employed to assist with moving and handling insulation materials in bulk to keep installation production levels up. A crew of two or three may be needed to set up and move scaffolding to work in high places. Certain foam applications require certified applicators (and companies) in order to comply with standards.

4.2 Productivity

Approximate factors are given in Table 1 for installation of each of the three main categories of insulation identified in Part 1.1. The assumption is made that work is being done by skilled personnel on commercial or institutional projects of average size and normal complexity.

5.0 Procedures

5.1 Preparation

Before commencing the work of this section, all obstructions, debris, and equipment not necessary for

Table 1
PRODUCTIVITY FACTORS FOR INSTALLING INSULATION

Type of Work	Area per Hour	
	m²	ft.²
Rigid boards:		
Loose in foundations	10	100
In sandwich floor slabs	5	50
On soffits of roof areas	4	40
On top of flat roofs	3	30
Glued to interior walls	2	20
Flexible batts:		
In floors and ceilings	8	80
In wall systems	10	100
With paper backings	12	120
Other types:		
Sprayed foam	20	200
Blown granules	15	150
Poured granules	10	100
Troweled coating	5	50

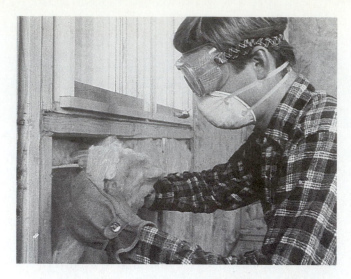

(a) Detailing

(b) Vapor barrier

Batt Finishing
Batts are carefully worked around interruptions (such as services) to ensure continuity of the insulation feature. Plastic vapor barrier is then spread, lapped, and stapled in position. (Owens-Corning Canada)

this work should be removed from areas to be insulated. In general, all roughing-in of electrical, plumbing, and mechanical work and supports for other services should be completed before insulation work commences. Dirt, dust, grease, oil, or paint should be cleaned up and removed. The installation of conduits, ducts, equipment, finishes, framing, or piping that might hinder the uniform installation or application of insulation should be deferred until the insulation is positioned. In some cases, scaffolding may need to be erected.

Wall Boards
Rigid panels of polyurethane or styrene can be adhered to wall or roof surfaces of buildings, depending on the heat-loss control system. On exteriors, some refer to it as "outsulation." (UBC Architecture)

5.2 Process

Installation of insulation in general is relatively simple and straightforward. Descriptions for specific types of materials follow.

Rigid Boards. These are either laid loose and dry, embedded into an adhesive of some sort, or mechanically clipped in position with a system of bars and bolts. Square edges of boards should be close-butted; shiplapped or tongue-and-groove edges should be coupled together. Knives and saws can be used to form cutouts for pipes or other protrusions passing through the insulated system. See Figure 2.

Flexible Batts. These are selected on the basis of their size relative to the spaces they are intended to fill. They are trimmed as necessary using knives or heavy-duty scissors and then simply placed into the spaces, where they stay in position because of gravity and friction. If they have paper or plastic backing, the backings are usually stapled to the building

Figure 2   Rigid Insulation

frame; separate vapor barriers can be installed as described in Section 06–100. See Figure 3.

Foamed Plastics. The ingredients are mixed at the site, then pumped into position through hoses with nozzles selected to suit the size of the apertures through which the foam has to be pumped.

Roof Stockpiles
Insulation can be raised to the roof by crane or hoist in bulk on wooden pallets and protected from the weather until installation on the roof deck. (UBC Architecture)

Loose Particles. These are manually shoveled or blown through an air pump into position between studs or joists or into the cavities of masonry bricks or blocks. Uniformity of thickness can usually be achieved by lightly hand raking the loose fill after initial placement. See Figure 4.

Sprayed Materials. These are machine mixed and then hand troweled or machine sprayed around structural steel or other building components requiring to be insulated.

During and upon completion of insulation work, tests should be conducted to determine that areas scheduled for treatment are completely insulated, that proper adhesion has occurred if foam is used, that specified thicknesses have been achieved, and that excess insulation has been neatly trimmed and removed.

Figure 3 Flexible Batts

Roof Boards

The roof boards are taken from stockpiles, cut or trimmed as necessary, manually placed in position, and secured in place with patented adhesives, clips, or both as required by specification. (Dow Chemical Corp)

Figure 4 Granules and Powders

5.3 Precautions

Insulation work is not inherently hazardous, although care has to be taken when working on ladders and scaffolds and on high or sloping roof surfaces. Because of their toxicity, insulation products having an asbestos base should not be used in buildings. Insulation products containing isocyanate compounds require special precautions during handling and installation. Some of the adhesives used to glue insulation products to the building frame are volatile and should not be inhaled in excessive amounts.

As most of the better insulation products have a porous characteristic, it is essential that they be stored in dry and well-ventilated places. If extensive amounts of fiberglass material will be handled, work gloves should be worn to prevent irritation of the skin. When using spray equipment to apply insulation, breathing masks and eye protection are advised. As most insulation materials are relatively fragile, care should be taken to temporarily protect them from damage until they can be finally covered with permanent protection, where necessary.

(a) Preparation

(a) Application

(b) Application

Roof Batts

Some flat roofs are insulated on the upper side. Wood frames are prepared to support and secure subsequent metal cladding, then felt or wool batts are carefully spread and lapped in place. (Selz, Seabolt & Associates)

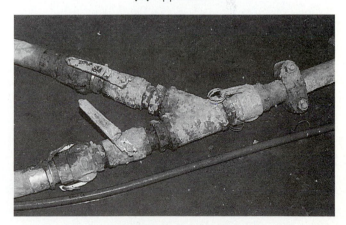

(b) Product control

Sprayed Fireproofing

The operator stands on a raised scaffold and directs a hose nozzle to spray fibrous insulation on concrete and steel soffits. Material is pumped through a system of hoses and gate valves. (UBC Architecture)

Section 07–300
Shingles and Tiles

1.0 Introduction

1.1 General Issues

Shingle, shake, and tile units of various types and sizes have been used to cover the exterior roofs and walls of buildings in virtually all cultures and climates of the world for centuries. There are two primary reasons for this: 1) the availability of materials appropriate to the system in most parts of the world, and 2) the suitability of the system to prevail against the natural dynamics of the atmosphere. The range of materials used to make such units include aluminum, asbestos, asphalt, bitumen, ceramics, clay, concrete, copper, fiberglass, plastic, slate, steel, wood, and other usually indigenous matter, from palm leaves in the tropics to ice blocks in the arctics.

1.2 Design Aspects

To avoid unnecessary repetition, the word *shingles* will be used throughout this section to cover references to shingles, shakes, slates, and tiles, except where specific issues affect either shakes, slates, or tiles. The words *exposure, lap,* and *weather* also require definition in this context. Figure 1 illustrates the first two concepts; in some regions, the word "weather" is used instead of "exposure."

The basic design of shingle systems involves placing and securing relatively small, thin, flat units on vertical exterior walls or sloping roof planes so that they overlap one another in the downward direction of the natural flow of water. Such systems are fairly resistant to weathering and the forces of nature such as rain and high wind, are generally pleasant in appearance, are comparatively economical to purchase and install, and permit flexibility in design. Because of the void spaces behind and between the shingle units, thermal expansion and contraction is minimized and readily absorbed, while the relatively small and varied sizes of the units can impart a high degree of visual texture and modeling potential to otherwise uninteresting building planes.

For roof slopes having a shallow rise-to-run ratio (up to 1:6), solid sheathing and roof felts below shingle systems are generally recommended. For slopes greater than 1:6, the sheathing may be spaced or battens may be used. Where overlaps occur between adjacent shingle units, it is good practice to have the overlap facing away from the direction of the prevailing winds.

1.3 Related Work

Work closely connected to this section is described in the following sections, to which reference should be made:

06–100   Rough Carpentry

07–600   Flashings

07–900   Joint Sealing

2.0 Products

2.1 Materials

Shingle units can be first categorized under two broad headings: those made from **natural** materials and those made from **manufactured** products. Typical units in both categories are described; within each, secondary classifications are identified.

Natural Materials.   These include **organic** and **inorganic** products.

1. Organic products. There are two main types:

   a. Wood shakes are hand-split, straight-split, or taper-split from cedar heartwood blocks;

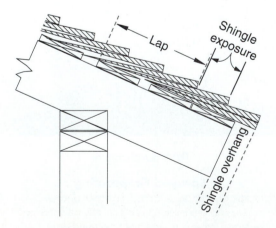

Figure 1   Exposure and Lap

lengths are 450, 600, and 800 mm or 18, 24, and 36 in.; thicknesses and widths vary. There is only one grade. Hand-split shakes can be re-sawn to produce a shake with a smooth back. Colors range from red to yellow.

b. **Wood shingles** are machine sawn from prepared quartered cedar bolts; lengths are 400, 450, and 600 mm or 16, 18, and 24 in.; thicknesses and widths vary. There are three primary grades, each labeled either blue, red, or black to indicate first, second, or third quality. A fourth grade is available for undercoursing. Colors range from yellow to white.

2. **Inorganic products.** There is one main type:

a. **Slate stones** are hand-split from natural slate beds: Lengths vary between 250 and 650 mm or 10 and 26 in.; widths vary between 150 and 350 mm or 6 and 14 in.; common thicknesses vary between 5 and 13 mm or $1/4$ and $1/2$ in. Slates having other dimensions are also available. Colors range from dark to light blue, green, gray, and red.

Manufactured Products. These include **fibrous, granular,** and **metallic** products.

1. **Fibrous products.** There are two main types:

a. **Asbestos shingles** primarily consist of a mixture of 30 percent asbestos fiber and 70 percent portland cement. Each manufacturer produces units of varying profiles, textures, and colors. Thicknesses are generally close to 6 mm or $1/4$ in.; lengths vary between 400 and 1,200 mm or 16 and 48 in.; widths vary between 200 and 400 mm or 8 and 16 in. Because of toxicity, asbestos products are being phased out of construction.

b. **Asphalt shingles** are made of thin, organic, asphalt-impregnated felts having colored mineral granules or chips bonded to one side. They are produced in either single or strip mode and with plain or interlocking tabbed corners. Singles are 300 × 300 mm or 12 × 12 in. in size; strips are 300 × 900 mm or 12 × 36 in. Common colors are black, blue, brown, green, gray, and red.

2. **Granular products.** There are two main types:

a. **Clay tiles** are produced in a manner similar to clay bricks; the clay is fired in kilns. Tiles may be glazed or unglazed. Because of their relatively heavy weight, units tend to be small (about 250 × 300 mm or 10 × 12 in.). They are available in a variety of profiles: flat, curved, ribbed, and interlocking. Colors depend on the clay or glaze used to make the tile, but

(a) Vaper barrier

(b) Installing shakes

Wood Shingles and Shakes

Rolled asphalt paper or sheet plastic is stapled in place. Shakes are nailed in position with regard to course alignment, weather exposure, overlaps, and roof interruptions. (UBC Architecture)

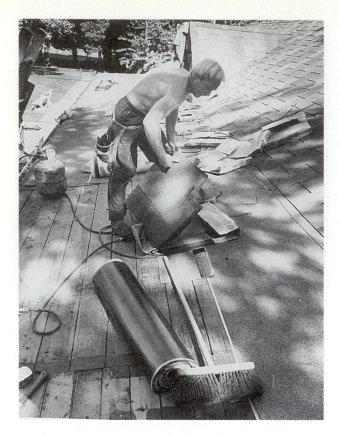

(a) Equipment used

(b) Metal shingles

(c) Fitting at ridge

Asphalt and Metal Shingles

Shinglers use hammers, knives, brooms, tin snips, propane heaters, and measuring tapes. Interlocking shingles have to be cut to fit at roof ridges, hips, eaves, and other irregular features. (UBC Architecture)

brown, purple, red, and yellow are common.

b. **Concrete tiles** consist of aggregate, sand, and portland cement, with integral color pigments added during manufacture. They are available glazed or unglazed. Like clay tiles, the units are relatively small (about 300 × 400 mm or 12 × 16 in.) because of their weight, and they are available in a similar variety of profiles. Many colors are available.

3. **Metallic products.** There are two main types:

a. **Aluminum shingles** are made from shaped sheet aluminum 0.5 mm or 0.02 in. thick, having colored mineral granules or a baked enamel finish bonded to one side. They are lightweight and durable and produced in sizes about 370 × 1,300 mm or 15 × 50 in. Each shingle weighs about 3 kg or 6 lb after coating. Most have interlocking features at edges. A wide range of colors is available.

b. **Steel shingles** are made from shaped, cold-rolled 30-gauge sheet steel, having a bonded colored porcelain-enamel coating on the exposed upper side and a rustproof primed coating on the rear face. Common overall dimensions are about 250 × 1,500 mm or 10 × 60 in., not including interlocking returns at edges and ends. Shingles weigh about 2.5 kg/m^2 or 0.5 lb./ft.^{2}. A wide range of colors is available.

2.2 Accessories

Shingle systems require to be installed in conjunction with a large number of accessories, such as building papers, roofing felts, roofing nails of galvanized or cadmium-coated steel, slater's nails of copper or brass, stainless steel or bronze screws, neoprene washers, metal or plastic flashings, and

(a) Cutting tiles   **(b)** Fitting tiles

Concrete Tile Units
The units are nailed to wood battens on roof slopes; mortar is used to weatherproof joints. Units are cut to fit at irregular roof features, using a heavy-duty saw with a carborundum blade. (UBC Architecture)

preformed trim to close open ends of shingle systems at corners, eaves, hips, and ridges. Most of these accessories are described in other sections.

3.0 Construction Aids

3.1 Equipment

As much of this work is done at roof level, ladders, scaffolds, and hoists are commonly utilized. Metal tiles and pans can be cut using a heavy-duty guillotine; they can be bent using a foot-operated device called a vice-bender. Forklift trucks are used to move heavy pallets of materials around the site. Roof jacks are frequently necessary.

3.2 Tools

Tools common to the carpenter, the roofer, and the sheet metal worker are required for the work of this section. These include a variety of axes, hammers, mallets, scribers, shears, tin-snips, and utility knives, among others.

4.0 Production

4.1 Crew Configuration

The most efficient crew for much of shingle work consists of two skilled tradespersons and a helper. On very large projects, two or more crews can be employed.

4.2 Productivity

Because of the large numbers of variables possible in shingle systems, arising from permutations of roof slope ratios and types, climatic conditions, availability of appropriate material and skilled labor, and so on, it is difficult to give accurate figures to cover generalities that will have valid application to specific situations. The factors shown in Table 1 represent typical installation on medium-sized commercial or institutional roof areas where normal work can proceed on an uninterrupted basis. For complex configurations, reduce factors by about 25 percent.

Table 1
PRODUCTIVITY FACTORS FOR INSTALLING SHINGLES

Type of Shingle	Area per Hour	
	m²	ft.²
Fibrous	6	60
Organic	5	50
Metallic	4	40
Granular	3	30
Inorganic	2	20

(a) Standard shingles

(b) Ornamental shakes

5.0 Procedures

5.1 Preparation

All shingle units and accessories should be stored in clean, dry, cool locations until ready for use. Wall and roof areas scheduled to receive shingle systems should be cleared free of debris and construction equipment not required for the work of this section. While it may be more pleasant to work in dry and mild weather, most shingle systems can be installed during cold or wet weather if necessary, provided care is taken not to entrap moisture within portions of the system. Virtually all shingle materials and accessories are delivered to the work-site ready for installation, with only minor cutting, drilling, or hole punching required to be done on the job.

5.2 Process

The installation of each of the various shingle products varies slightly because of the characteristics of the materials of which they are made.

1. Aluminum and steel pans (Figure 2). Wood battens must first be set out to panel manufacturer's directions. In general, these shingle systems are installed from the top down, by raising the bottom

Roof Patterns
Shingles and shakes of every kind can be arranged in various patterns to enhance architectural themes. In these two pictures, one can see both very simple and extremely complex arrangements. (UBC Architecture)

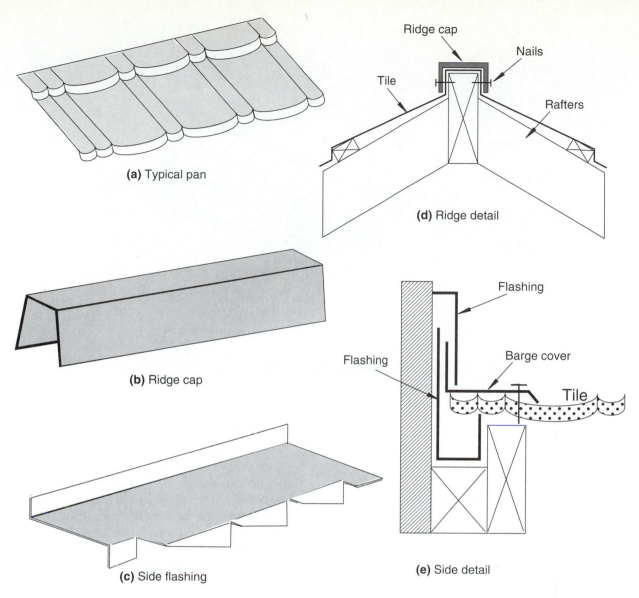

(a) Typical pan

(b) Ridge cap

(c) Side flashing

(d) Ridge detail

(e) Side detail

Figure 2   Metal Pans

edges of upper pans and slipping the top edges of lower pans underneath; both pans are then face-nailed together to the batten below.

2. Asphalt strip shingles (Figure 3). These are generally nailed or stapled along their top edges to solid sheathing covered with felt or paper. Some types have self-sealing asphalt spots and interlocking cuts at their lower edges to prevent minor windlift. Most have factory-printed markings intended to determine their correct positioning on the roof.

3. Concrete and clay tiles (Figure 4). These can be attached to spaced battens, with the pre-formed tabs at the head of every course hooked over a batten and every fourth course secured by nails to the building structure.

4. Slate and asbestos tiles (Figure 5). Slates are laid like concrete or clay tiles, but with the head of every unit drilled for and fastened with two nails to battens or sheathing below and installed to produce an exposure of about 100 mm or 4 in. Asbestos tiles are usually applied over a layer of roofing felt,

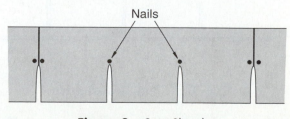

Figure 3   Strip Shingles

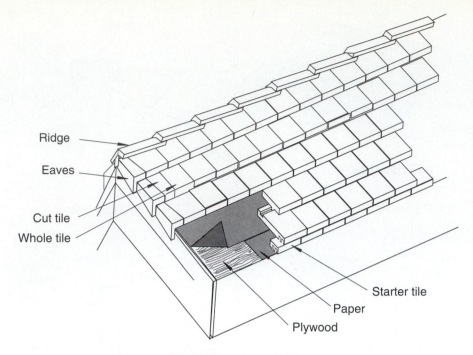

Figure 4 Concrete Tiles

drilled and fastened as described for slates, but with an overlap of about 100 mm or 4 in., resulting in varying exposure lengths.

5. Wood shakes and shingles (Figure 6). In general, it is best to attach these units to battens, to permit air circulation around and below each unit. The battens are spaced at the same distance and the intended exposure. Every unit is nailed with two large-headed roofing nails to every batten.

5.3 Precautions

Shingle work is almost always done at high elevations on the outsides of buildings; there are therefore some risks inherent in the work because of wind and weather. In most localities, regulations require that crawl boards and ladders be securely fastened in position, that roofer's toe-holds and safety belts be provided for work on steep roofs (1:3 slope), and that consideration be given to the provision of temporary

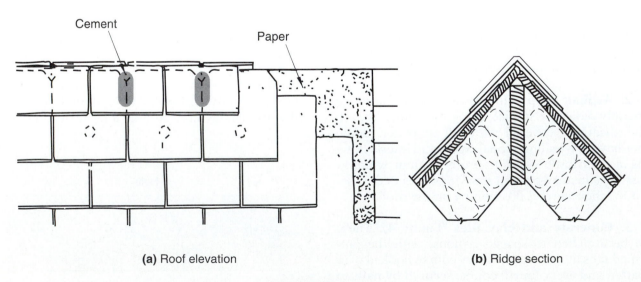

(a) Roof elevation

(b) Ridge section

Figure 5 Slates

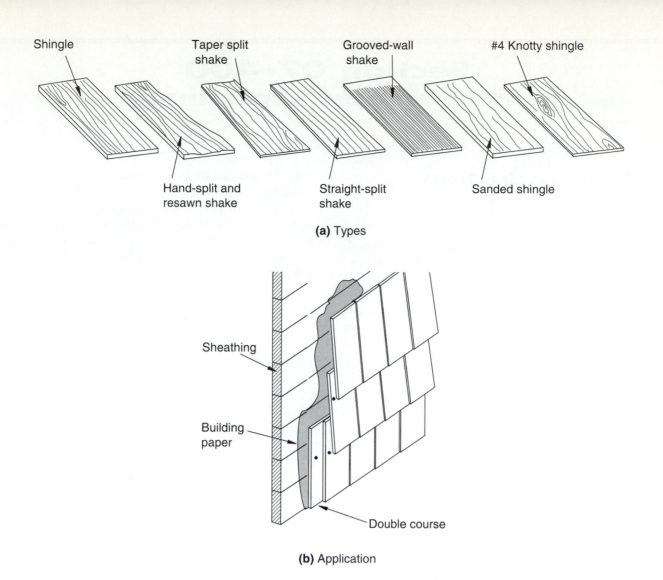

(a) Types

(b) Application

Figure 6 Wood Shakes and Shingles

boards to span weak areas of the roof structure, where personnel, materials, or equipment might be at risk.

While there is a small risk of damage occurring to other parts of the building from tools, equipment, or materials falling from or being blown off roof levels, most aspects of protection in this section are di-rected at preventing damage occurring to the shingle units themselves, during and after installation. The products involved in shingle systems are not par-ticularly hazardous, although normal precautions must be exercised when using sharp tools and heavy materials.

Section 07–400
Preformed Cladding

1.0 Introduction

1.1 General Issues

Preformed cladding consists of large, factory-shaped, interlocking, corrugated or ribbed sheets or panels, usually installed vertically on the outsides of buildings. While generally more expensive than shakes or shingles in unit cost, preformed cladding does not normally require sheathing or backing and can therefore be used to cover large areas of roof and wall framing rapidly and effectively. Most preformed cladding units are exceptionally durable and relatively attractive, provided they are not subjected to physical wear or abuse.

Preformed cladding should not be confused with two similar systems: 1) sheet metal roofing, in which large plain sheets of aluminum, copper, lead, or steel are specially cut, shaped, and fitted onto sheathed or battened roof surfaces, or 2) sheet metal siding, in which factory-shaped lengths of coated aluminum are secured horizontally to solid or sheathed walls and eave soffits of buildings. In this book, sheet metal roofing is described in Section 07–600 together with metal flashings. Sheet metal siding is described in Section 06–200 together with wood siding and trim; such work is usually considered to be part of the finish carpentry trade.

1.2 Design Aspects

When cladding units are being manufactured, various longitudinal profiles such as rounded corrugations, rectangular ribbing, beveled battens, and hemmed edges are imparted to them by passing them through rollers. The purpose of these configurations is to improve the strength, simplify the installation, and enhance the appearance of units. Some typical profiles are shown in Figure 1.

To use preformed cladding effectively, care must be taken in setting out the spacing of the supporting framing members to suit the lengths and widths of the cladding materials and the intervals at which they must be fastened. Allowance must be made for expansion and contraction to avoid buckling or warping of the cladding units. In general, the principles of shingle application (detailed in Sec-

tion 07–300) apply to the installation of preformed cladding units with respect to overlapping ends of units in the direction of the downward flow of water, to arranging vertical joints to face away from the direction of prevailing winds to minimize leakage, and to trimming or flashing openings or ends to conceal cut edges. See Figure 2.

1.3 Related Work

Work closely connected to this section is described in the following sections, to which reference should be made:

05–100   Steel Framing

06–100   Rough Carpentry

07–900   Joint Sealing

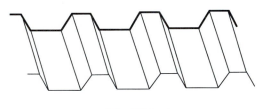

(a)   Ribbed

(b)   Wide ribbed

(c)   Vee beam

Figure 1   Preformed Profiles

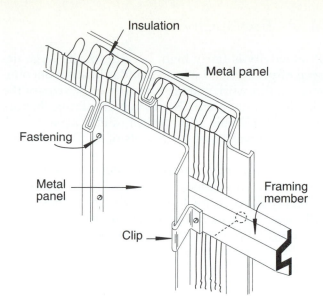

Figure 2 Cladding Section

2.0 Products

2.1 Materials

Materials for cladding can be categorized into **metal** and **nonmetal** products.

Metal Products. Two common metals are used: aluminum and steel. Aluminum cladding is available in panels up to 1 m or 3 ft. wide, 12 m or 40 ft. long, and about 1 mm or 0.04 in. thick. Steel cladding is available in panels of the same width, but half as long and half as thick. Both types are supplied with a factory-applied baked enamel or acrylic paint finish in a range of attractive colors; plain primed panels are also available.

Nonmetal Products. Four common materials are used: asbestos cement, fiberglass, plain or reinforced glass, and polyvinyl chloride (PVC) plastics. Each is available in sheets up to 1.2 m or 4 ft. wide, up to 3 m or 10 ft. long, and in various thicknesses between 0.5 and 10 mm or 0.02 and 0.4 in. Most are produced with a range of factory-applied integral colors, as well as plain. Wood siding is described in Section 06–200.

2.2 Accessories

The accessories which accompany cladding panels consist of an assortment of fasteners, such as bolts, clips, plates, screws, and metal and plastic washers, as well as matching preformed flashings and trim for use as corners, eaves, hips, ridges, valleys, and open edges.

3.0 Construction Aids

3.1 Equipment

Power-operated guillotines and extrusion machines are occasionally used to cut and shape metal for use in conjunction with cladding systems.

3.2 Tools

As this work involves shaping and cutting of sheet metal, glass, and plastic, the tools used are those of the

(a) Stockpile

(b) Installation

Standard Panels
Most standard panels are supplied preprofiled and prefinished. They are saw-cut to length, manually raised into position, and secured with neoprene-headed sheet-metal screws. (UBC Architecture)

sheet metal worker, the carpenter, and the glazier. Chase wedges, clamps, hardwood dressers, glasscutters, hammers, mallets, seaming pliers, shears, tinsnips, wedges, and wrenches are used, among others.

4.0 Production

4.1 Crew Configuration

A crew will normally consist of one or two sheet metal workers and a helper. On large projects, two or more teams may be combined and placed under the direction of a working foreman.

(a) Application

(b) Finishing trim

Custom Panels
Preformed panels can be supplied in virtually any desired profile, color, or finish. Panels are secured to metal or wood backing and finished with customized ridge, hip, and eaves trim. (Selz, Seabolt & Associates)

4.2 Productivity

Productivity is fairly high, because of the large degree of prefabrication and standardization encountered in this work and the relatively large sizes of the cladding units used. Some representative factors are listed in Table 1 for typical uninterrupted work on vertical walls and steep roofs of medium to large projects.

For lightweight products, such as aluminum, plastic, and fiberglass, factors can be increased by about 10 percent; for heavyweight products such as asbestos and steel, factors can be decreased by about 10 percent. For work on fairly flat roof decks, factors can be increased by about 10 percent; for work in complex areas, factors can be reduced by up to 25 percent.

5.0 Procedures

5.1 Preparation

Work areas should be cleared of all debris and construction equipment not required for the work of this section. Work should not proceed in wet or freezing weather, as moisture may get trapped beneath the cladding units. Adequate supplies of cladding units and accessories should be located near the work at hand.

5.2 Process

Installation is simple. Work commences at the bottom of areas and proceeds upward and laterally against the direction of the prevailing winds. Cladding units are manually handled and held in place during fastening procedures. Fasteners should normally be placed on the ridges of battens, corrugations, or ribs and not in the valleys, to avoid leakage. Fasteners are usually located at intervals

Table 1
PRODUCTIVITY FACTORS IN CLADDING WORK

Type of Work	Area per Hour	
	m²	ft.²
On wood framing	10	100
On steel framing	8	80

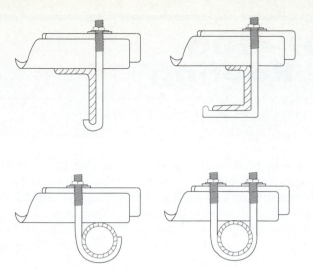

Figure 3 Cladding Connections

(a) Metal roofing shingles

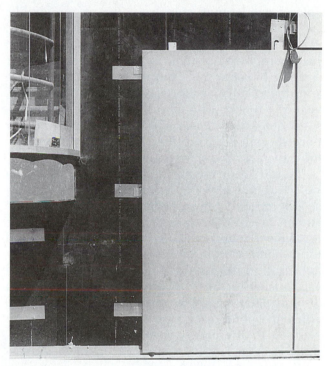

(b) Porcelain enamel panels

between 30 and 60 cm or 12 and 24 in. Waterproof washers and fastening cover caps colored to match the panels are available. See Figure 3.

5.3 Precautions

Many cladding products are supplied with factory-applied finishes; care must be taken to protect such finishes from accidental damage or discoloration. Cladding products are also susceptible to damage from distortion and cracking if fasteners are tightened or driven beyond manufacturers' recommendations. Cutting and drilling of units or accessories is best done at grade or floor level and not on ladders or scaffolds. Panel edges are particularly vulnerable to distortion or chipping.

Patented Systems

A wide range of specialty systems is available. Some are installed like regular shingles; others require special clips to secure their panel components to the building frame. (BCIT Building Technology)

Section 07–500
Membrane Roofing

1.0 Introduction

1.1 General Issues

Weatherproof membranes are used on essentially flat or simply curved roofs of commercial and institutional buildings. Where consistently sloped roofs are required, a different technique using the principle of overlapping shingles is usually preferable. For shingle systems, refer to Section 07–300.

Membrane systems can be classified as follows: those comprising a single or double layer of plastic sheeting of some sort (**simple systems**) and those comprising triple or more layers of asphalt and felt, usually covered with gravel (**multiple systems**). Both categories are described in this section. Other more specialized (and therefore less common) systems, such as fluid membranes, are not included.

Plastic sheet membranes are often utilized on roofs that may have curved, sloped, or other irregular features, whereas asphalt and gravel membrane systems are most frequently used on roofs that are nominally flat and level. The word *nominally* is used in this context because most such roofs are deliberately built to have a slight fall or inclined plane toward the drain lines. If any roof should be built absolutely flat or level, problems may be experienced with water ponding and perhaps freezing because it is unable to drain away properly. While most membrane systems involve some heat in their application, some are installed cold.

1.2 Design Aspects

First, it should be realized that the **value** of a roofing system selected for any building far outweighs its **cost**, relative to the consequences of damage that might be caused to the building's structure, its occupants, and its contents should the roof system substantially fail. Second, the larger the roof area, the greater the potential for problems. Consequently, for any building having a specifically required floor area, highrise or multistory design will produce less area of roof exposure than lowrise or single-story design, although the quality of roof exposure at higher levels can be more severe than that at lower levels. Third,

the materials used in most roofing systems are relatively inexpensive, compared to the other materials of construction. For the foregoing reasons, consideration should always be given to providing and installing the best type and quality of roofing system that the construction budget can afford. With respect to initial capital outlay, maintenance cost, and user satisfaction, it is false economy to put a cheap or inadequate roof on any worthwhile building.

Although even the best of roofing materials can fail, the more common causes of roof failure are faulty installation of otherwise appropriate materials and improper design of the structural roof frame or of the roofing membrane system itself. In particular, penetration and condensation of moisture within the roofing system is especially destructive. Wherever significant levels of moisture are likely to be present within a building, a positive vapor barrier should be placed between the inside of the building and the roofing membrane. Blisters caused by air entrapped between layers in the membrane system can also lead to system failure.

It should be understood that, when specifying any built-up asphalt and gravel roofing system, it is primarily the amount of asphalt (and not the number of plies of felt) that really determines the waterproofing quality of the system. Although the felts do impart some moisture protection, their main purpose is to permit the buildup of the required amount of asphalt and to hold the roof system together.

Designers should consider the value of having roofing specifications and procedures reviewed by an independent and qualified roofing inspection agency. They should request the submission of a written guarantee in the form of a bond from the contractor (or its roofing association) that the roofing system will perform as expected for a stated period.

It may be noted in passing that although many designers, roofers, and others may still refer to "tar and gravel" roofs, tar is not now used in good-quality roofing systems in North America. Furthermore, as tar and asphalt are not compatible, they should not be used in conjunction with each other on any one roof, such as might happen during renovation work or repairs. A similarly incorrect colloquialism also encountered in the roofing trade is the use of the term "galvanized iron" flashings, when what is really meant is galvanized steel flashings.

1.3 Related Work

Work closely connected to this section is described in the following sections, to which reference should be made:

03–300   Cast-in-Place Concrete

05–300   Steel Decking

06–100   Rough Carpentry

07–100   Water and Dampproofing

07–200   Insulation

07–600   Flashings

2.0 Products

2.1 Materials

Membrane materials, as stated, can be classified as **simple systems** *or* **multiple systems.**

Simple Systems.   There are two main groups of materials used in these systems:

1. **Prefabricated sheets** used for roofing systems frequently consist of a single thickness (1.5-mm or 0.06-in.) of heavy-duty PVC or styrene-butadiene black plastic material, reinforced with glass fibers or polyester fabrics. Typical roll sizes are 2 m wide by 20 m long or 6 ft. wide by 65 ft. long.

2. **Rubberized asphalt** or plastic must be preheated before being placed in position. It must be used in conjunction with a compatible primer-sealer to ensure a good bond with the roof deck and with reinforcing sheets at joints or points of possible stress. Manufacturers of such systems normally provide all components necessary for their system to be properly installed.

Multiple Systems.   Multiple systems are comprised of three main categories of materials used in conjunction with each other:

1. **Asphalts.** Bitumens, a group of naturally occurring hydrocarbon deposits found in solid, semisolid, and liquid forms in various parts of the world were formerly popular in roofing systems (and are still used in parts of Europe but have been largely superseded by the use of asphalts in North America. Asphalt is a manufactured product, consisting of a combination of petroleum oils and particles of carbon produced through the cracking process used to make refined oils and gasolines from crude oil. Asphalt is marketed in solid hexagonal blocks wrapped

(a) High rise

(b) Low rise

Materials Handling

On high-level roofing jobs, materials can be rapidly raised by electric cable hoists. On lower work, materials may be raised either manually or by light-duty gas-powered inclined hods. (UBC Architecture)

Table 1
ASPHALT TYPES AND USES

Type Number	Softening Temperature		Roof Slopes
	°C	°F	
1	60	130	1:12 or less
2	75	165	1:8 exactly
3	90	200	1:4 or more

in heavy-duty paper and weighing about 40 kg or 80 lb. per block. Controlled oxidization during manufacturing determines the viscosity or softness of asphalt. This results in three types or grades commonly used in construction. Each type is designated by its softening point as shown in Table 1, for use on roofs having slopes not exceeding certain ratios of rise to run:

Primers used with asphalt consist of asphalt which has been cut back (or thinned) with a solvent; they are used to seal surfaces and to improve adhesion between the roof deck and the roofing membrane system.

2. Felts are a group of products, made from organic or inorganic fibers, manufactured into large thin sheets which are cut and rolled for convenience. Each roll is about 1 m or 3 ft. wide and 45 m or 144 ft. long, and can weigh approximately 15, 30, or 40 kg or 32, 60, or 80 lb., depending on asphalt penetration. Other sizes and weights are available.

Some commonly encountered types of felts are listed in Table 2, with a brief comment on their main feature.

Some additional notes on felt types: Asbestos felts are seldom used now, because the disadvantage of the toxicity of asbestos outweighs the advantage of its fire-resistive qualities. Base felts are used in conjunction with plastic insulation materials. Coated felts and dry felts are sometimes used to form a slipsheet between a rigid deck and a built-up roof system. In glass felts, the asphalt only coats the fibers, which are impermeable. Mineral-surfaced felts are also available in narrow strips for use as cant strips. Organic felts tend to absorb the asphalt into their fibers. Organic felts can be attacked by vermin and fungi, whereas glass felts are immune to such attacks.

3. Gravel or other ballast is used to protect asphalt and felt roof membranes from several adverse conditions: ultraviolet light, physical damage, heat gain, and wind lift. Colored gravel is also used on occasion for aesthetic reasons, to improve the appearance of a roof. In general, gravels used for roofing should be clean, well graded between 5 and 15 mm

or $1/4$ and $1/2$ in. in size, sound and solid, and opaque to ultraviolet light. A common type of material used for this purpose is called torpedo gravel. Crushed rock, blast-furnace slag, and a number of ceramic materials are also available for this purpose.

Fluid Systems. Materials used in less common elastomeric or other plastic roofing systems are excluded from this review.

Measurement

Roofing is measured in metric units by the square meter and in imperial measure by a unit called the "square," comprising a square area having sides 10 ft. long and enclosing 100 sf. A roll of felt (3 ft. wide and 144 ft. long) covers 432 sf, which equals four "squares" of 100 sf each, plus 32 sf for overlaps. Roofing felts are identified by a number corresponding to their weight per square in pounds; for example, a #15 felt weighs approximately 15 lb. per square (or about 0.75 kg/m²).

2.2 Accessories

The first three items referenced below are not, strictly speaking, accessories. They are systems commonly used in conjunction with roofing membranes. They are described in more detail elsewhere in this

Table 2
ASPHALT FELTS AND FEATURES

Type	Main Feature
Asbestos	20% wood fiber plus about 80% asbestos fiber, impregnated with asphalt.
Base-sheet	Organic or glass felt with a continuous or intermittent asphalt coating applied to the underside.
Coated	Dry felt saturated with asphalt on one or both sides.
Dry	Untreated wood fiber sheets.
Glass	Asphalt-coated glass fiber.
Mineral-surfaced	Glass or organic felt, coated with asphalt-bonded colored sand particles on one side.
Organic	Asphalt-impregnated animal or vegetable fiber.
Perforated	Glass or organic felt, punctured with a pattern of tiny holes to release air and vapor during laying processes.

book; they are listed here for convenience of reference. Fastenings and adhesives are true accessories to roofing systems.

Vapor barriers: Refer to Section 07–100.

Insulation: Refer to Section 07–200.

Flashings: Refer to Section 07–600.

Fastenings:

1. Galvanized roofing nails, fastening bars, and metal clips: Refer to Section 05–050.
2. Specialty adhesives encountered in roofing work: Refer to Section 06–050.

Filter fabrics. Wherever an IRMA (Inverted Roof Membrane Assembly) roof is encountered, a thin, porous plastic filter fabric sheet is usually installed on top of the insulation to protect it.

3.0 Construction Aids

3.1 Equipment

Roofing equipment consists of two main groups of items: those used for **transportation** from plant to site and from ground to roof levels, and those used for **installation** of roofing systems.

Transportation

Ladder hoists consist of a metal ladder frame, having an electrical or gasoline-powered motor winch attached to the frame, and arranged to raise a wheeled bucket, skip, or platform by means of a cable wound around a drum.

Light cranes or **pulleys** are also used to raise materials and equipment to roof levels.

Tankers are large-capacity, temperature-controlled, insulated trucks, specially designed to safely handle and deliver heated liquefied asphalt in bulk to several job-sites in one day.

Installation

Asphalt kettles are large insulated tanks or containers, suitable for holding liquefied asphalt, mounted on wheeled carts or trailers, and equipped with a propane- or kerosene-fired burner to generate and control heat. They are available in a range of capacities, from 200 to 400 liters or 40 to 80 gallons. They can be equipped to let the asphalt pour out by gravity or to pump the asphalt upward through a system of pipes.

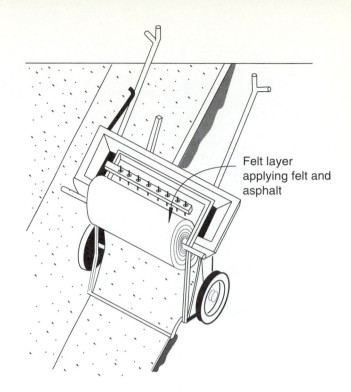

Felt layer applying felt and asphalt

Figure 1 Laying Machine

Laying machines are designed to easily handle and lay the felt rolls efficiently and continuously on the prepared roof deck, while simultaneously applying a uniform coating of hot asphalt from a small reservoir on the machine to the roll surface. See Figure 1.

Pourers are wheeled devices, consisting of a small tank with a manual release mechanism, used to safely and conveniently pour hot asphalt into flood coats during the roofing process. See Figure 2.

Spreaders are wheeled devices, consisting of a hopper with a manual release mechanism, used to uniformly distribute roofing gravels of various types on top of finished membranes, not unlike lighter but similar machines used to spread fertilizer on garden lawns. Some of the larger of these machines are self-propelled. See Figure 3.

In addition to machines designed to actually lay roofing materials, there are machines designed to facilitate the work in other ways, such as by hoisting felts and gravels from grade to roof levels. One such device is shown in Figure 4.

3.2 Tools

The common tools used in roofing are as follows:

Buckets may be simple metal containers having a capacity of about 10 liters or 2 gallons, manually carried with a short handle, or they may be safety

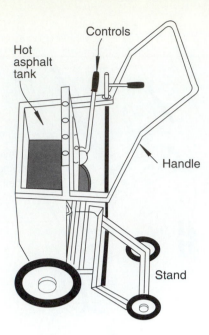

Figure 2 Pouring Machine

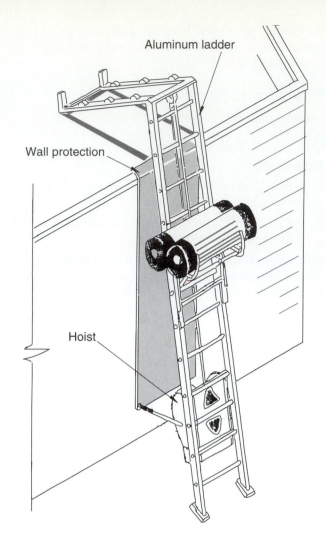

Figure 4 Roof Roll Hoist

mounted on a small metal frame equipped with castors or wheels and a long pull handle. Safety-wheeled buckets hold about 25 liters or 5 gallons.

Dippers are small ladles with long handles, used occasionally to place small amounts of hot asphalt in difficult-to-reach places.

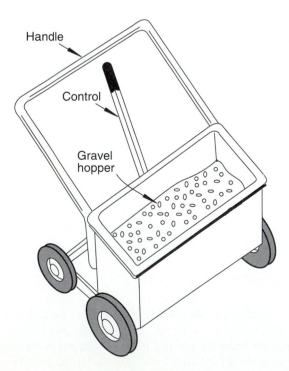

Figure 3 Spreading Machine

Mops consist of coarse rag-mop heads with long wood or metal handles; they are used to spread the hot asphalt. They are usually used in conjunction with a dipper, used to scoop out some hot asphalt from the bucket, ready for the mopper to spread it.

Pouring cans are similar in style to ordinary garden watering cans, and are used for pouring the flood coat of asphalt onto the membrane in a controlled fashion. They are sometimes used in conjunction with dippers and mops.

Pushers consist of a wide, double-sided metal blade, attached to a long wood or metal handle, and used in a manner similar to a garden rake to shove gravel particles around on the roof to eliminate irregularities in gravel thickness.

4.0 Production

4.1 Crew Configuration

A typical roofing crew for a roof of average size and complexity will normally comprise about five operators, each with a distinctive title. The kettleman tends the asphalt kettle; the pourer handles the hot asphalt in bulk; the feltman lays and nails felts; the mopman spreads the hot asphalt; and the helper moves materials and equipment around as necessary. The feltman or the mopman may be designated as foreman and made responsible for directing activities in an orderly manner. Roofing work is generally hot and dirty. It requires a considerable amount of patience, coordination, experience, and dexterity on the part of the crew members to achieve satisfactory results at economic prices.

4.2 Productivity

As roofs occur on the tops of buildings, the height above ground level is obviously a major consideration in productivity. It simply takes more time and effort to raise materials and equipment to higher levels than to lower levels. Figures given in Tables 3 and 4 are for simple flat roofs on lowrise buildings; for highrise, sloped, or complex configurations, they can be reduced by up to 25 percent. Table 3 shows time for preparation of various roof deck surfaces; Table 4 shows time for procedures on roofs having various numbers of plies. Both tables show production in square meters and in "squares" of 100 square feet.

5.0 Procedures

5.1 Preparation

Roofing work should proceed after all extraneous debris and construction equipment have been re-

Table 3
PRODUCTIVITY FACTORS FOR PREPARATION OF ROOF SUBSTRATES

Deck Type	Area per Hour	
	m²	squares
Concrete	50	5.0
Insulated	60	6.0
Steel	50	5.0
Wood	60	6.0

Table 4
PRODUCTIVITY FACTORS FOR VARIOUS ROOFING SYSTEMS

Roofing System	Area per Hour	
	m²	squares
Plastic layers:		
1-ply	40	4.0
2-ply	35	3.5
Asphalt and gravel:		
3-ply	30	3.0
4-ply	25	2.5
5-ply	20	2.0

moved from the roof areas. The structural deck should be checked for dryness, continuity, solidity, and soundness. Cant strips should be secured in position at perimeters between the horizontal planes of the roof deck and surrounding vertical planes. Membrane roofing should not proceed in freezing, raining, or snowing weather; care must be exercised to avoid trapping water under the membrane.

There are four types of roof deck substrates commonly encountered, as shown in Figure 5:

1. For **concrete** decks, the surface should be cured for at least 3 weeks, be dry and free of dust, and have a good, lightly textured, wood-float or steel-trowel finish. It should also be free of grooves, ridges, hollows, or other imperfections that might interfere with the roof membrane. Asphalt primer should be mopped or sprayed on at the approximate rate of 0.5 liter/m² or 1 pint/yd.².

2. For **insulated** decks, there are two preparatory processes: one for use with asphalt-impregnated **fiber** insulations made of wood or glass and one for use with foamed or beaded **plastic** insulations made of urethane or polystyrene. The installation procedures for these insulation materials are described in detail in Section 07–200; only the additional preparation of such insulated surfaces for roofing is described below:

a. For **fiber** insulations, proceed as for wood decks.

b. For **plastic** insulations, a coated base sheet should be applied to cover the insulation and to protect it from the effects of the hot asphalt mopping for the first layer of the roofing membrane.

3. For **steel** decks, the surface should be solid and free of excessive rust or loose particles. The deck should be primed with a proprietary rubber-based adhesive primer, specially formulated for such use and applied according to the manufacturer's instructions. Special care must be taken not to deform

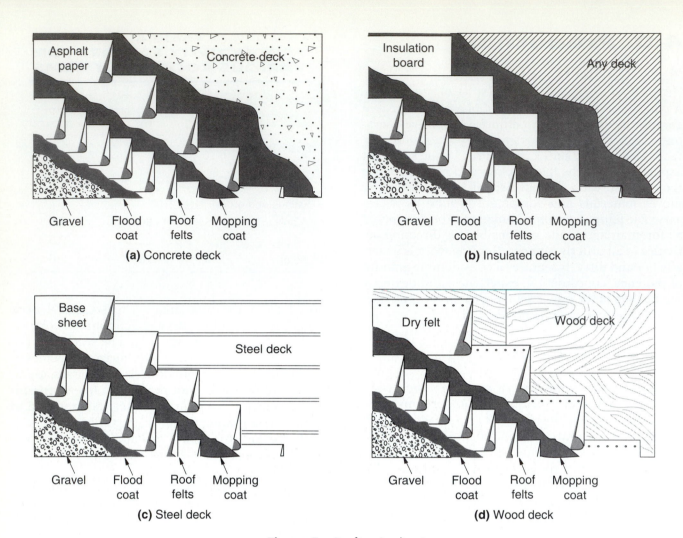

(a) Concrete deck

(b) Insulated deck

(c) Steel deck

(d) Wood deck

Figure 5   Roofing Applications

the flutes or corrugations of steel decks during roofing procedures, as this might weaken their structural characteristics.

4. For **wood** decks, the surface should be checked to remove or secure all cracks, loose boards, protruding nailheads, splinters, damp spots, or voids. Any small openings can be closed by tacking on a small piece of galvanized sheet steel. Asphalt primer should be mopped or sprayed on at the approximate rate of 0.25 liter/m² or 0.5 pint/yd.² Alternatively, a layer of dry felt can be stapled in position over the wood deck, overlapping the felt 50 mm or 2 in. at all edges. Follow with two layers of asphalt-impregnated felt, laid dry, stapled in position.

The point of all preparation is to bring every different type of roof deck surface to a condition appropriate to proceed with installation of the selected membrane system without further adjustment. It is important that the first layer of the roof membrane be separated from the substrate by a primer base coat or first mopping of asphalt or bitumen.

If asphalt and gravel roofing procedures have to be temporarily interrupted, as often happens on large projects at the end of the working day, it is a good practice to apply a glaze coat of asphalt at the rate of approximately 1 kg/m² or 2 lb./yd.² over the felt layers already placed, to minimize the absorption of moisture into them overnight. The glaze coat can then be prime-coated the following morning before work proceeds.

5.2 Procedure

As stated earlier, two common membrane systems are detailed in this section: **simple** systems (one or two layers), and **multiple** systems (three or more layers). These have been selected as being typical of many similar systems, with respect to their general characteristics and procedures. The primary determinants as to system choice will be the owner's needs and the construction budget. The primary determinant as to specific procedure will be the size of the

(a) Single ply

(b) Multiple ply

Membrane Distribution

After the structural roof has been prepared, the roofing material is unrolled and positioned. In all roofing systems, roll edges are overlapped and ends are trimmed as necessary. (UBC Architecture)

about 100 mm or 4 in., and the overlapped joints are either welded by the application of gas heat or hot air or sealed with asphalt adhesive.

2. In **double-layer** systems, bulk rubberized asphalt or plastic is used. The substrate deck is primed as before, then expansion joints or areas of stress are reinforced with long narrow strips of rubberized sheet embedded in a mopping of the membrane material. The roofing product is uniformly mopped or broomed into place and allowed to cure; a second layer is applied as necessary. In special situations, the second layer can be colored to improve its aes-

(a) Coated base sheet

(b) Regular roll roofing

Membrane Attachment

Depending on the specific system, roll roofing products are either torched or hot-mopped to sub-base systems. In some cases, mechanical fasteners may be used; others use synthetic adhesives. (BCIT Building Technology)

project: if small and complex, then mostly manual labor will be used; if large and straightforward, then more mechanized equipment will be used. Patented fluid roof systems are not included in this book.

Simple Systems. These consist of one or two layers of solid or liquid plastic being placed over the prepared deck. Such simple systems are frequently covered with rigid insulation boards laid on top of the membrane system and then covered with gravel.

1. In **single-layer** systems, the roof deck is primed by spraying or mopping the primer as recommended by the manufacturer of the system. The sheet membrane is then uniformly spread over the roof surface and overlapped at edges and ends by

Figure 6 Manual Felt Mopping

thetic appearance if required. A polyethylene separation strip is often laid on top of the system, followed by installation of rigid insulation and ballast gravel.

Multiple Systems. Multiple-layer roofing membranes are developed by building up alternate layers of asphalt and felt until the desired amount of asphalt is achieved in a sandwich-like form. The temperature of the asphalt during mopping or pouring operations should be approximately 175 degrees C or 350 degrees F.

1. To start the **manual** process (see Figure 6), about 3 m or yd. of felt are rolled out dry and aligned into position along the low side of the roof area. The mopman then spreads about 1 m² or yd.² of hot asphalt ahead of the roll, into which the feltman rolls the felt, adjusting the alignment as necessary, and so they continue along the length of the roll. The mopman will then return to mop in the starting area which was originally left dry. Asphalt should be applied at the rate of approximately 1 kg/m² or 2 lb./yd.² per layer.

2. To start the **machine** process, the feltman pulls out about 2 m or yd. of felt, then the machine operator starts applying the hot asphalt to the felts and the felts to the roof, moving along the row at a slow but steady speed. The mopman then mops the starter area and brooms the felt on top to ensure good adhesion as the machine progresses.

The process is repeated for all succeeding rows. At the end of each roll, the continuing roll should overlap the preceding roll by about 150 mm or 6 in. Along the edge of each roll, the amount of overlap is as shown in Table 5 for various numbers of plies.

An additional 25 mm or 1 in. is allowed in the overlap to ensure that the end result really does have

(a) Trimming at eaves

(b) Preparing for drains

Roof Detailing

Every roof membrane has to be worked to conform to the roof planes and other features. Special care must be taken at open edges and at openings passing through the membrane system.

Table 5
OVERLAP OF PLIES

Number of Plies	Amount of Overlap
3	$2/3$
4	$3/4$
5	$4/5$

three, four, or five plies as desired at every point in the roof membrane. If the roof slope exceeds a ratio of 1:12, the top edge of each felt layer should be secured to the substrate roof deck with roofing nails at 600-mm intervals, 50 mm from the top edge, or at 24-in. intervals, 2 in. from the top edge of the roll.

The next element in this roofing system is called the flood coat. This involves the application, either manually or by machine, of a layer of hot asphalt at

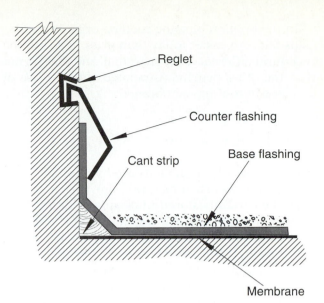

Figure 7 Base Flashing

the rate of approximately 3 kg/m² or 6 lb./yd.² over the entire system area. While the flood coat asphalt is still warm, the selected gravel is then spread, either manually or by machine, at the rate of approximately 18 kg/m² or 36 lb./yd.², to uniformly cover the flood coat. It is not uncommon to spread additional gravel at corners of the roof, to compensate for wind loss. Excess gravel which may spill over the edges of flat roof areas should be cleaned up and removed from the site.

At sloping faces of cant strips and upstanding edges of base flashings (see Figure 7), long strips of mineral-surfaced felt can be placed in position, overlapped at ends as necessary, interfaced with the roofing system, and glued in position, using roofing asphalt as the adhesive and tacking the top edge with roofing nails as described above.

(a) Flood coat kettle

(b) Gravel distribution

Roof Finishing
Most built-up roofing systems are finished with a thin flood coat of hot asphalt, onto which the roofing gravel is distributed by hand or machine. (Dow Chemical Canada Inc.)

In the opinion of some roofers, organic and asbestos felts are easier to lay than glass felts, but the procedural differences are marginal, and they do not offset the other benefits associated with the use of glass felts in roofing membranes.

5.3 Precautions

As many types of roofing felts are hygroscopic (that is, they can absorb moisture from the air), they should be carefully stored in clean and dry or low-humidity areas before use. Asphalt products should not be applied in temperatures below 5 degrees C or 40 degrees F. If it is necessary to do installation below this temperature, then the products and the surfaces should be carefully heated before application. Spraying of asphalt should be avoided in windy conditions, to avoid accidentally splattering adjacent areas.

Because of the risk of damage and the consequent cost of cleanup, particular care should be taken when handling asphalt products to avoid splashing other exterior surfaces or parts of the building, such as facing brick, stucco veneer, wood siding, or door and window frames. Protection in the form of large plastic sheets or canvas tarpaulins should be provided to cover such building elements wherever necessary.

If it is proposed to use machines to install the roofing membrane, then consideration must be given to the ability of the roof frame to support such temporary live loads. Similarly, large concentrations of stored roofing materials should not be permitted on the roof unless the roof frame is strong enough to withstand the stress. If rainwater gutters and down-pipes have already been installed at eaves before roofing commences, then precautions should be taken not to rest equipment on such fragile components which can be distorted or disturbed.

(a) Sand or gravel stockpile

(b) Fire isolation protection

Special Features

Some buildings require special roof features. For example, on steel decks, sand or fine gravel is laid in rows at right angles to the deck flutes to restrict the spread of fire gases. (Dow Chemical Canada Inc.)

Section 07–600 Flashings

1.0 Introduction

1.1 General Issues

Issues relative to both the perimeter edges and the central fields of metal roofing, waterproofing, and cladding systems are described in this section. The edges, joints, and changes of plane of many such systems normally require to be made weatherproof in some positive way. One way to achieve this is to provide a covering system called a *flashing*. The flashing may be made of waterproof metal, plastic, or fibrous materials. Flashing materials are usually produced and installed in long narrow strips of various profiles or configurations. They may be applied before, during, or after the roofing, waterproofing, or cladding system, depending on the configuration selected.

If one was to consider extending the perimeter metal flashing system over the entire roof, then a sheet metal roofing system would be achieved. As such systems are occasionally encountered on high-quality commercial and institutional buildings, a short description of metal roofing methods is included in this section.

1.2 Design Aspects

Good design should result in satisfactory performance of flashing and sheet metal roofing systems. Allowance must be made for physical movement due to temperature differences, coefficients of expansion, and building settlement or vibration. Positive drainage should be provided to deflect water away from flashing and joint locations; flashings should also be located above any elevation to which free-standing water may rise.

Avoid the inclusion of sharp corners or tight bends in continuous flashing systems; form unavoidable corners with molded capping pieces. Secure flashing systems to solid structural bearings. Design the flashing system so as to prohibit the ingress of water through capillary action. Avoid locating porous wall surfaces above flashings or water may bypass the flashing system. Avoid widths in excess of 60 cm or 24 in. in flashing systems. Conceal all fastenings from weather exposure. Avoid direct contact between dissimilar metals. Arrange for proper joints between adjacent pieces of flashing materials. In general, base flashings should be integrated with the roofing or waterproofing system,

and extended at least 150 mm or 6 in. out or up at perimeters.

It is customary to provide a counter- or cap-flashing to overlap the base flashing. Flashing and sheet metal roofing materials should be selected on the basis of compatibility with other related products, durability with respect to weathering, flexibility to accommodate some movement, and permanence of impermeability. Some typical arrangements are shown in Figure 1.

1.3 Related Work

Work closely connected to this section is described in the following sections, to which reference should be made:

07–100   Water and Damp Proofing

07–300   Shingles and Tiles

07–400   Preformed Cladding

07–500   Membrane Roofing

07–900   Joint Sealing

2.0 Products

2.1 Materials

Materials commonly used for flashings can be classified under four broad headings: **metals, felts, plastics,** and **composites.** Only the first relates to sheet metal roofing:

Metals. These include aluminum, copper, lead, steel, and zinc, among others such as monel.

1. Aluminum is durable, lightweight, inexpensive, and compatible with most other building products, but it is relatively difficult to work. Two types (#1100–O and #3003–O) are manufactured in sheet form for use in flashings. Aluminum is available in mill finish form, anodized, or coated with colored vinyl paint. Applied finishes may be damaged during shaping and installation operations. Aluminum gauge thicknesses of 24 and 26 (about 0.5 mm or 0.02 in.) are common. Strips are produced in widths of 15, 30, and 45 mm or 6, 12, and 18 in., and in various lengths.

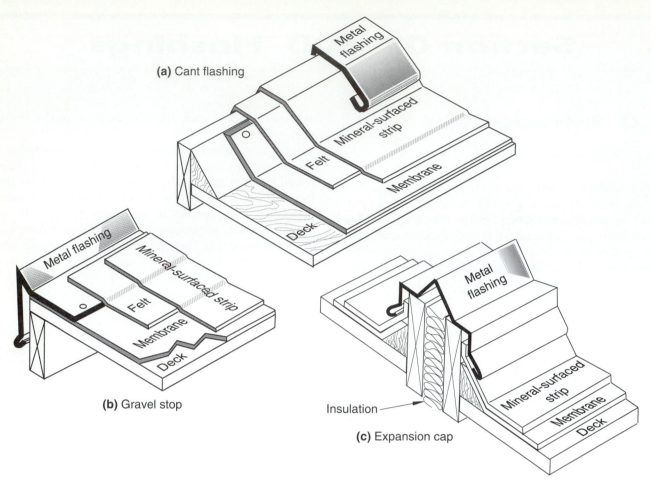

(a) Cant flashing

(b) Gravel stop

(c) Expansion cap

Figure 1 Flashing Arrangements

2. Copper is very durable and of medium weight, but it is fairly expensive and may react with other materials, such as concrete, plaster, and cedar wood. It is produced in a cold-rolled form (described as cornice-tempered) for use in flashing, and it can be naturally aged by weather exposure to form a patina or skin of pale green copper oxide having a pleasant appearance. It can also be more rapidly artificially aged using acid washes, although these often produce darker colors. Copper flashings are usually designated by weight: 4.5 and 5.7 kg/m² or 16 and 20 oz./ft.² weights are popularly selected. Sheets are available in widths of 60, 75, and 100 cm or 24, 30, and 36 in., and in various lengths. Thicknesses are approximately 0.5 and 0.6 mm or 0.02 and 0.03 in.

3. Lead is very heavy, very durable, and very expensive, but it is easy to work and is compatible with most other construction materials. There are several lead alloys and steel/lead combinations (such as terneplate) that are similar in flashing function to plain lead. Lead flashings are usually designated by weight: 11 kg/m² (1 mm thick) or 2.5 lb./ft.² (0.04 in. thick) are common for flashing. Sheets are available in widths of 30, 45, and 60 cm or 12, 18, and 24 in., and lengths of up to 6 m or 20 ft.

4. Steel (made from iron) is used in three forms:

a. Galvanized steel consists of mild steel sheet, coated with zinc at the rate of 0.6 kg/m² or 2 oz./ft.². It is fairly durable, of medium weight, very inexpensive, and easy to work, provided precautions are taken not to create sharp bends that may damage the zinc coating. Cut ends must be rustproof primed. Steel gauge thicknesses of 22 to 26 (about 0.8 mm or 0.03 in.) are common. Sheets are available in widths up to 1.5 m or 60 in. and in lengths up to 5 m or 16 ft.

b. Coated steel consists of mild steel sheet, coated with vinyl or enamel paint baked on. It is otherwise similar to galvanized steel described above.

c. Stainless steel is extremely durable and relatively attractive. It is slightly heavier than plain steel and is very expensive and difficult to work. Special types (#301 and #302) of stainless steel, some having slightly textured surfaces, are specifically produced for use in flashing systems for buildings.

Table 1
PROPERTIES OF ZINC FLASHING

Gauge	Thickness		Weight	
	mm	in.	kg/m²	lb./ft.²
10	0.51	0.020	3.66	0.75
12	0.71	0.028	5.13	1.05

Seven different finishes are available, ranging from dull to bright. Steel gauge thicknesses of 20 to 24 (about 0.8 mm or 0.03 in.) are common. Widths are usually 60 cm or 24 in.; lengths vary.

5. Zinc is used in both pure and alloyed forms for flashings. It is rolled into strips, machine cut, and shaped to required profiles. Gauges for zinc sheet products range from 3 which is paper-thin to 28 which is 25 mm or 1 in. in thickness; two gauges commonly used for flashing are shown in Table 1.

Felts. These include a range of mineral-surfaced, asphalt-impregnated strips of building paper or glass fiber, as more fully described in Section 07–500.

Plastics. These include a range of tough polyvinyl chloride or butyl rubber materials, as described in Section 07–500.

Composites. These consist of laminations of thin sheets or coatings of metal, plastic, and asphaltic materials, factory bonded to produce a thick sandwich-like product, capable of being cut, shaped, and joined similar to sheet metal flashing.

2.2 Accessories

The accessories used in conjunction with flashings consist of a variety of clips, nails, reglets, screws, and tapes.

3.0 Construction Aids

3.1 Equipment

Sheet metal is factory cut using an electric slitter, which is a small steel blade attached to the end of a long rotary shaft. Sheet metal is factory bent in a powered device called a brake-former or bending brake. See Figure 2.

3.2 Tools

As much of this work involves cutting and shaping sheet metal, the tools are generally those of the sheet metal worker, consisting of tin-snips and shears, markers and scribers, hole-punches and mallets, and a variety of set squares.

Typical Installation
Most flashing details involve positioning long strips of brake-formed galvanized or vinyl-coated steel and securing them in place, with allowances made for movement and storm restraint. (Dow Chemical Canada Inc.)

Openings and Vents
Flashing materials often have to be worked around openings in roof systems, such as at chimneys, skylights, plumbing vents, and so on. These sheet metal boxes will support roof exhausters. (BCIT Building Technology)

Figure 2   Bending Brake

Table 2
PRODUCTIVITY FACTORS IN FLASHINGS AND SHEET METAL ROOFING

Type of Work in Flashings	Output per Hour	
	m	ft.
Preparing grooves	3	10
Metal ridge flashing	4	15
Metal base flashing	5	20
Metal counter flashing	7	25
Metal eaves flashing	7	25
Metal cap flashing	9	30
Felt or plastic flashing	11	35
In Sheet Roofing	m²	ft.²
Working aluminum	4.0	40
Working steel	3.0	30
Working copper	2.5	25
Working lead	2.0	20

4.0 Production

4.1 Crew Configuration

Flashing and roofing crews are usually small, consisting of one skilled worker and one helper, except on the largest of projects. The skilled worker may be a sheet metal worker (sometimes called a tinner), a roofer, or even a carpenter or mason on occasion on small nonunion projects. It should be remembered that, where metal flashings are specified, much of the fabrication can be done at the sheet metal worker's shop, using powered equipment, in preference to doing such work at the site.

4.2 Productivity

Accuracy in estimating productivity relative to flashings and sheet metal roofing involves consideration of a number of components: the type of materials to be used, the complexity or simplicity of design, the quantity of work to be done, the location on the building of the flashing systems being installed, and the season and weather, among other items. While it is not practical to present factors for every possible type of work connected with flashing systems, some representative figures are given in Table 2 for typical installation work done on buildings of average size and complexity under normal weather conditions. Prior to installation of flashing, grooves (called reglets or raggles) often have to be formed or cut in concrete or masonry walls, to receive the top edge of the flashing system. If such cutting can be done be-

fore concrete or mortar cures, the factors given for this work can be doubled.

Prefabricated metal corner or end caps can be installed at the rate of about three or four per hour. Scuppers or drain boxes can be installed at the rate of about one per hour. Normal residential chimneys can be flashed in about 2 hours each. Simple plumbing vents passing through roof systems can be flashed in about 15 minutes. Figure 3 shows a typical chimney flashing detail.

5.0 Procedures

5.1 Preparation

Before commencing work, work areas should be cleared of construction debris and equipment not required for the work of this section. The surfaces to which flashing and roofing systems will be secured should be checked for completion, soundness, and fitness; all sharp projections and loose particles, dust, and dirt should be removed. Open edges of all sheet metal strips should be hemmed about 13 mm or 1/2 inch to improve rigidity and straightness of the exposed edge. Much of this work is done off site at the sheet metal worker's shop and brought to the building site ready for installation.

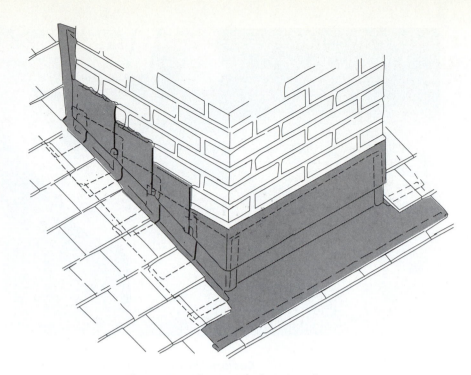

Figure 3 Chimney Flashing Detail

5.2 Process

In this part, **flashings** will be described first, followed by **sheet metal roofing**.

Flashing. Procedures for installing flashing systems in metals, felts, plastics, and composites naturally vary. Furthermore, because of the almost infinite variety of building design problems requiring flashing solutions, this section can only present an outline of the main features of some typical work in each generic grouping. Some details are illustrated.

1. **Metals and composites.** In general, these products require to be measured, cut, shaped, fitted, and securely installed in position, using a variety of reglets, clips, and other fastening devices to accommodate the principles of design articulated earlier in this section. See Figure 4.

2. **Felts and plastics.** In general, these products require to be measured, cut, tacked in place, and secured into final position using adhesives as recommended by the manufacturers of the felts and plastics. See Figure 5.

Roofing. Procedures for installing sheet metal roofing systems are essentially the same regardless of the metal being used for the process.

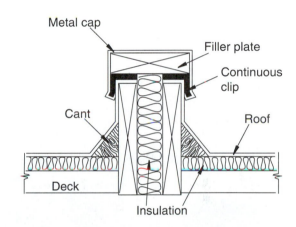

Figure 4 Rigid Flashing

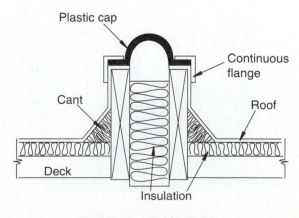

Figure 5 Pliable Flashing

Custom Work
Many parts of roof flashing systems (such as scuppers, hoppers, and down spouts) require sheet metal or plastic to be cut and fit to special shapes, on site or at the factory. (BCIT Audio-Visual Production)

(a) At concrete scuppers

(b) At change of direction

Detailing
As these examples show, flashing detailing is skilled work. It requires knowledge of tools, equipment, material properties, building science, codes, and contracts. (UBC Architecture)

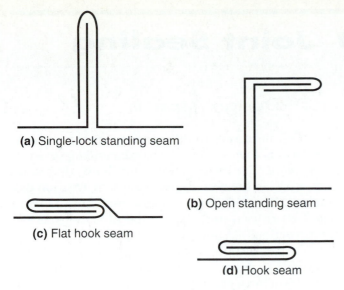

(a) Single-lock standing seam

(b) Open standing seam

(c) Flat hook seam

(d) Hook seam

Figure 6 Seaming Types

1. **Seams.** Sheet metal panels are installed using either batten seam, flat seam, lock seam, hook seam, or standing seam techniques. On roof slopes having a rise-to-run ratio of less than 1:4, flat seams can be used. The structural substrate should be covered with a layer of roofing felt, tacked in position before roofing commences. See Figure 6 for typical seam details.

2. **Fastenings.** Panels are formed into the shape of a small trough and secured at the sides to clips or battens. Joints are completed using snap-on covers or by turning over the top edges of seams to form locked joints of various configurations. Open ends are capped with purpose-made matching pieces, held in place with lock seams. All fastenings should be concealed from view and from weather exposure. See Figure 7 for typical fastening details.

5.3 Precautions

As many of the materials used in flashing and sheet metal roofing processes are quite valuable and subject to damage, care must be taken to provide ade-

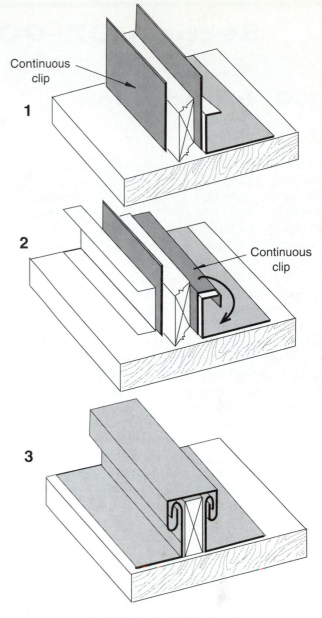

Figure 7 Fastening Details

quate security for temporary storage. Materials should be stored in clean, dry places, with rolled products stood on end in their vertical axis and sheet goods laid flat in the horizontal plane.

Section 07–900 Joint Sealing

1.0 Introduction

1.1 General Issues

In the not-too-distant past, the whole issue of caulking and sealing of buildings had a much lower profile in construction design and implementation. Builders were expected to produce reasonably weatherproof buildings, but there was not a general expectation that there would be no leaks in the exterior fabrics. However, during the past 25 or 30 years, with the advent of the so-called Space Age and the spin-off of resultant technology, a much higher degree of weatherproof performance of building systems has developed and is now expected, because the products capable of achieving better results are now more readily available. Out of this, in business terms, a whole new subdivision of the construction industry has emerged, and it is now quite common to find many companies specializing exclusively in the caulking and sealing of exterior building fabrics and components on a contract basis.

In economic terms, while the total volume of new construction has maintained a fairly steady percentage of the gross national product over the past 20 years, that part of the industry attributable to caulking and sealing has grown at a rate of approximately 50 percent per year in dollar value. Corresponding losses (for other reasons) are being experienced in some of the former traditional trades, such as plastering and masonry. Such shifts in the construction industry would make an interesting study regrettably beyond the scope of this book.

Caulking and sealing systems should be selected on the basis of satisfactory performance for both the short and the long term. However, it should be realized that all such elements of any building constitute a relatively expensive component, both in first cost and continued maintenance. As with roofing membrane systems, the costs arising from water damage caused by the use of poor materials or faulty installation clearly offset the high but lesser costs of doing the right thing in the first place. The results of good products properly placed are generally preferable to the continuous irritation and expense of leaks caused by improper design, inadequate materials, or faulty application.

1.2 Design Aspects

It is first necessary to differentiate among ambiguous terminology such as the words *caulking*, *glazing*, and *sealing*. For the purpose of this book, the reader is referred to the definitions in any construction dictionary. For the purpose of this section, the word *caulking* is used to designate the filling of joints in construction to render them waterproof.

The general object of design in this regard is to prevent air, water, or particles in vapor, liquid, or solid form from passing directly through the exterior building fabrics, around the edges of components such as doors and windows in exterior surfaces, and through construction cracks, whether deliberately formed, such as occurs where a door frame meets a masonry wall, or accidentally formed, such as might occur between a wall footing and a foundation or basement wall. The general approach is to seal exterior surfaces, caulk exterior joints of the building envelope, and install waterstop barriers in foundations. Although good-quality caulking, sealant, and waterstop materials tend to be expensive on a price-per-unit basis, it will be realized that good design of building surfaces and joints can ensure that relatively small quantities of material are required.

The remainder of information in this section deals only with caulking and joint sealants. Waterstop joints in concrete are described in Section 03–300; glazing systems are described in Section 08–800; surface sealers are described in Section 09–900.

There are two principal types of joints to be caulked: **butt joints** and **lap joints**; both are illustrated in Figure 1. Design criteria for joints include consideration of the elasticity of the caulking compound, the nature of the adjacent surfaces to which the caulk must adhere, and the anticipated amount of movement in related building components. When selecting materials to caulk joints in buildings, consideration should be given to the ability of such materials to be compressed and stretched, to recover their original dimensions, and to remain in a non-hardened state for a prolonged period, as well as to the probable life expectancy of the product once installed. The ability of the material to properly adhere to adjacent surfaces without leaking onto or staining surrounding components should also be examined, together with any limitations, such as flammability, limiting temperatures or curing times imposed on the product by its manufacturer, or the advisability

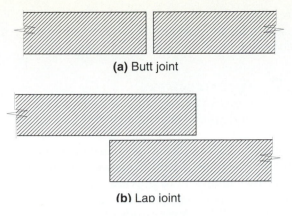

(a) Butt joint

(b) Lap joint

Figure 1 Joint Types

of applying paint or other finishes on top of the caulking material.

With respect to the ratio between the width and depth of the joint to be filled, most authorities recommend that the depth or thickness of filler never exceed the width, nor be less than half of the width if substantial movement of the adjacent components is anticipated, as shown in Figure 2. Consideration must also be given to the conditions of the joint at the time of application, relative to the conditions which will optimally prevail, so as to allow for forces likely to develop from subsequent expansion, contraction, shear, or torsion.

1.3 Related Work

Work closely connected to this section is described in the following sections, to which reference should be made:

03–300   Cast-in-Place Concrete

04–200   Unit Masonry

08–100   Metal Doors and Frames

08–400   Storefront Systems

08–500   Metal Windows and Frames

2.0 Products

2.1 Materials

This topic is dealt with in two parts: **compound types** and how they work and attributes of the **materials.**

Compound Types.   Most caulking compounds fall into one of three categories:

1. **Solvent-release** compounds, which cure by the evaporation of the solvent.
2. **One-part** compounds, which cure through chemical change upon exposure to air.
3. **Two-part** compounds, which cure through the addition of a catalyst to a base compound to start a finite chemical reaction.

The advantage of the solvent-release and one-part compounds is that they come from the factory premixed and ready for application; they also have a longer curing time and thus impose less pressure on the applicant to work quickly. The advantage of the two-part compounds is that, if properly handled, they generally result in sealed joints of superior quality, appearance, and color, although there is usually a shorter time frame in which to store and apply them after adding the catalyst.

Materials.   Caulking materials can be categorized under three headings:

1. **Oil-based compounds.** These include a variety of mastic oil putties and other oleoresinous prod-

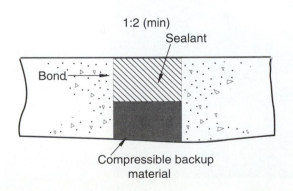

1:2 (min)

Sealant

Bond

Compressible backup material

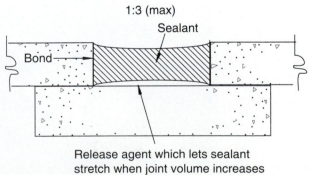

1:3 (max)

Sealant

Bond

Release agent which lets sealant stretch when joint volume increases

Figure 2   Joint Proportions

ucts, most of which are now obsolete because superior materials are readily available.

2. **Rubber derivatives.** These include butadiene, butyl, neoprene, Thiokol, and other synthetic rubber products which remain flexible after curing and can be painted.

3. **Synthetic materials.** These include polyurethane and silicone products, as well as vinyl and acrylic water-based latexes. All have generally good adhesive and flexible qualities.

The polyurethane products tend to be more difficult to apply but, if properly handled, can produce excellent results. The silicones, though expensive, are easy to work with and permit the greatest amount of movement. The latexes are inexpensive, but they tend to pick up dirt and they are slower to cure. Paint should not be applied on top of any of these products; most can be ordered to be integrally precolored.

2.2 Accessories

These include materials under two broad categories:

Primers. These consist of volatile products, such as toluene or xylol, intended to prepare joint surfaces to improve adhesion, to provide separation between caulking and packing materials, and to clean excess or spilled caulking compounds off adjacent surfaces.

Packing. These consist of lengths of woven or extruded flexible materials, in solid ropes made of hemp, oakum, or rep yarn, or in foamed tapes made of mastic, synthetic rubber, or plastic products such as urethane, intended to be inserted into narrow but deep joints to reduce the dimensions of the spaces to be sealed with more expensive caulking material. Semirigid products made of sheet cork, fiberboard, and styrofoam, as well as hollow rubber and plastic tubes of various configurations and dimensions, are also used to fill larger or wider joints.

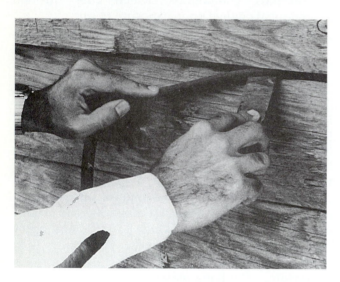

(a) Packing

Basic System
In most situations requiring joint sealing, the joint is first filled with packing material, compound is applied by gun, and the surface is finally smoothed by hand or with tools. (Dow Chemicals Canada Inc.)

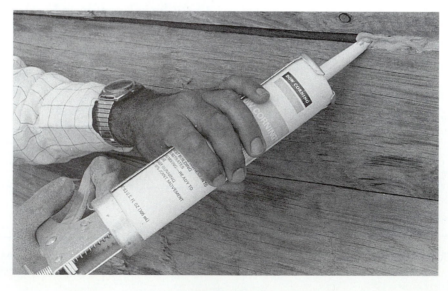

(b) Caulking

3.0 Construction Aids

3.1 Equipment

As much of this work is done above eye level, a variety of ladders and light movable scaffolding are frequently necessary for work done at grade or floor level. For work done on the outside of highrise or multistory buildings, swing staging may be necessary on large projects, although such equipment is usually provided under a back-charge arrangement between the caulking specialist and the general contractor or project manager. Light-duty air compressors are occasionally required to pump caulking compounds in bulk from containers to final locations, as well as to provide compressed air to operate certain types of caulking guns. Some caulking compounds, such as the acrylic-based types, may require to be heated before application; factory-made heating chests are available, although simple insulated wood or metal boxes with lightbulbs inside may also serve the purpose (see Figure 3). A number of pails or buckets are used for mixing compounds, while whisk brooms and hand brushes may be required for cleanup.

3.2 Tools

Caulking work requires the use of a number of small hand trowels, putty knives, utility knives, caulking guns to hold the tubes of compound, paintbrushes to apply primers and solvents, and clean cloths to clean off excess material. Some caulking guns are manually operated by squeezing a trigger connected to a piston which forces the compound out through a nozzle; others are operated by pressing a trigger which releases compressed air into a cylinder, thus forcing the compound out. Some guns are front-loaded by suction through the nozzle, while others are made for top-loading by cartridge or rear-loading by spatula or trowel. Components are often mixed together in a pail or drum using a metal or plastic paddle attached to the end of a slow-speed electric drill. Some examples are shown in Figure 4.

4.0 Production

4.1 Crew Configuration

Most joint caulking is done by skilled persons, such as carpenters or glaziers, either working alone or in pairs, except on the very largest of projects.

4.2 Productivity

Working on a normal project, under good conditions, with good access and with a reasonable amount of work to be done, a skilled operator should prepare, pack, seal, and clean up about 25 m or 75 ft. of

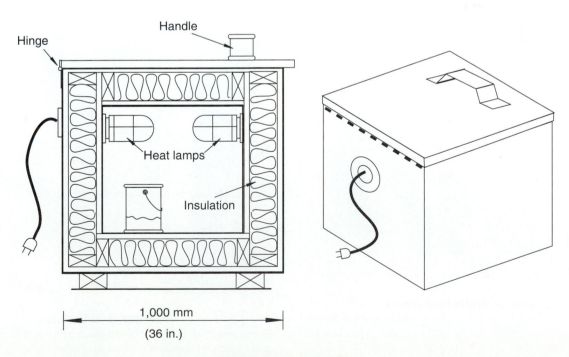

Figure 3   Warming Box

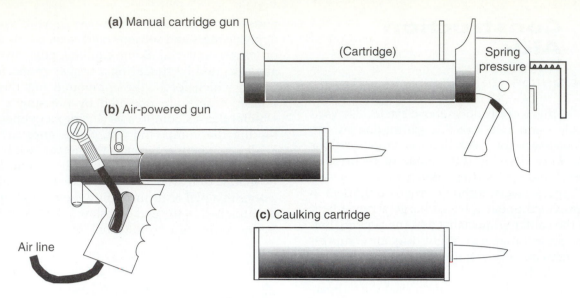

(a) Manual cartridge gun

(Cartridge)

Spring pressure

(b) Air-powered gun

Air line

(c) Caulking cartridge

Figure 4 Caulking Guns

straight joints between major wall panels per hour. Work around windows and doors will be less productive, resulting in about 15 m or 50 ft. per hour.

5.0 Procedures

5.1 Preparation

Prior to start of work, remove all construction debris and equipment not necessary for the work of this section. Ensure that all surfaces to be caulked are

Exterior Walls and Doors
Before external wood-framed walls are raised or door thresholds positioned, it is considered good practice to apply a thin bead of caulking compound to prevent the passage of moisture. (BCIT Audio-Visual Production)

Window Installation
Before installing windows or storefront systems, it is considered good practice to apply a thick bead of caulking compound to the outside perimeter of the frame. (BCIT Building Technology)

clean and dry and free of oil, wax, grease, or loose coatings or particles. Work should be done in temperatures between 4 and 20 degrees C or 40 and 70 degrees F. Where possible, avoid work in direct or strong sunlight, as this might raise the temperatures of the caulking materials as well as the materials to which the compounds are being applied. Temporary shades can usually be rigged where necessary. Unit masonry and concrete work should be dried and cured, as considerable moisture can be retained in such systems, especially at temperatures around freezing. In general, caulking compounds will not satisfactorily adhere to damp surfaces.

5.2 Process

The overall process of caulking joints can be reduced to three main components:

Packing. Packing (or backing) materials are used to reduce the depth of the joint to be sealed. Flexible materials are usually compressed to about half their original size, inserted into the joint, and then allowed to expand to try to recover their original dimensions, thus ensuring a snug fit. A simple depth gauge can be made using a wood float with a small strip of wood fastened to its underside. The packing is inserted, and the float is used to compress the packing while ensuring that the surface of the packing will be at the correct depth or level for the caulking compound. As caulking compounds should not adhere to the bottom of the joint or to the packing, a release agent such as a narrow strip of polyethylene plastic, masking tape, or chemical film is placed on top of the packing. See Figure 5.

Caulking. Brushes are used to apply solvents and primers to the sides to which the compounds have to adhere. The compound is then compressed into the prepared joint by pushing (rather than pulling) the caulking gun along as the compound is extruded from the gun. The object is to avoid imparting tension or permitting gaps or voids in the compound during application. Before curing occurs, the surface of the caulked joint should be neatly compressed and tooled with a small hand trowel or spatula and excess material removed.

Miscellaneous. Some products, such as the butyl rubber caulks, do not require joint surfaces to be primed; they adhere well enough on their own. Most caulking compounds should be applied when their own temperature is between 10 and 50 degrees C or 50 and 120 degrees F. Latex compounds are particularly well suited for sealing very small joints.

Other Applications

Caulking is required at many other places both inside and outside of buildings. Some examples are at skylights, exterior concrete or metal cladding panels, and around toilet fixtures. (BCIT Audio-Visual Production)

Figure 5 Packing and Backing

(a) Normal joint — Wall surface, 10 mm, 10 mm

(b) Large joint — Wall surface, Foam backing

(c) Stress failure — Wall surface

5.3 Precautions

Caulking products should be stored in clean, dry, cool, and safe locations. Shelf life of such products should be determined; outdated products should be discarded. Many caulking products contain ingredients in the uncured state that can irritate the skin; applicators should not expose bare skin directly to caulking compounds for extended periods of time. Avoid inhaling any fumes or vapors given off by curing compounds or solvents; work only in well-ventilated and well-lighted areas.

Retro Caulking
If it is necessary to caulk after building components are in place, the surfaces on each side of the joint can be protected with masking tape, making for neater work and easier finishing. (BCIT Audio-Visual Production)

CHAPTER 08
Openings

Section 08–100
Metal Doors and Frames

1.0 Introduction

1.1 General Issues

Although there is a very large variety of metal doors available on the market, manufactured by literally hundreds of different companies, for the purposes of this book all such doors can be grouped under four representative headings: those installed in companion frames, in assembled tracks, in storefront systems, and specialty doors.

The first two categories are described in this section; the third category is described in Section 08–400. In the fourth category, there is a large variety of specialty doors, such as airlock doors, bank vault doors, freezer locker doors, mechanical-access doors, and revolving sectional doors, among many others, which are less frequently encountered and which in any event require special investigation to ensure their suitability for particular uses. As the installation procedure for specialty doors is peculiar to each door type, such specific methodology is not described in this book on general procedures. With respect to the first two categories of metal doors, those installed in companion **frames** include all typical hollow or filled metal doors mounted on hinges, butts, or pivots, whereas those installed in assem-

bled **tracks** include side-sliding and vertical-lift doors in one-piece or sectional form. To avoid repetition, this section deals with doors made of steel. For aluminum doors in frames, refer to Section 08–400, Part 2.0; for aluminum doors in tracks, refer to Section 08–700, Part 5.0.

1.2 Design Aspects

Doors in buildings are similar to valves in a water-pipe system; they control the flow of traffic, just as valves control the flow of water. Like valves, they are also operable, in that they have moving parts, all of which are subject to wear and tear. Many doors, particularly in public buildings such as offices, schools and stores, are subjected to very heavy-duty use. Consider just one example: the doors to a college classroom may be opened and closed by as many as 50 individual students coming in at the beginning of each one-hour classroom session, of which there may be five or six per day scheduled for that room. This could result in as many as 500 opening and closing cycles per day, a process that will continue week after week, month after month, and year after year. It would be an economic error to select poorly made doors or shoddy hardware for such an application.

Doors also serve to separate various parts of the building, and may be required for reasons of access, privacy, security, acoustical separation, thermal conservation, and simply appearance, in some cases. Doors can move in a number of different ways: horizontally, vertically, or rotationally. They can swing through an arc, pivot on a point, slide or fold in any direction, or roll into cylindrical sections. Some of these primary movement functions are illustrated in Figure 1.

With respect to door swing (the way in which a hinged door moves when opened), there are a number of configurations to comprehend:

1. The convention has been adopted that to describe the swing of a door, the door is to be viewed from the **outside** of the building, room, or area enclosed by the door.

2. If the door opens away from the viewer, it is described as a **forward** swing; if it opens toward the viewer, it is described as a **reverse** swing.

3. If a door can swing both toward and away from the viewer from a closed position, it is described as a **double-acting** door.

4. The way a door opens is usually referred to as the **hand** of the door; that is, the door is described by either the right or left hand used to open it, as follows: When facing the door, if the hinging de-

vices, such as door butts or pivots, are on the right-hand side, it is described as a **right-hand** door, and vice versa, the reason being that to open the door, one would most likely put one's right hand across to operate the doorknob or handle located at the **left-hand** side of the door.

5. If a door is divided into two equal parts vertically, it is called a paired, double, or **French** door; if divided horizontally near the middle, it is called a split or **Dutch** door.

6. If the vertical outside edges of a door are worked to an angle to prevent the door from binding in the frame, the door is said to be **beveled**.

Some of these primary functions are illustrated in Figure 2.

All doors and frames should be selected on the basis of appropriate size and use for the proposed opening; experience indicates that many problems arise out of failure to make such an obvious connection. The sizes of certain egress doors, such as those required for fire safety, are dictated by building codes.

1.3 Related Work

Work closely connected to this section is described in the following sections, to which reference should be made:

03–300   Cast-in-Place Concrete

04–200   Unit Masonry

05–100   Steel Framing

06–100   Rough Carpentry

08–700   Finish Hardware

09–900   Painting and Decorating

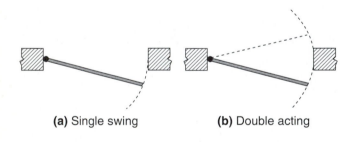

(a) Single swing   **(b)** Double acting

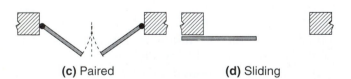

(c) Paired   **(d)** Sliding

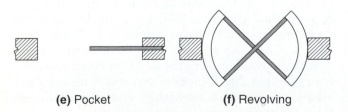

(e) Pocket   **(f)** Revolving

Figure 1   Door Swing Functions

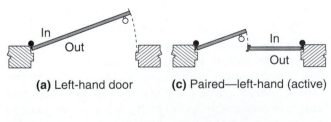

(a) Left-hand door   **(c)** Paired—left-hand (active)

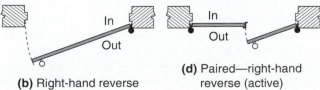

(b) Right-hand reverse   **(d)** Paired—right-hand reverse (active)

Figure 2   Door Hand Functions

2.0 Products

2.1 Materials

The materials used in connection with the work of this section can be considered under two broad headings: doors installed in companion **frames,** and doors installed in assembled **tracks.** Doors of various types are described in this part (see Figures 2 and 3 for some typical configurations); frames and related components are described in Part 2.2 Accessories.

Doors in Frames. There are four common types of metal doors encountered in conjunction with frames: **hollow, filled, kalamein,** and **fire-rated.** All are made of stretcher-leveled hot- or cold-rolled steel panels, welded to internal stiffeners, and all are usually galvanized or prime-coat painted with zinc chromate or other rustproofing material at the factory after fabrication. All good-quality metal doors have factory-welded internal solid metal reinforcement at hinge and lock locations. The doors are made from steel of three different thicknesses for different use conditions: 20 gauge for light-duty, 18 gauge for standard-duty, and 16 gauge for heavy-duty. Doors for residential use often have ornamental metal trim or indentations applied to the surfaces to simulate the paneling found in traditional wood doors. See Figure 3. Features specific to the four types are as follows:

1. **Hollow** metal doors have only some sound-deadening paint material applied to their inner surfaces to reduce noise.

2. **Filled** doors are similarly made, but instead of paint, they have a central core of cellular paper fiber, plastic foam, or mineral wool insulation bonded to the inner surfaces of the hollow metal exterior panels.

3. **Kalamein** doors are essentially solid wood doors with a thin sheet metal outer skin factory bonded to the wood core.

4. **Fire-rated** doors are similar to filled doors, but are specifically tested and independently labeled to establish their resistance to the passage of fire for certain stated periods, usually between $3/4$ hour minimum and 3 hours maximum, as required by various building codes.

(a) Standard frames

(b) Custom frames

Prefabricated Frames

For economy, prefab frames are usually standardized into a few styles and sizes, shipped to the site in bulk, and stockpiled ready for use. Note removable spreaders at jamb bottoms. (UBC Architecture)

16-gauge door end channels

24-gauge steel stiffener laminated to door skin

Semirigid insulation

18-gauge galvanized steel door skin

Section

Figure 3 Typical Metal Door Construction

Metal doors in frames have three general classifications:

1. **Seamless**, which have no visible seams.
2. **Flush**, which may have fine neat seams visible down the vertical stile edges.
3. **Panel**, which may have either flush or recessed panels to provide a visual feature in the field of the door.

All such doors may be manufactured with special features such as louvers and glazed panels, as well as in Dutch or French configurations. They may also be factory finished with baked-on paint, or provided with special laminated coverings of wood, plastic, or fabric.

Doors in Tracks. There are three types of metal doors commonly encountered in conjunction with tracks: **one piece, sectional overhead,** and **roller shutter.** The composition and manufacture of all three is generally similar to the metal doors described above. There are also other types of doors utilizing tracks, such as accordion and open-trellis types. As these are less frequently encountered and as their general method of installation is similar to the doors under review, they are not further detailed.

1. **One-piece** doors are made by assembling a number of smaller hollow or solid panels into one large piece, designed to slide or swing upward or

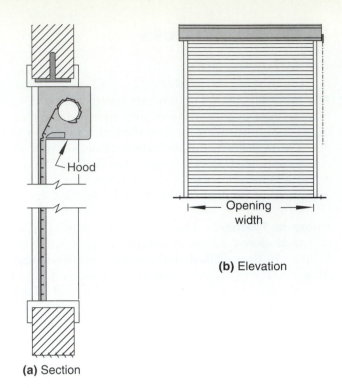

(a) Section

Figure 5 Roller Shutter Door

to one side as a single unit in (usually but not necessarily) straight parallel tracks.

2. **Sectional overhead** doors are made in hinged hollow or solid sections designed to slide vertically up the wall then horizontally across the ceiling in (usually) curved parallel tracks, to conserve headroom space. See Figure 4.
3. **Roller shutter** doors are made of interlocking horizontal steel slats (each between 50 and 75 mm or 2 and 3 in. in height), designed to slide upward in tracks and to wind around a rotating axle contained in a metal housing. See Figure 5.

All three types have their mass counterbalanced by torsion-spring or counterweight mechanisms, to permit the doors to be easily opened manually or electrically at controlled speeds and travel distances. All three can be supplied with glazed vision panels as required by circumstances.

2.2 Accessories

Accessories for doors can be categorized under two broad headings: **frame** components and **track** components. Hardware accessories necessary for the operation of doors are described in Section 08–700.

Frames. Frames for metal doors are usually made of 16-or 18-gauge cold-rolled steel, shaped to a

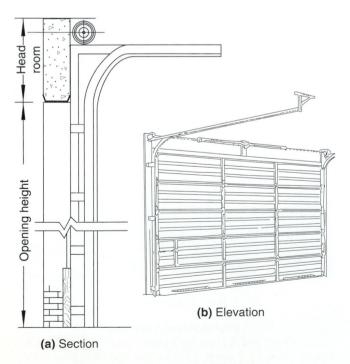

(b) Elevation

Figure 4 Sectional Overhead Doors

predetermined profile. They consist of four primary **components** and some related **accessories,** described as follows:

Components comprise two vertical jambs, one horizontal head rail, and (usually) a bottom spreader. In knockdown assemblies, all components are separate and require to be mechanically fastened together; in one-piece assemblies, the jambs and headrail are miter cut and factory welded at the top corners, with the spreader bolted across the bottom to keep the frame square and true. Holes for hinges and locks are machine punched before delivery.

Accessories comprise a number of wire or sheet steel anchors to secure the doorframes in position, as well as some small metal devices to connect jambs

and headers, to provide reinforcement for hinges and at locks, and to make tension adjustments to the finally installed frame. Small rubber buttons, called mutes, are also inserted into the locking doorstop to deaden the sound of impact when the door is closed. See Figure 6.

Tracks. Tracks for aluminum patio doors are described in Section 08–700, Part 5.0 and Figure 7.1. Tracks for steel doors are usually made of 20- or 22-gauge cold-rolled steel, shaped to a predetermined profile. They consist of two primary groups of components and some related accessories, described as follows:

Components comprise pieces of either straight or curved steel door track having a C- or U-shaped profile, axle shafts, torsion springs, and lifting cables or chains. Electric motorized operators (with automatic reversal feature) and metal stiffeners are also available for doors with greater than average width or weight.

Accessories comprise items of fixed hardware, such as plates and brackets, to secure the tracks and shafts in position and to connect the door sections together, along with items of moving hardware, such as rollers and latches, to permit the assembly to move up and down properly in the installed tracks.

Other accessories include neoprene or vinyl weatherstripping at sides and bottoms, antirattle devices to reduce noise from movement of the door in the frame, and sheet metal covers to house the operating mechanisms. Sectional overhead doors can also be equipped with safety devices to reverse the direction of travel if interrupted, similar to the doors in most passenger elevators.

3.0 Construction Aids

3.1 Equipment

The work of this section requires the use of industrial-type stepladders and some light movable scaffolding. In some cases, a light-duty tack welding machine is required.

3.2 Tools

This work entails the use of handheld electric drills and saws, powder-operated nailing guns, an assortment of wrenches, and screwdrivers with various bits, as well as some clamps and grips.

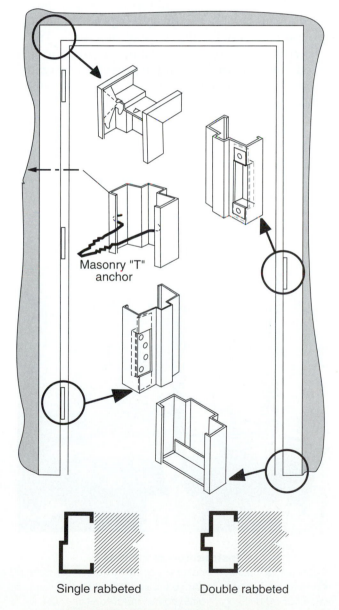

Masonry "T" anchor

Single rabbeted   Double rabbeted

Figure 6 Typical Metal Door Frames

4.0 Production

4.1 Crew Configuration

A typical crew for metal door installation might consist of two carpenters skilled in this work. On large projects there might be two crews, with some helpers to move the packaged door components to their final locations.

4.2 Productivity

Factors given in Table 1 relate to the types of doors and frames described in this section, for crews doing normal work in typical commercial and institutional buildings.

5.0 Procedures

5.1 Preparation

Before installing doors, frames, and tracks of any kind, check the door opening location and surrounding workspace to ensure that all is ready for this work to commence. The area should be clean, dry, free of obstructions, and reasonably well lit. Door frame and track kits should be opened, checked for integrity and completeness, and laid out for assembly close to their point of final installation.

Frames.   Frames for swing doors can be installed in one of two ways: either **before** or **after** the surrounding wall is built.

1. If **before**, then the frame has to be accurately located and temporarily braced in position while the wall is built.

Table 1
METAL DOOR
INSTALLATION TIMES

Type of Installation	Man-Hours per Unit
Preassembled door frame	1
Unassembled door frame	2
Single swing door	2
Paired swing doors	3
Tracks for vertical-lift door	3
Vertical-lift one-piece door	3
Tracks for sectional overhead door	4
Sectional overhead door	4

2. If **after**, then the frame must be selected and arranged to be properly secured to the jambs of the existing opening.

In general, one-piece welded frames are more often used before the wall is built, whereas three-piece knockdown frames are often used for insertion into existing openings. Preparation involves accurately marking the proposed location of the door frame and the location of the temporary braces if required.

Tracks.   Tracks for sliding doors are best (and usually) installed after all structural work creating the opening for the doorway is complete. Preparation involves accurately marking out the fixing points for the track mounting brackets using templates and dimensions supplied by the door manufacturer. Most track door assemblies require to be installed on a channel or angle steel subframe, usually put in place at the jambs of door openings by the general contractor, ready for the work of this trade. Tracks for vertical-lift doors are usually secured to prepared, solid, dressed (and often preservative-treated) wood plates fastened to the structural frame of the building.

Installation of Frames

In concrete or masonry locations, steel door frames are normally erected and temporarily braced before other work occurs. In wood-framed buildings, frames can be installed at any time. (BCIT Building Technology)

(a) Commercial pivot door

(b) Residential sliding door

Installation of Doors

Metal doors are delivered ready to install. Hinged or pivoted doors are mounted according to hardware requirements. Simple sliding doors are secured by nailing or screwing. (UBC Architecture)

5.2 Process

The installation procedures for **frames**, **tracks**, and **doors** follow.

Frames. There are two basic possibilities:

1. For **one-piece** welded frames, locate the door position on the floor, then fasten strips of rough lumber at right angles above or to the sides of the proposed door location, clear of future work. Temporarily wedge a strip of wood into the header so that it extends 200 mm or 8 in. on each end, and raise the frame into position. Secure the bottom spreader accurately in final position; then brace the headrail to the rough lumber strips using additional strips of wood or steel straps. Check the frame for accuracy in both vertical and horizontal planes. Install anchor devices and rubber bumpers, and leave ready for the wall to be built up around the frame and anchors. Remove temporary braces as structural wall work proceeds.

2. For **three-piece** knocked-down frames, install rubber door mutes as necessary, and position jamb anchor screws ready for adjustment. Put the header in position, temporarily secure, and immediately follow with both right and left jambs. Rotate the anchor screws until the jambs are secure at the top, then adjust the bottoms using a level, and fasten base anchors; finally, tighten the centerpoint anchors. Check and adjust the final installation for accuracy in both the vertical and horizontal planes. Some types of knockdown frames use a wedge-locking feature instead of screws for quick and positive assembly.

Both one-piece and three-piece frames can be built into framed walls consisting of wood or steel studs, by drilling holes in the studs and door anchors and connecting them with bolts.

Tracks. There are two basic configurations:

1. For **vertical-lift** or **side-sliding** tracks, raise the tracks into their approximate final positions and temporarily secure in place. Insert assembled door unit hardware into tracks, adjust as necessary, and tighten all fastenings.

2. For **sectional overhead** tracks, temporarily support the horizontal overhead tracks in their approximate position using metal straps or nylon ropes. Raise the assembled door (as described below) in its vertical tracks, and connect the tracks. Secure drop angles to the overhead soffit and to the horizontal tracks, using sway bars as necessary to provide

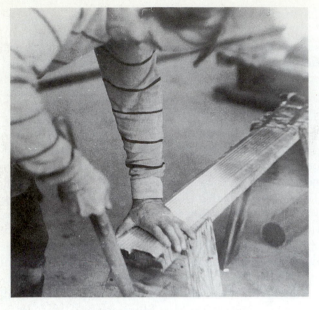

(a) Cutting and finishing

(b) Drilling and securrng

Thresholds

Most exterior doors require a wood or metal threshold. These are normally cut to length from stock moldings or extrusions, prepared to fit the frames, and bolted or screwed in position. (BCIT Building Technology)

rigidity. Ensure that both tracks are at the same height, are parallel, and have a uniform slope of 6 mm in 30 cm or $1/4$ in. in 12 in. Finally, secure vertical track components to the inner wall face, using purpose-made adjustable mounting brackets. **Roller shutter** tracks are installed in a similar fashion.

Doors. These may be installed in either frames or tracks; for installation of hardware, see Section 08–700.

1. For doors in **frames**, install hinges and raise the door into position, shimming underneath to line up hinge leaves with their corresponding locations on door jambs. Secure the top hinge first, then the lower ones. Install the lock strike assembly in the striking jamb, and then install the lock or latch set into the striking stile. Finally, install the door closer if required.

2. For doors in **tracks**, lay out door sections, mark locations for hardware, drill holes for screws and bolts, and attach hardware, weatherstripping, and trusses as necessary. Insert the hardware for the bottom section of the door into its tracks, and shim the section level. Tighten hardware into final position, then insert the remaining sections of the door,

(a) Stockpiled components

(b) Attaching hardware

Overhead Doors

The components for warehouse or garage doors arrive at the site as a kit. The various pieces are then assembled according to specification, ready for installation where desired. (UBC Architecture)

(a) Erection

(b) Connection

Frame Assembly
The overhead door frame tracks are erected into position, temporarily braced, and secured with heavy-duty bolts to the building frame. Door panels are then inserted into their tracks. (UBC Architecture)

ensuring that hardware is properly installed and engaged in its proper track.

For vertical-lift or sectional overhead doors, locate the torsion spring near the centerline of the door and secure it to the door shaft. Attach lifting cable drums, secure same to ends of the shaft, and attach one end of lifting cables to same. Secure the other end of cables at the bottom, and induce tension in the spring, following the manufacturer's instructions.

Lightly oil and clean all moving parts. Open and close doors several times to confirm correct operation. Make adjustments to tension in springs and to the spacing or operation of hardware components as necessary.

5.3 Precautions

There are specific regulations in building codes in every part of the continent governing doors of particular types, such as fire doors and required exit doors, to which designers and contractors must give careful attention. Such design data is beyond the scope of this book. Careful coordination between the selection of doors, frames, and hardware is also of critical importance to the proper functioning of the building as a whole. Keep door components and accessories clean and dry. Take precautions against loss, theft, or accidental damage to parts or finishes. The work of this section is not particularly hazardous.

Operation
Despite the fact that the mass of most vertical lift or sectional doors is counterbalanced with springs or weights, they usually have some mechanical assistance to open them. (UBC Architecture)

Section 08–200
Wood Doors and Frames

1.0 Introduction

1.1 General Issues

This section deals with both the factory assembly and the site installation of wood door and frame units, from which the separate techniques involved in erecting the frame and hanging the door will be easily deduced.

1.2 Design Aspects

Although one might still encounter the traditional methods of making and fitting wood doors and frames at the building site, it is now much more common for wood doors and frames to be delivered as preassembled units, ready for simple and rapid installation as a composite whole. For further discussion of specific aspects of design relative to doors (such as handing and swing), see Section 08–100, Part 1.2.

1.3 Related Work

Work closely connected to this section is described in the following sections, to which reference should be made:

06–100   Rough Carpentry

06–200   Finish Carpentry

08–700   Finish Hardware

2.0 Products

The components of this section logically fall under three headings: **doors** (described in Part 2.1 Materials), **frames** (described in Part 2.2 Accessories); and **hardware** (described in Section 08–700).

2.1 Materials

Although there are many kinds of wood doors (such as batten doors, louvered doors, framed and braced doors, bifold doors, pocket doors, and plank doors), those normally selected for use in modern buildings can be classified under two main headings: **panel** and **flush** doors.

Panel Doors. These consist of an arrangement of thick solid wood vertical stiles and horizontal rails, enclosing thinner solid or plywood panels, secured in place with narrow wood moldings called sticking (see Figure 1). The joints between the stiles and rails are usually strengthened and stiffened by using either mortise-and-tenon construction or by the insertion of round hardwood or plastic dowels or pins, all glued in place. Panels can be arranged for glazing, complete with perimeter wood beading miter-cut at corners.

Flush Doors. These consist of an interior concealed solid or hollow wood frame, with doweled or splined glued joints, covered on both faces with parallel and continuous composite panels of veneered plywood (see Figure 2). Solid cores consist of either an arrangement of glued or unglued vertical wood strips or blocks, or a uniform filling of plastic foam

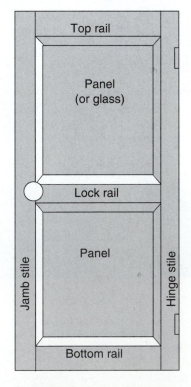

Figure 1   Panel Door

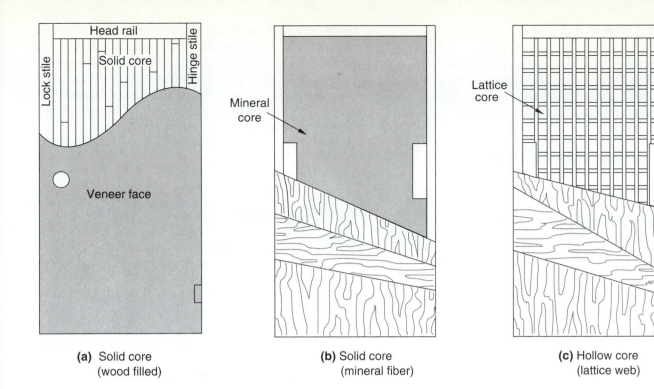

(a) Solid core
    (wood filled)

(b) Solid core
    (mineral fiber)

(c) Hollow core
    (lattice web)

Figure 2 Flush Door

or mineral fiber. Hollow cores consist of wood or fiber spacers, arranged in an open grid, honeycomb, or ladder pattern and glued in position to provide internal support to the face panels.

Both solid- and hollow-core doors are completed by having one or two layers of thin plywood glued to each face of the core frame, finally covered with a thin hardwood veneer, plastic laminate, or melamine resin skin bonded to the plywood, with the finished grain positioned vertically. Matching strips of veneer are then applied to the vertical edges of the door; in good-quality work, strips are also applied to the top and bottom edges of the door.

Both panel and flush doors are available with glazed panels of various sizes for light, vision, and appearance purposes, with wood or metal louvers for ventilation, or with lead foil laminated to one face for acoustical or medical purposes, as well as in single, double, or triple (or additional) combinations for use in closets and movable partitions.

2.2 Accessories

Accessories can be classified under three headings: **frames, trim,** and **hardware.** Wood trim is described in Section 06–200 and hardware in Section 08–700.

Frames.   There are two main types of frames for wood doors:

1. **Assembled** frames are factory-produced combinations of jambs, headers, and spreaders, prepared ready to receive a companion single, double, or pocket door.
2. **Unassembled** frames consist of stock door frame profiles in standard lengths, requiring to be measured, cut, and fitted at the job-site.

Both types involve the use of clear, kiln-dried softwood or hardwood stock. Common softwoods include cedar, fir, and pine; common hardwoods include ash, birch, and mahogany. All stock is run through a planer at the millwork shop, to produce appropriate profiles suitable for door frame use.

3.0 Construction Aids

3.1 Equipment

Electric routers are commonly used to prepare frames and doors for hinges and locksets.

3.2 Tools

As the installation of wood doors and frames is essentially carpentry work, the tools are those of the carpenter; wood planes, chisels, scribes, braces, and bits are frequently used to do this work.

4.0 Production

4.1 Crew Configuration

A crew for a small project might consist of one carpenter and two helpers. On medium-sized jobs, crews might consist of two or three carpenters and one helper, with one of the carpenters acting as foreman. On large sites, several crews could be used simultaneously or consecutively.

4.2 Productivity

Table 1 shows output factors for repetitive work done by an experienced crew hanging single doors under good conditions on a medium-sized commercial or institutional project. Double the labor time to fit and hang double doors.

5.0 Procedures

5.1 Preparation

Locations scheduled to receive wood doors and frames should be checked to ensure that they are clean, dry, and free from obstructions that might impede installation. Walls framed with wood or steel studs should have rough door openings reinforced with vertical cripples adjacent to each jamb, horizontal lintels overhead, and weatherproof thresholds or sills secured at door openings in exterior walls. Concrete or masonry walls should have galvanized steel or treated wood nailing blocks or inserts properly positioned and installed, ready to receive nailed fastenings to secure the frames in position.

5.2 Process

Wood Door Frames.   Proceed as follows:

1. With **preassembled** frames, the hinge jamb is nailed onto the plate or cripple next to it, after being plumbed vertical and shimmed as necessary. The head is then leveled, shimmed, and nailed to the lintel. Finally, the lock jamb is leveled, shimmed, and nailed to its corresponding plate or cripple. In frames for pocket doors, the appropriate spreaders, tracks, and stops have to be positioned ready to accommodate the door or doors (see Figure 3).

Typical Doors

Most residential buildings are now equipped with regular factory-made door and frame composites. These are available in all normal sizes, ready for installation as a complete unit. (UBC Architecture)

Table 1
WOOD DOOR
INSTALLATION TIMES

Type of Installation	Man-Hours per Unit
Factory combination	0.5
Unassembled frame	1.0
Preassembled frame	0.5
Door track unit	1.0
Light swing door	3.0
Heavy swing door	4.0
Light sliding door	2.5
Heavy sliding door	3.5
Bifold door	2.0
Pocket door	4.0

Preparation

There are several things to consider before installing wood door (or window) frames: check that the opening is square, check that jambs are plumb, and check dimensions and preparedness. (Wood Door and Window Institute)

Nontypical Units

Many commercial and institutional buildings require special custom-made doors and frames. The illustration shows a door finished with veneer to match adjacent frames and trim. (UBC Architecture)

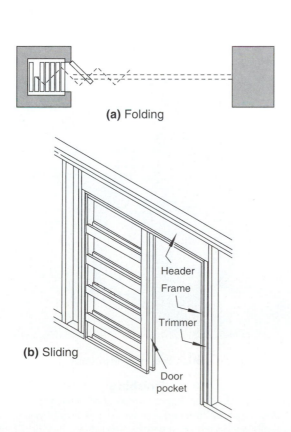

(a) Folding

(b) Sliding

Header
Frame
Trimmer
Door pocket

Figure 3   Pocket Doors

2. With **unassembled** frames, the head is first leveled, shimmed, and nailed into position beneath the lintel. Then both jambs are butted up to the underside of the head, tacked into position, shimmed, plumbed vertical, and nailed to secure them to their adjacent plates or cripples.

Wood Doors in Wood Frames. Proceed as follows:

1. Fit the door against the installed frame to check for size. Plane the edges to ensure a clearance of 5 mm or $^3/_{16}$ in. at head and jambs and 13 mm or $^1/_2$ in. at bottom. Using the plane, form a back-bevel on the outside edge of the locking stile, to prevent the door from binding in the frame as it opens (see Figure 4).

2. Using hardware templates, mark the positions for hinges, locksets, or rollers. Using a power router, cut holes for hardware and install as described in Section 08–700. Hang the door on its hinges and check for plumbness; adjust as necessary. Open and firmly close the door a few times to check that everything is in order.

(a) Shimming frames

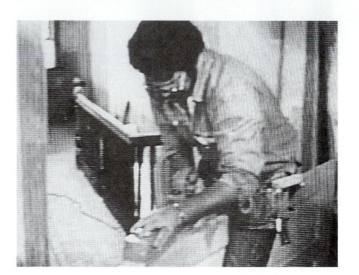

(a) Planing door edges

(b) Checking swing

Installation
After the door has been installed, frames are often shimmed to ensure perfect alignment between the frame and the door. The door swing and balance is checked before final fastening. (BCIT Building Technology)

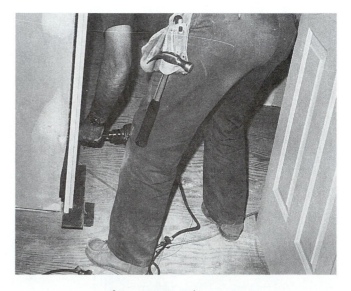

(b) Securing door stops

Finishing
If necessary, doors are lightly planed at edges to ensure a proper fit. Door stops are fastened with finishing nails and perimeter trim is usually applied to complete the installation. (Wood Door and Window Institute)

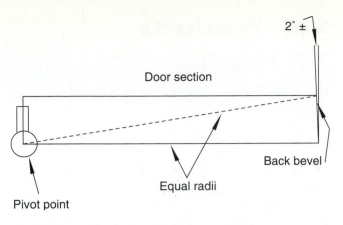

2° ±

Door section

Back bevel

Equal radii

Pivot point

Figure 4 Back-Beveled Edge

Wood Doors in Metal Frames. The process is similar to that described above for wood frames. The main difference is that the holes, slots, and reinforcement for attaching door hardware to the frames should already be prepared in the frames at the factory.

5.3 Precautions

Arrange to keep all components clean and dry, and take the usual precautions against loss, theft, or accidental damage to factory-finished parts or surfaces. Frames may be carefully stacked horizontally; doors should be stored vertically on end. All components should be stored close to their final locations for a few days to allow for acclimatization.

Section 08–400
Storefront Systems

1.0 Introduction

1.1 General Issues

It is a common practice to enclose the street-level entrance lobbies of commercial buildings with an assembly of metal framing incorporating glazed doors, windows, and spandrel panels. These assemblies are generally called *storefront systems*, because they are frequently used to create the front of commercial retail store buildings. They are also often used on institutional buildings (such as museums and schools) which are not stores in the commercial sense. They are occasionally used inside buildings to create special effects in offices, reception areas, or showrooms. They are seldom encountered in individual private residential buildings, except of the largest and most expensive type, where they may enclose a swimming pool or sundeck.

1.2 Design Aspects

There are three reasons why designers choose storefront systems: the suitability of the system for the required purpose; the opportunity for an almost infinite selection of design arrangements; and the general availability of appropriate systems. The **pur-poses** embrace characteristics such as weather protection, property security, personnel access, inviting appearance, and the passage of light. **Selection** embraces a wide choice of materials, finishes, and configurations of finely made main frame components, door and window units, perimeter trim, and operating hardware, to create almost any desired architectural effect, depending on the owner/client requirements. **Availability** embraces aspects of supply and economics; there are many excellent systems available in a fairly competitive market, resulting in good value for the consumer and economy in the construction budget.

There are some limitations placed on designers who select the storefront solution to an architectural design problem. One constraint is the general inability and inadvisability to mix and match components from different systems or sources; another constraint is that there are always some size limitations with respect to the individual components and to the overall assembly. A third constraint arises out of the difficulty of rendering an exterior glazed wall system (having so many small joints) entirely waterproof and wind resistant. Care must be taken with the reinforcing, glazing, and caulking systems selected for use in conjunction with any storefront system. A fourth constraint concerns the incompatibility of the materials from which many storefront systems are made with the materials of the building structural frame to which they are attached; positive separation, using paints or plastics, is often necessary, together with allowances for movement.

The design usually develops from considerations of the size, type, and position of the entrance doors to permit people (or vehicles) passage through the system. The spaces on either side and above the door openings are framed with (usually) symmetrically placed storefront structural members, and the doors, panels, and trim are then selected for best utility and appearance to complete the system. A typical arrangement is shown in Figure 1.

It is prudent for building owners to insist on tests for moisture and air penetration on the assembled system components. It is also a good practice to specify that the contractor must provide engineered shop drawings and notarized letters of compliance with the specifications.

1.3   Related Work

Work closely connected to this section is described in the following sections, to which reference should be made:

03–300   Cast-in-Place Concrete

04–200   Unit Masonry

06–100   Rough Carpentry

07–900   Joint Sealing

08–700   Finish Hardware

08–800   Glass and Glazing

2.0 Products

2.1 Materials

The materials for storefront systems fall into four categories.

Aluminum.   Most aluminum storefront system frames are made from commercially produced hot-extruded 6063–T5 (or 6060–T51) aluminum alloy, in hollow, rectangular, straight, tubular sections, having metal thickness of approximately 3 mm or $1/8$ in., and having surfaces either clear or color anodized and lacquered for appearance and protection. Vinyl-coated and porcelain-enameled systems in a wide variety of attractive colors are also available. Some typical profiles are shown in Figure 2.1.

Steel.   Most steel storefront system frames are made from commercially produced, cold-rolled, low-carbon mild steel, either 14- or 16-gauge thick, in hollow, rectangular (and occasionally circular), straight, tubular sections, and either galvanized or bonderized for rust prevention. They are available either factory finished with baked enamel paint or prepared ready for site painting. Some typical profiles are shown in Figure 2.2.

Glass.   The types of glass most commonly encountered in storefront systems are clear float, heat-tempered, and wire-reinforced. For detailed descriptions, see Section 08–800, Part 2.1.

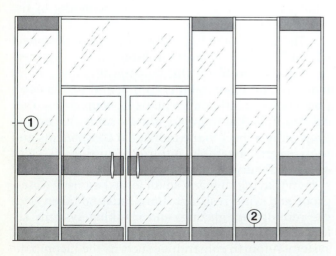

Figure 1   Typical Storefront System Elevation

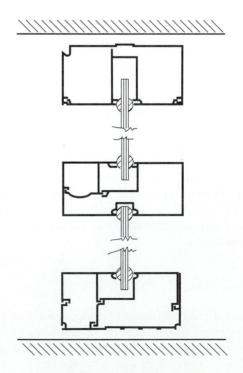

Figure 2.1   Aluminum Profile

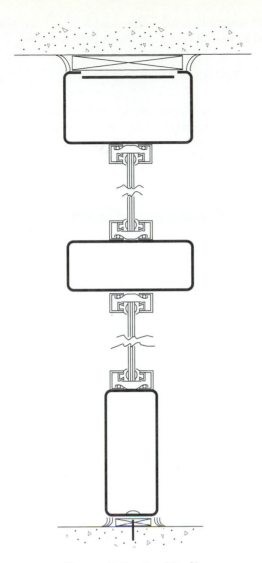

Figure 2.2 Steel Profile

(a)   Main entrance

(b)   Side entrance

General View

Storefront systems usually comprise an assembly of hollow aluminum, steel, or bronze framing members, with matching door components, louvered vents, and plain or ornamental glazing. (UBC Architecture)

Others.   In the most expensive or prestigious of buildings, storefront systems made of stainless steel or bronze components are occasionally specified. Their manufacture is similar to the mild steel and aluminum sections, respectively, described above; their installation generally follows the methods described later in this section for typical steel and aluminum systems.

2.2   Accessories

The accessories for storefronts fall into seven categories:

Connectors.   Each storefront system manufacturer provides a series of steel or aluminum clips, plates, reinforcing devices, screws, shims, bolts, and the like, to permit field connection and erection of the framing components and thermal movement.

Panels. Openings in or between storefront frame systems (not filled with doors or clear glass panels) are often filled with thin sandwich spandrel panels, made of sheet aluminum, asbestos, glass, hardboard, plastic, plywood, steel, or other decorative material, usually treated with paint to enhance appearance and resistance to weathering, and often bonded to an internal core of fiberglass, mineral wool, gypsum, or other insulating material.

Trim. Open-frame members are usually closed with a matching metal plate clipped, riveted, or welded in position. Openings at doorways are usually trimmed with an extruded aluminum threshold plate, bolted to the structural frame of the building, often mill finished but occasionally colored to match the rest of the storefront framing members. Glazed and spandrel panels are usually set in continuous, flexible, neoprene or rubber perimeter beading, secured in place with snapped-on or screwed-in, continuous, rigid, hollow, metal perimeter trim.

Caulking. This work is often part of a larger contract to seal the entire building and not just the storefront system. Regardless of contractual arrangements, for details of caulking, see Section 07–900.

Doors. Manufacturers of storefront systems usually make a variety of doors appropriate for installation in their framing systems. For details of other metal doors, see Section 08–100.

Hardware. Specific items of hardware used on doors and opening windows or vents in specific storefront systems are usually recommended by the system manufacturer. For details of hardware, see Section 08–700.

Glazing. Glazing systems used in conjunction with storefronts usually involve the use of long lengths of specially profiled butyl rubber or neoprene glazing bead to secure and seal the glazed portions of the assembly in position. For details of glazing, see Section 08–800.

3.0 Construction Aids

3.1 Equipment

Power saws capable of cutting through the aluminum or steel sections and power drills capable of making holes in the concrete, metal, or wood structural frame of the building are necessary for this work. Light-

weight movable scaffolding and ladders are also required to install components at higher levels.

3.2 Tools

As this work is essentially a combination of carpentry and glazing work, with occasional elements of sheet metal work, the tools used are those of the sheet metal worker, the carpenter, and the glazier.

4.0 Production

4.1 Crew Configuration

Depending on location, this work may be done by qualified mechanics who may also be carpenters, glaziers, or sheet metal workers. A typical crew might consist of two mechanics and one helper; on large projects, such as shopping malls with many retail stores, two or more crews might be used, with one mechanic delegated to act as foreman.

4.2 Productivity

Because of the large number of variables involved in the assembly of storefront systems and their components, it is difficult to list simplified figures that are truly representative without being possibly misleading. The factors shown in Table 1 are typical for the midrange of good-quality work done in medium-sized commercial or institutional projects, based on commonly encountered retail store widths of about 10 m or 35 ft. and heights of about 3 m or 10 ft., and having one pair of normal single-acting doors centrally located. For wider continuous fronts, decrease frame factors by about 20 percent; for higher fronts, increase frame factors by about 15 percent; for multiple doors side by side, decrease door factors by

Table 1
PRODUCTIVITY FACTORS FOR INSTALLATION OF STOREFRONT COMPONENTS

Type of Work	Man-Hours per 10 m² or 100 ft.²
Straight framing	30
Angled framing	40
Curved framing	50
Installing doors	10
Installing glass	7
Installing spandrels	5

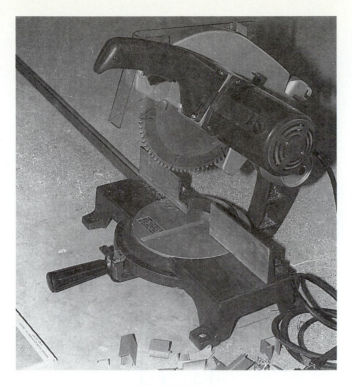

(a) Table saw

(b) Securing corner blocks

Assembly

The factory-fabricated components are delivered to site and saw-cut to size if necessary. After anchors and other accessories are secured, the frame is ready for insertion into the opening. (UBC Architecture)

Installation

The composite assembly is erected and inserted into the opening. A heavy-duty drill is used to cut bolt hole openings, and the unit is secured to the building frame. (UBC Architecture)

about 10 percent. The factors include measuring, cutting, fitting connectors and reinforcing bars, and installing completed frames and other components in their final positions.

5.0 Procedures

5.1 Preparation

Work spaces should be clean, reasonably dry, and free of construction debris or equipment not related to the work of this section. Portions of the structural frame of the building to which the storefront system will be attached should be complete, cured, solid, and ready to receive the system according to the requirements of the system manufacturer. All installation dimensions should be taken in the field from the actual structure and not estimated, calculated, or scaled from drawings. Hardware packages should be opened just prior to their use and checked for completeness. Appropriate equipment and tools should be assembled on site, ready for use.

5.2 Process

Frame components for aluminum systems are usually delivered in stock lengths, slightly oversized and ready to be cut to precise lengths at the site. Steel assemblies are best shipped to the site prewelded ready for installation, except where assembled sizes are greater than shipping limitations. Wherever possible, perimeter frame components should be installed in one piece full length from end to end. Intermediate vertical members are best installed in one piece for the full height, with intermediate horizontal members being cut, fitted, and clipped into position between the vertical members. In general, plain butt joints between frame members are simpler and cheaper to form and seal than mitered joints, where joints have to be made in the field. Jamb members next to masonry or concrete abutments should be fully grouted with mortar; those next to wood or steel abutments may be back-coated with asphalt paint. Typical installations are shown in Figures 3.1 and 3.2.

The installation procedure is as follows:

1. Fixing plates, clips, or expansion bolt shields are secured to the structural frame of the building in predetermined positions according to the system manufacturer's directions.

2. Frame members are measured and cut to length as necessary. The perimeter frame members are usually installed first, followed by the intermediate members. All frame members are shimmed, connected, leveled or plumbed as necessary, and tightened into final position.

3. Glass, vents, and spandrel panels are installed and beaded as described in Section 08–800.

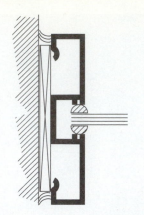

Figure 3.1 Jamb Section

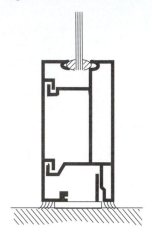

Figure 3.2 Sill Section

(a)   Installing bead by hand

(b)   Trimming bead at corners

Finishing

Once the assembly is secure in position, neoprene beading is inserted into the glazing grooves, ready to receive and support single- or double-glazed panels. Metal surfaces are wiped clean. (UBC Architecture)

4. Threshold plates are secured at door sills, and door hardware is installed on doors and frames as described in Section 08–700.

5. Doors are hung and tested as described in Section 08–100.

6. Finally, the whole storefront system is cleaned and the assembly is checked for defects and adjusted as necessary.

5.3 Precautions

As the components involved in storefronts are usually factory prefinished and finely machined, care must be taken during delivery and handling procedures not to permit damage or loss to occur. All components should be stored in a clean, dry, secure place. If temporary storage is required, framing bars, beads, and hardware should be placed horizontally in the delivery wrappings or cartons; door, window, glass, and other panel components should be stored vertically, with paper or plastic separators to prevent damage to finishes. Work gloves are recommended for mechanics.

Alternative Systems
This picture shows that not all storefront systems need be metal. This is a custom-made wood and glass system for a retail outlet in an urban shopping mall; many variations are possible. (UBC Architecture)

Section 08–500
Metal Windows and Frames

1.0 Introduction

1.1 General Issues

Residential metal windows and frames are customarily prefabricated in a factory and delivered to the site completely assembled and usually fully glazed. Commercial metal windows are also prefabricated, but they are often delivered to the site in knocked-down packages for later assembly and glazing. Window manufacturers produce many standard or stock sizes, specifications of which are usually described in detail in catalogs of various types and qualities. Most manufacturers will produce customized units to special order and at additional cost.

1.2 Design Aspects

The following criteria will influence the success of any metal window frame system: adequate accommodation of anticipated thermal expansion and contraction of metal and glass, avoidance of direct glass-to-metal contact at any point, resistance to the passage of moisture through perimeter joints or at frame corners, acceptable aesthetic appearance, and predictable economics with respect to both materials and installation costs.

Metal windows are classified by **use** into commercial, industrial, institutional, and residential. They are classified by **frame configuration** into awning, casement (pivoted or projected), double-hung sash and case, hopper, jalousie or louver, and vertical or horizontal slide types, some shown in Figure 1.

1.3 Related Work

Work closely connected to this section is described in the following sections, to which reference should be made:

05–050   Metal Fastening

07–900   Joint Sealing

08–800   Glass and Glazing

09–900   Painting and Decorating

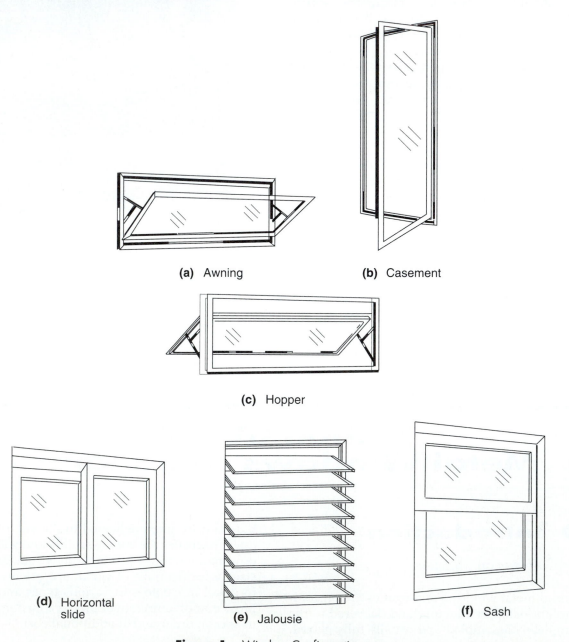

(a) Awning   (b) Casement

(c) Hopper

(d) Horizontal slide   (e) Jalousie   (f) Sash

Figure 1 Window Configurations

2.0 Products

2.1 Materials

Although theoretically almost any metal could be used to make the frames of metal windows, the majority are made from extruded aluminum of various qualities and finishes; a minority are made from mild carbon steel. Other metals, such as stainless steel and bronze alloys, are not common, though they are occasionally encountered on high-quality institutional work. For types and quality of aluminum and steel, see Section 08–400. For typical cross-sectional profiles, see Figure 2.

Aluminum. Aluminum windows are made from aluminum extrusions, manufactured by forcing molten aluminum continuously through a preformed die, which produces extrusions of any given profile. The extrusions are cleaned, cut to industry standard lengths, packaged, and delivered mill finished to the window manufacturer. Most better-quality extrusions are then finished either by painting or anodizing, although some cheaper frames are left as mill finish or treated with a clear lacquer coating.

Steel. Steel windows are made from mild steel bars, forced hot or cold through configuration rollers set to produce a predetermined cross-sectional profile. The shaped bars are then cleaned and cut, ready for further remanufacture usually by the same company, to form the perimeter and interior frames for windows of various configurations. Most steel frames are factory prefinished with a rustproof treatment, followed by a baked-on acrylic finish in a variety of standard colors.

2.2 Accessories

These can be categorized as those used **within** the frame and those used **around** the frame.

(a) Installation

(b) Fastening

Residential Windows

Most residential metal windows are easily handled by a crew of two. One works outside to raise the window into place; the other works inside to hold the unit during the fastening process. (UBC Architecture)

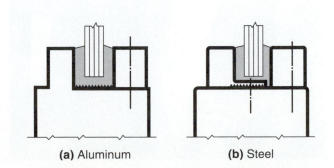

(a) Aluminum   **(b) Steel**

Figure 2 Metal Window Frame Cross Sections

Within frames:

1. **Beads.** Used to hold glazing compounds against the glass.
2. **Glass.** See Section 08–800.
3. **Setting blocks.** Used to separate glass from metal.

Around frames:

1. **Building paper.** Used to improve resistance to passage of water vapor at edges of rough wood openings. See Section 06–100.
2. **Nails.** Used to secure frames to structure. See Section 05–050.
3. **Screws.** Used to assemble frames. See Section 05–050.
4. **Sills.** Used to trim bottoms of rough openings.
5. **Wood shims.** Used to true up frames in rough openings.

3.0 Construction Aids

3.1 Equipment

The equipment necessary to install metal windows is normally selected from among the following items:

(a) Fitting framing

Commercial Windows

Many commercial installations utilize prefabricated windows similar to residential units. However, it is equally common for components to be custom-cut and site-assembled. Note shims. (UBC Architecture)

extendable ladders, lightweight scaffolds, and safety belts.

3.2 Tools

The tools used are selected from among carpenter's hammers, builder's levels, hard rubber mallets, variable-speed electric drills, screwdrivers with assorted bits, glazier's clamps (suction cup devices), hacksaws, pinch bars, staple guns, and caulking guns.

4.0 Production

4.1 Crew Configuration

Metal windows are usually installed by glaziers, although many finish carpenters also have the skill and (in some regions) union jurisdictional authority to do so. Such work is best done using small teams of two workers, one a skilled journeyman, the other a semiskilled helper; some jurisdictions require pairs of glaziers working together.

4.2 Productivity

Times will naturally vary, depending on the size and complexity of the project, specification and building

(b) Checking glass

Table 1
PRODUCTIVITY FACTORS FOR
WINDOW INSTALLATION

Type of Work	Minutes per Window
Preparation:	
New work	10
Renovations	20
Installation:	
Simple residential	30
Complex commercial	60
Double-hung/projected	90
Pivot/combination	120
Removal:	
Simple residential	15
Simple commercial	30
Complex commercial	60

code requirements, the weather and time of year, the skill of the teams, and the amount of preparation to be done. Table 1 gives some representative crew time factors for both new work and renovations.

As the installation of metal windows invariably occurs on the outside of buildings, the weather plays a significant role in productivity factors. During good (dry and warm) weather, one may deduct about 10 percent from the above values; in poor (wet or cold) weather, add about 15 percent to the values.

5.0 Procedures

5.1 Preparation

One common problem is the difficulty of fitting an essentially rectangular metal frame into a wood, concrete, or masonry opening which itself is not exactly rectangular. Proper preparation of an accurate opening is essential for rapid installation of acceptable quality.

Windows above ground floor levels will usually require some scaffolding or staging to permit their installation. However, if frames are not glazed before installation (as most commercial windows are not), they can often be installed from inside the building, thus avoiding the need for ladders or scaffolds. Care must be taken to select a frame profile that will permit subsequent glazing also from inside the building, although it should be noted that such frames are more difficult to render watertight than externally glazed profiles because of wind pressure on the glass pane.

5.2 Process

The procedures for the installation of residential windows differ in some respects from those for commercial windows. Both are described next.

Residential.   This involves both **new** and **replacement** work.

1. New work. Check the rough window opening for dimensions and squareness. The opening should be about 25 mm or 1 in. taller and 20 mm or 0.75 in. wider than the frame dimensions. Insert the new window frame headrail first, and slide the frame into the sill at the bottom, tapping lightly with a rubber mallet on all sides. Check levelness, plumbness, and squareness, shimming as necessary. Then screw the headrail first, jambs next, and the sill last.

2. Replacement work. Carefully remove old wood or metal window frames and discard. Check the rough opening for dimensions and squareness; remove and replace any loose, rotted, or rusty components. Measure and cut the extruded preformed metal sill to fit over the old wood frame at the bottom of the opening. Extend sill ends beyond the window opening 50 mm or 2 in. at each end; form closed returned ends on the sill. Screw the new sill to the old wood frame in such a way that the screwheads will be covered by the new metal frame. See Figure 3. Then continue as for new work described above.

Commercial.   This primarily involves new work. Install spigots or brackets at ends of headrail and sill members. Locate jambs to conceal brackets and screw to same. In concrete or masonry structures, install expansion shields into predrilled holes at

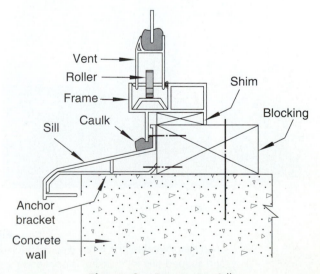

Figure 3   Renovation Sill

(a) Drilling

Fastening

Most residential window units are fastened to the building by nailing through a perimeter flange. Heavier commercial frames need to be drilled and then screwed at jambs and sills. (BCIT Building Technology)

(b) Screwing

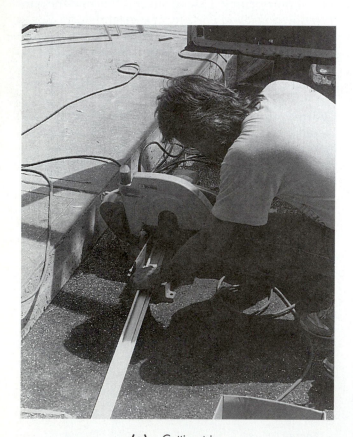

(a) Cutting trim

(b) Applying caulking

Finishing

Most metal windows have some sort of perimeter metal trim or beading. The material is cut to length and shaped on-site, caulking is applied to the rear face, and the trim is secured in position. (UBC Architecture)

heads, jambs, and sills. Alternatively, provide and install wood nailing blocks or crimped sheet metal nailing inserts at intervals around the perimeter of the opening. Use a high-speed electric drill with carbide-tipped bit to drill holes for screw fastenings. Drill the first holes about 50 mm or 2 in. from the member ends and intermediate holes at about 300-mm or 12-in. intervals in between the end holes. Raise and install the assembled frame into the prepared opening; level and plumb the frame using a carpenter's level, shimming as necessary. Insert screws through frame holes into expansion shields or to contact wood or metal nailers, and tighten with an electric power driver, taking care not to deform frame metal or to scratch the surface finish. The frame is now ready for glazing, for which see Section 08–800.

5.3 Precautions

The most obvious aspect of safety in handling glazed windows is first to prevent the windows from getting broken, and secondly, if the windows do get broken, to avoid or minimize injury to the workers. Prevention of the first possibility can be ensured by providing adequate packing or crating of windows to industry standards; prevention of the second involves care and attention to duty, as well as the use of protective work gloves, proper industrial clothing, and correct footwear.

Care must be taken with the delivery of metal windows, whether glazed or not, to avoid breakage or warpage. They are best transported in a more or less vertical configuration in vehicles specially prepared for the purpose, having inclined, padded metal A-frames to which the window frames can be temporarily secured by clamps or straps. At the site, window frames should also be handled and stored in an essentially vertical plane, to avoid distortion or breakage.

Section 08–600
Wood Windows and Frames

1.0 Introduction

1.1 General Issues

Most wood windows are prefabricated in factories and delivered to the site completely assembled and usually fully glazed. Wood window manufacturers produce many standard or stock sizes, specifications of which are usually described in detail in catalogs of various types and qualities. Most manufacturers will also produce custom units to special order and at additional cost. Many factories also produce plastic-coated wood windows, primarily for the residential market.

1.2 Design Aspects

The following criteria affect wood window and frame systems:

1. Adequate accommodation of expansion and contraction of wood due to moisture and of glass due to temperature changes.

2. Avoidance of direct glass-to-wood contact at any point.

3. Resistance to the passage of moisture through the frame or at the joints.

4. Acceptable aesthetic appearance.

5. Predictable economics with respect to both materials and installation costs.

The classification of configurations of wood and plastic windows is identical to that described in Section 08–500 for metal windows. For a cross section through a typical frame, refer to Figure 1.

1.3 Related Work

Work closely connected to this section is described in the following sections, to which reference should be made:

06–200   Finish Carpentry

07–900   Joint Sealing

08–700   Finish Hardware

2.0 Products

2.1 Materials

The species of wood used most often for wood windows is either hemlock or western pine; cedar is occasionally encountered. The grade of wood is always clear (that is, free of significant knots or other defects), and the type of wood is always kiln-dried. There are three levels of quality in clear-grade wood used for window frames: low, intended for utility installations, such as in basements or storage areas; medium, intended for general commercial and residential installations, such as offices, houses, and stores; and high, intended for top-quality institutional and residential installations. The kiln-dried

(a) Residential

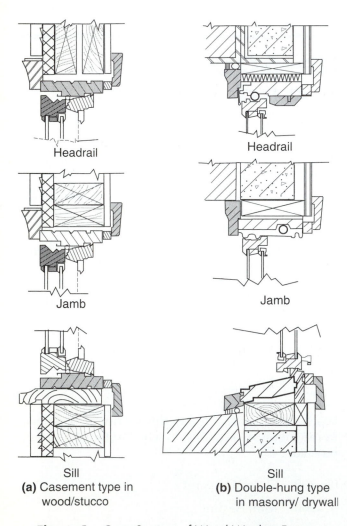

(a) Casement type in wood/stucco

(b) Double-hung type in masonry/ drywall

Figure 1 Cross Sections of Wood Window Frames

(b) Commercial

Types of Windows

The appearance of many buildings can be enhanced by the use of standard wood windows. One nonstandard example is this side-hinged, top-hung, open-out, wood-framed, double-glazed, twin-vent sash. (UBC Architecture)

wood stock is purchased in bulk by the window manufacturer from the lumbermill for remanufacture.

Approximate efficiency factors for factory utilization of the three qualities of milled stock are about 90 percent for high, 75 percent for medium, and 60 percent for low quality. The wood is kiln-dried to minimize warpage, to improve resistance to decay, and to enhance workability and fineness of finishes.

2.2 Accessories

These consist of fastening devices, hardware, and glass. For more specific details on each, refer to the sections indicated below:

Fastenings: Section 05–050

Hardware: Section 08–700

Glass: Section 08–800

3.0 Construction Aids

3.1 Equipment

Major equipment used to make wood windows includes heavy-duty planer-shapers, double-end tenoners, radial arm saws, pneumatic staplers and pointers, electric hand drills, sanding machines, and adjustable jigs and templates. All such equipment is located in factories; it is seldom encountered on site.

3.2 Tools

As this work is essentially carpentry work, the tools used are those of the carpenter: hammers, mallets, levels, measuring tapes, glue brushes, wrenches, plumb bobs, and nail-sets.

4.0 Production

4.1 Crew Configuration

To install most single wood window and frame units, the crew will consist of one qualified carpenter and one helper, with occasional assistance required from a second helper if the work involves double or triple units or very heavy single units.

4.2 Productivity

Productivity will vary, depending on whether the windows being installed are singles, doubles, or triples, and whether they are of double-hung sash or casement sash construction.

For ordinary commercial construction, an experienced crew will install about 10 to 12 preassembled units of single-frame sash in one 8-hour day, excluding trim. For doubles and triples, or for top-quality institutional work, productivity will be reduced by about 15 percent or to about one unit per hour per crew.

5.0 Procedures

5.1 Preparation

Check the rough window opening for dimensions and squareness. The opening should be about 25 mm or 1 in. taller and 20 mm or 0.75 in. wider than the frame dimensions. Check and sort the frames as

Checking
Before installing wood, metal, or vinyl windows, the rough openings must be checked to ensure they are square, plumb, level, correctly dimensioned, and ready to receive the window unit. (UBC Architecture)

they are delivered to the site. Temporarily store frames under cover until they are installed.

5.2 Process

Wood windows are installed in one of two ways: by way of an applied nailing flange or by nailing directly through the sash or frame. The new window frame is inserted into the prepared opening headrail first and slid into the sill at bottom, tapping lightly with a rubber mallet on all sides. Check levelness, plumbness, and squareness, shimming as necessary. Then nail (or screw) the headrail first, jambs next, and sill last.

For other aspects, refer to the following sections:

Perimeter trim: Section 06–200

Replacement work: Section 08–500

Glazing: Section 08–800

5.3 Precautions

Precautions are the same as for metal windows described in Section 08–500, Part 5.3.

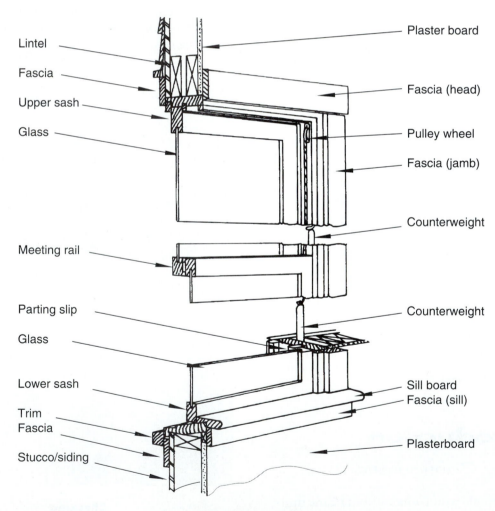

Wood Window Details

Like all other building components, there is a lexicon of terms to describe various parts and features of wood windows. Each manufacturer produces components machined to unique profiles. (Rehau Incorporated)

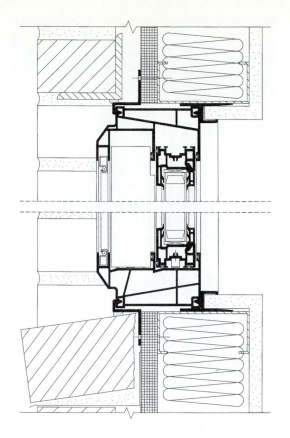

(a) Sliding window

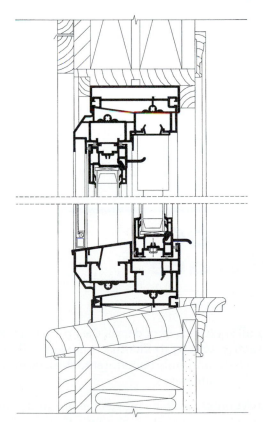
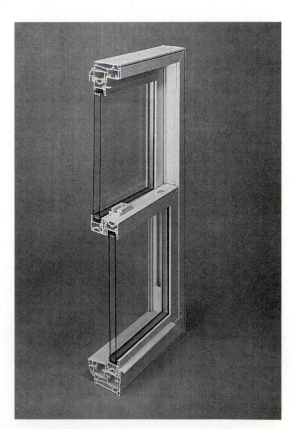

(b) Double-hung window

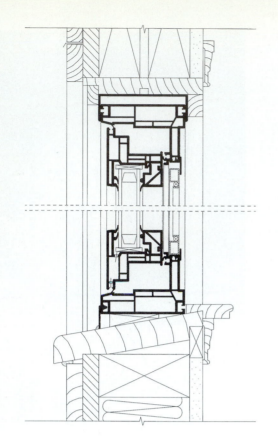

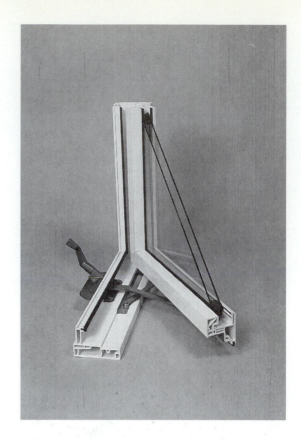

(c) Casement window

Window Sections

Some manufacturers produce vinyl components made to emulate wood windows. Like all other building components, wood and vinyl windows use special terms to describe various parts and features. (Rehau Incorporated, Virginia)

Section 08–700
Finish Hardware

1.0 Introduction

1.1 General Issues

The range of hardware devices available for doors, windows, cabinets, and general purposes is truly enormous. There are hundreds of manufacturers producing thousands of different kinds of devices by the million, in some cases. As it is impossible to cover all such variety in detail, the approach taken in this section will be to identify some general characteristics of commonly encountered devices in each of four major categories:

1. **Movement,** such as hinges, pivots, and rollers.
2. **Security,** such as locks and latches.
3. **Convenience,** such as closers and push-plates.
4. **Utility,** such as hooks and brackets.

Before proceeding with the study of description and installation of hardware devices, a distinction should be made between the terms *rough* hardware and *finish* hardware. **Rough** hardware consists of bolts, nails, screws, straps, and similar static devices, most of which are intended to be concealed from view in the finished work; some of the more common of these are described in Section 05–050. **Finish** hardware consists of hinges, latches, locks, rollers, push or pull handles, and similar operable devices, parts of which are intended to be visible in the finished work; these are described in this section. Manufactured specialties (such as toilet accessories like soap dishes and towel bars) are described in Section 10–001.

1.2 Design Aspects

Because of the enormous number of permutations of features available in items of finish hardware, many designers and contractors delegate this part of construction to independent architectural hardware specialists. However, it is appropriate for those involved in design and construction to have some concept of the more significant design issues involved, such as **function, selection, keying,** and **finishes.**

Function. This involves the reason for the hardware selection. For example, with regard to door latches and locks, the degree and type of security required to be provided by the door to which they are attached will limit the number of choices. One may wish to be able to perform one (or more) of the following functions:

1. Open the door by simply turning a doorknob on either side, such as in a residential living room.
2. Lock the door with a key from one side, while still being able to open it from the other side, such as the entrance door to a residence.
3. Lock the door from one side using a key and from the other side by pressing a button, such as in a private office.

4. Use a key to lock and unlock the door from both sides, such as in a bank or store entrance.
5. Press a button on one side to lock the door on the other side, such as in a washroom or toilet.

Other possible functions may require the use of combinations of blank plates, deadbolts, doorknobs, push buttons, thumb-turns, and the like. Some options are shown in Figure 1.

Selection. Selection of finish hardware devices should be made on the following bases: sound construction, reliable performance, attractive appearance, and competitive price. Bear in mind that most items of finish hardware are subject to high factors of wear and tear, and are usually intended to be in use for the life of the building; cheap or shoddy products will quickly develop problems and cause additional expense for repair or replacement. It is generally good practice to select all finish hardware items for any one purpose in one building from any one manufacturer, to simplify installation, maintenance, and the placement of responsibility for defects.

Keying. This is the term given to the hierarchy of locks that any given key can operate. A lock may be keyed-differently, keyed-alike, master-keyed, grand-master-keyed, or indeed, great-grand-master-keyed, depending on the perceived need for security and access at various levels of authority.

To give a simple example, consider a small department in a college organization. Each faculty office will be keyed-differently for privacy; each classroom will be keyed-alike for ease of access by all faculty; the key used to open each faculty office door might also open all classroom doors. Each storage room within the department could be keyed-differently or keyed-alike to the other storage, class, or office rooms, depending on the need for access or security. The department head would have a master-key which would open all door locks in the department. The cleaning staff might have a grand-

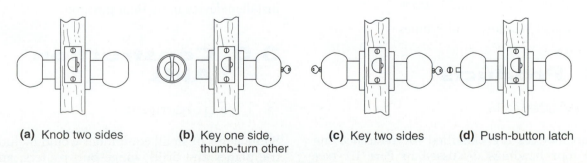

(a) Knob two sides   (b) Key one side, thumb-turn other   (c) Key two sides   (d) Push-button latch

Figure 1   Door Hardware Examples

Table 1
EXAMPLES OF FINISH CODES

Finish	BHMA*	USSF†
Brass, bright	605	3
Brass, satin	606	4
Bronze, satin	612	10
Bronze, oiled	613	10B
Chrome, bright	625	26
Chrome, satin	626	26D

*Builders Hardware Manufacturers Association.
†United States Standard Finishes.

master-key that would open all locks in the college, except the vault room where the records of the bursar or registrar are kept. The security staff administrator might have a great-grand-master-key. And so on.

Finishes. Finishes encountered on finish hardware items fall into seven basic categories, known by their trade names: mill, dead or flat, mat, dull, satin, polished, and bright. These finishes are achieved by a variety of factory-applied techniques involving brushing, buffing, dipping, etching, plating, or varnishing, to name a few, as well as no finish. In addition to these basic types, many hardware manufacturers offer specialty finishes, involving colors, textures, and patterns. Most manufacturers designate their finishes using industrywide alphanumeric systems. Some examples are shown in Table 1.

1.3 Related Work

Work closely connected to this section is described in the following sections, to which reference should be made:

06–400   Architectural Woodwork

08–100   Metal Doors and Frames

08–200   Wood Doors and Frames

08–400   Storefront Systems

08–500   Metal Windows and Frames

08–600   Wood Windows and Frames

2.0 Products

2.1 Materials

Hardware devices are classified for reference under the four headings discussed in Part 1.1 (see Figure 2):

Typical Units
Permutation of combinations of typical hardware on doors and windows is probably infinite. The illustration shows two of many door units: a thumb-turn dead-bolt at top and a latch-set. (UBC Architecture)

1. **Movement.** A variety of glides, guides, hinges, pivots, pulleys, roller bearings, slides, and tracks are used, among others.
2. **Security.** A variety of bars, bolts, hooks, latches, locks, rods, and strike plates are used, among others.
3. **Convenience.** A variety of closers, doorstops, kickplates, mail slots, nameplates, peepholes, and push- and pull-plates are used, among others.
4. **Utility.** A variety of brackets, clips, hooks, rails, and weatherstrips are used, among others.

2.2 Accessories

Most hardware devices are supplied in a crate or carton, together with some printed instructions for installation and use, and usually some accessories in the form of mounting templates or jigs of some sort and concealed brackets, screws, or clips to secure the installed device in its final position.

3.0 Construction Aids

3.1 Equipment

Some items of small equipment would include electric planes and drills, hinge butt routers, and lock mortisers.

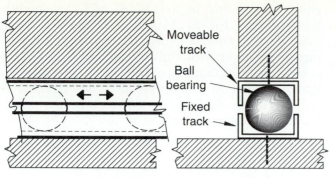

(a) Movement (roller track)

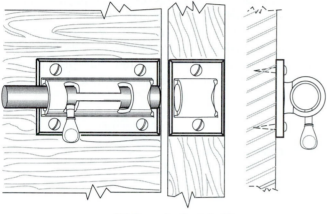

(b) Security (lock-bolt)

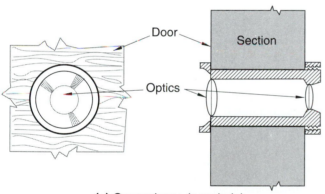

(c) Convenience (peephole)

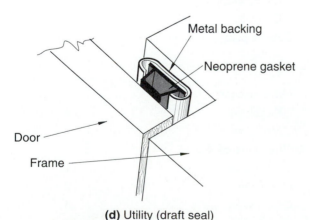

(d) Utility (draft seal)

Figure 2 Hardware Functions

Nontypical Units

Commercial and institutional buildings invariably have some customized window or door openings. This photo shows the entrance to a hotel ballroom; note the large number of heavy-duty pivots. (UBC Architecture)

3.2 Tools

As much of this work is generally classified as carpentry work, the tools used are those of the carpenter, such as chisels, drills, levels, mallets, screwdrivers, and set squares.

4.0 Production

4.1 Crew Configuration

In general, crew sizes for the installation of hardware at the job-site are small, consisting usually of one experienced tradesperson such as a carpenter. On large projects, two carpenters and a helper might be involved. In factory situations, where mass production using powered equipment is available, a variety of configurations of specialty help is possible.

4.2 Productivity

Factors given in Table 2 are representative of times that it might take experienced personnel working on typical commercial or institutional buildings to install ordinary hardware devices at the site, by hand and using appropriate power tools and jigs. Consistent with the rest of this section, some typical items have been selected from each of the four main groups of hardware devices. The figures given are for installing one unit, kit, or set of the hardware devices only, not the appliance or component they go with. For high-quality manual work, decrease productivity by about 25 percent; for factory mass-produced installation, productivity can be easily doubled.

5.0 Procedures

5.1 Preparation

Surfaces of building components scheduled to receive finish hardware devices should be clean, firm, smooth, and dry. The correct devices, tools, and equipment should be assembled and conveniently located, ready for use. Proposed locations of hardware devices should be accurately determined by measurement or template and carefully marked for cutting, drilling, planing, or routing as necessary. An understanding of the operating characteristics of each hardware device is essential for proper installation of all these devices.

5.2 Process

It is neither practical, possible, nor necessary to detail the installation process of every type of available hardware. Simple procedures to install typical groups of hardware devices on selected common building components are described below under the four main headings. The selected examples are representative of general procedures applicable to many

Table 2
PRODUCTIVITY FACTORS FOR INSTALLATION OF FINISH HARDWARE

Type of Hardware	Units per Hour	Type of Hardware	Units per Hour
Movement:		**Security**—Continued	
Door hinges:		Cabinet catches:	
On wood	6	Door latches	6
On metal	12	Drawer locks	8
Pivots:		Panic devices:	
Door	4	Surface	1
Window	6	Concealed	1
Window hinges:		**Convenience:**	
Casement	8	Closers:	
Projected	4	Surface	2
On cabinets:		Concealed	1
Door hinges	8	Doorstops:	
Drawer glides	4	On doors	6
Sliding track:		On walls	4
For exterior doors	1	Cabinet pulls:	
For interior closets	1	Surface	8
Security		Recessed	4
Door locks:		Miscellaneous:	
Quick-set	4	Kickplates	4
Mortised	2	Mail slots	2
Window latches:		**Utility (sets of 4):**	
On wood	6	Shelf brackets	1
On metal	4	Mirror clips	2
		Coat hooks	3
		Closet rails	1

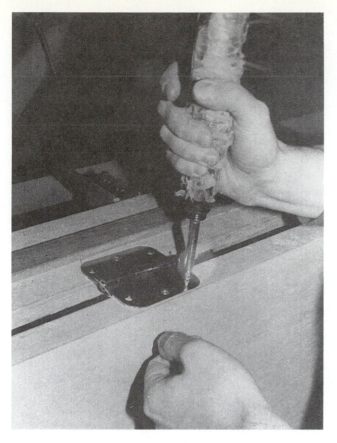

(a)   Door hinge

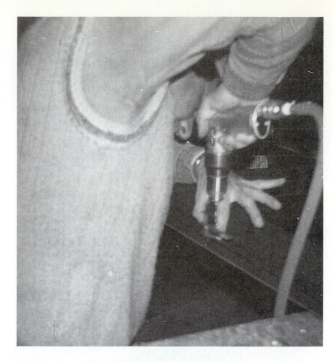

(b)   Window latch

Factory Installation

On large projects, it is usually better, quicker, and cheaper to install as much hardware at the factory as possible before delivery of doors and windows to the site. (BCIT Building Technology)

(a)   Door hinge

(b)   Window latch

Site Installation

Although the end result (with respect to hardware function) may be the same, site installation is proportionally more labor-intensive and subject to problems and delay than factory work. (BCIT Building Technology)

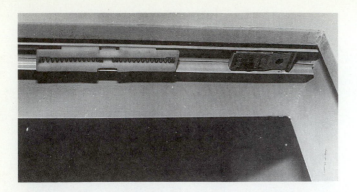

(a) Top track

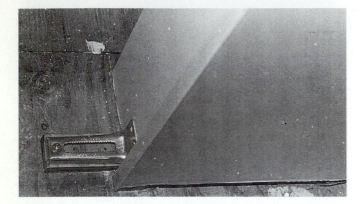

(b) Bottom pivot

Closet Hardware

Closets and cupboards in many buildings have bifold doors, to conserve space and ease operation. Such doors are mounted on adjustable pivots and attached at top to a spring-loaded guide. (BCIT Building Technology)

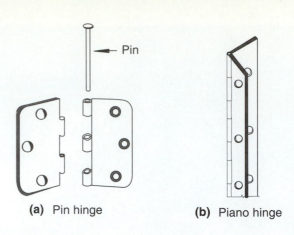

(a) Pin hinge   **(b)** Piano hinge

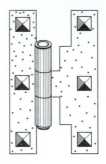

(c) Ornamental hinge   **(d)** Plain butt hinge

Figure 3.1   Wood Door Hinges

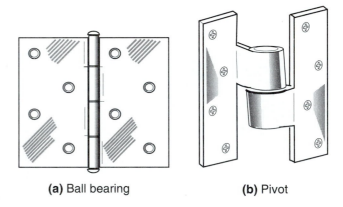

(a) Ball bearing   **(b)** Pivot

Figure 3.2   Metal Door Hinges

similar devices within each group. An illustration of one example in each group is shown as a general guide to the type.

Movement. This includes hinges, pivots, glides, and tracks.

Door Hinges

1. On wood doors (see Figure 3.1). There are three techniques used to install hinges on wood doors: by hand, by electric router, and by prehung door machine. In each case, the location of the hinge is determined, a template is attached to mark its location, and a shallow recess is cut on the hinge stile and hinge jamb, ready to receive the hinge.

2. On metal doors (see Figure 3.2). The hinge recesses in metal doors and frames must be precut in the correct position at the factory, with reinforc-

ing plates welded in position and predrilled ready to receive hinge screws.

Pivot Devices

1. On doors (see Figure 4.1). The location of the pivots must be marked, then recesses are cut and holes are drilled as necessary to receive and secure the pivot devices.

2. On windows (see Figure 4.2). On wood windows, the procedure is the same as for wood doors.

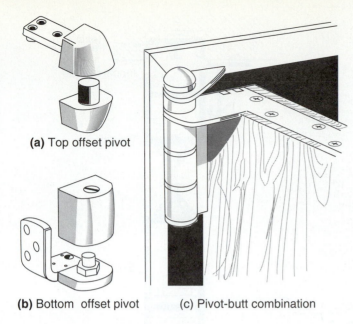

(a) Top offset pivot

(b) Bottom offset pivot   **(c)** Pivot-butt combination

Figure 4.1   Door Pivots

Figure 4.2   Window Pivots

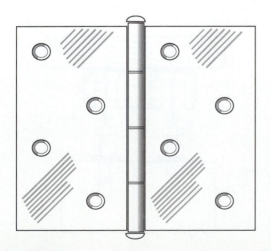

Figure 5.1   Wood Casement Hinge

On metal windows, the pivot casings are usually formed as an integral part of the sash and frame; they require simple assembly.

Window Hinges

1. On casements (see Figure 5.1). On wood windows, the procedure is the same as for wood doors. On metal windows, the procedure is the same as for metal doors.

2. On projected types (see Figure 5.2). Locations for screw holes are marked, slots are cut as necessary to accommodate the arms of the hinge mechanism, and the devices are manually installed and adjusted for tension and friction.

Cabinet Hardware

1. Door hinges (see Figure 6.1). The variety of cabinet hinges includes simple butt (exposed, semi-exposed, or concealed), pivot, continuous piano-type, and European swivel, among others. Some are surface mounted, some are semirecessed, and others are fully recessed. Virtually all are factory installed, using specialized power equipment.

2. Drawer glides (see Figure 6.2). There are two basic forms: plastic bottom or corner guides and metal side rollers. The drawers must be dimensioned to allow for the space taken up by these devices, most of which are surface mounted and stapled or screwed in position.

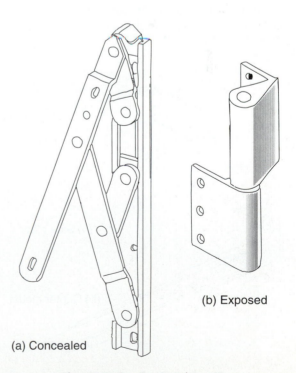

(b) Exposed

(a) Concealed

Figure 5.2   Projected Hinges

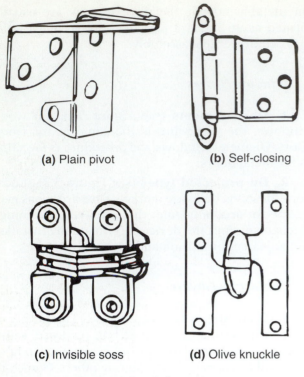

(a) Plain pivot   **(b)** Self-closing

(c) Invisible soss   **(d)** Olive knuckle

Figure 6.1   Cabinet Hinges

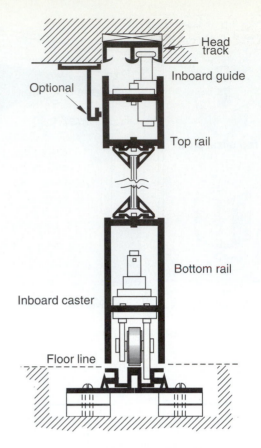

Figure 7.1   Exterior Door Track

Sliding Track

1. For exterior doors (see Figure 7.1). For aluminum or wood patio-type doors, the tracks are usually mounted underneath the door with an overhead guide to maintain alignment. Tracks are measured, cut to length, hand located, and screwed or bolted into position. For aluminum patio door components, see Section 08–400, Part 2.0; these doors are made using materials and methods virtually identical to storefront doors. For wood patio door components, see Section 08–200, Part 2.0.

2. For interior closets (see Figure 7.2). For wood or steel closet doors, the tracks are usually mounted above the door, with a bottom guide to

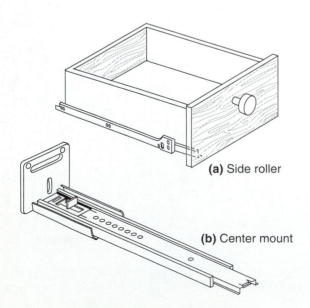

(a) Side roller

(b) Center mount

Figure 6.2   Drawer Glides

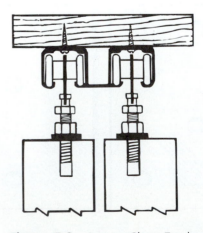

Figure 7.2   Interior Closet Track

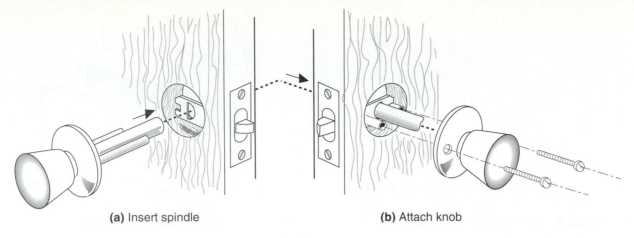

(a) Insert spindle   **(b)** Attach knob

Figure 8.1   Quick-Set Lock

maintain alignment. Installation is similar to that for exterior door tracks.

Security. This includes locks, latches, catches, and panic devices.

Door Locks

1. Quick-set (see Figure 8.1). To install this type, one large hole is drilled through the face of the door, and a second smaller hole is drilled through the edge of the locking stile of the door, using specialized jigs and drill bits. Then a shallow recess is cut to receive the lock plate. The strike plate is mounted in a shallow recess opposite the lock plate.

2. Mortised (see Figure 8.2). To install this type, one deep hole is routed out of the edge of the locking stile, a smaller hole is drilled through each face for the knob shaft, and a shallow recess is cut

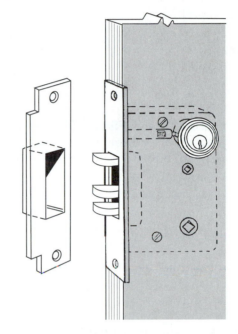

Figure 8.2   Mortised Lock

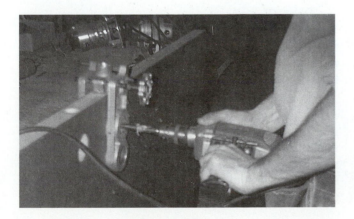

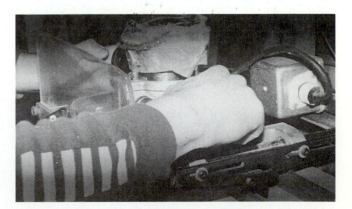

(a)   Hinge router   **(b)**   Latch-set jig

Factory Preparation

Wherever possible, doors and windows are prepared at the factory ready to receive selected hardware units. This permits mass-production and maximum mechanization for economy. (BCIT Building Technology)

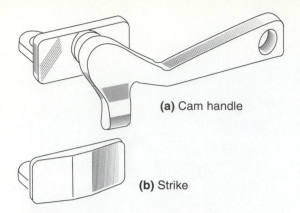

(a) Cam handle

(b) Strike

Figure 9 Wood or Metal Window Latch

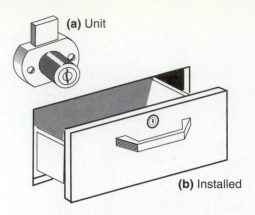

(a) Unit

(b) Installed

Figure 10.2 Drawer Lock

for the lock plate. The strike plate is mounted as described above.

Window Latches

1. On wood (see Figure 9). Positions are marked, holes are drilled, and latches and strikes are installed by hand, either at the factory or the site.

2. On metal (see Figure 9 also). Same as for wood windows, but usually factory installed.

Cabinet Catches

1. Door latches (see Figure 10.1). There is a large variety of such devices, some of which rely on magnetic attraction, or spring-loaded ball bearings or hooks, or simple hook-and-eye combinations, or rocker or thumb-turn operation, among others.

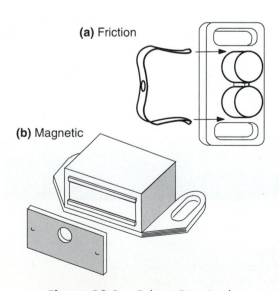

(a) Friction

(b) Magnetic

Figure 10.1 Cabinet Door Latch

2. Drawer locks and latches (Figure 10.2). Drawer locks consist mostly of small cylinder locks with keys. Latches may be indentations worked into tracks or glides to keep the drawer shut.

Panic Devices

1. Surface portions (see Figure 11.1). Positions of latching and guiding devices are marked, holes are drilled, and units are installed by hand.

2. Concealed portions (see Figure 11.2). In every case, the concealed portions of the operating mechanism for panic devices must be installed at the factory, into door and frame components specially modified for the purpose. Only the surface trim and bars are installed at the site.

Convenience. This includes closers, stops, pulls, and knobs.

Door Closers

1. Surface portions (see Figure 12.1). Positions of mounting plates and brackets are marked, holes are drilled, and devices are installed by hand.

2. Concealed portions (see Figure 12.2). In every case, the concealed portions of the operating mechanism for door closers must be installed into apertures in door and frame components specially modified at the factory for the purpose. Closers and surface trim such as cover plates are installed at the site.

Doorstops

1. On doors or floors (see Figure 13.1). The position of the stop is marked, holes are drilled, and the device is attached. Hollow metal doors are usu-

Figure 11.1 Panic Bar, Exposed Portion

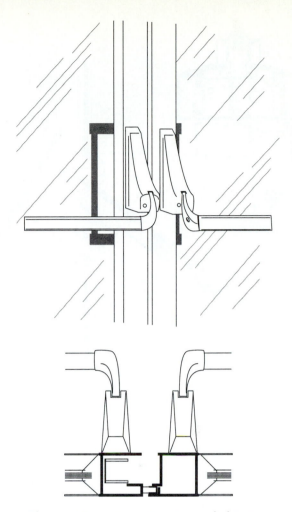

Figure 11.2 Panic Bar, Concealed Portion

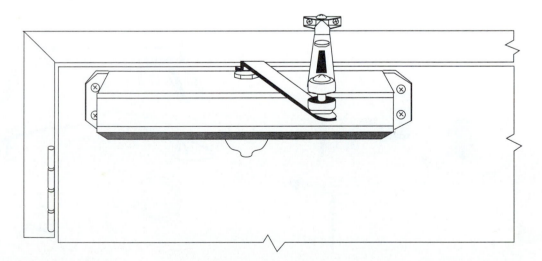

Figure 12.1 Closer, Exposed Portion

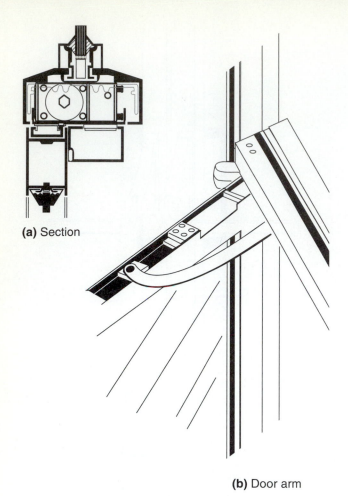

(a) Section

(b) Door arm

Figure 12.2 Closer, Concealed Portion

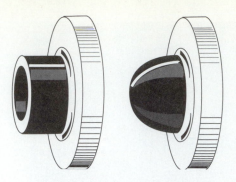

Figure 13.2 Wall Stops

Cabinet Pulls

1. Surface mount (see Figure 14.1). These can be selected from a large variety of shaped wood, metal, porcelain, or plastic knobs, bow handles, and continuous bars of various designs. Locations are marked, holes are drilled, and devices are attached by hand.

2. Recessed (see Figure 14.2). Isolated slots or continuous grooves are routed out to predetermined depths and shapes, ready to receive the devices.

Miscellaneous

1. Kickplate (see Figure 15.1). This device is typical of many that are simply surface mounted to doors, windows, and cabinets. Holes for screws are marked and drilled, and the device is secured in position.

2. Mail slot (see Figure 15.2). This device is typical of many that require a slot or hole to be cut in a door or other panel, using a keyhole saw or similar tool, before simple insertion and securing of the device together with any cover plates or trim.

ally reinforced with a small internal steel plate to provide a secure attachment.

2. On walls (see Figure 13.2). The process is the same as for doors, ensuring that there is a solid backing inside the wall to which the screws can be attached.

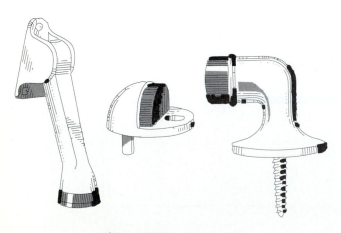

Figure 13.1 Doorstops

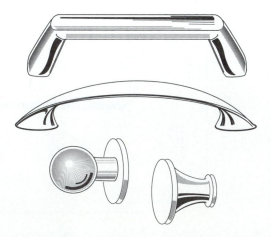

Figure 14.1 Surface-Mounted Cabinet Pulls

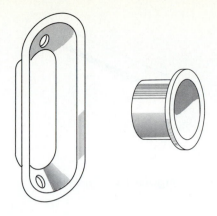

Figure 14.2 Recessed Cabinet Pulls

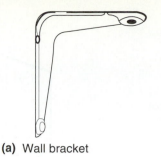

(a) Wall bracket

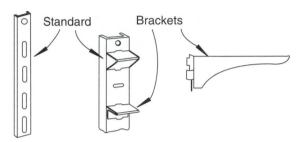

(b) Standards and brackets

Figure 16 Shelf Brackets

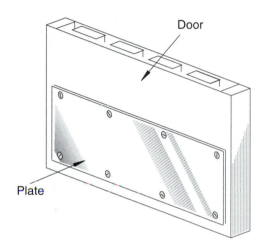

Figure 15.1 Kickplate

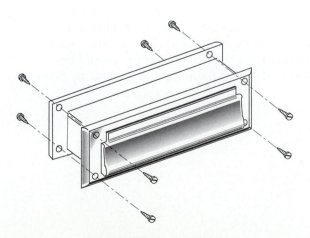

Figure 15.2 Mail Slot

Utility. Four commonly encountered items have been selected to be representative of such hardware devices:

1. Shelf brackets (see Figure 16). These consist of two basic components: the standards and the brackets. There are two basic types of standard: surface mounted and recessed. For recessed types, slots must be routed into the panels or walls to which the standards are to be attached. Some shelf kits are supplied with shelf hold-down clips to prevent subsequent movement or accidental dislodgment of the shelf units.

2. Mirror clips (see Figure 17). These devices are usually made of metal or plastic, and are prepared for either concealed or exposed mounting. Installation is usually a simple matter of marking out locations, drilling, temporarily supporting the mirror in place, and inserting and tightening the screws.

3. Coat hooks (see Figure 18). There is a large variety of designs for metal and plastic coat hooks, involving single, double, or multiple hangers, with exposed or concealed fastenings. One feature of such devices is that they are usually installed in multiple groupings. Fixing is simple: Mark screw holes with a template, drill, and install.

4. Closet rails (see Figure 19). There are two basic models of rails: one which comes in the form

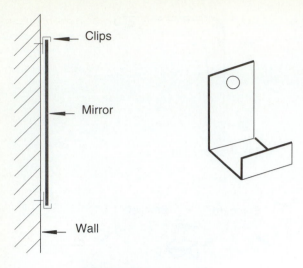

Figure 18 Coat Hook

Figure 17 Mirror Clips

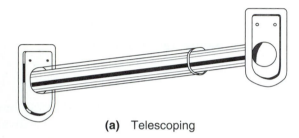

(a) Telescoping

Preformed
metal stripping

Shelf

(b) Fixed

Figure 19 Closet Rails

of a wood rod or plastic or metal tube (perhaps tele-scoping), intended to be cut to length and mounted on small end clips or cups; and one which comes in the form of a continuous sheet of preformed metal, intended to be secured to the underside of a wood or metal shelf. Fixing is simple, as for coat hooks.

5.3 Precautions

There are relatively stringent regulations in most building codes regarding the careful selection and correct installation of hardware for specific purposes, such as in emergency exits and stairwells. Instructions provided by manufacturers for the correct installation and use of their products should be read, understood, and followed.

Finish hardware should be stored in a clean, dry, warm, secure place at the building site. Packages should not be opened until the contents are required for use; contents should be carefully checked before use, for absence of damage and for completeness. Care should be taken not to damage the finish on parts of hardware or other building components which will be exposed to view or to the weather upon completion of work. Such items should be covered or removed during painting and decorating procedures.

Section 08–800
Glass and Glazing

1.0 Introduction

1.1 General Issues

For the purposes of this book, the word *glass* refers to materials; the word *glazing* refers to processes, involving glass and other materials. The process consists of installing glass and related glazing materials into specially framed windows, doors, or other openings made of wood, steel, or aluminum. The principles of the process are ancient, dating back to early Egyptian times; the practices of the process are as modern as the Space Age.

1.2 Design Aspects

The consideration given by designers to the placement of windows in buildings is called *fenestration*, a word derived from the Latin *fenestra,* meaning windows. There are two primary issues involved in fenestration: aesthetics, concerning the size, type, and placement of windows in the building; and mechanics, concerning the operation and efficiency of the selected window system to perform its required functions. These functions include control of the passage of light and air, resistance to the passage of heat and moisture, and the embodiment of structural integrity and adequate protection in both the framing and glazing systems. In general, all glass of any one type in any one location or on any one elevation of a building should be purchased from one manufacturer to ensure uniformity of appearance, color, reflectance, and quality of the glass panels.

Another important issue arises out of the option of arranging window and door frames to be glazed either from the inside or the outside of the building (see Figure 1). In most new construction work, either option is equally appropriate from a first-cost point of view. However, if a damaged pane of window glass has to be replaced in a window located on one of the upper floors of a multistory building, then interior glazing offers some advantages by eliminating the need for exterior scaffolding or staging.

Consideration must be given to the general configuration of the glazing system. **Single** glazing (the provision of a single panel of glass in the frame) is common in construction where low budget or utility is of importance and where minimal control of light, heat, or sound energy is desired. **Double** glazing (the provision of two parallel but separate glass panels in the frame) is necessary where a greater degree of control of energy is considered necessary, such as in air-conditioned office buildings, shopping malls, and better-quality residences. In exceptional cases, **triple** glazing (the provision of three parallel glass panels) can be incorporated, where virtually total control of energy of every sort requires to be exercised, such as in a radio or TV station control booth, the operating theater of a hospital, or a scientific laboratory.

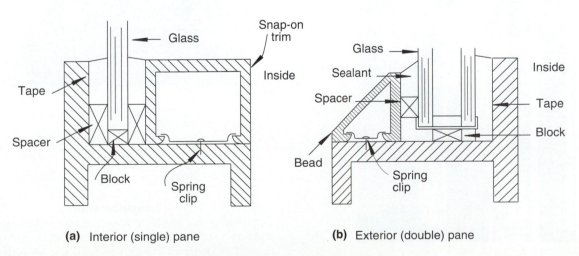

(a) Interior (single) pane   (b) Exterior (double) pane

Figure 1 Glazing Configurations

Allowance must be made in the design for 1) the anticipated expansion and contraction of the glass, the glazing materials, and the perimeter frame, having regard to the coefficients of expansion of all components of the selected glazing system, and 2) resistance to expected deflection arising from positive and negative wind loads. A major consideration is the maximum size of glass panels recommended for use in exterior frames subject to wind loadings. Some representative values are given in Tables 1.1 (metric) and 1.2 (imperial) as a guide to maximum dimensions; for more precise information (required for actual design or installation) the reader is advised to refer to local building codes and to glass manufacturers' guides. A distinction should be made, of course, between maximum sizes of panels permitted in openings by code (as suggested in Tables 1.1 and 1.2) and the maximum sizes of panels available from manufacturers as listed later in Table 2.

Other important design considerations involve elimination of condensation on glass and frames, the effects of building shading characteristics on fenestration systems, and calculation of heat loss and gain through window and/or curtain wall systems. These topics are all beyond the scope of this book.

1.3 Related Work

Work closely connected to this section is described in the following sections, to which reference should be made:

08–100   Metal Doors and Frames

08–200   Wood Doors and Frames

08–400   Storefront Systems

08–500   Metal Windows and Frames

08–600   Wood Windows and Frames

08–900   Curtain Walling

2.0 Products

2.1 Materials

Glass can be considered under five headings: **ingredients, forms, types, sizes,** and **grades.**

(b) Carrying in

(a) Vehicle loading

Transportation
Glass, being very fragile, requires special handling during transportation. Glaziers' vehicles are usually equipped with adjustable padded metal frames in which the glass can be secured. (BCIT Building Technology)

Ingredients. Glass is a mixture of oxides derived from specially selected stocks of three common ingredients: sand, soda, and lime. Although some glass does occur naturally, virtually all glass used in construction is manufactured. Different kinds of glass are made by varying the proportions and types of the three basic ingredients and by altering the manufacturing processes to achieve a variety of results. Approximate typical proportions are 75 percent sand, 15 percent soda, and 10 percent lime. Virtually all glass produced commercially for construction purposes has some impurity, incorporated either accidentally or deliberately; for example, most common glasses contain small amounts of iron, which produces the characteristic greenish tinge seen in most clear glass panels; minute amounts of lead will enhance the brilliance of the surfaces.

Chemically speaking, glass is not a solid; it is a supercooled inorganic liquid; as a result of this characteristic, it is relatively easy to dissolve other ingredients (such as lead or color pigments) in the molten glass to change its physical properties, and also possible to mold glass into almost any shape. Because of its ingredients, glass is relatively heavy, weighing approximately 2,600 kg/m³ or 150 lb./ft.³. Glass is not significantly affected by any of the chemicals associated with normal construction operations. Glass is strong in tension and compression, but weak in shear and bending.

Recent research in glass technology is disclosing some interesting characteristics of glass; for example, strands of glass thinner than human hairs have been discovered to be stronger in tension than strands of steel of comparable diameter. Depending on thickness and composition, clear glass will permit the passage of between 60 percent and 90 percent of intended visible light; deliberate tinting of glass with pigments can reduce this percentage to as low as 25 percent for any practical purpose, and to zero if necessary.

Forms. Glass is used in the construction industry in the following basic forms:

1. Glass **blocks** are occasionally used in masonry work to form loadbearing and partition walls and also for purely decorative screening purposes.
2. Crushed glass **chips** are often used as dash coats on stucco and plaster finishes.
3. Glass **fibers** are used primarily for thermal and acoustical insulation and separation, in the form of prefabricated batts or tiles.
4. Glass **plates** are used for large windows and for desks, tables, and countertops.
5. Glass **powders** are used as fillers in certain types

Table 1.1
MAXIMUM RECOMMENDED GLASS PANEL AREAS (METRIC)

Wind Speed (km/h)	Maximum Area (m²)* by Glass Thickness			
	3.0 mm	6.0 mm	10.0 mm	12.5 mm
60	3.5	13.5	23.0	N/A
80	2.5	9.0	20.0	26.0
100	1.5	6.5	15.0	22.5
120	1.0	4.5	10.0	18.0
140	0.5	3.5	7.5	14.0

*Rounded to nearest 0.5 m².

Table 1.2
MAXIMUM RECOMMENDED GLASS PANEL AREAS (IMPERIAL)

Wind Speed (mph)	Maximum Area (ft.²)* by Glass Thickness			
	1/8 in.	1/4 in.	3/8 in.	1/2 in.
40	35	145	250	N/A
60	20	85	190	200
80	10	50	110	190
100	5	30	65	115

*Rounded to the nearest ft².

of acoustic tiles, resilient flooring, specialty paints, and plastics.

6. Glass **sheets** (in plain, patterned, or corrugated styles) are used for windows, skylights, mirrors, and picture frames.

Types. The main types of glass encountered in typical buildings are as follows:

1. **Bent** glass can be formed from virtually all of the other glasses listed below, by heating relatively thin glass sheets and allowing gravity to bend them around metal mandrels or molds. There are some practical restrictions on the maximum thickness of the glass and the minimum radius to which it can be bent.

2. **Colored** glass is produced by the introduction of pure metals or metallic oxides into the basic ingredients. For example, cobalt oxide is used to make glass blue, cadmium sulfide for yellow, chromium oxide for green, and manganese oxide for red, among many others.

3. **Corrugated** glass is made of plate or float glass that has been passed through rollers to imprint an obscuring pattern on one side and to shape the flat glass sheet into a wave-form profile. It is available in wired and unwired forms.

4. **Float** glass is produced by passing a fluid mixture of the glass ingredients, called *frit,* over a shallow bath of molten tin. The ingredients are liquefied by heat, resulting in an exceptionally smooth and blemishfree end product. For these reasons, as well as lower cost, float glass is now the most common type of glass used in most applications in normal construction.

5. **Heat-absorbing** glass is specially formulated with ingredients that enhance the absorption of heat energy coming primarily from the sun, thereby reducing the direct transmission of such energy to the inside of the building during daylight hours. The energy absorbed in the glass is then slowly released during the night, partly to the inside but also partly to the outside of the building. Such glass is available in tempered or nontempered forms and is usually tinted to some degree because of its manufacture.

6. **Heat-strengthened** glass consists of (usually) flat sheets of float glass, on one side of which a colored ceramic material has been fused under a reheating process. The end result is similar to tempered glass.

7. **Insulating** glass is technically a misnomer, as all glass has insulating properties to a limited extent. This term usually refers to composite glazed units, consisting of two (and sometimes three) parallel panes of glass of various types separated by a small airspace, and secured and hermetically sealed around the perimeter by a continuous metal or glass bead.

8. **Laminated** glass consists of a sandwich configuration of two sheets of glass, one on each side of a central clear or colored vinyl plastic core panel, to which the outer sheets are carefully factory glued. Additional laminations can be incorporated to create so-called bulletproof glass.

9. **Lead** glass is manufactured from specially selected proportions of sand, soda, and lime, to

(a) Glass panels

(b) Glazing bead

Stockpiling

Glass units are distributed throughout the building areas to be stacked on and secured to movable wood or metal A-frames. Other supplies (such as setting blocks and beading) are required. (UBC Architecture)

418

which specific amounts of lead are added to create glasses having a variety of known and measurable resistance to the passage of X-radiation.

10. Leaded glass is plain or stained glass, cut into small decorative shapes and installed in a framework or system of lead-covered copper cames or wires.

11. Mirror glass is float glass specially selected for its uniform surfaces, freedom from blemishes, and suitability for coating on the rear surface with an electrolytically deposited reflective coating of metal alloys, such as chromium, silver, gold, or bronze. The metallic coating can be opaque for regular mirrors or semitransparent for one-way viewing. Such viewing panels are often incorporated into jails, clinics, retail stores, and other public buildings where one area requires to be visually supervised from an adjacent area. Opaque mirror coatings are usually protected with a backing coat of paint or varnish.

12. Nonreflective glass is manufactured by treating plain or float sheet glass with a light wash of acid or by mildly abrading the glass surface with very fine sand to microscopically remove the smooth surface, thus reducing light reflection. It is often used to protect art works, such as paintings.

13. Optical glass is available in a number of types, each specially composed to enhance a number of visual or energetic effects. One type consists of glass having a minimal angle of refraction, resulting in minimal distortion to light passing through the glass at an acute angle to its surface. Such glass is sometimes used in the portals of film projection booths in movie theaters. Another type of optical glass contains minimal levels of iron to enhance the passage of light in the ultraviolet region of the radiation spectrum; higher levels of iron increasingly prohibit ultraviolet transmission.

14. Ornamental glass is produced by treating high-quality float, plate, or sheet glass with acid etching or sandblasting to permanently incise custom designs on the glass surface.

15. Patterned glass is formed by passing medium-quality sheet or float glass in a semimolten state through rollers which impart a predesigned figured pattern to one or both sides of the glass surfaces. It can be tempered after rolling. Patterns can be in the form of ribs, squares, circles, hammered or pebbled surfaces, or stylistic representations of animals, birds, sailboats, and the like.

16. Plain glass, also known as **drawn** glass, was formerly the industry standard for most glazing applications. The glass was drawn by dipping a metal bait into a crucible of molten glass and then raising it up in the vertical plane to create a con-

trolled sheet of glass. Such glass is seldom used in modern buildings.

17. Plate glass is made by pouring a thin layer of molten glass or laying a softened layer of sheet glass onto a horizontal heated metal table or plate, having raised edges to prevent the glass from spilling over the sides. The hardened plate blanks are removed from the table and ground and polished to produce clear plate glass. The process is largely obsolete now, because of its cost.

18. Polarized glass requires the surface application of a fine layer of an organic crystalline called tourmaline, which causes polarization of light transmission through a single pane into a single plane, thus offsetting and reducing glare.

19. Reflective glass is sheet or float glass treated with a microscopically thin reflective film of gold or other metal, to reflect predicted amounts of heat and light energy impinging on its exterior surfaces and thus reduce energy transfer. Nonreflective coatings, made from magnesium fluoride, are used to enhance energy transfer, especially the passage of light.

20. Safety glass is a general term for glass panels which have been designed to reduce the hazards usually associated with the breakage of panels not so designed. The safety is imparted in one of three ways, described under *laminated*, *tempered*, and *wired* glass in this alphabetical list.

21. Solar glass, also known as **glare-reducing** glass, was generally described above under *heat-absorbing* glass. Some of the newer types of such glass are surface treated with pyrolytic or sputtered coatings, as well as being integrally formulated to reduce or eliminate radiation in the infrared and ultraviolet bands at each end of the visible spectrum. Some of these glasses are referred to as "low–e" glass (for low emissivity).

22. Stained glass consists of sheet or float glass, usually (but not necessarily) lightly acid etched or sandblasted, and then superficially decorated with specially formulated colored stains for primarily aesthetic purposes. It can be distinguished from colored glass in that the colors are not integral, that is, not uniform throughout the glass thickness.

23. Structural glass is made from heavy sheet or float panels, heat treated to increase strength and rendered opaque by the introduction of metallic oxides as described under *colored* glass. Like all tempered glasses, it cannot be cut or drilled after manufacture. It is usually used as infill spandrel panels in areas of curtain wall systems between windowlights; for this reason, it is sometimes called **spandrel** glass.

24. Tempered glass consists of float glass which has been passed through a heat chamber to bring it close to its melting point temperature and then exposed to jets of cold air on the surfaces and edges of the glass panel, to develop tension between the surfaces and the central core. After treatment, it is twice as strong as nontempered glass, but it cannot be cut or drilled.

25. Window glass is a nonspecific term for medium-weight float or sheet glass intended for use in windows of residential buildings.

26. Wired glass consists of float, plate, or sheet glass in which a layer of fine woven or soldered wire netting has been embedded in the central plane. The object is to prevent portions of the glass from falling out of the frame in the event of damage (as distinct from tempered glass, where the object is to improve the strength of the glass). The netting pattern is usually square or hexagonal.

27. Many more specialized types of glass exist, such as those exhibiting unique thermal or other properties. Others are being developed as science and technology make new discoveries.

Sizes. In general, the thickness of glass is designated in millimeters or fractions of inches; panel dimensions of glass are designated in united centimeters or united whole inches. The word *united* in this context means the sum of the dimensions for length and breadth. Tables 2.1 and 2.2 give approximate maximum dimensions for some of the types of glass encountered in normal construction; refer to glass manufacturers for more precise data. In Table 2.1, the maximum size for single strength glass is 50 × 40 in. or 90 united inches. If a sheet of this glass is cut to 36 × 36 in., its size would be 72 united inches. Additional thicknesses, sizes, and types are also available.

Grades. There are three grades of window glass commonly used in construction:

1. "AA" grade is intended for work of the highest quality.
2. "A" grade is recommended for work of better than average quality.
3. "B" grade is adequate for general glazing where blemishes such as minor waves or miniscule air bubbles would not be objectionable.

There are two strengths of window glass: single and double (as shown in Table 2.1).

2.2 Accessories

In general, materials used for glazing must maintain control of water and air leakage, while allowing for movement and acting as a separator between the glass and the frame. They must also be relatively inert to avoid staining or reacting with surrounding materials, unaffected by solar radiation, and reasonably durable.

Beads are narrow strips of solid or hollow wood or metal which, when secured to the window frame, restrain the glass and glazing materials in position. See Figure 2.

Blocks are small pieces of hardwood, soft lead, or dense plastic, placed at intervals along the bottom edge of glass panels to keep the glass edge away from the frame, to evenly distribute the glass load to the frame at known points, and to provide clearance between the bottom of the glass and the surface of the frame rabbet. See Figure 3.

**Table 2.1
APPROXIMATE DIMENSIONS
OF SHEET GLASS PANELS**

Glass Type	Thickness		Maximum Dimensions	
	mm	in.	cm × cm	in. × in.
Single strength	2.5	$3/32$	127 × 102	50 × 40
Double strength	3.0	$1/8$	203 × 152	80 × 60
Thick sheet	5.0	$3/16$	305 × 213	120 × 84
	5.5	$7/32$	305 × 213	120 × 84
	6.0	$1/4$	305 × 213	120 × 84
	9.5	$3/8$	406 × 213	160 × 84
	11.0	$7/16$	213 × 152	84 × 60

Table 2.2
APPROXIMATE DIMENSIONS
OF FLOAT GLASS PANELS

Glass Type	Thickness		Maximum Dimensions	
	mm	in.	cm × cm	in. × in.
Clear	3.0	1/8	244 × 305	96 × 120
	6.0	1/4	305 × 508	120 × 200
	10.0	3/8	305 × 508	120 × 200
	12.5	1/2	330 × 508	130 × 200
	16.0	5/8	305 × 457	120 × 180
	19.0	3/4	305 × 457	120 × 180
Tinted	3.0	1/8	244 × 305	96 × 120
	6.0	1/4	305 × 610	120 × 240
	10.0	3/8	305 × 457	120 × 180
	12.5	1/2	305 × 457	120 × 180
Tempered	6.0	1/4	117 × 244	46 × 96
Wired	6.0	1/4	152 × 366	60 × 144
	10.0	3/8	183 × 330	72 × 130

Gaskets are strips of extruded profiled butyl rubber or neoprene plastic, usually having a zipper-locking feature, used to install single or double sheets of glass in simply framed openings. See Figure 4.

Glazing tape is frequently made of butyl rubber, coated on both faces with an adhesive formulated to

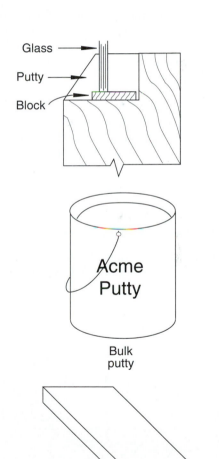

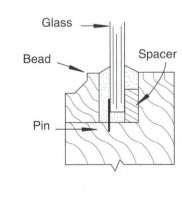

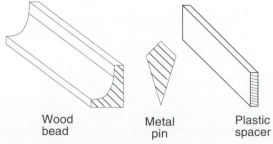

Figure 2   Beads; Pins; Spacers

Figure 3   Blocks; Putty

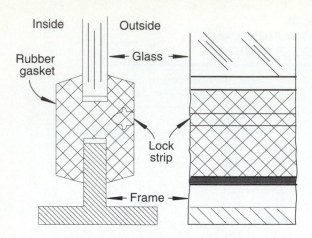

Figure 4 Gaskets and Sealers

permanently adhere to the metal and glass surfaces with which it comes in contact.

Pins, also called **points,** are small, flat, diamond-shaped pieces of galvanized or blued steel, used to hold glass panes in place in wood frames before the application of putty to the external face of the glazed system (as in Figure 2).

Putties generally consist of a mixture of lead oxide and linseed oil; they cure by the slow and controlled oxidization of the oil. When used for glazing, they are specially composed and selected for each specific purpose, depending on whether the frame to be glazed is made of wood, steel, or aluminum. It is critical that the selected putty will adhere properly both to the glass and to the frame and bead materials with which it will be used (as in Figure 3).

Silicone adhesives are factory made and used to make watertight glass-to-glass connections. They are

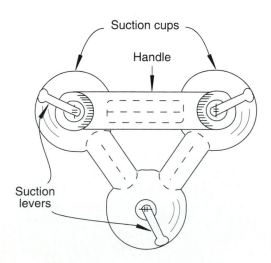

Figure 5 Suction Cup Device

also often used to seal the space between the top edges of glazing tapes and the sight line.

Spacers are small flat strips or blocks of neoprene plastic, used to keep the surface of the glass pane a uniform distance away from the frame in which it is placed, to permit the application of sealing compounds between the glass and the frame. They are also used to keep field-fabricated inboard and outboard panes of glass in insulated systems at a uniform distance apart (as in Figure 2).

3.0 Construction Aids

3.1 Equipment

Some common equipment encountered in this trade is as follows:

Air compressor. This device is used in the ornamental sandblasting process.

Bevelers. These are used to bevel or smooth the cut edges of glass panels. They consist of heavy-duty electric belt sanders, having emery or silicon carbide belts.

Suction cups. Also called **glaziers' clamps,** these consist of small metal cups, having a hard rubber lining, capable of creating a vacuum between the cup and the glass surface when a small hand pump is activated on the metal casing. They are available in configurations of two, three, and four. They are used to pick up and carry sheets of glass by hand. See Figure 5.

Glass carts. These consist of a variety of metal A-frames, arranged to support sheets or plates of glass, mounted on a rectangular base frame attached to castor wheels; these carts are used to move heavy sheets of glass from the delivery truck to the final window frame position. See Figure 6.

3.2 Tools

The tools are those of the glazier:

Cutters. There are two types: wheel and diamond; both have a short shaft handle of wood or metal. The wheel cutter is made of hardened steel about 5 mm or $1/4$ in. in diameter; the diamond cutter is a small piece of industrial diamond mounted on the end of a short shaft.

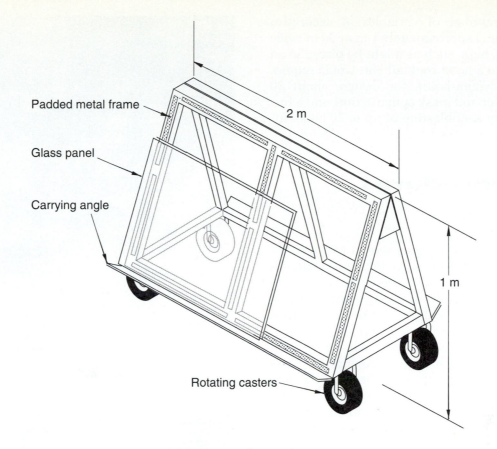

Figure 6 A-frame Glass Cart

Putty knives. These consist of broad, flat, thin stainless or carbon steel blades, attached to a wood or metal shaft handle; they are available in a variety of sizes.

Vinyl roller. This is a small hand tool, consisting of a short shaft wood or metal handle supporting a steel stirrup in which a hard plastic or wood wheel is mounted. It is used to smooth and compress glazing compounds.

Zippers. This is a hand tool used to force preformed hard rubber or neoprene zipper gaskets between frames and glass.

4.0 Production

4.1 Crew Configuration

The primary issue in regular glazing work is whether the work is done at the factory or at the site. Other factors involve number and sizes of panels to be glazed, the nature of the frame and bead system, and the type of glazing materials proposed for use. Glazing teams will vary between one qualified glazier on a small job to five or six glaziers with helpers on large jobs.

4.2 Productivity

For regular glazing work, a team of two qualified glaziers working in a typical factory glazing wood sash window or door frames with plain putty should be able to install about 30 m² or 300 ft.² of plain glass per day. The same team working on similar frames made of metal with removable metal glazing beads, glazing tape, and steel sash putty will install about 15 m² or 150 ft.² per day. A larger team of about five glazier journeymen should glaze about 25 m² or 250 ft.² of metal storefront system in one 8-hour day.

If the same work is done at the site instead of the factory, the foregoing values should be reduced by about 15 percent. If the work is done outside in the wintertime, another 10 percent can be deducted. Furthermore, the larger the glass panel united dimensions (that is, length plus breadth), the more glaziers and helpers will be required, from less than two for small panels having united dimensions of less than 250 cm or 100 in., such as are found in typical residences, to more than ten for large panels exceeding united dimensions of 750 cm or 300 in., such as are found in retail storefronts.

For ornamental or design work on glass, it is difficult to tabulate precise productivity factors, because of the number of variables. A decorative frosted glass panel approximately 1 m or 36 in. wide by 2 m or 72 in. high, such as might be placed in an entrance door to a hotel cocktail bar, would require about 8 journeyman-hours for design, about 30 hours for transfer and mask construction, and a further 10 hours for sandblasting or up to 20 hours for the acid-etching process.

5.0 Procedures

5.1 Preparation

In general, glass is cut by being scored with a cutter on one surface, placing the score line over a fulcrum or divider of some sort (such as the edge of a workbench), and then carefully applying sharp and sudden pressure to either side of the score line, thus causing the glass to snap along the line.

While this procedure works well for straight lines which extend from edge to edge of the glass panel, less-than-full-length straight lines or any curved lines require a more cautious approach, involving a score line of the correct configuration dictated by the design, the removal of as much glass as possible by straight-line cutting, and the final shaping of internal corners or curved shapes using glass nippers specially designed to do this work.

Glass can also be cut by burning, but this is not a common technique in glass used for construction. Application of heat in connection with cutting mainly arises out of the need to make cut edges smooth, such as along the exposed edges of shelf panels made of glass or at the open edges of glass panels used at tellers' wickets in bank counters and at ticket booth windows in theater lobbies. Such smoothing of edges is usually done with a small blowtorch or an acetylene burner.

5.2 Process

Glazing.   The process of installing glass in frames is called glazing. There are two basic approaches to glazing: "wet" using tapes and/or putty; and "dry" using pins and/or beads. Each type of frame requires its own process; the most common ones are detailed below. The principle objectives are to ensure that the glass is held securely in the frame without touching it, that the glass is not under undue tension or compression, and that leakage of moisture or air around or through the perimeter glazing system will not occur. It is also critical that the depth of the rabbet in the frame be sufficient to provide the required bite on the glass. A typical installation of glass into a wood window frame is shown in Figure 7.

(a)   Cutting glass

(b)   Nibbling edges

Preparation
Glass panels are measured, cut with a glass cutter, snapped to line, and "nibbled" where necessary to ensure an accurate fit. Movement of the finished pane in its frame must be considered. (UBC Architecture)

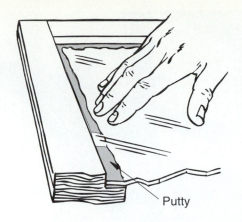

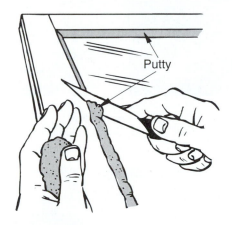

Figure 7 Installing Glass

Aluminum Windows (see Figure 8a)

The sash frame should be cleaned with a solvent, such as toluene, and allowed to dry. Glazing tape is carefully cut to size and neatly installed against the back frame; corners should be miter-cut and glued. The glass is placed after setting blocks have been located at quarter points along the bottom edge. Side and top spacers are placed as necessary. Additional tape is placed around the panel edges, and the perimeter bead is snapped on or screwed in place. A bead of silicone is often placed on top of the edges of the butyl glazing tape to ensure full moisture seal.

Steel Windows (see Figure 8b)

The sash frame should have a prime coat of a rust-inhibiting paint and then be prime-painted, ready to receive glazing materials. A thin layer of steel sash putty is pressed into the rabbet, followed by the glass pane, which is lightly pressed into the putty bed. If the frame design permits it, small spring clips are installed to secure the glass in place, and additional

putty is placed on the glass, lightly compressed, and struck off to a bevel between the sight line and the edge of the frame on both sides of the glass panel.

Wood Windows (see Figure 8c)

The sash frame rabbet should be lightly coated with boiled linseed oil and then wiped dry. A thin layer of wood sash putty is placed in the rabbet and around the edges of the glass pane. The pane is then lightly pressed into position in the frame to cause the putty to slightly squeeze out. Next, glazier's points are installed, using pneumatic dispensing guns, at not

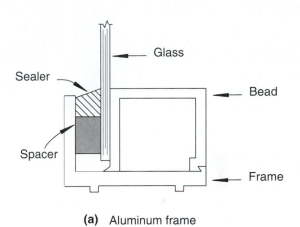

(a) Aluminum frame

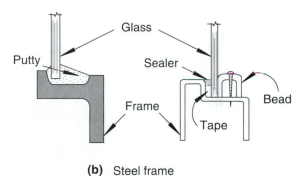

(b) Steel frame

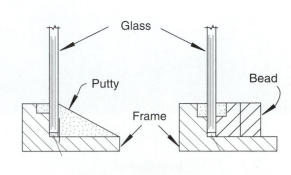

(c) Wood frame

Figure 8 Glazing in Frames

(a) Vertical window

(a) Pre-insertion

(b) Sloping skylight

Installation

Most glass panels are easily lifted by two (or three) workers using patented suction cups. The precut panels are carefully inserted into prepared frames and secured as specified. (UBC Architecture)

(b) Post-insertion

Perimeter Beading

In some instances, it is expedient to position the perimeter beading before the glass units are installed. Elsewhere, beading can be inserted after the glass, by using an appropriate tool. (BCIT Audio-Visual Production)

more than 600-mm or 24-in. intervals around the perimeter of each pane, to hold the glass firmly against the putty in the rabbet. The remaining process is as described above for steel sash windows.

Ornamental Work. It is a common practice to do ornamental work of various types on glass, for hotel lobbies, pubs and taverns, shopping malls, and so on. While most ornamentation techniques are applied in glass shops or factories, a brief outline of two common processes, sandblasting and acid etching, is presented in this section to give readers some insights and ideas. Actual factory production processes are beyond the scope of this book, as are some other methods of glass ornamentation, such as grinding, engraving by hand or by machine, or the fusion of multiple layers of glass.

First, a distinction should be made between patterned glass which is usually factory produced for general use, and ornamental glass which is usually custom decorated to a special design. Second, regardless of the ornamental technique to be selected, there are three steps involved: development of the **design** to be used, **transfer** of the design to the glass, and **implementation** of the ornamentation process.

Design

A concept is developed by the customer or glass designer, drawn to scale, and produced on transparent film using felt-tip pens. (See Figure 9.1.)

Transfer

The transparency is projected to produce a full-size working drawing. The drawing is taped to an adjustable table to permit work to conveniently proceed. A clean sheet of glass is then secured on top of the drawing and masking commences. In sandblasting, the masking process involves application of special adhesive tape; in acid etching, the masking is achieved by acid-resistant inks and wax dikes. (See Figure 9.2.)

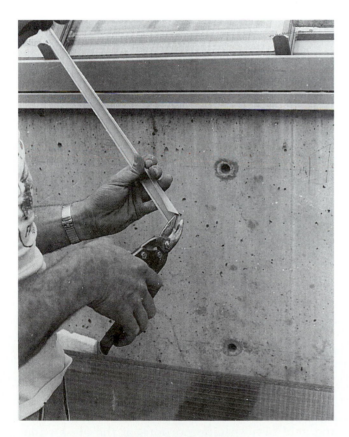

(a) Cutting beading

(b) Fitting beading

Finishing

Wood or metal beads are selected, cut to length, and then installed in several ways. The illustrations show vinyl-coated aluminum trimming bead being precut and snapped into position. (UBC Architecture)

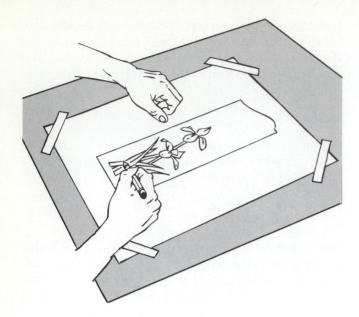

Figure 9.1   Design Concept

Implementation

As suggested by the masking processes, the techniques for sandblasting and acid etching are different.

1. *Sandblasting.* There are two techniques commonly used to sandblast glass. The first is called *frost* or *surface blasting,* and as its name implies, it is a light surface treatment. The second is called *stage* or *grave blasting,* in which different areas of the glass panel are worn down by sandblasting to establish separate depths of cut. On completing of blasting, the surfaces are wiped with a clean cloth, soaked in spirits, washed and dried, and the whole panel is then set

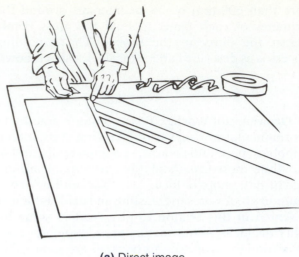

(a) Direct image

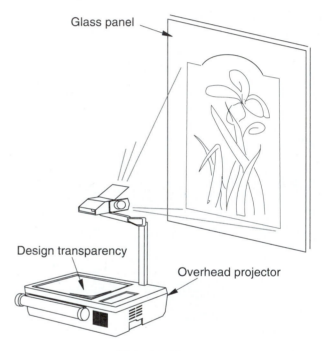

(b) Indirect image

Figure 9.2   Design Transfer

aside for further treatment, such as coloring, or for delivery to the site. (See Figure 9.3.)

2. *Acid Etching.* A common technique, called *bossing,* uses an acid-resistant ink to impart the design, with small wax dikes to control the flow of ink and acid over specific portions of the glass panel. The panel is leveled and the acid (in cream form) is carefully poured onto the fields contained within the wax dikes. The acid burns away the glass exposed to it. After a precalculated time, the panel is tilted to remove the acid and, if necessary, the process is re-

Figure 9.3   Sandblasting

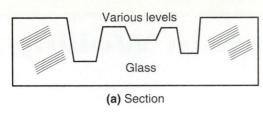

(a) Section

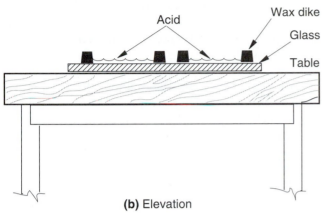

(b) Elevation

Figure 9.4   Acid Etching

(a)   Setting block

(b)   Speak-through

peated. When the desired etching effect has been achieved, the dike is stripped off, the ink resist is removed with a solvent, and the panel is washed clean and dried with a soft cloth. A variety of textures and finished are available on either one or both sides of the glass. (See Figure 9.4.)

Some disadvantages of acid etching are its higher cost compared to sandblasting, the hazards of using dangerous and toxic chemicals, the risk of nonremovable imperfections in the finished work, and the difficulties of obtaining the correct type of glass for best results.

5.3 Precautions

Most building codes place type, thickness, and size restrictions on the use of glass in certain locations because of potential hazards to the building occupants. It is common knowledge that most types of glass are easily broken, and that broken pieces of glass have sharp and dangerous edges and points. It is therefore necessary to take care in handling glass to avoid breakage and the chance of injury. Appropriate clothing should be worn, together with safety boots, eye-protection, and tough leather mitts to protect the hands when manually moving sheets of glass. Glass panels should be stored upright along their longer edges in wooden or padded metal racks to facilitate the easy removal of individual sheets, one at a time.

Accessories

Many accessories are used in glazing systems; most are described in the text. Some improve structural or aesthetic qualities of the installation; others enhance its usefulness. (BCIT Building Technology)

Ornamental Work

Glass can be treated for decorative effect by chiseling, acid etching, or by heating and bending, among other methods. Here, a panel is shown being sandblasted to produce a textured finish. (BCIT Building Technology)

Section 08–900 Curtain Walling

1.0 Introduction

1.1 General Issues

Curtain walling is so named because it consists of systems of metal and glass that are literally hung like fixed, flat, rigid curtains on the outside of framed buildings otherwise made of concrete, steel, or wood. It is most often encountered on highrise commercial buildings, such as office towers and apartment blocks, although it is occasionally included mainly for decorative purposes in lower-rise projects such as shopping malls and institutional buildings such as banks, hospitals, and schools. It is seldom used in residential work.

In general, curtain walling can best be considered as a composite of parts of the following sections, detailed more fully elsewhere in the book:

07–200   Insulation

07–600   Flashings

07–900   Joint Sealing

08–400   Storefront Systems

08–500   Metal Windows and Frames

08–800   Glass and Glazing

For this reason, references will be made to these other sections wherever appropriate, to minimize repetition in this section. It may be noted in passing that on some construction projects, the curtain wall system may be specified, bid, and contracted on an all-inclusive package basis, whereas on other projects, each of the primary elements of the system (such as the framing, the glass and glazing, the opening windows or doors, and the sealing) may all be separately contracted, with consequent problems of coordination and responsibility.

1.2 Design Aspects

Curtain wall systems usually consist of a horizontal and vertical assembly of hollow, rectangular metal tubes, secured to the main building frame with steel or aluminum adjustable clips and profiled to receive clear glass windows or translucent or solid spandrel panels as infill. Figure 1 shows a typical arrangement. Such systems may be insulated or uninsulated, and arranged for single or double glazing as necessary. Most require to have some internal steel reinforcement to resist anticipated wind and other loads.

Allowance must also be made for thermal movement within the system and between the building frame and the system frame. Well-designed curtain wall components permit equalization of air pressure between the inner and outer parts of the system, to prevent ingress of moisture. In cold climates, the metal components may be thermally broken, that is to say, the outer colder parts of the metal system are separated from the warmer inner parts by the inclu-

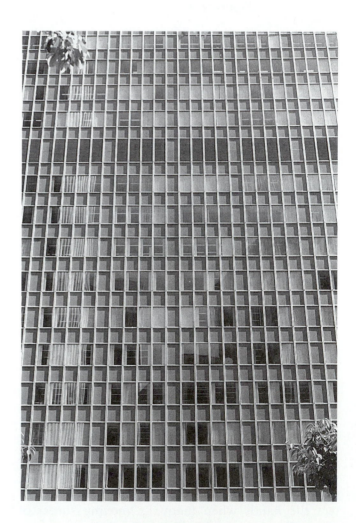

General View
Curtain wall is a system of metal, glass, and caulking that is literally hung on and secured to the exterior of framed buildings. There are many possible variations of components. (UBC Architecture)

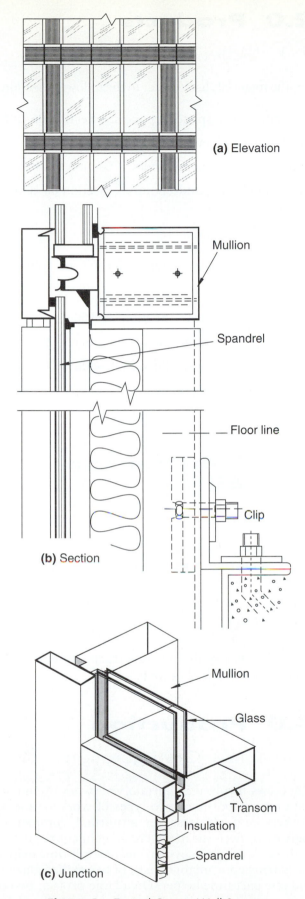

(a) Elevation

Mullion

Spandrel

Floor line

Clip

(b) Section

Mullion

Glass

Transom

Insulation

Spandrel

(c) Junction

Figure 1 Typical Curtain Wall System

sion of insulated plastic separation strips and devices which hold the parts together. The sealing of joints within the system is usually specified to be part of the system; sealing at edges or points where the system abuts other building systems is frequently specified in sections other than the curtain walling section.

There are a number of advantages to the designer in selecting curtain walling to complete the exterior skin element of a building, given the fact that this element usually represents one of the largest in the budget and one of the most complex in the design. Curtain walling offers a wide range of possible solutions to design problems of building enclosure, planar configuration, light transmission, heat loss or gain, cost, and exterior and interior aesthetic appearance.

Curtain walling is usually fixed in such a way that few if any of its components are movable or operable. Wherever opening windows or doors are required in curtain wall systems, such as at ground-level entrances or upper-level mechanical louvers, they are designed and installed as described

Assembly

Metal and glass components are precut, either at the factory or on site, then assembled with simple hand tools to produce necessary configurations of framing, opening, or venting. (UBC Architecture)

in other appropriate sections of this book. It might be noted in passing that there is an increasing amount of research being done on the mental and physical health of people who live and work in such closed buildings, although it is beyond the scope of this book to investigate this topic. The problem does not appear to stem from curtain wall systems per se (although this could on occasion be the case), but rather from the difficulties of efficiently handling large volumes of recirculated air in buildings having such sealed exterior elements.

1.3 Related Work

Work closely connected to this section is described in the following sections, to which reference should be made:

Sections noted in Part 1.1

03–300   Cast-in-Place Concrete

05–100   Steel Framing

06–100   Rough Carpentry

Stockpiling

Individual glass and metal components are raised to various levels in the buildings and stockpiled, ready for installation. (UBC Architecture)

2.0 Products

2.1 Materials

For the materials listed, refer to the following sections:

Wood or plastic spandrel panels: Section 06–200

Insulation products: Section 07–200

Aluminum framing members: Section 08–400

Glass panels or spandrel units: Section 08–800

2.2 Accessories

For the accessories listed, refer to the following sections:

Metal reinforcement: Section 05–100

Metal clips and connectors: Section 05–500

Flashing accessories: Section 07–600

Joint sealants: Section 07–900

Glazing materials: Section 08–800

3.0 Construction Aids

3.1 Equipment

For equipment commonly utilized to do the work of this section, see Part 3.1 of Sections 08–400 and 08–800.

3.2 Tools

For the tools required for this trade, see Part 3.2 of Sections 08–400 and 08–800.

4.0 Production

4.1 Crew Configuration

The crews involved in curtain wall work often consist of a composite of two types of workers: metalworkers and glaziers. On a normal commercial highrise project, the metal crew might consist of two or three skilled journeymen and one full-time helper; the glazing crew might consist of two skilled glaziers and one part-time helper. On a large project, two or even more composite crews might be utilized for speed and efficiency. On every project, one journey-

Table 1
PRODUCTIVITY FACTORS FOR INSTALLATION OF CURTAIN WALL COMPONENTS

Type of Work	Man-Hours per 10 m² or 100 ft.²
Straight framing	20
Angled framing	30
Curved framing	40
Single glazing	4
Double glazing	6
Spandrel panels	5
Louvers and doors	10

man should be designated as foreman, to supervise the field operations.

4.2 Productivity

Table 1 shows data representative of probable installation times by well-equipped and experienced crews working continuously under good conditions on typical projects of average complexity. As conditions deteriorate, such as for work done in inclement weather, on unusual configurations of walling, or on an intermittent basis, the factors will of course increase.

It will be noted that the time figures given for the installation of curtain wall components are slightly lower (meaning that productivity is higher) than those given elsewhere for the installation of storefront systems and ordinary glazing. The primary reason for the difference is the probability that in curtain walling, the building surface areas to be completed are generally much larger than corresponding areas of storefront or ordinary glazing and productivity usually improves as the system progresses toward completion, because of the so-called learning curve. In the example given in Figure 2, if the average estimated price of curtain walling is (say) $200 per unit of surface area, then initially the unit price may appear to be high, but as the work progresses and workers learn the installation procedure, the unit price should fall below the estimated average. The object is to ensure that the shaded area above the average price line is never greater than the corresponding area below the line.

5.0 Procedures

5.1 Preparation

Preparation for curtain walling is essentially the same as that described in Sections 08–400 for storefront systems and 08–800 for glazing.

5.2 Process

The process for installing curtain wall components is essentially the same as that described for storefront systems in Section 08–400. Mounting clips are

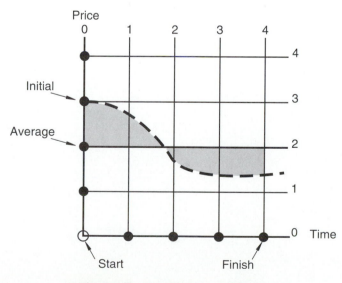

Figure 2 Sample Learning Curve

Installation
Composite units are then brought to the edge of the building floors, loaded onto suspended gantries, and installed on the building frame according to codes and specifications. (UBC Architecture)

selected, positioned, and secured; the metal framing members are cut to length, manually installed and aligned, and then connected or fastened to the clips.

The process for installing clear or tinted glass or solid spandrel panels is essentially the same as that described in Section 08–800 Glass and Glazing. The panels are cut to size, placed in position, and sealed by normal glazing methods, using sealants or beads. Cover trim is cut to length and then either snapped on or screwed into position where necessary to conceal joints and fastenings.

Most curtain wall systems are installed piece by piece, usually (but not necessarily) working from the top of the building downward on a floor-by-floor basis. It is occasionally practical to assemble a composite unit consisting of the framing and infills within one bay or between two or more grid-line spacings of the building elevation, and then to raise the composite unit into position. However, this process requires more equipment to lift the heavier loads into place and entails greater risk of damage to the panels, their mounting assemblies, and the building frame during installation.

5.3 Precautions

Safety considerations for curtain walling are essentially the same as those described for Section 08–400 and Section 08–800.

CHAPTER 09
Finishes

Section 09–100
Metal Support Systems

1.0 Introduction

1.1 General Issues

In many buildings, there is a need to leave some space between the primary horizontal plane at the underside of the structural floor or roof frame and the secondary plane or level of finished ceilings. This space is required to house and conceal mechanical, electrical, and other functional systems within the building volume. Such spaces also come about through differences in building floor or ceiling elevations, or through the need to close off the bottoms of ducts or shafts. To achieve a framework suitable for supporting finishes at such secondary building planes, a suspension system (often called *furring*) is utilized. The resultant composite ceiling system is variously referred to as a *dropped, furred*, or *suspended ceiling*. Such systems may consist of metal or wood components. This section describes metal systems; for wood systems, see Section 06–100.

1.2 Design Aspects

There are two basic arrangements for metal support systems. One is intended to carry a continuous gypsum or metal lath system to which plasterboard or acoustical tiles may be adhered (see Figure 1). The other is intended to carry an assembly of spacer bars with prefabricated tile or panel inserts of one sort or another (see Figure 2). These arrangements may be installed horizontally or inclined, in flat planes or with curves or steps, in continuous or intermittent fashion. They are usually integrated with the terminal fixtures required for lighting, heating, public address, and other building systems.

1.3 Related Work

Work closely connected to this section is described in the following sections, to which reference should be made:

03–300   Cast-in-Place Concrete

05–200   Steel Joisting

06–100   Rough Carpentry

09–200   Lath and Plasterwork

09–500   Acoustical Treatments

435

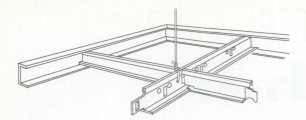

Figure 1 Suspended Continuous Support

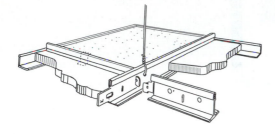

Figure 2 Suspended Panel Support

2.0 Products

2.1 Materials

The main components are **runners** and **cross-channels**; both are described.

Runners. Cold-rolled, galvanized, light steel channels, having a narrow flange and a wider web, in sizes and weights as noted in Table 1.

Cross-channels. Essentially the same as runners, but smaller and lighter in weight, as shown in Table 1.

2.2 Accessories

Accessories used in this work are as follows:

Pencil rods. Short lengths of thick mild steel wire, 10 mm or ³/₈ in. in diameter, used to form the grid to support furred systems.

Hanger wire. Long lengths of thin mild steel wire, 9-gauge or thicker, used to support suspended ceilings.

Spring clips. A wide assortment of purpose-made wire clips, used to positively and securely connect the system members.

Tie-wire. Fine steel wire, 16-gauge or thicker, used to connect system members to the building frame or to each other.

Others. An assortment of nails, screws, and staples is also used in this work.

3.0 Construction Aids

3.1 Equipment

Movable, self-braced scaffold units or powered scissor-lift platforms are used to raise workers and equipment to working levels.

3.2 Tools

Tools used are essentially those of the carpentry and metalworking trades, as well as the following:

Hacksaw. A short, bow-backed frame supporting a stretched, toughened steel, fine-tooth saw blade, suitable for cutting metal.

Wire cutters. Plier-like devices for snipping hanger and tie-wire to length.

Table 1
SIZES AND WEIGHTS OF RUNNERS AND CROSS-CHANNELS

Component	Web Depth		Approximate Weight	
	mm	in.	kg per 100 m	lb. per 1,000 ft.
Heavy runner	50	2.00	90	600
Light runner	38	1.50	70	475
Cross-channel	19	0.75	50	300

Installation
Mobile scaffolding or staging is erected in the general area where support systems are required. Workers mount ladders on the staging to get convenient access to final elevations. (UBC Architecture)

Basic Grid
The selected suspended system is attached to hanger wires with arrangements made to incorporate electrical and mechanical fixtures into the grid to suit the designer's specification. (UBC Architecture)

4.0 Production

4.1 Crew Configuration

A typical hanger crew might consist of one mechanic and one helper. On large projects, two or more crews might be utilized. Mechanics may be carpenters, metalworkers, or others skilled through experience or training to do this work.

4.2 Productivity

In large unobstructed areas, a crew installing a metal grid system consisting of hangers, main runners, and cross-channels (excluding gypsum or metal lath) should normally complete about 10 m² or 100 ft.² of ceiling area per hour. In small or confined areas, decrease normal productivity by about 30 percent; in complex sloped, stepped, or curved areas, decrease normal productivity by up to 50 percent. To include fastening gypsum or metal lath to the suspension system, installation (whether plane, sloped, or complex) will take about twice as long, compared to simply installing the supporting framework.

5.0 Procedures

5.1 Preparation

The areas to be suspended should be examined for obstructions, both temporary (such as stored builder's equipment and supplies) and permanent (such as mechanical ducts, lighting fixtures, and other irregularities), in the structural frame or shape of the building. The centers for the location of holes, hooks, or ties requiring to be installed in wood, steel, or concrete should be determined and delivered to those responsible for their proper placement ahead of time.

The layout of the pattern for the hangers should be determined with reference to the local building code. In general, spacing of hangers along the length of the main runners will be dictated by the size of the channel and the proposed lateral spacing of the main runners. Some typical spacings are indicated in Table 2.

5.2 Process

Starting. There are three common types of structural frame from which suspended metal systems are hung:

1. From concrete. Hanger ties or hooks are secured

Table 2
SPACING FOR RUNNERS AND HANGERS

Size of Runner (web depth)		Space between Runners		Space between Hangers	
mm	in.	mm	in.	mm	in.
50	2.00	120	48	180	60
38	1.50	90	36	120	48
19*	0.75*	60	24	90	36
10†	0.38†	30	12	60	24

*Cross-channel.
†Pencil rod (diameter).

to reinforcing steel within the concrete before the concrete is poured or cast (see Figure 3a).

2. **From steel.** Hanger wires are wound around the bottom chord of open web joists or inserted through holes predrilled in wide-flange joists or steel decking (see Figure 3b).

3. **From wood.** Holes may be drilled through the neutral axis of the joist, or spikes may be driven through to provide points to which the hangers may be secured (see Figure 3c).

Finishing. There are two elements to this part of the process:

1. The rigid hangers or hanger wires are hung from the prepared structure down to a point just below the intended level of the finished suspension system and cut off. The main runners are measured and cut to length, shaped or leveled as necessary, and then fastened in place by twisting the hanger wire around them at predetermined intervals. There should always be one main runner placed within 150 mm or 6 in. of vertical wall surfaces along every side of the system area.

2. Cross-channels or pencil rods are then measured, cut, and fastened to the main runners, using tie-wire or special clips, to produce an accurate rigid rectangular grid, ready to receive the proposed lath or acoustical system. No part of the suspension system should touch the perimeter enclosing vertical surfaces.

5.3 Precautions

As much of this work is done overhead and over-hand, and usually at some height above floor levels, eye protection, hard hats, and good nonslip footwear are recommended. There is little protection necessary for the materials or accessories used, except to keep them clean and dry.

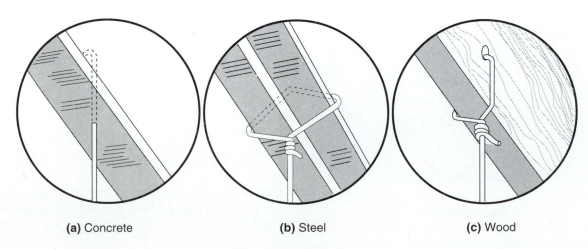

(a) Concrete   **(b)** Steel   **(c)** Wood

Figure 3 Soffit Mounts

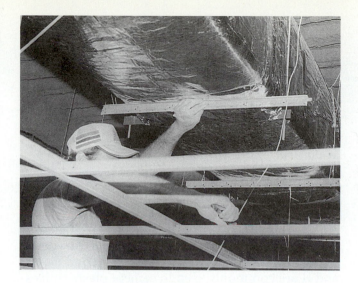

(a) In center

Special Features

Where hanger wire patterns are interrupted by other building components, special stirrups have to be incorporated to maintain correct grid spacing. Vertical finishes terminate at grid level. (UBC Architecture)

(b) At perimeter

Section 09–200
Lath and Plasterwork

1.0 Introduction

1.1 General Issues

Society is experiencing the end of a long and honorable era with respect to the use of traditional lath and plasterwork in construction. Lime, gypsum, and cement plasters have been used to finish the insides and outsides of buildings for many centuries, from before the time of the ancient Greeks and Egyptians up to the middle of the current century. However, in recent years, plastering has experienced a significant decline in popularity, primarily arising from competition by less expensive finishes, such as gypsum plasterboard as well as plastic, wood, or metal paneling, which are considerably less labor intensive. Plastering, like painting, is one of the few building finish trades where skill acquired through years of experience by the person doing the work has a direct effect on the quality of the finished product. This contrasts with other finishes which are factory pro-

duced, more or less ready for simple, errorfree installation by semiskilled workers.

1.2 Design Aspects

Plaster finishes still offer designers a number of advantages, such as flexibility to choose flat or curved surfaces, modeling and sculpting possibilities, good fire, sound, and thermal separation, and a durable, high-quality, plain or textured finish. Plaster finish systems are also more resistant to damage from moisture than are gypsum plasterboard systems.

Like many words, *plaster* has several meanings; the one significant to construction means a substance having a paste-like composition. Plaster finishes are applied in successive layers (called *coats*) pasted over prepared bases (called *substrates*) to build up to required thicknesses. One-coat plastering is seldom used, except for parging flue linings or coating concrete foundations prior to dampproofing. In two-coat work, the brown coat is omitted, although the scratch coat is often applied to double thickness by applying a second layer immediately on top of the first layer, before the finish layer is applied. In three-coat work, the first coat is called the *scratch* coat, so named because its surface is deliberately roughened ready to bond to the next coat called the *brown* coat, so named because of its usually dark color. The third coat is called the *finish* coat. The basic system is shown in Figure 1.

Care should be taken with the proper design and placement of sheet metal flashings used in conjuction with external stucco or plaster systems, to ensure the deflection of water away from the system. Similarly, thought should be given to the appropriate placement of metal expansion and separation joints, to minimize the extent and effect of the inevitable cracking of cured plasterwork, caused by movement of building components.

1.3   Related Work

Work closely connected to this section is described in the following sections, to which reference should be made:

05–400   Steel Stud Systems

06–100   Rough Carpentry

09–900   Painting and Decorating

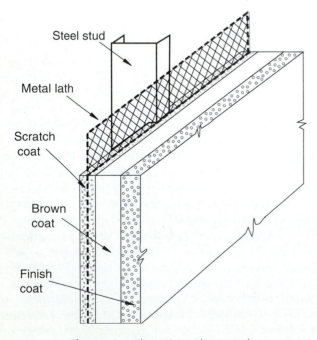

Steel stud

Metal lath

Scratch coat

Brown coat

Finish coat

Figure 1   Three-Coat Plasterwork

2.0 Products

2.1 Materials

Material Categories.   The materials used in plasterwork fall into three broad categories: **plasters, aggregates,** and **water.** Each is described below; they are mixed together to produce different forms of plaster.

Plaster Ingredients

1. Cement.   This is a factory-produced mixture of limestone and selected clays, fired and powdered; for details, refer to Section 03–300. Portland Types I and II are commonly used in cement plaster mixes.

2. Gypsum.   This is scientifically hydrous calcium sulfate ($CaSO_4 \cdot H_2O$); for details, refer to Section 09–250. When heated and dried, it forms anhydrous calcium sulfate ($CaSO_4$). In this form, with additives to form slow-setting or quick-setting types, it is mixed with lime putty to form Keene's cement and used where a hard, solid, smooth, dense plaster surface impervious to moisture is required.

3. Lime.   Dry calcium oxide (CaO) is called quicklime; water is added to form calcium hydroxide ($CaOH_2$), which is a putty-like mixture called slaked lime. The chemical reaction is exothermic (i.e., it produces heat). After cooling and curing for about two weeks, lime putty is ready for use in plastering. Under factory conditions, calcium hydroxide is also produced and packaged in two powder forms called hydrated lime: Type N for normal use (requiring lengthy soaking before use) and Type S for special use (ready for immediate use after adding water).

Aggregates

1. Aggregates, coarse.   Both heavyweight aggregates (such as crushed stone, gravel, and sometimes small glass particles) and lightweight aggregates (such as perlite, expanded shale, and vermiculite) are used.

2. Aggregates, fine.   This is clean, well-graded, fine stone sand; for further detail refer to Section 03–300, Part 2.1.

3. Dashes.   These consist of a large variety of commercially prepared small colored glass, marble, quartz, or stone chips; they are used for final decoration of exterior stucco surfaces.

4. Fillers.   In earlier times, horse hair was used to strengthen certain types of plasters, and although asbestos fiber was also once popular, it is seldom used now for reasons of health. Currently, wood and glass fibers are occasionally introduced into plaster mixes to improve strength and resilience while reducing weight.

Water

Clean potable (drinkable) water is used in most plaster mixes.

Plaster Types. There are several combinations of ingredients used to form different types of plaster:

Acoustic plaster. A mixture of gypsum, lime, and lightweight aggregates.

Base-coat plaster. Lime or gypsum, used in scratch and brown coats.

Bond-coat plaster. A mixture of lime or gypsum with selected bonding agents, used to chemically bond scratch coats to concrete substrates.

Cement plaster. A mixture of cement, water, and fine aggregate, used most often in exterior applications.

Fiber plaster. A factory-made mixture of gypsum plaster and selected wood or glass fibers, used in locations subject to increased physical wear.

Gauging plaster. A mixture of lime putty and finely powdered hydrated gypsum, used where increased hardness is desired in the finished surface.

Molding plaster. A fine, white, hydrated gypsum powder which, with the addition of water, produces a dense plastic material ideal for producing ornamental molded or sculpted plasterwork.

Ready-mix plaster. A factory-made mixture of fine (usually lightweight) aggregate and hydrated gypsum powder, bagged ready for immediate use upon the addition of water.

Stucco plaster. Similar to cement plaster, but often having an aggregate dash coat applied to the surface.

2.2 Accessories

Accessories for plasterwork fall into three broad categories:

Plaster Lath. These can be either **gypsum-based** or **metal-based**, as follows:

1. **Gypsum based.** Consisting of a paper covered gypsum core, and available in the following forms:
   a. **Plain.** Ordinary gypsum plasterboard in small sizes (400 × 1,200 mm or 16 × 48 in.).

(a) Stucco lath

(b) Corner bead

Metal Lath and Trim

Stucco mesh is stapled over building paper or vapor-wrap to form a mechanical key to which the plaster/stucco can attach. Corner and casing beads are stapled on over the metal lath. (UBC Architecture)

(a) Gas-powered mixer

Mixing Stucco

Stucco is mixed like concrete, though usually in fairly small batches. It is then transported in wheelbarrows or power buggies to a location where it can be hoisted to the workers. (UBC Architecture)

(b) Materials handling

b. **Long length.** Same as plain, but in lengths up to 3,600 mm or 12 ft. (and longer on special order).

c. **Insulating.** Same as plain, but with aluminum foil factory laminated to one face.

d. **Perforated.** Same as plain, but having a system of holes, 19 mm or ³/₄ in. in diameter, drilled at 100-mm or 4-in. intervals in both directions, as a means to improve bonding of plaster finishes.

e. **Fire-resistive.** Having a perlite/gypsum core.

2. **Metal based.** Generally consisting of a galvanized steel base, and available in the following forms:

a. **Expanded metal.** Sheet steel, slit and stretched to form diamond-shaped openings; available in sheets 600 to 725 mm or 24 to 29 in. wide and up to 3,600 mm or 144 in. long.

b. **Rib lath.** Same as expanded metal, but having stiffening ribs incorporated into the manufacture.

c. **Sheet lath.** Flat sheets of copper-bearing steel, perforated with small circles, rectangles, or squares to improve the mechanical bond of plaster.

d. **Stucco lath.** 18-gauge steel wire, woven and stretched to form an open diamond-shaped mesh, having apertures approximately 38 mm or 1¹/₂ in. in size. The wire is crimped at intervals to provide a self-furring feature.

e. **Wire lath.** 16-, 17-, 18-, or 19-gauge steel wire, woven or welded to form an open square or hexagonal patterned mesh, having apertures about 50 mm or 2 in. in size. One form of this lath incorporates a layer of heavy-duty, waterproof kraft building paper woven between the wires.

Some examples of lath are shown in Figure 2.

Metal Trim. This generally consists of galvanized sheet steel with expanded metal flanges for fastening, and is available in the following forms:

Casing beads of J profile, used to trim open edges.

Control beads of V profile, used to form expansion joint features in large plastered areas.

Corner beads of L profile, used to reinforce corners.

Picture molds of U profile, used to create a small concealed recess to facilitate the hanging of pictures.

Plaster boxes, used to keep plaster clear of electrical or other components set into walls to be plastered.

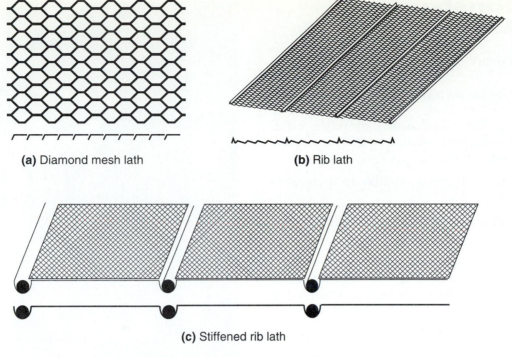

(a) Diamond mesh lath

(b) Rib lath

(c) Stiffened rib lath

Figure 2   Examples of Metal Plaster Lath

Rods and clips, used to provide separation of plaster lath from supporting frames for acoustical purposes.

Some examples of trim are shown in Figure 3.

Related Components.   An assortment of building papers, nails, staples, screws, and tie-wire is also utilized in the work of this trade. Most of these are described in other sections of this book.

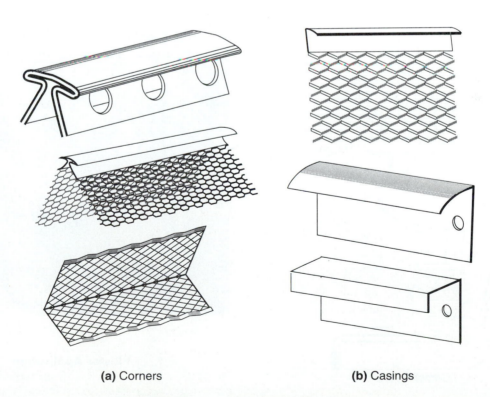

(a) Corners

(b) Casings

Figure 3   Examples of Metal Plaster Trim

3.0 Construction Aids

3.1 Equipment

Equipment used in this trade includes the following:

Darby. A long, flat, wooden or lightweight metal bar, attached to handles; used to roughly level plasterwork between screeds.

Mixer. A motorized device, similar to a concrete mixer.

Scaffolding. Fixed and movable scaffolding is used in many phases of plasterwork.

Sprayer. A power-operated pump and hopper, connected to hoses and nozzles, through which plaster is forced to produce various texture finishes (see Figure 4).

3.2 Tools

Tools used in this trade include the following:

Brush. A short handle with a wood cross-head, holding bristles of varying stiffness; used to prepare and finish various coats of plaster, as well as for applying textures.

Float. A wood handle, to which can be attached a wood slab, a steel plate, a firm sponge, or a cork, rub-

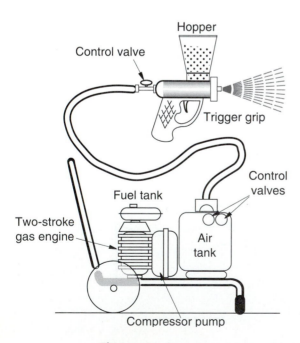

Figure 4 Sprayer

(a) Troweling

(b) Derbying

Plaster Application

The plaster or stucco mix is liberally applied in one, two, or three coats, depending on specifications. The mix is quickly spread with a hand trowel and straightened with a long derby. (UBC Architecture)

ber, or carpet pad; used to spread and level plaster coats.

Hawk. A flat sheet of aluminum, approximately 30 mm or 12 in. square, with a handle fixed to the center of the underside; used to carry small amounts of plaster.

Scratcher. A stiffened strip of metal with short teeth; used to roughen plaster surfaces to enhance the bond with subsequent coats.

Stapler. A pneumatic-powered, heavy-duty stapler.

Trowel. A flat, tempered or stainless steel blade, attached to a short handle; used to compress and finish surfaces. There are four basic blade shapes: rectangular, pointed, margin, and angle.

4.0 Production

4.1 Crew Configuration

A typical crew consists of two plasterers and one helper, with one of the plasterers acting as foreman. On large projects, two or more crews might be employed, with one general foreman.

4.2 Productivity

The following productivity factors are suggested for work done by an experienced crew operating on large, plain, unrestricted, and vertical wall areas. For horizontal or sloping flat surfaces of ceilings and soffits, decrease productivity factors by about 10 percent; for work done to circle or curve, decrease factors by about 30 percent; in small or complex areas, decrease factors by about 50 percent.

Gypsum plaster lath can be installed at the rate of about 20 m² or 200 ft.² per hour. Metal lath can be installed at the rate of about 15 m² or 150 ft.² per hour. Metal trim can be installed at the rate of about 10 m or 30 ft. per hour.

Table 1
PRODUCTIVITY FACTORS
FOR APPLICATION OF
PLASTER COATS

Type	Area per Hour	
	m²	ft.²
Scratch coat	10	100
Brown coat	12	120
Finish coat	8	80

Plaster coats may be installed by hand at the rates shown in Table 1. For machine application on larger jobs, increase factors by about 20 percent for scratch coats, 30 percent for brown coats, and 40 percent for finish coats.

5.0 Procedures

5.1 Preparation

Solid Substrates. Surfaces to receive wet plaster finish must be clean and free of dirt, dust, rust, grease, oil, paint, efflorescence, laitance, loose particles, or other impediments to good bonding. Concrete or masonry surfaces should be dampened if necessary and primed with a bonding compound or a thin dash coat of one part cement and two parts sand, applied with a stiff brush.

Lathing. There are several different conditions with which to contend:

1. In **solid sheathed construction,** breather-type building paper is first stapled over external sheathing, starting from the bottom and working upward with 50-mm or 2-in. overlaps at edges and ends. Then ribbed lath for plaster or stucco mesh for stucco is secured to the face of the substrate. See Figure 5.

2. In **exterior open frame construction,** 18-gauge line wire is stretched across and fastened to the framing members at 150-mm or 60-in. vertical intervals, and a heavy-duty, waterproof building paper is secured by staples to the studs, again working from the bottom up. Alternatively, a factory-made wire and paper combination lath as described in Part 2.2 Accessories may be installed. Stucco mesh is then secured with staples over the building paper as before (the building paper layer is not necessary with the wire and paper combination lath). See Figure 6.

3. In **interior open frame construction,** ribbed metal lath is secured with its long dimension at right angles to the direction of the framing. Alternatively, gypsum lath is clipped to studs, with small spaces left between lath panels to allow for movement and to enhance the mechanical key or bond of the subsequently applied plaster coats. Wire and paper combination lath can also be used.

Trim. Metal, plastic, or plaster preformed corner beads, edge beads, picture molds, reinforcing strips, expansion joints, plaster boxes (used to create recesses for light switches and power outlets) and similar accessories are then positioned as necessary.

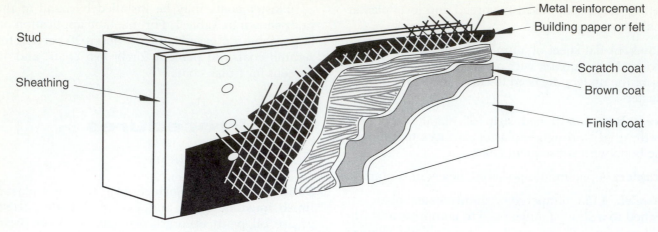

Figure 5 Solid Sheathed System

5.2 Process

Once the surfaces to be plastered have been properly prepared, plastering can commence. The procedures described below encompass two basic systems of work: **interior plaster** and **exterior stucco.** These are followed by an explanation of some specific plastering features. Common thicknesses of finished plaster and stucco systems recommended for various structural surfaces (or substrates) are shown in Table 2.

Interior Plaster.   Plaster on gypsum lath or other smooth surfaces requires at least a two-coat system.

Plaster on metal lath or rough and uneven substrates requires a three-coat system.

1. Two-coat system. Base-coat plaster is applied by hand or machine and then spread between screeds to a thickness just less than the proposed overall finished thickness of the system, to allow for the finish coat. The base coat may be applied to its full thickness in one operation, or it may be applied to half its thickness in one sweep with the other half thickness immediately applied before the first half has set or cured. The surface of the base coat is roughened to form a good bond with the finish coat, then allowed to set and cure for a few days. Later, the

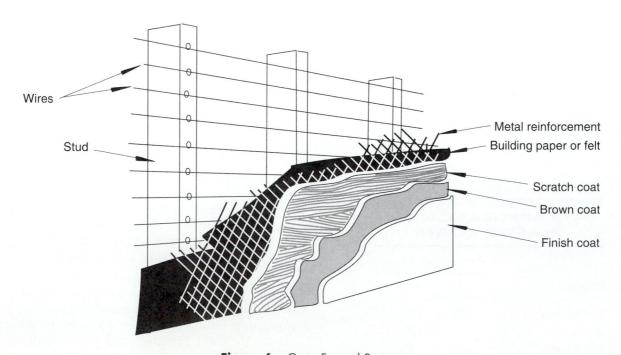

Figure 6 Open Framed System

Chapter 09   Finishes

Table 2
THICKNESSES FOR PLASTER AND STUCCO

Substrate	Thickness	
	mm	in.
Gypsum lath	13	$1/2$
Masonry/concrete	16	$5/8$
Metal/wire lath	19	$3/4$

finish coat is applied to required thickness, as described below.

2. Three-coat system. Scratch-coat (also called *render-coat*) plaster is applied by hand trowel, forced into the openings or crevices of rough surfaces or metal lath backing, leveled by darby, filled if necessary by trowel, lightly and uniformly scratched, and allowed to set and cure. This imparts stiffness to the more flexible lath. The brown coat is then applied in two stages: first a thin application to ensure a good and uniform bond with the scratch-coat surface, followed by a thicker application to bring the thickness out to a plane ready to receive the finish coat. The surface of the brown coat is roughened to form a good bond with the finish coat and allowed to set

and cure for a few days. Later, the finish coat is applied to required thickness, as described below.

3. Finish coat. The brown coat is dampened and covered with the finish coat, applied by trowel. Depending on the designer's choice, the surface of the finish coat may be troweled smooth, manually stippled with sponges, mechanically textured with a dash coat of fine sand or other granules, or decorated with motifs or in other ways.

4. Angles and beads. Internal and external corners can be formed using shaped templates or planted using precast inserts. Simple angles, splays, and curves can be selected, as well as more complex quirks or ova.

Exterior Stucco. Stucco work normally involves a two-coat system, with a final surface treatment of some sort.

1. Two-coat system. A base coat plaster mixed with damp loose sand is applied by hand or machine to the stucco mesh and lightly but firmly compressed to ensure a good mechanical bond and to fill about half the required finished thickness of the stucco. It is then slightly roughened and allowed to set and cure for a few days. Later, the base coat is lightly dampened and a second coat of matching material is applied on top to complete the full finished thickness.

(a) Brush stippling

(b) Steel finishing

Surface Texturing

The wet plaster or stucco is easily textured by sponging, dashing with small pebbles, swirling with a trowel or brush, then left to cure. Later, the surface can be washed and sealed. (BCIT Building Technology)

2. Surface finish. Before it finally sets, the surface of the stucco can be finished in a number of ways:

a. Smoothed by steel hand trowel.

b. Stippled using synthetic sponges.

c. Formed to selected profiles using shaped templates.

d. Textured with a dash coat of fine sand.

e. Rendered with a uniform sprinkling of larger glass, marble, quartz, or selected stone particles, dry cast onto the uncured stucco surface by hand or by machine.

5.3 Precautions

Cementitious plaster products and metal accessories should be stored where they will not be adversely affected by dampness, heat, or contamination. Another consideration involves temporary protection of surfaces not scheduled to receive plaster finishes, such as windows or floors, but which could be damaged by careless handling of plastering equipment, tools, or materials. Care should be taken to ensure chemical compatibility between substrate surfaces and succeeding plaster coats. Slaked lime should not be used before it is properly cured.

Section 09–250
Gypsum Plasterboard Systems

1.0 Introduction

1.1 General Issues

About 100 years ago, gypsum plasterboard was developed as a substitute for the wood lath then used as a base for plaster finishes. The thin plasterboards were cast in shallow forms, one sheet at a time. They were then nailed to wall or ceiling framing, and either covered with a thin skim coat of wet plaster or left exposed with the joints covered with wood battens. About 60 years ago, the idea was conceived to cover these boards with paper, leading to the development of the modern gypsum plasterboard. Such boards are commonly referred to as drywall boards, although they are not installed only on walls; some go onto ceilings and elsewhere. Other common names are gypsumboard, gypboard, gyprock, and sheetrock.

1.2 Design Aspects

There are several design advantages to using gypsum plasterboard. Because the system is principally installed in a dry state, there is no time lost waiting for this component of the building to dry out; there is also no transfer of moisture to the frame of the building. From an economic point of view, both in first cost and in speed of installation, gypsum plasterboard systems compare favorably with almost any

other system available to the designer's choice. The gypsum core, consisting of calcium sulfate, is essentially nonflammable and thus provides a good measure of fire safety in any building where it is extensively used. The boards are relatively lightweight, and they are ready for site finishing with paint or simply applied wallcoverings.

The only design drawbacks of any consequence are that the boards are fairly fragile, they are available in a large but finite range of sizes that do not always fit the building module, and the finished appearance of the basic wallboard system is relatively plain and uninteresting. The relationship between the spacing of support members and the thickness of the plasterboards should be determined as noted later in this section.

As gypsum is affected by water, moisture from any source can have adverse effects on the end use of such a finishing system, causing sagging, blistering, discoloration, or outright failure. Similarly, gypsum plasterboards should not come into direct contact with exterior metal window or door frames, because condensation will cause rapid deterioration of the board at the points of contact.

1.3 Related Work

Work closely connected to this section is described in the following sections, to which reference should be made:

05–400   Steel Stud Systems

06–200   Rough Carpentry

09–900   Painting and Decorating

2.0 Products

2.1 Materials

A typical gypsum plasterboard is made by sandwiching a core of semiliquid commercial gypsum ($CaSO_4 \cdot H_2O$) between two continuous layers of specially treated kraft paper, and then curing the whole under controlled heat and pressure to produce large stiff boards of predetermined appearance, rigidity, length, width, and thickness.

Types of Boards. Some of the more common types of boards encountered in general construction are described below; many companies produce more specialized boards for more specific applications.

Plain. Standard gypsum core and paper sandwich, having a fine, ivory-colored, sized paper on the front face, regular gray kraft paper on the rear face, edges taped, and ends unfinished.

Fire resistive. Similar to plain board, but having 15 percent fiberglass incorporated in the core to improve fire resistance.

Insulating. Similar to plain board, but having a sheet of thin aluminum foil laminated to the rear face to reflect heat.

Perforated. Similar to plain board, but having kraft paper on both faces and a series of holes, 19-mm or $3/4$-in. diameter, drilled every 100 mm or 4 in. on center (oc) in a regular pattern over the surface, intended to improve the adhesion of applied plaster finishes.

Edges. Boards are available with a variety of edge profiles as shown in Figure 1: square, round, tapered, beveled, shiplap, and tongue-and-groove are common. Ends are square cut or plain butt.

Dimensions. There are three aspects of dimensions:

1. **Thickness.** Boards are generally available in standard thicknesses of 10, 13, and 16 mm or $3/8$, $1/2$, and $5/8$ in. Special-core boards are made 25 mm or 1 in. thick; other thicknesses can be ordered. Boards 10 mm or $3/8$ in. or less in thickness should be supported at not less than 400 mm or 16 in. oc; thicker boards can be supported at 600 mm or 24 in. oc.

2. **Width.** Most boards have a standard width of 1,200 mm or 4 ft. Plaster lath drywall boards are 400 mm or 16 in. wide.

3. **Length.** Lengths are generally available from 2.5 m or 8 ft. up to 5 m or 16 ft., in 600-mm or 24-in. increments, although other lengths can be specially ordered.

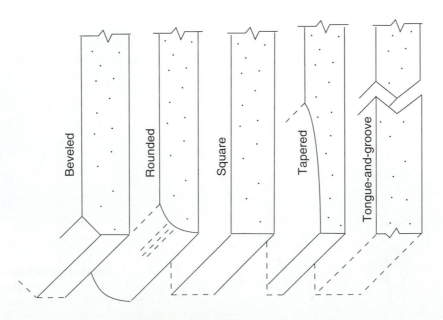

Figure 1   Plasterboard Edges

2.2 Accessories

Accessories for plasterboards fall into two broad categories:

Fastenings. These consist of nails, screws, and glues, all specially made for the purpose. Nails and screws are usually about 30 mm in length; nails are barbed-shank, annular-ring, or cement-coat type, while screws have special smooth, round heads prepared for driving using a Phillips- or square-head bit and have two different thread configurations, depending on whether fastening will be to wood or steel studs. Glues are gun-applied, contact-bond type and are quick curing.

Finishings. These consist of two subgroups:

1. **Metal trim** is in the form of thin galvanized steel corner and edge beads, profiled as shown in Section 09-200, Figure 3.
2. **Fillers** are available in bags of powdered mix weighing 40 kg or 80 lb. which produce a smooth, plastic, putty-like compound applied in conjunction with 50-mm or 2-in.-wide kraft paper tape, available in rolls 150 m or 500 ft. long, used for reinforcement.

3.0 Construction Aids

3.1 Equipment

Some typical pieces of equipment are listed below:

Bazooka. A colloquial term for a tape applicator (see Figure 2).

Board lifter. A manually operated pneumatic jack, on which boards can be initially loaded in the verti-

Figure 2 Gypsum Equipment

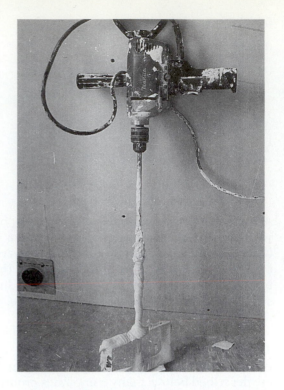

(a) Mixing paddle

(b) Tape bazooka

Tools and Equipment

Like all trades, drywallers have specialized tools made to speed up and simplify their work. The two shown here are typical of those used to mix finishing compound and apply paper tape. (BCIT Building Technology)

cal position, swung to the horizontal position, and then raised up to normal ceiling heights by a simple pumping action.

Jigsaw. An electrically powered, handheld motor, equipped with a reciprocating jig and bit to which a small narrow saw blade is secured at one end; used to cut out small openings, such as for electrical boxes, pipes, and the like. Also called a saber saw.

Scaffolding. Usually a stationary self-braced framed system; if movable, it should be equipped with positive locking castors or wheels.

Screw gun. An electrically powered, handheld drill, having a slip-clutch and a special bit made to receive the various types of screws used to secure plasterboards to framing.

Tape applicator. A pole-like device, having accommodation for a roll of joint tape on the outside and a charge of joint compound on the inside, used to simultaneously apply both.

Tape shaper. A pole-like device, having two sets of small steel rollers set at right angles, used to press and smooth tape and compound into final position.

Taper. A pole-like device, having a trowel-like blade at one end, used to remove excess joint compound and to feather or flare out edges of filled joints to create a smooth transition between the joint and the fields of the boards on each side of the joint.

Toe lifter. A small metal fulcrum, used to slip under the edge of a plasterboard and move it into position against the wall frame.

3.2 Tools

The tools are those of the carpenter and drywaller:

Applicator's axe. A short wood-handled tool, having a rounded hammer head combined with a small axe-head having a slot for removing nails.

Circle cutter. A small metal device, similar to a compass fitted with an adjustable centering pin and a small sharp blade, used to cut out holes to any given radius in plasterboards.

Keyhole saw. A saw with a short, narrow, tapered steel blade, used to cut small openings in plasterboards.

Leather tool pouch. Used to hold small hand tools.

Sharpening stone. A small Carborundum block for maintaining blades at peak cutting efficiency.

Trowels. Small hand trowels of various sizes.

Utility knife. A short, sharp, heavy-duty cutting device, usually having interchangeable blades.

4.0 Production

4.1 Crew Configuration

A typical plasterboard (or drywall) crew might consist of three persons: the applicator (sometimes called the boarder), the finisher, and a helper. The applicator measures and places the boards and trim; the finisher does the taping and filling at joints and corners. The helper is employed generally moving materials around the site and particularly assisting the boarder and finisher as necessary. On large projects, two or more crews may be utilized.

4.2 Productivity

On fairly large, unobstructed walls, an experienced plasterboard crew should apply approximately 35 m² or 125 ft.² of each single ply of plain gypsum plasterboard in one hour. Such productivity will be reduced on large plain ceilings by about 10 percent; in small or irregular areas, such as closets, alcoves, or other recesses, productivity may decline by as much as 50 percent.

Metal trim can be manually applied at the rate of about 20 m or 50 ft. per hour. Finishing tape and joint compound can be applied manually at the rate of about 10 m or 30 ft. per hour, or by special machine at the rate of about 50 m or 150 ft. per hour.

5.0 Procedures

5.1 Preparation

Before starting work in this section, the planes of wall studs, ceiling joists, and strapping and other supporting components or accessories should be checked for alignment. If any part is found to be inadvertently more than 6 mm or $1/4$ in. out of line or plane, it should be rectified. A check should be made to ensure also that there will be solid backing along all edges of all boards for fastening. All plumbing and electrical roughing-in and inspection should be complete, with wires and pipes positioned so as not to be at risk during the nailing of the boards. It is a good practice to mark the position of wall studs on the subfloor before installing the wallboards, so as to facilitate discovering their locations for subsequent fastening work.

Plasterboards are delivered to the site by truck, off-loaded by a forklift, and manually distributed by

(a) Scoring

Preparing Boarding

Plasterboard sheets are measured, scored, and snapped to reduce them to sizes or shapes to fit into the building features. (BCIT Building Technology)

(b) Snapping

(a) Raising boards

(b) Securing boards

Installing Boarding

While one or two workers can place boards on vertical wall framing, it takes two or three workers to efficiently raise and secure gypsum board panels of average size on ceiling soffits. (BCIT Audio-Visual Production)

helpers to their final locations, according to a schedule prepared by the estimator for each room or area. Boards should be stacked flat and off the floor, in their horizontal plane to prevent warpage or cracking; personnel should not be permitted to walk across such stored boards.

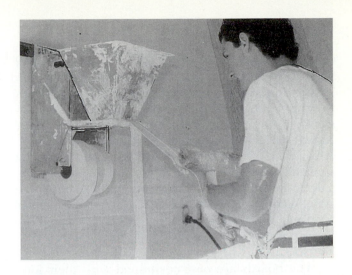

(a) Special shapes

Applying Compound
One technique used to apply filling compound to paper tape is to secure a small hopper to the wall, with the tape passing under a small opening in the hopper base. Tape is then manually applied. (BCIT Audio-Visual Production)

(b) Waste and debris

Special Features
Gypsum board can be successfully modified to suit unusual architectural features. Excessive use of nonstandard detailing results in excessive waste and higher labor costs. (BCIT Audio-Visual Production)

Measurements are taken to determine the numbers and sizes of full and partial boards required for each location. These measurements are then transferred to the boards to be installed. Whole boards are installed without cutting; partial boards are marked and cut straight or to irregular line as necessary. Straight, full-width cuts are performed by scoring the board on the rear face, snapping the board at the cut, and then neatly cutting through the face paper with a sharp knife. Irregular cuts can be easily made with a coping, keyhole, or saber saw. Small holes for pipes or wires can be drilled by hand brace or machine bit.

5.2 Process

Gypsum plasterboard is applied on wood or steel framing to create vertical walls and horizontal ceilings. It can also be easily applied on sloping frames to produce inclined flat planes, and with some adjustment, on circular barrel vault or similar simply curved surfaces by scoring the rear face at frequent intervals and bending the board to radius. It can be applied in single, double, or triple layers and in nominally solid or hollow configurations. It can also be installed over masonry or concrete substrates, either directly or attached to wood or metal strapping. Some typical configurations at corners are shown in Figure 3.

The boards are best positioned with their long axes at right angles to the direction of the supporting frame members. Ceilings and boards at upper levels are best installed before walls and boards at lower levels, to avoid potential damage in case a piece of material or equipment is accidentally dislodged during operations. Boards with dissimilar edge profiles should not be used adjacent to each other.

There are two common ways in which plasterboards can be fastened: **mechanically** and with **adhesive**; **finishing** procedures are also described.

Mechanical Fastening. Boards can be installed using nails, heavy-duty staples, or screws, set out 180 mm or 7 in. apart on walls and 200 mm or 8 in. apart on ceilings; if double nailing is used, set nails 300 mm or 12 in. apart, with the second nail 50 mm or 2 in. from the first nail.

Fastenings along edges of boards should be not less than 10 mm or ³/₈ in. and not more than 13 mm or ¹/₂ in. from the edge. Fastening should start in the center of each board and work out toward the edges.

(a) Applying compound

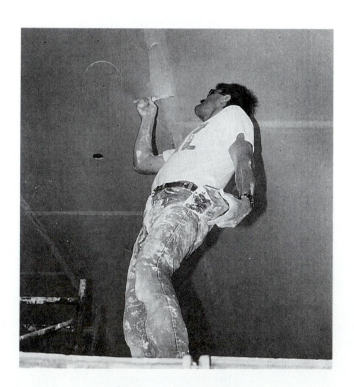

(b) Troweling compound

Finishing Joints

The finishing compound is liberally applied to completely cover the taped joints, then immediately smoothed over with a broad steel trowel and left to cure for a few hours. (UBC Architecture)

(a) Pencil

(b) Round

(c) Splay

(a) Square

Metal corner strip

Figure 3   Typical Configurations of Applied Plasterboard

The tops of all nails, staples, and screws should be recessed slightly below the surface of the board.

Boards can also be installed using metal clips made for this purpose; some systems permit the edges of boards to "float," thus accommodating the movement of supports to which they are attached.

Adhesive Fastening. Boards can be installed using glue specially made for this purpose. A continuous bead of glue, having a cross-sectional area of at least 6 mm or $^1/_4$ in., is applied by caulk gun to the stud or joist frame members, either in a straight line on intermediate members or in a long, lazy S-curve on members where the edges of two adjoining drywall sheets are to be fastened. When the boards are firmly pressed against the glue beads, the beads will compress to one quarter of their thickness and four times their width. Temporary nailing or bracing may be necessary until the adhesive has properly cured.

Finishing. There are four elements in finishing plasterboard systems:

1. Metal trim is measured, cut to length with shears or saws, and secured with galvanized nails or staples, using a J-profile bead at open edges and an L-profile bead at external corners.

2. At joints, a layer of joint compound is applied, joint tape embedded along the central axis of the seam, and more compound applied to fill the recessed joint up to the plane of the board on either side. When dry, a second coat of compound is applied, feathering the edges out over the surfaces of the adjacent boards; in top-quality work, a third application of compound may be made beyond the second one. The process may be done by hand or by machine.

At internal corners, the process is similar, except that the tape is folded along its longitudinal axis before installation. At plain butt joints, the ends (or edges) of the boards adjacent to the joint can be cut with a sharp utility knife to form a small "vee" joint running the width of the board and extending about 6 mm or $^1/_4$ in. on each side of the joint; the resulting valley is finished as before.

3. A small amount of joint filler is spread by trowel over nailheads and screwheads, with excess struck off flush with the surface of the board.

4. After the compound has cured, the surfaces are lightly sanded as necessary to remove any rough imperfections, taking care not to sand so hard as to disturb the natural nap of the plasterboard paper face.

Some general aspects of finishing are shown in Figure 4.

5.3 Precautions

In work associated with this trade, there are some commonsense admonitions about taking care when handling heavy loads, using sharp or powered tools, and working off scaffolding. Protective toe coverings, eye shields, and hard hats are recommended.

Because gypsum plasterboards are relatively fragile, they require care in handling. Boards are packaged in pairs, with the two fine paper sides face to face. Protective bindings prevent damage to the edges of boards. Boards and accessories should be stored in cool, dry, secure locations. Boards should be stored flat; boards stored vertically on edge or end should be secured from falling or blowing over.

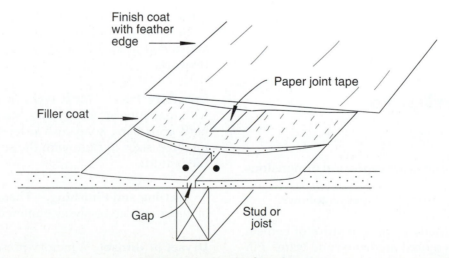

Finish coat with feather edge

Paper joint tape

Filler coat

Gap

Stud or joist

Figure 4 Details of Finishing

Section 09–300
Ceramic Tile Work

1.0 Introduction

1.1 General Issues

The term *ceramic tile work* used in this context generally refers to a durable finish covering on floors or walls consisting of a series of relatively small ceramic, clay, or glass units arranged in (usually) regular patterns. Such units are available in an almost infinite variety of styles, depending on material composition, manufacturing process, type of finish, and degree of kiln firing.

1.2 Design Aspects

Ceramic tiles can be installed wherever their characteristics of durability, ease of cleaning, resistance to moisture, and pleasant appearance may serve the function of the room or space. Because of its rigidity, tilework should not be installed in locations subject to significant structural movement, such as on wood floors in old buildings.

1.3 Related Work

Work closely connected to this section is described in the following sections, to which reference should be made:

03–300 Cast-in-Place Concrete

06–100 Rough Carpentry

09–100 Metal Support Systems

09–250 Gypsum Plasterboard Systems

2.0 Products

2.1 Materials

The main considerations are **types** and **dimensions**.

Types. There are five main types as follows:

1. **Cement tiles.** Made from a mixture of cement, fine aggregate, colored pigments, and water. Finishes may be plain, textured, or polished.

2. **Ceramic tiles.** Made from specially selected clays, formed into thin biscuits by extrusion, molding, or pressing, then fired in kilns. Available white or colored, patterned or plain, glazed or unglazed, with or without setting nibs.

3. **Clay pavers.** Similar to quarry tiles, but usually thicker.

4. **Mosaic tiles.** Similar to ceramic and quarry tiles, but much smaller. There are three common forms: glass, porcelain, and clay, all of which are usually mounted on mat or paper backs for ease of handling and installation.

5. **Quarry tiles.** Made from natural clays or shales, usually in natural earth tones of browns, reds, or grays. They are usually quite thin and are made by being either extruded or pressed, fired, then machined.

Dimensions. All types of tiles are made in a large variety of sizes, shapes, and thicknesses. The most common shape is square or rectangular, and the most common sizes are shown in Table 1. Ceramic and mosaic tiles are usually between 6 mm or $1/4$ in. and 8 mm or $5/16$ in. thick. Clay and quarry tiles are more commonly manufactured to be between 8 mm or $5/16$ in. and 13 mm or $1/2$ in. thick. Cement tiles are made in 19-mm or $3/4$-in. and 32 mm or $1 1/4$-in. thicknesses.

2.2 Accessories

These consist of a variety of specialty tiles intended to be used in conjunction with the tiles described above and other materials used to set or finish the tilework.

Specialty Tiles. Most types of tiles are produced with matching accessory tiles, such as tile edge trim, bath grab bars, soap dish inserts, and the like, in modular sizes to fit in with the surrounding general tile pattern.

Setting and Finishing. There are several groups of materials commonly encountered in these processes:

Dryset or thinset. A factory-premixed composition of latex or acrylic fluids and cement, sand, and a

Table 1
Typical Sizes of Commonly Used Tiles

Tile Type	Common Sizes	
	mm	in.
Cement	230 × 230	9 × 9
	300 × 300	12 × 12
Ceramic	100 × 100	$4^1/_4 \times 4^1/_4$
	150 × 150	6 × 6
Clay	100 × 100	4 × 4
	100 × 200	4 × 8
Mosaic	25 × 25	1 × 1
	25 × 50	1 × 2
Quarry	150 × 150	6 × 6
	230 × 230	9 × 9

bonding agent, used to glue tiles to floors and walls in heavy-duty applications.

Grout. Factory-premixed grout powders, some containing varying proportions of fine sand. It is mixed with water to form a thick paste, used to fill joints between tiles.

Mastic. A factory-premixed synthetic adhesive, used to glue tiles to walls in light-duty applications.

Mortar. A site-prepared mixture of cement, fine sand, lime, and water, sometimes with an epoxy or latex bonding agent added, used to form a solid bed for floor and wall tiles in heavy-duty applications.

Sealants. A variety of synthetic proprietary products intended to inhibit fungal growth in damp or humid applications.

Water. Fresh, cool, and potable.

3.0 Construction Aids

3.1 Equipment

Equipment used by this trade is limited in scope:

Concrete mixer. A motorized six-sack machine, used to mix mortar for bedding.

Cutter. An industrial diamond-edged cutting machine to score and snap tiles along straight lines.

Placement grid. A metal frame with handles, used to simplify setout and regular placement of tiles on walls or floors.

3.2 Tools

The tools are those of the tilesetter:

Drills. Power or manually operated, with toughened bits used for boring holes through tiles.

Level. A carpenter's level, used to determine lines and planes of tilework.

Nippers. Carbide-tipped sharp pliers used for working irregular shapes at edges of tiles.

(a) Tile products

(b) Mortar bedding

Stockpiling
Some ceramic tile products are individually packaged; others come preassembled on backing materials for accurate installation. Various mortars and grouts are available in bulk or by the bag. (UBC Architecture)

Section 09–300   Ceramic Tile Work

457

(a) Cutting tile

(b) Installing floor tile

Floor Tile
Subfloors are swept clean and damp-mopped; tile centers and joint lines are laid out; perimeter joints and special cutting and fitting at recesses and projections are considered. (UBC Architecture)

Sponges. Organic or plastic type, used to remove minor spillage of grout or adhesive from tile surfaces.

Straightedge. A long, stiff, wooden or metal bar, having one edge planed true to line, used to establish straight lines or planes.

Trowels. Tilesetters use as many as six different types of trowels, some with square, flat, or notched edges for spreading mortars and adhesives, and some made of foam or rubber for spreading grout.

4.0 Production

4.1 Crew Configuration

A typical crew consists of one tilesetter and two helpers on simple projects. On more complex work, two tilesetters and one helper might be better. On large jobs, two or more crews might be utilized.

4.2 Productivity

Productivity will vary, depending on the size of the job, whether work is being done on floors or walls, whether the crew is installing tiles or mosaics, and

the nature of the base fastening, whether of adhesive, dryset, or mortar. Some representative hourly figures for completed dryset applications are about 1.5 m² or 15 ft.² for work on floors and about 1 m² or 10 ft.² for work on walls. These factors can be increased by about 15 percent for adhesive applications and decreased by about 30 percent for mortar bed applications. Trim tiling at coves and bases can be installed at the rate of about 5 m or 15 ft. per hour, while unit accessories such as soap dishes take about 30 minutes each to locate and install, with about another 5 minutes for a tilesetter to come back and check the installation later.

5.0 Procedures

5.1 Preparation

Surface Preparation. Surfaces to receive tiling of any sort should be solid, true to plane or curve, fairly smooth though not polished, and free from oil, paint, wax, grease, or debris. By applying a long straightedge to surfaces, high and low spots can be located; high spots can be ground off or sanded level and low spots can be filled with material compatible with the adhesive proposed for the tilework. Con-

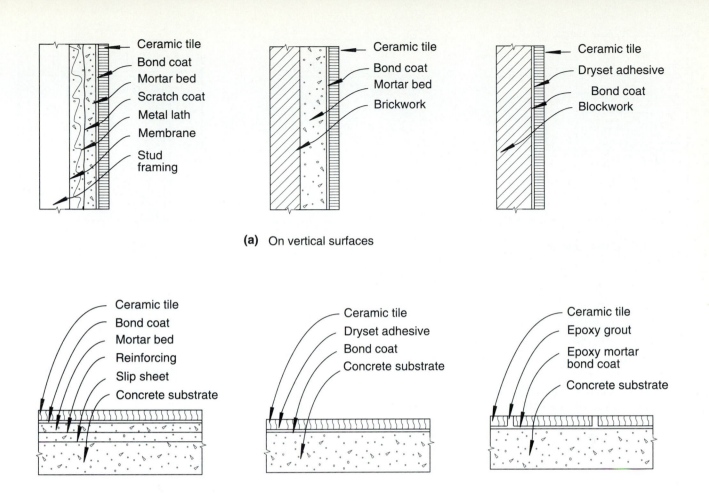

(a) On vertical surfaces

(b) On horizontal surfaces

Figure 1 Typical Configurations of Tile Application

crete surfaces should be properly cured; wood surfaces should be cleaned and slightly dampened; metal lath surfaces should be neatly overlapped at edges and securely fastened in position. Some typical details are shown in Figure 1.

In renovation work, one solution for unsuitable surfaces is to secure a thin plywood or particleboard underlay over the existing surface before installing adhesives for tilework. On old stripwood floors, a layer of felt may be glued down to serve the same purpose, provided care is taken to eliminate any air pockets under the felt.

Layout.   Measure the area to be tiled to determine its central axes. Snap a chalk-line to mark the axes. Tiles can be laid at either 90 or 45 degrees to the axis. For 90-degree layouts, adjust the axes lines to ensure that border tiles will be at least half a tile in width. Some layouts are shown in Figure 2.

For both 90- and 45-degree layouts, the installation procedure is the same. Reference lines are laid out on the substrate, and the adhesive or mortar is spread in limited areas (taking care not to obliterate the guide lines).

5.2 Process

In tile installation, there is a choice of **methods,** a **technique** to be used with each, and a finishing process called **grouting.**

Method.   There are primarily three methods used to install tiles on walls or floors:

1. **Adhesive** is spread on the substrate and on the back of the tiles by smooth-edge trowel and allowed to cure. Then tiles are installed by simply pressing them in order against the prepared substrate.

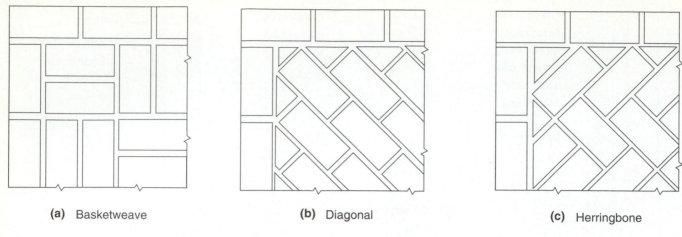

(a) Basketweave   (b) Diagonal   (c) Herringbone

Figure 2 Typical Floor Tile Layouts

2. **Dryset** (or thinset) is spread on the substrate surface by notched trowel, and the tiles are then pressed into the dryset before it cures.

3. **Mortar** is prepared, spread over the substrate after treatment with a chemical bonding agent where necessary, screeded to required levels, and allowed to cure to a point just before its initial set. Tiles are lightly dampened and then evenly pressed into the surface of the mortar bed.

No matter which method is used, tile trim pieces are installed as follows: Required lengths are measured, the product is cut as necessary, mortar or adhesive is applied, and the pieces are pressed into position, with corner accessories where necessary.

Technique. In each method, the first of the field tiles are carefully laid along the layout lines on the adhesive or mortar bed, and the process is repeated

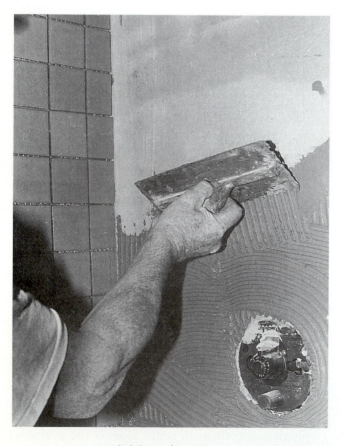

(a) Spreading mortar

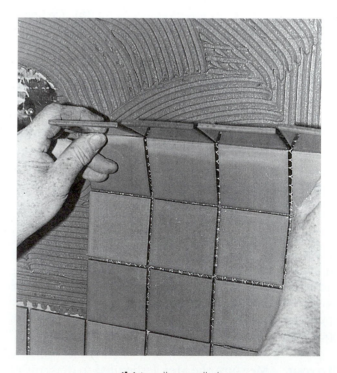

(b) Installing wall tile

Wall Tile

Setting bed mortar is applied by serrated trowel to prepared wall surfaces. Tile mats are raised by hand into position and lightly tapped to embed tile backing into mortar bed. (UBC Architecture)

(a) At entrance

Custom Work
Many public and private buildings have certain areas of floors or walls finished with marble or other specialized units. Detailed design layout drawings are often prepared in advance. (UBC Architecture)

(b) On stairs

until the central field is complete. Then the border tiles are scribed, cut, tested for size, and placed in position. The area is now ready for grouting. If the area perimeter line is unusually irregular, as may occur in a bathtub or shower recess, its outline can be scribed onto a piece of felt or paper and then the line can be transferred to the tiles to be cut. Tiles with integral setting nibs are automatically aligned in position. Tiles without nibs require to have small temporary cardboard or vinyl spacers placed during setting to establish uniform joint lines; these are withdrawn before grouting.

In every case, tiles and trim should not be pressed into the bedding or adhesive so firmly that excess material is squeezed up into the joint, thus displacing some grout space. Because there is a curing time of several hours with all the glues, mastics, and mortars used for this work, it is a fairly easy task to make minor final adjustments to spacing or cuttings on tiles after their initial placement. This is frequently necessary, as tiles have to be removed to cut out circular openings for plumbing pipes and the like and then replaced.

Grouting. Grout mix is evenly spread over the fixed tile surface using a soft foam trowel or rubber

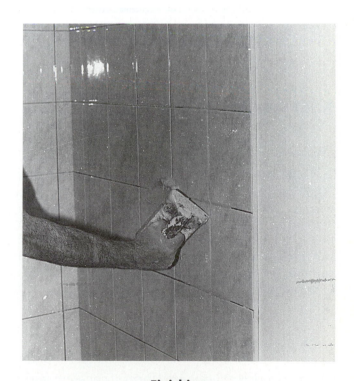

Finishing
After tile or marble units are securely positioned, grout is spread to fill the joints, lightly struck off at an angle, then neatly worked in with a damp cloth, and finally wiped clean. (UBC Architecture)

squeegee, taking care to uniformly fill all the joints between the tile pieces. Excess grout is immediately removed by wiping or sponging, and the installation is then allowed to cure for several hours. Loose tiles can be discovered by lightly tapping on the surfaces, which will produce a hollow sound; they should be removed and reglued. Later, the tilesetter returns to wipe down grouted areas with a sponge, dampened with clean water, to remove grout residue from tiled surfaces. A narrow margin trowel, a knife, or a sharp screwdriver may be used to loosen minor accumulations of grout, provided care is taken not to scratch the tile or grouted joint surfaces.

5.3 Precautions

The tile materials are quite brittle and fragile; they should therefore be handled carefully to avoid accidental breakage. They are also usually factory finished with a glaze or other finely textured surface; care should be taken not to damage or disfigure units. The tiles are best left in their delivery packages until close to the time of actual installation. Precautions normal to the handling and application of mor-

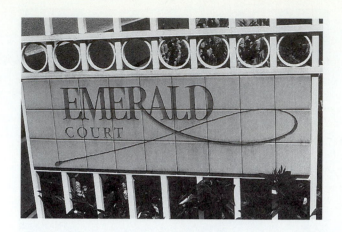

Custom Orders
If a project is large enough, the cost of having some custom-made decorative tiles is negligible, and they can add interest and distinction to otherwise utilitarian building elements. (UBC Architecture)

tars, adhesives, and fillers should also be observed to avoid deterioration or other harm before or after installation or application. Tilesetters usually wear protective kneepads when installing floor tiles.

Section 09–400 Terrazzo Work

1.0 Introduction

1.1 General Issues

The word *terrazzo* is Italian in origin and means a terrace or balcony. The root of the word is *terra*, Latin for earth. In English, this word means a form of concrete topping, widely used as a floor finish in the public areas of institutional buildings, such as courthouses and museums, swimming pools and commercial kitchens, and suburban shopping malls for decorative effect and durable service.

1.2 Design Aspects

Terrazzo work is a specialized form of concrete work. Like concrete, the primary ingredients of terrazzo consist of cement, sand, water, and aggregate. Unlike concrete, the aggregate is usually made of colored

marble or quartz chips instead of plain gravel or granite chips, and the surface of the finished product is ground and polished. One other distinction from ordinary concrete topping is that in terrazzo, a synthetic resin may be substituted for the cement. Terrazzo can be either poured in place or precast, with a smooth finish, a nonslip finish, or a sparkproof finish. Figure 1 shows a typical installation.

The overall quality of work of this trade is largely influenced by recommendations of the National Terrazzo and Mosaic Association (NTMA). The color and pattern of terrazzo finishes are dictated by the selection and proportions of matrix and aggregate ingredients. The NTMA has produced a series of numbered colored photographic plates representing the probable appearance of selected composite finishes, depending on ingredients and ratios, intended to assist designers in making their selection. It might be noted that terrazzo topping is not recommended for areas subject to spills of strong acid or alkaline solutions.

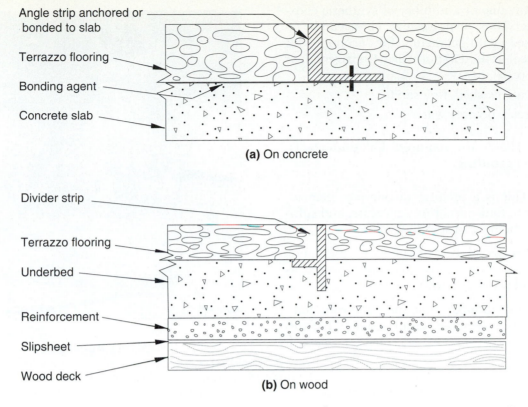

Angle strip anchored or bonded to slab

Terrazzo flooring

Bonding agent

Concrete slab

(a) On concrete

Divider strip

Terrazzo flooring

Underbed

Reinforcement

Slipsheet

Wood deck

(b) On wood

Figure 1 Terrazzo Installation

1.3 Related Work

Work closely connected to this section is described in the following section, to which reference should be made:

03–300 Cast-in-Place Concrete

2.0 Products

2.1 Materials

Materials can be considered under three headings:

Ingredients. These consist of **cement, aggregates,** and **other materials.**

Cement. Both normal Portland and white cements are used; for specific descriptions, see Section 03–300, Part 2.1.

Aggregates. Virtually all types of calcareous stone are used, such as marbles and quartzites, usually selected on the basis of aesthetic appeal. Chip sizes shown in Table 1 are established by the NTMA.

Other materials. These include the following:

1. **Carbon black.** In fine powder form, used to produce an electrically conductive topping.

2. **Carborundum.** In fine granule form, used to produce a nonslip finish.

3. **Color pigments.** Limeproof, nonfading, mineral-based types.

Table 1
TERRAZZO PARTICLE SIZES

Chip #	Size	
	mm	in.
0	4	0.07
1	7	0.13
2	10	0.25
3	13	0.38
4	16	0.50
5	19	0.63
6	22	0.75
7	25	0.88
8	28	1.00

4. **Resins.** Any one of a number of synthetic epoxies, polyacrylates, or polyesters. These can be either mixed with cement (for economy or appearance) or used in pure form (for strength or chemical resistance).

5. **Sand.** Clean, washed, fine sand.

6. **Water.** Fresh, potable water.

Mixes. These are required for **underbeds, toppings,** and **grouting.**

Underbed. This is a mixture of one part cement, two parts sand, four parts fine aggregate, and sufficient water to achieve proper hydration.

Topping. This is a mixture of one part cement, two parts selected terrazzo chips, coloring pigments as necessary, and water as above.

Grouting. This is a mixture of one part proprietary paste, two parts proprietary grout powder, and sufficient water to activate chemical reaction between the ingredients.

Forms. Terrazzo can be made in any one of at least six types:

1. **Plain** terrazzo consists of a homogeneous mixture of the ingredients, cured and then ground smooth as described later.

2. **Conductive** terrazzo is the same as plain terrazzo, except that it has electrically conductive acetylene carbon black added to the matrix, and the topping is usually applied more thinly than plain (10 mm or $3/8$ in. instead of 13 mm or $1/2$ in.).

3. **Mosaic** terrazzo consists of a bed or matrix into which small pieces of glass, pottery, or colored stone are embedded and tamped flat.

4. **Resilient** terrazzo consists of plain terrazzo with a rubber latex base added to the matrix. Although having some marine applications, it is not often used in buildings.

5. **Rustic** terrazzo is identical to plain terrazzo, except that it is not ground smooth.

6. **Venetian** terrazzo involves the placement of the marble chip aggregates manually into the surface of the underbed matrix. Because of the high labor cost, it is not common in North America.

2.2 Accessories

These fall into three categories:

1. **Divider strips.** These are usually made from bronze, colored hard vinyl plastic, or white zinc

Mixing Aggregates
Selected aggregates are provided in the correct proportions and then mixed by hand or machine to produce the desired visual appearance in the finished work. (UBC Architecture)

Spreading Terrazzo
The terrazzo base is placed and troweled into position between pre-set metal or plastic divider rails. These rails act as screeds during installation and as dividers in the finished work. (UBC Architecture)

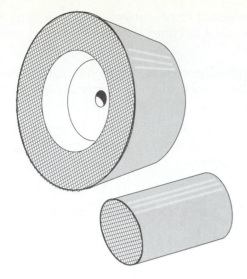

(a) Grinding stones

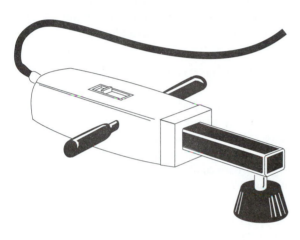

(b) Grinding machine

Figure 2   Terrazzo Equipment

3.0 Construction Aids

3.1 Equipment

As this work is similar to concrete work, most of the equipment (such as concrete mixers, barrows, and chutes) is as described in Section 03–300. The following specialized equipment is also used:

Grinding machine. There are two basic types: handheld single disc and floor-operated double disc. Depending on size, four to eight grinding stones can be mounted on each disc.

Grinding stones. There are two basic grades: rough (having a grit size between #24 and #46) and fine (having a grit size between #80 and #120). There are also two types, shown in Figure 2.

Vacuum cleaner. The heavy-duty, wet-and-dry, industrial type is used.

Drill mixer. This is a $1/2$-horsepower, rotary-blade type.

Spreading Aggregates
Mixed aggregates are evenly cast by hand and simultaneously worked by trowel into the terrazzo mortar bed, taking care to distribute the topping mix into corners and around projections. (UBC Architecture)

alloy. Though once popular, pure brass and half-hard brass are now seldom used for this purpose. Strips are usually 3 mm or $1/8$ in. thick and 32 mm or $1\frac{1}{4}$ in. tall, although thicker and taller strips are available. They are available in a variety of shapes for various purposes; some typical profiles are shown later in Figure 3.

2. **Reinforcement.** This is a 14-gauge galvanized wire netting having a 50-mm or 2-in. mesh; sometimes referred to as "chicken netting."

3. **Underlay.** This is an asphalt-impregnated, heavy-duty kraft paper, used as a separation sheet.

3.2 Tools

The tools are similar to those of the concrete finisher (Section 03–350) and the plasterer (Section 09–200):

Brooms. Used to sweep up slurry and debris.

Measures. Metal vessels used to proportion mixes of matrices, grouts, and sealers.

Pails. Used to transport water and to rinse tools and cloths.

(a) Grinding machine

(b) Washing surfaces

Finishing

After the terrazzo mix has been leveled and properly cured, the surface is lightly ground by hand-held or wheeled grinders, then it is pressure washed and scrubbed with stiff brooms. (UBC Architecture)

Squeegees. Hard rubber strips on long wooden poles, used to control the flow of water around the floor.

Straightedges. Long wooden or metal boards with handles, used to align dividers and screed tops of terrazzo panels.

Trowels. Small steel blades of various shapes with handles, used to spread and consolidate underbeds and toppings.

4.0 Production

4.1 Crew Configuration

A typical terrazzo crew consists of two journeymen and two helpers, with one journeyman acting as foreman. Larger projects might use an additional journeyman and helper. It is not usual to employ more than one crew on a project.

4.2 Productivity

In typical commercial or institutional buildings having fairly large unobstructed areas of plain terrazzo topping, a good terrazzo crew should install about 40 m² or 400 ft.² of terrazzo laid in square panels having 600-mm or 24-in. sides, or 50 m² or 500 ft.² in square panels, having 1,200-mm or 48-in. sides. For smaller obstructed areas or areas with more complex divider patterns, a decrease in productivity up to 25 percent may be expected.

Each journeyman should be able to grind about 10 m² or 100 ft.² of plain terrazzo topping per working day. Terrazzo curbs can be installed at the rate of 3 m or 10 ft. per hour and can be finished at about the same rate.

5.0 Procedures

5.1 Preparation

The subfloor must be free of dust, dirt, loose particles, openings, sharp ridges, paint, oil, grease, or wax. For best results, the subfloor should also be properly pitched for natural drainage. The elevation at the top of the subfloor should be about 45 mm or 1³/₄ in. below the proposed elevation of the top of the finished terrazzo topping.

Concrete floors should be properly cured, slightly roughened, and lightly dampened. If necessary, shallow saw cuts may be made to permit slight thermal movement of the concrete substrate without cracking the topping. Metal floors should be free of bond-inhibiting agents, such as smooth paint finishes. Wood floors should be covered with a membrane impervious to moisture. All of this preparatory work is usually done by persons other than the terrazzo crew.

5.2 Process

There are four distinct parts to the process of laying terrazzo floor systems: **underbeds, dividers, topping,** and **finishing.**

Underbeds.   There are two methods used to install underbeds for terrazzo toppings:

1. Bonded, where little or no structural movement is anticipated. The concrete substrate is first covered with a light wash of fine cement slurry or a proprietary bonding agent made for the purpose. Next, a plain concrete underbed (about 30 mm or $1^{1}/_{8}$ in. thick) is uniformly poured over the substrate and screeded level. Into this bed, the divider strips are placed according to their pattern, predetermined as described below, so that the tops of the strips will be coincident with the elevation proposed for the top of the finished floor. The system is now ready to receive the topping.

   2. Separated, where there may be significant structural movement. There are two methods used to separate terrazzo applications from their subfloors in such situations:

  a. Sand cushion. On concrete substrates, a thin bed of clean sand (about 6 mm or $^{1}/_{4}$ in. thick) is uniformly placed over the subfloor and then covered with building paper, carefully laid so as not to disturb the sand. Wire net reinforcement is then laid on top of the paper.

  b. Slip sheet. On wood, building paper is neatly stapled to the subfloor, then wire net reinforcement is stapled on top of the paper.

   The substrate is then ready for the underbed to be poured as described above.

Dividers.   Divider strips can be considered under two headings:

Purposes

1. They permit large areas of topping to be interrupted to minimize the possibility of cracking due to structural movement.
2. They permit ornamental patterns to be introduced into the system.

3. They act as screeds to establish thickness of topping and uniformity of finished plane.

Layout

1. They should be located over points or lines of probable stress or movement in the substrate.
2. They should be continuous to the outside edges of finished areas.
3. They should present a pleasing and usually grid-like symmetrical pattern. Refer to Figure 3 for typical layouts.

   For cement-based terrazzo, in areas of heavy traffic, the dividers should establish rectangular panels having sides not exceeding 600 mm or 24 in., whereas in light traffic areas, panels may have sides up to 1,200 mm or 48 in. For resin-based terrazzo, panels may have sides up to 10 m or 30 ft. in length, regardless of traffic conditions.

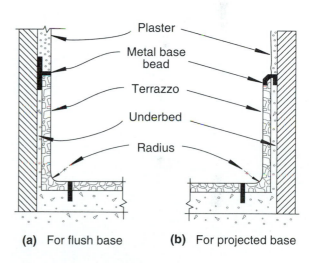

(a) For flush base   **(b)** For projected base

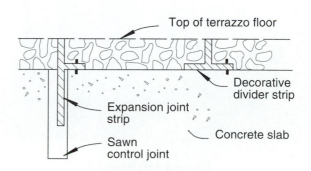

(c) Floor applications

Figure 3 Layout of Dividers

Topping. The surface of the underbed should be lightly dampened and cleaned free of dust, dirt, and debris. While the underbed is still green (not fully cured), its surface should be lightly broomed, and then the topping matrix (about 13 mm or ½ in. thick) is placed, screeded level with the tops of the divider strips, and allowed to cure to the point where it can be walked upon without damage. Grout is then applied by trowel to fill any minor pinholes or voids, and the whole system is allowed to cure for two or three days, depending on the weather.

Finishing. There are two types of finish: **ground** and **unground.**

Ground

Ground finish involves grinding the surface of the terrazzo system by machine. There are two methods of grinding:

1. In **dry** grinding, the first cut is made using a grinding machine fitted with rough-grade stones, to produce a floor showing about 65 percent of the aggregate chips and about 90 percent of the tops of the divider strips. The second cut is made using fine-grade stones, to produce a floor showing about 70 percent of chips and 100 percent of divider tops. As considerable dust is generated by dry grinding, areas being treated should be carefully sealed off from the rest of the building.

2. In **wet** grinding, areas to be ground are flooded with water, with additional water applied to the process by the grinding machine as it operates, creating a slurry or paste on top of the surface as work proceeds. This slurry is removed by wet-vacuuming; it should not be allowed to dry onto the surface of the topping. To prevent water damage to toppings or adjacent areas, water should be applied only where work is about to commence or is already underway.

After grinding is complete, grout is again worked over the surface with a trowel, scraped off, and allowed to cure for two days. A third cut is made using fine-grade stones, just enough to remove excess grout to expose the color and pattern of the topping. Defective spots are regrouted and reground. The floor is then rinsed, vacuumed, sealed with three coats of a clear silicone or polyurethane sealer, and is then ready for use.

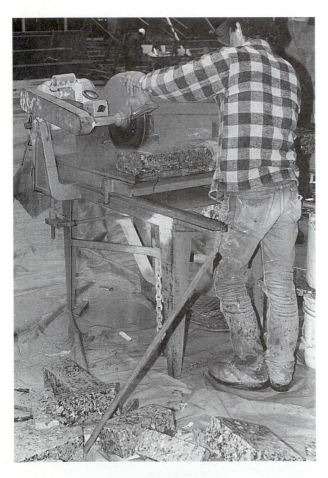

Precast Terrazzo
Terrazzo can be precast into large or small blocks to create desired decorative effects in courtyards and plazas. The blocks are cut with a carborundum masonry saw to site-specific shapes. (UBC Architecture)

Installation
The precast, prepolished, and precut terrazzo units are placed on a mortar bed, set to proper planes by lightly tapping with a wooden trowel, and the joints are grouted and cleaned off. (UBC Architecture)

Unground

Unground finish involves washing the rough topping surface with a dilute solution of muriatic (hydrochloric) acid, rinsing with clean water, stiff-brooming the surface to disclose the color and texture of the aggregate granules, and rinsing again with water to which a mild detergent may be added. The surface is then wet-vacuumed to remove water and any loose particles still lodged in minute crevices in the topping.

Curbs. The installation of curbs or coved bases is essentially identical to that of topping. A thin (6-mm or 1/4-in.) layer of grout is applied to the vertical substrate surface and allowed to cure. A terrazzo mix, slightly drier than that used for floors, is troweled on and left to cure. Grinding is done by machine where possible, by hand in areas not accessible to the machine. Sealing and finishing proceed as for floor toppings.

5.3 Precautions

The only regulations of significance applying to terrazzo installations relate to conductive toppings, intended for use in hospitals or other buildings where flammable gases or electrical sparks may cause problems. In such installations, determination of the conductivity characteristics of the finished floor system must be made, with copies of reports furnished to the owner, the contractor, and the supplier of the topping materials.

Although terrazzo work is not particularly hazardous, there is always risk of flying particles, considerable dust and noise, and slippery surfaces underfoot, so that proper footwear, protective clothing, eye goggles, ear plugs, and breathing masks are recommended. Furthermore, the grinding equipment used is capable of causing injury if improperly assembled or handled.

Section 09-500
Acoustical Treatments

1.0 Introduction

1.1 General Issues

Noise is a sure sign of activity. Unwanted noise can also be a source of irritation and distraction. As the physiological and psychological effects of exposure to noise become better understood, so greater attention is being paid by the owners, designers, and occupants of buildings to the means and methods of controlling noise, not only to mask, suppress, or eliminate unwanted noise, but also to propagate and enhance desirable sound transmission.

This sector of the construction industry has responded to the challenge of noise by producing a very large variety and range of proprietary products and systems for use in the solution of acoustical problems in buildings. It is neither practical nor necessary to describe all of these products and systems in detail, as there are some general characteristics of all of them that can be fairly quickly reviewed and easily understood, sufficient for the purpose of this book.

1.2 Design Aspects

There are at least four issues (among others) to consider with regard to the control of sound energy in buildings:

1. **Location** of the building or parts of it to be remote from known and objectionable sound sources, such as traffic outside the building.

2. **Control** of noise sources, such as motors, fans, lights, moving equipment, and the like inside the building.

3. **Prevention** of transmission of sound energy through the frame, ductwork, or openings of the building.

4. **Absorption** of sound energy within each part of the building by the adroit selection and installation of appropriate materials.

These general issues are illustrated in Figure 1.

To prevent the passage of sound through a floor, wall, or ceiling system, components having suffi-

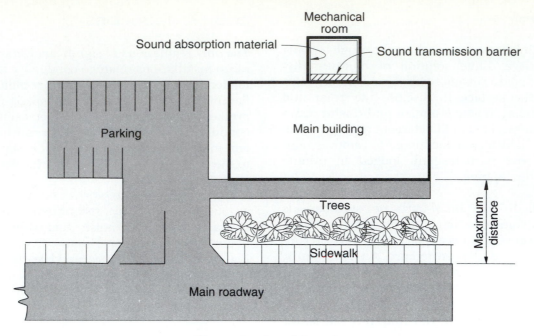

Figure 1 Sound Control

cient mass or resilience must be incorporated into the system to absorb the sound energy. To control sound energy within a confined space, components having soft and absorptive properties have to be strategically positioned in relationship to hard impervious surfaces.

Of the four issues mentioned above, only the last is considered in this section. Within that category, only materials permanently positioned in buildings for acoustical purposes are included. The use of heavy drapes, stuffed furniture, and movable acoustic baffles or absorption clouds such as encountered in theaters and auditoriums is excluded.

1.3 Related Work

Work closely connected to this section is described in the following sections, to which reference should be made:

06–100   Rough Carpentry

09–100   Metal Support Systems

2.0 Products

2.1 Materials

These can be grouped under two headings: **tiles and panels** which are generally exposed to view and **sheets and batts** which are generally concealed

from view. Consideration should be given to acoustical characteristics, modular dimensions, fire resistance, potential smoke generation, thickness, weight, and (for exposed products) light reflectance, before final selection.

Tiles and Panels

Tiles and panels usually have a perforated, textured, or fissured surface beneath a factory-applied finish of white or light-colored reflective paint. Edges of tiles or panels may be plain butt, beveled, tongue-and-groove, kerfed, or otherwise profiled. They are manufactured in either square or rectangular shapes, usually in combinations of modular dimensions ranging from 30 cm or 12 in. up to 120 cm or 48 in.

1. Acoustic **tiles** are usually made of either blown-slag mineral fiber, cellulose cane fiber, or fine glass fiber, mixed with a resin binder, compressed and cut to standard sizes.
2. **Panels** consist of a lightweight, shallow, aluminum or steel pan, perforated to permit sound to pass, and filled with an absorbent mineral, cellulose, or glass fiber core.

Sheets and Batts

1. One common **sheet** material used for acoustical purposes is thin sheet lead, weighing about 9 kg/m² or 2 lb./ft.² (approximately 1 mm or

$^1/_{32}$ in. thick), manufactured into sheets 2.4 × 6 m or 8 × 20 ft., and draped from battens to absorb sound energy. Sheets of less than half this weight are used for laminations on gypsum plasterboard or in door cores, while sheets up to 25 mm or 1 in. thick are used for vibration absorption pads under steel column bases.

2. Acoustic **batts** are made from either semistiff mineral wool or soft glass fiber wool in various thicknesses, ranging from 50 mm or 2 in. up to 150 mm or 6 in., and usually in standard-width rolls 400 mm or 16 in. wide and 6 m or 20 ft. long. Unlike batts made for thermal insulation, acoustic batts are not enclosed in paper.

2.2 Accessories

Acoustic materials are either fastened with adhesive to a solid surface or they are inserted into a prepared wood or metal frame. Accordingly, consideration of the accessories associated with the materials are so classified.

Adhesives. These are always as recommended by the manufacturer of the acoustic materials to be glued—often an oleoresin, synthetic rubber, or asphalt-based type. See Section 06–050 for further detail.

Framing. These components are usually made in long lengths of either extruded or shaped sheet aluminum having either a C, H, L, T, or Z cross-sectional profile, depending on the manufacturer and the proposed installation arrangement. Parts exposed to view can have a factory-applied paint or vinyl finish.

Related Components. A large assortment of nails, screws, staples, splines, and special clips are also utilized by the work of this trade. See Section 05–050 for further detail.

3.0 Construction Aids

3.1 Equipment

The following equipment is of particular concern to the work of this trade:

Laser transit. This is a device that emits a narrow beam of coherent (i.e, very sharply "focused") light; it is set on a tripod, leveled, activated, and then rotated through 360 degrees. The point where the light strikes the surrounding areas is marked and can then be used as a datum for other measurements.

Scaffolding. A movable, self-braced scaffold or powered scissor-lift platform is used to facilitate access of workers, equipment, and materials to ceiling levels.

3.2 Tools

The tools used for this work are essentially those of the carpenter and metalworker, plus the following:

Powder-activated gun. A device for driving or firing fastening pins or hooks into wood or concrete substrates.

Tin-snips. (also called **aviation shears**). A lightweight plier-like device, capable of cutting through plastic trim and thin sheet metals.

4.0 Production

4.1 Crew Configuration

A typical crew consists of one or two mechanics and a helper. On large projects, two or more crews might

Acoustic Plaster
This common finish is sprayed onto prepared gypsum board ceiling soffits, partly to provide some acoustical absorption, but also to obscure minor imperfections in the boarded ceiling. (UBC Architecture)

Table 1
PRODUCTIVITY FACTORS FOR ACOUSTICAL WORK

Type of Work	Area per Hour	
	m²	ft.²
Soft batts	15	150
Sheet lead	2	20
Tile goods:		
Lay out	10	100
Install	5	50
Panel units:		
Lay out	10	100
Frame	5	50
Install	8	80

Tee-Bar System

This suspended exposed metal system has acoustical tile panels inserted and clipped in place, with cutouts for pot lights, smoke detectors, and sprinkler heads as necessary. (UBC Architecture)

be utilized, with one mechanic working as foreman to oversee the work of each crew.

4.2 Productivity

Productivity naturally varies depending on the nature, quality, and complexity of the work to be done. Figures given in Table 1 are representative of output for work done by experienced crews operating in fairly large, unobstructed, simple areas. For small, obstructed, or complex areas, decrease productivity by up to 50 percent.

5.0 Procedures

5.1 Preparation

Spaces to be finished with an acoustical treatment should be cleared of temporary obstructions and should be clean, dry, warm but not hot, and well lit. Surfaces to be covered should be cured as necessary and should be free of dirt, dust, loose particles, oil, wax, grease, or paint residues.

Consideration should be given to the pattern or appearance proposed for the finished assembly. This can often be achieved by developing a drawing showing a wall elevation or a reflected ceiling plan to indicate the configuration of framing and panels of the acoustical system and their relationship to other fixtures, such as lights, duct vents, and the like, to be incorporated into the wall or ceiling surface.

All framed systems are set out on an essentially rectangular grid pattern, with main runners usually located at 1,200 mm or 48 in. on center along the

longer axis of the area, and cross-channels located at closer modular centers along the shorter axis and clipped into preformed slots at intervals along main runners. Main runners and cross-channels are cut to required lengths, using a hacksaw for aluminum products and tin-snips for steel products.

For Tile Goods. First, check the backing surface or substrate to ensure that it is sound and solid and level or true to plane; grind off or shim out to correct planar defects. To set out a rectangular area for tiles, locate the center lines of the area, offset the starting line by the width of about half a tile, and mark on the substrate with a chalk-line. For butt-edge tiles, start in the center and work out to the edges; for flange-edge tiles, start along one side with cut tiles, and work toward the opposite side. Make allowances for working around preinstalled lights or mechanical fixtures.

For Panel Systems. First, check existing hanger connections to ensure that they are properly secured and correctly located; adjust or add as necessary. Next, determine the room size, and add the width or length of one panel to the dimensions. Locate the center lines in each direction and offset by half the width or length of one panel, to ensure that panels at principal perimeter edges will be at least half wide. Adjust layout patterns as necessary to accommodate electrical, mechanical, and other fixtures. Mark chalk-lines to show the location of the main runners.

For Frame Assemblies. There are three basic systems available: fully concealed, semiexposed, and fully exposed, two of which are shown in Figure 2. Each uses a selection of bars of C, H, L, T, or Z profile, and all can be either hung directly from the building structure or secured by wire clips to a prehung metal suspension system.

In a fully exposed system, all supporting parts of the grid frame (except for hanger wires) are visible on completion. In a fully concealed system, no part of the frame is visible. In a semiexposed system, usually only the main runners in one direction are visible, although various manufacturers have devised different solutions to the problem of concealment.

5.2 Process

There are four distinct installation processes that are encountered in acoustical work.

For Tile Goods. These can be either glued to gypsum or plaster surfaces or stapled or nailed to wood strapping. Gluing is done by applying small dabs of adhesive to the back of each tile and firmly pressing it into position against the substrate. Stapling is done through the concealed flanged edge of tiles specially selected with this feature. Nailing is done

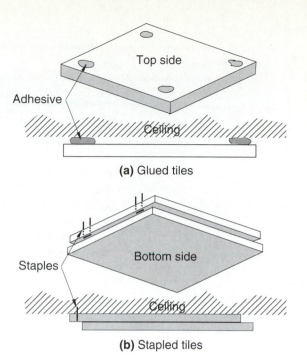

(a) Glued tiles

(b) Stapled tiles

Figure 3   Tile Installation

through the face of tiles specially selected with a prepared nailing hole in each corner. See Figure 3.

For Panel Systems. Acoustic panels are selected on the basis of their suitability for insertion into concealed, semiexposed, or fully exposed framed systems as described above. The panels are manually laid or clipped into position in the preassembled and installed framing system. The frame should be set out to accommodate as many whole modular-sized panels as possible; where necessary, panels are cut to fit at irregular shapes or along perimeters of paneled areas. See Figure 4.

Tiles and panels to be cut should be placed face up, the line to be cut marked but not drawn, a metal straightedge placed on the side of the line to be kept, and a sharp knife quickly and firmly drawn along the straightedge once or twice. The part to be removed can usually be bent or snapped off cleanly. Minor rough edges can be trimmed clean with a sharp knife.

For Soft Batts. Mineral or glass fiber batts are measured, cut to size, and inserted into the spaces between framing members, so as to completely fill all voids in the area to be acoustically treated, but to avoid undue compression of the fiber material. See Figure 5.

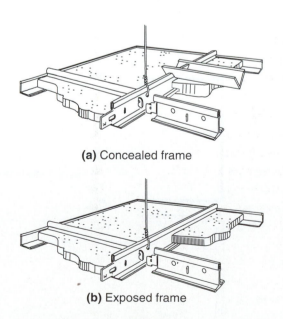

(a) Concealed frame

(b) Exposed frame

Figure 2   Typical Frame Systems

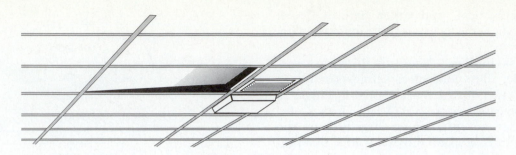

Figure 4 Panel Insertion

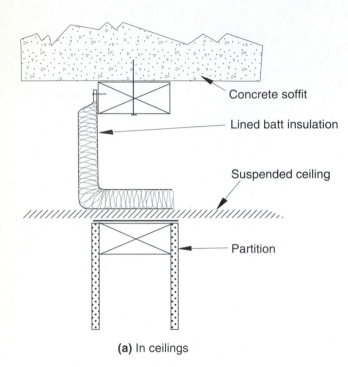

Concrete soffit

Lined batt insulation

Suspended ceiling

Partition

(a) In ceilings

For Lead Sheets. Panels of manageable size are measured and cut, and the tops are lapped and turned over wood or metal battens which are then secured to the substrate or structural frame of the building. Take care to overlap sheets at edges by about 50 mm or 2 in. See Figure 6.

5.3 Precautions

As much of this work is done above eye level, eye protection, hard hats, and good nonslip footwear are recommended for use. The materials and accessories should be properly packaged and stored in clean, dry, cool, secure locations until required for installation.

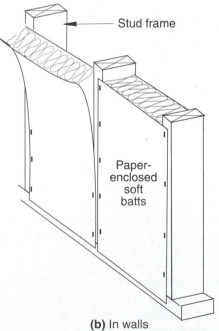

Stud frame

Paper-enclosed soft batts

(b) In walls

Figure 5 Soft Batt Insertion

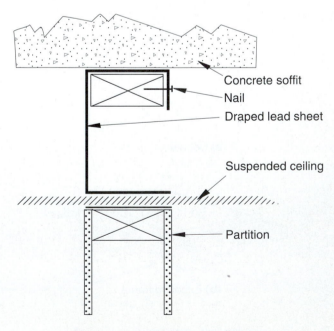

Concrete soffit

Nail

Draped lead sheet

Suspended ceiling

Partition

Figure 6 Lead Sheet Installation

Integrated Systems

Such systems come factory prefabricated to accommodate lighting fixtures, heating and ventilating components, and large drop-in acoustical panels. Grids are coordinated with columns. (UBC Architecture)

Composite Systems

The public areas of many large commercial and institutional buildings utilize composite systems of suspended acoustical tiles and plaster surrounds to create special decorative effects. (UBC Architecture)

Patented Systems

Many highly specialized systems are available, such as this one which shows interlocking linear metal panels used to conceal mechanical and electrical services in a shopping mall. (UBC Architecture)

Section 09–550
Finished Wood Flooring

1.0 Introduction

1.1 General Issues

Finished wood floors are frequently installed in commercial buildings such as dance halls and exercise clubs, in public buildings such as school and college gymnasiums, and in private buildings such as residences and apartment blocks. Such floors are used for many reasons, including the good wearing qualities of properly selected wood materials for specific activities (like basketball, dancing, racquetball, squash, and other indoor recreations), the enhancement of acoustics in a room or area by the provision of hard materials and resilient mountings, and the aesthetic or visual appeal of the finished appearance of natural wood products. Furthermore, many people have allergic reactions to other floor finishes, such as carpets or vinyl, so wood may be specified for reasons of health.

1.2 Design Aspects

Wood floors are available in three basic forms: **block, plank,** and **strip.** Such floors may be installed either on solid surfaces (see Figure 1.1) such as sheathing, slabs, and decks, or else on furred systems (see Figure 1.2) such as strapping, joists, or resilient bars. When used for game courts, they are usually decorated with painted lines and letters to delineate game boundaries, and finished with tough clear natural or synthetic varnished coatings. They also often have brass, steel, or plastic accessories set

flush into their surfaces, to secure and support apparatus (such as net posts) for a variety of games. Wood floors are usually installed in a truly horizontal plane, with space left around the perimeter to permit movement because of thermal or moisture changes, and, where necessary, the movement of air under the system.

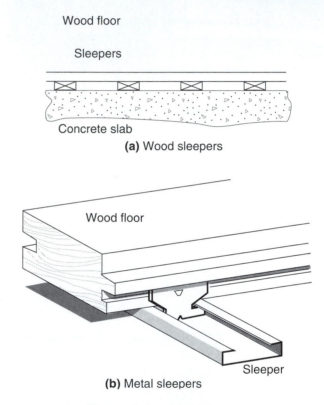

(a) Wood sleepers

(b) Metal sleepers

Figure 1.1 Solid Substrate

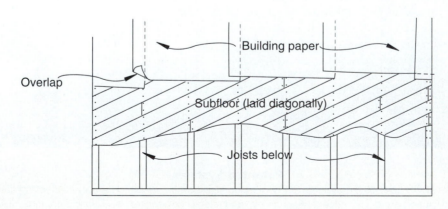

Figure 1.2 Furred Substrate

In recent years, with restoration of older buildings becoming more popular, ornamental features in wood floors, such as borders and perimeter trim, are coming back into vogue. Also, recent studies have shown that properly installed wood floors can improve acoustical separation between stories by as much as 25 decibels compared to competing hard finishes.

Wherever wood floors are placed on grade slabs or in potentially damp areas below grade, special precautions must be taken to deal with significant movement in the wood system caused by the absorption and evaporation of moisture. Where wood floors are used in conjunction with radiant heating systems embedded in the slab, allowance must also be made for movement of the slab and floor, by use of a floating or slipping type of installation. In general, tongue-and-groove products should not be used in such situations of excessive dampness, dryness, or movement. Floor design should endeavor to ensure a moisture content level in the finished wood system of approximately 12 percent.

1.3 Related Work

Work closely connected to this section is described in the following sections, to which reference should be made:

03–300   Cast-in-Place Concrete

06–100   Rough Carpentry

09–900   Painting and Decorating

2.0 Products

2.1 Materials

These can be considered under three headings: **species, types,** and **grading.**

Species. Wood species used for finished wood flooring fall into two categories: **hardwoods** (from deciduous trees) and **softwoods** (from coniferous trees). Hardwoods are usually selected for areas anticipating heavy-duty wear and tear, such as gymnasium or dance floors, living rooms, and lobbies; softwoods may be selected for light-duty areas such as residential bedrooms and the floors of store windows. The most common species are listed below:

1. **Hardwoods.** Ash, beech, birch, maple, oak, and walnut. Some more expensive exotic or tropical woods, such as jarrah, are occasionally encountered. Block, plank, and strip products should be flat-sawn or quarter-sawn. (See Figure 1, Section 06–200.)

2. **Softwoods.** Fir, hemlock, larch, and pine. Block products should be end-grain; plank and strip products should be edge-grain.

Types. There are three basic types of products: **block, plank,** and **strip.** All are available with edges tongue-and-groove or plain and surfaces factory finished or plain.

Block

This is for commercial or residential use, in forms as follows:

In **hardwood,** in three forms:

1. **Parquetry,** being short, narrow pieces of wood, between 13 and 25 mm or $1/2$ and 1 in. wide, 230 and 300 mm or 9 and 12 in. long, and 6 and 13 mm or $1/4$ and $1/2$ in. thick, arranged into square tiles usually on a paper backing.

2. **Unit block,** being small, solid wood squares cut from plank or strip flooring decribed below.

3. **Laminated block,** being small, factory-made squares consisting of three layers of wood, crossbanded, glued, and bonded together under heat and pressure.

In **softwood** for industrial use: short, squat pieces of wood, between 50 and 100 mm or 2 and 4 in. wide, 100 and 230 mm or 4 and 9 in. long, and 32 and 100 mm or $1 1/2$ and 4 in. thick.

Plank

These are long, narrow pieces of wood, between 100 and 150 mm or 4 and 6 in. wide and about 13 mm or $1/2$ in. thick, in random lengths up to 2.4 m or 8 ft. and longer on special order.

Strip

These are long, narrow pieces of wood, between 40 and 80 mm or 1.5 and 3 in. wide and about 13 mm or $1/2$ in. thick, in random lengths up to 1.2 m or 4 ft..

Both plank and strip types are available in solid or laminated form.

Grading. Industrywide grades of flooring material usually apply only to unfinished wood products; most factory-prefinished material is ungraded, other than by each individual manufacturer. There are two grades commonly encountered: firsts and seconds. First-grade flooring is free from all defects; second-grade flooring permits sound, tight knots, minor pinholes, small streaks, and unobstrusive machining imperfections to show on the surface. Other selection considerations are based on wood color and whether or not clear-faced pieces are totally and exclusively required. Care should be taken to order all pieces for any one installation from the same source and of the same grade.

2.2 Accessories

Some accessories are necessary to install and secure the floor in position; other accessories are used to make the floor system operable for sport activities. Both groups are described.

Installation. Nails are usually either finish or spiral-screw type; steel or brass screws are used only with plank flooring. Adhesives are usually rubber-based mastic type; resilient pads or bars are made of hard rubber or neoprene extrusions. Baseboards and shoe molds are usually factory profiled from the same species of wood as selected for the floor, although purpose-made, preformed, profiled plastic baseboard and shoe mold combinations are also available in long lengths.

Operation. There are a number of purpose-made, factory-fabricated metal and plastic inserts available for installation into finished wood floors used in gymnasiums, intended to secure or support posts and guy wires for volleyball nets, basketball backstops, and the like. These operational accessories are selected from catalogs of companies specializing in such units.

3.0 Construction Aids

3.1 Equipment

The following equipment is of particular concern to the work of this trade:

Power nailer. A pneumatically or electrically operated heavy-duty staple or nail gun, designed to cinch boards tightly and to drive nails of any selected size to any required depth.

Sanding machines. Electrically operated devices; both disc and belt sanders are used to finish wood flooring.

3.2 Tools

The tools used for this work are those of the carpenter. Refer to Sections 06–100 and 06–200 for further detail.

4.0 Production

4.1 Crew Configuration

A typical floor-laying crew consists of one or two carpenters and a semiskilled helper. On large projects, two or more crews might be utilized.

Flooring Tools
Many of the tools used to prepare and install wood flooring are those of the carpenter. Additional equipment shown here includes a pneumatic nailer and staple gun, as well as a mallet. (UBC Architecture)

Table 1
PRODUCTIVITY FACTORS FOR WOOD FLOORING

Type of Work	Area per Hour	
	m²	ft.²
Laying vapor barrier	40	400
Spreading mastic	15	150
Setting sleepers	20	200
Laying strip floors	3	30
Laying block floors	4	40
Laying parquet floors	5	50
Sanding floors	6	60
Finishing floors	12	120
Installing baseboard	6 m	20 lf
Finishing baseboard	12 m	40 lf

4.2 Productivity

Productivity factors given in Table 1 represent good-quality commercial installation by an experienced crew, working in fairly large rectangular areas, such as gyms, lobbies, or living rooms. In small or complex areas, decrease factors by 15 to 20 percent.

5.0 Procedures

5.1 Preparation

Areas scheduled to receive finished wood flooring should be clean, dry, well lit, reasonably warm, and free of loose particles, dust, and debris. Materials and accessories should be brought to the site and stored for a few days in the areas where they will be installed, so that they will become acclimatized. Care must be taken to keep kiln-dried wood products away from sources of moisture. Typical substrates capable of receiving finished wood flooring include open joists, sheathed plywood subflooring, wood strapping or sleepers, concrete floors, and metal decking.

Open joists should be level and firmly braced. Tops should be relatively free of hard knots or other defects impeding nailing. Sheathed subfloors should be covered with one layer of asphalt-impregnated kraft building paper, lapped 100 mm or 4 in. at all edges and neatly stapled in position. Wood strapping or sleepers should be treated with a clean impreg-

nated wood preservative, cut to lengths, laid in a staggered pattern at right angles to the proposed direction of the finished wood floor pattern, shimmed level, and nailed to wood subfloors or power-pinned to concrete or metal deck subfloors (see Figure 2). Concrete subfloors should be smooth, level, and properly cured (at least 50 to 60 days). Metal decking should be smooth, level, free of rust, and prime-coat painted.

Tests should be conducted on wood and concrete subfloors to determine whether or not a vapor barrier is necessary. One simple test is to apply a strip of duct tape to the floor and leave it for a few days; if there is dampness, it will show on the underside of the tape. If a barrier is necessary, one of two procedures may be adopted:

1. A thin coat of asphalt paint (or similar product) is applied by brush or spray to the substrate, into which a thin sheet of polyethylene is embedded and covered with a layer of asphalt mastic, applied by trowel, into which the sleepers are embedded.

2. Preserved wood sleepers are secured to the subfloor structure by nailing or gluing, a thin sheet of polyethylene is stretched and stapled on top, and a second row of sleepers is then nailed through to the lower layer of sleepers.

Block and parquetry tile flooring can be installed at either 90 or 45 degrees to the primary axis of the room or area to be covered. In each case, a center line or diagonal is determined, a chalk-line is marked, and blocks or tiles are set out to be displaced by about one-half the width of the block or tile being installed. This ensures that perimeter tiles will be of reasonable size.

5.2 Process

There are four aspects of this process to understand:

Adhesive. There are two techniques for spreading mastic adhesives:

1. **Hot.** The mastic is carefully heated in kettles within known temperature limits, then uniformly spread by squeegee and trowel in small portions over the areas to be covered, with the blocks embedded by hand before the mastic cools.
2. **Cold.** The mastic is softened by the addition of controlled amounts of solvent, then uniformly spread as above, with blocks embedded before the solvent evaporates.

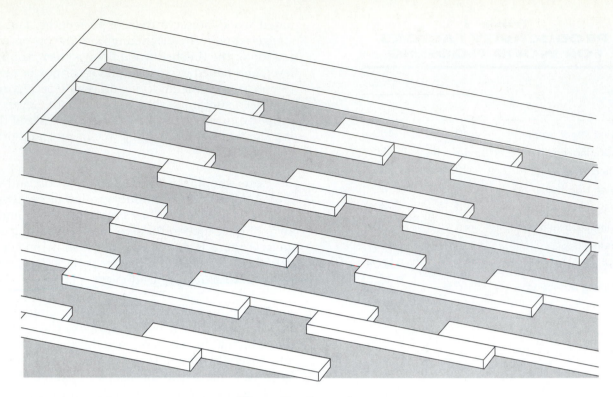

Figure 2 Sleeper Layout

Nailing. There are two techniques for nailing flooring (see Figure 3):

1. Face nailing. Nails are driven perpendicularly through the upper face of each floor piece, close to one tongued edge, and set with a nailset just below the surface of the wood. Face nailing is usually limited to the first few and last few strips, as well as at ends of rows, where feather nailing is not possible because of space limitations.

2. Feather nailing (or blind nailing). Nails are driven at a 50-degree angle through the top edge of the tongue of each floor piece and set flush with the wood surface. Feather nailing is usually done throughout the field of each area, sometimes by hand but usually by power nailer.

In either technique, nails are spaced 30 to 60 cm or 12 to 24 in. apart, or spaced to coincide with sleepers or joists along the length of each piece, with none closer to ends than 50 mm or 2 in. Nail lengths vary between 38 and 75 mm or 1½ and 3 in., depending on the thickness of the flooring material.

Installation. Once preparation is complete, installation of flooring may commence. As three basic flooring products (**block, plank,** and **strip**) are available, the process for each is described.

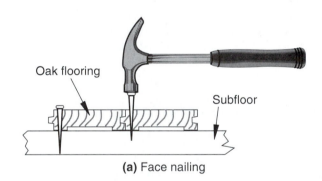

Oak flooring

Subfloor

(a) Face nailing

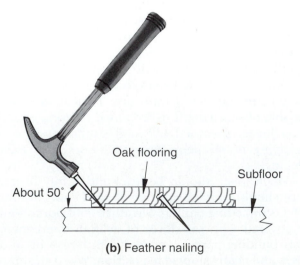

About 50°

Oak flooring

Subfloor

(b) Feather nailing

Figure 3 Nailing Types

(a) Nailer

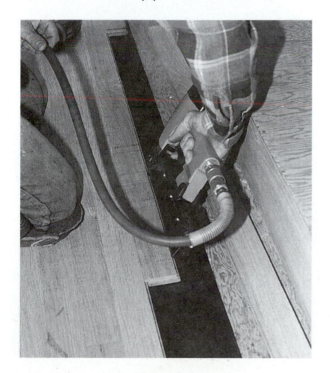

(b) Stapler

Installing Flooring

The punch nailer is used to secure main areas of the floor. The stapler is used where working space is restricted, such as at perimeters. (UBC Architecture)

Filling

After installation is complete, nail holes, knots, and other imperfections are hand-filled or otherwise prepared for machine sanding. Minor stains and debris are also removed. (UBC Architecture)

  1. Block. There are two types of block installation:

a. For **industrial** block, rows of block are fastened together with small metal or wood splines set into grooves cut in the sides of the blocks, then these rows are set (with edge-grain vertically positioned) into a hot or cold mastic adhesive base, with each row in close contact with its neighboring row.

b. For **commercial** block, such as unit block and laminated block, flooring pieces are usually set into hot or cold mastic, although they can both be face or feather nailed into position. Parquetry tiling is almost always glued down to a solid wood or concrete subfloor, allowing for movement by leaving a small gap around the perimeter of each area tiled. Tiles are glued down with the paper backing upward, for later removal after the adhesive has properly cured.

2. Plank. Laying procedure for plank flooring is similar to that given for strip flooring below, with the exception that holes are usually drilled in the ends of each plank for concealed screw fastening. These holes are drilled about halfway through the thickness of the plank and have a diameter of 13 mm or ¹/₂ in., into which a matching circular wood pellet or plug can be glued after the screws have been driven.

3. Strip. On open joist floors, select or cut strips to ensure that all end joints fall on top-centers of joist lines in a staggered regular pattern; install strips at right angles to joist lines. On sheathed wood or sleepered subfloors, select strips to ensure that joints form a staggered random pattern, not necessarily coinciding with joist or sleeper lines, but with not more than one end joint between joist or sleeper lines in any one row of strips; install strips at right angles to joist lines. On concrete floors or metal decks, uniformly spread mastic adhesive and firmly embed strips into mastic.

In each situation, lay the first strip with its grooved edge parallel to and against one side of the floor area to be covered, leaving a gap of 13 mm or ¹/₂ in. to allow for movement, and secure in position. Lay the next row tight against the first row, lightly tapping it into place and protecting the floor tongue with a small piece of scrap flooring, and secure into position. Repeat the laying operation across the area until the opposite wall is reached. The last row of strips may have to be scribed and ripped longitudinally to ensure a uniform fit, allowing for 13 mm or ¹/₂ in. clearance for movement at all edges of flooring.

Finishing. Perimeters of wood floors are best finished with two components: baseboard and shoe mold. A factory-profiled wooden baseboard is secured to the surrounding wall, and then a quarter-round shoe mold is secured by nailing or gluing it to the baseboard, allowing the floor to move slightly beneath both pieces (see Figure 4). On both components, end joints should be bevel-cut, and corners should be miter-cut.

(a) Belt sander

(b) Cove sander

Finishing

Floor surfaces are machine sanded using a flat-belt sander for large central areas and a cove sander around the edges. Sanding is done parallel to the wood grain, prior to staining. (UBC Architecture)

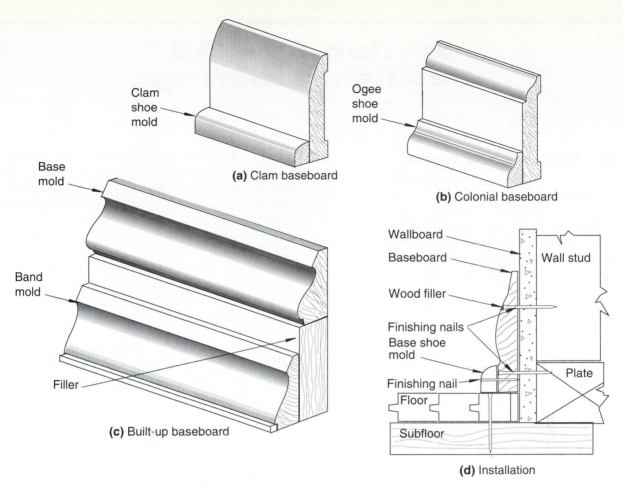

Clam shoe mold

(a) Clam baseboard

Ogee shoe mold

(b) Colonial baseboard

Base mold

Band mold

Filler

(c) Built-up baseboard

Wallboard

Baseboard

Wood filler

Finishing nails
Base shoe mold

Finishing nail

Floor

Subfloor

Wall stud

Plate

(d) Installation

Figure 4   Baseboard Sections and Installation

Flooring and perimeter trim are then cleaned free of debris, machine sanded, vacuumed, damp-mopped, stained if required, painted with game lines if necessary, and then most often finished with one or two (and sometimes three) coats of a synthetic polyurethane varnish in semi- or high-gloss finish. Some natural wood floors are hot-waxed and mechanically buffed; other floor products are prefinished with factory-impregnated acrylic compounds intended to improve color and enhance wearing characteristics. For additional finishing information, see Section 09–900.

5.3 Precautions

Workers should wear protective kneepads when installing flooring, eye shields when using power nailers, and face masks when using sanding machines and vacuums. The materials and accessories for wood flooring should be stored in secure, dry locations before installation. Before installation, subfloors should be tested for dampness as described in Section 09–650, Part 5.0; after installation, finished areas of flooring should be closed to traffic or be protected by spreading large loose sheets of kraft building paper or polyethylene, secured with masking or duct tape in areas where other workers may have to walk.

Section 09–650
Resilient Flooring

1.0 Introduction

1.1 General Issues

For the first half of the current century, the term *resilient flooring* generally referred to a product known as linoleum. The word *linoleum* originally was the patented name of a flooring material. It was made by coating a woven burlap or linen base with a solid mixture of linseed oil, powdered cork, rosin, and colored pigments, and by coating the cured mixture with a hard lacquer finish for protection. The root of this word is two Latin words: *linum* (meaning flax) and *oleum* (meaning oil). It is a another example of many such invented words (such as aspirin, masonite, and nylon) which permanently enter our vocabulary to describe everyday things.

Since World War II, there has been phenomenal development in new flooring products involving the use of natural and synthetic rubber, plastics, and other materials, together with appropriate accessories such as adhesives and trim. Some of them have superseded linoleum in popular use though similar in appearance, function, and style to the original.

The term *resilient flooring* refers to floor coverings which are to some extent resilient under the weight of a normal person and which exhibit a good degree of recovery from indentation after removal of loads, such as furniture or equipment. One distinction to note is that the term *resilient flooring* is not usually applied to carpeting or other forms of applied floor finishes, such as porch paint or seamless plastic coatings.

1.2 Design Aspects

There are two primary design considerations in the selection of a resilient flooring system: the overall appearance of the completed area (or **field**) to be covered and the treatment of **joints** in the fields, at edges and perimeters.

The Field. Because of the fashionable nature of flooring products, there is an extensive and rapid turnover of available patterns and designs, with many changes being introduced on an annual basis. Designers should therefore check with local manufacturers' representatives for availability, styles, and patterns of current products. For heavy-duty installations, such as in cafeterias, hotel lobbies, offices, schools, shopping centers, and the like, consideration should be given to selecting flooring products having an integral (as distinct from an applied) color and pattern, for longer wear and better appearance.

The Joints. Where floor finishes of different types, patterns, or colors are used in adjoining spaces, consideration should be given to the best location and appearance of the unavoidable joint between the finishes.

It is best not to have joints occurring at the center of fields, at random locations, or too near the edges of finished areas. Joints at doorways are best located directly beneath the center line of doors in the closed position, if doors are used to separate the areas, otherwise the joints can be located at some logical point, such as midway through an opening.

Sheet Goods

When laying out resilient sheet goods, care should be taken to have longitudinal joints laid parallel to (and not at right angles to) the general direction of traffic on the floor. In most rooms, a suitable roll length can be selected to avoid the necessity of having intermediate joints between one end of the area and the other.

Tile Goods

When laying out resilient floor tiles, the joint lines should be arranged to be square with or parallel to the principal axis of the room or area. The joint layout should be arranged so as to ensure that cut tiles at perimeters of areas should be at least one-half of a tile in width. This will avoid unsightly narrow or thin strips of tile flooring around the edges. A typical arrangement is shown in Figure 1.

1.3 Related Work

Work closely connected to this section is described in the following sections, to which reference should be made:

2.0 Products

2.1 Materials

Flooring materials can be considered under two headings: **types** and **sizes.**

Types.   Some of the more common of the current resilient flooring products are alphabetically listed and generically described as follows:

Asphalt. Made from a mixture of asbestos fibers, fillers, and pigments, bound together in an asphaltic base under pressure.

Cork. Made from a mixture of compressed natural cork granules, wood flour, and pigments, bound with animal or vegetable glues under pressure and treated with a thin polyurethane coating for protection and appearance.

Rubber. Made from natural or synthetic rubber, with mineral filler and pigments incorporated.

Vinyl. Made from mineral fillers, stabilizers, and pigments, bound together in a colorless polyvinyl chloride base under heat and pressure.

Vinyl-asbestos. Made from vinyl as above, with asbestos fibers and mineral fillers added to reduce cost and improve wearability.

Vinyl chip. Made by suspending small chips of pure colored vinyl in a matrix of molten colorless or tinted vinyl, then rolling the resultant solution to produce a three-dimensional effect.

In general, the asphalt-based products produce darker colors and are less expensive than the vinyl-based products. Vinyl sheet is available in two forms: backed or unbacked. The backed form has a layer of felt or asbestos fiber glued to the back and is used in light traffic areas.

Sizes.   Resilient flooring materials are available in two basic forms: in large sheets or cut into small tile-sized pieces. Sheet sizes vary, but widths of 2 m or 6 ft. are common, with lengths varying from 12 to 30 m or 50 to 100 ft. Square tile sizes are usually either 30 cm² or 12 in.² or else 25 cm² or 9 in.². Larger sizes are available. Thicknesses for most products include 1.6, 2.4, 3.2, 4.0, and 4.8 mm or $^1/_{16}$, $^3/_{32}$, $^1/_8$, $^1/_4$, and $^3/_8$ in. Criteria for selecting thickness include cost, probable wear, and the likelihood of "ghosting," which is the tendency of irregularities in the flooring substrate to make an impression through the finish material.

2.2 Accessories

Accessories used are **trim, adhesives,** and **other application products.**

Trim.   There are three main types:

1. **Base trim.** This is made of extruded synthetic rubber or vinyl, in three basic sizes (heights): 65, 100, and 150 mm or 2.5, 4, and 6 in.; and in three basic profiles, as shown in Figure 2:

   a. **Butt-cove.** The bottom edge is shaped to finish flush with the flooring.

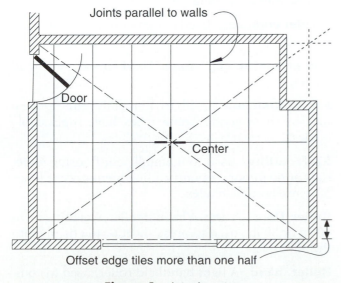

Figure 1   Joint Location

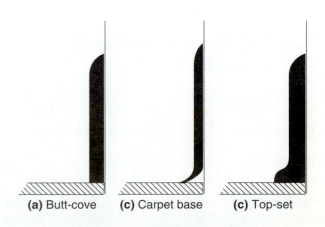

(a) Butt-cove   (c) Carpet base   (c) Top-set

Figure 2   Typical Base Profiles

b. Carpet-base. The bottom edge is shaped to curve out over the top of the carpet.

c. Top-set. The bottom edge is rounded for placement on top of the floor finish.

2. **Edges.** Narrow strips of solid-colored vinyl are available in most colors, to form feature strips, letters, or geometric patterns within any given field of resilient flooring. Standard widths are 6, 13, and 25 mm or $1/4$, $1/2$, and 1 in.

3. **Treads.** Stair treads are made of patterned synthetic rubber or vinyl, in two forms, square nose and round nose, and two thicknesses, 3.2 and 4.8 mm or $1/8$ and $3/16$ in.

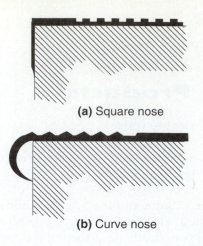

(a) Square nose

(b) Curve nose

Figure 3 Typical Tread Profiles

Adhesives. These should always be as recommended by the manufacturer of the selected resilient flooring for the intended application on wood, concrete, or metal. There are two basic categories of flooring adhesives:

1. **Plastic,** such as asphalt base and sulfite liquor.
2. **Elastic,** such as rubber cement and contact bond.

Plastic adhesives are preferred where dampness is a problem. There are two basic types of adhesives:

1. "**Wet**," implying that flooring has to be applied before the adhesive has cured.

2. "**Dry**," implying that the adhesive is allowed to cure to a tack state before flooring is applied.

Related Products. Fillers, primers, and solvents should all be as recommended by the adhesives manufacturer.

3.0 Construction Aids

3.1 Equipment

The equipment used by this trade is as follows:

Floor sander. A heavyweight, electrically powered device for smoothing out rough wood substrates.

Floor stripper. Similar to the sander, but having reciprocating blades to remove old resilient flooring from existing substrates.

Kneepads. Used to protect workers' knees as they move around on hands and knees during installation operations.

Moisture testing. A variety of devices as described in Part 5.1.

Tile cutter. A device for scoring and snapping resilient floor tiles to accurate lines and angles.

3.2 Tools

Some of the tools used in this work are described below:

Base lifter. Used to loosen and lift wood or plastic baseboards, prior to installation of flooring materials.

Chalk-line. Used to mark location of layout lines on floors, prior to installation.

Divider compass. Used to mark out points of equal distance or to scribe curved lines to desired radii.

File or **sharpening stone.** Used to sharpen hand knives.

Knife, linoleum. Used to manually cut flooring tiles or sheet goods; some types have replaceable blades.

Knife, utility. Used to manually cut flooring materials or do minor carpentry adjustments; some types have replaceable blades.

Roller, floor. A heavy manual roller, weighing up to 40 kg or 80 lb., used to press sheet or tile firmly into the adhesive.

Roller, hand. A light handheld roller, used to compress seams and joints while adhesives are curing.

Scriber, corner. Used to mark outside corners on flooring goods before cutting and fitting.

Scriber, universal. Used to mark inside corners and irregular outlines on flooring goods before cutting and fitting.

Spreader, adhesive. A trowel used to spread adhesive over the flooring substrate.

Straightedge. A flat metal bar used to permit straight lines to be cut on sheet goods.

Trowel, filler. Used to spread and level filling composition material, used prior to installation to eliminate minor depressions and irregularities in flooring substrates.

4.0 Production

4.1 Crew Configuration

A typical floor-laying team consists of two skilled installers working together, occasionally with a helper. On large projects, two or more teams might be utilized.

4.2 Productivity

Factors given below assume an experienced team working on commercial projects under normal conditions, unless otherwise stated.

1. For tile goods, a good team should install approximately 80 m² or 800 ft.² per working day.
2. For sheet goods, productivity is about 50 percent that of tile goods, with only about 40 m² or 400 ft.² being laid per day.
3. In small, confined, and complex areas (such as closets and alcoves), productivity may be reduced by as much as 25 percent.
4. Base trim and edge strips can be installed at the rate of about 10 m or 35 ft. per hour.
5. Normal-sized residential stair treads take about 10 minutes each to install.

5.0 Procedures

5.1 Preparation

The length of service to be expected from any resilient flooring system will depend in large measure on the quality of preparation before installation. Subfloors must be cleaned free of dirt, dust, debris,

paint, oils, grease, and wax. Cracks, depressions, ridges, mounds, or other imperfections must be removed or rectified by filling or grinding.

New concrete floors below grade should be primed, using floor adhesive which has been thinned with solvents. Concrete floors above grade should be thoroughly cured and dry. New wood floors should be vacuumed. Old wood floors should be sanded and sealed. In renovation work, one solution for unsuitable substrates is to put down a thin plywood or particleboard underlay before installing floor finishes, securing the underlay to the subfloor with ring-groove or cement-coated nails. On old stripwood

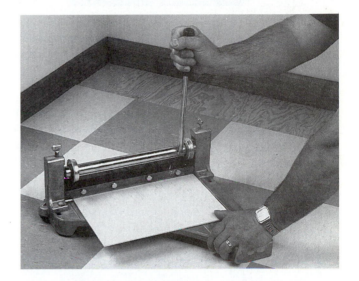

(a) Cutting tiles

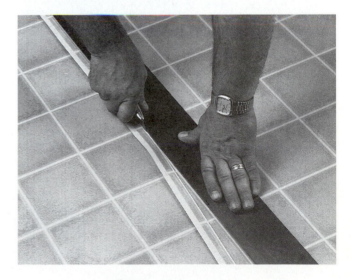

(b) Cutting sheet goods

Cutting Flooring

Guillotines, metal straightedges, and utility knives are used to trim tiles and sheet goods at straight line edges and joints in floor areas. (Resilient Floor Covering Institute)

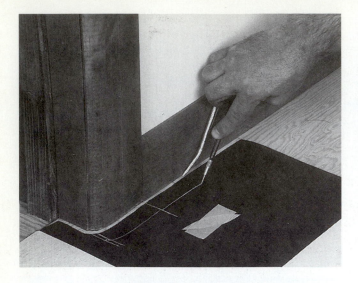

(a) Scribing tile goods

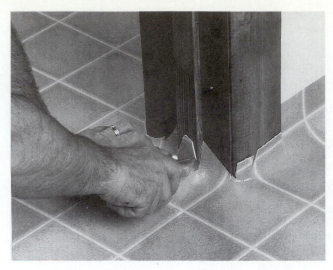

(b) Scribing sheet goods

Scribing Flooring

Dividers can be used to mark patterns on paper templates from which tiles can be cut to fit irregular locations. Sheet goods can be trimmed to fit with heavy duty knives or scissors. (Resilient Floor Covering Institute)

floors, a layer of felt may be glued down to serve the same purpose, provided care is taken to eliminate any air pockets under the felt.

The subfloor must be tested for moisture content. Flooring should never be laid on an untested floor; to do so may void any manufacturer's warranties. The optimum water content should be less than 1.5 kg per 100 m² or 3 lb. per 1,000 ft.². With the exception of plain asphalt and vinyl-asbestos tiles, no resilient flooring should be laid if moisture is pre-

(a) Bulk supply

(b) Installed trim

Base Trim

The cut edges at the perimeter of resilient floor coverings can be concealed with a continuous base trim, usually applied with adhesive and complete with preformed matching corner pieces. (UBC Architecture)

sent in the subfloor or underlay. There are four simple tests that can be used to ascertain if moisture exists:

1. Using **calcium chloride:** A small quantity of this dry chemical is weighed, placed on the floor, and covered with a plastic box sealed around the edges with putty. After three days, the chemical is removed and reweighed; the difference in weight indicates the amount of moisture present.

2. Using a kit with **carbide granules:** A small hole is drilled into the concrete substrate, powdered concrete from the hole is mixed with the carbide and deposited into a small vial or tube, and the tube is sealed. A gauge on the tube registers any change in pressure and thus indicates the degree of moisture present in the sample.

3. Using **rubber mats:** A small solid rubber mat is placed on the floor to be covered. After 24 hours, the underside of the mat is examined for moisture. If the underside indicates dampness, then a more precise test may be required.

4. Using a **moisture meter:** This electrical device consists of an ammeter, a battery for energy, and two sharp probes. The probes are inserted into the subfloor at a fixed distance apart, the power is switched on, and the resistance between the probe points is automatically expressed as a percentage of moisture on the calibrated dial.

Dry adhesives can be spread over the entire area to be covered in one working day. Wet adhesives should only be spread over as much area as can be covered before the adhesive dries.

5.2 Procedure

Techniques for installing **sheet** goods differ from those for **tile** goods:

Sheet Goods.   Measure the room to determine the number of roll widths required. If the room is slightly larger than an even multiple of roll widths, a border strip can be installed. Snap a chalk-line where the joint seams will be located. Cut the roll, allowing an additional 25 mm or 1 in. for trimming at uneven edges. Lay out the cut pieces in their final positions, and glue the center field pieces first, then the perimeter trim. Gluing is done by folding the piece back in half, spreading the glue on the subfloor, and then replacing the folded piece in its final position; repeat for the other half. Scribe the border strips using a wall scriber, fit in position, then cut off overlapped material. Miter-cut at corners. Cutting is done by holding a linoleum knife vertically and cutting down through the center of overlapped edges. Remove the excess material and glue the final joint using a seam sealant. Press the entire floor with a

Ornamentation
Designs and logos can be worked into most resilient flooring installations by cutting the flooring material to special shapes, as shown in this mosaic example in an entrance hallway. (UBC Architecture)

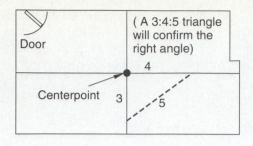
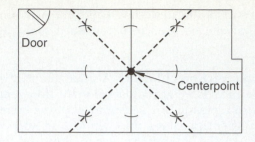

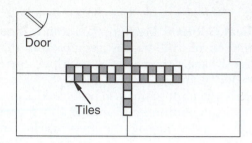
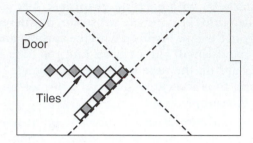

Figure 4 Tile Flooring Layout

heavy roller to ensure uniform and tight adhesion; pin-prick to eliminate air pockets.

Tile Goods.   Measure the room to determine its central axes. Snap a chalk-line to mark the axes. Tiles can be laid at either 90 degrees (square) or 45 degrees (diagonal) to the axis. For square layouts, adjust the axes to ensure that border tiles will be at least half a tile in width. For both square and diagonal layouts, the installation procedure is the same. Reference lines are laid out on the subfloor, the adhesive is spread in limited areas (taking care not to obliterate the guide lines), the field tiles are laid on the adhesive, and the process is repeated until the central field is complete. Then the border tiles are scribed, cut, and glued in position, and the entire floor is rolled with a heavy roller. If the perimeter wall line is unusually irregular, its outline can be scribed onto a piece of felt or paper and then the line can be transferred to the flooring tiles. Some installation aspects are illustrated in Figure 4.

Base and Trim.   Perimeter baseboard trim, reducing strips at open edges of resilient flooring, and stair treads are simply installed. Required lengths are measured, the product is cut with knives or scissors, glue is applied by gun or trowel, and the pieces are pressed into place, with corner accessories positioned where necessary. Sandbags can be used to apply local pressure for a short period.

5.3 Precautions

Ordinary commonsense precautions regarding the use of heavy rollers, sharp utensils, and toxic and volatile products should be taken. While few applicators wear work gloves or hard hats, most will benefit from the use of kneepads and steel-toed shoes. Materials and accessories should be carefully handled and stored to prevent accidental damage from occurring. Avoid incorporating cracked or broken sheets or tiles in finished work.

Section 09–680
Carpets, Underlay, and Trim

1.0 Introduction

1.1 General Issues

Carpets are incorporated into buildings for many reasons: to improve foot comfort, to enhance decor, to alter acoustical characteristics, to create psychological moods, to reduce maintenance costs, to cover unsightly or uneven substrates, and to meet budgets, among other reasons. Carpeting made from natural fibers such as wool and cotton has had a long and interesting history; in recent years, the development of new and useful synthetic fibers and improved carpet accessories has given added impetus to the increased use of carpeting in modern public and private buildings.

1.2 Design Aspects

Carpets can be installed with or without underlay, depending on conditions of service and budget. The purpose of the underlay is to absorb shock by increasing resilience, to minimize the wearing effect of minor irregularities in the substrate on the underside of the carpet, and to improve the removal of dirt during cleaning.

Most carpets are installed with concealed fastenings; face nailing or exposed tacking should not be accepted in work of any significant quality. Seams and joints should not be located in areas of heavy traffic and they should generally run parallel to the flow of traffic and not at right angles to it. Changes of color or pattern should normally occur at doorways or other definite lines or points relative to the shape of the area being carpeted. As there can be variations of color or pattern in carpets selected from different factories or batches, care should be taken to order and place sufficient carpet material of any one type from one batch and from one source to avoid problems in this regard. Consideration should also be given to the possibility of colors fading due to exposure to light or due to dampness from steam cleaning. Laboratory tests can predict such aspects of service.

1.3 Related Work

Work closely connected to this section is described in the following sections, to which reference should be made:

03–300 Cast-in-Place Concrete

06–100 Rough Carpentry

06–200 Finish Carpentry

09–650 Resilient Flooring

2.0 Products

2.1 Materials

Carpets used in modern buildings can be considered under two headings: **types** and **forms**.

Types. There are two basic types, as shown in Figure 1:

1. **Woven.** The face yarns are woven into the back yarns; these include Axminster, velvet, and Wilton weaves.
2. **Tufted.** The face yarns are not woven into the back yarns; these include shag, bonded, knitted, and some loom weaves.

Both types may be made of either natural or synthetic yarns or fibers.

Forms. There are two basic forms:

1. **Area rugs** and **mats** are not usually included in construction contracts, and therefore will not be further described in this section.
2. **Broadloom** (also called wall-to-wall) **carpet** is so called because it is manufactured on a loom about 4 m or 12 ft. wide. It is intended to be installed in a wall-to-wall fashion in large rooms or other open areas.

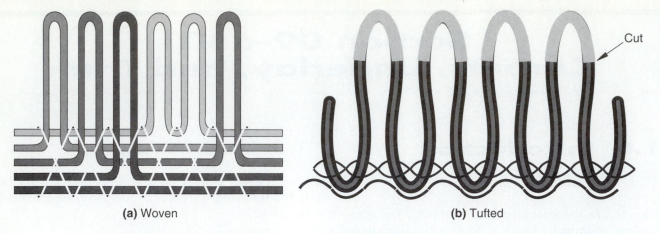

(a) Woven   (b) Tufted

Figure 1   Two Main Carpet Types

2.2 Accessories

These comprise **underlays, trim,** and **adhesives**:

Underlays.   There are four main types:

1. **Felt padding.** Made of organic hair material, steamed and pressed then rolled into smooth thin sheets. Weights vary between 1 and 3 kg/m² or 32 and 86 oz./yd.²; typical width of rolls is 5 m or 15 ft.

2. **Foam rubber.** Made by mechanically introducing air bubbles into a liquid rubber latex base then rolling into thin sheets; also available in bonded chip form. Weights vary between 0.9 and 2.2 kg/m² or 28 and 65 oz./yd.²; typical roll width is 4 m or 12 ft.

3. **Foam urethane.** Made by chemically inducing air bubbles in a pure or densified urethane polymer base, then after expansion and curing under slight pressure, it is cut into plain sheets and bonded to a reinforcing backing layer. Weights are comparable to foam rubber; typical roll width is 2 m or 6 ft.

4. **Sponge rubber.** Made by chemically inducing air bubbles in a liquid rubber latex base then forming the expanded foam material into continuous sheets of waffled, rippled, ribbed, or plain configuration. A cotton or linen facing material is then bonded to one side to protect the rubber from wear. Weights vary between 1.4 and 4 kg/m² or 40 and 120 oz./yd.²; typical roll width is 4 m or 12 ft.

Lengths of the foregoing underlays vary from 10 to 30 m or 30 to 100 ft. Thicknesses vary from 6 to 19 mm or ¼ to ¾ in.

Trim.   There are four main types:

1. **Baseboard.** Long lengths of profiled solid wood, rubber, or vinyl, used to trim edges of carpets at wall perimeters or other abutments to vertical planes; for details see Sections 06–200 (for wood trim) and 09–650 (for other trim).

2. **Bond tape.** Long rolls of fiberglass tape, having a thick wax coating applied to one side, used with heat to bond adjacent edges of carpet together.

3. **Edge strip.** Strips of plywood, 1.2 m or 4 ft. long, 25 mm or 1 in. wide, and 6 mm or ¼ in. thick, having two staggered rows of sharp pins driven through from the underside; used to catch and hold the edges of broadloom carpet in position. There are two types: standard and prenailed.

4. **Edge trim.** Long lengths of extruded or molded metal or hard vinyl, used to trim edges of carpets at doorways or other openings.

Adhesives.   Always use those recommended by the carpet and underlay manufacturers for use with their products.

3.0 Construction Aids

3.1 Equipment

Some of the equipment used in this work is described below:

Carpet roller. A steel drum, weighing up to 10 kg or 20 lb., attached to a wooden or metal pull handle, and used to secure the bond between the carpet and the adhesive.

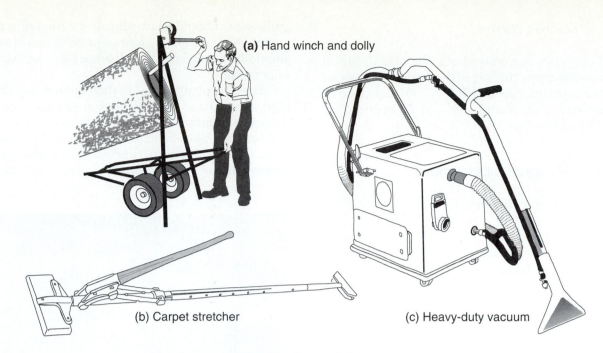

(a) Hand winch and dolly

(b) Carpet stretcher

(c) Heavy-duty vacuum

Figure 2 Carpet Equipment

Heat-seaming irons. An electric iron having a specially shaped flat blade and capable of generating heat up to 230 degrees C or 450 degrees F, used to melt the wax on carpet bond tape.

Knee kicker or **carpet stretcher.** A metal device having a plate with adjustable pin settings at one end to grip the carpet and a padded push plate at the other end; used to stretch carpet tightly over edge strips.

Stud driver. A power-operated pistol, used to drive "studs" (hardened steel nails) through edge strips into concrete substrates.

Winch and dolly. Heavy carpet rolls can easily be moved about on a wheeled cart onto which they have been lifted using a small manual winch (see Figure 3).

3.2 Tools

Some of the tools used in this work are described below:

Carpet knife. A hand knife having interchangeable, stiff, razor-sharp, stainless steel blades, used for general cutting of carpets and underlay materials.

Flex-blade knife. A hand knife having a tempered, flexible, carbon steel blade, used for trimming around curves and corners.

Porcupine roller. A small handheld roller, having points molded into the roller face, used to compress carpets firmly onto the edge strips.

Rubber mallet. Used to operate the stair tool or to press down edges of metal trim.

Stair tool. A broad-bladed, steel, chisel-like device, used to tuck edges of carpet into place.

Staple hammer. A heavy-duty stapler, balanced to hold about 150 rear-loaded staples at one end to offset the weight of the machine end, and capable of one-hand operation by a simple beating action on the underlay.

Wall trimmer. A small, handheld, cutting device, having an adjustable handle and heel plate, to permit cutting carpet and underlay under toe spaces or in restricted corners.

4.0 Production

4.1 Crew Configuration

A typical carpet-laying crew consists of one or two carpet-layers and one helper. On very large projects, two or more crews might be utilized, with one journeyman appointed as foreman.

4.2 Productivity

A good carpet-laying crew should be able to install carpet components in large unrestricted areas at about the rates indicated in Table 1. For confined or complex areas, the factors should be reduced by about 25 percent.

5.0 Procedures

5.1 Preparation

Areas to be carpeted require to be cleaned free of dirt, dust, dampness, debris, or equipment that might adversely affect the work in process or the end result. Preparation involves two further main activities: **planning** and the use of **accessories.**

Planning. Areas to be carpeted should be accurately measured and a plan drawn on graph paper to show the precise configuration of each room or area. A clear plastic template can then be prepared to represent the carpet roll and moved about over the plan to determine the most economical arrangement of rolls and joints. Carpets and underlays are then cut, with an allowance of between 50 and 100 mm or 2 and 4 in. to allow for room irregularities. If patterned carpet is involved, then the repeat (or "drop") of the pattern may require additional allowances to be made. Arrows are drawn with felt-tip marker on the back of each piece of carpet to indicate the direction of the pile, so that adjacent pieces will have their pile lying in the same direction. Before starting installation work, subfloors scheduled to receive carpeting should be checked to ensure that they are solid, clean, and dry.

Accessories. Edge strips are positioned close to but not touching the perimeters of the areas to be carpeted. A small space, called the "gully," is left to permit the edge of the carpet to be tucked down; the

gully width should be two-thirds the thickness of the carpet. Metal trim at doorways or other openings should be cut to length with a hacksaw and secured in position.

The precut underlay is then spread out and either stapled to wood subfloors or glued to concrete subfloors. If staples are used, a strip of self-adhesive padding tape should be fixed along the line to be stapled. Overage along perimeters is trimmed with a carpet knife to within 6 mm or $1/4$ in. of the inside of

(a) Floor preparation

(b) Carpet edge strip

Preliminaries

Floor surfaces are cleaned, scraped, and filled as necessary. Tack edge strip is cut and fitted around perimeters to secure the carpet in position. (UBC Architecture)

Table 1
CARPET-LAYING PRODUCTIVITY

| Component | Units per Hour | |
	Metric	Imperial
Edge strip	10 m	30 lf
Underlay	15 m²	150 ft.²
Inexpensive carpet	10 m²	100 ft.²
Expensive carpet	8 m²	80 ft.²
Base trim	10 m	30 lf

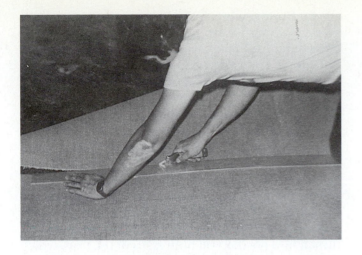

(a) Cutting underlay

Underlayment

Some carpets require a resilient underlay. If so, the appropriate material is measured, cut, and carefully fitted into the specified areas, then glued down or stapled to the subfloor. (BCIT Building Technology)

(b) Stapling underlay

the edge strip. Excess adhesive, scraps, and debris must be removed.

If edge strips and underlay are not to be used, all holes and cracks in subfloors should be filled with latex patching compound, and ridges should be removed by grinding or sanding. The area should be vacuumed, dampmopped, and then left ready for the carpet.

5.2 Process

In laying carpets, there are three main elements: **laying the carpet, treating the joints**, and **cleaning up.**

Laying Carpets. There are three possibilities.

Carpet with Underlay

The first piece of carpet is attached to the edge strip in one corner of the area and then spread and stretched out from that corner along the adjacent wall lines and toward the opposite corner. A knee kicker is used to secure the edges of the carpet to the edge strips, making sure that the rows of pins fully penetrate the carpet. The procedure is illustrated in Figure 3. The technique of heat seaming is described later.

Carpet without Underlay

Where foam-backed carpet is used, edge trim and

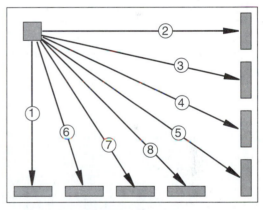

(a) Stretch directions

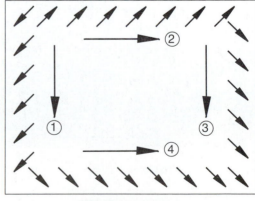

(b) Kicking patterns

Figure 3 Typical Carpet Installation

underlay are not required. Locate the center lines of the room or area and snap a chalk-line to mark them. Lay two pieces of carpet, one on each side of the line and overlapped by 50 mm or 2 in. Using a straight-edge and a carpet knife, cut through both layers of carpet and remove the trimmings. Lay the carpet back to about half its width on each side of the line, spread the adhesive, and return the folded carpet onto the glued areas. Lay the opposite side of the carpet back, spread the adhesive, and return the carpet to its final position. Using the knee kicker, carefully butt the cut edges of carpet tightly at joint lines, and heat-seam as described below. Trim perimeter edges using a sharp carpet knife or wall trimmer, and tuck minor frayed ends down out of sight along the edges, using an awl. Finally, roll the entire installation with a carpet roller.

Carpet on Stairs

The process is similar to that for floors. With underlay, edge strips are applied, and underlay is stapled or glued on tread and halfway down risers. Then carpet is cut sufficiently large to cover one tread and one riser in one piece with overage, placed in position from the center out, stretched and hooked to the edge strips, the excess trimmed off, and edges tucked into gullies using a stair tool. Without underlay, carpet is cut, glued, and trimmed to fit.

Two methods of connecting carpet edges at joints are the following:

1. **Handsewing.** In earlier times, joints between pieces of carpet were handsewn using a variety of cross-stitching. Such work is seldom encountered now, because of the high labor cost and the availability of better and cheaper techniques to achieve the same result.

2. **Heat seaming.** It is now more common to use a wax bond tape and a heat-seaming iron to make virtually invisible carpet joints. The edges of the two pieces of carpet to be joined are folded back about 30 cm or 12 in. A strip of wax bond tape is placed along the center line of the joint and glued to the subfloor. The heat-seaming iron is placed at one end of the tape and the edges of the carpet are returned into position on both sides of the iron, which is then moved slowly, deliberately, and uniformly along the line of the seam. The carpet edges are pressed firmly down into the melted wax immediately after the iron has passed. Some simple equipment used in the system is shown in Figure 4.

Cleaning Up. Upon completion of carpet-laying operations, all debris arising from this work should be picked up and removed. Carpet surfaces should be thoroughly vacuumed, with loose pieces resecured. Areas subject to access by following trades should be protected by spreading a layer of heavy-duty plain kraft building paper over the surface of the carpeted areas, secured in position with masking tape.

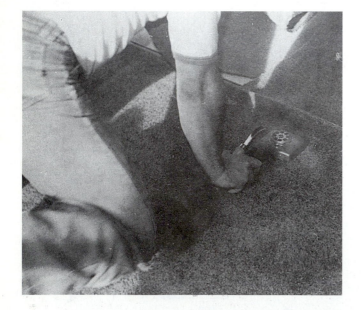

(a) Knee kicking

(b) Heat seaming

Carpet Laying

Carpets are measured, cut, and fitted into specified areas. Perimeters are hooked over edge-strips using a knee-kicker. Seams may be sewn but are more likely to be glued with a seaming iron. (BCIT Building Technology)

(a) Preparing

(b) Carpeting

Stairs

Edge-strips and underlay are cut, fitted, and secured in place to conform to the stair risers and treads. Carpets are installed using shears, knee-kickers, and broad-blade chisels. (BCIT Building Technology)

(a) Stockpiles

Carpet Tiling

Carpet tiles are rapidly becoming a popular floor finish. They are easily installed, with simple cutting and fitting at perimeters and by lightly gluing tile units to the subfloor. (UBC Architecture)

(b) Installation

Section 09–680   Carpets, Underlay, and Trim

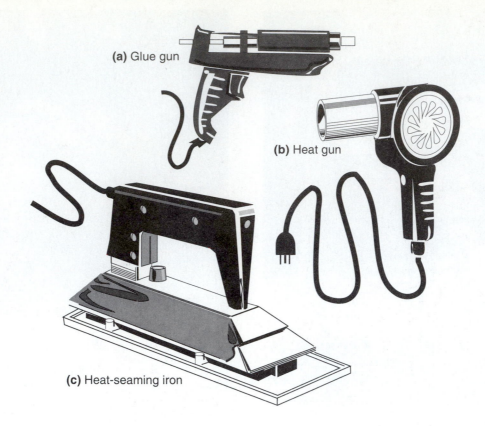

(a) Glue gun

(b) Heat gun

(c) Heat-seaming iron

Figure 4 Heat-Seaming Tools

5.3 Precautions

This work is not particularly hazardous, but the usual precautions should be observed when handling heavy loads, sharp tools, and toxic and flammable products, to avoid injury to people or damage to property. Clothing appropriate to the work should be worn, with particular reference to kneepads and toeguards. The materials and accessories should be protected from damage or dampness during delivery, handling, and storage.

Section 09–900
Painting and Decorating

1.0 Introduction

1.1 General Issues

Relatively few building materials are left in their natural unfinished states; the majority of products used in construction have some kind of protective or decorative finish applied to their surfaces, either at the factory or at the site. With few exceptions, untreated wood will rot, untreated metal will rust, untreated asphalt will oxidize, untreated concrete or clay products may permit moisture to penetrate into them. Furthermore, it should be realized that maintenance of protective and decorative finishes is an ongoing process that will likely be continued for the life of the building. In general, the better the initial installation and subsequent program of care, the lower will be the costs of maintenance and the longer will be the life of all or parts of the building, including the finishes.

1.2 Design Aspects

With respect to types of treatment, applied decorative finishes can be categorized as being opaque, translucent, or transparent. In general, where it is intended to conceal the underlying surface, paints are used for opaque finishes, while natural or synthetic stains or varnishes are used for translucent or transparent finishes where it is desired that some characteristics of the underlying surface remain visible after treatment.

With respect to color selection, the designer has a number of difficulties and also a number of aids. The difficulties stem from the subjective nature of color perception (being a combination of propagation of and response to light waves and the quality of personal vision), whereby every individual reacts to specific colors in a slightly or even substantially different way. A whole new field of psychology is arising out of the study of this particular aspect of human experience.

The aids to color selection derive from the ability of science to distinguish (from the entire spectrum of energy radiation) the limited range of frequencies that constitute visible light, and to analyze that range into its components, relative to their respective frequencies. Radiation of low frequency produces colored light in the brown and red range, of medium frequency in the orange and yellow range, and of high frequency in the green and blue range. The so-called **primary** colors of red, yellow, and blue are located near the middle of each range of frequencies. If these colors are arranged in a circular pattern, then three **secondary** colors can be interspersed between them. A third or **tertiary** group of colors can now be inserted between the secondary colors, and so a color chart of any desired complexity can be developed, as shown in Figure 1.

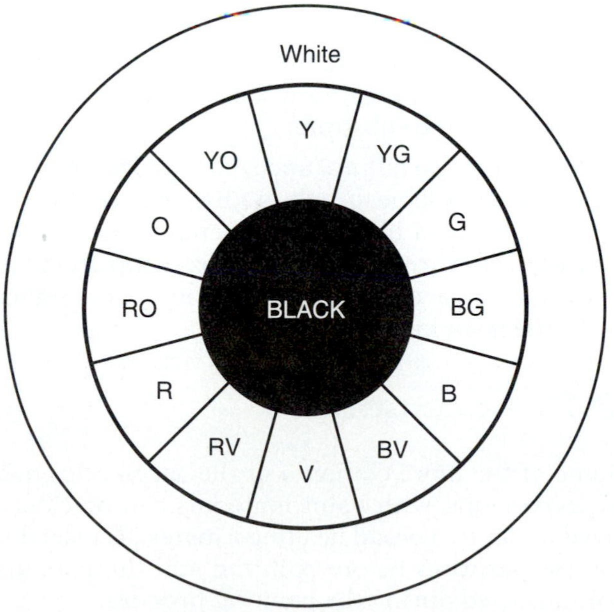

An additional value can be added, wherein each color can be tinted from white (which is the simultaneous presence of all color) to black (which is the total absence of all color). These hues or tints can then be numbered for identification, and in this manner information can be conveyed between the owner, designer, and painter to determine the colors that have been selected for use. Paint pigments are usually manufactured in a variety of black, brown, red, yellow, green, blue, and white colors, which can then be mixed in various proportions to produce an infinite number of variations.

With respect to color use, low-frequency colors such as reds and browns are generally considered to be "warm," midfrequency colors such as oranges and yellows tend to be "neutral," whereas high-frequency colors such as greens and blues are considered to be "cool." High ceilings can be made to appear lower by applying darker colors to them than on the adjacent walls. Conversely, low ceilings can be given the illusion of height if they are light-colored. It is also possible to enhance feelings of spaciousness with lighter colors and feelings of closeness or intimacy with darker colors. The procedural objectives of this book preclude further discussion of this important topic here.

1.3 Related Work

Work closely connected to this section is described in the following sections, to which reference should be made:

04–200	Unit Masonry
05–100	Steel Framing
06–200	Finish Carpentry
06–400	Architectural Woodwork
09–200	Lath and Plasterwork
09–250	Gypsum Plasterboard Systems
09–550	Finished Wood Flooring

V = violet   R = red   O = orange
Y = yellow   G = green   B = blue

Figure 1 Color Wheel

2.0 Products

2.1 Materials

The materials for this work can be categorized under three broad headings: **paints, stains,** and **varnishes.**

Paints.   One can consider **ingredients, types,** and **finishes:**

   1. Ingredients. True paints have four primary ingredients:

a. The **pigment** may be white or colored; white pigments usually consist of oxides of lead, zinc, or titanium while colored pigments usually consist of natural clays such as ocher, sienna, or umber, and chromates or oxides of antimony, copper, iron, lead, and other selected metals. The main purpose of the pigment is to hide the surface of the substrate.

b. The **extender** is usually an inexpensive fine sand, clay, barite, mica, or fiber product incorporated to reduce expense, enhance coverage, and improve workability.

c. The **vehicle** is a liquid solvent, intended to bind the pigments and extenders in suspension and to carry them onto the substrate and then to evaporate; various types of volatile liquids, petroleum and other spirits, and water are used.

d. **Additives** are mixed with paints to assist the curing process, to minimize foaming during mixing, to control chemical reactions, and to extend shelflife, among other reasons.

   2. Types. Paints are available in a wide variety of types; some of the more common ones are alphabetically listed in Table 1, with their main feature described.

   3. Finishes. Paints are available in a wide variety of surface finishes from dull to shiny, some of which are known as flat, matte, eggshell, semigloss, gloss, and high-gloss. Mottled, textured, and stippled finishes are also available.

Stains.   True stains consist of two primary ingredients:

1. **Vehicles** may consist of alcohol, various fine oils, or water, depending on the application.

2. **Pigments** are similar to those described above under paint, but in stain their purpose is not to hide the substrate but rather to enhance its natural appearance. Although white is available, the pigments are usually colored.

Table 1
PAINT TYPES

Type	Feature
Acrylic	Polymer base of acrylic acid.
Alkyd	Glycol resin vehicle.
Asphalt	Water-based asphalt emulsion.
Cement	Portland cement pigment.
Emulsion	Liquid suspended in liquid.
Enamel	Varnish vehicle, with thinners.
Fire retardant	Tumescent or expanding pigment.
Fluorescent	Fluorescing pigment.
Latex	Rubber latex vehicle.
Luminous	Fluorescing pigment.
Masonry	Cement base with sand.
Metallic	Metal particle pigment.
Mold resistant	Antifungal solvents.
Oil based	Oil vehicle, with thinners.
Primer	Paint thinned with spirits.
Rustproof	Usually containing zinc dust.

Varnishes.   True varnishes consist of one ingredient: the **vehicle**. It may be one of a number of products:

1. In natural varnish, the vehicle consists of a combination of mineral spirits and natural resins or waxes.

2. In synthetic varnish, the vehicle may be polyurethane or some similar polyester product.

3. In both types, the vehicle evaporates to leave a residue in the form of a hard, tough, clear skin bonded to the substrate.

4. There are also natural and synthetic lacquers and shellacs available, usually with plasticizers added, and which act like and are therefore used on occasion as varnishes. Lacquer is a nitrocellulose resin in an acetate solvent; shellac is a natural lac beetle resin in an alcohol solvent.

2.2 Accessories

Some of the more common of the accessories used in conjunction with paint materials can be categorized under two broad headings: materials used during **preparation** before painting and thinners and solvents used during the painting **process.**

Preparation.   Self-adhesive masking tape, white-lead putty, and white or tinted synthetic wood filler are used.

Process. Acetone, alcohol, butyl acetate, concentrated colors-in-oil, ketone, mineral spirits, toluene, turpentine, and water are used.

3.0 Construction Aids

3.1 Equipment

Some of the equipment used in this trade is described below:

Paint sprayers. There are two types:

1. In **compressed air** sprayers, the air is used to either push or suck the paint through an adjustable nozzle while simultaneously mixing with it to form a fine spray. See Figure 2.
2. In **airless** sprayers, liquid paint is forced through an adjustable nozzle either by gravity or by a pump.

Other equipment. Painters also use a variety of ladders, small mobile scaffolds, dropcloths, buckets, and brooms in their work.

3.2 Tools

Some of the tools used in this work are described below:

Brushes. Good-quality brushes will have natural or synthetic flagged or split-end bristles of differing lengths, trimmed to square or beveled ends. Brushes are available in a large variety of sizes and shapes to facilitate specific painting tasks.

Rollers. There are three basic types in use: pan, fountain, and pressure. All are used manually and can be attached to wood or lightweight metal extension poles for reaching above arm's reach. The rollers are made of nylon, lambswool, or mohair, mounted on a stiff paper core, and are available in different diameters and lengths to suit different painting procedures.

Other tools. Painters also use an assortment of putty knives, utility knives, small hand scrapers, wirebrushes, scissors, screwdrivers, paddles and sticks for mixing and stirring paint, and caulking guns for applying sealers.

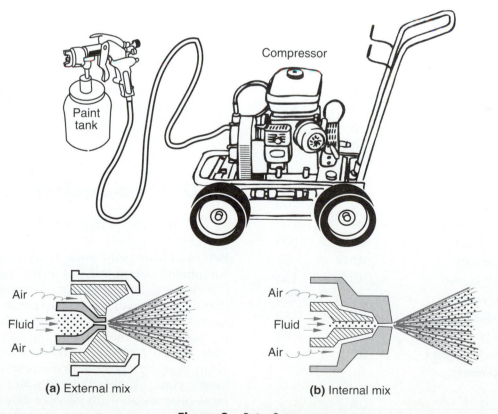

Compressor

Paint tank

Air

Fluid

Air

(a) External mix

Air

Fluid

Air

(b) Internal mix

Figure 2   Paint Sprayer

4.0 Production

4.1 Crew Configuration

On a typical commercial or institutional building project, a paint crew might consist of two painters and a helper. On large projects, two or three crews might be utilized, with one painter designated as foreman.

Table 2
PRODUCTIVITY FACTORS FOR PAINTING

Type of Work	Area per Hour	
	m²	ft.²
Preparatory work:		
Cleaning, general	10	100
Concrete and brick	8	75
Putty and fill	20	200
Remove old paint	5	50
Sand plaster areas	30	300
Sand wood surfaces	15	150
Tape and fill drywall	10	100
Exterior application:		
Brick, painted	10	100
Concrete, painted	15	150
Doors, painted	15	150
Fences, painted	13	125
Fences, stained	15	150
Flashings, painted	15	150
Siding, painted	10	100
Siding, stained	8	75
Stucco, painted	10	100
Waterproofing	10	100
Windows, painted (gross)	10	100
Interior application:		
Doors, painted	15	150
Drywall, painted	20	200
Floors, concrete, painted	20	200
Floors, wood, painted	30	300
Floors, wood, stained	40	400
Plaster, textured, painted	10	100
Wall paneling, stained	20	200
Windows, painted (gross)	12	120
Wiped finishes	8	75
Wood, varnished or waxed	15	150
Trim painted (linear):		
Exterior	50 m	150 lf
Interior	60 m	200 lf

4.2 Productivity

Because of almost infinite variety, it is not practical to list productivity factors for every type of painting preparation and finishing work that could be encountered in residential, commercial, or institutional projects. Instead, some representative factors are listed in Table 2 to indicate average output for fairly typical and normal kinds of work that may be routinely encountered in medium-sized projects.

Factor adjustments for Table 2 are as follows:

1. For simple **preparatory** work and for the first **brush** coat application for exterior and interior finishes, the figures in the table are reasonably representative and may be used as given.

2. For **roller** applications, increase factors by 25 percent.

3. For **sprayer** applications, increase factors by 100 percent.

4. For **very large** plain areas, increase factors by 20 percent.

5. For **smaller complex** areas, decrease factors by 20 percent.

6. For **exterior** work, because of the extra care usually taken to properly apply the first coat for protective reasons, factors for **subsequent** applications beyond the first coat can be increased by about 20 percent on **smooth** surfaces and about 40 percent on **textured** or rough surfaces.

7. For **interior** work, because greater care is usually taken with subsequent applications for aesthetic reasons, factors for **subsequent** applications beyond the first coat can be decreased by about 20 percent on **smooth** surfaces and about 30 percent on **textured** surfaces.

5.0 Procedures

5.1 Preparation

Before starting paint work, remove all furniture and equipment not required for the painting process from areas to be treated. Remove and store all finish hardware, metal or plastic cover plates, and light fixtures. Cover factory-prefinished surfaces.

Remove all loose scale, dirt, dust, and debris. This can be done by hand using wirebrushes and scrapers or by machine using power tools, such as needle guns, sandblasters, or water jets. Wash surfaces as necessary with alkali or detergent solutions, and rinse with clean water. Apply mordant (etching) primers where necessary to create a good bond between the surface to be treated and the preparatory coats of paint or stain.

Fill all minor cracks with appropriate filling compound, after applying primer. Lightly sand and clean all surfaces to be finished as necessary. Cover surfaces, items, and fixtures (which cannot be moved and are not to be painted) with masking tape or plastic covers. Cover floor areas with dropcloths.

Prepare new wood surfaces by drying, sealing if necessary (especially open-grain hardwoods), and prime-coating. Prepare new metal surfaces by abrasion, acid pickling, and priming. Prepare new cementitious or clay surfaces by curing, wirebrushing, and filling minor holes and cracks.

The general sequence for painting any area is to start at the highest level of horizontal or inclined ceilings or soffits, continue with the vertical walls, followed by fittings and fixtures, such as balustrades, cupboards, doors, trim, and windows, and finishing with the floor or stair areas. Cutting-in at perimeters of areas should precede filling in fields of areas.

5.2 Process

There are four considerations regarding procedure: the nature of the **surface** to be finished, the type of finish **system** to be applied, the method of **applica-**

Preparation
Surfaces to be painted have to be cleaned, filled, and sealed as necessary. Surfaces not to be painted have to be covered with plastic sheeting or masking tape. (BCIT Building Technology)

Area Setup
Areas to be painted have to be cleared of obstructions, materials have to be stockpiled, equipment assembled, and appropriate environmental conditions established. (BCIT Building Technology)

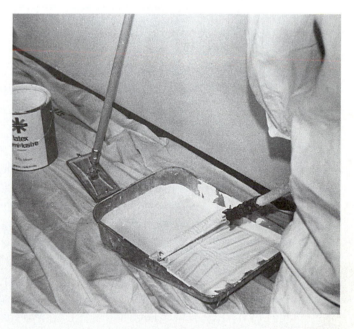

Paint Supply
Paint can be applied by roller either manually (as shown here) or continuously through a hose attached to a compressor and reservoir connected to a handle controlled by the painter. (BCIT Building Technology)

tion of the finish materials, and **completion.** Each is described below.

Surfaces. These may be interior or exterior, old or new, smooth or textured, porous or nonporous, solid or perforated, hot or cold, and wet, damp, or dry. They can be horizontal, vertical, or inclined, as well as domed, dished, plain, or erratic. They may be made of asphalt, cloth, concrete, fabric, glass, masonry, metal, paint, paper, plaster, plastic, stucco, or wood. Each requires special consideration regarding preparation, type, and application of proposed finish systems.

Paints and stains are usually manufactured specifically for either exterior or interior use; exterior paints or stains should not be used internally, and vice versa. Table 3 shows some suggested paint and stain applications.

Systems. In general, paint systems are applied in three coats for new work, two coats for renovation work, and one coat for stained or rubbed work. On new surfaces, a primer/sealer is usually applied first, allowed to cure, then lightly sanded and wiped free of dust. Then the first topcoat is applied and allowed to cure, usually overnight. After correction of minor blemishes, the final topcoat is applied and allowed to cure for about eight hours.

Application. This is usually done by **brush, roller, spray,** or **rubbing,** often in combination with each other. Each is described below.

Brushed Work (see Figure 3.1)

Line work at trim, sashes, and corners is done with fine brushes, held in the hand like a pencil. Field work to cover larger areas of doors, walls, and ceilings is done with broad brushes, held in the hand like a knife. Paint is loaded onto the brush by dipping the brush bristles about halfway into the paint in a deep circular paint can, then tapping the loaded brush gently against the inside edge of the rim of the paint can. Paint is liberally applied to the wall in short, smooth, overlapping, vertical strokes, spreading the paint uniformly to cover the substrate, taking care not to overwork the paint.

Rolled Work (see Figure 3.2)

Line work is done with a brush as described above. Field work is done with a paint roller, either hand-

Table 3
FINISH APPLICATIONS

Product	Application
Acrylic paint	Wood and metal paneling and trim.
Alkyd paint	Wood and metal paneling and trim.
Asphalt paint	Basement walls and furred floors.
Cement paint	Bare concrete floors.
Chlorinated rubber	Exterior concrete, stucco, or asphalt.
Enamel paint	Wood and metal paneling and trim.
Fluorescent paint	Marking mechanical/electrical systems.
Lacquer	Finishing wood cabinets and panels.
Latex paint	Gypsum or plaster walls and ceilings.
Masonry paint	Coating concrete or brick walls.
Metallic paint	Radiator or convector grills.
Porch paint	Exterior wood decks, railing, and trim.
Rustproof paint	Priming exterior steelwork.
Shellac	Finishing furniture and cabinets.
Silicone paint	Waterproofing exterior masonry.
Stain	Wood shingles, siding, paneling, and trim.
Urethane	Finishing wood paneling and trim.
Varnish	Finishing wood paneling and trim.
Vinyl paint	For resistance to corrosion.

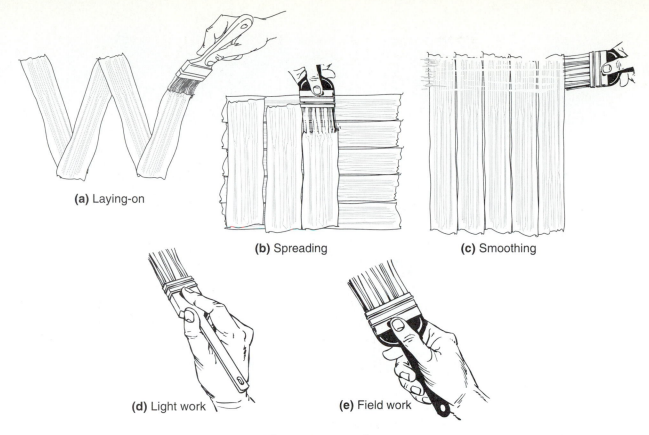

(a) Laying-on

(b) Spreading

(c) Smoothing

(d) Light work

(e) Field work

Figure 3.1 Brushing

(a) Plain wall application

(b) Accessing remote areas

Rolling

Rolling is often used to cover large areas quickly. Paint is rolled onto prepared surfaces in long lazy "M" strokes in one direction on ceilings and usually vertically on walls. (BCIT Building Technology)

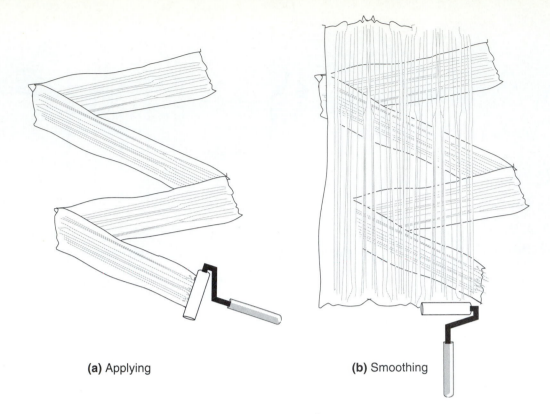

(a) Applying   **(b)** Smoothing

Figure 3.2   Rolling

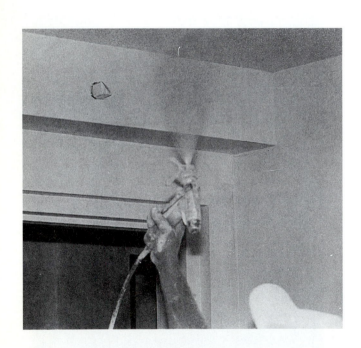

(a) Soffits

Spraying

Spraying can be an efficient technique to use, particularly on textured surfaces of plaster or stucco. The spray gun is held a short distance from the surface and moved in steady strokes. (BCIT Building Technology)

(b) Sides

held or attached to an extension pole. Paint is loaded onto the roller by rolling it in paint placed in a shallow, sloped, rectangular paint pan, with excess paint removed by rolling the roller on the exposed sloped end of the pan. Paint is liberally applied to the wall or ceiling surface in a large "W" or "M" pattern stroke, quickly doubling back without removing the roller from the surface, to spread the paint out evenly and to feather painted areas at the edges. Work should proceed at a constant speed and pressure to avoid creation of air bubbles or other blem-ishes. On wood, generally work parallel to the grain. On plaster or gypsum, avoid splatter or spray by rolling slowly.

Sprayed Work (see Figure 3.3)

Line work is usually done by masking areas not to be sprayed with the color to be applied to the line, and then uniformly spraying along the line. Paint is loaded into a reservoir, the compressor or pump is

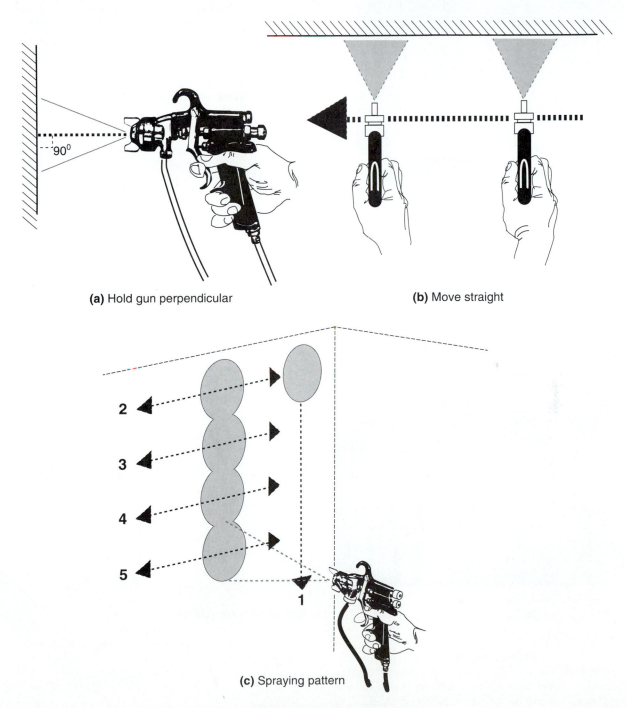

(a) Hold gun perpendicular

(b) Move straight

(c) Spraying pattern

Figure 3.3   Spraying

(a) Exterior siding

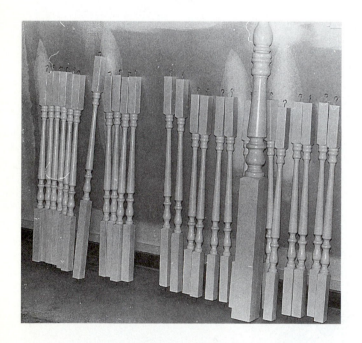

(b) Stair balusters

Pretreatment

It is often good practice to apply paint on hard-to-reach surfaces of building components before their installation. Here, exterior siding and stair balusters are being pretreated. (BCIT Building Technology)

connected and started, the spray gun nozzle is adjusted as necessary, and a few trial shots are made on scrap material to ensure that everything is in order.

Paint is then applied to the field surface by holding the spray gun nozzle perpendicularly to the surface, at a distance of between 150 and 250 mm or 6 and 10 in., and steadily moving the nozzle laterally for a distance of about 1 m or 3 ft., then doubling back with an overlapping pass below the first stroke. Each move is started before the gun trigger is pressed, to avoid a buildup of paint at the starting point. When spraying open work, such as fence pickets or stair balusters, adjust the nozzle to produce a spray wider than the picket or baluster, and hold the nozzle at an angle to minimize the amount of paint shot through the openings.

Rubbed Work (see Figure 3.4)

Stain or paint is liberally applied to the surface by brush, allowed to soak in for a short period, and then wiped off (usually across the grain) using a clean, soft, tight-weave cloth (two coats may be necessary to achieve the desired tone). A coat of wax, varnish, or lacquer may then be uniformly brushed or sprayed on top of the cured rubbed stain and allowed to cure. Painters sometimes use mittens made of lambswool to do this work.

Completion. The following recommendations apply to rapid removal of paint or stain droppings or splatters before they have set and cured, using

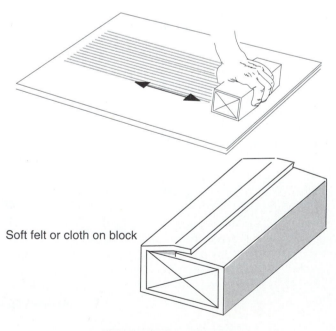

Soft felt or cloth on block

Figure 3.4 Rubbing

solvent products recommended by the paint or stain manufacturer, unless otherwise stated. **Never use gasoline** for cleaning surfaces or equipment.

To clean building **surfaces**, use one of the following techniques:

On **asphalt**, wipe up excess with a cloth and remove residue with a wirebrush; do not use solvents.

On **cloth or carpet**, physically remove excess with a scraper, blot affected area with a clean rag soaked in solvent, and rinse with clean water; repeat as necessary.

On **glass**, if smooth: let paint dry, then remove with a razor blade; if textured: remove excess immediately and wipe residue off with a solvent-soaked rag.

On **resilient flooring**, remove excess, firmly wipe affected area with a solvent-soaked rag, then rinse with clean water. Do not scrape surface of flooring.

On **metal or wood**, remove excess, and dilute the remainder with a solvent-soaked rag, wiping along the grain; on unfinished surfaces, lightly wirebrush if necessary, then resand.

To clean **equipment**, use one of the following techniques:

Thoroughly clean brushes, rollers, and small hand tools with solvent (see below), wash with warm soapy water, rinse, then carefully dry.

Using solvents: **Never use gasoline**; use water for water-based paint, turpentine for oil-based paint, and alcohol for shellac and lacquer.

Flush spray equipment with paint thinner immediately after use, remove excess thinner, then carefully wipe off and dry all surfaces.

5.3 Precautions

Gasoline should **never** be used as a paint thinner or remover. Paint products and many accessories used must be handled with care, as many of them are poisonous and almost all of them are flammable. Many paint products give off volatile or explosive vapors or particles during the curing process. All spills and leaks should be cleaned up immediately. Safety regulations are usually quite specific about the kinds of protective clothing and masks that painters and helpers must wear and about maintaining a high level of personal and site cleanliness. Workers should

Brushing
Fine work and cutting to line are still done with a good brush of the right type in the hands of a skilled painter. (BCIT Building Technology)

wear coveralls, good nonslip footwear, caps or hard hats, eye protection, work gloves, and face masks, particularly when engaged in spray painting. Hands and faces should be washed after painting and before eating. Good ventilation and lighting levels are necessary wherever painting work is being done.

Caution should be exercised regarding smoking and other open flames, pilot lights, or sparks wherever paint work is going on. All tools and equipment should be in good working condition. Parts of the building not to be painted should be covered with protective sheets, and accumulations of debris should not be permitted. Paint should not be applied in direct sunlight or during periods of rain. Ideally, paint work should not be done in temperatures below 10 degree C or 50 degree F or above 35 degrees C or 90 degrees F, in conditions of very low or very high humidity, or in strong winds, particularly when spray painting.

Paint products should be neatly stored together in a secure, clean, well-ventilated, and well-lit location at the site. Empty paint or solvent containers should be promptly removed off site, and paint-soiled or oil-soaked dropcloths should be properly aired until dry.

CHAPTER 10
Specialties

Section 10–001
Manufactured Specialties

1.0 Introduction

1.1 General Issues

Specialties is the title of Division 10 in *MasterFormat* categorizing a wide range of composite products which are factory produced ready for installation in buildings. Within Division 10 there are a number of sections, covering information on composite items such as fireplaces, flagpoles, grills, guards, louvers, postal accessories, scales, signs, sun control devices, and so on. Four of these sections commonly encountered in commercial and institutional building projects are shown below, each dealing with a separate product or item:

10–100   Chalkboards and Tackboards

10–150   Compartments and Cubicles

10–500   Lockers and Cabinets

10–800   Toilet and Bath Accessories

These four separate *MasterFormat* sections are described together in this composite section of this book. Although these specialty products show little

relationship to each other from a functional point of view, all have some common attributes with respect to the manner in which they are

1. **Produced** by manufacturers,
2. **Selected** by designers from individual manufacturer's trade catalogs,
3. **Delivered** by suppliers to the job-site in cartons or packages, and
4. **Installed** by contractors following the manufacturer's directions.

Each of these sections in Division 10 would be treated separately in a construction contract; it is only because there are so many elements common to all that they have been consolidated into one section in this book for convenience of reference and to minimize repetition. Each will be elaborated separately only to the extent that it is necessary to show significant distinctions relative to each one.

1.2 Design Aspects

The design of manufactured specialty items is virtually exclusive to the manufacturers of the products.

Owners and designers of buildings have little input to such design, beyond the general pressures they can exert as consumers in the marketplace. As a result, the extent of latitude in matters of design available to building owners and designers is limited to making selections from a variety of similar devices produced by competitive manufacturers, and also to making choices from a limited number of options available within the product range of any one manufacturer.

There are of course some creative possibilities in the manner in which the selected products and options can be set out or arranged in the building spaces. For example, if a building requires to be provided with storage lockers, then the space where the lockers will be located can be designed around the lockers selected, and the appearance and features of the lockers can themselves contributed to the overall design effect. Similarly, a public washroom in a building such as a school or hotel can be designed to accommodate the products of a particular manufacturer of toilet accessories, with respect to shape, color, and scale. Allowances must be made for the inclusion of specialty items used by the physically disadvantaged, by providing ramps, extra-wide openings, secure grab bars, and safety rails, and by placing operable items at levels easily accessed by people with restricted movement or reach. Manufacturers are naturally keen to sell their products, so they make items that building owners and designers are likely to want to have in their buildings, with respect to the variables of appearance, color, economy, maintenance, quality, serviceability, style, and utility. New models are developed and marketed each years, as new technology, consumer demands, or industry requirements make improvements possible or necessary.

Most manufacturers (and some manufacturers associations) prepare, produce, and distribute literature outlining or detailing the technical and other attributes of their product line, in the form of catalogs, flyers, and pamphlets. They also advertise in professional, technical, and trade journals at the local and national levels and in special construction compendiums or encyclopedias arranged and distributed annually by publishing companies such as *Sweet's General Building Renovation Catalog File* published by McGraw-Hill, Inc., in both Canada and the United States. Architectural and engineering design offices develop extensive specification libraries in which to store and retrieve all this information.

1.3 Related Work

Work closely connected to this section is described in the following sections, to which reference should be made:

03–300	Cast-in-Place Concrete
04–200	Unit Masonry
05–100	Steel Framing
06–100	Rough Carpentry
06–200	Finish Carpentry
09–200	Lath and Plasterwork
09–250	Gypsum Plasterboard Systems
09–300	Ceramic Tile Work
09–400	Terrazzo Work
09–900	Painting and Decorating

2.0 Products

2.1 Materials

The word *materials* is not the best word to use in this context in this section, because most if not all of the specialty items described below consist of a composite arrangement of several different kinds of materials and finishes. All are factory made and preassembled, although they may be supplied in knocked-down form for site reassembly by skilled workers. Primary materials of the products in the four *MasterFormat* sections chosen for discussion are as follows:

Chalkboards and Tackboards (see Figure 1). These consist of panels having a plywood or fiberboard backing and either a porcelain-enameled metal face (with matte finish for chalking or semi-gloss finish for felt pen) or a layer of cork, felt, or textured vinyl (for tacking) adhered to the backing. Edges are usually trimmed with continuous anodized aluminum channels, miter-cut at corners. Sizes vary up to 1,200 × 3,600 mm or 48 × 144 in.; larger units can be assembled from series of smaller units. Units can be either plain or curved, fixed or demountable, and vertically or horizontally sliding on spring balances or rollers, respectively.

Compartments and Cubicles (see Figure 2). These consist of panels, pilasters, and doors made of either welded hollow sheet metal with solidly insulated cores and trimmed edges, plywood or particleboards, plastic or marble slabs, or combinations of these and other products. There are three basic configurations available: floor mounted, overhead braced, and ceiling hung. Typical component thicknesses are about 25 mm or 1 in.; other approximate dimensions are shown in Table 1; specific manufacturers will quote actual sizes.

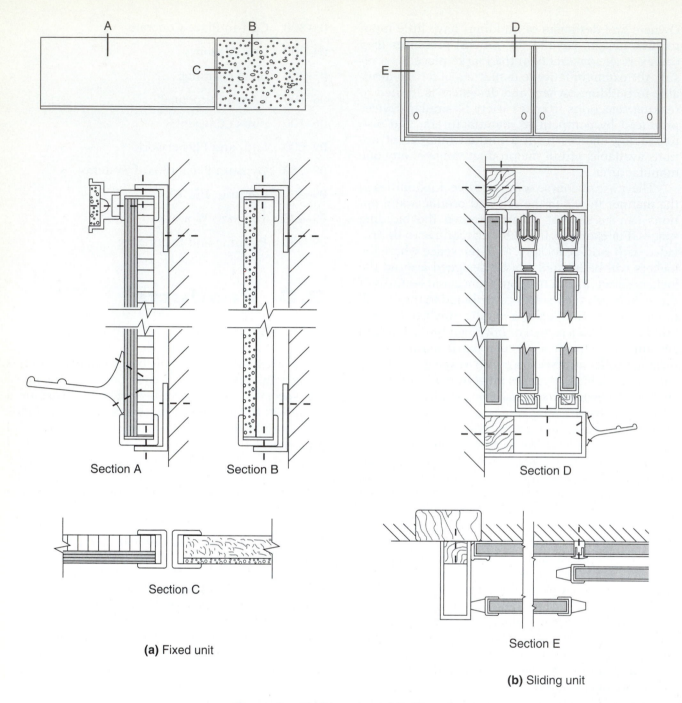

(a) Fixed unit

(b) Sliding unit

Figure 1 Chalkboards and Tackboards

Lockers and Cabinets (see Figure 3). These are storage compartments and cabinets, usually made of sheet steel and consisting of 24-gauge bodies, 20-gauge doors (usually reinforced and either slotted or perforated for ventilation), and 16-gauge angle steel door frames, all factory finished with baked acrylic or enamel paint in designer colors. Locker trim is either shaped, chrome-plated steel or molded, colored, polypropylene plastic. They are available in vertical, single, double, triple, and multiple tiers (up to six), and are usually assembled and then horizon-

Table 1
COMPARTMENT DIMENSIONS

Item	Length		Height	
	mm	in.	mm	in.
Doors	600	24	1,500	60
Panels	1,500	60	1,500	60
Pilasters	250	10	2,000	80

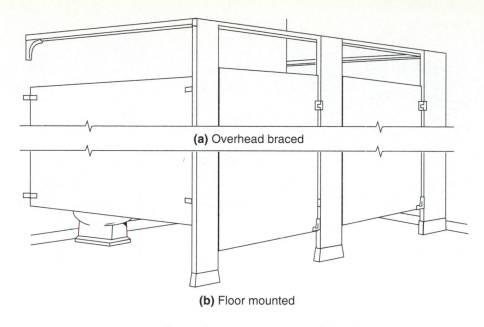

(a) Overhead braced

(b) Floor mounted

Figure 2   Compartments and Cubicles

(a) Preparation

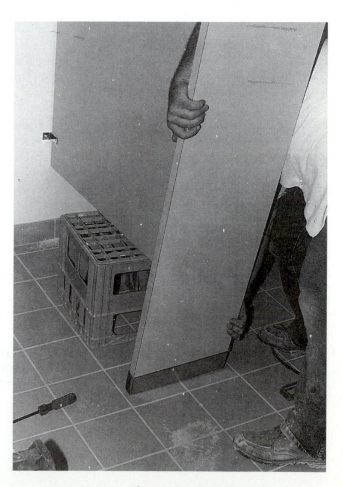

(b) Installation

Toilet Partitions

Toilet cubicle locations are measured and marked out, holes drilled through floors and walls as necessary, partition brackets are secured in position, and panels and doors are assembled. (UBC Architecture)

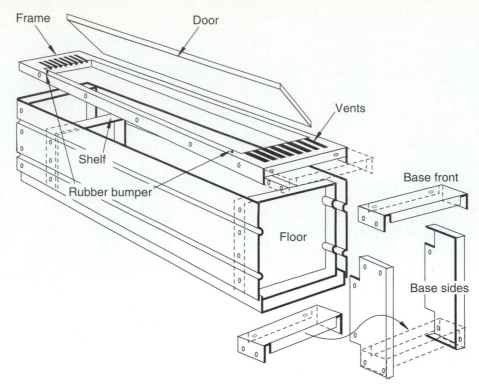

Figure 3 Lockers and Cabinets

tally ganged together with pop-rivets into composite banks of three- or four-unit widths at the factory before shipment. Some typical dimensions of lockers and cabinets are given in Table 2; other sizes are available.

Toilet and Bath Accessories (see Figure 4). These consist of individual items such as ashtrays, bars for towels, dispensers for soap and toilet paper, disposal bins for sanitary napkins, trash cans, medicine cabinets, mirrors in either single or multiple sections, racks for drinking glasses and toothbrushes, and rails for shower drapes, among other things such as bottle openers and retractable clotheslines. Depending on their design, they may be made of glass, metal, plastics, or wood, or combinations of these materials, and they may be designed and prepared for surface or recessed mounting.

2.2 Accessories

Accessories for specialty items usually take the form of additional items such as mounting hardware, cover plates, ornamental trim, and other optional features. A few representative items are listed below as a guide to the general nature of such accessory components; reference to manufacturers' trade catalogs is recommended for more specific detail.

Chalkboards and Tackboards. These include wood or metal chalk rails, map and tack rails, display hooks and clips, intermediate painted steel or anodized aluminum trim, counterbalancing weights or springs for double-hung units, removable shelf units, and locking devices.

Table 2
LOCKER APPROXIMATE DIMENSIONS

Item	Width		Height		Depth	
	mm	in.	mm	in.	mm	in.
Single-tier	300	12	1,800	72	550	22
Double-tier	300	12	900	36	550	22
Multiple-tier	300	12	300	12	550	22

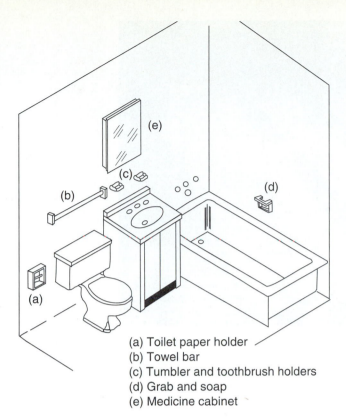

(a) Toilet paper holder
(b) Towel bar
(c) Tumbler and toothbrush holders
(d) Grab and soap
(e) Medicine cabinet

Figure 4 Toilet Accessories

Compartments and Cubicles. These consist of panel mounting hardware in the form of finished metal adjustable H-, T-, and U-clips; door hardware, such as pivot hinges and latches; and miscellaneous trim, such as combination coathooks and door bumpers, pilaster footing cover plates, overhead braces, and the like.

Lockers and Cabinets. Doors can be fitted with recessed latches for separate padlocks, coin- and key-operated locks, and tamperproof pin hinges. Most manufacturers offer a range of optional features, such as additional interior shelves, towel bars, clothes rods, coathooks, identification number plates, legs (instead of bases), and assorted perimeter base, end, and top trim.

Toilet and Bath Accessories. These consist mostly of an assortment of adhesives, bolts, brackets, caps, clips, nails, plugs, screws, shims, and the like, appropriate to the device to be installed.

3.0 Construction Aids

3.1 Equipment

As this work is not unlike metal and carpentry work in many respects, the equipment used in conjunction

(a) Toilet paper dispensers

Toilet Accessories
A wide assortment of surface-mounted and recessed devices is available. Most manufacturers offer choices of finishes, colors, coin-operation, and other useful or safety features. (Bobrick Washroom Equipment Inc.)

(b) Napkin dispenser and disposal

Section 10–100   Manufactured Specialties

515

(a) Locker assemply

(b) Panel riveting

(c) Installed bank

Storage Lockers
Standard components are manually assembled at the shop, fastened together with pop-rivets, and delivered in composite units (or "banks") to the site for final fastening in position. (BCIT Building Technology)

with it is similar to equipment described in Sections 05–500 and 06–100.

3.2 Tools

For a detailed description of hand tools common to this work, such as chalk-lines, clamps, drills, hammers, mallets, measuring tapes, pliers, levels, rollers, screwdrivers, and the like, refer to Section 01–525 Construction Aids.

4.0 Production

4.1 Crew Configuration

Small items, such as towel rails and bars, can usually be installed by one skilled tradesperson such as a carpenter, while larger units, such as chalkboards and toilet partitions, may require up to three people, two semiskilled workers to hold the unit temporarily in position while the third skilled person does the actual fastening. On large projects, it may be appropriate to utilize two or more crews to speed up the work.

4.2 Productivity

Some representative factors are given in Table 3 for the placement of common specialty items installed in repetitive fashion by skilled workers employed on typical commercial or institutional projects.

Table 3
PRODUCTIVITY FACTORS FOR SPECIALTIES

Type of Unit	Minutes per Unit
Chalkboards and tackboards:	
Simple fixed	20–30
Complex sliding	40–60
Compartments and cubicles:	
Panels and pilasters	60–80
Doors and braces	40–60
Lockers:	
Individual units	20–30
Ganged banks of four	30–40
Toilet and bath accessories:	
Simple surface mount	10–15
Complex recessed	20–30

5.0 Procedures

5.1 Preparation

Areas scheduled to receive manufactured specialties should be clean and free of debris and equipment not required for the installation of the specialties.

The wall or structure to which the specialty item is to be attached should be checked for soundness and for blockings or backing supports as necessary to secure the product in position. Battened wood walls should have the battens cut, removed, or otherwise adjusted so that specialty items can fit flush against the main wall plane. Plain masonry walls should have holes drilled and fiber or plastic plugs inserted corresponding to the locations and sizes of the screwed or bolted mountings on the specialty unit. Walls having irregular surfaces such as rough stone or ornamental block masonry should have the areas required for specialty items prepared ready to receive them.

Shop drawings, layout drawings, and templates are almost always necessary to ensure proper fastening methods and correct positioning of manufactured specialties. Specialty items should be removed from delivery packaging, checked for completeness and serviceability, and prepared for installation. In the case of metal lockers and cabinets, it is usually less costly to have the final assembly mostly done at the factory and not at the site, because of the higher availability of efficient powered equipment and cheaper manual labor in factories and shops than at job-sites.

5.2 Process

Installation of typical units in the four sections of *MasterFormat* Division 10 selected for inclusion in this book are briefly described below; they are presented as being representative of many similar items or units.

Chalkboards and Tackboards. Units are positioned against the wall to which they will be fastened on temporary wood or metal supports previously cut to the required height. Perimeter trim is straightened with a rubber mallet. Screws are driven through predrilled holes, starting at the bottom center of the unit and working out and up around the sides. There are three basic installation methods: exposed fastenings, concealed fastenings, and demountable boards. Finally, intermediate trim, chalk rails, and map rails are added if required and fastened in place. Figure 5 shows the layout.

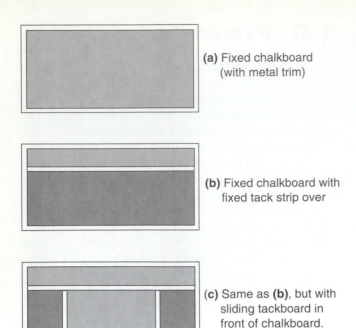

(a) Fixed chalkboard (with metal trim)

(b) Fixed chalkboard with fixed tack strip over

(c) Same as (b), but with sliding tackboard in front of chalkboard.

Figure 5 Layout for Boards

Compartments and Cubicles. Locate the center lines of the pilaster and panel lines from the approved shop drawings and mark them off on the floors and walls. The width of toilet stalls varies between 800 and 900 mm or 32 and 36 in. Drill holes for and install adjustable floor and wall brackets according to approved templates. Install pilasters and headrails; then install division panels and doors, temporarily resting them on wood or concrete blocks about 300 mm or 12 in. high to establish the correct elevation of these components. Check and adjust as necessary, then install remaining trim, such as pilaster shoes, door latches, and coathooks. Finally, adjust the gravity hinges on doors to hold doors in the correct position when not latched closed, by adjusting the hinge nut assembly. See Figure 6.

Lockers and Cabinets. Lockers can be installed either against existing walls or back to back in free-standing central locations. The units are usually mounted on a preconstructed, level wood, concrete, or masonry base about 100 mm or 4 in. high, intended to provide a solid foundation and to create a small toe recess; some assemblies have an integral

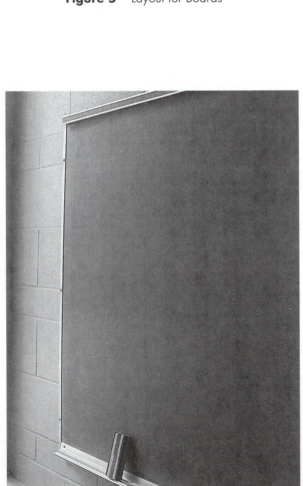

(a) School chalkboard

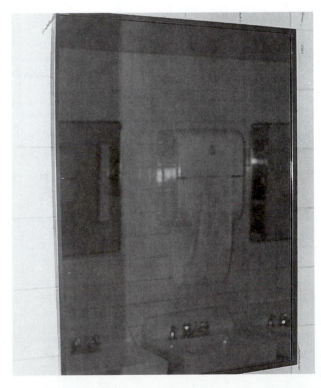

(b) Tamperproof mirrors

Miscellaneous Units

As mentioned in the text, Division 10 of *MasterFormat* lists a wide variety of manufactured building products. The two shown here are simply representative of that wider range. (UBC Architecture)

Chapter 10   Specialties

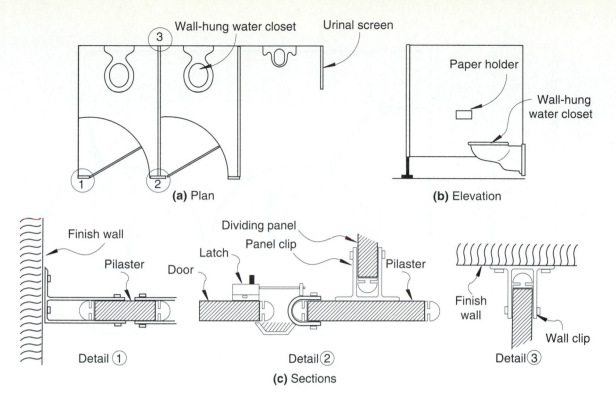

(a) Plan

(b) Elevation

(c) Sections

Figure 6 Layout for Cubicles

or separate preformed and prefinished metal base. As most lockers have perforated backs for ventilation, they have to be mounted at least 25 mm or 1 in. away from the wall or other lockers in back. Solid wood or metal channel strapping accomplishes the correct spacing behind the units. The units are leveled, shimmed if necessary, and screwed into posi-

tion in accordance with manufacturers' instructions. Prefabricated metal end and corner trim, colored to match the rest of the units, can be fastened using pop-rivets, and if required, a continuous sloping top cap complete with end gussets can be installed to deter the accumulation of garbage and dust. Figure 7 shows the layout.

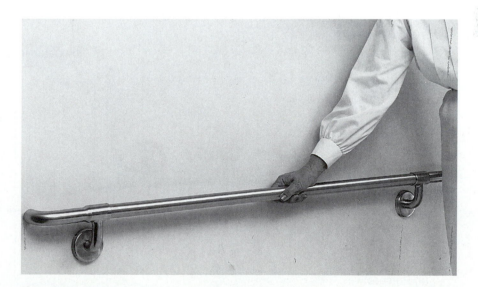

Safety Rails

In many buildings, customized safety grab rails must be provided where required by codes or common sense. As shown here, these need not be unattractive nor difficult to install. (Bobrick Washroom Equipment Inc.)

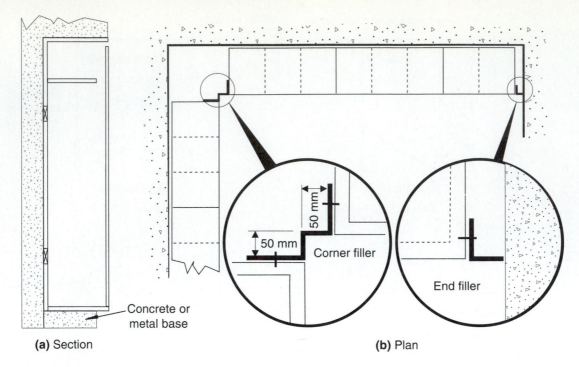

(a) Section
(b) Plan

Figure 7   Layout for Lockers

Toilet and Bath Accessories. There are three significant aspects to consider; each has two components:

Installation

1. Surface mounted (see Figure 8.1). Such items require simple measurement to establish their location and level. Depending on method of fasten-ing, they may require marking and drilling of suit-able holes, insertion of plugs, placing of the unit, and tightening of screw or bolt fasteners; alternatively, an adhesive may be required to be used.

2. Recessed (see Figure 8.2). Such items re-quire measurement and marking of portions of walls or other fixtures (such as countertops or sides), a hole to be cut out, and rough bearers or mounting blocks to be inserted to receive the fastening devices.

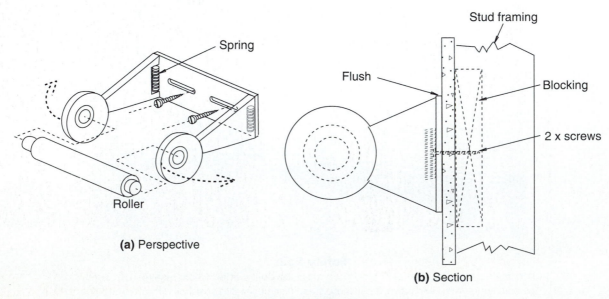

(a) Perspective
(b) Section

Figure 8.1   Surface Mounting

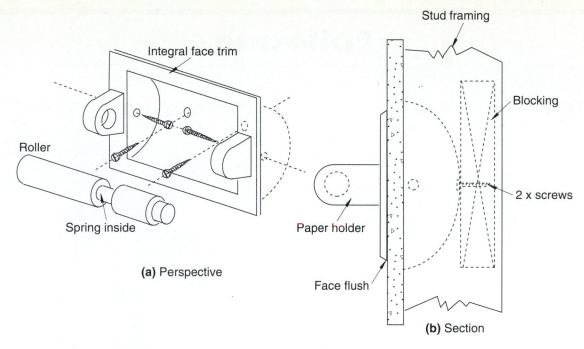

Figure 8.2   Recessed Mounting

Fastening

1. Exposed. The tops or ends of the fastening devices are visible after the unit is installed; the fastenings are therefore usually finished to match the units.

2. Concealed. Most units are mounted on clips or brackets which are previously attached to walls or other fixtures and then covered with the base or trim of the accessory in its final position.

Stocking

1. Liquids. Soap and other fluid dispensers should be filled with liquids as recommended by their respective manufacturers.

2. Solids. Paper towels, packaged soap tablets, toilet tissue, sanitary napkins, condoms, or other solid contents of the correct type and size should be installed into dispensers. All manual or coin-operable toilet accessories should be tested by the general contractor to ensure correct function in the given circumstances, prior to handing over the building to the owner.

5.3 Precautions

Although there are some regulations governing the design and manufacture of manufactured specialties, there are few regulations governing their installation and use. Such work is not (for the most part) particularly hazardous.

As most specialty items are supplied from the factory prefinished, particular care must be taken not to damage the finishes during installation, as in most cases it is not possible to make satisfactory site repairs; the unit usually has to be replaced in whole or part. Furthermore, as most specialty items are relatively delicate, expensive, and prone to theft, they should be temporarily stored after delivery to the site in clean, dry, and secure locations. The work involved in installing specialties does not normally involve the use of any special protective clothing or masks. Care should be taken not to damage other installed finishes, such as anodizing, carpeting, painting, paneling, or tilling, during installation procedures.

Epilogue

And so we come to the end of this book. Although it is an end in one sense, it also can be considered just the beginning of what may become a lifelong journey for many young readers. The breadth, depth, and range of the many facets of the construction industry in North America have only been hinted at in the various sections of the book, which detail some aspects of the work of the more commonly encountered building trades and the kinds of constraints that govern them. Students are encouraged to use this book as a foundation on which to build their growing knowledge of the construction world.

Four ingredients (among others) essential to any successful technical career in the construction industry are knowledge of building **materials,** construction **methodology,** contractual **procedure,** and development **costs.** The proper absorption of selected components of the first two of these four ingredients into the minds of properly motivated young people has been the main objective of this book; the latter ingredients have been covered previously in two other books by this author:

1. *Construction Specifications and Contracts* (Reston, VA: Reston Publishing Co., 1981).
2. *Construction Estimating Techniques* (Englewood Cliffs, NJ: Prentice Hall, 1981).

Persons responsible for the preparation and presentation of college courses on construction materials and methods are reminded that a companion *Instructor's Manual* is available from the publisher. More general application of the book abounds in architectural and building technology courses on contracts and procedures, construction economics and estimating, project costing and management, and site layout and processes. These also form the basis for term assignments, classroom discussions, pop

The Process in Action
Another building nears successful completion as a result of many of the construction procedures described in this book. (UBC Archive)

quizzes, course tests, and formal or professional examinations.

It is hoped that students, instructors, and others find the book to be reliable, useful, readable, and, indeed, enjoyable. It would also be gratifying if the book contributed to understanding and cooperation in the construction industry.

"The art of building, or architecture, is the beginning of all the arts that lie outside the person."
Havelock Ellis, in *The Dance of Life*

522

Glossary

First, while extensive, this glossary is not exhaustive; it includes only words or phrases used in the book. Second, many common words (such as *beam, column, nail, post, roof,* etc.) have been excluded to keep the list concise. Finally, there will be some differences of opinion as to the correct definition of technical terms used in various parts of the continent; the meanings given are considered to be appropriate for most regions.

absorption: ability of material to retain moisture or absorb sound energy.

active leaf: the leaf of a door to which the operating hardware is attached.

additive: a mixture added to another mixture, usually to alter chemical characteristics.

adhesion: the ability of one material to stick to another.

adze: a small hand axe, used for rough cutting lumber surfaces.

aging: the process of artificially curing a product.

air-dried: material naturally seasoned by exposure.

air-entrainment: the introduction of millions of microscopic air bubbles into concrete by the use of special effervescents.

allan-key: a short, bent shaft used to tighten socket-head screws.

ambient: the surrounding or prevailing normal condition.

anhydrous: material containing no water.

annealing: the process of tempering or cooling metal under control to relieve stresses.

anode: an electrode giving off positive ions or attracting negative ions.

anodize: to electrically deposit protective film on a metal base.

applied stop: a surface-mounted member intended to arrest the travel of a door or window through a framed opening.

architrave: the moldings or trim around a door or window frame.

argillaceous: clay-like.

arris: an external corner formed at the junction of two planes.

artisan: a skilled tradesperson.

ashlar: a type of cut stone masonry bond pattern.

astragal: a small molding intended to support glass panels in a door or window; also, a molding used to close the small gap between the meeting edges of a pair of doors.

auger: a corkscrew-like drilling tool.

awl: a manual tool with a sharp pin, for making small holes.

axial: parallel to the long axis.

axis: the central line of any symmetrical area or body.

axminster: a type of carpet weave.

backset: the horizontal distance from the center of a lockset to the vertical outside edge of the locking stile.

backsplash: a sheet of protective material placed vertically behind a horizontal work surface, such as a kitchen counter.

ballast: heavy material placed over lighter material to hold it in place, such as gravel on top of roof insulation.

balloon frame: a structural wood system having outer vertical studs continuous from foundation to roof elevations.

ball peen: a type of hammer having a rounded striking head.

baluster: the small vertical supports in a balustrade.

balustrade: a railing consisting of balusters and a top rail.

baseboard: trim placed at the join of floor and wall planes.

basement: the portion of a building below grade.

bat: a cut brick, having one uncut end.

batten: a continuous piece of square-sawn lumber to which sheet metal panels can be attached; also, a wood or metal covering strip, to conceal joints from view and from the weather.

batter: the slope of inclination of a surface from the vertical plane, measured in degrees.

batts: flexible insulation material which has been cut into specific dimensions to fit between studs or joists.

beading: a painting technique used to produce a clean, sharp bead of paint to form a demarcation line between surfaces painted in two different colors.

bearing plate: a flat plate, intended to spread load from a column to the foundation, to provide for fastening and to permit leveling of the column base.

bed: the substrate or level on which masonry work is built.

bedding: the act of placing a material (such as glass) to be secured in another material (such as putty).

bench mark: a predetermined point used to establish layout and elevation of new construction.

bent: a piece of timber shaped to a curve by steaming.

bevel: the join of two surfaces at an angle other than a right angle; e.g., cutting the vertical edge of a door to a slight angle to prevent the door from binding in the frame.

bit: a small interchangeable cutting point used in a drill.

bite: the amount by which the edge of a pane of glass overlaps the edge of the wood or metal frame in which it is set.

blanked: a mortise hole cut out of a metal door frame for hinges or locksets.

blank-plate: an inoperable ornamental plate secured over the face of unused holes drilled for hardware components.

bleeding: the extrusion of adhesive, cement paste, creosote, or resins from building components.

blemish: a visual (but not structural) defect in any material.

blind: a light-duty sun shade; also, anything concealed, such as blind nailing.

blinding: to cover compacted gravel sub-bases with fine sand to produce a smooth bed for waterproofing or vapor barriers.

blind-nailed: nails driven at 45 degrees through the root of the siding tongue.

blocking: solid wood filling in between two adjacent members.

board foot: a piece of wood 12 in.² x 1 in. thick (US).

board meter: a piece of wood 1 m² x 25 mm thick (UK).

boasting: chipping small pieces of stone off a larger piece to improve fitting.

bolster: a continuous support for a group of parallel reinforcing steel bars or rods; also, a short, broad-bladed, blunt trowel used for shaping masonry units and joints.

bolt: a solid cylindrical fastener having a threaded shank and a securing nut; also, a short section cut from a long log.

bolt, dead: a solid bolt, usually having a square end, extended and retracted by means of a key.

bolt, latch: a solid bolt, usually having a beveled end, extended by means of a spring and retracted by pressure against the strike plate or by operation of the door knob.

boxing: to encase or enclose in wood or metal cabinetry; also, forming an opening in a proposed concrete component.

brad: a short square-section nail.

breakback: a weakened point in a form tie that permits the tie to be easily broken at that point.

breast: a projection, such as a chimney, standing out from the face of the wall plane.

bridging: blockings between joists used to distribute loads and stiffen framing.

bright: usually means new, unmarked, unstained.

brooming: working a surface with a stiff brush or broom.

brown coat: the second layer of a three-layer plaster system.

Btu: an imperial unit of energy (one Btu equals the energy required to raise one pound of water one degree Fahrenheit).

buck: a rough stud forming the frame for vertical jambs at openings in wood-framed walls.

buckle: in structural terms, failure by deflection; also to connect two ends of a belt or wire together (turn-buckle).

buff: to polish to a dull finish.

bulkhead: continuous blocking forming a deliberate break or construction joint usually within a formwork configuration.

bullnose: a masonry or tile unit having one curved end.

bush hammer: a specially shaped hand tool used for dressing or finishing stone blocks.

butt: another name for a hinge; also, the line where two materials touch without overlapping; also, the lower edge or end of a shingle or shake.

buttering: the application of mortar to the sides or ends of a masonry unit.

calcareous: containing lime or calcium.

calk: to seal joints or cracks with a mastic material.

camber: the upward curve of a surface or a beam, usually invoked to offset deflection or induce drainage.

cant strip: a continuous block of treated wood or plastic, cut in cross-section at 45 degrees and installed at the perimeter of built-up roofing membranes to deflect water.

capillary: (from the Latin, *capilla*, "a hair"); very fine threads or tubes.

capillary action: the movement of water along fine passages caused by differences in surface tension.

carcass: an unfinished skeleton frame.

carriage: an intermediate stringer, usually placed along the underside of the center line of the flight.

casework: factory-made wood or metal cabinets.

casing: wood trim around doors and windows.

cathode: an electrode giving off negative ions or attracting positive ions.

catwalk: a light gangway to provide access over a roofed area or through a system of roof trusses.

catalyst: a substance used to alter, initiate, or improve a chemical reaction without itself being affected.

caulk: see *calk*.

celsius: metric temperature scale.

cell: the hollow core of a block or brick in masonry.

cellular: a material characterized by having a system of small compartments or cells throughout its structure.

cement factor: the percentage of cement in a volume of concrete.

centering: curved formwork and falsework used to make arches.

chain: carpet yarns running longitudinally to restrain lateral shot yarns.

chair: an individual support for reinforcing steel bars or rods; chairs can be high or low.

chalking: oxidization of paint over time due to weathering.

chalk-line: retractable cotton cord, powdered to leave marks.

chamfer: a small continuous shaped fillet of wood intended to form splayed or rounded corners on concrete components.

chargehand: the factory equivalent of a site foreman.

chord: the upper or lower member of a truss, usually absorbing the primary forces of tension and compression.

chroma: the purity, clarity, or strength of any specific color (high chroma colors are strong; low chroma are subdued).

cladding: a non-load-bearing skin forming an exterior wall.

clean-out: a small aperture left in a masonry wall to facilitate the removal of excess mortar from cavities.

clear: usually means without significant visual or structural blemish; also, without interruption, as in a "clear" span.

clear span: horizontal unsupported distance between bearings.

cleat: a protrusion (or system of protrusions) intended to improve the attachment of any material to its substrate.

cleavage: the plane along which materials are easily split.

clerk of works: a field engineer usually hired to look after the owner's interests on site.

clinker: an overburned brick.

closer: an adjustable spring-loaded oil- or air-damped device exerting controlled and steady pressure on a door to return it to the closed position.

closure: a cut brick inserted to maintain brick bonding patterns.

coat: a single layer of paste, cream, or liquid covering applied to a surface, usually for protection.

cohesive: to stick together (e.g., soils like clay).

coin: in stone masonry, a corner.

collar: a sectional circular, wedge-shaped sleeve which fits over the ends of reinforcing tendons to maintain tension; also, a horizontal tie between sloped rafters.

color: spectral evaluation of reflected or transmitted light.

come-along: a leverage device, used to impart tension to straps.

compression: the state of being pressed or condensed by forces.

condensation: the formation of water out of moisture vapor because of reduced temperature.

conductivity: the ability of any material to conduct energy.

conduit: a metal or plastic tube that allows wires to be threaded through construction systems.

construction economist: a firm or person retained as a consultant to advise on economic and contractual matters of construction.

cope: to cover, such as with wood or stone at joints or edges; also, to shape one piece to fit the profile of another piece.

corbel: a portion of a wall that projects outward and upward in successive layers or courses.

cornice: ornamental molding installed on the upper parts of external walls or between internal walls and ceilings.

corrugate: to bend sheet material into a series of parallel folds to produce a regular pattern of furrows and ridges.

cost plus: a type of construction contract in which costs are billed to the owner as they arise, together with a fee.

course: a horizontal row of masonry units.

coverage: the amount of paint necessary to cover a given surface area; also, the number of laps or plies in a shingle system.

creep: deformation of a material under stress.

cribbing: an assembly of heavy wooden members to retain earth.

cricket: a small shaped metal hood, usually located at the upper side of chimneys or similar projections through roofs, to deflect water around the projection.

cripple: any support that is shorter than normal full length.

critical path: the most efficient sequence of events and activities to complete construction within a predetermined time and budget.

cross-bridging: lateral stiffening between joists or rafters.

cross-cutting: cutting across the grain.

cull: to select and clear out undesirable pieces.

cup-shake: a defect in flat grain lumber caused by shrinkage along the annular rings.

curing: the period during which chemical materials (such as cement, paint, or preservatives) gain rated characteristics.

curtain wall: a non-load-bearing envelope wall hung on the external structural frame of a building.

cutout: a piece removed to create a small opening.

cutting in: the establishment of a clean, sharp border at the edges of surfaces painted in contrasting colors.

C-value: amount of heat conducted through one square foot of surface area per unit thickness of any specific material.

cylinder: a rotating spindle, containing adjustable tumblers, forming the operable security element in a door-lock.

dado: a small groove cut into the face of a wood panel; also, a continuous permanent vertical wainscot wall panel partially covering a full-height wall (from floor to shoulder level).

damp course: a horizontal layer of material impervious to the passage of moisture.

damp-proofing: the exclusion of water in its vaporized form.

decibel (dB): a unit on a logarithmic scale used to measure sound pressure or intensity. The scale starts at the threshold of hearing (0 dB) and increases in increments of 10 db to finish at the threshold of pain (130 dB).

decking: system used to form a wood or metal horizontal platform.

defect: a natural or machining fault that detracts from the servicability or appearance of a piece of material.

deficiency list: identification by the designer of minor defects to be rectified by the contractor before a construction contract can be declared complete.

deflection: downward displacement of a beam or truss because of loading.

delamination: the separation of layers of glued material.

deluging: to flood with liquid.

derrick: a hoisting device consisting of a vertical mast, an inclined rotating boom, and pulleys, cables, and hooks.

designer: the firm or person responsible for the building design.

detailer: a person with the knowledge and skill to prepare schedules for the fabrication of reinforcing steel.

diffusion: the gradual permeation of a region by a fluid.

double time: payment of wages at twice the normal rate.

dovetail: a type of interlocking joint.

dowel: a cylindrical pin used to join two components.

dressed: planed, machined.

dressing: working the surfaces of brick or stone masonry.

drift pin: a short tapered hardened steel rod used to align corresponding holes in adjacent steel members.

drip: a small groove formed under an overhanging projection on the outside of a building to deflect water.

drop cloth: a large sheet of tight-weave cotton or thin polyethylene used to protect surfaces from paint splatters.

drowned mortar: mortar having an excess of water.

dry rot: a type of wood decay caused by a fungus.

dry stone: masonry built without the use of mortar.

dunnage: scrap wood or metal used to temporarily raise stored products above mud or water at a building site.

dunnage beam: a temporary beam used to strengthen the structure during steel erection operations.

durability: characteristic of materials that determines how long they will last under expected conditions of service.

dutch: the term used to describe a door cut in half horizontally.

ease: to take the sharp edge or corner off a piece of material.

efflorescence: a powdery gray-white salt residue brought to the surface of masonry by the action of moisture.

electrode: a metal rod consisting of the material to be deposited during a welding process.

elevation: a drawing of or the actual vertical face of a building or a portion or component of a building; also, the height or depth of any part of a building relative to a fixed datum.

emery: a hard abrasive powder consisting of carborundum and other ingredients available in varying grades of fineness.

emulsion: an oil suspended in another liquid.

end-pan: a specially formed unit intended to close the open end of a cellular deck pan unit.

escutcheon: an ornamental plate secured by the rose of a lock-set.

esthetic (aesthetic): pertaining to beauty; having primarily to do with appearance.

etch: to slightly erode the surface of glass using acid, usually for decorative purposes.

expansion joint: a location where construction systems are interrupted to permit movement of the building.

exposure: the amount by which each shingle is exposed to the weather, or the distance from one butt to the next butt.

extensions: the results of multiplying quantities or materials or work by unit prices.

extras: items of work not included in the original contract.

fabric: an interwoven and/or welded arrangement of wire that produces an open sheet of reinforcing material; also, woven cloth material.

fabricator: usually a company that makes building components to special order.

face: the surface exposed to view.

Fahrenheit: imperial (or English) temperature scale.

faience: ornamental clay tile with a colored, glazed ceramic face.

failed set: the delayed hydration of cement.

fall: the slope or decline of a deck toward a drainage opening.

false set: the apparent but incorrect hydration of cement.

fascia: a long, flat band of wood or metal forming an architectural feature at eaves or gables of roofs.

fat mortar: mortar with an excess of cementitious ingredients.

feather: a small tapered or sloping feature along the edge of a piece of material.

fieldstone: naturally occurring uncut blocks of stone.

file: a rough, flat steel bar used to wear down materials; also, a means of sorting and storing information either manually or electronically; also, a row (as in single file).

fillet: a narrow strip of wood used to fill the internal joint between two planes of material.

finger joint: an interlocking glued assembly (resembling the interface of fingers when hands are clasped together).

finishing: the final treatment in any building process.

fire stop: a built-in component designed to resist the passage of flame and heat.

fixture: anything that is attached to a building and thereby legally fixed to the real property.

flagstone: large, thin, irregularly shaped pieces of slate or shale laid flat as paving stones.

flammable: combustible; easily set on fire.

flange: the peripheral plates along the outermost edges of the central web of a steel beam.

flashing, base: that part of the flashing system that connects the horizontal roof or waterproof membrane to the adjacent vertical wall or parapet.

flashing, cap: a continuous piece of metal, snapped on to complete a weatherproof system at edges, ridges, or expansion joints in roof systems.

flashing, counter: that part of the flashing system that overlaps the base flashing.

flash set: the premature setting of cementitious mixtures before complete hydration or bonding has occurred; usually caused by excessive heat or cold.

flight: a continuous series of steps between two building levels.

flitch: a half-log of hardwood before cutting veneers.

floating: working the surface of concrete in its plastic state to produce a homogeneous and solid finish of cement paste.

flood coat: the final thick coating of asphalt poured onto the built-up system prior to the spread of gravel.

flue: a (usually) vertical duct or vent for hot gasses and smoke.

flush: two components having surfaces lying within one plane.

fluting: ornamental curved hollowed grooves cut into a surface exposed to view.

flux: a nonmetallic substance (such as borax) used to prevent oxidization of metal during welding processes.

f.o.b.: free on board (the financial status of material ordered for a building project, e.g., f.o.b. truck).

fogging: creating a water vapor mist using a fine nozzle.

foil: sheet metal less than 0.2 mm or 0.04 in. thick.

forward: the term given to the direction of swing of a door away from the viewer.

french: the term given to any door cut in half vertically.

frequency: vibration or oscillation of particles, measured in cycles per second, called Hertz (Hz).

frieze: a decorative horizontal band on a building surface.

froe: a special axe used to split shakes.

frog: a small indentation formed in one or both flat planes of the width of a brick which makes the unit easier to grasp and handle, and provides a mechanical key for the mortar.

frontage: the length of the property adjoining the street line.

fungus: a tiny plant organism devoid of chlorophyll, such as mildews, molds, and some rusts (plural: *fungi*).

furan: a colorless liquid adhesive [C_4H_4O].

furring: light framing used to support a false front or soffit.

gable: the end panel of a cabinet or the upper triangular area formed by the sloping roof at the end wall of a building.

galleting: filling a stone masonry joint with small chips of matching rock.

ganged: assembled in groups, as in ganged forms.

gel: the colloidal dispersion of a solid, such as cement, with a liquid, such as water.

girder: a horizontal or slightly inclined main beam.

girt: a horizontal intermediate support.

girth: the distance measured around some building member.

glazing: the process of securing glass panels into prepared door or window frames.

glides: metal or plastic slides on which cabinet drawers are mounted for ease of movement without binding.

gloss: light reflected from a surface.

glulam: glued laminated wood members.

going: the horizontal distance covered by a sloping member.

grade: a standard of quality for materials or performance established by legislation or by industrial agreement.

grade beam: a horizontal foundation that transmits loads to vertical piles.

grain: the characteristic natural cell pattern showing on the cut face of a piece of lumber. (This word always requires an adjective to delineate a specific aspect of grain.)

grain, edge: lumber in which the grain runs at an angle greater than 45 degrees to the surface.

grain, flat: lumber in which the grain runs at an angle less than 45 degrees to the surface.

grain, vertical: same as *edge grain*.

green: unseasoned; uncured; freshly placed.

grille: an open slatted or perforated ventilator.

ground: the earth; also, a rough base of some sort.

grout: a mixture of cement, fine sand, and water used to fill minor voids in concrete or masonry work.

grub screw: a short headless machine screw.

guniting: spraying a fine cement/sand mix to stop soil erosion.

guy: a steel wire stay or brace usually capable of having its tension adjusted by means of a turn-buckle.

hand: the method of designating which side (left or right) of any building component will have a special feature, such as doors, hinges, or handrails.

handrail: the inclined or level rail often secured to a system of balusters and newels to provide support for the hand.

hanger: any metal or plastic device used to suspend building components.

hardware, finish: catches, hinges, hooks, latches, locks, etc.

hardware, rough: bolts, clips, nails, screws, washers, etc.

haunch: a sloping collar that eliminates abrupt changes of plane.

hawk: hand tool used by plasterers and masons to hold paste.

header: a masonry unit laid horizontally with its length perpendicular to the wall plane; also, the horizontal frame member at the top of an opening.

heel: the point where two chords of a truss meet.

hemmed edge: where the cut edge of sheet metal is folded back to form a small neat border.

hickey bar: a long-handled metal lever used manually to bend light steel bars or rods.

hiding power: the ability of paint to obscure the substrate.

hinge: a three-part metal device invariably used (in pairs or threes) to hang doors and to permit their movement. (The three parts are joined by a fixed or removable pin.)

hinge stile: the stile to which hinges are secured.

hip: the intersection of sloping planes at the top of a roof.

hod: a small container, used to carry loads on the shoulder.

honed: finely polished stone.

hopper: a metal enclosure usually constrained at either end by quadrants and intended to deflect the movement of air passing though an open window vent.

hue: property of light that distinguishes one color from another.

humidity: the amount of moisture in the atmosphere, usually expressed as a percentage.

hydration: the chemical conversion of cement powder to crystals by the addition of water.

hydrostatic pressure: the pressure exerted on a structure by the weight of still water having a depth of any given value.

impact insulation class: a numerical factor, between 30 and 90, indicating the ability of a floor or wall system to isolate impact sounds generated on one side from the other side. The higher the factor, the better the isolation.

in situ: built or cast in place.

insulation: any material that will not easily conduct energy in the form of heat, sound, or electricity.

IRMA roof: inverted roof membrane assembly in which roof insulation is placed on top of the system, not beneath it.

item: a unit of labor, material, or work in an estimate.

jack: a mechanical, pneumatic, or hydraulic levering device used to exert pressure on or lift an object (a common example is the automobile jack).

jack rafter: a shortened rafter between a hip and a valley.

jack stud: a shortened stud below a sill plate.

jamb: the vertical side of any opening.

jimmy: a short steel bar, pointed at one end and flattened at the other, used to take building components or packaging apart.

jig: a clamping device used to hold materials in a specific position during fabrication processes.

joiner: a finish carpenter.

joint: the point of contact between two components.

joint compound: slow-setting topping paste for plaster board.

jointer: a small metal hand tool used to compact and shape mortar joints to a slight veed or concaved recess.

joint filler: fast setting material used with plaster board.

joist: horizontal structural member supporting decks and floors.

joule: a metric unit of energy (one joule equals one kilogram per meter squared per second squared).

journeyman: a qualified tradesperson who has completed a recognized course of training.

kerf: a small cut, not wider than the width of the saw blade, made on the edge of any building component.

kerosene: oil solvent distilled from petroleum.

key: many meanings; generally letting one component into another; also, a continuous tongue and groove feature intended to transfer shear between concrete components.

kicker: a falsework brace used to support formwork panels.

knocked-down: delivered unassembled.

knocked-up: a slang term meaning damaged or defective.

knock-out: a small removable (and disposable) panel usually encountered in electrical accessories like switch boxes.

knot: a defect in the cut surface of lumber, caused by a former branch; knots may be tight, loose, or void.

knuckle: the part of a hinge that houses the pin.

kraft paper: a heavy duty unbleached, unsized coarse paper used for a variety of building processes.

k-value: amount of heat conducted through one inch per unit area of any specific material.

label: frequently refers to a certificate required to be attached to building products or components having a specific fire-resistance rating.

laborer: an unskilled helper.

laitence: a milky cream that rises to the surface of concrete or plaster that has been overworked.

laminate: to apply a thin layer on top of another layer.

landing: an intermediate rest platform in a flight of stairs.

lath: a wood or metal base for stucco or plaster finish.

lean mortar: mortar deficiency in cementitious ingredients.

level: horizontal; also, a device used to determine elevations.

lewis: a wedge-shaped split-metal device used to lift blocks of stone.

lifter: a shaped metal bar used as a lever to raise heavy loads.

light (also lite): a division in a window equal to one pane of glass; also, the opposite of heavy (as in light duty or heavy duty); also, an illuminating device.

light reflectance: a percentage factor indicating the ability of an applied finish to reflect light.

lintel: a horizontal member used to distribute forces above an opening.

lite: see *light* (window).

local authority: a regulatory agency, such as the government of a region, state, province, county, municipality, city, town, village, or other public body having jurisdiction, such as a water or gas utility board.

lock, mortise: a lock recessed into a door or window.

lock, rim: a lock mounted beside and covering part of the locking stile of the door.

lock stile: the stile to which the door lock is secured.

lock, surface: a lock mounted on the outside surface of a door or window.

lookout: an overhanging rafter, usually at right angles to other rafters, used to support a cantilevered portion of the roof.

lot: a quantity of material; also, a small piece of urban real estate on which buildings are usually built.

louver: a slatted ventilation opening.

lumber: timber split or sawn into boards or planks.

lumber, dressed: rough lumber after planing.

lumber, rough: timber as cut from the saw.

lump sum: a type of construction contract in which the contractor offers to construct a building for a stipulated or precalculated sum of money.

make good: to repair, to restore to a former condition.

mallet: a short-handled hardwood weight used to beat metal.

manhour: the amount of work done by one person in one hour.

masking: protection of a surface from minor damage.

MasterFormat: a system for organizing construction information.

mastic: oil- or cement-based paste used to fill minor holes and cracks in buildings.

meeting stile: stiles that become adjacent when pairs of double doors are closed.

membrane: a thin pliable sheet or layer of (usually waterproof) material used as a liner in parts of buildings.

mesh: woven metal material (an incorrect name for welded fabric).

mildew: a whitish fungal coating, often appearing on damp paper or plaster surfaces.

mineral wool: a light-weight porous material made from expanded slag, shale, or other mineral material.

miter: a joint in which the components meet at 45 degrees.

miter box: a device used to guide saw blades at specific angles as they cut through wood.

module: a standardized but variable unit of length or area used to facilitate building planning and construction.

moisture content: the percentage of water in any given volume of material.

molding: trim or ornamental cover.

mortgage: a loan secured by title to real property.

mortise: a slot cut into a piece of material to create a joint utilizing a tenon or tongue.

mounting: the method of attaching acoustical systems to the building frame. The Acoustical Materials Association has designated eight standard mountings, of which #2 indicates solid backing and #7 indicates a suspension system.

mudsill: a continuous heavy timber plank used to distribute loads from supports to the ground or slab below the mudsill.

mullion: the main perpendicular members that divide the lights of a window.

muntin: see *mullion*.

muriatic: dilute hydrochloric acid used to clean concrete and masonry surfaces.

mute: a small rubber bumper installed in door frames to deaden the sound made by closing the door.

mylar: a tough, semitransparent plastic sheet or film.

nailing flange: a thin protrusion of metal around the perimeter of the frame to permit nailing or screwing the frame to the building structure.

nail-set: a small pointed steel probe used to drive the heads of finishing nails below the material surface.

nap: short fuzzy ends of fibers on the surface of kraft paper.

naphtha: a colorless volatile petroleum distillate used as a solvent.

neat cement: a paste made with portland cement and water.

needle: a short stiff beam inserted into and used to support upper walls during alterations to lower walls.

neoprene: a plasticized membrane. (The word *neoprene*, like the word *aspirin*, was originally a proprietary name; now it is used in a generic manner.)

nesting: to fit one component into another.

newel: the end post in a staircase balustrade.

nibble: to improve or remove rough or jagged metal edges.

nippers: sharp-edged pliers used to trim ceramic or brick tiles.

noise reduction coefficient (NRC): a percentage used to indicate the ability of a material to absorb sound energy.

noncohesive: not sticky (e.g., dry sand, boulders).

nosing: the leading open edge of a stair tread or landing.

nut-driver: similar to a screwdriver, but shaped to fit nuts.

offset: a change of vertical plane.

opaque: impenetrable by light.

organic: derived from living organisms; carbon compounds.

osmosis: the diffusion of fluids through porous membranes.

outrigger: a cantilevered beam or joist end.

overhang: the distance a joist or chord extends beyond the bearing point.

overtime: payment for working extra hours.

owner: the person or organization for whom the building is being constructed.

padlock: a loose lock with key or combination security, with a loop passing through the staple of a hasp and staple latch.

pan: a particular type of prefabricated metal form used to form rib or waffle slabs; also, a unit of metal decking.

panel: a flat board, plate, or pane inserted into a frame.

panic bar: activating lever on an emergency fire-exit door.

panic bolt: the operating rod that disengages from the door frame upon operation of the panic bar.

parapet: a low wall projecting above the roof level.

parging: a single application of masonry cement used to cover minor blemishes in concrete or masonry walls; also used to line brick chimney vents.

parquetry: a term applied to small wood block flooring laid in basket-weave or other mosaic patterns.

partition: a non-load-bearing wall separating two areas of a building.

pattern drop: the amount by which the pattern at one edge of a roll of wallpaper is offset by its matching pattern at the edge of the adjacent roll.

peeling: the separation of adhesive from glued surfaces.

penny-weight: traditional method of designating U.S. nail sizes.

permeability: ability to permit (or resist) the passage of water.

phillips head: a type of screw head having a cross-shaped slot.

pier: a vertical portion of wall between openings, also a free-standing short or stubby column.

pilaster: a flat rectangular column projecting from but attached to a structural wall.

pile: the texture of the carpet surface; either looped, cut, or a combination of both.

pin: a small rod that connects the two leaves of a hinge; they may be loose (removable) or tight (nonremovable); also, any small fastening device.

pitch: natural resin; slope or angle; tone; (plus other meanings).

pith: the hard, dry center of a log.

plan: the diagrammatic horizontal layout of a floor or building.

plasticizers: materials added to soften hard pigments and extenders to form pliable paint films.

plane: a cutting tool; also, a smooth surface.

plate: a flat horizontal member in a framed wall.

platform frame: a structural wood system in which the outer vertical studs rest on a plate secured to a framed platform between floors, ceilings, and roofs.

plumb: vertical; also, a weighted string device used to establish plumbness.

point: small diamond-shaped pieces of flat blued or galvanized steel used to secure panes of glass in wooden frames.

pointing: filling existing masonry joints with fresh mortar.

polymer: a plastic compound having high molecular weight.

ponding: the accumulation of water in low areas of nominally flat roof decks or paved areas.

popping: the loosening of cover over concealed nail heads caused by thermal or moisture movement in framing.

pop-rivet: a small fastening device capable of being pushed through two materials (to be fastened together) from one side, then retracted from that same side to cinch tight.

porous: a surface permeable by water or air.

post-forming: the action of heating and bending plastic laminate sheeting around a curved metal bar to create a change of plane direction, such as at a counter edge or splash-back.

post-tensioned unit: precast concrete in which compressive forces are induced *after* placement of the concrete.

potable: fresh clean water, suitable for drinking.

poultice: a paste made with solvents and fillers, used to remove stains from masonry.

powder-driver: a pistol-like device used to drive fasteners.

pozzolans: powdered volcanic material used to reduce the likelihood of heat and expansion in concrete.

precast unit: concrete formed, poured, and cured in a location other than its final location.

prestressed unit: precast concrete in which compressive forces are induced *before* placement of the concrete.

pretinning: preparing metal surfaces for solder adhesion.

priming: preparation of a surface by coating it with material compatible with subsequent coats.

proprietary: a product manufactured under patent.

proud: just above the surface; protruding.

provisional sum: a cash allowance included in a contract to cover the estimated cost of supplying and installing a component.

punch: to produce a hole in a metal component by striking.

punchlist: a list of deficiencies in a building.

purlin: a secondary horizontal beam in a roof-framing structure.

push-button: a spring-loaded device used to permit a doorknob to be locked by pressing the button.

push stick: a small safety device used to manually feed material through electric saws and planers.

quadrant: a metal bracket used to constrain an opening vent.

quantity surveyor: see *construction economist*.

quarterpoint: location for placing setting blocks at the bottom of large glass panels; specifically, halfway between the midpoint and the ends.

quirks (and ovules): finely tooled, S-shaped recessed lines run into plaster work, usually for ornamentation but sometimes used to divide large areas into smaller areas to reduce cracking.

raggle: a small groove or chase either cut or inserted into the vertical face of a wall or parapet to receive the top edge of either a base or counterflashing.

rail: any intermediate frame component in a door or window.

rake: a tool for raking; also, a slope or incline.

ramp: an inclined plane.

ramps-and-twists: the curved portions of handrails, usually carved from solid wood.

real estate: tangible property, such as land and buildings.

real property: tangible property plus intangibles, such as rights and restrictions.

ream: to enlarge or clean a punched hole by fine scraping.

rebate: see *rabbet*.

reciprocating: moving backward and forward (like a saw).

refusal: the point beyond which a nut cannot be tightened without damage either to itself, to the bolt threads, or to the materials being fastened.

reglet: similar to a raggle.

reshoring: the act of replacing vertical falsework supports after formwork has been removed from under slabs and beams.

resist: a tough durable film made of wax, plastic, or rubber used during acid-etching or sandblasting processes to protect surface areas of glass not to be etched or blasted.

resistance: the ability of any material to resist the passage of energy.

retempering: the attempt to make stiffening concrete more workable by the addition of more water.

return: a change of planar direction, usually at right angles.

reveal: to set back to form a different plane, such as a reveal at the jamb of a window; the distance between the face of a frame and the face of the adjacent wall plane.

reverse: the term given to the swing of a door toward the viewer.

ribband: a horizontal band inserted into the vertical studs in balloon frame construction to support upper floor joists.

ridge: the uppermost edge of a roof plane; the upper apex between two adjoining roof planes.

ripping: cutting along the grain.

rise: the vertical dimension of a sloping member or system.

riser: the vertical component of a step, intended to prevent the feet from slipping beyond the tread.

rising butt: a hinge in which the knuckle slots are cut on a bevel or bias so that one leaf rises relative to the other leaf as the door is opened.

rivet: a device used to fasten two components; consists of a short metal shank with a preformed head on one end, the other end being hammered to form a head after insertion.

rod-buster: a slang term for an ironworker.

roof jack: a device used as a temporary platform by roofers; consists of a metal strip bent to support a short plank and drilled at one end for spiking to the roof frame.

rose: a simple circular plate used to secure a lock-set to the door.

rout: to gouge with a cutting tool.

rowlock: a masonry unit positioned horizontally with its end exposed vertically.

rubble: natural stones of irregular sizes and shapes used in masonry walls and embankments.

run: the horizontal dimension in a sloping member or system.

runners: horizontal framing that supports acoustic tile panels.

R-value: resistance (in imperial units: Btu/hr/ft²/°F; in metric units: watts/m²/°C).

saddle: in framing, similar to a cricket; also, a purpose-made metal shoe prepared to secure the base of a vertical post; another name for a reinforcing chair.

sailor: a masonry unit positioned vertically with its broader face exposed laterally.

salamander: a portable temporary heating device, usually powered by propane.

sandblasting: abrading or eroding buiding surfaces with particles of sand expelled through controlled high-pressure nozzles.

sandstone: a naturally cemented sedimentary stone consisting of a mixture of clay and quartz.

sandwich floor: a precast floor slab formed horizontally as one of a vertical series and, when cured, raised to a higher horizontal elevation and secured in place.

sash: the movable part of an opening window frame.

saw, keyhole, or saber: a hand-held electrically powered saw with a short, thin, reciprocating blade; suitable for cutting irregular or rectangular holes in wood or plastic.

sawn, plain: lumber cut tangentially.

sawn, quarter: lumber cut radially.

sawn, rotary: lumber cut concentrically.

scab: a small block of wood or metal used to connect two larger pieces; also, a pejorative term used to describe a worker who crosses a union picket line.

scaffold: a temporary wood or metal platform frame used to support workers or materials.

scarf: a type of joint wherein the ends of two components are beveled and fitted together.

schist: a type of hardened slate.

scotia: an S-shaped profile run on the sides of wood members.

scow: a large mobile garbage container.

scratch coat: the first layer of a plaster system.

screed: a device used to establish the thickness of layers of concrete, plaster, or terrazzo; usually long pipes or boards.

screeding: the act of using screeds.

screw: a fastening device consisting of a pointed pin with a helical or spiral thread machined into its shank, and having a slotted or indented head to facilitate its placement.

scribe: to cut to shape to fit an irregular line or contour.

scriber: a knife-like device having a guide fitted to one side.

sealants: products used to seal joints that have been packed with weatherproof materials.

sealers: waterproof products used to coat or prepare surfaces or areas to inhibit moisture penetration.

sealing: the process of applying sealers over surfaces of areas.

seconds: anything of second quality, particularly in reference to bricks or tiles.

secret: concealed from view; e.g., secret nailing.

segregation: the separation of the components of concrete through the action of gravity.

serpentine: snake-like; undulating; gently curving, as in a wall.

serrated: having edges notched or toothed.

set: to drive or sink a nail or screw beneath the surface.

setting: the crystallization of concrete to form a solid mass.

setting blocks: small blocks or pads of hard neoprene or lead, used to separate glass from frames to allow for deflection.

setting nibs: small protrusions molded onto the side of a tile unit so as to automatically align the tile with its neighboring tiles to create uniformly spaced joints.

shade: the degree to which a color is darkened by adding black.

shake: a shingle split (not cut or sawn) from a wood block; also, defects in lumber having origins in the living tree.

shear: to cut in a straight line; also, the tendency of forces to cause a transverse fracture across a member.

sheathing: usually rough wood or plywood boarding used to enclose a space and impart structural integrity to a wood or metal frame, such as a floor, wall, or roof.

shelf life: the period during which a product can be stored before it spoils.

shim: a small wedge-shaped plate of wood or metal, used to finely align framing members secured to uneven substrates.

shiner: see *sailor*.

shingle: a thin piece of wood cut or sawn from a wood block.

shiplap: lumber profiled to have one-half the thickness cut from one edge to fit a similar profile on an adjacent edge.

shop drawing: diagrams and data produced by a contractor or supplier to show manufacturing details of a building system.

shore (shoring): temporary vertical metal or wood devices used to support horizontal falsework or formwork.

shot yarn: carpet yarns running laterally so as to bond pile to backing chains.

SI: Système International (the metric system).

siding: overlapping long, narrow, thin boards of wood or metal attached horizontally or vertically to the outside of buildings to improve weather protection and appearance.

sill: the lowest horizontal part of any opening through a wall.

size: a gelatinous or glutinous paste used to seal porous paper or plaster surfaces before further treatments, such as painting or printing; also, magnitude.

skewed: angled, oblique, off center.

skintled: irregular masonry made using deformed units.

skip: an area where surface treatment is defective or missing; also see *scow*.

slag: a crust that forms on top of a weld, usually caused by the fluxing material.

sleeper: long, narrow strips of wood intended to raise the finished floor above the substrate and to provide a good nailing base.

slicker: a long wood or metal straight-edge board used to quickly screed plastered areas to a level plane.

slides: similar to glides.

slip form: a form that is moved without removal from the concrete surface.

slump: the amount by which the height of a concrete cone of known volume sags or falls below its original height upon removal of constraint; a measure or test of concrete consistency.

slurry: a thin paste made of cement, sand, and water.

smoke generation: a factor by which the ability of material to produce smoke in the event of fire is measured relative to smoke generated by a known standard material, such as wood.

snap-tie: a form-tie having a special break-back feature at each end, for quick release using a small twist clamp.

sneck: a small, squared piece of stone fitted in between larger squared pieces to complete a bonding pattern.

soffit: the exposed underside of any building surface.

soldier: a masonry unit positioned vertically with its narrower edge exposed laterally.

sole: the lowest horizontal part of wood-framed walls.

sound: sensations detected by the hearing organs when energy of various pressures and pitches impinges on the ear at the speed of 1150 km/h or 720 mph; also, of good quality.

sound transmission class (STC): a ratio used to indicate the ability of a material to permit sound energy to pass.

spline: a small metal, fiber, or plastic plate inserted into the kerfed edge of tiles or panels to ensure alignment.

spacer: a small insert, usually of hardwood or plastic, used to keep adjacent building components permanently separated.

spandrel: the vertical plane between the head of one opening and the sill of an opening directly above.

specification: detailed description of materials and workmanship standards.

spigot: a small peg or bracket used to join two frame members.

spine: see *carriage*.

splatter: to carelessly spill or splash liquids or pastes.

splice: a device to form a join between two components.

spud: a wrench having a short open end and a long tapered handle.

square: a carpenter's tool for right angles; also, an imperial measure, comprising an area of 100 square feet.

squeegee: a tool having a thin but wide rubber blade suitable for sweeping water or other fluids in any desired direction.

stagger: to arrange components in an alternating sequence, such as staggered studs.

staging: see *scaffolding*.

stanchion: see *stantion*.

stantion: a light-weight upright steel post or support.

stapler: a spring-loaded triggered device used to drive staples.

step: a combination of one tread and riser in a stair system.

sticking piece: a small piece of metal, plastic, or wood used as a spacer to establish uniform separation between components.

stiffness: the degree of workability of concrete.

stile: vertical outside components of a door or window unit.

stile, hinging: the vertical portion of an opening door or window frame that meets a mullion or jamb, to both of which hinges are attached.

stile, meeting: the vertical portion of an opening door or window frame that meets a mullion or jamb when the window is closed.

stipple: to decorate by small touches or dashes, as with the tip of a brush or side of a sponge.

stirrups: light-weight bent steel rods used to link heavier steel reinforcing bars to spread tensile loads more evenly.

stop: any device used to limit travel, e.g., to stop a door bumping against an adjacent wall.

storey pole: a long, thin piece of wood with marks placed at intervals to indicate the required spacing of materials (such as plank siding) installed on a repetitive basis.

story (also storey): the usable portion of a building between one floor and the one above it.

straight-edge: a long stiff wood or metal device, used to mark lines for cutting materials or to establish planes.

strapping: continuous wood strips or metal battens secured to the building frame at right angles to the direction of material (such as shingles) which will be attached.

strength: the characteristic of a material that determines its ability to resist or impart forces.

stretcher: a masonry unit laid horizontally with its length parallel to the wall surface.

striated: a grooved or finely furrowed surface having a striped appearance.

strike: a small metal plate that catches and retains the bolt of a door lock when the door is closed.

stringer, housed: treads and risers are housed in dadoes or grooves cut into the face of an otherwise plain stringer.

stringer, plain: the primary inclined continuous support for the treads and risers in a flight of stairs.

stripping: to remove temporary work, such as forms or molds; also, to remove old paint or varnish.

strongback: a support used to stiffen a formwork panel.

stuffers: yarns added to form an interwoven backing in carpets.

subcontractor: a firm or person who contracts to construct a part of the whole building project.

substrate: the surface beneath a finishing layer or coating.

suction: the property of a surface to absorb moisture.

supplier: a person or firm that supplies materials not worked to a specialized design for a specific project.

swatch: a sample of (usually) soft material, like cloth.

sway-brace: a diagonal brace inserted to resist lateral movement of framed members; sometimes called lacing.

tar: a black, heavy, sticky viscous liquid consisting of hydrocarbons, phenols, sulfur, and other chemicals.

tagline: a light cord attached to components being raised by crane and used to guide them safely.

tarp (tarpaulin): a large waterproof oiled canvas or reinforced plastic temporary cover.

tell-tale: any device that indicates slight movements.

temperature steel: a layer of welded wire fabric positioned in a wall or slab to minimize the effects of movement due to thermal expansion and contraction.

template: a pattern, usually full size, of a building component.

tenon: the tongued or male portion of a mortise and tenon joint.

tension: forces tending to stretch or elongate an object.

terrazzo: a mixture of cement paste and marble chips, ground and polished after curing.

threshold: see *sill*.

thumb-turn: a rotational device used to permit a doorknob to be locked when the device is turned by hand.

tie: a wood or metal device used to hold formwork panels at a predetermined distance apart; also, small pieces of twisted wire used to hold reinforcing steel members together.

tier: a row or a range; one unit of a vertical stack.

tile: a thin, shaped slab of metal or baked clay.

tilt-up wall: a precast wall panel, formed horizontally on a prefinished concrete floor slab and, when cured, raised to the vertical position and secured in place.

timber: very large pieces of roughly processed wood; sometimes used to refer to forested areas.

tin-snips: heavy-duty scissors.

tint: that amount by which a color is lightened by the addition of white or darkened by the addition of black.

toluene: a colorless liquid solvent [$C_6H_5CH_3$].

tone: modification of a given color ("blue with a green tone").

tooled: worked surfaces of stone work.

tooling: the finishing of mortar or caulked joints using a shaped tool to produce compaction, profile, and texture.

topping: a thin layer of fine concrete laid on top of and bonded to a thicker substrate of structural concrete.

torque: a device used to measure rotational tension.

trade: a major subdivision of the construction industry, such as masonry, painting, or roofing.

translucent: transmitting light in a diffuse or distorted manner.

transom: a small glazed opening vent or panel above a door.

transparent: transmitting light clearly and undistorted.

tread: the horizontal component of a step.

trim: long, narrow strips of shaped and finished wood, metal, or plastic used to conceal joints of building components.

trimmer: a piece of dimension lumber or steel inserted to support the ends of joists or rafters at openings.

trowel: a short-handled steel blade used to smooth plaster work.

troweling: the manual or machine finishing of concrete or plaster to produce smooth, textured, or featured surfaces.

truss: a structural frame, usually part of a roof structure.

tucking: see *pointing*.

tumbler: a small adjustable spring-loaded pin in a cylinder lock.

turn-buckle: a sleeve with an internal screw thread capable of being rotated to change tension in a brace or guy wire.

united dimensions: the sum of the width and breadth of a pane of glass, expressed in centimeters or inches.

unsound: not solid; loose; defective.

U-value: in imperial units, the number of Btu/hr passing between two sides of a building system for each degree F difference between sides. In metric units, the number of watts passing for each degree C difference between sides.

valance: a vertical drop panel of wood or gypsum board intended to conceal drapery tracks and runners at interior window heads.

valley: the line where two inclined planes of a roof surface meet, and to which water will be directed.

valley, closed: where two planes of a roof meet with the roofing material touching at the join to form a concealed gutter.

valley, open: where two planes of a roof meet with the roofing material cut back at the join to expose the gutter beneath.

value: the amount of white or black in any given color. Light colors have high value; dark colors have low value.

veneer: a thin layer of wood, masonry, or metal applied for primarily cosmetic effect.

vent: the hinged opening portion of a window.

viscosity: internal resistance to flow within a liquid.

vise-grips: pliers with an adjustable locking device.

void: missing; wanting; a hole.

volatile: readily evaporated, such as fluid gasoline.

waler: a horizontal stiffening member used to support and align adjacent formwork panels.

wane: lumber cut so as to include a portion of the bark.

warp: a significant and unwanted deviation from an intended true plane; also, interlaced yarns running lengthwise in the weave or loom of carpets.

waste: excess material not required or used for construction.

waterblasting: cleaning surfaces with compressed water jets.

waterproofing: the exclusion of water in its liquid form.

watt: a metric unit of power (joules per second).

weather: same as *exposure*.

weatherbar: a small metal plate vertically inserted across and beneath a window or door sill.

weave: the interlacing of yarns or threads to form a fabric.

web: the central vertical plate between outer beam flanges.

wedge: a small tapered piece of wood, metal, or hard plastic used to tighten up assemblies of components.

weep holes: small spaces left in mortar joints or concrete walls to permit moisture to escape.

weft: interlaced yarns running crosswise in the weave or loom.

wilton: a type of carpet weave.

winder: a wedge-shaped tread intended to change the direction of stair travel.

winning: obtaining original supplies, such as gravel from a quarry or aluminum from bauxite.

wood: (latin: *xylem*) a hard, fibrous natural cellulose substance comprising the main trunk and branches of trees, often suitable for conversion to lumber.

wood, hard: lumber produced from deciduous timber.

wood, soft: lumber produced from evergreen timber.

woof: similar to *weft*.

workability: the ease or difficulty with which materials can be applied, cut, molded, or shaped.

work-apron: a leather or cotton pouch strapped around the waist.

wrenches: devices used to tighten or loosen nuts and bolts.

wythe: in masonry, width; usually the width of one brick, as is a wall or veneer one wythe thick.

X-ray: radiation of very short wavelength, capable of penetrating material objects.

xylene: a colorless benzene solvent $[C_6H_4(CH_3)_2]$.

yarn: threaded fibers of natural (cotton, hemp, jute, wool) or synthetic (acrylic, nylon, polyester, polypropelene, rayon) materials.

yoke: a U-shaped clamp having a collar secured with bolts.

zipper lock: a type of patented rubber gasket used to secure panels of glass into metal window frames, consisting of an "H" section profile and having a removable pressure strip.

zoning: subdivision of a building structure or city area into portions of specialized performance or use.

Bibliography

The bibliography identifies some contemporary American, British, and Canadian books that deal with building technology, construction procedures, materials manufacturing, and production processes in a more general and comprehensive manner. Students are encouraged to read or at least refer to some of these books to broaden their knowledge of the construction industry and its many interesting and important processes. Books dated earlier than 1970 have been excluded from the list.

Section 01-001   Prologue and Objectives

Allen, Edward. *Fundamentals of Building Construction: Materials and Methods*. New York: John Wiley & Sons, 1985.

Cannon, Kenneth F., and Hatley, Frederick G. *Building Construction Technology*. Ontario: McGraw-Hill Ryerson, Ltd., 1982.

Ching, Francis D. K. *Building Construction Illustrated*. New York: Van Nostrand Reinhold, 1975.

Dagostino, Frank. *Materials of Construction*. Reston VA: Reston Publishing Company, 1982.

Ellison, Donald C., Huntington, Whitney C., and Mickadeit, Robert E. *Building Construction: Materials and Types of Construction*. New York: John Wiley & Sons, 1987.

Herubin, Charles. *Basic Construction Materials*. Reston VA: Reston Publishing Co., 1977.

Hornbostel, Caleb. *Construction Materials—Types, Uses, and Applications*. New York: John Wiley & Sons, 1978.

Hornbostel, Caleb, and Hornung, William J. *Materials and Methods for Contemporary Construction*. New York: Van Nostrand Reinhold, 1982.

Huntington, W. C., and Mickadeit, R. *Building Construction: Materials and Types*. New York: John Wiley & Sons, 1975.

Maguire, Byron W. *Construction Materials*. Reston VA: Reston Publishing Co., 1981.

Peurify, Robert L. *Construction Planning, Equipment, and Methods*. New York: McGraw-Hill, 1970.

Reiner, Laurence E. *Methods and Materials of Residential Construction*. Englewood Cliffs NJ: Prentice Hall, 1981.

Shoemaker, Morrell M., and McLurg, William M. *The Building Estimator's Reference Book*. Chicago IL: Frank R. Walker Company, 1979.

Smith, Ronald C. *Materials of Construction*. New York: McGraw-Hill, 1979.

Smith, Ronald C. *Principles and Practices of Light Construction*. Englewood Cliffs NJ: Prentice Hall, 1970.

Smith, Ronald C. *Principles and Practices of Heavy Construction*. Englewood Cliffs NJ: Prentice Hall, 1986.

Spencer, A., Powell, G., and Hudson, D., *Materials for Construction*. Reston VA: Reston Publishing Co., 1982.

Technical Literature. *Canadian Wood-Frame House Construction (Metric Edition)*. Ottawa, Ontario: Canada Mortgage and Housing Corporation, 1981.

Watson, Donald A. *Construction Materials and Processes*. New York: McGraw-Hill, 1984.

Section 01-002   MasterFormat and Layout

Hardie, Glenn M. *Construction Contracts and Specifications*. Reston VA: Reston Publishing Co., 1981.

Technical Literature. *MasterFormat*. Washington DC: Construction Specifications Institute, 1988.

Section 01-003   The Design/Build Process

Barrie, D. S. and Paulson, B.C. *Professional Construction Management*. New York: McGraw-Hill, 1974.

Collier, Keith F. *Managing Construction Contracts*. Reston VA: Reston Publishing Co., 1982.

Ferry, Douglas J. *Cost Planning of Buildings* (4th Ed.). St. Albans: Granada Publishing, 1980.

Fisk, Edward R. *Construction Project Administration* (4th Ed.). New York: Simon & Schuster, 1992.

Hardie, Glenn M. *Construction Estimating Techniques*. Englewood Cliffs NJ: Prentice Hall, 1987.

Helyar, Frank W. *Construction Estimating and Costing*. Toronto: McGraw-Hill Ryerson, 1978.

Nunnally, S. W. *Construction Methods and Management* (2nd Ed.). Englewood Cliffs NJ: Prentice Hall, 1986.

Mansfield, G. L. *Bidding & Estimating Procedures for Construction*. Reston VA: Reston Publishing Co., 1983.

McNulty, Alfred P. *Management of Small Construction Projects*. New York: McGraw-Hill, 1982.

Ramus, J. W. *Contract Practice for Quantity Surveyors*. London: William Heinemann Ltd., 1981.

Roberts, Joseph M. *Construction Management: An Effective Approach*. Reston VA: Reston Publishing Co., 1980.

Royer, King. *The Construction Manager in the 80's*. Englewood Cliffs NJ: Prentice-Hall, 1981.

Russell, James E. *Site Planning*. Reston VA: Reston Publishing Co., 1984.

Seeley, Ivor H. *Building Economics* (2nd Ed.). London: MacMillan Press, 1976.

Stillman, W. J. *Construction Practice*. Reston VA: Reston Publishing Co., 1978.

Section 01-004   Dimensioning

Technical Literature. *How to Write SI*. Metric Commission, Ottawa, ON K1S 5G8

Technical Literature. *Moving to Metric*. Metric Commission, Ottawa, ON K1S 5G8

Technical Literature. *The International System of Units (SI)*. Washington DC: U.S. Department of Commerce, National Bureau of Standards.

Section 01-005   Inspection and Safety

Technical Literature. *Canadian Labor Code*. Toronto: Butterworth's Ltd., current edition.

Technical Literature. *Construction Industry Safety and Health Standards* (Publication 2207). Washington DC: OSHA, 1991.

Technical Literature. *Construction Inspection Manual*. Los Angeles: Building News Inc., current edition.

Technical Literature. *Workers Compensation Board Regulations* in every State and Province.

Section 01-050   Field Engineering

Alexander, Christopher et al. *A Pattern Language—Towns, Buildings, Construction*. New York: Oxford University Press, 1977.

Cannon, Kenneth F., and Hatley, Frederick G. *Building Construction Technology*. Toronto: McGraw-Hill Ryerson Ltd., 1982.

Smith, Ronald C., and Andres, Cameron K. *Principles and Practices of Light Construction* (4th Ed.). Englewood Cliffs NJ: Prentice-Hall, 1993.

Section 01-500   Temporary Facilities

Chudley, R. *Building Siteworks, Substructure, and Plant*. London: Construction Press, 1982.

Ratay, Robert T. *Handbook of Temporary Structures in Construction*. New York: McGraw-Hill, 1984.

Stillman, Robert. *Construction Practices for Project Managers and Superintendents*. Reston VA: Reston Publishing Co., 1975.

Section 01-520   Construction Aids

Hassig, L., and Freni, A. *The Home Tool Kit*. Alexandria VA: Time-Life Books, 1976.

Hunt, B. J. *Review of Technical Information on Scaffolds*. Washington DC: National Bureau of Standards, 1987.

Kogan, Josef. *Crane Design—Theory and Calculations*. New York: Halstead Press, 1976.

Shapiro, Howard I. *Cranes and Derricks*. New York: McGraw-Hill, 1980.

Strakosh, George R. *Elevators and Escalators*. New York: John Wiley & Sons, 1983.

Technical Literature. *Hydraulic Cranes*. Pennsylvania: Grove Manufacturing Company, 1980.

Technical Literature. *Steel Scaffolding*. Ontario: Mills Steel Products, Ltd., 1982.

Section 02-100   Preparation

Conway, Steven. *Logging Practices*. San Francisco: Miller Freeman Publications, 1978.

Horowitz, Eleanor C. J. *Clearcutting*. Washington DC: Acropolis Books, 1974.

Nichols, Herbert L. *Moving the Earth: The Workbook of Excavation*. Greenwich CT: North Castle Books, 1976.

Wood, Stuart. *Heavy Construction Equipment and Methods*. Englewood Cliffs NJ: Prentice Hall, 1977.

Section 02-140   Dewatering

Debo, Harvey V. *Construction Superintendent's Job Guide*. New York: John Wiley & Sons, 1980.

Powers, J. Patrick. *Construction Dewatering*. New York: John Wiley & Sons, 1981.

Ratay, Robert T. *Handbook of Temporary Structures in Construction*. New York: McGraw-Hill, 1984.

Section 02-150   Protection

Technical Literature. *Workers Compensation Board* and *O.S.H.A.* Regulations in every State and Province.

Section 02-200   Earthwork

Church, Horace K. *Excavation Handbook*. New York: McGraw-Hill, 1981.

McClimon, Alan S. *Estimating Manual for Hydraulic Excavators*. Milwaukee: Keohring Company, 1971.

Wood, Stuart. *Heavy Construction*. Englewood Cliffs NJ: Prentice Hall, 1977.

Section 02-500   Paving

Asphalt Institute, The. *Drainage of Asphalt Pavement Structures* College Park MD: Author, 1984.

Scherocman, J. A. *Asphalt Pavement Construction*. ASTM Special Technical Publication 724, 1979.

Section 02-700   Drainage

International Institute for Land Reclamation. *Drainage Principles and Applications* (Vol IV). Washington DC: Author, 1974.

Payne, Rolf. *Drainage and Sanitation*. New York: Longman Press, 1982.

Wiley, John. *Seepage, Drainage, and Flow Nets* (2nd Ed.). New York: John Wiley & Sons, 1977.

Section 03-100   Formwork

Hurd, M. K. *Formwork for Concrete*. Detroit: American Concrete Institute, 1981.

Kenny, Michael F. *Concrete Estimating Handbook*. New York: Construction Publishing Co., 1975.

Richardson, John G. *Formwork Construction and Practice*. London: Cement and Concrete Association, 1977.

Waddell, Joseph J. *Concrete Construction Handbook* (2nd Ed.). Toronto: McGraw-Hill, 1974.

Section 03-200   Reinforcement

Limbrunner, George F., and Speigel, Leonard. *Reinforced Concrete Design* (2nd Ed.). Englewood Cliffs NJ: Prentice Hall, 1986.

McCormac, J. C. *Design of Reinforced Concrete*. New York: Harper & Row, 1978.

Technical Literature. *Metric Design Handbook for Reinforced Concrete Elements*. Toronto: Canadian Portland Cement Association, 1980.

Technical Literature. *Placing Reinforcing Bars*. Washington DC: Concrete Reinforcing Steel Institute, 1972.

Technical Literature. *Reinforcing Steel—A Manual of Standard Practice*. Willowdale: Reinforcing Steel Institute of Ontario, 1977.

Technical Literature. *Specification CSA A23.3*. Ottawa: Canadian Standards Association, 1977.

Section 03-300   Cast-in-Place Concrete

Avery, Craig (Editor). *Concrete Construction and Estimating*. (2nd Ed.) Carlsbad CA: Craftsman Book Co., 1981.

Illingworth, J. R. *Movement and Distribution of Concrete*. New York: McGraw-Hill, 1972.

Orchard, D. F. *Concrete Technology*. New York: Halsted Press, 1973.

Technical Literature. *Proportioning Concrete Mixes*. Detroit: American Concrete Institute, 1974.

Technical Literature. *Specification C 175*. Washington DC: American Society for Testing Materials, current.

Technical Literature. *Specification CAN 3 A23-1*. Ottawa: Canadian Standards Association, current.

Wardell, Joseph J. *Concrete Construction: Concrete Mixing*. Novato CA: McGraw-Hill, 1974.

White, George R. *Concrete Technology*. New York: Litton Educational Publications, 1977.

Section 03-350   Concrete Finishing

Huff, Darrell. *How to Work with Concrete*. New York: Popular Science Publishing Co., 1968.

Perkins, Phillip. *Concrete Structures: Repair, Waterproofing, and Protection*. New York: Applied Science Publishers, 1977.

Technical Literature. *Color and Texture in Architectural Concrete*. Chicago: Portland Cement Association, 1980.

Wilson, J. Gilchrist. *Exposed Concrete Finishes*. New York: John Wiley & Sons, 1964.

Section 03-370   Concrete Curing

Gilson, George. *Concrete Flatwork Manual*. Carlsbad CA: Craftsman Book Co., 1982.

Technical Literature. *Design and Control of Concrete Mixtures*. Ontario: Canadian Portland Cement Association, 1981.

Technical Literature. *Standard 308-71: Recommended Practices for Curing Concrete*. Washington DC: American Concrete Institute, 1971.

Section 03-400   Precast Concrete

Allen, A. H. *An Introduction to Prestressed Concrete*. Wexham Springs: Cement and Concrete Association, 1978.

Ferguson, Phillip. *Reinforced Concrete Fundamentals*. New York: John Wiley & Sons, 1981.

Gerwick, Benjamin C. *Construction of Prestressed Structures*. New York: John Wiley & Sons, 1971.

Waddell, Joseph J. *Precast Concrete: Handling and Erection*. Ames: Iowa State University Press, 1974.

Section 04-100   Mortar and Accessories

Kreh, R. T. *Advanced Masonry Skills*. Ontario: Litton Educational Publishing, Ltd. 1978.

National Building Code. Part 9, Section 20. Ottawa: National Research Council, 1985.

Technical Literature. *Blok-Lok Products Catalog*. Weston, Ontario: Blok-Lok Ltd., 1984.

Technical Literature. *Brick Veneer*. Reston VA: Brick Institute of America, 1983.

Technical Literature. *Mortars for Concrete Masonry*. Herndon VA: National Concrete Masonry Association, 1984.

Technical Literature. *Masonry Cement Mortars*. Skokie IL: Portland Cement Association, 1983.

Technical Literature. *Masonry Report—Mortar*. Vancouver: The Masonry Institute of British Columbia, 1984.

Technical Literature. *Wall Ties for Cavity Walls*. Herndon VA: National Concrete Masonry Association, 1984.

Section 04-200   Unit Masonry

McGuire, Byron W. *Masonry and Concrete*. Reston VA: Reston Publishing Co., 1978.

Sahlin, Sven. *Structural Masonry*. Englewood Cliffs NJ: Prentice Hall, 1971.

Self, Charles R. *The Brickworker's Bible*. Blue Ridge Summit PA: TAB Books, 1981.

Sunset Books. *How to Build Walks, Walls, Patios, and Floors*. Oakland CA: Lane Publishing Co., 1977.

Telford, Thomas. *Reinforced and Prestressed Masonry*. England: Thetford Press, Ltd., 1982.

Section 04-400   Stone Masonry

Kicklighter, Clois. *Modern Masonry*. South Holland IL: Goodheart-Willcox Co., 1977.

Nickey, J. M. *The Stoneworker's Bible*. Blue Ridge Summit PA: TAB Books, 1979.

Self, Charles R. *The Bricklayer's Bible*. Blue Ridge Summit PA: TAB Books, 1981.

Technical Literature. *Stone Catalog*. New York: Building Stone Institute, 1975.

Section 05-050   Fasteners

Althouse, A. et al. *Modern Welding*. Chicago: Goodheart-Willcox, Inc., 1976.

Baker, Glenn. *Carpentry Fundamentals*. New York: McGraw-Hill, 1981.

Feirer, John Louis. *General Metals* (6th Ed.). New York: McGraw-Hill, 1986.

Giachino, Joseph W., and Weeks, William. *Welding Skills and Practices*. Chicago: American Technical Society, 1976.

Griffin, I. et al. *Welding Processes*. New York: Reinhold Publishing Co., 1978.

Parmley, Robert O. *Standard Handbook of Fastening and Joining*. Toronto: McGraw-Hill, 1977.

Self, Charles R. *Fasten It!*. New York: Tab Books, 1984.

Technical Literature. *Welding Equipment*. Belmont MI: Jackson Products, 1979.

Wagner, Willis H. *Modern Woodworking—Tools, Materials, and Processes*. New York: Goodheart-Willcox Co., 1978.

Section 05-100   Metal Framing

Rapp, William G. *Construction of Structural Steel Building Frames*. New York: John Wiley & Sons, 1980.

Technical Literature. *Code of Standard Practice for Structural Steel*. Ontario: Canadian Institute of Steel Construction, 1980.

Technical Literature. *Metric Structural Steel Design Data*. Ontario: Canadian Institute of Steel Construction, 1979.

Technical Literature. *Structural Steel Detailing*. Chicago: American Institute of Steel Construction, 1979.

Section 05-200   Metal Joisting

Technical Literature. *Standard Specifications and Load Tables*. Myrtle Beach SC: Steel Joist Intitute of America, 1970.

Section 05-300   Metal Decking

Kuzmanovic, Bogdan, and Willems, Nicholas. *Steel Design for Structural Engineers*. Englewood Cliffs NJ: Prentice Hall, 1977.

Canadian Institute of Steel Construction. *Handbook of Steel Construction*. Toronto: Universal Offset Ltd., 1970.

Section 05-400   Metal Stud Systems

Technical Literature. *Cold Formed Steel Design Manual*. Columbus Ohio: American Iron and Steel Institute, 1986.

Technical Literature. *Lightweight Steel Framing Manual*. Willowdale, Ontario: Canadian Sheet Steel Building Institute, 1987.

Section 05-500   Metal Fabrications

Doyle, Lawrence E. *Manufacturing Processes and Materials for Engineers* (3rd Ed.). Englewood Cliffs NJ: Prentice Hall, 1985.

Feirer, John L. *General Metals* (6th Ed.). New York: McGraw-Hill, 1986.

Section 06-050   Adhesives

Bateman, D. L. *Hot Melt Adhesives*. New York: Noyes Data Corporation, 1978.

Gillespie, Robert H. *Adhesives in Building Construction*. Washington DC: U.S. Dept. of Agriculture, 1978.

Katz, Irving. *Adhesive Materials: Their Properties and Uses*. New York: Foster Publishing Co., 1971.

Lees, W. A. *Adhesives in Engineering Design*. London, England: The Design Council, 1984.

Section 06-100   Rough Carpentry

Technical Literature. *Canadian Wood-Frame House Construction*. Ottawa: Canada Mortgage and Housing Corporation, 1981.

Technical Literature. *Of Note: General Construction*. Tacoma WA: American Plywood Association, 1976.

Technical Literature. *Plywood Construction Manual* (3rd Ed.) Vancouver: Council of Forest Industries, 1976.

Section 06-170   Prefabricated Wood

Schroeder, Roger and Sobon, Jack. *Timber Frame Construction*. Pownal VT: Garden Way Publishing Co., 1984.

Technical Literature. *Post and Beam Construction*. Ottawa: Canadian Wood Council, 1986.

Technical Literature. *Product Manual*. Boise ID: Trus-Joist Corporation, 1985.

Section 06-200   Finish Carpentry

Ball, John E. *Exterior and Interior Trim*. New York: Delmar, 1975.

Ching, Francis D. K. *Building Construction Illustrated*. New York: Van Nostrand Reinhold Co., 1975.

Galvin, Patrick J. *Finishing Off*. Detroit MI: Structures Publishing Co., 1977.

Geary, Donald. *Roofing and Siding: a Practical Guide*. Reston VA: Reston Publishing Co., 1978.

Litchfield, Michael W. *Renovation: A Complete Guide*. New York: John Wiley & Sons, 1982.

Technical Literature. *Roofs and Siding*. Alexandria VA: Time-Life Books, 1977.

Wagner, Willis H. *Modern Carpentry*. South Holland IL: The Goodheart-Willcox Co., 1987.

Section 06-300   Wood Treatment

Morrell, J. J. *The Safe Use of Treated Wood* (short title). Eugene: Oregon State University, 1988.

Nicholas, Darrel D. *Wood Deterioration and its Prevention by Preservative Treatments*. Syracuse NY: Syracuse University Press, 1973.

Smith, R. S. *Protection and Preservation of Wood in Service*. Vancouver: Forintek Canada Corporation, 1980.

Technical Literature. *Facts about Pressure Treated Wood*. Ontario: Timber Specialties Ltd., 1979.

Technical Literature. *Pressure Treated Timber*. Ottawa: Canadian Institute of Timber Construction, 1971.

Section 06-400   Architectural Woodwork

Christ, James N. *The Complete Guide to Modern Cabinet Making*. Englewood Cliffs NJ: Prentice Hall, 1988.

Jones, Peter. *Shelves, Closets, and Cabinets*. New York: Van Nostrand Reinhold Co., 1988.

Mannes, Willibald. *Designing Staircases*. New York: Van Nostrand Reinhold Co., 1982.

Mowat, W., and Mowat, A. *A Treatise on Stairbuilding and Handrailing*. Fresno CA: Linden Publishing Co., 1985.

Section 07-100   Water and Damproofing

Product Literature. Fiberglas Canada Inc., Toronto, Ontario.

Product Literature. Dow Chemical Canada, Inc., Sarnia, Ontario.

Section 07-200   Insulation

Product Literature. Dow Chemical Company, Ontario.

Product Literature. Fiberglas Canada Incorporated, Ontario.

Product Literature. Grace Construction Products, Massachusetts.

Technical Literature. *Fundamentals of Building Insulation*. Insulating Board Institute, Chicago, Illinois.

Technical Literature. *Wool Building Insulation*. Mineral Wool Association, New Jersey.

Section 07-300   Shingles and Tiles

Technical Literature. *Decrasystems*. AHI Roofing International, New Zealand and California. 1980

Technical Literature. *Red Cedar Shingles and Shakes*. Forest Industries Council, British Columbia. 1979

Wagner, Willis H. *Modern Carpentry*. South Holland IL: Goodheart-Willcox Co., 1976.

Section 07-400   Preformed Cladding

Technical Literature. *Roofing and Siding*. Ontario: Westeel-Rosco Ltd., 1986.

Section 07-500   Membrane Roofing

Griffin, Charles W. *Manual of Built-Up Roofing Systems*. New York: McGraw-Hill, 1982.

Watson, John A. *Commercial Roofing Systems*. Reston VA: Reston Publishing Co., 1984.

Section 07-600   Flashings and Sheet Metal

Griffin, C. W. *Manual of Built-up Roof Systems* (2nd Ed.). New York: McGraw-Hill, 1982.

Watson, John A. *Commercial Roofing Systems*. Reston VA: Reston Publishing Co., 1984.

Section 07-900   Joint Sealing

Beech, J. C. *Selection and Performance of Sealants*. England: Information Office, Building Research Establishment, 1981.

Cook, John P. *Construction Sealants and Adhesives*. New York: John Wiley & Sons, 1970.

Technical paper. *Adhesives and Sealants*. Ottawa: Canadian Wood Council, 1981.

Section 08-100   Metal Doors and Frames

Feirer, J. L., and Hutchings, G. R. *Carpentry and Building Construction*. New York: Charles A. Bennett Co., 1981.

Section 08-200   Wood Doors and Frames

Talbot, Anthony (Ed.). *Handbook of Door Making, Window Making, and Stair Casing*. Alexandria Bay, NY: Argus Books, 1980.

Section 08-400   Store Front Systems

Sweets Catalog. *Construction Data (Division 08)*. Ontario: McGraw-Hill Ryerson Information Systems, Inc. (current edition).

Section 08-500   Metal Windows and Frames

DeCristofor, B. *Dwelling House Construction*. New York: Harper & Row, 1977.

Wagner, W. *Modern Carpentry*. South Holland IL: Goodheart-Wilcox Co., 1976.

Section 08-600   Wood Windows and Frames

Diats, Albert. *Dwelling House Construction*. Boston: M.I.T. Press, 1973.

Anderson, L.O. *Wood Frame House Construction*. Washington D.C.: U.S. Government Printing Office, 1975.

Section 08-700   Finish Hardware

Jones, Peter. *Shelves, Closets, and Cabinets*. Ontario: Van Nostrand Reinhold, 1977.

Popular Mechanics. *Do It Yourself Encyclopedia*. New York: Hearst Corporation, 1979.

Wagner, H. Willis. *Modern Carpentry*. South Holland IL: Goodheart-Willcox Co., 1976.

Section 08-800   Glass and Glazing

Duthie, Arthur L. *Decorative Glass Processes*. Corning NY: Corning Museum of Glass, 1982.

Nord. *Etching and Sandblasting Glass*. Gainsville FL: Chrome Yellow Private Press, 1980.

Norman, Barbara. *Glass Engraving*. New York: Arco Publishing Co., 1981.

Section 08-900   Curtain Walling

Technical Literature. *Guide Specifications*. Chicago IL: Architectural Aluminum Manufacturers Association.

Technical Literature. *World Wall*. St. Louis MO: Cupples Products, 1983.

Section 09-100   Metal Support Systems

U.S. Gypsum Company. *Lathing and Plastering Handbook*. Chicago: Author, 1972.

Section 09-200   Lath and Plaster Work

Taylor, J. B. *Plastering*. London: George Godwin Ltd., 1970.

Section 09-250   Gypsum Plasterboard Systems

Canadian Standards Association. *Gypsum Board Products*. (A82-27-M) Ottawa: Author, 1985.

Harris, Robert. *Drywall: Installation and Applications*. Washington DC: American Technical Society, 1979.

Kozloski, Arnold. *Do Your Own Drywall*. Blue Ridge Summit PA: Tab Books, 1985.

Technical Literature. *Gypsum Construction Handbook*. United States Gypsum Company, Inc., 1982.

Section 09-300   Ceramic Tile Work

Ceramic Tile Installation. Princeton NJ: Tile Council of America, 1976.

Construction Techniques. Newtown CT: Taunton Press, 1986.

Section 09-400   Terrazzo Work

Martin, David (Ed.). *Specification 84, Building Methods and Products* (vol. 3). London: The Architectural Press, Ltd.

Terrazzo Technical. Virginia: National Terrazzo and Mosaic Association, 1973.

Section 09-500   Acoustical Treatments

Donn Products. *Data Catalogs*. Ontario: Donn Canada Ltd., 1982.

Olin, Harold B. *Construction Principles and Practices* (3rd Ed.). Chicago: The Institute of Financial Education, 1975.

Section 09-550   Wood Flooring

Badzinski, Stanley. *Carpentry in Residential Construction*. Englewood Cliffs NJ: Prentice Hall, 1972.

Section 09-650   Resilient Flooring

Schuler, Stanley. *The Floor and Ceiling Book*. Toronto: McClelland & Stewart, 1976.

3-M Company. *The Home Pro Floor & Carpeting Installation and Repair Guide*. Minnesota Mining & Mfg. Co., 1975.

Section 09-680   Carpeting, Underlay and Trim

Brann, Donald R. *Carpeting Simplified*. New York: Directions Simplified, 1973.

Garstein, A. S. *The How-To Handbook of Carpets*. Monsey, NY: Author: 1979.

Wagner, Dorothy. *What You Should Know About Carpet*. New York: Popular Library, 1973.

Section 09-900   Painting and Decorating

Banov, Abel. *Paints and Coatings Handbook*. Michigan: Structures Publishing Co., 1973.

Goodier, J. H., and Hurst, A. E. *Painting and Decorating*. London: Griffen & Co., 1980.

Weismantel, Guy E. *Paint Handbook*. New York: McGraw-Hill, 1971.

Weiss, Jeffrey. *How to Paint Interiors*. New York: Simon & Schuster, 1981.

Section 10-001   Specialties

Technical Literature. *Washroom Equipment*. Bobrick Washroom Equipment, Inc., California, 1994.

Technical Literature. *Decorative Bath Hardware*. Ajax Hardware Company, Inc., California, 1985.

Technical Literature. *Chalkboards & Bulletinboards*. Claridge Products & Equipment, Inc., Arkansas, 1980.

Technical Literature. *Lockers*. Shanahan's Manufacturing Limited, British Columbia, 1980.

Technical Literature. *Toilet Compartments*. Westeel-Rosco Ltd., Ontario, 1987.

NOTE: The reason some Sections have only one or a few references listed is because information on these specific topics is obtainable from many of the other more general references listed in other Sections.

Index

NOTE: To avoid repetition and speed reference, the contents of entire Parts of Sections can be located by their uniform book Part Title and Number, listed below. For example, to find "Productivity" for any of the trade Sections listed in the Table of Contents, look in Part 4.2 of that Section.

1.0 INTRODUCTION
1.1 General Issues
1.2 Design Aspects
1.3 Related Work

2.0 PRODUCTS
2.1 Materials
2.2 Accessories

3.0 CONSTRUCTION AIDS
3.1 Equipment
3.2 Tools

4.0 PRODUCTION
4.1 Crew Configurations
4.2 Productivity

5.0 PROCEDURES
5.1 Preparation
5.2 Process
5.3 Precautions

accessories (see note)
acoustic:
  batts 470,473
  frame, assemblies 473
  frame, concealed 473
  frame, exposed 473
  frame, systems 472
  lead sheet 470,474
  panels 470,472
  plaster 471
  systems 475
  taping 241
  tiles 470,472
  treatment 469
acronyms:
  AIA 16
  AISC 213
  ASTM 107
  CCDC 16
  CISC 213
  CSA 107
  CSC 5
  CSI 5
  BCIT vii
  IRMA 347
  MIA 195
  NBS 259
  NIST 259
  NLGA 259
  NTMA 462
  OSB 260
  OSHA 38,39
  OSHB 38,42
  OWB 260
  PCA 140
  PET 259
  PVC 321
  SI 5
  SJI 221
  UBC vii
  VPS 259
  WCB 42
  WCLIB 259
  WWPA 259
addenda 16, 19
adhesives, features:
  application 250
  compatability 249
  classification 249

adhesives, features (*Contd.*)
  cleavage 249
  color of 249
  creep 248
  curing 250
  definition 248
  dispensers 251
  moisture resistance 250
  peeling 249
  removal 254
  selection 250
  solvents 254
adhesives, types:
  contact cement 253
  elastomeric, one-part 253
  epoxy, two-part 252
  flooring 486
  glazing 421
  glue, animal 253
  glue, casein 253
  glue, white 252
  inorganic 249
  liquid asphalt
  melamine 253
  natural 249
  neoprene 253
  organic 249
  phenolic resin 253
  polymers 254
  polyvinyl acetate 252
  resorcinal 253
  rubber-based 252
  solvent-based 252
  starch 249
  synthetic 249
  thermoplastic 251
  thermosetting 251
  urea formaldehyde 253
  water-based 252
aggregates
  asphalt 107
  concrete 142
  coarse 107,440
  fine 107,440
  grades 142
  paving 107
  terrazzo 463
  types 107,142
  sizes 107
  storage 138
aluminum:
  formwork 118
  storefront 384
allen key 72
allowances:
  cash 8,15
  slope 104
ammonium phosphate 306
asphalt:
  application 110
  basic 107
  cutback 107
  fillers 107
  in membranes 345
  rubberized 345
  sealers 107
  sealing 110
  texturing 106
  transport 107
  types 107,346
  uses 346
associations:
  American 5
  Canadian 5
auger 102
awl 72
axe 47

backhoe 77,97
bar charts 23
bazooka 450
beads:
  casing 442
  control 442
  corner 442
  glazing 420
  picture 442
  profiles 442
beams:
  concrete 149
  formwork 122
  steel 217
  wood 274
bending brake 358
bevel 73
bevelers 422
bid:
  acceptance 22
  form 18
  process 17
  procurement 21
  strategy 17
bit 72
blasting:
  earth 103
  stone 196
  tree stumps 77
blinding, gravel:
  paving 111
  sub-bases 323
blocking:
  studs, steel 241
  wood framing 270
blocks:
  glass 188
  concrete 183
  pulley 78
blockwork 189
board feet 262
board lifter 450
boards:
  hard 260
  lumber 259
  particle 260
  pulp 260
  wafer 260
bobcat 97
bolts:
  anchor 201
  carriage 201
  expansion 201
  field 201
  high strength 201
  machine 201
  methodology 202
  stove 202
  toggle 202
  unfinished 202
bolster 132
bonding:
  adhesives
  cement 139
  mortar 171
  patterns 179,193
  reinforcement 131
bonds:
  contract 16
  unit masonry 179
  stone work 198
book:
  applications 3
  contents 3
  epilogue 522
  objectives 1
  prologue 1

book (*Contd.*)
scope 2
structure 2
bracing:
masonry 93,189
post & beam 282
shoring 90
steel framing 218
steel joists 225
steel studs 241
temporary 93
wall framing 269
brazing, features:
materials 207
process 207
temperatures 207
brazing, methods:
dip 207
furnace 207
induction 207
resistance 207
torch 207
bricks, *see* masonry
brickwork 190
broadscope 6
broom 73
brushes:
general 73
paint 501
budgets 14
buckets:
concrete 144
in general
roofing 347
buildings:
codes 214
commercial 2
highrise 430
inspection 36
institutional 2
lowrise 430
papers, *see* paper
residential 2
types 2
wooden 255
bulldozer 77,98
burning debris 84

cabinets 511,518
cable 77
Canada:
building codes 214
contract forms 16
grades, lumber 259
grades, plywood 260,286
sand, dry 170
steel shapes 214
studs, steel 233
cant strip 353
carpentry, finish:
definition 283
exterior 283
interior 283
laminates 292,298
paneling 291
siding 291,292
trim 292
carpentry, framing:
balloon 255,256,269
cross-bridging 265
floor system 264,269
frame & brace 255
platform 255,256,264
post & beam 255,274,279
roof, sloped 265
roof, flat 269
seismic control 273
wall system 265,269
carpentry, rough:
boards 270
blocking 266
definition 254
firestopping 266
flooring 264
furring 270

carpentry, rough (*Contd.*)
gables 266
girts 266
hips 266
headers 264
joists 264,266
openings 266
panels 270
plates, floor 269
plates, sill 264
plates, top 257
riband 269
sheathing 266,270
strapping 272
studs 266,269
valleys 266
carpet, features:
adhesives 492
colors 491
gullies 494
laying 494
layout 496
pile 494
patterns 491
planning 494
seaming 496
sewing 496
stair 496
trim 492
underlays 492
wall-to-wall 491
carpet, types:
area rugs 491
broadloom 491
foambacked 495
forms 491
tiling 497
tufted 491
woven 491
carts:
concrete 144
glass 422
hand 71
cement:
in concrete 142
in mortar 173
in terrazzo 463
caulk (calk):
process 367
retro 368
storefronts 386
ceilings:
dropped 435
furred 435
suspended 435
certificate:
of completion 26
of occupancy 24
chains:
clearing 77
survey 44
chainsaw 79
chalkboards 511,517
chalkline 73
changes 18
chemicals:
asphalt 345
cement 142
glass 417
gypsum 440
lime 440
chisel 72
choker 79
chords 274
chutes:
concrete 144
garbage 54
cladding:
aluminum 341
asbestos 341
connections 343
curtain wall 430
definition 340
fiberglass 341
finishes 341

cladding (*Contd.*)
glass 430
metal 341
non-metal 341
plastic 341
preformed 340
profiles 340
steel 341
wind direction 342
wood siding 291
clamps:
glazier 422
grips 72
clamshell 98
clay:
bricks 181,183
pipes 113
clean-out:
studs, steel 241
clean-up:
adhesives 254
carpet 496
cleared areas 82
for concreting 137
for safety 38
clearing 103
coats:
paint, *see* paint
plaster, *see* plaster
coffee breaks 26
color:
adhesives 249
agents 142
carpets 491
concrete 142,154
cool 499
darker 499
flooring 485
frequency, high 499
frequency, low 499
laminates 284
lighter 499
mortar 171
nature of 499
masonry 181
pigment 500
primary 499
psychology of 499
secondary 499
sealants 363
terrazzo 463
tertiary 499
treated wood 303
warm 499
wheel 499
columns:
concrete 141
formwork 122
steel 217
wood 279
come-along 71
compaction:
earth 96
paving 108
compactor 98,108
compartments 511,518
compass 73
computer:
applications 27
document generation 16
images 29
concrete, curing:
artificial 159,162
chemical 159
cold weather 160
covering 159,160
dry heating 162
hot weather 160
fogging 161
natural 159,160
ponding 161
steaming 162
concrete, design:
air entrainment 141,142
appearance 138

concrete, design (Contd.)
 cutting 158
 discarding 151
 durability 138,141
 hydration 130,139
 in compression 130,139
 in tension 130,139
 measuring 139
 proportions 139
 ratios 139
 slump 140
 strength 138,140
concrete, finishes:
 abrasion 156
 applied 151,153
 brushing 155
 bushhammering 156
 chemical 152,154
 dashing 154
 formed 154
 grinding 156
 integral 154
 molding 155
 paints 153
 physical 152,154
 sandblasting 157
 surface 154
 toppings 153
 treatment 138
 troweling 155
 waterblasting 157
concrete, ingredients:
 accelerators 142
 additives 142
 aggregates 142
 cement, types 142
 cement, factor 139
 coloring 142
 damproofer 142
 hardener 143
 ingredients 139
 pozzolan 142
 reducers 142
 retarder 142
 water, see water
concrete, mixing:
 batching 141,148
 hand 148
 machine 148
 quality control 141
 retempering 141
 workability 141
concrete, placing:
 bucketing 149
 carting 149
 chuting 149
 conveying 149
 delivery 143
 floating 150
 handling 149
 identification 149
 placing 143,148,149
 pumping 151
 screeding 147,150,151
 spreading 150
 toppings 153
 vibrating 151
concrete, setting:
 failed 159
 false 159
 final 159
 flash 159
 initial 158
concrete, types:
 cast-in-place 138
 posttensioned 164,166
 precast 163,165
 prestressed 164,166
 topping 151,153
connectors:
 cladding 343
 storefront 385
construction, types:
 categories 2

construction, types (Contd.)
 commercial 2
 disciplines 2
 fireplace 190
 heavy 281
 horizontal 2
 industrial 2
 institutional 2
 light 278
 non-residential 2
 post & beam 279,280
 residential 2
 vertical 2
construction, processes:
 aids 63
 facilities 53
 materials 3
 methods 3
 people in 4
 planning 22
 procedure 22
 sandwich lift 164
 scheduling 22
 tilt-up 164
contract, constituents:
 consideration 19
 genuine intention 20
 lawful object 20
 legal capacity 20
 mutual agreement 19
contract, contents:
 bonds 16
 close-out 24
 disputes 16
 documents 16
 elements of 20
 guarantees 24
 inspections 16
 insurance 16
 parties to 17
 permits 17
 progress 17
 taxes 17
 time 17
contract, processes:
 award of 19,20
 changes to 16,18,27
 completion of 24,26
 deficiencies in 24
 payments 17,23
 process 15
 performance of 24
 records 24
contract, types:
 cost-plus-fee 15
 hybrid types 16
 oral 20
 stipulated sum 15
 target price 16
 unit price 16
 written 20
contractors:
 general 22
 subtrade 22
controls:
 energy 30
 pollution 30
conveyors 64,144
copper:
 arsenate 306
 chromate 306
 flashings 356
 naphthenate 306
 sulfate 306
costs:
 concrete 139
 equipment 117
 formwork 116
 in general 4
 material 117
 precast 163
 roofing 344
 waste 453
crafts, building 2

cranes 64,65,214
creosote 306
crew configuration (see note)
cubicles 511,518
curbs 110
curing:
 adhesives 250
 asphalt 106
 concrete 158
curtain wall:
 definition 430
 masonry 179
 composition 430
 process 433
 thermal break 430
custom-made items 247
cutters:
 circle 451
 glass 422
 tile 457
cutting:
 concrete 158
 decks, steel 229
 glass 424
 masonry 186
 metal 211
 laminates 292
 steel bars 134
 steel members 216
 thresholds 376
 wood 258

dampproofing:
 definition 320
 foundations 324
 floors 324
 openings 325
 paints 321
 papers 321
 plastics 321
 roofs 324
 walls 324
darbies 73, 444
dashes:
 stucco 440
 terrazzo 465
decking:
 steel 226
 wood 280
delivery (see note)
demolition 77
derricks 216
design aspects (see note)
design, process:
 architectural 2
 development 13
 documentation 13
 program 13
 schematics 13
 structural 2
design/build 12
development 13
dewatering 84,103
dew point 321,322
dimensions, general:
 actual 30
 applications 31
 conversions 34,35
 equivalents 35
 examples of 34
 general 5
 imperial 30,32
 metric 30,31
 nominal 30
 relationships 31,32
 stairways 315,316
dimension lumber 259
dimensions, materials:
 acoustic products 470
 ashlar, stone 195
 barriers, vapor 261
 blocks 183
 bricks 183
 carpet, broadloom 491

dimensions, materials (*Contd.*)
  carpet, underlay 492
  cladding 341
  felts 346
  flooring, resilient 485
  flooring, wood 477
  glass types 420,421
  gypsum boards 449
  hardboard 260,286
  hardwoods 285
  laminates, plastic 284
  lumber 262,263
  masonry units 183
  metal lath 442
  panel boards 287,288
  papers, building 261
  particle board 260
  plaster board 441
  pulp board 260
  plywood 260,286
  roofing products 345,346
  shingles, metal 334
  shingles, wood 333
  siding, wood 287
  slates 333
  softwoods 262
  steel decking 227
  steel studs 233,234
  tiles, ceramic 456
  tiles, clay 333
  tiles, concrete 334
  underlay, carpet 492
  wafer board 260
dippers 348
disposal:
  garbage 54
  earthwork 103
  toxic 30
divider 73
documentation 13
dolly 493
doors, categories:
  framed 369,371
  metal 369
  storefront 369,386
  specialty 369
  tracked 369,372
  wood 378
doors, frames:
  assembled 379,380
  steel 372,374
  tracks 373,374
  unassembled 379,380
  wood 379
doors, functions:
  beveled 370,383
  handing 370
  in general 369
  left hand 370
  right hand 370
  swings 370
  tracks 375
doors, types:
  double 370
  dutch 370
  filled 371
  fire 371
  flush 372,378
  french 370
  hardware, *see* hardware
  hollow 371
  kalamein 371
  nontypical 381
  panel 372,378
  pocket 380
  rated 371
  roller 372
  seamless 372
  sectional 372
  sliding 375
  typical 381
  vertical lift 375
dragline 98
drainage 114

drains:
  open 114
  french 114
  permanent 112,115
  pipes 113
  sanitary 112
  sewer 112
  storm 112
  temporary 112
drawings:
  architectural 14
  electrical 14
  engineered 384
  mechanical 14
  site 14
  shop 198,215,228,311
  structural 14
  survey 43
  working 14
drift pin 119
drills 72,85
drilling 104
drywall 448
durability:
  asphalt 106
  concrete 138,141

earth 96
earthwork:
  backfilling 104
  bank measure 102
  definition 96
  filling 103
  finishing 103
  grading 103
  loosening 103
  slopes 104
economics of:
  curtain walling 433
  door hardware 401
  formwork 116
  roof membranes 344
  sealing joints 362
  wood buildings 255
  work (see note)
edger 72
electrical work 2
energy control 30
engineering, field 43
entrainment, air 141,142
equipment (see note):
  administrative 63
  ancillary 64
  definition of 63
  operating 63
  safety 38
estimating:
  activity 17
  textbooks 118,148,164
excavation:
  bulk 103
  machines 100,101
  processes 103
  protection 103
  stripping 103
  trenching 103
  trimming 103
explosives 77

fabrication, metal:
  assembly 247
  bending 244
  burning 245
  drilling 245
  examples 247
  finishing 247
  forming 245
  general 241
  machining 245
  pressing 246
  punching 246
  reaming 246
  rolling 246
  sawing 246

fabrication, metal (*Contd.*)
  shearing 246
falsework:
  definition 116
  precedent 120
  reshoring 128
  subsequent 121
  shores 128
  supports 128
fans 78
fasteners:
  concealed 200
  crimping 211
  decking 228
  devices 201,293
  exposed 200
  metal 200
  patented 211
feasibility study 13
feet:
  board 262
  imperial 33
felts:
  flashings 357
  membranes 346
fences 58,60
fenestration 415
field offices 60
file 72
filling 103
financing, sources 13
finish hardware, *see* hardware
finishes:
  concrete 151
  paint 504
  paving 110
  plasterboard 450
  plasterwork 446
  stucco 447
  suspension systems 438
  terrazzo 468
fireplace 190
first aid 37,53
flashing, features:
  at chimneys 359
  at openings 357
  base 353,355
  cant 356
  cap 355
  composites 357
  custom work 360
  definition 355
  expansion 356
  fastening 361
  gravel stop 356
  reglets 353
  seams 361
flashing, types:
  aluminum 355
  chimney 359
  copper 356
  counter 355
  felts 357
  lead 356
  metal 355
  plastic 357
  steel 356
float 73, 444
flooring, resilient—features:
  adhesives 486
  bases 485,490
  definition 484
  edges 486
  field 484
  layout 490
  moisture test 489
  ornamental work 489
  scribing 488
  treads 386
flooring, resilient—types:
  asphalt 485
  cork 485
  linoleum 484
  resilient 484

flooring, resilient—types (*Contd.*)
  rubber 485
  sheet 484,489
  tile 484,490
  vinyl-asbestos 485
  vinyl-chip 485
  vinyl-filled 485
flooring, wood—features:
  adhesives 479
  baseboard 483
  finishing 482
  hardwood 477
  sleepers, wood 476
  sleepers, metal 476
  softwood 477
  species 477
  substrates 476
flooring, wood—types:
  block, laminated 476
  block, unit 476
  commercial 481
  industrial 481
  parquetry 477
  plank 477,482
  strip 477,482
forming, metal 246
formwork, features:
  accessories 119
  chemicals 119
  erection 121
  fabrication 120
  failure 129
  inspection 127
  liners 119
  openings 122
  reuse 116
  setbacks 123
  steel 118
  stripping 127
formwork, types:
  aluminum 118
  bases 121
  beams 122
  columns 122
  falsework 117, 120
  footings 122
  foundations 122
  fly 122
  gang 123
  ornamental 130
  plastic 118
  rib slab 122
  slabs 123,125
  slip 123,129
  stairs 125
  steel 118
  waffle 125
  walls 127,128
  wood 119
foundations:
  formwork for 122
  stone 198
  treated wood 303
frames:
  assembled 375,379
  door, aluminum 386
  door, steel 372
  door, wood 379
  knocked down 375
  unassembled 375,379
  window, aluminum 391
  window, steel 391
  window, wood 398
framing:
  custom 245
  floors 265
  lumber 259
  metal 212
  roofs 268
  systems 255
  walls 266
  wood 264,269
front-end loader 98
furring:
  metal suspension 435

furring (*Contd.*)
  studs, steel 241
  wood framing 270

gallon 33,34
gantries 67
garbage disposal 54
gauge (gage):
  aluminum 355
  steel door frames 372
  wire, hanger 436
  wire, tie 436
  zinc flashing 357
gender 5
geopaction 76
girders 212
glass, forms:
  blocks 417
  fibers 417
  plates 417
  powders 417
  sheets 418
glass, types:
  bent 418
  colored 418
  corrugated 418
  drawn 419
  float 418
  glare reducing 419
  heat-absorbing 418
  heat-strengthened 418
  insulating 418
  laminated 418
  lead 418
  leaded 419
  mirror 419
  nonreflective 419
  optical 419
  ornamental 419
  patterned 419
  plain 419
  plate 419
  polarized 419
  reflective 419
  safety 419
  solar 419
  spandrel 419
  specialized 420
  stained 419
  structural 419
  tempered 420
  tinted 420
  window 420
  wired 420
glazing, features:
  beads 420
  blocks 420
  burning 424
  chemistry 417
  configurations 393,415
  cutting 424
  definition 415
  double 415
  dry 424
  functions 415
  gaskets 420
  grades 420
  ingredients 416
  nibbling 424
  pins 421
  points 421
  putties 421
  single 415
  sizes 416
  spacers 422
  tapes 420
  triple 415
  wet 424
  windows 425
  zippers 421
glazing in:
  aluminum 425
  steel 425
  wood 425
glazing, ornamental:

glazing, ornamental (*Contd.*)
  acid etching 428
  design 427
  implementation 428
  sandbalsting 428
  transfer 427
glue, *see* adhesives
  gun 498
grading, materials:
  aluminum 384
  glass 420
  hardwoods 285
  laminates 284
  masonry units 182
  marble types 195
  plywood 260
  softwoods 259
  steel 213
  wood flooring 477
  wood in windows 396
  woodwork 309
gravel:
  gradation 107
  paving 106
green chain 258
grinding:
  concrete 157
  terrazzo 465
grout:
  mortar 174,175,177
  steel 217
  tile 457,461
gypsum:
  board 449
  chemical 440
guns:
  caulking 366
  glue 498
  heat 498
  powder 471
  screw 234
  spray 501

hacksaw 72,234
hammer 72
handcarts 71
hangers:
  metal suspension 436
  stud systems 239
hardwoods, *see* wood
hardware, functions:
  appearance 401
  categories 401
  concealed 411,412
  convenience 400,406
  exposed 411
  finishes 402
  function 401
  keying 401
  movement 400,405
  performance 401
  price 401
  recessed 412
  security 400,409
  selection 401
  surface 412
  utility 400,413
hardware, finish:
  cabinet 407
  casement 407
  catches 410
  closers 410
  closet, doors 405
  closet, rails 414
  coat hooks 414
  definition 401
  door 405
  drawer glides 408
  handles 412
  hinges, cabinet 408
  hinges, door 405
  hinges, window 407
  kick plate 412
  latches, window 410
  locks, door 409

hardware, finish (*Contd.*)
    locks, drawer 410
    mail slot 412
    mirror clips 413
    morticed 409
    olive knuckle 408
    panic bars 410
    pivots 405
    pulls 412
    quick-set 409
    shelf bracket 413
    soss 408
    stops, door 412
    stops, wall 412
    track 408
    window 407
hardware, rough:
    bolts 201
    definition 401
    hangers, joist 266
    nails 202
    rivets 204
    screws 205
    seismic 273
    staples 206
hawk 73,444
header 180
heaters:
    asphalt 108
    temporary 108
hickey bar 132
history of:
    adhesives 248
    carpentry 254
    flooring 484
    glass work 415
    joint sealing 362
    masonry walls 179
    plasterboard 448
    plasterwork 439
    shingles 332
    steel studs 230
    stone in masonry 192
    wood in buildings 255
    wood treatment 302
hod:
    in general 73
    masonry 178
hoists 66,348
holdback 24
hoppers 144
housekeeping 40
hydraulic shovel 98

imperial:
    conversions 35
    dimensions 32
    measurement 33
    relationships 32
inspection:
    building 36
    formwork 127
    safety 36
installation (see note)
instructor's manual 5
insulation, features:
    heat loss 326
    measurement 326
    purpose of 326
insulation, types:
    batts 326,329
    boards 326,329
    cork 326
    diatomaceous earth 326
    expanded shale 326
    foamed 326
    flexible 326,329
    glass fiber 326
    granules 326
    loose 326,330
    mica 326
    perlite 326
    polyurethane 326
    polystyrene 326
    rigid 326,329

insulation, types (*Contd.*)
    sawdust 326
    slag 326
    sprayed 326,330
    vermiculite 326
iron, heat-seaming 493

jack-hammering 323
janitors 24
jig 72
jimmy 72, 102
jointer 73
joints:
    butt 362
    brazed 207
    control 180
    finishing 175
    in carpets 496
    in flooring 484
    in mortar 177
    in trim 299
    lap 362
    sealing 362
    soldered 207
    welded 210
joists:
    composite 221,225
    open-web 221
    solid-web 220
    steel 220
    stud 238
    unified 221
    wood 256

kettles
    asphalt 108
    roofing 347
keyhole saw 453
keying 401
kiln-dried 274,396
kneekicker 493
kneepads 486
knives:
    carpet 493
    flexblade 493
    linoleum 486
    putty 251,423
    utility 73,486

labor:
    organization of 28
    productivity of (see note)
    proportions of 29
ladders 66
laitence, concrete 143
laminates:
    beams 276
    decks 276
    plastic 297
    posts 276
    sheets 284
land:
    clearing 103
    grading 103
    owning 13
    title to 13
laser transit 471
lath:
    expanded 442
    fire-resistive 442
    gypsum 441
    insulating 442
    long 441
    metal based 442
    perforated 442
    plain 441
    rib 442
    sheet 442
    wire 442
layout:
    of book 6
    of buildings 50
    of carpeting 494
    of flooring 484
    of plot plans 12

layout (*Contd.*)
    of sites 21,22
lead, sheet 474
levels:
    automatic 46
    builders 45,50
    carpenters 73
    electronic 51
    transit 46
    tube 44,51
liens 24
lifter, board 450
lime:
    in mortar 173
    in plaster 440
loads:
    dead 117
    eccentric 281
    live 117
lockers 522,518
lumber:
    appearance 259
    boards 259
    construction 259
    dimensions 259
    dry 255
    economy 259
    grades 258
    green 255
    joist 259
    light framing 259
    measurement 262
    planks 259
    seasoned 255
    selects 259
    sheathing 259
    shop 258
    structural 258,259
    stud 259
    timber 259
    yard 258

machines:
    asphalt 109
    curbing 108
    digging 97–99
    paving 108
    trenching 101
machining, metal 245
mallet 72,493
manual:
    project 7
    tools 63
masonry, bonds:
    american 180
    ashlar 193
    composites 187
    english 180
    flemish 180
    garden wall 180
    modular 181
    rubble 193
    running 180
    stacked 180
masonry, features:
    bond patterns 179,191
    bracing 189
    control joints 180
    cutting 186
    loadbearing 179
    monolithic 179
    mortar, *see* mortar
    nonloadbearing 179
    patterns 179
    spelling of 170
masonry, units:
    adobe 182
    blocks 183
    bricks 183
    clay 181
    colors 181,182
    cured 182
    drypress 181
    engineered 183
    facing 190

masonry, units (*Contd.*)
  fire 190
  fired 181
  glass 181
  gypsum 181
  hollow 181
  modular 179
  norman 183
  orientation 180
  roman 183
  salvaged 190
  sand-lime 181
  soft mud 181
  solid 181
  stiff mud 181
  specialty 180,184
  tiles 189
  used 190
MasterFormat:
  division 6
  in general 5,6,8
  list of titles 8–11
  section 6
materials (see note):
  bulk 35
  disposal 40
  handling 40
  in general 3
  storage 40
measures:
  acre 33
  bank 102
  bushel 33
  feet 33
  foot board 262
  gallon 34
  gill 34
  hectare 35
  imperial 32
  inch 33
  liter 35
  lumber 262
  meter 35
  metric 31
  peck 33
  pint 33
  pound 34
  quart 33
  tape 46
  ton 35
  yard 34
measurement:
  angular 33
  area 33
  dry 33
  drywall 453
  field 46
  general rule 283
  imperial 32
  linear 33
  liquid 33
  metric 31
  miscellaneous 33
  roofing 346
  systems 30
  time 33
  volume 33
  weight 33
mechanical work 2
membranes:
  roofing 344
  waterproofing 323
meter 31
metals:
  aluminum 354,384
  copper 242,356
  lead 356,470
  painting of 503
  steel, *see* steel
  zinc 242
methods, construction 3
metric:
  basis 31
  conversions 31,35

metric (*Contd.*)
  measurement 31
  prefixes 31
  relationships 31
miter box 72
mixers 144
models:
  architectural 3
  instructional 4
moisture content:
  in substrates 479,488
  in wood 255
  tests for 489
mop, asphalt 348
mortar, features:
  additives 174
  appearance 171
  buttering 174,199
  color in 171
  description 170
  discarding 176
  embedding 171
  ingredients 170
  purposes 171
  retempering 176
  slushing 199
  strength 171
  uses 170
  workability 171
mortar, types:
  beds 177,188
  dryset 456
  fat 171
  for stone 198
  grout 174,177
  lean 171
  lime 171
  thinset 456
mud 138
mud-capping 82

nails, features:
  categories 203
  heads 202,203
  lengths 203
  points 202,203
  shanks 202
  sizes 203
nails, types:
  annular ring 203
  box 203
  brad 203
  casing 204
  common 204
  cut 202
  double-head 204
  finishing 204
  masonry 204
  panel 204
  powder-set 204
  roofing 204
  spikes 204
  tacks 204
  wire 202
nailing:
  concealed 296
  exposed 296
  face 480
  feather 480
  machines 478
  patterns 454
  techniques 204
  toe 273
narrowscope 6
needs:
  developer 13
  owner 13
nipper 72,457
noise 469
nuts 202

occupancy 24
owners 13,24
ova 447

pails 466
paint, features:
  additives 500
  coats 504
  color 499
  extender 500
  ingredients 500
  line work 504
  pigment 500
  systems 504
  surfaces 504
  vehicle 500
paint, processes:
  application 504
  asphalt 110
  cleaning 509
  brushing 504
  pretreatment 508
  rolling 504
  rubbing 508
  spraying 507
paint sprayers 501
paint types 500
panel board:
  particle 260
  gypsum 449
  wood 287
paneling, wood:
  fielded 295,296
  plank 295,296
  sheet 295,296
paper, building:
  asphalt sheathing 261
  black waterproof 261
  dry kraft 261
  plastic coated 261
  reinforced 261
particle board:
  hardboard 260
  pulpboard 260
  waferboard 260
paving:
  asphalt 109
  brick 111
  categories 105,106
  concrete 106
  curing time 106
  definition 105
  durability 106
  gravel 111
  quality 106
  stone 111
  types 105
payments:
  applications 27
  holdback 24
  process 23
  schedules 26
pentachlorophenol 306
people 4
pipes:
  accessories 113
  asbestos 112
  concrete 113
  clay 113
  metal 113
  plastic 113
plane 72
planning 22
plant 63
plasterboard, features:
  cutting 453
  edges of 449
  fastening 450,454,455
  finishing 455
plasterboard, types:
  fillers 450
  fire-resistive 449
  insulating 449
  perforated 449
  plain 449
plaster, coats:
  base 441
  bond 441

plaster, coats (*Contd.*)
  brown 440
  dash 440,447
  finish 440,447
  one 439
  scratch 440
  three 440,447
  two 440,446
plaster, features:
  angles/beads 447
  aggregates 440
  boxes 442
  definition 439
  fillers 440
  ingredients 440
  lathing 445
  substrates 445
  trim 446
  work 439
plaster, types:
  acoustic 441
  board 449
  cement 400
  dashes 447
  fiber 441
  gauging 441
  gypsum 440
  lime 440
  molding 441
  parging 439
  ready mix 441
  stucco 441
plaster, lath:
  gypsum base 441
  metal base 442
  trim 442
plastic:
  flashings 357
  forms 118
  laminate 284
  membranes 323
  panels 292
  pipes 113
  protection 89
  sheet 89,93
  solid 298
platforms 68
plier 72
plumb-bob 73,234
plywood, types:
  categories 260
  exterior 260
  hardwood 260
  interior 260
  overlaid 260
  softwood 260
  specialty 260
  veneers 286,287
plywood, veneers:
  book match 286
  butt match 286
  center match 286
  patterns 287
  running match 286
  slip match 286
  types 286
poison 77
posts, wood 275
posthole digger 100
pourers 347
power shovel 100
precautions (see note)
precedence 23,24,25
preloading 77
preparations (see note)
pressing, metal 246
prevention:
  accident 38
  fire 39
prices:
  alternate 20
  separate 20
  unit 21
procedures (see note):

procedures (see note) (*Contd.*)
  building 21
  industry 12
processes (see note)
procurement 21
productivity (see note):
  in general 7
program 13
proportions:
  in concrete 139
  in mortar 171
  in terrazzo 464
protection:
  breathing 39
  earthwork 103
  embankments 92
  eye 39
  head 40
  hearing 40
pulverizer 108
pumps:
  concrete 85,144
  sump 85
punch:
  fasteners 234
  list 24
  tool 72
punching, metal 246
pushers 348

quarrying 196
quinolinolate 306
quirks 447

rain screen 232
rakes:
  blade 78
  garden 73
  hand 73,147
rasp 72
ratios:
  in concrete mixes 139
  rise-to-run, roofs 332
  rise-to-run, stairs 316
reaming, metal 246
record keeping 24
references 5
reinforcement, features:
  bending 131,135
  blocking 136
  connections 132
  cutting 134
  delivery 135
  fabrication 133
  installation 133,136
  mill marks 131
  openings in 136
  rust 131
  spacing of 131
  supports
reinforcement, types:
  bar 132,136
  bolsters 132,136
  chairs 132
  fabric 132
  knots 137
  masonry 174,176
  mats 136
  mesh 443
  rod 132,136
  sheets 136
  terrazzo 465
  wire 137
related work (see note)
ripper 100
risers:
  stairs 315
  wells 85
rivets:
  blind 205
  button-head 204
  chemical expansion 204
  counter-sunk 204
  flat-head 204

rivets (*Contd.*)
  pop-type 204
  solid 205
  tubular 205
riveting 204
road oil 107
rollers:
  carpet 493
  floor 486
  hand 486
  paint 501
  paving 108
  porcupine 493
  spreading 73
  vinyl 423
  wheeled 108
rolok 180
roofing, features:
  moisture in 344
  slopes 332,346
  squares 346
  value of 345
roofing, systems:
  built-up 352
  decks, concrete 349
  decks, insulated 349
  decks, steel 349
  decks, wood, 350
  fluid 346
  metal 361
  system, simple 345,352
  system, multiple 345,352
  tar & gravel 344
roofing, materials:
  bitumens 345
  fabrics, filter 347
  felt, coated 346
  felt, glass 346
  felt, organic 346
  felt, surfaced 346
  flood coat 353
  gravel 346
  hygroscopic 354
  membrane 351
  sheet, base 346
  sheet, prefab 346
  sheet, rubber 345
  softening point 346
root-hook 79
router 72
rust:
  prevention 384
  on reinforcing 131

safety, equipment:
  belts 41
  components 37
  hardhats 40
  harness 38
  scaffolding 41
  shoes 37
  signs 41
  specifics 39
safety, standards:
  activities 37
  concerns 29
  illumination 40
  in general 7,37
  inspections 36
  in trades 37
  legislation 38
  noise level 41
  on sites 37
  signals 41,225
sand:
  in concrete 142
  in mortar 173
  in stucco 440
  in terrazzo 424
sandblasting:
  concrete 158
  for waterproofing 323
  glass 428
sander, floor 486

sawing:
    flat 477
    half round 286
    plain slice 286
    quarter 286,477
    rotary cut 286
saws:
    hack 72,436
    keyhole 451
    masonry 185
    radial arm 234
sawing, metal 246
scaffolds:
    for carpentry 290
    for masonry 185
    for metal support 457
    for painting 501
    for plastering 444
    for steel studs 234
    in general 66,
    safety 41
scarifier 108
schematics 13
scissor 72
scows 67
scraper 73,100
scratcher 445
screeds:
    concrete 147
    plaster 446
    terrazzo 467
screw, features:
    heads 205,206
    methods 205
    shanks 205,206
screw, types:
    drywall 205
    general use 205
    lag 205
    machine 205
    masonry 205
    self-tapping 205
    wood 206
screwdriver 72
scriber 73,487
sealants:
    compounds 363
    oil-base 363
    one-part 363
    packing 364,367
    primers 364
    rubber base 364
    solvent release 363
    synthetic 364
    two-part 363
sealing:
    asphalt 110
    backing 367
    caulking 362
    definition 362
    joints 362
    objectives 362
    paving 107
    terrazzo 468
services:
    free 53
    temporary 53
    user pay 53
setting, see concrete
shakes, wood 333,338
sharpening stone 451
shearing, metal 246
shears 72
sheathing:
    boards 271
    panels 272
sheeting, closed 89,90,92
shiner 180
shingles:
    aluminum 334
    asbestos 333,337
    asphalt 333,337
    exposure 332
    fibrous 333
    granular 333

shingles (Contd.)
    split 339
    inorganic 332
    lap 332
    metallic 334
    organic 332
    pans 337
    patterns 336
    steel 336
    strip 337
    terminology
    weather 332
shoring:
    closed 91
    open 89,92
shotcrete 89,93
shovel:
    hydraulic 99
    manual 73
    power 100
shredder 78
shrub removal 82
siding:
    aluminum 295,341
    bevel 287
    board & batten 287
    channel 287
    diagonal 294
    horizontal 294
    nondirectional 295
    tongue & groove 288
    trim 288
    vertical 294
    wood 287
sills:
    mud 120
    window 392,396
site:
    layout 22
    offices 62
    start-up 21
skips 67
slate 333,337
sodium silicate 306
soffit:
    definition 295
    framing 239
    mounts 438
    paneling 295
    plasterboard 452
softwood (see wood)
soil pincer 114
soils:
    classification 96,
    categories 104
    cohesive 96
    imported 96
    native 96
    non-cohesive 96
    shrinkage 96
    swelling 96
soldering, features:
    materials 207
    process 207
    temperatures 207
soldering, types:
    cold 207
    iron 207
    sweat 207
    torch 207
soldering, process 207
soldier 180
spacing:
    channels 438
    fasteners 236
    joists, ceiling 266
    joists, floor 264
    runners 438
    sleepers 479
    ties, masonry 190
    tiles, ceramic 461
    tiles, stone 199
    studs, steel 237
    studs, wood 266
spades 73,114

spandrel panels 430
specialties, features:
    attributes 510
    definition 510
    fastenings 521
    recessed 520
    selection 511
    surface mounted 520
    stocking, liquids 521
    stocking, solids 521
specialties, types 511-518
species, see wood
specifications:
    roofing 344
    sections 6
sponge 73,458
spreaders 108,347,487
spreadsheets 17
square:
    check for, building 49
    check for, doors 380,
    check for, windows 397
    marking tool 73
    roofing measure 346
squeegee 466
staging 67
stair:
    carpet tool 493
    formwork 127
    wells 315
stairs, wood:
    assembly 318
    balustrades 318
    balusters 317
    basement 318
    components 318
    configurations 317
    construction 316
    design 315
    finial 317
    flight 315
    handrails 318
    landing 317
    manufacture 316
    newel post 317
    porch 318
    terminology 317
    spiral 318
    sundeck 318
staple hammer 493
staple, features:
    finishes 206
    methods 206
    points 206
staple, types:
    chisel-point 206
    divergent-point 206
    spear-point 206
steel, decking:
    cellular 227
    configurations 227
    description 226
    fastening 229
    installing 229
    longspan 227
    regular 227
    shop drawings 228
    single sheet 227
    trim 228
steel, features:
    connections 217
    drawings 215
    flashings 356
    gauges 371,384
    guy wires 218
    shapes 213,214
    slings 217
    taglines 217
    tiers 217
steel, joists:
    bracing 225
    composite 221
    designations 222
    installation 224
    preparation 223

steel, joists (*Contd.*)
    positioning 224
    types 221
    unified 221
steel, studs:
    ceilings 237
    channels 237
    components 233
    features 230
    hangers 237
    openings 237
    runners 237,238
    soffits 239
    standards 233
    studding 236
    tracking 236
steel, types:
    alloy 212,213
    axle 132
    billet 132
    carbon 212,213
    coated 356
    grades 132
    mild 213
    rail 132
    rolled 213,371
    stainless 356
    strecher-leveled 371
steel, work:
    beams 218
    bolting 215
    columns 217
    coping 212
    custom 246
    cutting 212,216
    forms 118
    delivery 216
    erecting 216
    fabrication 216
    framing 212
    measurement 217
    ornamental 246
    painting 217
    riveting 215
    shoring 89
    storefront 384
    welding 215
stirrup, post 245
stockpiling:
    carpentry, rough 263
    concrete, precast 166
    countertops 312
    curtain walling 432
    formwork/falsework 129
    frames, door 371
    glass, supplies 418
    glass, units 418
    insulation, roof 329
    masonry units 182
    paint products 503
    steel framing 215
    steel decking 228
    steel studs 233
    stone materials 194
    wood, architectural 311
    wood flooring 479
    wood, prefabricated 278
    wood paneling 291
stone, types:
    building 194
    granite 194
    field 194
    flag 194
    geologic origin 194
    granite 194
    igneous 192
    limestone 194
    marble 194
    metamorphic 192
    monumental 194
    pumice 192
    sandstone 194
    schist 195
    sedimentary 192
    slate 195

stone, types (*Contd.*)
    tiles 199
    traprock 195
    travertine 195
stone, work:
    ashlar 193
    boasting 197
    bonding 193,198
    cutting 196
    drilling 196
    finishing 197
    heating 196
    polishing 198
    quality 192
    rubble 193
    setting up 198
    sculpturing 197
    tooling 197
    trial panels 199
    wedging 196
storage sheds 61
storefront:
    aluminum 384
    connectors 385
    definition 383
    doors 386
    framing 388
    glass 384
    glazing 386
    hardware 386
    panels 386
    steel 384
    wood 389
story pole 185
straightedge 73,458
strapping:
    steel 241
    wood 272
stretcher:
    in carpeting 493
    in first aid 37
    in masonry 180
stringers:
    closed 316
    cut 316
    housed 316
    plowed 316
    shoring 92
    stair 316
stripping:
    floors 486
    formwork 128
stucco:
    definition 441
    finishing 447
    mixing 442
    two coat 447
stud driver 493
studs:
    steel, *see* steel
    wood, *see* carpentry
stump grubbing 81
substrates for:
    carpets/underlay 494
    ceramic tilework 459
    paint finishes 504
    plastering 445
    stonework 199
    terrazzo 467
    toppings 154
    resilient flooring 487
    wood flooring 479
    water/damp proofing 323
sumps 86
supports, metal:
    definition 435
    channels 436
    clips 436
    finishing 438
    hangers 426
    rods 436
    runners 436
    soffit mounts 438
surfaces, painting 504
survey, features:

survey, features (*Contd.*)
    back sight 52
    batter boards 44
    bench marks 48,52
    chains 44
    elevation 50,52
    fore sight 52
    investigation 43
    levels 47,51
    lines 45
    location 49,51
    markers 45
    plans 21
    rods 45
    squares 45
    triangles 46
    tubes 50
surveying:
    building 48
    instruments 44–47
    land 43
    layout 21,43
    preliminary 43
    property 48
    topography 48
surveyors:
    land 43
    quantity 530
systems:
    acoustical 472
    color 499
    concreting 149
    cladding 340
    curtain walling 430
    dampproofing 321
    dimensional 30
    flooring, wood 265,476
    formwork/falsework 121
    framing, wood 256
    glazing 415
    joint sealing 364
    joist placement 224
    organizational 6
    painting 504
    plasterboard 448
    plastering 446
    post & beam 275
    roofing, membranes 350
    roofs, wood 268
    shingles 332
    steel erection 217
    storefronts 383
    support, metal 435
    terrazzo 463
    walls, wood 267
    waterproofing 321
    welding 209

tables of contents 15
tackboards 511,517
tamper 100,102,108
tapes:
    applicators 451
    measuring 73
    shapers 451
    survey 46,47
template 73
temporary services:
    barricades 59
    braces 218
    facilities 53
    fences 59
    heat 54
    light 54
    offices 62
    phone 55
    power 55
    signs 56
    supports 218
    toilets 56
    water 57
tendons 164,166
terrazzo, features:
    curbs 469
    definition 462

terrazzo, features (*Contd.*)
    divider strips 464,467
    finishes 468
    grinding 465
    grouting 464
    ingredients 463
    layout 467
    mixes 464
    pigments 463
    resins 464
    sand cushion 467
    slip sheet 467
    underlay 465
terrazzo, types:
    bonded 467
    conductive 464
    mosaic 464
    nonslip 463
    plain 464
    reinforced 465
    resilient 464
    rustic 464
    separated 467
    topping 464,468
    venetian 464
    underbed 464
thresholds:
    door 376
    storefront 389
ties:
    formwork 119
    masonry 187
    removers 119
    snap 119
tiers, steel 217
tiles, ceramic:
    custom work 461,462
    grouting 461
    layout 459
    methods 459
    techniques 460
    types 457
tiles, features:
    designs 489
    finishing 462
    mastic 457
    mortar for 460
    setting 460
    sealants 457
tiles, types:
    acoustical 470
    carpet 497
    cement 456
    ceramic 456
    clay 456
    concrete 334
    custom 461
    drainage 113
    flooring 485
    masonry 189
    mosaic 456
    pavers 456
    quarry 456
    resilient 485
    roofing 334
timbers 259
tin snips 72,234
toe lifter 451
toe nailing 273
toilet:
    accessories 514
    partitions 513
tolerances:
    manufacturing 30
    in lumber 30
    in blocks 30
toxic products 331
tools, types (see note):
    clamping 71
    cutting 72
    definition of 63
    manual 63
    marking 73
    miscellaneous 73

tools, types (see note) (*Contd.*)
    power 72
    safety 42
    spreading 73
trade names:
    Aspenite 288
    Aspirin 484
    Boliden 304
    Cafco 304
    CelCure 304
    Chemonite 304
    GluLam 274
    Greensalt 304
    Koppers 304
    Linoleum 484
    Masonite 288
    MicroLam 274
    Nylon 484
    OsmoSalt 304
    Paralam 274
    Tanalith 304
    Timber Specialties 304
    TrusJoist 274
    Velcro 248
    Wolman 304
    Wood-Tek 304
trades, building 2
tree:
    cutters 78
    felling 80
    removal 81
trencher 101
trenching 103
trim:
    carpet 492
    curtain wall 434
    flooring 485
    joints in 299
    metal 288
    plaster 442,445
    plastic 288
    running 299
    siding 288
    storefront 386
    tile 456
    wood, exterior 283
    wood, general 288
    wood, interior 283
trimming 103
tripod 48
trowels:
    in flooring 487
    in general 73
    in gypsum work 454
    in masonry 174
    in plastering 444
    in terrazzo 466,
    in tiling 458
trucks:
    dump 69,71
    panel 69,71
    pick-up 69,71
    pup 69,71
trusses:
    categories 277
    closed web 276
    fabricated 276
    open web 276

underlay, carpet:
    felt 492
    foam 492
    laying 494
    rubber, foam 492
    rubber,sponge 492
    urethane 492
underpinning 89,92
United States:
    building codes 214
    contract forms 16
    grades, lumber 259
    grades, plywood 260,286
    sand, damp 170
    steel shapes 214

United States (*Contd.*)
    studs, steel 233

vacuums, floor 493
valid contract 19
vans 69
vapor:
    barrier 261
    control 261,272
    retarders 261
vegetation 76
veneers:
    masonry 179
    plywood 286
    stone 197
vibrators 108,109,145
vibroflotation 76

walers 117,128
wall trimmer 493
walls:
    composite 187,192
    curtain 179,
    in general 179
    loadbearing 179
    masonry 179
    nonloadbearing 179
    stone 192
    wood framed
warming box 365
warranties 17
washers:
    plain 202
    spring 202
    tooth 202
waste:
    plasterboard 453
    stonework 196
water, features:
    fresh 142
    in concrete 142
    in construction 320
    in mortar 173
    in plasterboard 448
    in plastering 441
    liquid 320
    presence of 84,320
    reducers 142
    salt 142
    solid 320
    stops 143
    vapor 320
water, proofing:
    coatings 321
    definition 320
    floors 323
    membranes 323
    sheet goods 321
    walls 323
webs:
    open 220
    plywood 274
    solid 213
wedge 79
weights of:
    asphalt 107
    cement 142
    earth, soil 96
    glass 417
    particle board 261
    plywood 261
    water 31,321
welding, features:
    arrangements 209
    characteristics 211
    processes 207,208
    symbols 211
    types 211
welding, methods:
    arc 208
    beam 210
    gas 210
    shop 208
    site 208

welding, joints:
  butt 210
  edge 210
  fillet 211
  groove 211
  lap 211
  plug 211
  stud 211
  tack 211
wells 86
wellpoints:
  equipment 85
  layout 87
winch 78, 493
windows, configurations:
  awning 390
  casement 390,399
  double-hung 396,399
  hopper 390
  jalousie 390
  pivoted 393
  projected 393
  sash 390
  sliding 390,399
windows, features:
  beads 392
  configurations 390
  fabrication 391
  frames 390
  glazing 393
  manufacture, metal 391
  manufacture, wood 396
  terminology 398
windows, types:
  aluminum 391
  classification 390
  commercial 393
  metal 389
  residential 393
  steel 391
  wood 395
winds:
  prevailing 342

winds (*Contd.*)
  loads 416
  speeds 417
wire:
  cutters 436
  guy 218
  tie, hangers 436
  tie, runners 234
withes 188
wood, architectural:
  definition 309
  balustrades 315,318
  box-framing 312
  cabinets 310,312
  case-work 312
  counters 312
  countertops 312,314
  custom 309,319
  finishing 313
  economy 309
  grading 309
  handrails 315,318
  manufacture 310
  molding/trim 289
  placing 314
  premium 309
  purpose made 319
  shelves 310,314
  siding 291
  sorting 313
  stairs 310,315,318
  wall units 314
wood, features:
  close grain 258
  edge grain 477
  end grain 477
  prefabricated 274
  shoring 89
  shrinkage 255
wood flooring, *see* flooring
wood, species:
  hardwoods 284,477
  softwoods 258,477

wood, treatment:
  chemicals 306
  decay 302
  diffusion 307
  dry rot 302
  ecology 302
  gas-borne 303
  generic titles 307
  impregnation 307
  oil-borne 304
  problems 303
  testing 307
  water-borne 304
  wet rot 302
work:
  force 17
  measurement of 17
  of trades (see Parts 5.0)
  pricing of 17
  quality of 17
workability:
  concrete 141
  mortar 171
wrench 72

x-axis 231
x-ray radiation 419

yard:
  measure 34
  side 28
y-axis 231

zinc:
  arsenate 306
  chloride 306
  coating 357
  flashing 357
  naphthenate 306
zippers 423
zoning 13,43